D0449587

Time Out Guides Limited
Universal House
251 Tottenham Court Road
London W1T 7AB
Tel + 44 (0)20 7813 3000
Fax + 44 (0)20 7813 6001
Email guides@timeout.com
www.timeout.com

Editorial

Editor Anne Hanley
Deputy Editor Peter Watts
Listings Checkers Patrizia Lerco, Chiara Barbieri
Proofreader Adam Barnes
Indexer Anna Norman

Editorial/Managing Director Peter Fiennes
Series Editor Ruth Jarvis
Deputy Series Editor Lesley McCave
Business Manager Gareth Garner
Guides Co-ordinator Holly Pick
Accountant Sarah Bostock

Design

Art Director Mandy Martin
Deputy Art Director Scott Moore
Senior Designer Tracey Ridgewell
Designers Oliver Knight, Tessa Kar
Junior Designer Chrissy Mouncey
Digital Imaging Dan Conway
Ad Make-up Charlotte Blythe

Picture Desk

Picture Editor Jael Marschner
Deputy Picture Editor Tracey Kerrigan
Picture Researchers Ivy Lahon, Monica Roche

Advertising

Sales Director Mark Phillips
International Sales Manager Ross Canadé
Advertising Sales (Venice) Fabio Giannini
Advertising Assistant Lucy Butler

Marketing

Marketing Director Mandy Martinez
US Publicity & Marketing Associate Rosella Albanese

Production

Production Director Mark Lamond
Production Controller Samantha Furniss

Time Out Group

Chairman Tony Elliott
Managing Director Mike Hardwick
Group Financial Director Richard Waterlow
Group Commercial Director Lesley Gill
Group General Manager Nichola Coulthard
Group Circulation Director Jim Heinemann
Group Art Director John Oakey
Online Managing Director David Pepper
Group Production Director Steve Proctor
Group IT Director Simon Chappell

Contributors

Introduction Anne Hanley. **History** Anne Hanley (*Austrian rule* Gregory Dowling). **Venice Today** Cat Bauer. **Painting in Venice** Frederick Ilchman. **Architecture** Anne Hanley. **Palladian Villas** Frederick Ilchman. **Literary Venice** Gregory Dowling. **Where to Stay** Nicky Swallow. **Sightseeing** Gregory Dowling (*Handle with care* Anne Hanley, *Nature trail: Flora & fauna* Gaby Lewin. **Eating Out** Lee Marshall, Michela Scibilia. **Cafés, Bars & Gelaterie** Jill Weinreich. **Shops & Services** Pamela Santini (*The cobbler of Venice* Anne Hanley). **Glass** Louise Berndt. **Festivals & Events** Gaby Lewin. **Children** Gregory Dowling, Patrizia Lerco. **Film** JoAnn Titmarsh. **Galleries** Chiara Barbieri (*YVAs* JoAnn Titmarsh). **Gay & Lesbian** Salvatore Mele. **Nightlife & Music** Kate Davies. **Performing Arts** JoAnn Titmarsh. **Sport & Fitness** JoAnn Titmarsh. **The Veneto: Getting Started** Anne Hanley. **Padua** JoAnn Titmarsh. **Verona** Michael Thompson. **Vicenza** Michael Thompson. **Treviso & the Northern Veneto** Michael Thompson. **Directory** Gaby Lewin (*Glossary, Vocabulary, Further Reference* Anne Hanley).

Maps LS International Cartography, via Sanremo 17, 20133 Milan, Italy.

Photography by Alys Tomlinson, except: pages 10, 17, 26, 28, 43 Bridgeman Art Library; page 13 AKG; page 41 MEPL. The following image was provided by the featured establishment/artist: page 208.

The Editor would like to thank the Dowling family, Roberta dal Carlo, Tudy Sammartini, and Lee and Clara Marshall.

Contents

Introduction

Finding words to express adequately the beauty and uniqueness of Venice has occupied writers and travellers through the centuries. It is the city's other-worldly, fairy-tale quality that attracts, keeping visitors flooding to its narrow *calli* and palazzo-packed *campi*. Not even the less picturesque manifestations of today's mass tourism – the shops full of plastic flashing *gondole* and the serried ranks of nylon football shirts on stalls around the Rialto – can really tarnish the romantic dream.

It's just as well, really. Were the magic to wear thin, what would Venice do?

Once the world's greatest trading empire and a major ship-building centre, the city of Venice now has an economy that relies to a huge extent on its tourist industry and the spin-offs from it. Under such circumstances, you might expect visitors to be treated as honoured guests. They're not. They pay 300% (and more) more than locals for using the city's transport system; they are regularly charged more than locals in restaurants; they find the doors of the city's main tourist office (where, by the way, there's not a single free map in sight) firmly shut after 3.30pm with no indication that there's another branch still open round the corner; they are charged for transport maps and for using public toilets. And they are bombarded by 'rules' on how to behave in the lagoon city on a ubiquitous poster that informs them – among other

things – that they will be fined for picnicking in St Mark's square... without mentioning that places in which picnics *can* be spread are remarkable only by their absence in this near-benchless city.

Yet tourists still love Venice. And they're right to do so.

Unique it may be, but Venice is also satisfyingly simple to get to grips with: go with the weirdness, walk and walk, and poke your nose into the dingiest courtyards and darkest churches. It's ten to one you'll find a glowing Madonna or splendidly carved arched doorway – it takes no time at all to build up your own private treasure trove of 'your' Venetian finds.

In this edition of our Venice guide, we set out to help visitors get to grips with another particular feature of Venice: its 'urban-ness'. Despite its precarious position at the centre of the world's largest wetland, apt to disappear (briefly and in part) under water at the whim of hostile winds and tides, there can be few cities where you feel further away from a bit of grass and some trees. But there *is* nature there, both in image and in fact, as our series of Nature trail features reveals.

The most important 'rule' for any successful trip to Venice is to accept it on its own, unique, terms, delving into the city beyond the clichés. And we can only hope that when visitors learn to do this, Venice will love – and respect – tourists as much as tourists love Venice.

ABOUT TIME OUT CITY GUIDES

Time Out Venice is one of an expanding series of travel guides produced by the people behind London and New York's successful listings magazines. Our guides are all written and updated by resident experts who have striven to provide you with all the most up-to-date information you'll need to explore the city, whether you're a local or first-time visitor.

THE LOWDOWN ON THE LISTINGS

Above all, we've tried to make this book as useful as possible. Websites, telephone numbers, transport information, opening times, admission prices and credit card details are all included in our listings. And, as far as possible, we've given details of facilities, services and events, all checked and correct at the time we went to press. However, owners and managers

can change their arrangements at any time. Before you go out of your way, we'd strongly advise you to call and check opening times, dates of exhibitions and other particulars.

Remember that there's nothing simple about finding your way around the Venetian labyrinth. To complicate matters, Venetians have a very flexible attitude towards spelling and will swing back and forth between Italian and dialect names for streets and *campi*; sometimes locals have no idea of the 'official' name of their street, preferring to use the traditional one. We have given the most commonly used names; be prepared, however, to have to do some guesswork.

While every effort has been made to ensure the accuracy of the information contained in this guide, the publishers cannot accept responsibility for any errors it may contain.

advice, so we always want to know if you've been badly treated or overcharged.

THE LIE OF THE LAND

We've divided Venice by *sestieri*, the city's 'quarters'. Note than house numbers don't begin and end in each street: they start at an arbitrary spot in each *sestiere* and continue, apparently at random, to the last house in that district. Venetian addresses are, therefore, almost useless for the purposes of locating your goal. To make your task easier, our listings include first the official address (*sestiere* and number), followed by the name of the street. Each listing also has a map reference, indicating the page and square on which it can be found on our maps that begin on p305.

TELEPHONE NUMBERS

The area code for Venice is 041. This code must always be dialled whether you're calling from outside or within the city.

To dial numbers given in this book from abroad, use your country's exit code (00 in the UK, 011 in the US), followed by the country code for Italy, 39, then the local code (*including* the 0) and number. For more details of phone codes and charges, *see p291*.

ESSENTIAL INFORMATION

For all the practical information you might need for visiting the city – including visa and customs information, disabled access, emergency telephone numbers, a list of useful websites, a glossary of art terms and the lowdown on the local transport network – turn to the Directory chapter at the back of this guide. It starts on p275.

MAPS

We've include a series of fully indexed colour maps to the city at the back of this guide – they start on p305 – and, where possible, we've printed a grid reference against all venues that appear on the maps.There's also a map of the Veneto region on p234 and a map of Venice's *vaporetto* routes on p320.

PRICES AND PAYMENT

We have noted whether venues such as shops, hotels and restaurants accept credit cards or not but have only listed the major cards – American Express (AmEx), Diners Club (DC), MasterCard (MC) and Visa (V). Some business will accept other cards, including Maestro or JCB. Many hotels will also accept travellers' cheques issued by a major financial institution (such as American Express).

The prices we've supplied should be treated as guidelines, not gospel. Fluctuating exchange rates and inflation can cause charges, in shops and restaurants particularly, to change rapidly. If prices vary wildly from those we've quoted, ask whether there's a good reason. If not, go elsewhere. Then please write and let us know. We aim to give the best and most up-to-date

LET US KNOW WHAT YOU THINK

We hope you enjoy *Time Out Venice*, and we'd like to know what you think of it. We welcome tips for places that you consider we should include in future editions and take notice of your criticism of our choices. You can email us on guides@timeout.com.

There is an online version of this book, along with guides to over 45 other international cities, at **www.timeout.com**.

In Context

Tintoretto's *Annunciation* in the Doge's Palace.

History

A city state built on water that ruled the waves until its inevitable, glorious decline.

Mainland Veneto cities with Roman and pre-Roman pedigrees – Verona and Vicenza, Padua and Treviso – try hard to look down their noses at Venice, the upstart on the lagoon: that watery city is a mere 15 centuries old, nothing compared to them. Yet Venice rises above their disdain. *La Serenissima* basks in the glory of its millennium and more as an independent city state; what other mini republic can claim to have had total control over the shipping routes of the eastern Mediterranean for almost six centuries?

But proud as the city is of its glorious past, it has to be said that Venice's origins were decidedly unheroic. What would become known as the Most Serene Republic was born of a far-from-serene exodus of terrified inhabitants from those longer-established cities on the mainland, fleeing before the barbarian hordes who invaded the collapsing Roman Empire in the fifth century.

The brutality of Visigoths, Huns, Ostrogoths and Lombards drove thousands of town dwellers out onto the muddy, flood-prone islets and sand banks of the lagoon. Enormous

public works were necessary almost from the beginning to shore up and consolidate the islands. Huge amounts of timber had to be cut down and transported from coastal forests to the islands. Here the trunks were sunk deep into the mud as foundations for the buildings – mainly wooden – of the villages scattered on islands all over the lagoon. But above all, the rivers, including the fast-flowing Brenta and Piave, which drain the eastern Dolomites and which threatened to silt up the lagoon, had to be tamed and diverted.

And yet this battle against nature helped to unite the early lagoon dwellers into a close-knit community and eventually into a republic that was to become one of the strongest and most stable states in European history. The fight against the sea never ended. Even in the 18th century, when the French army was advancing on the lagoon and the Venetian Republic was near the end of its own decline and fall, the government invested its last resources in the construction of the *murazzi*, the massive sea walls that run between the Lido, Pellestrina and Chioggia.

Until the collapse of the Roman Empire, the islands of the lagoon hosted only transient fishing hamlets. The surrounding mainland, however, was one of the richest areas of the empire. Padua, Verona, Aquileia and Altino were among the most prosperous cities in Roman Italy; many smaller towns – among them Vicenza, Concordia and Belluno – were of almost equal importance. With the final disintegration of any semblance of public order and security in the late sixth century, their inhabitants finally fled for their lives. Those from Aquileia and Concordia gravitated towards the islands of the Grado lagoon, between Venice and Trieste. The inhabitants of Altino and Treviso made for the islands of Murano, Burano, Mazzorbo and Torcello in the northern section of the lagoon. Paduans pitched up on the central island of Rivo Alto ('high banks'), soon abbreviated to Rialto, the first nucleus of historical Venice. Chioggia drew fugitives from Este and Monselice.

'This battle against nature helped to unite the lagoon dwellers.'

These influxes were meant to be temporary, but as economic life on the mainland collapsed, the lagoon islands came to be thought of as permanent homes. They offered enormous potential in the form of fish and salt, commodities that even in times of chaos were basic necessities. Once settled in the lagoon, the fugitives could also enjoy the relative peace and tranquillity that would be denied to the peoples of mainland Europe for centuries to come.

BARBARIAN INTERVENTION
In 552 Justinian I, the emperor of Byzantium, was determined to reconquer Italy from the barbarians. His first object was the city of Ravenna. But his troops were confronted with an almost insuperable problem: they had made their way overland, via the Dalmatian coast on the eastern side of the Adriatic, but were blocked by the barbarian Goths who controlled the mainland to the north of Venice. The only way they could attack and take Ravenna was to bypass the Goths, crossing the lagoon from the town of Grado. Justinian's commander Narsete requested help to transport his men. Already by this time, the lagoon communities had adopted a practice that was to mark Venetian diplomacy through its 1,250-year history: staying as far as possible from – and, where possible, profiting by – other people's quarrels. Justinian's request presented a dilemma: helping would be seen as a

declaration of war against the Ostrogoths in Ravenna, with whom the lagoon communities had reached a comfortable *modus vivendi* assuring safety on the mainland for their traders. Yet the Eastern emperor was offering vast monetary and political rewards for transporting his troops.

The communities eventually threw in their lot with Byzantium. Justinian conquered Ravenna and marched on to Rome. From this time on the communities of the lagoon became vassals of the Eastern Empire, with its capital in Constantinople. Venice would remain technically subject to the Byzantine emperors until well after the Sack of Constantinople – an attack led by Venetians – during the Fourth Crusade in 1204.

THE DUCHY AND THE DOGE
It was not until AD 697, under the growing threat of the barbarian Lombards who then controlled the mainland, that the communities scattered around the lagoon – now officially recognised by Byzantium as a duchy – decided to convert their fragile confederation into a stronger, much more centralised, state. In this year (or maybe not: some historians have dismissed the story as a Venetian myth) they elected one Paoluccio Anafesto to be their first doge, as the dukes of Venice became known. Yet right from the beginning *il Doge* was very different from the other feudal strongmen of Europe.

In the first application of a system that would be honed into shape over the centuries (*see p12* **Machinery of state**), the doge was elected for life by a council chosen by an assembly that represented all the various social groups and trades of the island communities. Technically, therefore, the leadership was elected democratically, although the strongest groups soon formed themselves into a dominant oligarchy. Yet democracy of a kind survived in the system of checks and balances employed to ensure that no single section of the ruling elite got its hands on absolute power. Venetians, fearing the creation of an immovable hereditary monarchy, hedged the office of doge with all kinds of limitations.

The first ducal power struggle took place in 729. The doge in question, Ipato Orso, achieved the duchy's first outstanding victory as a military power when he dislodged the Lombards from Ravenna. Success, though, went to Orso's head, and he attempted to transform the doge's office into a hereditary monarchy. Civil war racked the lagoon for two years, ending only when a furious mob forced its way into Orso's house and cut his throat. Troubles continued with the two succeeding doges: both were accused of tyranny, and were not only deposed and exiled but also ceremonially blinded.

'Civil war racked the lagoon for two years.'

Despite moments of near-anarchy, the lagoon dwellers were already becoming a major economic power in the upper Adriatic, the eastern Mediterranean, the Black Sea and North Africa. Craftsmen were sent abroad to Dalmatia and Istria to study the art of shipbuilding; they learnt so swiftly that by the seventh century the construction and fitting-out of seagoing vessels had become a thriving industry. Mercantile expansion and technical advances went hand in hand, as tradesmen brought back materials and techniques from far-flung places – especially from the Middle and Far East, where technical and scientific culture was far in advance of the West.

In 781 Pepin, son of the Frankish king Charlemagne, invaded Italy and attacked the Lombards. Wariness of involving the lagoon in mainland struggles still dominated the duchy's policy and it played for time, unsure whether to sacrifice the alliance with Byzantium to this new and powerful player on the European scene. In the end, however, Pepin's designs on Istria and Dalmatia – part of the Venetian sphere of influence – caused relations to turn frosty. Exasperated by the duchy's fence-sitting, Pepin attacked its ally Grado on the mainland, executing its cardinal by hurling him from the town's highest tower. He then proceeded to take all the mainland positions around Venice, and besieged the lagoon communities from the sea.

In the mid eighth century the confederation had moved its capital from Heraclea in the northern lagoon to Malamocco on the Adriatic coast, where it was now at the mercy of Frankish naval forces. At this crucial juncture, in 810, a strong, effective leader suddenly

Machinery of state

The longevity of the Venetian republic was due to a large extent to a finely honed system of checks and balances that kept the powerful merchant aristocracy closely involved in the machinery of state without allowing any one person or dynasty to lord it over the others. The main ruling bodies were:

Collegio dei savi (College of Wise Men) – a group of experts, elected by the *senato*, who staffed special committees to oversee all aspects of internal, marine and war policy.

Consiglio dei dieci (Council of Ten) – appointed by the *senato*, the council's extensive network of spies brought any would-be subversives to a closed-door trial in which defence lawyers were forbidden. In time, the increasingly powerful *Consiglio dei dieci* would have the Inquisition to assist it in its task.

Il doge (the Duke) – elected for life in a complicated, cheat-proof system of multiple ballots, the sumptuously robed Duke of Venice was glorious to behold. He could not, however, indulge in business of his own, receive foreign ambassadors alone, leave Venice without permission, or accept personal gifts. If his city state tired of him, he could be thrown out of office. With his whole extended family banned from high office for the term of his reign, many doges hailed from less politically adept Venetian clans. Most, moreover, were old and tired

by the time they donned the *biretta*, the distinctive horned hat – the average age of doges between 1400 and 1570 was 72. However, the doge was the only official privy to all state secrets and eligible to attend meetings of all state organs; he could, if he played his cards right, have a determining effect on Venetian policy.

Maggior consiglio (Great Council) – the Republic's parliament, with around 500 elected members, which in turn elected (and provided the candidates for) most other state offices, including that of doge.

Minor consiglio (Lesser Council) – elected by and from the *maggior consiglio*, this six-man team advised – or kept tabs on – the doge.

Pien collegio (Full College) – made up of the *minor consiglio* and the *collegio dei savi*, this became Venice's real government, eventually supplanting the senato.

Quarantie – the three supreme courts; the 40 members were chosen by the *senato*.

Senato (Senate) – known until the late 14th century as the *pregadi*, the *senato* was the upper house of the Venetian parliament; by the 16th century it had some 300 members.

Serenissima signoria (Most Serene Lordships) – made up of the *minor consiglio*, the heads of the three *quarantie* courts and the doge, this body was vested with ultimate executive power.

emerged in the form of an admiral, Angelo Partecipazio. He immediately abandoned the besieged capital of Malamocco; almost overnight, the capital was moved to the island archipelago of Rialto in the centre of the lagoon.

Partecipazio's next move was a stroke of military genius. He ordered his fleet to head out of the lagoon through the strait of Malamocco to attack Pepin's ships, then to feign terror and head back into the lagoon. In hot pursuit, the deep-keeled Frankish ships ran aground on the sandbanks of the lagoon, allowing the locals, with their intimate knowledge of deep-water channels, to pick off the crews with ease until thousands had been massacred.

THE CITY IS NAMED

After his great victory against the Franks, Partecipazio was elected doge. During his reign, work began on a ducal palace on the site of the current one, and the confederation of islands that made up the lagoon duchy was given the name 'Venetia'. Around the same time, the flourishing city of Torcello began to decline, as the surrounding lagoon waters silted up and malarial mosquitoes took over.

This was also when Venice set about embroidering a mythology worthy of its ambitions. After local merchants stole the body of St Mark from Alexandria and brought it to Venice – traditionally in the year 829 – the city's previous Byzantine patron, St Theodore, was unceremoniously deposed and the Evangelist – symbolised by a winged lion – set up in his place. A shrine to the saint was erected in the place where St Mark's basilica would later rise (see p17 **Illustrious remains**).

Angelo Partecipazio's overwhelming success in both military and civic government led to another tussle for power. Before he died in 827, he made certain that his son Giustiniano would succeed him. When Giustiniano died two years later, his younger brother Giovanni was elected doge, despite mounting dissent and jealousy from rival families. It was a measure of Partecipazio's importance that his surname was to feature repeatedly in the ducal roll of honour over the next century, but the family was never allowed to achieve the hegemony that the Medici dynasty enjoyed in Renaissance Florence. In Venice, any sign of dynastic ambition was greeted either with banishment or worse; one doge with aspirations beyond the role assigned to him, Pietro Candiano, was thrown to the dogs at the end of the tenth century.

EXPANDING THE EMPIRE

The development of the vast Venetian empire grew out of the mercantile pragmatism that dominated Venetian political thinking.

Justinian: a dilemma for Venice. *See p11.*

Expansion was embarked upon for two main reasons: to secure safe shipping routes and to create permanent trading bases. Harassed by Slav pirates in the upper Adriatic, the Venetians set up bases around the area from which to attack the pirate ships: gradually they took over the ports of Grado and Trieste, then expanded along the coastlines of Istria and Dalmatia. In some cases, Venetian protection against pirates was requested; in others, 'help' arrived unbidden.

With the coast well defended, the Venetians rarely bothered to expand their territories into the hinterland. There was, for many centuries, a certain mistrust of terra firma; Venetian citizens were not even allowed to own land outside the lagoon until 1345.

The crusades presented Venice with its greatest opportunity yet for expanding trade routes while reaping a profit. Transporting crusaders to the Holy Land became big business for the city.

More importantly, the naïve crusaders were easy prey for the professional generals – the *condottieri* – who commanded Venice's army of highly trained mercenaries: the eager defenders of the faith were, as often as not, used to extend and consolidate the Venetian empire. Never was this truer than in the case of the Fourth Crusade, which set off proudly from

Venice in 1202 to reconquer Jerusalem. The Venetian war fleet was under the command of Doge Enrico Dandolo who, though 80 and completely blind, was a supremely cunning leader, outstanding tactician and accomplished diplomat. Other European crusader leaders were persuaded to take time out to conquer the strategic Adriatic port of Zara, thus assuring Venice's control of much of the Dalmatian coastline. Even more surprisingly, they allowed themselves to be talked into attacking Constantinople.

'The crusades presented Venice with its greatest opportunity yet.'

Venice's special relationship with the Eastern Empire had always had its ups and downs. In 1081 and 1082, Venice had done the Byzantine emperor a favour when it trounced the menacing Normans in the southern Adriatic. In return, it was granted duty-free trading rights throughout the Empire. But in 1149 those trading privileges were withdrawn in disgust at Venetian arrogance during a siege of Corfu.

As the Fourth Crusade set out, Dandolo saw that this was an ideal opportunity to remove the Byzantine challenge to Venetian trade hegemony once and for all. He pulled the wool over his fellow crusaders' eyes, with the noble argument that the Eastern emperor must be ousted and replaced by someone willing to reunite the eastern Orthodox and western Roman churches.

They acquiesced, but there was nothing noble about the brutal, bloody, Venetian-led sacking of the city on 13 April 1204, nor about the horrendous pillaging that ensued. Far outstripping their colleagues in greed and callousness, the Venetians looted the city's greatest treasures, including the celebrated quartet of antique Greek horses that was transported back to Venice and placed above the main entrance of St Mark's basilica (*see p 79*). Innumerable other artefacts – jewellery, enamels, golden chalices, statuary, columns and precious marbles – were plundered: they are now an inseparable part of the fabric of the *palazzi* and churches of Venice.

But the booty was only a minor consideration for the Venetians and their pragmatic doge: the real prize was the one handed out when the routed Byzantine empire was carved up. The Venetians were not interested in grabbing huge swathes of territory that they knew they couldn't hold. This was left to the French and German knights, who, indeed, lost it within a few decades. Putting their intimate knowledge

of eastern trade routes to excellent use, the Venetians hand-picked those islands and ports that could guarantee their merchant ships a safe passage from Venice to the Black Sea and back. These included almost all the main ports on the Dalmatian coast, certain strategic Greek islands, the Sea of Marmara and a number of strategic Black Sea ports.

For many years after the conquest of Constantinople, Venetian ships could sail from Venice to Byzantium without ever leaving waters controlled by the city. The Serene Republic, *La Serenissima*, had finally become a major imperial power. The city marked the turn of events by conferring a new title upon its doge: *Quartae Partis et Dimidiae Totius Imperii Romaniae Dominator* – Lord of a Quarter and Half a Quarter of the Roman Empire.

MEMBERS ONLY

In 1297, in what came to be known as the *Serrata del Maggior Consiglio*, the leaders of the Venetian merchant aristocracy decided to limit entry to the Grand Council to those families already in the club. Membership of the *maggior consiglio* was restricted to those who had held a seat there in the previous four years, or to descendants of those who had belonged at any point since 1172. Under these rules, only around 150 extended families were eligible for a place, but the number of council members leapt to some 1,200.

Up-and-coming clans were understandably indignant at the thought of being forever excluded from power and from a coveted place in the *Libro d'oro* – the Golden Book – of the Venetian aristocracy. In 1310 a prosperous merchant, Baiamonte Tiepolo, harnessed the growing discontent in a rebellion against the aristocratic oligarchy. Had Tiepolo's standard-bearer not been felled by a loose brick knocked carelessly out of its place by an old lady watching the shenanigans from her window in the Mercería, the uprising may have succeeded. But his troops fled in panic, the uprising was savagely crushed, and the much-feared Council of Ten was granted draconian police and judicial powers. An extensive network of spies and informers was set up to suppress any future plots.

In 1354 Doge Marino Faliero made a bid to undermine the powers of the Venetian oligarchy while increasing and consolidating his own powers as a permanent hereditary leader. This plot too, was mercilessly suppressed and Faliero was beheaded.

The Council of Ten – along with the Venetian Inquisition that was also set up after the Tiepolo plot of 1310 – wielded its special powers most effectively after the Faliero incident, ensuring that this was the last serious attempt to attack the principle of rule by elite. It was at this time that lion's-head postboxes first appeared at strategic points around the city: Venetians were encouraged to drop written reports of any questionable activity through their marble mouths.

'An extensive network of spies and informers was set up to supress any future plots.'

While Venice's mercantile power was at its zenith from the 13th to the 15th centuries, vast fortunes were built up and lavished on building, furnishing and decorating great *palazzi* and churches. It was at this time that the city took on the architectural form still visible today. For sheer luxury, Venice's lifestyle was unequalled anywhere else in Europe.

In the 14th and 15th centuries, Venice was one of the largest cities in Europe, with an estimated population of between 150,000 and 200,000, many connected with the city's booming mercantile activities. International visitors were astounded by *La Serenissima*'s legendary opulence and phenomenal economic dynamism.

The salt which had been the mainstay of Venice's economy in the early days had long ceased to be Venice's main trading commodity. When ships set sail from Venice for the Middle East, their holds were crammed with Istrian

Dressing down

Venice's role as Europe's major provider of luxury goods from the Orient gave the inhabitants of the Most Serene Republic a head start where sumptuous decking-out – of houses, means of transport and personal apparel – was concerned. But the shameless flaunting of conspicuous wealth caused some qualms among church and state authorities, so much so that attempts to curb it were made from the 13th century onwards in a series of sumptuary laws; special magistrates, called *Provveditori sopra le pompe*, were appointed to implement them.

Perhaps the best-known of the sumptuary laws was introduced in 1562: it ordained that gondolas – flashy jobs which had been reaching canal-blocking dimensions – should be painted a uniform black and be 11 metres (35 feet) long and 1.75 metres (six feet) wide – more or less the same dimensions of today's boats.

But most sumptuary laws were created by Venice's powerful men to limit the freedom of the city's disempowered sectors: Jews, prostitutes and women.

After the creation of the Ghetto (*see p104*) in 1516, Jewish men were obliged to wear a yellow hat to distinguish them when they left their enclave, and to steer clear of fine furs. (In fact, the Jewish community had its own sumptuary laws, banning the kind of garish get-ups that they considered degradingly gentile.)

Women, however, were the main target of the style police. In 1437 Venice's patriarch threatened to excommunicate any woman

wearing brightly coloured silk, lengthy trains, excessively long sleeves, sleeves ornamented with pearls and hair adorned with gold, silver, pearls or false tresses. Extravagant buttons and showy jewellery were repeatedly forbidden. In 1443 the senate banned dresses made of gold and silver textiles, a ban that Venice's wily ladies got around by lining their sleeves with it, then slashing them and pulling bits of the precious fabric through the holes; in 1472 sleeve-slashing was added to the list of no-nos.

'Nice' ladies had various ways of making their riches known, despite the sumptuary legislation. They rarely ventured out in public anyway, and when they did, they wore hugely high pattens – a kind of platform shoe – so high that they needed a helper on each side to keep them from toppling over. The extra fabric – of high quality, however sombre the hue – needed to cover the pattens and sweep down to the ground was a sign of healthy cash flow. When, as in 1459, Venice's ladies were called upon by the senate to dazzle a bevvy of visiting French ambassadors with their outfits, they always happened to have just the thing to hand.

Their less genteel sisters – whether they were prostitutes or high-class courtesans – were, in theory, meant to wear trademark yellow veils. The sumptuary laws were applied to them in a more haphazard fashion. The fact that the only jewellery that they alone were barred from wearing was pearls suggests that just about anything else may have been tolerated.

pine wood, iron ore, cereals, wool and salted and preserved meats. These were traded for finely woven textiles, exotic carpets, perfumes, gold and silverware, spices, precious stones of all kinds, ivory, wax and slaves: with a virtual monopoly on all these sought-after commodities, Venice was able to sell them on to the rest of Europe at enormous profit.

The Venetian aristocracy liked to live in comfort. 'The luxury of any ordinary Venetian house,' wrote one traveller in 1492, 'is so extraordinary that in any other city or country it would be sufficient to decorate a royal palace.' Domestic luxury was not confined to the city. The Venetians were also investing huge amounts of money in their summer villas on the mainland, which often surpassed their city establishments in magnificence, designed and decorated as they were by the leading Veneto architects and painters.

Venetians lavished the same kind of attention on their appearance (*see p15* **Dressing down**). Fortunes were spent on the richest and most gorgeous textiles and jewellery. Venetian women were famous for the unbridled luxury of their clothing, of their furs and of their fabrics woven with gold and silver thread. Their perfumes and cosmetics were the envy of all Europe, as were the beauty and fascination of the estimated 12,000 courtesans who dominated much of the social and cultural life of the city in the 15th century.

So dedicated were Venetians to the cult of love and earthly pleasures, that the Patriarch, Venice's cardinal, had to issue orders forbidding the city's nuns from going out on the town at night in ordinary clothes.

Sumptuous festivals of music, theatre and dance were almost daily occurrences. The visit of a foreign ruler, a wedding or funeral of a member of the nobility, a religious festival, a naval or military victory, or delivery from an epidemic were all excuses for public celebrations involving days of festivities and huge sums of money. The city's foreign communities – Jews, Armenians, Turks, Germans, French and Mongols, many of them permanent residents in this truly cosmopolitan city – would celebrate their national or religious feast days with enormous pomp.

Despite the wealth of the city and the full employment created by its trades and industries (at full stretch, the shipyard was capable of launching one fully equipped ship every day), life was not easy for the city's poor, who often lived in damp, filthy conditions.

Epidemics were frequent: more than half the city's population is estimated to have died in the Black Death of 1348-9. Social tension and discontent were rife.

GENOA GETS MAD

The enormous wealth of the Venetian Republic and its rapidly expanding empire inevitably provoked jealousy among the other trading nations of the Mediterranean – above all with the powerful maritime city state of Genoa, Venice's main rival in its trade with the East.

In 1261 the Genoese had clashed with the Venetians when the former obliged the Byzantine emperor by helping to evict Venice's high-handed merchants from Constantinople. Skirmishes between the two Italian powers continued throughout most of the 14th century, regularly flaring up into major battles or periods of open warfare, and often resulting in disastrous defeats for Venice.

By 1379 the situation had become desperate for *La Serenissima*. The Genoese fleet and army had moved into the Gulf of Venice in the upper Adriatic and, after a long siege, had taken Chioggia, at the southern end of the lagoon. From here the Genoese attacked and occupied much of the lagoon, including Malamocco and the passage to the open sea. Venice was under siege and began to starve.

> ## 'Genoa's days as a great naval power were over, and Venice exulted.'

Then, in 1380, the city worked another of its miracles of level-headed cunning. Almost the whole of the Genoese fleet was anchored inside the fortified harbour of Chioggia. Vittor Pisani, the admiral of the Venetian fleet, ordered hundreds of small boats to be filled with rocks. Panicked by a surprise Venetian attack on the mouth of the port, the Genoese failed to notice that the small boats were being sunk in the shallow port entrance, preventing any escape. The tables had been turned, and Venice besieged the trapped Genoese fleet until it surrendered unconditionally. Genoa's days as a great naval power were over, and Venice exulted.

Ironically, however, this victory was to spell the beginning of the end for *La Serenissima*. For though the Republic had reached the climax of its prosperity and had re-acquired its supremacy in the East, concentrating its energies on fighting Genoa was to prove a fatal foreign policy mistake. Venice's leaders badly underestimated the threat posed by the emergence of the Turks as a military power in Asia Minor and the Black Sea area. Convinced – wrongly and ultimately fatally – that diplomacy was the way to deal with the threat from the East, Venice turned its attention to conquering other powers on the Italian mainland.

Illustrious remains

Whose is the much-revered body buried in St Mark's basilica? St Mark's, we have long been led to believe; but one historian — Alexander the Great specialist Andrew Chugg – begs to differ. In an article which sent shock waves through Venice, the British expert asked for DNA testing on the illustrious remains which, he insists, are those of Alexander.

This Macedonian warlord conquered a swathe of territory stretching from Greece to Pakistan before dying suddenly in 323 BC at the age of 33 in Alexandria, the Egyptian city he founded. He was buried there, in a gold sarcophagus. Worshipped as a divinity during his lifetime, Alexander was no less highly considered after his death, and for many centuries his tomb was a place of pilgrimage.

It wasn't, in fact, until Christians began getting the upper hand in the fourth century AD that all trace of the pagan remains vanished. But Chugg believes that they didn't so much disappear as change identity.

Various early Christian sources report that the body of Mark the Evangelist was burnt directly after his death. Yet at the very point in time when Alexander's remains disappeared, here was St Mark's corpse, buried at the same central crossroads where the Macedonian had for so long rested in peace. There 'St Mark' remained for 400 years, until some wily Venetian merchants nabbed what they thought was the saint's body, wrapped it up in pork to stop Muslims

and Jews from probing too closely into the contents of their swag bag, and brought it triumphantly back to Venice in 829.

Already bridling at the very suggestion that the relics may not be those of Mark, church authorities in Venice may be loathe to permit the exhumation of the saintly bones. But the discovery in 1970 of the remains of Philip II, Alexander's father, means DNA testing *could* lay this ghost to rest once and for all.

St Mark's body in St Mark's?

STAYING IN NEUTRAL

For centuries Venice had followed a conscious policy of steady neutrality towards the various powers that had carved up the Italian mainland. The European political upheavals from the end of the 12th century to the end of the 14th century put paid to that neutrality. The bitter rivalry between Venice and the other Italian maritime states, especially Pisa and Genoa, inevitably brought it into conflict with their powerful mainland allies: the Pope, the Scaligera dukes of Verona and a succession of Holy Roman emperors.

The defeat of the vast Scaligera empire (which included much of the Venetian hinterland) by Count Gian Galeazzo Visconti of Milan in 1387 brought the Milanese much too close to the lagoon for comfort. It was not only Venetian security which was under threat, but also access to all-important trade routes through north-eastern Italy and across the Alps into northern Europe beyond. Venice began a series of wars that led to the conquest of Verona and its enormous territories in 1405, and also of Padua, Vicenza and a number of other significant towns.

By 1420 Venice had annexed Friuli and Udine; by 1441 *La Serenissima* controlled Brescia, Bergamo, Cremona and Ravenna. The land campaign continued until 1454, when Venice signed a peace treaty with Milanese ruler Francesco Sforza. Though Ravenna soon slipped from Venice's grasp, the rest of the republic's immense mainland territories were to remain more or less intact for almost 300 years.

THE DECLINE STARTS HERE

Even as Venice expanded on the mainland, events were conspiring to bring *La Serenissima*'s reign as a political power and trading giant to a close. In 1453 the Ottoman Turks swept into Constantinople, and Venice's crucial trading privileges in what had been the Byzantine Empire were almost totally lost. In 1487 Vasco da Gama rounded the Cape of Good Hope; in 1489 he became the first European to reach Calcutta by sea, shattering Venice's monopoly on the riches of the East. The arrival of Portuguese ships laden with spices and textiles in Portuguese ports caused a sensation in Europe and despair in Venice. The Venetians hastily drew up plans to open a canal at Suez to beat the Portuguese at their own game, but the project came to nothing.

Instead, cushioned by the spoils and profits of centuries and exhausted by 100 years of almost constant military campaigns, the city sank slowly over the next two centuries into dissipation and decline.

But, as was only to be expected from a city as lavish as Venice, the decline was glorious. For most of the 16th century few Venetians

The Uskoks of Zengg

The Uskoks were probably of Croatian origin. Harried by Ottoman invaders, they were driven to the area around the fortified town of Zengg in Habsburg-controlled Dalmatia where they turned to piracy. Yet these were pirates with a twist: never averse to a bit of looting and pillaging, it was all done in good faith and firmly in defence of Christianity against Muslim Ottoman Turks.

Supported and funded by Austria's Habsburgs, the Uskoks proved a handy bulwark against the encroaching Turks who continued to be perceived as a threat to the Austro-Hungarian Empire, even after the Ottomans and Habsburgs signed the Treaty of Adrianople in 1568.

When war flared up once again between Austria and the Turks in 1593, Venice's help was sought by the Habsburgs and the Pope. Never one to put religious ideals before commercial advantage, *La Serenissima* weighed up the pros and cons, and decided that smug neutrality was the safest option.

For the uncomplicated Uskoks, this was no better than a declaration in favour of the Infidel. For Austria, it was yet another slap in the face from the supercilious, grasping Venetians; with the Uskoks' idealistic rage directed towards both Turks and Venetians, the Habsburgs were only too delighted to back the righteous marauders.

Hostilities came to an end in 1606, when Habsburg-Ottoman relations entered a new, happier phase with the Treaty of Zsitva-Torok... much to the disgust of the Uskoks who were keen to continue waging their Holy War.

These pirates remained a thorn in the side of the stability-bent Austrians for almost a decade. Until, that is, the War of Gradisca in 1615-7 at the end of which Austria bowed rather too hastily to Venetian demands that the Uskoks be relocated from their stronghold at Zengg and banished to some far-off corner of the empire where Venetian ships would no longer be at their mercy.

behaved as if the writing were on the wall. Such was the enormous wealth of the city that the economic fall-out from the Turks' inexorable progress through the Middle East went almost unnoticed at first. Profits were not as massive as before, but the rich remained very rich and the setbacks in the East were partly counter-balanced by exploitation of the newly acquired terra firma territories.

As revenue gradually declined through the 16th century, spending on life's little pleasures increased, producing an explosion of art, architecture and music. Titian, Tintoretto, Veronese and Giorgione were hard at work in the city (*see pp26-32*). Palladio, Sanmicheli and Scamozzi were changing the face of architecture (*see pp38-42 and pp33-37*). The city rang out to the music of the Gabriellis.

'But, as was only to be expected from a city as lavish as Venice, the decline was glorious.'

Meanwhile, on the mainland, Venice's arrogant annexation of territory had not been forgotten by the powers that had suffered at her hands. When Venice took advantage of the French invasion of Italy in the final years of the 15th century to extend its territories still further, the Habsburgs, France, Spain and the papacy were so incensed that they clubbed together to form the League of Cambrai, with the sole aim of annihilating Venice.

They came very close to doing so. One Venetian rout followed another, some Venetian-controlled cities defected to the enemy, and others that did not were laid waste. Only squabbling within the League of Cambrai stopped Venice itself from being besieged. By 1516 the alliance had fallen to pieces and Venice had regained almost all its territories.

ATTACK OF THE OTTOMANS
Its coffers almost empty, its mainland dominions in tatters, Venice was now forced to take stock of the damage that was being done by the Turks. A short-sighted policy of trying to keep the Ottoman Empire at bay by diplomacy had already had devastating effects on Venice's once-supreme position in the eastern Mediterranean.

In 1497, as the Ottomans stormed through the Balkans, coming almost within sight of the bell towers of Venice, *La Serenissima* had been obliged to give up several Aegean islands and the port of Negroponte; two years later it lost its forts in the Peloponnese, giving the Turks virtual control of the southern end of the

Adriatic. And if Venice felt jubilant about securing Cyprus in 1489 by pressuring the king's Venetian widow Caterina Cornaro into bequeathing control of the island, the legacy involved the Republic in almost constant warfare to keep the Turks off this strategically vital strip of land.

In 1517 Syria and Egypt fell to the Turks; Rhodes followed in 1522; and by 1529 the Ottoman Empire reached across the southern Mediterranean as far as Morocco. The frightened European powers turned to Venice to help repulse the common foe. But mistrust of the lagoon republic was deep, and, in their determination to keep Venice from deriving too much profit from the war against the Turks, the campaign itself was botched.

In 1538 a Christian fleet was trounced at Preveza in western Greece; in 1571 Venice led a huge European fleet to victory against hundreds of Turkish warships in the Battle of Lepanto, in what is now the Gulf of Corinth. But despite the massive propaganda campaign of self-congratulation and self-glorification that followed, it became apparent that the victory was hollow and that the Turks were as strong as ever. In a treaty signed after the battle in 1573, Venice was forced ignominiously to hand over Cyprus, its second-last major possession in the eastern Mediterranean. (Crete, the final one, held out until 1669.)

ACCEPTING THE INEVITABLE
By the 17th century the Venetian government was no longer under any illusion about the gravity of its economic and commercial crisis. In a report issued by the *Savi alla Mercanzia*, the state trading commission, dated 5 July 1610, it was noted that, 'Our commerce and shipping in the West are completely destroyed. In the East only a few businesses are still functioning and they are riddled with debt, without ships and getting weaker by the day. Moreover, and this must be emphasised, only a small quantity of goods is arriving in our city, and it is becoming increasingly difficult to find buyers for them. The nations which used to buy from us now have established their businesses elsewhere. We are facing the almost total annihilation of our commerce.'

'Venice was down but not quite out.'

Venice was down but not quite out, however, and some heroic attempts were made to regain the empire that had been so disastrously mauled in the 16th century by the Turks. In 1617 a successful campaign was fought against the Uskoks (*see p18* **The Uskoks of Zengg**), pirates financed by the Austrian Habsburg rulers in Istria and along the Dalmatian coast; in the process, some resounding blows were struck against the Turks of the region too. Between 1681 and 1687 Francesco Morosini, the brilliant strategist then in command of the

Venetian fleet, succeeded in reconquering much of the territory that had been taken by the Turks in the preceding century, including Crete and the Peloponnese. But these moments of glory, celebrated with colossal pomp and ceremony in Venice itself, were invariably short-lived.

Austrian rule

Austria ruled Venice for nearly 60 years during the 19th century – far longer than the Napoleonic occupation (a mere nine years). Yet while Napoleon remains a dirty name, few Venetians seem to feel any rancour towards the longer-lasting rulers.

In some ways, it's only to be expected: Napoleon, after all, not only brought about the collapse of the Venetian Republic but made great rents in the city's constitutional, social and architectural fabric. The Austrians, on the other hand, did very little at all.

The Treaty of Campoformio (1797) gave Venice to the Austrians who held it until 1805 – eight years of quiet stagnation. Napoleon then wreaked his reforms, until he met his Waterloo (1815) and Venice bounced back to Austria for a further 51 mainly eventless years. With just one significant interruption.

Almost all 19th-century accounts and images of Venice are foreign ones. Visitors flocked here: this was Romantic Venice, the unreal, insubstantial city depicted as a shimmering illusion by such artists as Turner, its decay part of its attraction.

In 1825,the Austrians granted Venice the status of a free port, which brought back some semblance of the city's former prosperity. The murazzi, the city's sea-walls, were restored and gas lighting was finally introduced in 1843.

It was the railway link to Milan, built in 1846, that made Venetians aware of new commercial possibilities… and of the fact that Italian Unification was a possibility. Suddenly, anti-Austrian feelings ran high in Venice. When an Austrian band struck up in piazza San Marco, Venetians would leave. All that was needed now was a leader.

Daniele Manin was a lawyer of Jewish descent. He was brought up a republican and patriot. With the support of Dalmatian scholar and patriot, Nicolò Tommaseo, he petitioned Vienna for an end to censorship. On 18 January 1848 the two men were arrested. When news came in March that the Emperor had promised a constitution, the whole city

flocked to the piazza. The governor, Count Aloys Palffy, listened in trepidation to cries of '*fuori Manin e Tommaseo!*' Terrified, Palffy released the prisoners. Manin became the leader of the insurrection.

On 18 March there was a riot in piazza San Marco. Austrian soldiers opened fire; eight people were killed and many wounded. Manin demanded the right to institute a mainly middle class civic guard, which could be used, among other things, to protect the lives and property of wealthier citizens. Count Palffy agreed.

Permission from the emperor to form a Venetian government failed to convince Manin that the occupiers were prepared to give in wholly. On 22 March Arsenale workers rioted, assassinating their overbearing Austrian supervisor. When Manin moved to take over the Arsenale (see p97), the Italian troops under Austrian command refused to open fire. The capture of Venice's fortress and arms-depot was achieved without further bloodshed.

The Venetian Republic was thus officially reborn. It was to last only a year and a half, defeated at last not by the insistent shelling of the Austrians but by starvation and cholera. The terms of surrender were surprisingly unvindictive: leaders of the revolution were to leave the city. Manin and his family boarded a steamer for exile. On the voyage Manin's wife died of cholera; his daughter died soon after in Paris. There Manin scraped a meagre living teaching Italian until his death in 1857, aged 53.

The Austrian occupation lasted another 17 lethargic years, during which tourism returned but commerce continued to decline. In 1866, Venice and the Veneto voted overwhelmingly to join the new Italian nation. Pragmatism, together with the new spirit of Italian nationalism, had put an end to all thoughts of a revival of the Venetian Republic.

In 1868 Daniele Manin's body was brought to Venice and placed in an ornate sarcophagus in the north wall of St Mark's.

Exhausted by debts and the sheer effort of its naval campaigns, the Venetian Republic lacked the resources needed to consolidate its victories and newly reconquered territories.

In 1699 the Treaty of Carlowitz had rewarded Francesco Morosini's naval and military victories, restoring much of Venice's possessions in the Easst and many of its trading privileges. But by 1718 the Republic was struggling to keep its head above water as the Austrians and Turks forced it to cede most of these same territories in the humiliating Treaty of Passarowitz.

By the time the Venezia Trionfante café (now Caffè Florian, *see p166*) opened for business in piazza San Marco in 1720, the republic was virtually bankrupt; its governing nobility had grown decadent and politically inert. But decadence was good for the city's growing status as the party capital of Europe.

Aristocratic women of all ages and marital states were accompanied in their gadding by handsome young *cisibei* (male escorts), whose professions of chastity fooled nobody. Masked nuns from fashionable convents were a common sight at the city's gambling houses and theatres; party-pooping church officials who tried to confine nuns to barracks at the convent by the church of San Zaccaria were met with a barrage of bricks on at least one occasion.

Priests, too, were not slow to join in the fun: composer-prelate Antonio Vivaldi's supposed affairs with members of his famous female choir were well-publicised. Father Lorenzo Da Ponte, Mozart's great Venetian librettist, was better known for his amorous conquests than for his sanctity. And though Giacomo Casanova, the embodiment of sexual excess, never actually donned a cassock, he had been a promising student of theology before he realised where his true vocation lay.

ONE LAST STAND

Bankrupt, politically and ideologically stagnant and no longer a threat to any of its former enemies, Venice directed its final heroic effort to survive not against those erstwhile foes but against the forces of nature. Even as Napoleon prepared to invade Venice in 1797, the city was spending the meagre funds left in its coffers on building the vast *murazzi*, the long stone and marble dyke designed to protect the city from the worst ravages of unpredictable Adriatic tides (*see pp137-139*).

On 12 May 1797 the last doge, Lodovico Manin, was deposed by the French who, even before the Republic bowed to the inevitable and voted itself out of existence, had handed control of the lagoon city over to Austria under the terms of the Treaty of Loeben (*see p20*

Torcello: site of an early settlement.*See p13*.

Austrian rule). Manin consigned his doge's cap to the victors, saying, 'Take this, I don't think I'll be needing it any more.'

In 1805 Napoleon reversed this state of affairs, absorbing Venice back into his Kingdom of Italy. Until 1815, when the French emperor's star waned and Venice once again found itself back under Austrian control, Napoleon's Venetian plenipotentiaries were given free rein to dismantle churches, dissolve monasteries and redesign bits of the city, including the wide thoroughfare now known as via Garibaldi and its adjoining public gardens.

The last, ill-fated spark of Venice's ancient independent spirit flared up in 1848, when lawyer Daniele Manin (no relation of the last doge) led a popular revolt against the Austrians. An independent republican government was set up, holding out valiantly against siege and bombardment for five heroic months. It was doomed to failure from the outset, however, and the Austrians were soon firmly back in the saddle, keeping their grip on this insignificant backwater until 1866, when a weakened Austria, badly beaten on other fronts by the Prussians, handed the city over to the newly united Italian state.

Italians do it better.

travelplan it
Done by Netplan, done by Italians.

www.travelplan.it

You're going to love the Italian portal **Travelplan.it** because it's just like having a guidebook at hand, free and always up to date.

That's why over 100,000 travelers like yourself log on every month and discover a passion for our country, along with absolutely everything needed to visit it.

Because there's only one way to see Italy: with those who really know it.

Venice Today

While tourists crowd San Marco, everyday life in Venice is harder to track down.

Living in Venice is part reality and part theatrical production, with the same stock characters appearing on stage through the centuries. Nothing and everything has changed since playwright Carlo Goldoni recorded the city's scandals and intrigues in the 18th century. The gondola glides across time, the passengers now strangers who pay plenty to peek through the curtain. Ask Venetians why they stay, nearly suffocated by mass tourism and rising water levels, and they will tell you that the tourists are supernumeraries, the *acqua alta* part of the scenery, and the play itself is still the greatest show on earth.

In the 12th century, the first three floors of Ca' Barzizza (*see p74*) were constructed: it is Venice's earliest Byzantine house. The next floor up is 14th century; the top floor probably dates from the 19th. Still visible in the walls of the 19th-century palazzo next door are traces of columns from a warehouse, conjuring up images of days when powerful merchants lived, worked and entertained in *La Serenissima*, the mistress of the Mediterranean.

Inside ancient buildings such as these, current events stream in over broadband connections and satellite television. At San Polo, an outdoor movie theatre blares the latest blockbusters (*see chapter* **Film**) in a campo where bullfights were once held. At the *pescaria* (*see p114*), the metallic tune of a mobile phone distracts a housewife as she haggles over the price of *branzino*. Inside the *piano nobile* of a palazzo, breakfast arrives on a silver platter, while the locals at the bar below confer on the nobleman's latest conquest and the latest developments in Iraq. Century upon century of history; layer upon layer of mystery; the past preserved in the present: this is Venice today.

Beyond island Venice is another world again, that of the Veneto. While *La Serenissima* continues to hold the world in her thrall, the terra firma side of the lagoon has come quietly but steadily into its own. And besides being one of Italy's biggest economic success stories, it now has a burgeoning tourist industry as well. According to Veneto region figures, more than 50 million visitors stayed in 2003; only a fraction of these stayed in Venice itself. In the next three or four years, annual arrivals are expected to rise to 70 million, making this the most visited region in all of Italy.

The success story of Venice and the Veneto is a very recent one. Venice had slipped far into decline before the city capitulated to Napoleon's troops in 1797, putting an end to the longest-running independent republic in history – more than 1,000 years. Under Austrian rule (1815-66), it was relegated to the status of a picturesque, inconsequential backwater. But if the city suffered, the fate of its former mainland territories was even worse: with no industry to speak of, and agriculturally behind the times, the Veneto ran the semi-feudal south a close race for the title of Italy's own Third World. Between 1876 and 1901, almost 35 per cent of the 5.2 million desperate Italians who sought a better life abroad were fleeing from the crushing poverty of the Veneto and the neighbouring Friuli region.

Massive industrialisation in Venice's mainland Porto Marghera area after World War I and – more extensively – World War II served to shift the more impoverished sectors of the population from agricultural to urban areas. But the poverty remained. As recently as 1961, 48 per cent of homes in the north-east had no running water, 72 per cent had no bathroom and 86 per cent had no heating.

What the people of the Veneto did have, however, was a deep-rooted attachment to their traditional crafts, and a cussedness of character unmatched anywhere else in Italy. In the past, both proved detrimental: in the age of heavy industry, small-scale manufacturing was a sure-fire loser; and when captains of heavy industry sought meek vassals to man the furnaces, many of the natives of the Veneto who protested were forcibly deported to populate Fascist new towns in the malarial swamps south of Rome.

It was not, in fact, until the 1970s that north-eastern determination came into its own. With a growing trend towards industrial downscaling, those family-run workshops that had tightened their belts and ridden out the bad times gradually became viable business concerns. Giuliana Benetton's humble knitting machine gave birth to a global clothing empire centered in Treviso; the metalworking lessons that Leonardo del Vecchio learned in an orphanage spawned Luxottica, the world's biggest producer of spectacle frames, based in Belluno; and Ivano Beggio progressed from tinkering with bikes in his father's cycle shop in Noale to running Aprilia, one of Europe's largest manufacturers of motorcycles and scooters. Indeed, in the last 40 years, employment in the Veneto has segued from mostly agricultural

to overwhelmingly industrial; moreover, the region boasts some of Italy's lowest unemployment – under five per cent.

Theories explaining the north-eastern miracle are as numerous as they are unconvincing. Most sociologists and economists agree, however, that the region's historical links across the Alps to Austria, Germany and eastern Europe, and its family ties to successful emigrants further afield gave it a vocation for export unmatched anywhere else in Italy. Through the mid to late 1990s, a third of the country's huge balance of trade surplus was generated in the north-east.

The 21st century has seen a slight tarnishing of the Veneto's Midas touch. The competitive edge for exports created by a weak lira has been lost since the introduction of the single European currency. Crippling labour costs have forced many businesses to relocate to eastern Europe. A manpower shortfall has been bridged by hiring immigrant workers, resulting in an unprecedented ethnic pot-pourri: learning to live with social and cultural differences is one of the challenges the famously insular Veneto must face if it is to maintain or increase its present level of development.

The post-war parabola described by island Venice – for so many centuries one of the richest and most prosperous commercial centres in the civilised world – was, if anything, bleaker. In the middle of the last century, the odd boat was still being constructed in small shipyards, a few glass-blowing workshops were still active on the island of Murano and a small fishing fleet was still operative. As the terra firma became increasingly industrialised, blue-collar workers looked across the water for employment. Then, realising that housing on the mainland was cheaper, drier and easier to park in front of, they moved out in an exodus that has brought the population of island Venice plunging from around 170,000 in 1946 to about 65,000 today.

For an area about the size of New York's Central Park, however, that's still a respectable figure. Few such small cities, moreover, can lay claim to a population comprising gondoliers, mask makers, glass-blowers, monks, nuns, fishermen, musicians, artists, writers, architects, historians, academics, restoration experts and many of Italy's rich and famous. Add to that a sizeable student population, a dedicated group of expats and part-time residents, plus the thousands of workers who commute to Venice from the mainland each day, and the result is a solid base of 'locals' that gives Venice its distinct flavour. The stalwarts who remain cite many reasons for their endurance.

Francesca Bortolotto Possati, president and CEO of the luxurious Hotel Bauer has a firm opinion about Venice's love-hate relationship with tourism. 'I provide information to my guests about the eccentricities of Venice and how to best navigate the city. People come here with a fantasy that they can have Venice all to themselves ; it's impossible. I live here because of the quality of life – the physical and psychological well-being that the city provides. I have invested my time and money in this city because I love it – otherwise I'd sell it all and move. Like anything, it is a balance, but the good far outweighs the bad. Yes, sometimes it's difficult, but this city is worth it.'

Native son Sergio Boldrin is a mask maker. His tiny shop, La Bottega dei Mascareri, shares a wall with the oldest church in town, San Giacomo di Rialto, in the tourist-crammed area by the Rialto bridge. With a weary eye, he has watched meat and milk give way to trinkets and T-shirts. 'It would be ridiculous for me to criticise tourists, since they are my livelihood – Venetians certainly don't buy masks. But the tourists are only on a few *calli*, the main arteries. Where I live, over in Santa Marta, many people never see a tourist except when they ride the vaporetto. There are people in my neighbourhood who get to piazza San Marco once a year. If they are honest, any Venetian will tell you they would rather live in Venice than in Mestre, but they just can't afford to buy an apartment. Why is life in Venice so expensive? Simple. Because it's better here.'

Better, but not perfect. There's much to put to rights: Venice is so busy that at times it can seem like one big construction site. A fourth bridge over the Grand Canal, designed by Spain's architectural superstar Santiago Calatrava (*see p34* **Shining path of light**) – was due to be unveiled late in 2004.

The world-famous La Fenice opera house (*see p219* **Phoenix from the flames**), gutted by fire in 1996, reopened for the 2004-5 season.

Plans are afoot to enlarge and restore the Gallerie dell'Accademia (*see p130*). All over town, canals are being dredged and *fondamente* raised in the ongoing war against *acqua alta*. And the controversial MoSE flood barrier at the *bocche* – entrances – to the lagoon now looks as if it will be built.

Over on the Lido, an international competition has been announced to find a design for a new Palazzo del Cinema three times the size of the current structure (*see chapter* **Film**). In Mestre , the piazza and *campanile* have been restored. Among the high-tech businesses attracted to the rapidly developing Venice Gateway for Science and Technology park (VEGA) at the northern end of Porto Marghera, is a nanotechnologies laboratory, placing Venice in the running for title of world leader in the technology that manipulates matter on a scale below 100 nanometres. Equally impressive, San Giuliano – a vast, verdant area on the mainland between Venice airport and the road and rail bridge across the lagoon – has been converted from a dumping ground for industrial and urban waste into the largest city park in Europe, with 11 miles of bike paths.

The real Venice – not the Venice of the day tripper – remains insular and strong, and is only slowly revealed to the newcomer. Ironically, mass tourism seems to affect tourists themselves more than residents, who have adjusted their lives around it, manoeuvring through the labyrinth of *calli* largely unobserved by visitors.

Much of Venetian life takes place behind closed doors, concealed from the casual observer. Venetians have always maintained their unique code of conduct and ethics, their particular sense of time. An isolated culture, hedged about by water, one that remained an independent republic for over a millennium, one that once lorded it over the entire Mediterranean, cannot be easily penetrated by an outsider, although everyone and anyone is welcome to try. Otherwise, feel free to sit back and enjoy the show.

Tintoretto's
Stealing of the body of St Mark.

Veronese's
Mystic Marriage of St Catherine.

Venetian Painting

Shimmering light effects and warm tonalities:
Venetian painting reflects the city itself

Of all the pleasures that lure visitors to Venice – the mid-afternoon *ombra* of local wine, gliding in a gondola, a concert featuring the wiry and insistent melodies of Vivaldi – perhaps the most consistent draw has been her great paintings. From the 15th century to the 21st, connoisseurs have come to Venice to take in acres of delectable pictures.

In 1557, a Venetian dialogue on art proclaimed that 'painting was invented primarily to give pleasure'. Those lucky enough to spend an hour in the church of the Frari (*see p120*) or the Scuola Grande di San Rocco (*see p123*) typically became addicted to the visual gratification Venetian painting provides. Even a visitor as tight-lipped as the Victorian critic John Ruskin (*see p44* **Throwing stones**) permitted himself paroxysms of delight when confronted with a picture by his beloved 'Tintoret' or 'John' Bellini.

Today, thanks to significantly longer opening hours in churches and museums, determined travellers can indulge their eyeballs as long as their feet hold out.

Visual pleasure in Venice is made more acute because many great pictures remain in the buildings for which they were painted. The attentive art pilgrim can maximise enjoyment by observing carefully a painting's technique and its setting, since the two are intertwined more in Venice than anywhere else on the globe. Leave the madding crowd at San Marco behind, and you'll soon come across superb pictures in obscure churches: glowing altarpieces and pulsating canvas *laterali* (paintings for side walls of chapels). Seeing these pictures in their original sites reveals how aware painters were of the relation of their works to the surrounding architecture, light and existing artwork. Yet, exceptionally, the paintings also relate to the physical context of Venice itself. What makes Venetian painting distinctive – the decorated surfaces, asymmetry, shimmering light effects and, above all, warm tonalities – can also be found in the lagoon environment. Venetian visual culture during the Renaissance encompassed the richness of Byzantine mosaics and Islamic art, the haphazard arrangement of streets and canals with their strong shadows, and light experienced through haze or reflected off moving water.

THE END OF ANONYMITY

Venetian church interiors were once covered with frescoes; the damp climate means that very few of these earliest works survive today. The official history of Venetian painting begins in the 1320s with the first painter to emerge from medieval anonymity, **Paolo Veneziano** (c1290-1362), who worked in egg tempera and gold leaf on wood panel. He championed the composite altarpiece, which would become one of the key formats of Venetian painting. His polyptychs, such as the newly-cleaned *The Coronation of the Virgin* in the Accademia (see p130), were ornately framed, compartmentalised works featuring sumptuous fabrics, a preference for surface decoration and pattern over depth, and a seriousness – or stiffness – derived from Byzantine icons. A love of drapery and textile patterns proved to be a Venetian constant, still visible in Veronese's paintings in the 16th century and in Tiepolo's in the 18th century.

'Technique and setting are more intertwined in Venice than anywhere on the globe.'

Although many painters worked in Venice in the century after Paolo, the next major legacy was that of a team, **Giovanni d'Alemagna** (John of Germany) and his brother-in-law **Antonio Vivarini**, active in the mid 15th century. Their three altarpieces in San Zaccaria (see p95; pictured p29, right) dated 1443, one in San Pantalon (see p123) and an imposing canvas triptych in the Accademia demonstrate the transition from Gothic to Renaissance.

All have benefited from recent restorations that recapture the original courtly elegance and three-dimensional details in *pastiglia* (raised ornament). Although Italian art historians give precedence to Antonio, the sudden decline in the quality of his works after Giovanni's death in 1450 indicates that his partner was the brains behind the operation. Antonio's younger brother **Bartolomeo**

Vivarini, who ran the family workshop from the 1470s until about 1491, learned Renaissance style from both painting and sculpture, as seen in the lapidary figures in the altarpiece (1474) in the Cappella Corner of the Frari (see p120).

By the next generation, the main players had become more clearly defined. From around 1480 **Giovanni Bellini** directed the dominant workshop in Venice. Most of Bellini's sizeable output, stretching from the late 1450s until his death in 1516, was painted on wood panel rather than the newer canvas. He cornered the market in small, devotional panels commissioned by cultivated private clients.

'Modern painting was born in Venice around 1500.'

The important group of early Bellini pictures in the Museo Correr (see p83) and the many variations on the Madonna and Child theme in the Accademia show how varied and moving these subjects could be. Equally impressive is Bellini's stunning series of altarpieces. In these he perfected the subject of the *Sacra conversazione* (Sacred Conversation), where standing saints flank a seated figure, usually the Virgin Mary, within a setting that evokes the gold mosaics and costly marbles of the Basilica di San Marco. The inner glow afforded by the new medium of oil paint allowed Bellini to model his figures with an astonishing delicacy of light and shadow. One can follow his progress through a series of altarpieces that remain in situ: in Santi Giovanni e Paolo (see p94), the Frari, San Zaccaria and San Giovanni Crisostomo (see p103). A letter home by German painter Albrecht Dürer in 1506 shows that Bellini's fame was great in his own lifetime: 'Giovanni Bellini is very old but he is still the best painter of all.' (Dürer would have agreed that Bellini deserved a cocktail named after him.)

Giovanni's elder brother, **Gentile Bellini**, enjoyed even greater official success: from 1474 until his death in 1507 he directed the decoration of the Palazzo Ducale, replacing crumbling frescoes with huge canvases. He also performed a diplomatic role for the Venetian government by travelling to Constantinople in 1479 to paint for the Ottoman sultan. Although his Palazzo Ducale canvases were destroyed by fire in 1577, his *Procession in Piazza San Marco* (1496), now in the Accademia, shows his ability to depict sumptuous public spectacle with choreographed verve.

> ▶ For artistic terms, see p295 **Glossary**

Getting into shape

Venetian painting can be better appreciated by studying the format – by which we mean the shape and size – of a picture. A building's architecture sometimes forced artists to adapt their compositions to take account of unwieldy spaces. Solutions could be rather ingenious: for instance, Tintoretto's *Christ before the People* is sandwiched above a door in the Scuola di San Rocco (*see p123*), and Palma il Giovane's own monument is wedged between the organ and a corbel in Santi Giovanni e Paolo (*see p94*).

Generally artists were asked to paint more orthodox shapes, however, and each format carried certain assumptions for Renaissance painters and viewers. For centuries, the most prestigious format available was the altarpiece, a picture decorating the altar table where Mass was said. In the 14th century, altarpieces were polyptychs, with tiers of painted compartments arrayed horizontally.

Altarpieces themselves had to relate in width to the altar table before them. Since by tradition these tables were supposed to replicate the table of the Last Supper and a sarcophagus, the only way altarpieces could grow was by going up. In the second half of the 15th century, altarpieces became vertical in orientation, and the polyptych was abandoned in favour of the *pala*, a large, single-field work.

If the altarpieces of Giovanni Bellini's era were sometimes monumental (eg Bellini's in San Zaccaria, *pictured below centre*), those of later generations – such as Titian's dramatic *Assumption* in the Frari (*see p120*) or Veronese's high altar in San Sebastiano (*see p125*) – could be gargantuan, rising to four metres or more in height. Artists then had to adjust their compositions to fit these larger vertical fields, typically filling the upper sections with architecture or figures perched in clouds.

The damp Venetian climate meant that the side walls of chapels were rarely covered in frescoes, the norm in the rest of Italy. Instead, large horizontal canvases called *laterali*, depicting narrative scenes, became the rule for mural decoration. Artists executing both altarpiece and *laterali* for a chapel, like Tintoretto's in San Cassiano (*see p118*), created a unified ensemble.

The vertical rectangle is so associated with altarpieces that it can come as a surprise when the format performs other functions. In Room VI of the Accademia, two Tintoretto canvases – featuring Saints George and Alvise, and Saints Andrew and Jerome – possess both the vertical shape and the sacred subjects customary for altarpieces. Yet these were executed for the Palazzo dei Camerlenghi, the headquarters of the State Treasures at the Rialto, and the saints commemorate the names of key officials in 1551-2: Giorgio Venier, Alvise Foscarini,

Andrea Dandolo and Girolamo Bernardo. Other paintings that look like altarpieces – for example Tintoretto's *St Peter's Vision of the Cross* and the *Execution of St Paul* in the apse of the Madonna dell'Orto – are the dismembered inner wings of organ shutters.

Ceiling paintings could be varied in shape, often octagonal or oval, as seen throughout the Palazzo Ducale. Thus paintings now in museums with these formats (and an off-centre point of view) might originally have been set into a Venetian wooden ceiling.

In the Renaissance, as today, the portrait format tended to be a vertical rectangle. The exceptions – in the 'landscape' format – are group portraits, or the unsettling individual portraits of Lorenzo Lotto, like the *Portrait of a Youth (pictured below left)* in the Accademia, which are greater in width than in height. By playing with assumptions about format, painters could challenge both rivals and viewers.

Three painters born in the second half of the 15th century and who were active in the 16th are worth seeking out. **Cima da Conegliano** (c1459-1517) offers a stiffer style than Bellini, with figures standing in dignified repose against crisp landscapes. Cima's best altarpieces, in the Accademia, and at San Giovanni in Bragora (*see p101*), the Madonna dell'Orto (recently restored, *see p108*) and the Carmini (*see p128*), all demonstrate a mastery of light.

Vittore Carpaccio (c1465-1525) specialised in narrative works for the *scuole* (*see p99* **Back to school**). These canvases tell a story from left to right, and offer enough miscellaneous detail to immerse the viewer in the daily life of Renaissance Venice. Two intact cycles from around 1500 are among the treasures of Venetian painting: the grand St Ursula cycle in the Accademia and that of St George and St Jerome in the intimate Scuola di San Giorgio degli Schiavoni (*see p101*).

Lorenzo Lotto (c1480-1556), active throughout the first half of the 16th century, spent much of his career outside Venice: he was an entrepreneur who knew how to create markets in provincial centres. His best altarpieces in Venice, in the Carmini and Santi Giovanni e Paolo, combine an uncanny accuracy in rendering landscape or cloth with a deeply felt spirituality. His impressive portraits, such as the *Portrait of a Youth*, displayed in the Accademia, employ an unusual horizontal format and convey a seemingly modern melancholy.

SECULAR SUBJECTS

At the beginning of the 16th century, Venetian painting took a dramatic turn. Three of Bellini's pupils – Giorgione, Sebastiano del Piombo and Titian – experimented with new secular subject matter and new ways of handling paint. **Giorgione** (c1477-1510) remains one of the great enigmas of art. No other reputation rests on so few surviving pictures. The hard contours and emphasis on surface pattern seen in earlier Venetian painting have softened in his work, and for the first time the atmosphere becomes palpable, like damp lagoon air. Two haunting pictures in the Accademia, *La Tempesta* and *La Vecchia*, may be deliberately enigmatic, more concerned with mood than story. It can be argued that the modern concept of the painting was born in Venice around 1500. For the first time, three conditions that we now take for granted were met: these works were all oil on canvas, painted at the artist's initiative, and not intended for a specific location.

Sebastiano del Piombo (c1485-1547) left his mark with a similar emphasis on softened

Tintoretto's *Birth of St John* in San Zaccaria.

contour and tangible atmosphere. His major altarpiece, which was painted in around 1507 and can still be seen in San Giovanni Crisostomo, shows a *Sacra conversazione* in which some of the figures are seen in profile, rather than head-on, and hidden in shadow. Even more exciting is a set of standing saints painted as organ shutters, now in the Accademia, which show an unprecedented application of thick paint (*impasto*).

TITIAN AND TINTORETTO

Events conspired to boost the early career of **Titian** (Tiziano Vecellio, c1488-1576) when, in the space of only six years (1510-16), Giorgione fell victim to the plague, Sebastiano del Piombo moved to Rome and Giovanni Bellini died. Titian soon staked his claim with a dynamic *Assumption of the Virgin* for the high altar of the Frari (1518). There he dominated the enormous space by creating the largest panel painting in the world. Although Titian gained fame throughout Europe for his portraits and mythological paintings, no examples of these survive in Venice.

The lagoon city is, however, the place to appreciate in situ the nearly 70-year span of the master's religious work. These include a second, glorious altarpiece in the Frari (the *Madonna di Ca' Pesaro*, which is a *Sacra conversazione* rotated on its axis), the virile St Christopher fresco in the Palazzo Ducale (*see p85*) and the ceiling paintings in the sacristy of the Salute (*see p132*).

For a decade (c1527-39) Titian had a true rival in **Pordenone** (1483?-1539), a painter of muscular figures engaged in violent action. Now, for the first time in decades, Pordenone's work can be appreciated in Venice. The recently restored *Saints Christopher and Martin* in the church of San Rocco (*see p123*) shows an urgent style that had great appeal. Even more interesting is the confrontation in the reopened church of San Giovanni Elemosinario (*see p115*), where Pordenone's bulging figures on the right altar square off against the soft contours of Titian's high altar. Yet once again Titian reaped good fortune when his adversary suddenly died.

By the 1560s, in works such as the extraordinary *Annunciation* in San Salvador (*see p88*), Titian's handling of paint had become so loose that forms were not so much defined by contours as caressed into being. Line was replaced by quivering patches of warm colouring. Canvas, which had originally been seen as a cheap and durable substitute for fresco or wood, was now a textured surface to exploit. Contemporaries swore that the old artist painted as often with his fingers as with the brush. Nowhere is this tactile quality more apparent than in Titian's final painting, a *Pietà*, originally intended for his tomb, and now in the Accademia. Left unfinished at his death during the plague of 1576, this picture summarises the Venetian artistic tradition, with its glittering mosaic dome and forms so dissolved as to challenge the very conventions of painting.

Instead of mourning Titian's death, Jacopo Robusti (c1518-94) – better known as **Tintoretto** – probably breathed a sigh of relief. Though he rose to fame in the late 1540s, he had to wait until he was 58 years old before he could claim the title of Venice's greatest living painter. Yet Tintoretto was canny enough to learn from his rival. He supposedly inscribed the motto 'The drawing of Michelangelo and the colouring of Titian' on the wall of his studio. Tintoretto's breakthrough work, *The Miracle of the Slave* (1548), now in

the Accademia, offered a brash attempt at this synthesis, combining Michelangelo's confident muscular anatomies with Titian's glistening paint surface. Borrowing the figure types and violent compositions of Pordenone, Tintoretto's aggressive and tumultuous canvases marked the end of the decorative narrative painting tradition perfected by Carpaccio.

As Ruskin noted in *The Stones of Venice*, Tintoretto, unlike Titian, is an artist who can only be appreciated in Venice. Among the dozens of works in his home town, the soaring choir paintings in the Madonna dell'Orto (c1560) or the many canvases at the Scuola Grande di San Rocco (*see p123*), executed 1564-87, amaze in their scale and complexity. Tintoretto offered his clients free pictures or discounts, revealing a knack for marketing.

His many workshop assistants, including two sons and a daughter, allowed him to increase production to unprecedented quantities. Like his contemporaries Bassano and Veronese, Tintoretto went even further than Titian in the liberation of the brush stroke. Rough brushwork and *impasto* served as a sort of signature for these artists. The tradition of bravura handling that goes from Rubens to Delacroix to De Kooning begins with the action painters of 16th-century Venice.

'Tintoretto, unlike Titian, is an artist who can only be appreciated in Venice.'

Paolo Veronese (1528-88) made his impact in Venice with a love of rich fabrics and elegant poses that contrast with Tintoretto's agitated figures. Veronese's savoir faire is best seen in the overpopulated feasts he painted for monastery refectories. The example now in the Accademia got its painter in hot water. When confronted by the Inquisition in 1573 over a *Last Supper* in which figures of 'buffoons, drunkards, Germans, dwarves' apparently insulted church decorum, Veronese cleverly got around the Inquisition's command to alter the picture by changing the title to *Feast in the House of Levi*. Veronese's wit can also be seen in one of the few great 16th-century mythological paintings remaining in Venice: *The Rape of Europa* in the Palazzo Ducale, with its leering, slightly comical bull. His supreme ensemble piece is in San Sebastiano (*see p125*), a church that features altars, ceilings, frescoes and organ shutters all painted by Veronese, as well as the artist's tomb.

Venetian painting was also practised outside Venice: **Jacopo Bassano** (c1510-92) was an artist based in a provincial centre who kept pace with the latest innovations. Although his work is best seen in his home town of Bassano del Grappa (*see p267*), canvases in the Accademia and an altarpiece in San Giorgio Maggiore (*see p136*) display characteristic Venetian flickering brush work and dramatic chiaroscuro.

With the following generation, the golden age of Venetian painting drew to a close. The super-prolific **Palma il Giovane** (c1548-1628), who completed Titian's *Pietà*, now in the Accademia, created works loosely in the style of Tintoretto. His finest pictures, such as the *Crucifixion* in the Madonna dell'Orto or those in San Giacomo dell'Orio (*see p118*) or the Oratorio dei Crociferi (*see p109*), all date from the 1580s. After the deaths of Veronese and Tintoretto it seems that the pressure was gone and the quality of Palma's work took a nosedive. The decline of Venetian painting at the end of the Renaissance can be seen at San Giovanni Elemosinario, finally open after decades *in restauro*. Although outsized canvases by painters active at the end of the 16th century crowd the church's walls, the aforementioned small altarpieces by Titian and Pordenone executed more than half a century earlier outshine their progeny and dominate the space.

BAROQUE AND ROCOCO

In the years that followed, the Baroque in Venice was represented largely by out-of-towners (**Luca Giordano**, whose restored altarpieces adorn the Salute) or by bizarre posturing (**Gian Antonio Fumiani**'s stupefying canvas ceiling in San Pantalon). Exaggerated light effects ruled the day. It was only at the beginning of the 18th century, as Venetian power slipped away, that Venetian painting experienced a resurgence. In the first half of the century, **Giambattista Piazzetta** (1683-1754) produced a ceiling painting in Santi Giovanni e Paolo and a sequence of altarpieces (particularly those in Santa Maria della Fava, *see p88*, the Gesuati, *see p133*, and San Salvador), all demonstrating restrained elegance and a muted palette of gold, black and brown. He enlivened otherwise static compositions by placing the figures in a zigzag arrangement.

Giambattista Tiepolo (1696-1770), the greatest painter of the Venetian rococo, adapted Piazzetta's zigzag scheme for use with warm pastel colours. In his monumental ceilings in the Gesuati, the Pietà (*see p99*) and Ca' Rezzonico (*see p127*), Tiepolo reintroduced frescoes on a large scale after more than two centuries of canvas ceilings. Perhaps the most satisfying place to view his work is the upper room of the Scuola Grande dei Carmini (*see p128*), where

the disproportionately low ceiling provides a close-up view of his technique. The depth of Venetian talent in the 18th century is demonstrated by the painters of impressive facility overshadowed by the dazzling Tiepolo, starting with his own son, **Giandomenico Tiepolo** (1727-1804).

Though frequently his father's top assistant, Giandomenico can be seen at his independent best in an eerie cycle of 14 *Stations of the Cross* in San Polo, which he executed as a 20-year-old. **Gaspare Diziani** (1689-1767) deserves credit for three gorgeous ceiling canvases on the life of St Helen, recently cleaned, in the former meeting room of the Scuola del Vin (wine merchants' confraternity), entered through the church of San Silvestro (*see p116*).

Above all, the essence of the Venetian rococo is to be found in the sites where architecture, sculpture and painting were employed to form a unified whole: the Gesuati, Santa Maria della Fava, San Stae (*see p119*) and the furnished rooms of Ca' Rezzonico.

> ### 'As political and economic power slipped away, Venetian painting experienced a resurgence.'

In the 18th century, both local and foreign collectors provided a constant demand for portraits and city views. A woman artist, **Rosalba Carriera** (1675-1757), developed a refined portrait style using pastels. **Canaletto** (1697-1768) and **Guardi** (1712-93) offered views of Venice, respectively in sharp focus and softly blurred. The popularity of these landscape paintings as Grand Tour souvenirs means that although examples exist in the Accademia and Ca' Rezzonico, both artists are seen at their best in Britain. A different aspect of 18th-century painting, and perhaps Guardi's masterpiece, can be seen in the astonishingly delicate *Stories of Tobias* (1750-3) decorating the organ loft in the church of Angelo Raffaele (*see p125*). **Pietro Longhi** (1702-85) was a sort of Venetian Hogarth, creating amusing, naïve genre scenes in which the social life of his day was gently satirised.

By the time of Napoleon's conquest in 1797, Venetian painting, like Venetian military power, was a spent force. The capital of the art world in the 19th century was Paris. Over the following 200 years, however, Venice's unique setting and lavish collections have remained a magnet for foreign visitors, including artists. Venice now exhibits painters, rather than producing them.

Italian pavilion at **La Biennale**. *See p36.*

Architecture

Inspiration for the Venetian cityscape comes from
far and wide.

Venice's architecture is based on borrowings,
assimilations and blatant theft. Not content
with drawing architectural inspiration from
Constantinople and Rome, and decorating its
palazzi with looted treasures, it also looked
beyond the lagoon for its architects. Of the four
who can altered the fabric of the city, three are
out-of-towners: Tuscan-born Jacopo Sansovino;
Vicenza-based Andrea Palladio (*see pp38-42*
Palladian Villas); and early Renaissance
master Mauro Codussi from Bergamo (*see p145*
Dark horse). The only native talent is Baroque
wonderboy Baldassare Longhena.

MEDIEVAL AND BYZANTINE

It all started in Torcello, where the Cathedral
of Santa Maria Assunta (*see p145*), founded
in 639, is the oldest surviving building on
the lagoon. It has been remodelled since then –
notably in the ninth and 11th centuries –
but still retains the simple form of an early
Christian basilica. Next door, the 11th-century
church of Santa Fosca (*see p144*) has a Greek
cross plan – also found in San Giacomo al Rialto

(*see p114*), traditionally considered the earliest
church in Venice. The portico of Santa Fosca
exhibits a feature that recurs in the first-floor
windows of 12th-century townhouses on the
Grand Canal – stilted arches, with horseshoe-
shaped arches supported on slender columns.

The history of Venetian architecture can be
charted by following the development of the
arch, the most typically Venetian of all
structural devices. This is understandable
in a city built on mud, where load-bearing
capabilities were a prime consideration. In the
latter part of the 13th century the pure, curved
Byzantine arch began to sport a point at the
top, under the influence of Islamic models –
an early example of this can be seen in the
heavily restored Albergo del Selvadego in
calle dell'Ascensione (San Marco). Soon this
point developed into a fully fledged ogee arch –
a northern Gothic trait.

Meanwhile, San Marco's basilica (*see p79*)
was into its sixth century of growth. Founded
in 829-32, the original church was modelled on

the Church of the Apostles in Constantinople. This first church burnt down, but had been rebuilt by 1075. The main body of the church – with its Greek cross plan surmounted by five domes – dates from the 11th century; but it was embellished extensively over the next four centuries, sometimes with curious results (note the curved Byzantine arches on the façade surmounted by hopeful Gothic ogees). Two humbler 12th-century churches, San Giacomo dell'Orio (*see p118*) and San Nicolò dei Mendicoli (*see p125*), both feature squat bell towers detached from the church – a key feature of the Veneto-Byzantine style.

GOTHIC & LATE GOTHIC

In the 14th and 15th centuries Venetian architecture developed an individual character unmatched before or since. It was at this time – when Venice had beaten Genoa for control of eastern Mediterranean sea routes, and when the Republic was engaged in large-scale *terra firma* expansion – that the city's own Arab-tinged version of Gothic came into its own.

By the mid 14th century the ogee arch (two concave-convex curves meeting at the top) had sprouted a point on the inside of its concave edge – producing the cusped arch, which distributes the forces pressing down

Shining path of light

Venetians have traditionally been content to paddle across their high street: until the mid 19th century, in fact, only the Rialto (built 1588-92) spanned the Grand Canal, joining the city's two halves. Perhaps this explains the lukewarm welcome given by Venetians to the much-heralded fourth bridge – due to be unveiled in late 2004 – described as a 'shining path of light' by its creator, Spanish architectural whizz Santiago Calatrava.

Venice's Austrian occupiers were responsible for bridging key points in the city: the rail link to the mainland was their idea, as were the iron bridges that stood where the *ponti* dell'Accademia and degli Scalzi now stand. The former was replaced in the 1930s by a wooden construction, an exact replica of which was contructed in the 1980s; the latter was substituted, in 1934, by the deceptively venerable-looking structure standing outside

the railway station today. Calatrava's latest creation (building site *pictured above*) will span the Grand Canal from a point near the railway station to piazzale Roma, Venice's road and bus hub.

Critics have questioned the need to link these two (alternative) points of arrival/departure; they've pointed out, moreover, that the new bridge cuts less than ten minutes off the existing hike. Also, citizens' rights groups are incensed that wheelchair access to the bridge was cobbled together by city council engineers after it was not included in the original plan.

Stunning as Calatrava's creation is, its siting in what passes for Venice's dingy outskirts begs the question: how serious is the council's boasted commitment to bringing contemporary design to this historic city?

on it so efficiently that John Ruskin (*see p44* **Throwing stones**) decreed that 'all are imperfect except these'.

'The Palazzo Ducale was a prime example of the Venetian faith in tradition'

By the beginning of the 15th century, this basic shape had been hedged around with elaborate tracery and trefoils (clover-shaped openings) and topped with Moorish-looking pinnacles in a peculiarly Venetian take on the flamboyant Gothic style, which reached its apotheosis in the façades of the Palazzo Ducale (*see p85*) and the Ca' D'Oro (*see p103*) – both completed by 1440. The Palazzo Ducale was a prime example of the Venetian faith in tradition: a design first initiated in the 1340s – was duplicated faithfully over the following century; the florid Porta della Carta (1438; *see p85*) marks this passage of time most dramatically.

CHURCHES AND SCUOLE

Outside of Saint Mark's, church architecture mainly reflected the traditional building styles of the orders which commissioned the work: the cavernous brick monuments of Santi Giovanni e Paolo (completed in 1430; *see p84*) and the Frari (1433; *see p120*) are classic examples of, respectively, the Dominican and Franciscan approaches. Both have a Latin cross plan, a façade pierced by a large rose window and a generous sprinkling of pinnacles. More individual are churches such as Santo Stefano (*see p90*), with its wooden ship's-keel roof, and the first *scuole* (*see p85* **Back to school**), such as the Scuola Vecchia della Misericordia (*see p107*), with its ogee windows and oddly Flemish-style roof gable. Both involved the collaboration of **Giovanni** and **Bartolomeo Bon**, who also worked on the Ca' D'Oro. These mid 15th-century sculptors and masons are among the first named 'architects'.

THE VENETIAN PALAZZO

Majestic Grand Canal palaces such as Ca' Foscari (begun in 1452) and Palazzo Pisani Moretta (for both, *see p74*) continued to indulge the yen for elaborate tracery windows, but behind the façade the structure went back centuries. The Venetian palazzo was not only a place of residence; it was also the family business headquarters, and the internal division of space reflects this, with loading and storage space below a magnificent first floor *piano nobile*.

On the roof, between those funnel-shaped chimneys, there was often a raised wooden balcony or *altana*, where clothes were dried

and Titianesque beauties bleached their hair in the sun. In a city where space was at a premium, courtyards were almost unheard of.

EARLY RENAISSANCE

Venetians were so fond of their own gracefully oriental version of Gothic that they held on to it long after the new classicist orthodoxy had taken over central Italy. For the second half of the 15th century, emergent Renaissance forms existed alongside the Gothic swansong. Sometimes they merged or clashed in the same building, as in the church of San Zaccaria (*see p95*), which was begun by **Antonio Gambello** in 1458 in the purest of northern Gothic styles but completed by **Mauro Codussi** in the local Renaissance idiom he was then elaborating.

Next to nothing is known about Codussi's background, save that he may have trained under Giovanni Bon. In 1469 he was appointed *protomagister* (works manager) for the church of San Michele in Isola (*see p140*), on what is now the city's cemetery island. Within ten years he had completed the first truly Renaissance building in the city. The austere Istrian marble façade with its classical elements has something Palladian about it, though the curves of the pediment and buttresses are pure Codussi, adapted from a late Gothic model.

LOMBARDESQUE STYLE

Codussi took over a number of projects begun by **Pietro Lombardo**, who represents the other strand of early Renaissance architecture in northern Italy. This was based on the extensive use of inlaid polychrome marble, Corinthian columns and decorated friezes. Lombardo's masterpiece is the jewel-like church of Santa Maria dei Miracoli (*see p110*), but he also designed – with his sons Tullio and Antonio – the lower part of the façade of the Scuola Grande di San Marco (*see p95*), with its trompe l'oeil relief. The Lombardesque style, as it was known, was all the rage for a while, producing such charmers as tiny, lopsided Ca' Dario (1487-92; *see p129*) on the Grand Canal.

HIGH RENAISSANCE

Codussi's influence lingered well into the 16th century in the work of architects such as **Guglielmo dei Grigi** and **Scarpagnino**, both of whom have been credited with the design of the Palazzo dei Camerlenghi (1525-8) next to the Rialto bridge. It was around this time that piazza San Marco took on the shape we see today, with the construction of the Procuratie Vecchie (*see p78*) and the Torre dell'Orologio (*see p87*), both to designs by Codussi and both demonstrating that in the centre of civic power, loyalty to the myth of Venice tended to override architectural fashions and impose a faintly antiquarian style harking back to the city's Veneto-Byzantine origins. It was not until the late 1520s that something really new turned up, in the form of **Jacopo Sansovino**, a Tuscan sculptor.

Perhaps it was the influence of his new-found friends Pietro Aretino and Titian (*see p89* **Poison pen**) that secured him the prestigious position of *protomagister* of St Mark's only two years after his arrival, despite his lack of experience; certainly the gamble paid off, as Sansovino went on to create a series of buildings that changed the face of the city. He began to refine his rational, harmonious Renaissance style in designs for the church of San Francesco della Vigna (begun in 1532; *see p83*) and Palazzo Corner della Ca' Grande on the Grand Canal, Venice's first Roman-style palazzo, with a heavy debt to Bramante.

'Palladio set the agenda for the 16th century.'

But it was in piazza San Marco that Sansovino surpassed himself, in three buildings planned in the course of 1536 and 1537. La Zecca (*see p87*) – the state mint – with its heavy rustication and four-square solidity, is a perfect financial fortress. The Biblioteca Marciana (*see p83*; completed in 1554, also known as the Libreria Sansoviniana) is his masterpiece, disguising its classical regularity beneath a typically Venetian wealth of surface detail. Finally, the little Loggetta (*see p83*) at the base of the Campanile showed that Sansovino was also capable of a lightness of touch that derived from his sculptural training.

PALLADIAN PRE-EMINENCE
Michele Sanmicheli, primarily a military architect, built the imposing sea defences on the island of Le Vignole, and two hefty Venetian *palazzi*, the Palazzo Corner Mocenigo (1559-64) in campo San Polo and the Palazzo Grimani (1556-75) on the Grand Canal. But it was another out-of-towner, **Andrea Palladio**, who would set the agenda for what was left of the 16th century (*see pp38-42* **Palladian Villas**).

A star in his adopted town of Vicenza, the man who invented the post-Renaissance found it difficult to get a foothold in a city that valued flexibility above critical rigour. But he did design two influential churches: San Giorgio Maggiore (begun in 1562; *see p135*) and the Redentore (1577-92; *see p135*). Anyone who considers Palladio's designs to be over-simplistic should observe the subtle play of levels and orders on the exterior. The church of the Zitelle (*see p134*), also on the Giudecca, was built to Palladio plans after the architect's death.

Palladio's disciple **Vincenzo Scamozzi** designed the Procuratie Nuove (*see p78*) to complete the north side of piazza San Marco. At the same time, **Antonio Da Ponte** was commissioned to design a stone bridge at the Rialto (*see p74*) in 1588 after designs by Michelangelo and Palladio had been rejected.

BAROQUE
The examples of Sansovino and Palladio continued to be felt well into the 17th century, though buildings such as Palazzo Balbi (1582-90) on the Grand Canal, by **Alessandro Vittoria**, showed the first signs of a transition to Baroque opulence. But it wasn't until the arrival on the scene of **Baldassare Longhena** in the 1620s that Venice got twirly bits in any abundance. Longhena was a local boy who first made his mark with the Duomo (*see p139*) in Chioggia. But it was with the church of Santa Maria della Salute (*see p132*) that he pulled out all the stops, creating perhaps the greatest Baroque edifice outside of Rome. Commissioned in 1632, and 50 years in the making, this huge, circular and highly theatrical church dominates the southern reaches of the Grand Canal.

Longhena was also busy designing a series of impressive *palazzi* for rich clients, including the huge Grand Canal hulk of Ca' Pesaro (begun in 1652; *see p116*). He also designed the façade of the Ospedaletto (1667-74; *see p94*), with its grotesque telamons.

This was a taste of things to come: the overwrought façade developed in the 1670s through the exuberance of the Scalzi (*see p104*) and Santa Maria Del Giglio (*see p91*) churches – both the work of Longhena's follower **Giuseppe Scalzi** – to the bombastic drama of San Moisè (*see p91*), a kitsch collaboration between **Alessandro Tremignon** and sculptor **Heinrich Meyring**.

La Biennale

Venice's best showcase for cutting-edge design is the Biennale di Architettura, where some of the world's hottest architects and installation artists present their visions for the future at the Giardini della Biennale (*see p97*) or in the spectacular exhibition space carved out of the Arsenale complex (*see p97*). This show runs from the second week of September to the first week of November in even-numbered years. For information call 041 521 8711 or consult www.labiennale.org.

In Context

NEOCLASSICISM

During the 18th-century decline, tired variations on Palladio and Longhena dominated the scene. **Domenico Rossi** adorned Palladian orders with swags and statuary in the façades he designed for the churches of San Stae (1709-10; *see p119*) and the Gesuiti (1715-28; *see p109*). Sumptuous palaces continued to go up along the Grand Canal; one of the last was the solid Palazzo Grassi (*see p90*), built between 1748 and 1772. It was designed by **Giorgio Massari**, the most successful of the city's 18th-century architects. Massari also designed the church of La Pietà (*see p99*) – the Vivaldi church – the oval floorplan of which strikes a rare note of originality (though it may have been copied from a church by Sansovino that was swept away by Napoleon). The Palazzo Venier dei Leoni – now home to the Peggy Guggenheim Collection (*see p130*) – also dates from the mid 18th century. If it had ever been finished, this huge palazzo would have been as boring as Palazzo Grassi, but funds ran out after the first storey, giving Venice one of its most bizarrely endearing landmarks.

Giannantonio Selva's La Fenice opera house (1790-2; *see p91*) – devastated by fire in January 1996 and finally reopened in 2004 – was one of the Serene Republic's last building projects. Napoleon's arrival in 1797 marked the destruction of many churches and convents, but also began a series of clearances that allowed for the creation of the city's first public gardens, the Giardini pubblici (*see p97*), and the nearby thoroughfare now known as via Garibaldi. Piazza San Marco took on its present-day appearance at this time, too, when the Procuratie Vecchie and Nuove were united by the neoclassical Ala Napoleonica (*see p79*).

Though one project – the railway bridge linking Venice to Mestre (1841-2) – put an end to the city's history of isolation, restoration rather than building dominated the Austrian occupation of Venice (1815-66). This trend was reinforced by John Ruskin in his influential book the *Stones of Venice* (1853). Ruskin set out to discredit 'the pestilent art of the Renaissance' in favour of 'healthy and beautiful' Gothic. Such was the clout of Ruskin and his stiff-collared Victorian cronies that the city became an architectural sacred cow, untouchable by the unclean hand of innovation.

SINCE THE RISORGIMENTO

Little wonder then, that the years when Venice became a part of modern Italy were also the years when it began to recreate its Gothic and Byzantine past. An example is the Palazzo Franchetti next to the Ponte dell'Accademia, a 15th-century edifice redesigned in neo-medieval style (1878-82) by opera composer and librettist **Camillo Boito**. One of the city's most elegant neo-Gothic constructions is the cemetery of San Michele (1872-81; *see p140*), the pinnacle-and-arch brick facing of which dominates the northern lagoon view. Another landmark from the same period is the Molino Stucky (1897-1920; *see p134*), a huge former pasta mill and grain silo at the western end of the Giudecca designed in turreted Hanseatic Gothic style by **Ernest Wullekopf**. The turn of the century was also a boom time for hotels, with the Excelsior on the Lido (1898-1908) setting the eclectic, Moorish-Byzantine agenda.

MODERN ARCHITECTURE

Venice's modern architecture is limited, though things are looking up. To date, only locally born modernist **Carlo Scarpa** (1906-78) – a master of multi-faceted interiors – has had a chance to build up a body of work, with the entrance and garden patio of the Biennale gardens (1952; *see p97*), the Olivetti showroom (1957-8) in piazza San Marco, the entrance lobby of the IUAV architecture faculty near piazzale Roma and the ground-floor reorganisation of the Museo Querini Stampalia (1961-3; *see p93*). Scarpa's student **Mario Botta** has recently overhauled the top-floor exhibition rooms of this last establishment.

The 1970s and '80s brought one or two adventurous public housing projects around outlying areas of the city or lagoon, such as **Giancarlo De Carlo**'s low-income housing on the island of Mazzorbo (1979-86), an asymmetrical arrangement inspired by the colourful domestic architecture of Burano.

A new high-tech airport terminal by local architect **Giampaolo Mar** was inaugurated in summer 2002, and, as this guide went to press, work was well under way on Santiago Calatrava's sleek new bridge over the Grand Canal (*see p34* **Shining path of light**).

Projects currently in the pipeline include an extension of the cemetery at San Michele by London-based architect David Chipperfield; the Venice Gateway hotel and convention complex by Frank O Gehry near the new airport; and a revamp by the Spanish-Italian team of Enric Miralles and Benedetta Tagliabue of the old port authority area near Santa Marta for the IUAV.

With all this activity, the usual excuse given for architectural stasis – shortage of space – becomes ever less convincing. The real stumbling block for Venice's vocation to innovation may well prove to have been resistance to change engendered by John Ruskin; resistance which now shows healthy signs of crumbling.

Villa Foscari. *See p40.*

Palladian Villas

The Veneto's grand houses are without equal.

Palladio's villas prove that all grand homes are not created equal. Of all the great country houses in the world – chateaux along the Loire, opulent English houses like Vanbrugh's Blenheim, mansions in Newport, Rhode Island – the villas by Andrea Palladio (1508-1580) in the Veneto are the easiest to imagine living in. Never overbearing in size or use of costly materials, these private homes instead make subtler points through the dignity found in classical vocabulary (columns, cornices, pediments), the harmony of their proportions both external and internal, and their human scale. Giorgio Vasari, a contemporary of Palladio, admired the elegance and comfort of these 'commodious' houses, lauding their 'many conveniences'. Vasari understood that the villas of Palladio offered something new.

Palladio's revival of ancient Greek and Roman architecture created a late Renaissance style popular throughout Europe. In the succeeding centuries, architects and patrons in dozens of countries saw Palladio's homes as a standard of excellence. Other architects have marvelled over their simplicity, practicality and economy. In the early 18th century, an English architect confirmed the success of Palladio's example: 'the Beauties of Architecture may consist with the greatest plainness of structure'. Less could indeed be more.

The authority of Palladio's domestic architecture, particularly in the English-speaking world, has in fact overshadowed his accomplishments as a designer of churches (in Venice), palaces and theatres (in Vicenza). Any architectural pilgrimage in the Veneto must include Palladio's public buildings in both cities. Yet his villas are famous for good reason. Although many Palladian villas are far from the city centre, effort spent finding them will be rewarded. Palladio himself spread the fame of his architecture by writing a treatise, *I quattro libri dell'architettura* (*The Four Books of Architecture*, 1570), one of the most influential books ever written on building. Yet his logical text and straightforward illustrations don't have the same impact as experiencing these marvellous buildings in person. Visiting these villas will convert sceptics, and make you reconsider what a great house should be.

Arguably the most influential architect in Western culture, Palladio had a lowly start. He was born in Padua on 30 November 1508 and baptised Andrea di Pietro della Gondola. His father, who milled grain and transported it for a living, apprenticed him at the age of 13 to a local sculptor and decorator. In 1524 Andrea moved to Vicenza and began working for Giovanni da Porlezza, a stonecarver. The workshop, recognising his talent, put up the money for Andrea's guild entrance fee. Palladio learned to design and carve church altars, tombs and architectural elements, many commissioned by the Vicenza nobility.

Between 1530 and 1538, while working on the decorative details of a villa on the outskirts of Vicenza, he met its owner, Count Giangiorgio Trissino, an influential and wealthy aristocrat who was the leader of a group of Humanist intellectuals dedicated to reviving all aspects of classical culture. This chance meeting was to change the course of Western architecture. Trissino, a poet and amateur architect, was immensely impressed with the young stonecutter and decided to take him under his wing, encouraging and funding his studies of the art and architecture of Rome.

Over the next few years, Trissino set about turning Andrea into a worthy heir to Vitruvius, the ancient architect whose treatise *De Architectura* underpinned the return to classical models in the Italian Renaissance. He began with finding a suitable name: 'Palladio' not only resonated with classical associations, but it was the name of a helpful angel in Trissino's epic poem *Italia liberata dai goti* (*Italy Liberated from the Goths*). In transferring the name to his protégé ,Trissino was expressing the hope that Andrea would liberate Italian architecture from the Gothic. Andrea was introduced to Humanist circles around the Veneto, given time off to study Roman antiquities in Verona and Padua and taken to Rome on three lengthy visits between 1540 and 1550. (Palladio made two more trips to the Eternal City on his own.) There he scrutinised, measured and sketched all the major classical remains; he also studied the buildings and plans of Renaissance greats throughout Italy, including Sanmicheli, Bramante, Raphael and Giulio Romano. In 1554 he published his Roman findings in a sort of early guidebook, *Le antichità di Roma*.

The result of this research and study was a fully developed and newly confident classical style that the architect had already begun to apply in a number of commissions. Palladio's early patrons were part of the Trissino circle, who made sure the architect received both work and intellectual stimulation after Trissino died in 1550. Among these enlightened Vicentine

nobles were Pietro Godi – whose villa at Lonedo di Lugo (*see p41*) was Palladio's first independent commission, in 1537 – and the Barbaro brothers, a pair of scholars and statesmen who dabbled in design themselves and whose collaborative encouragement of the young architect generated one of his country house masterpieces, the Villa Barbaro (1550-7, *see p42*) at Maser. Girolamo Chiericati, another of Palladio's patrons, was on the board of commissioners who gave the architect his first big break in 1549, when his plans for the reconstruction of Vicenza's town hall (the Basilica Palladiana, *see p259*) were accepted. This revolutionary design, in which the Gothic structure was wrapped in a huge, unifying, two-storey classical loggia, established Palladio as one of the leading architects of his day.

As an architect of villas, Palladio also benefited from good timing. In the 16th century the Venetian government insisted that nobles build houses and develop farms on terra firma in order to boost agricultural production and increase *La Serenissima*'s control over the countryside. As a result of this policy, Palladio and his contemporaries received commissions for villas throughout the Venetian mainland. Palladio's villas – which uniquely managed to be both practical farmhouses and elegant country residences – soon became the most famous. Palladio's own writings furthered the fame of commissions both built and never completed. In 1570 he moved to Venice, where he enjoyed the unofficial status of chief architect. The construction of prominent churches in Venice like San Giorgio Maggiore (*see p135*) and the Redentore (*see p134*) reinforced his fame. By the time of his death in August 1580, his influence was beginning to be felt from London to Moscow.

Palladio never simply copied ancient Roman models: he elaborated classical motifs, creating a style that was entirely his own. The most recognisable feature of his buildings was the use of the Greco-Roman temple front as a portico; equally innovative, though, were the dramatic high-relief effects he created on façades. He frequently employed the thermal window (a semicircular opening divided by two vertical supports) to evoke the monumentality and grandeur of Roman bath complexes. The floor plans usually emphasised a strong central axis and symmetrical wings. The proportions of the rooms were determined mathematically to create harmonic spaces, typically with high ceilings. Though always unmistakably his, each of Palladio's buildings is startlingly different. He was capable both of the stark simplicity to be found at the Villa Pisani Ferri (*see p264*) at Bagnolo di Lonigo, which is almost totally devoid of decorative elements, and of the immense complexity of the statue-crowned Palazzo Chiericati in the centre of Vicenza (*see p260*). Much decoration was also functional: the gracious entrance ramp at the Villa Emo (*see p42*) may also have been used as a platform for threshing grain. Palladio preferred thrifty building materials for his villas and most walls are plaster over brick.

But Palladio's inventiveness and sensitivity were not limited to the buildings themselves. He was also obsessed with the smallest details of the natural environment in which his buildings were to be inserted. Building near a river or canal was highly recommended by the architect; as well as allowing easy access by boat, water guaranteed cool breezes during the hot summer months and irrigated the gardens, and, not incidentally, 'will afford a beautiful prospect'. However, patrons should avoid building near standing waters, or in valleys, since both lack good air circulation. Naturally, Palladio also had opinions on where certain functions – stables, cellars, granaries – should be located within the compounds.

Palladio thus saw his own villas in practical terms, as the centrepieces of prosperous farms, as opportunities for physical exercise on foot and horseback, and especially as beautiful retreats. The villa was conceived as an antidote to the stresses of urban life. In his *Four Books of Architecture*, he wrote that a country house offered a setting where the mind, 'fatigued by the agitations of the city, will be greatly restored and comforted, and be able quietly to attend to the studies of letters, and contemplation'. Palladio's very same motives still obtain today.

What follows is a critical selection of the most important visitable villas designed entirely or mostly by Palladio. For the Basilica Palladiana and the townhouses in Vicenza, *see pp257-64*. Note that the names of villas change when they pass from one family to another, though the original owner's surname is generally retained, and occasionally some of the intermediate ones. In the listings below we refer to the villas by their most commonly accepted names. Since the following are mostly private homes, the opening hours change frequently; phoning in advance is recommended. Many villas, such as the Villa Pisani in Montagnana (*see p264*), are not open to the public and can only be admired from the outside.

Venice province

The splendid classical proportions of the **Villa Foscari 'La Malcontenta'** – set on a dramatically high platform – together with its imposing position on a curve of the Brenta canal close to its entrance to the Venetian lagoon, have made this villa, designed in 1555, one of Palladio's most celebrated creations. The name of the village (and nickname of the villa) refers to the land disputes of discontented peasants in the 15th century, and not – as legend claims – to an unhappy ('*malcontenta*') wife exiled from the fun in Venice. With its double staircase and elegant Greek temple façade, the Villa Foscari has been the model and inspiration for thousands of buildings in Europe and America. The rear façade is remarkably inventive, revealing in its detailing the interior spaces. Although the graceful frescoes by Battista Franco and Giambattista Zelotti are damaged and faded (and despite the present proximity to Marghera's oil refineries), the villa remains one of the most attractive and pleasant country houses in the world. It can be visited as part of the Burchiello boat excursion down the Brenta (*see pp235-45*).

Villa Foscari 'La Malcontenta'
Via dei Turisti 10, Malcontenta (Apr-Oct 041 547 0012/Nov-Mar 041 520 3966/studiofoscari @libero.it). Bus 53 *from piazzale Roma*. **Open** *Apr-Oct* 9am-noon Tue, Sat; other times by appointment. **Admission** €7 Tue, Sat; other times €8; groups, students €6. **No credit cards**.

Padua province

Villa Cornaro is one of the most satisfying and elegant of Palladio's free-standing, two-storey villas (as opposed to the elongated farmhouse style of the Villa Barbaro or Villa Emo). Probably completed between 1560 and 1570, it features a double-tiered Greek temple-style front porch with genetically evolved Corinthian columns (they of the acanthus-leaf capitals) above more primitive Ionic ones, with scrolled volutes. The interior has some drab 18th-century frescoes by Mattia Bortoloni and rather inventive stucco statues of members of the Cornaro family by Camillo Mariani.

Villa Cornaro
Via Roma 92, Piombino Dese (049 936 5017). SITA *bus from Padua (piazzale Boschetto) for Trebaseleghe*. **Open** *May-Sept* 3-6pm Sat; other times by appointment for groups only. **Admission** €5. **No credit cards**.

Vicenza province

Palladio's first villa, **Villa Godi Valmarana ora Malinverni** was built before he ever set foot in Rome and completed by 1542. In some ways it's one of his most radical, pared-back designs. Its matter-of-fact solidity reminds us that most of these villas were built as working farms. Set in a vast park, the villa has some good 16th-century frescoes as well as a former owner's collection of 19th-century art, artefacts and fossils (including a palm tree 5m/16ft high).

Villa Pisani was an early commission (begun in 1542), and shows Palladio honing his style and experimenting with features such as rusticated arches that he later abandoned. Looking at the building-block simplicity of the façade, it's hard to appreciate how revolutionary this must have seemed at the time. The revolution continues inside, where the division of rooms and design details such as the thermal windows are purely classical in inspiration.

Now the town hall of the otherwise unremarkable town of Quinto Vicentino, the imposing **Villa Thiene** is only a fraction of what was to be an even more immense villa designed by Palladio in 1546. The interior was frescoed in the mid 16th century by Giovanni De Mio and Bernardino India.

Villa Pojana is a Palladian bungalow, or one of the architect's most original creations, depending on your point of view. Dating from around 1550, the villa offers no projecting temple portico for once, and the façade is dominated by a serliana arch (in which a central arched opening is flanked by two rectangular ones) topped by telephone-dial openings – giving an oddly contemporary feeling and suggesting that Palladio was the original post-modernist. The interior has perfectly symmetrical rooms, with frescoes by Bernardino India and Anselmo Canera.

Andrea Palladio.

Until a few years ago, the lovely **Villa Saraceno** was in a state of disrepair, in use as a barn. Then, in 1988, it was bought up by the British Landmark Trust and restored, opening as self-catering accommodation in 1994 and offering a unique chance to stay in a Palladian villa. The designs reveal two wings that failed to materialise. Its farmyard fate was at least in keeping with the building's original function: like many of Palladio's villas, it was built for a gentleman farmer, with an attic-granary lit by large grilled windows, so that the wheat was kept ventilated. As this guide went to press, Landmark was fighting to prevent a motorway sliproad being built nearby.

Perhaps the best-known of the Veneto villas, **La Rotonda** – designed by Palladio between 1567 and 1570, but not completed until 1606 – was the first to be given a dome, a form previously associated with ancient temples or Renaissance churches. The successful reconciliation of the circle and the square resolved a problem that had baffled generations of architects. The Rotonda (officially called the Villa Almerico-Capra Valmarana) was planned not as a family home but as a pleasure pavilion for retired cleric Paolo Almerico; thus although the structure has a huge footprint it actually comprises relatively few rooms. The four temple-like façades still face out on to lush green countryside on three sides, despite the site's proximity to the city centre. Scholars (or talented bluffers) keen to examine the inside of one of the most famous buildings in Western architecture may be granted permission to visit the Rotonda's lavish interior outside the limited opening times. Those left outside need not complain: the building's exterior was far more influential and walking around it offers the visitor extraordinary aesthetic pleasure.

Villa Piovene may have been one of the architect's last commissions. The formulaic Palladian style – the portico, the colonnaded wings, the theatrical double staircase out front – is proof for some that self-parody was beginning to set in (or that Palladio's followers were not up to the level of the master). Only the central block is plausibly by Palladio; the rest may be by his follower Vincenzo Scamozzi.

All transport instructions apply from central Vicenza; unless otherwise stated, services depart from the rural FTV bus service terminal (information 0444 223 115/fax 0444 327 422/ www.ftv.vi.it) in front of Vicenza station.

Villa Godi Valmarana ora Malinverni

Via Palladio 44, Lonedo di Lugo (0445 860 561/fax 0445 860 806/www.villagodi.com). Bus to Thiene; change at Thiene to hourly bus for Lugo di Vicenza. **Open** *June-Sept* 3-7pm Tue, Sat, Sun. *Nov-Mar*

2-6pm Tue, Sat, Sun. Mornings and other days available for groups with reservations. **Admission** €6; groups of 10-plus €5. **No credit cards**.

Villa Piovene

Via Palladio 51, Lonedo di Lugo (0445 860 613). Bus to Thiene; change at Thiene to hourly bus for Lugo di Vicenza. **Open** *Gardens only* Apr-Oct 2.30-7pm daily. Nov-Mar 2-5pm daily. **Admission** €4.20. **No credit cards**.

Villa Pisani

Via Risaie 1, Bagnolo di Lonigo (0444 831 104/fax 0444 835 517). Bus for Cologna Veneta. **Open** by appointment. **Admission** €6; €5 groups of 15-plus; €4 under-14s. **No credit cards**.

Villa Pojana

Via Castello 41, Pojana Maggiore (0444 898 554/ cpojana@tin.it). Bus for Noventa Vicentina. **Open** *Apr-Oct* 10am-12.30pm, 2-7pm Tue-Sun. *Nov-Mar* 10am-12.30pm, 2-5pm Tue-Sun. **Admission** €4; €2.50 groups of 15 or more, under-14s. **No credit cards**.

Villa Rotonda

Via della Rotonda 45 (0444 321 793). Bus 8 or 13. **Open** *Gardens* Apr-Oct 10am-noon, 3-6pm Tue-Sun. Nov-Mar 10am-noon, 2.30-5pm Tue-Sun. *Interior* mid Mar-Oct 10am-noon, 3-6pm Wed. **Admission** *Gardens* €5. *Interior* €10. **No credit cards**.

Villa Saraceno

Via Finale 8, Finale di Agugliaro (0444 891 371). Bus for Noventa Vicentina; change at Ponte Botti for local service. **Open** *Apr-Oct* 2-4pm Wed. *Nov-Mar* by appointment. **Admission** by donation. For weekly rental (sleeps 12) call Landmark Trust UK (01628 825 925/www.landmarktrust.co.uk).

Villa Thiene

Piazza IV Novembre 2, Quinto Vicentino (0444 584 224/fax 0444 357 388/biblioteca@comune. quintovicentino.vi.it). Bus 5 (for Quinto or Lanzé) from Vicenza (piazza Matteotti). **Open** 9.30am-12.30pm, 3-7pm Mon, Thur; 9.30am-12.30pm Tue, Wed, Fri. Other times/days by appointment. **Admission** free.

Treviso province

The **Villa Barbaro a Maser** is deservedly among the most famous of all Palladian villas. The charm of this out-and-out exercise in rural utopianism derives partly from Palladio's intellectual communion with the Barbaro brothers for whom it was designed and built between 1550 and 1557, and partly from the quality of the decoration: for only in this villa did the architect find a painter, Paolo Veronese, capable of matching his genius. The natural setting is superb, with a rising, wooded hill behind tamed into classical symmetry by the semicircular lawn with its classical statuary in front. Two traditional parts of the Veneto

farmhouse have been dressed up in a new classical disguise: those two arcaded wings flanking the main porticoed building are actually two *barchesse*, or farmhouse wings; while the mirror-image, sundial-adorned chapel fronts on either end are in fact dovecotes. Behind is a nymphaeum – a semicircular pool surrounded by statues. Even this served a practical function: the water flowed from here into the kitchen, from there into the garden for irrigation, and ultimately to the orchard on the far side of the road. Veronese's trompe l'oeil frescoes inside – including the magnificent ceiling in the central Hall of Olympus – are in the same playful classical tradition as their frame. The meeting of minds is completed by Alessandro Vittoria, a pupil of Sansovino, who designed and carved all the statues and ornamental details. Although some of the decorative encrustation may reflect the patrons' wishes more than Palladio's, the total effect is extraordinary.

By the side of the road in front of the villa is the Tempietto Barbaro, designed in the late 1570s as a memorial to Daniele Barbaro. This – Palladio's last church – is also one of his most geometrically ambitious, despite its small scale: looking back past the architect's own Redentore in Venice to the Pantheon in Rome, the design ingeniously reconciles the circle-in-a-square plan with the Greek cross layout, a satisfying resolution of paganism and Christianity.

In the same mould as the Villa Barbaro but a tad more rustic, with more recognisable dovecotes at the end of the long *barchesse*, the surprisingly intimate **Villa Emo** was one of the first properties built as part of a Venetian scheme to encourage landowners to develop uncultivated land and exert greater government control over the terra firma. The striking beauty of the exterior resides in its austerity and proportions rather than its decoration. Still owned by the Emo family, it has joyous frescoes by Giambattista Zelotti, one of the major fresco artists of the late Italian Renaissance.

Villa Barbaro a Maser

Via Cornuda 7, Maser (0423 923 004/fax 0423 923 002/www.villadimaser.it). Autoservizi La Marca bus from Treviso bus station to Maser. **Open** *Mar-Oct* 3-6pm Tue, Sat, Sun. *Nov-Feb* 2.30-5pm Sat, Sun. Other days by appointment for groups only (min 20 persons). **Admission** €5; €4.50 groups (by appointment). **No credit cards**.

Villa Emo

Via Stazione 5, Fanzolo di Vedelago (0423 476 414/ fax 0423 487 043/villaemo@apf.it). Autoservizi La Marca bus from Castelfranco Veneto station for Montebelluna. **Open** *Apr-Oct* 3-7pm daily. *Nov-Mar* 2-6pm Sat, Sun. **Admission** €5.50; €5 groups; €3 concessions. **No credit cards**.

Melodramatic:
the Bridge of Sighs.

Literary Venice

Authors and poets have long been transfixed by the
city's singular personality.

Venice produced great architects, painters,
sculptors and musicians but rarely great
writers. Only **Carlo Goldoni** and **Giacomo
Casanova** have become household names,
the one for his lively comedies of Venetian
mercantile life and the other for his equally
lively accounts of his own sexual escapades.
Nonetheless, if the city couldn't produce its
own home-bred literary artists, it was always
more than hospitable to writers from elsewhere,
particularly if their writings would help to
promote the city's image.

One important recipient of such hospitality
was the 14th-century poet **Petrarch**, who
left his library to the city. The city lost it,
which speaks volumes about Venice's literary
sensibility. It was not, in fact, till the advent of
printing (Aldo Manuzio set up his Aldine Press
here in 1495) and its lucre-generating potential,
that Venice really awoke to the virtues of books.
By the 16th century, partly thanks to the laxity
of its censorship, Venice was one of the most
important centres of the European printing
trade, with over 100 active presses producing
books in dozens of different languages. Apart
from anything else, printed books were then
objects of great beauty – and catching the eye
was (and still is) Venice's speciality.

Countless writers have had their eyes caught
in just this way over the centuries – though
they have not always been pleased with what
they saw. English writers in particular have
swayed between love and loathing, romantic
admiration and puritan disapproval, ever since
Venice first became a major tourist attraction.

The city really enters English literature
with **William Shakespeare**. The Bard never
actually set foot here, but nonetheless the city
of *The Merchant of Venice* and *Othello* is a
more fully realised place than, say, the Sicily
of *Much Ado About Nothing*. Clearly, Venice
was already as powerful an icon as New York
is today; the Rialto bridge and gondolas could
be mentioned as casually as Brooklyn Bridge
and yellow cabs. Shakespeare's Venice is very
much a mercantile city. There are no sunsets
over the lagoon, no gondola serenades. Venice
is the city of deals, exchanges and bonds. But
it is also a place of licentiousness and scheming,
where people are not necessarily always
what they seem. To use Iago's definition of
Desdemona, the typical citizen of the Republic
is a 'super-subtle Venetian'.

The first detailed description by an English
visitor was that of insatiable literary traveller
Thomas Coryat, who set out on foot from

Throwing stones

John Ruskin first came to Venice in 1835 at the age of 16. Obsessed by the city, he would return at regular intervals – sometimes for as long as a year or more – for the rest of his life. Yet when, in old age, he came to write his autobiography, he described his work there as 'byework' and the city 'a mere temptation'… astoundingly dismissive comments from the man who more than any other influenced our way of seeing Venice.

Ruskin's relationship with the lagoon city was always ambivalent, if not tortured. It is generally assumed that this arbiter of Victorian artistic and archaeological taste considered Venetian Gothic good and everything that followed bad. Ruskin was, however, forever changing his mind, and even holding contradictory opinions: some of his highest praise goes to the Venetian colourists of the High Renaissance, from earnest Tintoretto to sensuous Veronese.

Ruskin's first serious study of Venice's art was made in 1845, while he was working on *Modern Painters*. Originally focused on the art of William Turner, Ruskin's studies drew him to Venice for an in-depth study of the colourists of the Venetian school. The high point of this visit was his discovery of Tintoretto. The downside was evidence of the 'modernisation' of the city – '*gas-lamps!*… in grand new iron posts of the last Birmingham fashion' – which squared badly with the critic's cartoon-like view of a medieval Venice peopled by figures of pure fantasy: 'Deep-hearted, majestic, terrible as the sea – the men of Venice moved in sway of power and war; pure as her pillars of alabaster, stood her mothers and maidens.' Not that such rose-tinted visions hampered Ruskin's acute observation of the material of which this city is made: the stones of Venice.

It was during a visit to Venice in 1849-50, accompanied by his high-spirited young wife Effie, that Ruskin began work on *The Stones of Venice*. There were few visitors to the city which was still recovering from the Austrian siege (*see p23*). Ruskin, clambering up ladders to inspect obscure cobwebby tombs and architectural ornaments, soon became a well-known eccentric. (Effie, with her husband's unruffled consent, took consolation in the social life offered by

Odcombe in Devon in 1608. *Coryat's Crudities* is one of the first gobsmacked-tourist descriptions of Venice: 'Such is the rarenesse of the situation of Venice, that it doth even amaze and drive into admiration all strangers that upon their first arrival behold the same.' He records the precious stones and marbles, assesses the bell towers, counts the churches. Everything is tested and measured, including the courtesans: 'As for herself, she comes to thee decked like the queen and goddess of love… Also the ornaments of her body are so rich, that except thou dost even geld thy affections… she will very near benumb and captivate thy senses.'

It's difficult not to see an association with the city here – enchantingly bedecked in riches. Just in case we were getting the wrong idea, he adds: 'Although I might have known them without my experience, yet for my better satisfaction, I went to one of their noble houses (I will confess) to see the manner of their life, and observe their behaviour.' The typical tourist, watching the glass-blowing but never buying.

In the more cynical 18th century, wariness predominated over bedazzlement. Venice was viewed less as a real place and more as a metaphor – usually a negative one. English travellers set their burgeoning sense of national self-importance against Venice's decline. This admonitory use of the city was to culminate in the works of **John Ruskin** (*see above* **Throwing stones**).

'In the cynical 18th century, wariness predominated.'

During the period of the Grand Tour the English came to Italy as to a great museum, picking up fragments of culture, works of art and Italian vices. Venice gets one contemptuous mention in **Alexander Pope**'s *Dunciad*, as a place of dissoluteness, while **Edward Gibbon** was even more dismissive: 'The spectacle of Venice afforded some hours of astonishment and some days of disgust… stinking ditches dignified with the pompous denomination of Canals; a fine bridge spoilt by two rows of houses upon it, and a large square decorated with the worst Architecture I ever yet saw.' And even those who came specifically in search of its dissolute pleasures were soon fed up. **James Boswell** wrote: 'For the first week I was charmed by the novelty and beauty of so

Austrian officers and administrators.) Ruskin was determined never to see anything through other people's eyes. When told by an 'expert' that there was not the slightest indication that the windows of the Doge's Palace without tracery had ever had any, Ruskin procured a ladder and found clear signs of former tracery. Ruskin always took the trouble to look, long and hard.

This hard staring led to his superbly detailed studies of the Doge's Palace, Torcello and St Mark's, together with numerous other examples of civic and ecclesiastic architecture. The culmination was the great chapter on 'The Nature of Gothic', which revolutionised attitudes towards Venetian architecture – and was to result (to Ruskin's disgust) in countless Doge's-Palace-inspired high schools, pubs and swimming pools throughout England.

With the same intensity that he loved one part of Venice's architecture, he hated the other. Yet even his lacerating criticism of the decadence of post-Gothic Venetian civilisation often reveals an unconfessed attraction to the sensual delights of certain aspects of its art. As critic Tony Tanner has said, Ruskin, unable to consummate his own marriage with Effie, seemed to compensate with a tormented love affair with the city; even as he attributes the decline of the city to its indulgence in 'the arts of delight' and in 'forbidden pleasures', he himself indulges in a prose of sensual verbal ecstasy which at times, Tanner says, borders on the orgasmic.

'Gothic ornament stands out in prickly independence, and frosty fortitude, jutting into crockets, and freezing into pinnacles... alternately thorny, bossy, and bristly, or writhed into every form of nervous entanglement,' wrote Ruskin, in a description that could equally well be applied to himself.

It is Ruskin's prickly independence of vision that is his greatest legacy. While it certainly did not make him happy and perhaps eventually led to insanity (his first bout of madness occurred in Venice in 1876), it helped all later visitors see Venice afresh. While we are bound to disagree with a good many of his opinions, we can never fail to admire the 'thorny, bossy and bristly' spirit that produced them.

---

singular a city, but I soon wearied of travelling continually by water, shut up in those lugubrious gondolas.'

Then suddenly, with the Romantics, decadence was the whole point. Writers such as **William Beckford**, **Lord Byron** and **Percy Shelley** thrilled. They sought shudders by visiting the prisons of the Palazzo Ducale; they saw romance in the mix of decay and splendour.

Byron's twofold reaction to Venice makes him the most interesting expatriate writer of the period. In his immensely fashionable poem *Childe Harold's Pilgrimage* – a sort of cross between *A Year in Provence* and *Fear and Loathing in Las Vegas* – he draws Venice as a dream; the city is seen at 'airy distance'. Its past is melodramatic: dungeons, the Council of Ten, vendettas. It's a purely literary creation, based more on a self-propagating writerly tradition than on observation. He continued to mine this Venetian seam in his lugubrious historical verse dramas *The Two Foscari* and *Marino Faliero* (both 1821).

But in *Beppo* Byron draws a very different picture, describing Venice at Carnevale time: a menacing Turk turns out to be a lost husband; and when this husband finds his wife has taken a lover, no knives are pulled; instead they discuss the situation over coffee and all three settle down to live together happily ever after.

Byron enjoyed the contrast with England, the 'tight little island', and appreciated the tolerance of Venetian society, where 'a woman is virtuous (according to the code) who limits herself to her husband and one lover – those who have two, three or more are a little wild.'

Throughout the 19th century travellers drifted through Venice in their closed gondolas. In their accounts of their visits, they fall into swoons or trances; the city mesmerises them. 'Je végète, je me repose, j'oublie,' murmurs **George Sand**. It's Turner's Venice they describe: a dreamscape where buildings seem less substantial than the dazzling light and shimmering water, where *palazzi* and churches merge mirage-like into their reflections.

In *Pictures From Italy*, **Charles Dickens** recounts the experience of floating through the city, even through St Mark's, which is described in terms of colour and perfumes. In the end, he gives up trying to describe and merely babbles: 'unreal, fantastic, solemn, inconceivable throughout...' Or, as he put it elsewhere: 'Opium couldn't build such a place...'

The strongest reaction to all this came from **John Ruskin** (*see p44* **Throwing stones**). He can be prejudiced, inconsistent and sometimes plain barmy. But the greatest contribution he made to Venetian studies was his continual emphasis on the physical reality of the place. In an age when most visitors saw it through a haze of romantic enchantment, Ruskin focused his attention on the stones of Venice – the crumbling bricks and marble.

Every major writer on Venice thereafter – **Marcel Proust, WD Howells, Henry James** – had to break free from Ruskin: it took some courage to like the Baroque with Ruskin's fulminations ringing in one's ears. Gradually a new taste arose, in which the ambivalence of Venice played a key role, attracting writers such as **John Addington Symonds** and **Frederick Rolfe** – the self-styled 'Baron Corvo' who described an androgynous city. The mysterious secrecy of the city was perfect for James, who wrote: 'Venice is the refuge of endless strange secrets, broken fortunes and wounded hearts.' He was perhaps also attracted by a city whose topography was almost as labyrinthine as his own syntax.

Playwright **Carlo Goldoni**. *See p43.*

'Modernist authors were divided between disgust and admiration.'

Modernist authors seemed torn between disgust and admiration. **DH Lawrence** and **TS Eliot** saw the city as irredeemably commercial and sordid. Lawrence pictures it as the 'Abhorrent green, slippery city'. Eliot describes a city where 'the rats are underneath the piles'. In **Ezra Pound's** *Cantos*, on the other hand, the Golden Age of Venice appears as one of the positive poles, an image of luminous splendour to set against the corruption of contemporary society based on usury. After he was released from a US hospital for the criminally insane, where he had been confined for his active wartime support for Mussolini's Fascist regime, Pound chose to divide most of his last years (1958-72) between Venice and Rapallo. As he put it: 'Venice is an excellent place to come to from Crawfordsville, Indiana.' He is buried on the cemetery island of San Michele (*see p140*).

Recent literature and cinema have mostly remained faithful to the *Childe Harold* version of Venice: sex, lies and dirty canals. The city is murky, treacherous and damp in novels by **Ian McEwan, Barry Unsworth** and **Lisa St Aubin de Téran**, and in **Nicholas Roeg's** manneristically melodramatic film *Don't Look Now* (from a short story by **Daphne du**

Maurier). The detective novels of American writer Donna Leon are equally melodramatic in plot, but are firmly set in workaday Venice: the aquatic dream-city seems almost down-to-earth.

Perhaps the finest summation of the two contrasting visions of the city can be found in the narrative poem *The Venetian Vespers* (1979), by the American poet **Anthony Hecht**, whose disturbed protagonist seems to have chosen the city as his place of residence precisely because its internal contrasts so perfectly match his own inner lacerations.

Romance returns in two more recent novels with Venetian settings. In *An Equal Music* **Vikram Seth** revives the dream vision, tempering it with Carpaccio-esque humour. The bestseller by **Sally Vickers**, *Miss Garnett's Angel,* gives us a refreshingly ungloomy Venice; awe prevails for the protagonist of this novel, who finds her rigid atheism shaken by the almost paradisiacal qualities of what appears to be a city of angels.

The lighter Byronic side of the city is celebrated in a verse-novel by **Anthony Burgess**, which is a clear homage to the Romantic poet, even in its title: *Byrne.* The American poet **William Logan,** in his recent volume *Macbeth in Venice*, sees the city in grotesque terms, taking as its symbol the figure of Punchinello.

It is clear enough that real writers are never going to be put off by the thought that there's nothing new to say about Venice. After all, you could say the same thing about falling in love.

Where to Stay

Where to Stay

It might be hard to find a bargain, but Venice does have plenty of choice.

Top attraction Venice may be, but the post-September 11 tourism industry crisis has hit here too. In response, many hoteliers have kept prices steady – or even dropped them – since the third edition of this guide. Despite this, the price of a bed in Venice remains higher than elsewhere in Italy; in the lagoon city, 'bargain' is a relative concept.

One significant development has been the proliferation of B&B establishments (*see p56* **Boat & Breakfast?**) and small guesthouses that are providing healthy, lower-cost competition for traditional hotels. These latter have responded with great, off-peak deals: in *bassa stagione* (August, and November to the pre-Lenten Carnevale, excluding Christmas) many hotels slash rates. Throughout the year, midweek stays can sometimes mean that even the swankiest five-star hotels approach affordability for many.

LOCATION

Choosing your location carefully will enhance your enjoyment of the city. Many of Venice's plushest hotels are in San Marco or on the riva degli Schiavoni but these can seem brash or overcrowded; if you're seeking peace and local colour, the northern reaches of Castello or Cannaregio provide a quieter alternative. Residential, artsy Dorsoduro is picturesque and quiet and has a high concentration of interesting spots to lay your head. See our Sightseeing section for more detail about the city's *sestieri*.

Like locations, hotels in Venice vary enormously – from grand, historic hotels such as the **Gritti** (*see p49*) and the **Danieli** (*see p53*) where plush rooms offer classic Grand Canal or lagoon views, to charming little B&Bs in family *palazzi* on tranquil backwaters, and no-frills, family-run, one-star jobs where the welcome is friendly and the hotchpotch rooms are basic.

WHAT YOU'LL GET

Price category and star rating give no real indication of what you'll find when you get there. For instance, the modern annexe or extreme refurbishment will provide more mod cons than the old palazzo with bouncy floors and cranky plumbing, but it may be a little short on Venetian magic.

For a city with no cars, Venice is surprisingly noisy; narrow alleys can throw your room into permanent penumbra and echoes bouncing off walls can be very loud if the alley happens to be an important thoroughfare. Rooms overlooking a garden, courtyard or terrace provide some relief from noise and heat.

Any kind of watery view will push up the price of your room. In some cases 'canal view' will actually mean *the* canal – but find out just how much of a view it is before paying a huge surcharge. In other cases, you may find yourself paying for a glimpse of narrow, murky water with an oppressive brick wall on the other side.

By and large, most hotels will exchange currency (although the rate will not be favourable) and, for an extra charge, organise babysitting, laundry and dry-cleaning. Baby cots or supplementary beds can often be squeezed into bedrooms, but expect to pay an extra 20 to 40 per cent on top of the room price.

Not all rooms in the lower price category hotels have their own bathroom. We have stated when this is the case, but check when booking that you have been given what you want – those without will obviously be cheaper. Facilities for the disabled are shamefully

The refined **Gritti Palace**. *See p49.*

lacking in Venetian hotels, though this is partly due to the nature of the buildings. Where we have stated that disabled rooms are available, this means that the room (and bathroom) is fully wheelchair accessible.

Don't take the term 'no-smoking room' at face value; Italians are inclined to flout any obstacles to puffing. Breakfast is usually included in the price of the room; if it's not, opt out of what will almost certainly be a disappointment and head to the local bar or pasticceria to start the day Venetian style, standing up (see pp165-73).

LAST-MINUTE OPTIONS

The best way to ruin your stay in Venice is to show up with no hotel room booked, even in what elsewhere would count as the low season.

If you have nowhere to lay your head, make for an AVA (Venetian Hoteliers Association) bureau at the Santa Lucia railway station, piazzale Roma or the airport: staff will help you track down a room, charging a small commission that you can claim back on the price of your first night.

If you're not fussy about the state of your room or don't mind a hike down the corridor to the bathroom, try the cheaper hotels in the area around the station (which, despite the plethora of tacky souvenir shops, is cleaner and safer than in most cities). If you're really desperate, there's always Mestre on the mainland – by no means a bad bet if you're travelling by car; hotels are usually cheaper and it's only a ten-minute hop across to Venice by train or bus. But don't let anyone try to convince you that it's the same as staying in Venice: it very definitely isn't. For last-minute bookings from home, AVA has a detailed online information and booking service as well: www.veniceinfo.it.

On the www.venicehotel.com site is a large directory of hotels, B&Bs and campsites that can be booked online.

CUTTING COSTS

Check hotel websites for off-peak and midweek offers. Some hotels such as **La Calcina** or **Messner** (for both, see p63) have apartments for longer stays, as do some of the B&Bs (see p56); these are true money-saving options, especially for groups or families. Cleaning and breakfast are not always included in the price: ask beforehand. Also, www.viewsonvenice.com and www.veniceapartment.com are good online resources if you fancy a more residential approach to the city. See also p289.

LOCATING YOUR HOTEL

Even old Venice hands get lost in the city. Make sure you obtain detailed directions before you arrive: ask your hotel for the nearest vaporetto stop, easily identifiable campo (square) and/or landmark (such as a church). Alternatively, you'll need an excellent map and a fiendishly good sense of direction.

San Marco

Deluxe

Gritti Palace ❶

San Marco 2467, campo Santa Maria del Giglio (041 794 611/fax 041 520 0942/www.luxury collection.com/grittipalace). Vaporetto Giglio. **Rates** €391-€503 single; €589-€755 double; €2,140-€3,692 suite. **Breakfast** €50. **Credit** AmEx, DC, MC, V. **Map** p311 B2.
Expect no postmodern frills, just a studied air of old-world charm and nobility in this suitably elegant 15th-century palazzo, former home of Doge Andrea Gritti. Refined and opulent, adorned with antiques and fresh flowers, each room is uniquely decorated; one that we saw is entirely lined with antique floor-to-ceiling mirrors. A courtesy boat ferries guests to the Starwood Group's sports facilities on the Lido. An aperitivo on the vast canal terrace is an experience in itself. When she was in Venice, Queen Elizabeth (the current one, that is) opted to stay here, which says it all really.
Hotel services Bar. Business centre. Concierge. No-smoking rooms. Restaurant. Room service. TV.

Luna Hotel Baglioni ❷

San Marco 1243, calle Larga dell'Ascensione (041 528 9840/fax 041 528 7160/www.baglioni hotels.com). Vaporetto Vallaresso. **Rates** €206-€373 single; €316-€620 double; €442-€1,520 suite. **Credit** AmEx, DC, MC, V. **Map** p311 B3.
Dating back to the 15th century, this hotel is located near Harry's Bar (see p166), but with the exception of original frescoes and stucco decorations in the conference room, little of the period decor remains after refurbishment. Elsewhere, kilometres of shiny marble, swathes of rich fabric and lots of Murano glass provide the backdrop for luxurious bedrooms and communal areas. Views from the rooms are of the Giardinetti Reali, the lagoon and San Giorgio Maggiore.
Hotel services Bar. Business centre. Concierge. Internet access. No-smoking rooms. Restaurant. Room service. Safe. TV.

Hotel Monaco & Grand Canal ❸

San Marco 1332, calle Vallaresso (041 520 0211/ fax 041 520 0501/www.hotelmonaco.it). Vaporetto Vallaresso. **Rates** €110-€290 single; €170-€510 double; €260-€725 suite. **Credit** AmEx, DC, MC, V. **Map** p311 B3.
Now owned by the Benetton group, this Grand Canal classic just across the road from Harry's Bar (see p166) is a curious hybrid. The lobby and bar area is a fussy mix of classic and modern, but the rooms in the main building are untouched by the design revolution; those along the calle Vallaresso side have a

www.veneziasi.it
Hotel Reservations

450

Hotels from 1 to 5 stars
in the Historic Centre of Venice,
Lido, Mestre, Marghera, Cavallino
and Brenta Riviera

21.000 Beds

7

Information Offices

Call Center open every day
from 9:00 a.m. to 9:00 p.m.

slightly tacky 1980s feel, while those on the Grand Canal frontage are ultra-traditional Venetian, brocade and all. More *charmant* are the rooms in the Palazzo Selvadego residence a minute's walk away, which comes without the lagoon views but with rooms done out in a modern, ethnic Mediterranean style with warm, colour-washed walls and cast-iron bedsteads. Best of all, though, is the Teatro Ridotto, reached via a flight of stairs off the entrance hall, which is worth a look even if you're not staying here. It comes on like a stuccoed, chandeliered and mirrored ballroom, but this 17th-century jewel was in fact Venice's first gambling hall, where Giacomo Casanova and other young rakes would come to lose money and win hearts. Newly restored, the Ridotto is today rented out for parties, receptions and society weddings.
Hotel services *Bar. Concierge. Conference facilities. Disabled rooms (6). Internet access. No-smoking rooms. Restaurant. Room service. Safe. TV.*

Palazzo Sant'Angelo sul Canal Grande ④

San Marco 3878B, fondamenta del Teatro a Sant'Angelo (041 241 1452/fax 041 241 1557/ www.palazzosantangelo.com). Vaporetto Sant' Angelo. **Rates** €396-€446 single; €492-€558 double; €773-€1,066 suite **Credit** AmEx, DC, MC, V. **Map** p311 A2.
While it certainly enjoys a stunning location with its own landing stage on the Grand Canal (although you have to pay a hefty supplement for a room overlooking it) not far from San Marco, and its facilities and traditional decor are nothing if not luxurious, this relatively new hotel is rather lacking in soul. All rooms have jacuzzi baths, fine bed linens, fluffy robes and slippers.
Hotel services *Bar. Disabled rooms. Internet access. No-smoking rooms. Room service.*

Expensive

Saturnia & International ⑤

San Marco 2398, via XXII Marzo (041 520 8377/ fax 041 520 7131/www.hotelsaturnia.it). Vaporetto Vallaresso. **Rates** €112-€280 single; €180-€450 double. **Credit** AmEx, DC, MC, V. **Map** p311 B2.
An old-fashioned and friendly atmosphere pervades this bustling hotel, which is housed in an original 14th-century building whose interior has been done up in a faux-Renaissance style with touches of Charles Rennie Mackintosh. The bedrooms vary considerably in their appearance; the majority are done out in fairly traditional Venetian style, but five have recently been given a more contemporary makeover in the retro style of Ca' Pisani (which is under the same ownership; *see p61*). A pleasant roof terrace has a view on to the basilica of Santa Maria della Salute.
Hotel services *Bar. Business centre. Concierge. Internet point. No-smoking rooms. Restaurant. Room service. TV.*

The best # Hotels

For victims of glitz overkill
DD 724 (*p63*); **Ca' Pisani** (*p61*); **Saturnia & International** (if you choose the right room, *left*); **Monaco & Grand Canal** (*p49*); **Locanda Novecento** (*p52*).

For getting away from it all
Locanda Cipriani (*p65*).

For value for money
San Samuele (*p53*); **Casa Verardo** (*p55*); **Ca' del Dose** (the room with the terrace, *p56*); **Eden** (*p59*); **La Calcina** (*p63*).

For celeb-spotting
Des Bains (*p65*); **Excelsior** (*p65*); **Cipriani** (*p64*).

For breakfast on the Grand Canal
Gritti (*p49*); **Monaco & Grand Canal** (*p49*).

For a home from home feeling
B&B San Marco (*p56* Boat & Breakfast?); **Palazzo dal Carlo** (*p56* Boat & Breakfast?).

For sporty types
Cipriani (*p64*); **San Clemente Palace** (*p65*); **Des Bains** (*p65*); **Excelsior** (*p65*); **Danieli** (*p53*).

For those with a musical bent
Locanda Vivaldi (*p55*); **Londra Palace** (*p53*); **Almaviva House** (*p56* Boat & Breakfast?); **Casa de' Uscoli** (*p56* Boat & Breakfast?).

For roof terrace views/elevated views
Locanda Vivaldi (*p55*); **Ca' Pisani** (*p61*); **Saturnia & International** (*left*); **Ca' dei Conti** (*p53*).

Moderate

Bel Sito & Berlino ⑥

San Marco 2517, campo Santa Maria del Giglio (041 522 3365/fax 041 520 4083/www.hotel belsito.info). Vaporetto Giglio. **Rates** €83-€125 single; €115-€192 double. **Credit** MC, V. **Map** p311 B2.
Equidistant from the Accademia and piazza San Marco, and near the restored Fenice (*see p219*), the Bel Sito's unpretentious rooms are decorated in faux 18th- and 19th-century style, half of them looking out on to the church of Santa Maria del Giglio.
Hotel services *Bar. No-smoking rooms. Room service. TV.*

De l'Alboro

*San Marco 3894B, corte dell'Alboro (041 522 9454/
fax 041 522 8404/www.alborohotel.it). Vaporetto
Sant'Angelo.* **Rates** €60-€150 single; €65-€250
double. **Credit** AmEx, DC, MC, V. **Map** p311 B2.
Set on a peaceful little campo sandwiched between
Palazzo Grassi and Palazzo Fortuny (for both, *see
p90*), this small hotel lies off the main tourist route
and yet is within easy reach of the Rialto bridge and
campo Santo Stefano. The spacious bedrooms are
plain but clean (about half have canal views), the
management is friendly and prices are reasonable.
Hotel services *Bar. TV.*

Do Pozzi

*San Marco 2373, via XXII Marzo (041 520 7855/
fax 041 522 9413/www.hoteldopozzi.it). Vaporetto
Giglio.* **Rates** €75-€135 single; €130-€230 double.
Credit AmEx, MC, V. **Map** p311 B2.
This hotel has a homely, friendly feeling and is very
appealing in spite of some rather cramped rooms
and tiny bathrooms. Although it's situated very near
to piazza San Marco, it is down a little alleyway and
off the main tourist track. In front of the hotel is a
lovely courtyard with an ancient well in the middle
where guests can eat breakfast or relax with a book.
Hotel services *Room service. TV.*

Flora

*San Marco 2283A, calle Bergamaschi (041 520 5844/
fax 041 522 8217/www.hotelflora.it). Vaporetto
Vallaresso.* **Rates** €90-€180 single; €130-€240
double. **Credit** AmEx, DC, MC, V. **Map** p311 B2.
Book well in advance if you want to stay at the
perennially popular Flora. Situated at the bottom of
a cul-de-sac near piazza San Marco, it offers a
dreamy, tranquil stay in the palazzo adjacent to the
so-called Desdemona's house. The decor is classic
Venetian, but bedrooms vary significantly from the
quite opulent to the relatively spartan; some are tiny.
Staff are helpful, there's a warm cosy bar and a
delightful, small garden with wrought-iron tables
and a fountain in the middle.
Hotel services *Bar. Internet access. TV.*

Locanda Art Deco

*San Marco 2966, calle delle Botteghe (041 277 0558/
fax 041 270 2891/www.locandaartdeco.com).
Vaporetto San Samuele or Sant'Angelo.* **Rates**
€70-130 single; €80-€170 double. **Credit** AmEx,
DC, MC, V. **Map** p311 B2.
This friendly, ten-room hotel is situated off campo
Santo Stefano on a busy street known for its antique
shops. The welcoming entrance hall and the simple
but stylish bedrooms are dotted with original pieces
of 1930s and '40s furniture, and other deco details.
There's a tiny breakfast area on a mezzanine floor.
Hotel services *Internet access. TV.*

Locanda Fiorita

*San Marco 3457, campiello Nuovo (041 523
4754/fax 041 522 0843/www.locandafiorita.com).
Vaporetto Sant'Angelo.* **Rates** €80 single; €110-€130
double. **Credit** AmEx, DC, MC, V. **Map** p311 B2.

Locanda Art Deco boasts 1930s features.

This cosy, family-run hotel between campo Santo
Stefano and campo Sant'Angelo has ten smartly
refurbished rooms (two with bathrooms in the corridor) with beamed ceilings; a couple have wonderful views through the hotel's vine-covered entrance
to the airy *campiello*. A newly opened annexe
nearby houses more upmarket (and pricier) rooms.
Hotel services *Internet access. Room service. TV.*

Locanda Novecento

*San Marco 2683/84, calle del Dose (041 241 3765/
fax 041 521 2145/www.novecento.biz). Vaporetto
Giglio.* **Rates** €150-€240 double. **Credit** AmEx, DC,
MC, V. **Map** p311 B2.
Wooden floors, ethnic textiles, oriental rugs,
Indonesian furniture, duvets on the beds and indi-
vidually-decorated rooms make a refreshing change
from the pan-Venetian style found in most of the
city's hotels. The cosy, nine-room Novecento is
owned by the same family as the Flora (*see above*)
and, with its friendly, helpful staff, reading and sitting rooms, tiny leafy courtyard and mellow background sounds, is a very special place to stay. Art
shows are regularly mounted in the public rooms.
Hotel services *Internet access. TV.*

Budget

Domus Ciliota

*San Marco 2976, calle delle Muneghe (041 520
4888/fax 041 521 2730/www.ciliota.it). Vaporetto
Sant'Angelo or San Samuele.* **Rates** €70-€85 single;
€100-€110 double. **Credit** MC, V. **Map** p311 B2.
A former convent (and still the property of the
church) with a lovely courtyard situated near campo
Santo Stefano, Domus Ciliota has 60 clean, modern
rooms distinctly reminiscent of university lodgings.

Being so big, there are often vacancies when everywhere else in Venice is packed, but prices are quite high for basic accommodation.
Hotel services *Disabled rooms. TV.*

Gallini 🔢

San Marco 3673, calle della Verona (041 520 4515/ fax 041 520 9103/www.hotelgallini.it). Vaporetto Sant'Angelo. **Closed** late Nov-mid Feb. **Rates** €30-€107 single; €70-€104 double. **Credit** AmEx, MC, V. **Map** p311 B2.

The Gallini has an omnipresent black cat and a great variety of rooms, ranging from some that are pretty expensive for this category to a few ultra-cheap ones with shared bathrooms. While spotlessly clean, all are done out in rather dreary browns with no-frills modern furniture. Some of those on the top floor have marvellous views over the rooftops; one even has a private (though not particularly glamorous) little roof terrace.
Hotel services *Room service. TV (in some rooms).*

San Samuele 🔢

San Marco 3358, salizada San Samuele (tel/fax 041 522 8045/www.albergosansamuele.it). Vaporetto San Samuele or Sant'Angelo. **Rates** €30-€45 single; €50-€100 double. **Breakfast** €4.50. **No credit cards.** **Map** p311 B2.

The sunny, pleasant rooms in this delightful little hotel are adorned with window boxes filled with cascading flowers. It is a clean and exceptionally friendly establishment with great prices and is a notch above most of its fellow one-stars, though all the single rooms have bathrooms in the corridor. No smoking is permitted in the hotel.

Castello

Deluxe

Danieli 🔢

Castello 4196, riva degli Schiavoni (041 522 6480/ fax 041 520 0208/www.starwood.com/italy). Vaporetto San Zaccaria. **Rates** €393-€426 single; €658-€880 double; €856-€3,300 suite. **Breakfast** €30-€50 extra. **Credit** AmEx, DC, MC, V. **Map** p312 B2.

Right next to the Doge's Palace, the Danieli (which numbers Balzac, Dickens, Wagner and Proust among past guests) is split between an unprepossessing 1940s building and the 14th-century Palazzo Dandolo: a room in the latter is definitely preferable if it's atmosphere and grandeur you're after. Even if you can't afford the high prices, take a twirl through the lovely old revolving door to gawp at the magnificent reception hall. The rooms are sumptuously decorated with Rubelli and Fortuny fabrics, antique furnishings and marble bathrooms. There are spectacular views across the lagoon from the stunning roof terrace. Guests can use the Starwood Group's sports facilities and beach on the Lido. A possible price rise of ten per cent in 2005 had yet to be confirmed as this guide went to press.

Hotel services *Bar. Business centre. Concierge. Disabled rooms. Internet access. No-smoking rooms. Restaurant. Room service. TV.*

Londra Palace 🔢

Castello 4171, riva degli Schiavoni (041 520 0533/ fax 041 522 5032/www.hotelondra.it). Vaporetto San Zaccaria. **Rates** €275-€685 double; €485-€790 suite. **Credit** AmEx, DC, MC, V. **Map** p312 B2.

Elegant but restrained, the Londra Palace offers traditional-style rooms furnished with antiques, paintings and the occasional piece of 19th-century Biedermeier furniture. Tchaikovsky composed his fourth symphony during a stay here in 1877; perhaps you can compose your own masterpiece while sunbathing on the roof terrace.
Hotel services *Bar. Concierge. Internet access. Restaurant. Room service. TV.*

Metropole 🔢

Castello 4149, riva degli Schiavoni (041 520 5044/ fax 041 522 3679/www.hotelmetropole.com). Vaporetto San Zaccaria. **Rates** €145-€306 single; €210-€580 double; €390-€740 suite. **Credit** AmEx, DC, MC, V. **Map** p312 B2.

This hotel's gorgeous garden offers a refuge from the tourist trudge of the riva degli Schiavoni: the only sounds are the occasional bells of neighbouring churches and water trickling in the fountain. Antiques from the owner's collection are dotted throughout the hotel, both in the elegant bedrooms and the sumptuous and spacious public rooms. There are views over the lagoon (if you are prepared to pay a hefty €100 or so extra), the canal, or on to the garden. The atmosphere is much less stuffy here than in some of the city's other grand hotels.
Hotel services *Bar. Concierge. Car park. Conference facilities. Internet access. No-smoking rooms. Restaurant. Room service. TV.*

Expensive

Ca' dei Conti 🔢

Castello 4429, fondamenta del Remedio (041 277 0500/fax 041 277 0727/www.cadeiconti.com). Vaporetto San Zaccaria. **Rates** €155-€310 single; €200-€413 double; €310-€620 suite. **Credit** AmEx, DC, MC, V. **Map** p312 B2.

In a historic palazzo situated on a quiet canal between Santa Maria Formosa and San Marco, this small, elegant hotel has all the comforts you'd expect from a four-star place. The rooms are tastefully decorated in Venetian style with particular attention paid to fabrics. There's a wonderful little terrace from which to survey the surrounding rooftops too.
Hotel services *Disabled room. Internet access. No-smoking rooms. Room service. TV*

Colombina 🔢

Castello 4416, calle del Remedio (041 277 0525/fax 041 277 6044/www.hotelcolombina.com). Vaporetto San Zaccaria. **Rates** €90-€270 single; €160-€420 double; €295-€800 suite. **Credit** AmEx, DC, MC, V. **Map** p312 B1.

Close to piazza San Marco but far from the crowds, the Colombina has decor that is a modern take on the usual Venetian: the Murano chandeliers are here, but the overall effect is understated. The bathrooms have loads of marble, and some rooms have balconies with views over the canal beneath the Bridge of Sighs. **Hotel services** *Bar. Concierge. Internet access. Room service. TV.*

Locanda Vivaldi ㉑

Castello 4150/52, riva degli Schiavoni (041 277 0477/fax 041 277 0489/www.locandavivaldi.it). Vaporetto San Zaccaria. **Rates** €130-€336 single; €180-€440 double; €340-€645 suite. **Credit** AmEx, DC, MC, V. **Map** p312 B2.

Located partly in the house where composer Antonio Vivaldi lived, and next to the church now devoted to his music, La Pietà (*see p96*), the Locanda offers tasteful rooms with lashings of modern comforts – many rooms have jacuzzis – and views of the island of San Giorgio from the magnificent roof terrace where breakfast is served in summer. **Hotel services** *Bar. Conference facilities. Disabled rooms. Internet access. Room service. TV.*

Savoia & Jolanda ㉒

Castello 4187, riva degli Schiavoni (041 520 6644/ 522 4130/fax 041 520 7494/www.hotelsavoia jolanda.com). Vaporetto San Zaccaria. **Rates** €130-€207 single; €190-€398 double; €320-€590 suite. **Credit** AmEx, DC, MC, V. **Map** p312 B2.

A hotel of two different but equally lovely halves, the Savoia offers rooms with balconies and views across the watery expanse of the Bacino di San Marco to Palladio's church of San Giorgio Maggiore (*see p135*) in one direction, or, on the landward side, facing back towards the glorious façade of San Zaccaria (*see p82*). The decor in both bedrooms and reception rooms manages to be pleasantly luxurious without going over the top. **Hotel services** *Bar. Concierge. Internet access. Restaurant. Room service. TV.*

Moderate

Bucintoro ㉓

Castello 2135, riva San Biagio (041 522 3240/fax 041 523 5224/www.hotelbucintoro.com). Vaporetto Arsenale. **Closed** Dec, Jan. Rates €62-€94 single; €125-€168 double. **Credit** MC, V. **Map** p312 B3.

A favourite choice for artists due to its proximity to the Biennale grounds, all the rooms in this friendly, family-run hotel have stunning views across the lagoon to the island of San Giorgio Maggiore with its Palladian church. It's amazingly good value given such a setting. Some bedrooms have no bathrooms of their own, but facilities on the same floor. **Hotel services** *Bar. Room service.*

Casa Fontana ㉔

Castello 4701, campo San Provolo (041 522 0579/ fax 041 523 1040/www.hotelfontana.it). Vaporetto San Zaccaria. **Rates** €60-€110 single; €80-€170 double. **Credit** AmEx, DC, MC, V. **Map** p312 B2.

It's a relief to leave the confusion of campo San Provolo behind you and enter this family-run hotel with its rather olde-worlde decor. Some rooms have balconies and some at the top have a view over the Romanesque campanile of San Zaccaria. **Hotel services** *Bar. No smoking rooms. TV.*

Casa Querini ㉕

Castello 4388, campo San Giovanni Novo (041 241 1294/fax 041 241 4231/www.locandaquerini.com). Vaporetto San Zaccaria. **Closed** 3wks Jan. **Rates** €73-€119 single; €124-€166 double. **Credit** DC, MC, V. **Map** p312 A1.

You will be greeted from a tiny reception area in this friendly hotel in a small square between bustling campo Santa Maria Formosa and San Marco. The stairs lead up to six comfortable bedrooms, all pleasantly decorated in sober Venetian style. The rooms are spacious, but be careful: some look over a rather uninspiring side alley. **Hotel services** *Internet access. Room service. TV.*

Casa Verardo ㉖

Castello 4765, calle della Sacrestia (041 528 6138/ fax 041 523 2765/www.casaverardo.it). Vaporetto San Zaccaria. **Rates** €60-120 single, €90-275 double. **Credit** AmEx, DC, MC, V. **Map** p312 B2.

Tucked away at the end of a narrow calle and across its own little bridge only a few minutes from piazza San Marco, the first impression of Casa Verardo is of cool and calm. Walls in the public areas are white and pale lemon while bedrooms are decorated in elegant, tasteful fabrics. There is a pretty courtyard at the back of the building and another terrace off the elegant salon where tables are laid for breakfast. The level of comfort and facilities is way above what one would expect at these prices, and staff are helpful. **Hotel services** *Bar. Internet access. Room service. Safe. TV.*

Locanda La Corte ㉗

Castello 6317, calle Bressana (041 241 1300/fax 041 241 5982/www.locandalacorte.it). Vaporetto Fondamente Nove. **Rates** €70-€130 single; €99-€250 double. **Credit** AmEx, DC, MC, V. **Map** p312 A2.

Housed in a small 16th-century palazzo far from the noisy tourist trails and set on a small canal, La Corte has 18 elegant bedrooms decorated in restful greens and a lovely little courtyard where breakfast is served in summer. **Hotel services** *Disabled room. Internet access. No-smoking rooms. TV.*

La Residenza ㉘

Castello 3608, campo Bandiera e Moro (041 528 5315/fax 041 523 8859/www.venicelaresidenza.com). Vaporetto Arsenale. **Rates** €50-100 single; €80-€160 double. **Credit** MC, V. **Map** p312 B2.

Housed in a grand (though slightly faded) Gothic palazzo, La Residenza possesses a genteel old-fashioned air and offers great value for money. It has the advantage of being away from the noisy crowds, but still within easy walking distance of

Boat & Breakfast?

Where to Stay

More and more visitors to this city of scary hotel prices are eschewing traditional accommodation options in favour of B&Bs. It was fears of an unhandle-able influx for the Jubilee Holy Year in 2000 that prompted city hall to encourage locals to open their homes to tourists. Five years down the line, the demand is still growing and business is booming.

Technically speaking, a B&B can have no more than three guest bedrooms, plus at least one bathroom exclusively for guests' use. Anything more ambitious than this falls into another hotel category – but many larger establishments call themselves B&Bs anyway, simply because it's sexy.

Venice's B&Bs range from simple yet clean rooms in relatively modern apartments to glorious antique-filled *palazzi*; you can even lay your head on a boat moored off the Giudecca. Prices reflect position and facilities; these latter can be spartan, so check when booking whether, for example, your room has a bathroom.

Below we have selected some of the most interesting places on offer. Our choice covers only bona fide B&Bs; small guesthouses are listed elsewhere in this chapter. The APT tourist office (*see p283*) has a complete list of Venice B&Bs; the excellent www.bed-and-breakfast.it website covers this kind of accommodation through Italy.

Roberta **dal Carlo**'s elegant palazzo-home on a quiet Dorsoduro backwater is filled with gorgeous heirloom-antiques and pictures. She has three bedrooms available to stay in, one of which has direct access to the roof terrace from where sunsets are pure magic. To round it all off, a generous breakfast is served off white linen in the living room.

Two of the bedrooms in **Casa de' Uscoli**, the eclectic home of Spanish nobleman Alejandro Suarez Diaz de Bethencourt, overlook the Grand Canal. Reached down a gloomy alleyway off campo Pisani and popular with an arty crowd, the palazzo is grand size but laid-back in atmosphere. Slightly faded

antiques rub along with huge contemporary pieces and quirky modern art. Passionate about classical music, the *padrone di casa* is often to be found at the grand piano in the living room.

Opera buff Arkadius Pstrong has named his stylish **Almaviva House** after the dastardly count in Mozart's Marriage of Figaro. The place is very relaxed: breakfast was being served at 11.30am when we visited.

Palazzo Soderini is minimalist and blindingly white – the ultimate relief from Venetian glitz or reminiscent of a doctor's waiting room. It's situated on a charming campo and two of the three spacious rooms look over a delightful garden with a lily pond in the middle.

Moving downscale a little, Marco Scurati's **B&B San Marco** is just behind San Giorgio degli Schiavoni. Three cosy, antique-filled bedrooms share a bathroom; there's also an apartment which sleeps four. Breakfast is served in Marco's own kitchen and guests are treated as part of the family.

Claudette is the friendly Brazilian owner of **Room in Venice**, situated down an unpromising-looking calle behind the riva del Carbon. Her three pleasant third-floor rooms are simple but spotlessly clean. They share two bathrooms and breakfast is served in the rooms.

Breakfast wherewithal is provided in the bedrooms at Sonia **degli Angeli**'s comfortable house, around the corner from the Arsenale. She rents out a double room, a studio flat and a two-bedroom apartment (with access to a pleasant garden), all of which are immaculate.

For a beach-side holiday, try **Villa Gabriella** on the Lido. This *faux*-Palladian villa with its grand entrance is impressive but the bedrooms are quite modest; there's a big terrace overlooking the sea where breakfast is served in summer.

But Venice's most unusual B&B experience is Shaula, Ava Cappellietti's lovely 1930s wooden yawl which is moored on the

San Marco. Breakfast is served at little tables set up in the vast, stucco-decorated salon on the first floor. The façade was being restored when we visited and the bedrooms have all been recently refurbished (sadly at the cost of their rather quirky character). It is a no-smoking hotel.

Hotel services *No-smoking rooms. TV.*

Budget

Ca' del Dose 29

Castello 3801, calle del Dose (tel & fax 041 520 9887/www.cadeldose.com). Vaporetto San Zaccaria or Arsenale. **Rates** €50-€75 single; €95-€120 double. **Credit** AmEx, MC, V. **Map** p312 B2.

Giudecca and sleeps seven in three cabins. Take a trip round the lagoon, eat dinner off piazza San Marco, sleep on board and have breakfast on deck.

Almaviva House

Dorsoduro 1348, fondamenta delle Romite (041 241 9659/fax 041 241 9659/ www.almavivahouse.com/www.palazzopompeo.com). Vaporetto Ca' Rezzonico or Zattere. **Rates** €90-€180 double. **Credit** AmEx, DC, MC, V. **Map** p311 B1.

B&B San Marco

Castello 3385L, fondamenta San Giorgio degli Schiavoni (041 522 7589/335 756 6555/www.realvenice.it/smarco). Vaporetto San Zaccaria. **Rates** €70-€100 double. **Credit** MC, V. **Closed** Jan; 2wks Aug; 2wks Christmas. **Map** p312 A2.

Boat with Breakfast

Moored in front of Ristorante Mistrà (see p162), Giudecca 212A (335 666 6241/ www.realvenice.it/shaula). Vaporetto Palanca. **Open** from Carnevale-end Oct; winter on request. **Rates** €50-€90 per person. **No credit cards**. **Map** p311 D1.

Casa de' Uscoli

San Marco 2818, campo Pisani (041 241 0669/fax 041 241 9659/ www.casadeuscoli.com). Vaporetto Giglio or Accademia. **Rates** €170 double; €400 suite. **Credit** AmEx, DC, MC, V. **Map** p311 B2.

Gli Angeli

Castello 2161, campo della Tana (041 523 0802/339 282 8501/www.gliangeli.net). Vaporetto Arsenale. **Rates** €70-€95 double; €120-€140 apartment. **Credit** AmEx, MC, V. **Map** p312 B3.

Palazzo dal Carlo

Dorsoduro 1163, fondamenta di Borgo (041 522 6863/www.palazzodalcarlo.com). Vaporetto Ca' Rezzonico or Zattere.

Rates €130-€140 double. **No credit cards**. **Map** p311 B1.

Palazzo Soderini

Castello 3611, campo Bandiera e Moro (041 296 0823/fax 041 241 7989/ www.palazzosoderini.it). Vaporetto San Zaccaria or Arsenale. **Rates** €120-€200 double. **Credit** AmEx, DC, MC, V. **Map** p312 B3.

Room in Venice

San Marco 4114A, calle S Antonio (tel/fax 041 522 9510/www.roominvenice.com). Vaporetto Rialto. **Rates** €50-€95 double; €70-€120 triple. **No credit cards**. **Map** p309 B2.

Villa Gabriella

Via Istria 12, Lido (041 731 426/347 915 1158/www.villagabriella.net). Vaporetto Lido. **Rates** €80-€139 double. **Credit** AmEx, MC, V. **Map** p307.

Palazzo dal Carlo.

This friendly guesthouse, on a quiet calle close to the busy riva degli Schiavoni, has six simple, stylish rooms on three floors. For a minimal extra charge, you can book the one at the top with its fabulous little roof terrace. Everything you need to make breakfast is supplied and you can order fresh croissants. **Hotel services** *No-smoking rooms. TV.*

Casa Linger ③⓪

Castello 3541, salizada Sant'Antonin (041 528 5920/fax 041 528 4851/hotelcasalinger@libero.it). Vaporetto Arsenale. **Closed** Dec. **Rates** €70-€120 double. **Credit** MC, V. **Map** p312 B3.

A steep, narrow flight of stairs leads up to this unassuming little hotel where the bedrooms (most of

History

Privacy

Qualified Staff......

Quietness

"Gardena style.....

Creative Sushi

which are spacious and airy) have recently been re-decorated; the two at the top of the house have great views. Breakfast is served in the rooms. It's on a busy street with a true downhome Venetian atmosphere, although it is quite a hike from the nearest vaporetto stop. Not all rooms are en suite.

Hotel Rio ③①
Castello 4356, campo Santi Filippo e Giacomo (041 523 4810/fax 041 520 8222/www.aciugheta-hotelrio.it). Vaporetto San Zaccaria. **Rates** €40-€130 single; €50-€170 double. **Credit** MC, V. **Map** p312 B2.
Under the same ownership as, and situated next door to, a lively, decent restaurant called Aciugheta, this hotel offers pleasant, modern rooms, which have been done out with a touch of originality; about half of them also have private bathrooms. If you want to pay a bit less, the hotel has simpler rooms in various adjacent buildings. Breakfast is served in the bar in the campo.
Hotel services *Internet access. TV.*

Locanda Silva ③②
Castello 4423, fondamenta del Rimedio (041 522 7643/fax 041 528 6817/www.locandasilva.it). Vaporetto San Zaccaria. **Closed** Jan. **Rates** €30-€70 single; €50-€110 double. **Credit** MC, V. **Map** p312 B2.
A large hotel with spacious, neat rooms and friendly staff, the Silva is situated on a picturesque canal just off the buzzing square of Santa Maria Formosa. About half of the rooms have private baths.

Cannaregio

Expensive

Giorgione ③③
Cannaregio 4587, campo dei Santi Apostoli (041 522 5810/fax 041 523 9092/www.hotel giorgione.com). Vaporetto Ca' d'Oro. **Rates** €105-€173 single; €150-€265 double; €185-€400 suite. **Credit** AmEx, DC, MC, V. **Map** p309 C2.
Just off the busy campo Santi Apostoli, the Giorgione exudes warmth and comfort rather than luxury and glitz. The older 15th-century palazzo joins the newer part around a flower-filled courtyard with a pretty, central lily pond. Some split-level rooms have terraces overlooking the rooftops and the courtyard below.
Hotel services *Bar. Concierge. Disabled rooms. Internet access. No-smoking rooms. Room service. TV.*

Locanda ai Santi Apostoli ③④
Cannaregio 4391/A, campo Santi Apostoli (041 521 2612/fax 041 521 2611/aisantia@tin.it). Vaporetto Ca' d'Oro. **Closed** 2wks Dec. **Rates** €150-€310 double. **Credit** AmEx, DC, MC, V. **Map** p309 C2.
A pair of handsome dark green doors on the busy strada Nuova leads through the courtyard of this palazzo (situated on the Grand Canal) from where a

lift will sweep you up to the third floor. Once inside, the atmosphere in the hotel is discreet and understated; it feels like an elegant private apartment. The 11 double rooms are individually decorated; the best are the two overlooking the Canal for which it is essential to book well in advance (and be prepared to pay extra). There is a comfortable sitting room overlooking the water, filled with antiques, books and magazines.
Hotel services *Bar. Internet access. No-smoking rooms. Room service. TV.*

Palazzo Abadessa ③⑤
Cannaregio 4011, calle Priuli (041 241 3784/fax 041 521 2236/www.abadessa.com). Vaporetto Ca' d'Oro. **Rates** €150-€230 single, €150-€350 double, €280-€490 suite. **Credit** AmEx, DC, MC, V. **Map** p309 C2.
A beautiful shady garden is laid out in front of this privately owned 16th-century palazzo, which is filled with family antiques, paintings and silver. Recently restored and opened to guests, a magnificent double stone staircase leads to the 12 impressive rooms, some of which are truly vast.
Hotel services *Internet access. No-smoking rooms. Room service. TV.*

Moderate

Eden ③⑥
Cannaregio 2357, campiello Volto Santo (041 524 4003/fax 041 720 228/www.htleden.com). Vaporetto San Marcuola. **Rates** €40-€115 single, €50-€170 double. **Credit** AmEx. DC. MC. V. **Map** p309 B1.
Situated on a tiny *campiello* just off busy rio terà della Maddalena and not far from the station, the 11-room Eden offers a genuinely friendly welcome, quiet and pretty rooms (all with orthopaedic matresses) and good value for money. There is a cheerful breakfast room, but you can order breakfast in your room free of charge.
Hotel services *TV.*

Locanda del Ghetto ③⑦
Cannaregio 2892-2893, campo del Ghetto Nuovo (041 275 9292, fax 041 275 7987/www.venezia hotels.com). Vaporetto San Marcuola or Guglie. **Rates** €100-€220 double. **Credit** AmEx, DC, MC, V. **Map** p308 B3.
The quiet, rather melancholy campo del Ghetto Nuovo is only five minutes' walk from heaving Lista di Spagna yet within easy reach of the peaceful Cannaregio backwaters. The building that houses this stylish, nine-room guesthouse dates from the 15th century and several rooms have original, decorated wooden ceilings. On the ground floor is a small breakfast room overlooking the canal while upstairs, the light and airy bedrooms are all done out with pale cream walls, honey-coloured parquet floors and pale gold bedcovers. Two have small terraces on the campo side.
Hotel services *Disabled rooms. No-smoking room. Room service. TV.*

Guerrini ㊳
Cannaregio 265, calle delle Procuratie (041 715 333/fax 041 715 114/www.hotelguerrini.it). Vaporetto Ferrovia. **Rates** €65-€100 single; €90-€150 double. **Credit** AmEx, DC, MC, V. **Map** p308 B3.

Set in a quiet alley, this two-star hotel is handy for the station without being too close to the noisy, crowded lista di Spagna. The bright rooms (about a quarter are without a bath) are perfectly clean and while the decor is simple, some effort has been made to cheer things up.

Hotel services *Room service.*

Rossi ㊴
Cannaregio 262, calle delle Procuratie (041 715 164/ fax 041 717 784/rossihotel@interfree.it). Vaporetto Ferrovia. **Closed** 6 Jan-Carnevale. **Rates** €53-€69 single; €75-€92 double. **Credit** MC, V. **Map** p308 B3.

For a one-star hotel near the busy, noisy and generally to be avoided area around Santa Lucia railway station, this is quite a find. At the end of an alleyway just off the touristy and noisy lista di Spagna, the basic rooms are acceptably clean; not all have private baths.

Hostels

Ostello Santa Fosca ㊵
Cannaregio 2372, fondamenta Daniele Canal (tel/ fax 041 715 775/www.santafosca.it). Vaporetto San Marcuola. **Rates** €18 per person in dormitory, €21 per person in double. **Credit** MC, V. **Map** p309 B1.

This student-run hostel is not best known for its efficiency, so make sure you have double confirmation of your booking before you turn up at midnight with a heavy bag in tow and find out they've never heard of you. Most beds are in multi-bed rooms (sleeping from 4-7), but there are a few doubles. From July-mid Sept there's a kitchen for guests' use.

San Polo & Santa Croce

Deluxe

Sofitel ㊶
Santa Croce 245, Giardini Papadopoli (041 710 400/fax 041 710 394/www.sofitel.com). Vaporetto Piazzale Roma. **Rates** €178-€400 single; €220-€490 double; €300-€600 suite. **Credit** AmEx, DC, MC, V. **Map** p308 C2.

We would normally avoid recommending hotels that are part of an international chain, but Venice's original Sofitel (there is another due to open on the island of Sacca Fisola shortly) is well placed for arrivals and departures both at piazzale Roma and the station and somehow avoids the total anonymity of hotels of this type. The modern building overlooks a canal and bustling campo Tolentini. There is an elegant cocktail bar and a restaurant housed in a lofty, plant-lined winter garden where breakfast is also served.

Hotel services *Bar. Conference facilities. Concierge. No-smoking rooms. Internet access. Parking. Restaurant. Room service. TV.*

Expensive

Marconi ㊷
San Polo 729, riva del Vin (041 522 2068/fax 041 522 9700/www.hotelmarconi.it). Vaporetto Rialto. **Rates** €55-€252 single; €70-€360 double. **Credit** AmEx, DC, MC, V. **Map** p309 D2.

With its enviable location right by the Rialto bridge, the Marconi welcomes you with a sumptuous, olde-worlde reception hall with dark wood panelling, velvet hangings and an impressive gold-embossed ceiling. The bedrooms are simpler, but still old-fashioned; two of them look out on to the Grand Canal, but the others are much quieter. There are some outdoor tables for morning coffee before a stroll through the Rialto market.

Hotel services *Internet access. Room service. TV*

San Cassiano – Ca' Favretto ㊸
Santa Croce 2232, calle de la Rosa (041 524 1768/ fax 041 721 033/www.sancassiano.it). Vaporetto San Stae. **Rates** €55-€242 single; €70-€360 double. **Credit** AmEx, MC, V. **Map** p309 C1.

A 14th-century Gothic building standing on the Grand Canal and facing the glorious Ca d'Oro *(see p103)*, the San Cassiano has its own private jetty, but if you're arriving on foot, get good directions as the hotel is difficult to find. While the place has a rather fusty feel to it, rooms are, on the whole, quite elegant. The airy breakfast room has huge windows overlooking the canal and there is a tiny but charming veranda right on the water.

Hotel services *Bar. No-smoking rooms. Room service. TV*

Moderate

Falier ㊹
Santa Croce 130, salizada San Pantalon (041 710 882/fax 041 520 6554/www.hotelfalier.com). Vaporetto Piazzale Roma or San Tomà. **Rates** €90-€210 double. **Credit** AmEx, MC, V. **Map** p308 D2.

This smart little two-star place is well located on busy salizada San Pantalon, just ten minutes' walk from the station. The rooms are done out in fairly restrained Venetian style and are surprisingly up-market considering the reasonable price; those on the second floor are newer. There is a comfy sitting area in the reception hall and a cosily beamed breakfast room.

Hotel services *Bar. Internet access. No-smoking rooms. Room service. TV*

Locanda Marinella ㊺
Santa Croce 345, rio terà dei Pensieri (041 275 9457/fax 041 710 386/www.locandamarinella.com). Vaporetto Piazzale Roma. **Rates** €50-€75 single; €75-€125 double. **Credit** AmEx, DC, MC, V. **Map** p308 D2.

On a tree-lined residential street near piazzale Roma, the Marinella offers six stylish, comfortable rooms done out in striking pale yellow and blue. There is a tiny garden at the back shaded by big white umbrellas. Given its location, this is a good choice for those with late arrivals or early departures. **Hotel services** *TV*

Locanda Sturion  46

San Polo 679, calle dello Sturion (041 523 6243/fax 041 522 8378/www.locandasturion.com). Vaporetto Rialto. **Rates** €70-€160 single; €120-€250 double. **Credit** MC, V. **Map** p309 D2.
Established in the late 1200s by the doge as an inn for visiting merchants, this hotel is still thriving – and it's not surprising, given the location. The Sturion has some of the best value Grand Canal-facing rooms (though there are only two of them), but the breakfast room shares the same view. The other spacious rooms give on to a quiet calle. It's a long haul up steep stairs, however, and there's no lift. Staff can be terse. **Hotel services** *Internet point. No-smoking rooms. Room service. TV.*

Budget

Casa Peron 47

Santa Croce 84, salizada San Pantalon (041 710 021/fax 041 711 038/www.casaperon.com). Vaporetto San Tomà. **Closed** 2wks Jan. **Rates** €45-€85 single; €70-€95 double. **Credit** MC, V. **Map** p311 A1.
The friendly Scarpa family and their vociferous parrot Pierino preside over this simple, clean hotel, very conveniently located in the university area with the shops, restaurants and bars of campo Santa Margherita nearby. Two rooms at the top of the house have private terraces; all have showers, though some are without toilets: check when booking.

Salieri 48

Santa Croce 160, fondamenta Minotto (041 710 035/fax 041 721 246/www.hotelsalieri.com). Vaporetto Ferrovia or Piazzale Roma. **Rates** €43-€85 single; €55-€145 double. **Credit** AmEx, MC, V. **Map** p308 D2.
This simple, family-run place between the railway station and piazzale Roma offers 11 bedrooms on three floors that have been recently smartened up; all now have en suite bathrooms and air-conditioning. Some rooms give on to the canal leading to the architecture university, others on to a quiet garden. A good choice if you get into Venice late.

Dorsoduro

Expensive

Accademia – Villa Maravege 49

Dorsoduro 1058, fondamenta Bollani (041 521 0188/fax 041 523 9152/www.pensioneaccademia.it). Vaporetto Accademia. **Rates** €80-€128 single; €130-€275 double. **Credit** AmEx, DC, MC, V. **Map** p311 B1.

This wonderful, secluded, 17th-century villa used to be the Russian embassy. It has two shady gardens, one of which surrounds a Palladian-style annexe. Breakfast is served in the front garden or in a wood-panelled breakfast area. The rooms are stylish, with marble or wood floors. Staff can be cold. **Hotel services** *Bar. Concierge. Internet access. Room service. TV.*

American 50

Dorsoduro 628, fondamenta Bragadin (041 520 4733/fax 041 520 4048/www.hotelamerican.com). Vaporetto Accademia. **Rates** €100-€180 single; €100-€300 double. **Credit** AmEx, MC, V. **Map** p311 C2.
Situated in the peaceful area of Dorsoduro, the American has recently refurbished and generally spacious rooms decorated in antique Venetian style, some of which have verandas adorned with fresh flowers, and face on to the delightful rio di San Vio. Try to secure one of the corner rooms where multiple French windows make for wonderful light. **Hotel services** *Bar. Concierge. Internet access. No-smoking rooms. Room service. TV.*

Ca' Pisani 51

Dorsoduro 979A, rio Terà Foscarini (041 277 1478/fax 041 277 1061/www.capisanihotel.it). Vaporetto Accademia. **Rates** €216-€354 double; €295-€400 suite. **Credit** AmEx, DC, MC, V. **Map** p311 C1.

Enjoy designer-chic luxury at **Ca' Pisani**.

Occupying a 16th-century palazzo painted a striking deep pink, Ca' Pisani's luxurious, designer-chic rooms in 1930s and 1940s style – a refreshing change from the usual fare of glitz, gilt and Murano glass – make this the best hotel in Venice if you like that sort of thing. It's conveniently located behind the Accademia (see p129), with friendly staff and large rooms. There's a restaurant with tables outside in the summer, a sauna, a roof terrace and a discount in the gym round the corner.
Hotel services Bar. Concierge. Disabled rooms. Internet access. No-smoking rooms. Restaurant. Room service. Spa. TV .

DD 724 52
Dorsoduro 724, ramo da Mula (041 277 0262/ fax 041 296 0633/ww.dd724.com). Vaporetto Accademia. **Rates** €200-€350 double, €300-€350 suite. **Credit** AmEx, DC, MC, V. **Map** p311 C2.
Several of the seven rooms at the newly opened DD 724 (it's the address) look over the Guggenheim Foundations' (see p129) garden; one has a little terrace. A design hotel in miniature, the place exudes understated contemporary luxury with art works and interesting objets dotted throughout the house. Bathrooms (done out in pale travertine stone) are super modern with big walk-in showers and delicious French bath goodies.
Hotel services Internet access. No-smoking rooms. Room service. TV.

Moderate

Agli Alboretti 53
Dorsoduro 884, rio terà Foscarini (041 523 0058/ fax 041 521 0158/www.aglialboretti.com). Vaporetto Accademia. **Closed** 3wks Jan. **Rates** €80-€105 single; €140-€180 double. **Credit** AmEx, MC, V. **Map** p311 C1.
The model ship in the window of the tiny, wood-panelled reception area of this friendly hotel lends a vaguely nautical air to the place. The simply decorated rooms are comfortable (if rather small) and well equipped; unusually for Italy, each has an electric kettle. The hotel also has its own restaurant and pretty outdoor eating area, where breakfast is served in summer. The staff are very helpful.
Hotel services Bar. Internet access. No-smoking rooms. Restaurant. Room service . TV.

Alla Salute da Cici 54
Dorsoduro 222, fondamenta Ca' Balà (041 523 5404/fax 041 522 2271/www.hotelsalute.com). Vaporetto Salute. **Closed** 2wks Dec, Jan-Carnevale. **Rates** €50-€115 single; €70-€140 double. **Credit** MC, V. **Map** p311 C2.
This extremely pleasant and large 50-room hotel has a pretty terrace garden and is just a stone's throw from most of the major sights, but also well away from the worst of the hubbub; indeed, it's perfectly situated for lovely, languid summer strolls along the Zattere. The design of rooms varies enormously between some rather plain ones with dated bath-

rooms in the main house and the much smarter doubles in the new annexe. Be warned, not all are en suite so it might be best to check in advance.
Hotel services Bar. No-smoking rooms

Ca' Zose 55
Dorsoduro 193B, calle del Bastion (041 522 6635/ fax 041 522 6624/www.hotelcazose.com). Vaporetto Salute. **Rates** €75-€160 single, €80-€210 double. **Credit** AmEx, DC, MC, V. **Map** p311 C2.
The enthusiastic Campanati sisters run this immaculate little 12-room guesthouse which is situated on a corner near the Guggenheim (see p129). There is a tiny, neat breakfast room off the cool white reception area; upstairs, bedrooms are done out in a fairly restrained traditional Venetian style with painted furniture. No smoking allowed in the hotel.
Hotel services Internet access. No-smoking rooms. TV.

La Calcina 56
Dorsoduro 780, fondamenta delle Zattere (041 520 6466/fax 041 522 7045/www.lacalcina.com). Vaporetto Zattere or Accademia. **Rates** €65-€106 single; €99-€186 double. **Credit** AmEx, DC, MC, V. **Map** p311 C1.
The Calcina, where Ruskin (see p44 **Throwing stones**) stayed in 1877 while writing St Mark's Rest, is in a great location: the Redentore church across the water can be admired while sipping cocktails (or, indeed, enjoying a full meal) on the floating terrace. It is also one of the best value – and unquestionably one of the most pleasant – hotels in this category. There is an air of cool and calm about the place, starting with classical music in the white-painted reception. Rooms have dark parquet floors, classic 19th-century furniture and a refreshingly uncluttered feel; one single is without private bath. Apartments are also available.
Hotel services Bar. Internet access. Restaurant. Room service. TV.

Locanda San Barnaba 57
Dorsoduro 2486, calle del Traghetto (041 241 1233/ fax 041 241 3812/www.locanda-sanbarnaba.com). Vaporetto Ca' Rezzonico. **Rates** €70-€110 single; €120-€170 double; €160-€210 suite. **Credit** AmEx, MC, V. **Map** p311 B1.
Situated at the end of a quiet alleyway with a welcoming atmosphere and 13 comfortable, individually decorated rooms (featuring an uncluttered mix of antique furniture and elegant fabrics), the San Barnaba is one of the best hotels in this price range in the area. There's a small courtyard and roof terrace, and no bridges to cross to get to the nearest vaporetto stop.
Hotel services Bar. No-smoking rooms. TV.

Messner 58
Dorsoduro 216, fondamenta Ca' Balà (041 522 7443/fax 041 522 6676/www.hotelmessner.it). Vaporetto Salute. **Closed** 3wks Dec. **Rates** €70-€100 single; €90-€160 double. **Credit** AmEx, DC, MC, V. **Map** p311 C2.

La Calcina. See p63.

The Messner's immaculate rooms may be too modern for many tastes, but the location, the shady garden and the warm staff make up for the lack of atmosphere. Between the main building and two annexes, there is a choice of rooms rom standards to 'de luxe junior suites'; prices vary. The hotel also manages some apartments in the area.

Hotel services *Bar. Internet access. No-smoking rooms. Restaurant. TV (in half the rooms).*

Seguso 59

Dorsoduro 779, Zattere (041 528 6858/fax 041 522 2340/www.pensioneseguso.it). Vaporetto Zattere or Accademia. **Closed** Dec-mid Feb. **Rates** €50-€150 single; €70-€180 double. **Credit** AmEx, MC, V. **Map** p311 C1.

A renowned hotel in traditional pensione style and with sunny outdoor seats and dark, cosy reception rooms, the Seguso has the air of a maiden aunt's house. Half board is no longer obligatory, although many regulars still choose to eat an evening meal 'in' in spite of rather mundane food. More than half the rooms are without private bath.

Hotel services *Bar. Restaurant. Room service.*

Budget

Antica Locanda Montin 60

Dorsoduro 1147, fondamenta delle Eremite (041 522 7151/fax 041 520 0255/www.locandamontin.com). Vaporetto Accademia or Zattere. **Rates** €50-€70 single; €110-€140 double. **Credit** AmEx, DC, MC, V. **Map** p311 B1.

It's difficult to get a booking in this charming 12-room locanda overlooking a delightful canal. It owes its popularity to the fact that it is also home to one of Venice's most famous – though very overrated – restaurants. Rooms house an eccentric mix of old and new furniture, but the overall feeling is homely and cosy.

Hotel services *Bar. Restaurant.*

Ca' Foscari 61

Dorsoduro 3887B, calle della Frescada (041 710 401/fax 041 710 817/www.locandacafoscari.com). Vaporetto San Tomà. **Rates** €62 single; €72-€93 double. **Credit** MC, V. **Map** p311 A1.

The delightful Scarpas have been running this wonderful little locanda and offering a genuinely friendly welcome since the '60s. The simple but cosy and homely rooms are on the second and third floors of the building (be warned, it's a bit of a climb); they are done out in cheerful colours and are spotlessly clean. The quietest of them have views over neighbouring gardens while others face the street; not all have private bathrooms.

La Giudecca

Deluxe

Cipriani 62

Giudecca 10, fondamenta San Giovanni (041 520 7744/fax 041 520 3930/www.hotelcipriani.com). Hotel launch from Vallaresso vaporetto stop. **Closed** end Oct-mid Mar. **Rates** €370-€755 single;

Where to Stay

€625-€1,300 double; €1,090-€3,945 suite; €4,700-
€8,045 Palladio Suite. **Credit** AmEx, DC, MC, V.
Map p312 D1.
Set in a verdant paradise on the eastern tip of the
Giudecca island, the Cipriani has great facilities as
well as a private harbour for your yacht and a
higher-than-average chance of rubbing shoulders
with a film star. Rooms are exquisitely decorated,
many with marble bathrooms. If this seems too hum-
drum, take an apartment in the neighbouring 15th-
century Palazzo Vendramin, complete with butler
service and private garden. Leisure facilities include
tennis courts, a pool, a sauna, a newly opened spa
and a gym. Despite the possibility of unlimited use
of the motorboat to San Marco, many guests choose
not to leave the premises, begging the question: do
they come here for Venice or for the Cipriani itself?
Hotel services *Bar (3). Concierge. Conference
facilities. Gym. Internet access. Restaurant (4). Room
service. Spa. Swimming pool. TV. Tennis court.*

Hostels

Ostello di Venezia ⑥³
(Youth Hostel)
*Giudecca 86, fondamenta delle Zitelle (041 523
8211/fax 041 523 5689/www.hihostel.com).
Vaporetto Zitelle.* **Closed** 2wks Dec. **Rates** €18.50
per person; €9 dinner. **Credit** MC, V. **Map** p311
D3/p312 D1.
A vaporetto ride away from the main island, this
youth hostel offers stunning and unique views
across the lagoon towards the church of Santa Maria
della Salute and San Marco. Written reservations are
needed, especially during the summer months.
Unadventurous but very cheap meals are served.

The Lido

Deluxe

Des Bains ⑥⁴
*Lungomare Marconi 17, Lido (041 526 5921/fax
041 526 0113/www.starwood.com/italy). Vaporetto
Lido.* **Closed** early Nov-mid Mar. **Rates** €192-€413
single; €440-€660 double; €580-€1,490 suite. **Credit**
AmEx, DC, MC, V. **Map** p306.
Thomas Mann wrote, and Luchino Visconti filmed,
Death in Venice in this glorious art deco hotel set in
its own park. Des Bains has a private beach just
across the street and access to tennis courts, a golf
course and riding facilities. A courtesy boat ferries
guests to San Marco every half hour.
Hotel services *Bar. Concierge. Conference
facilities. Gym. Internet access. No-smoking rooms.
Parking (free). Pool (outdoor). Restaurant. Room
service. TV.*

Excelsior ⑥⁵
*Lungomare Marconi 41, Lido (041 526 0201/fax
041 526 7276 /www.starwood.com/italy). Vaporetto
Lido.* **Closed** early Nov-late Mar. **Rates** €484-€846
double €432-€884; €1,111-€3,254 suite. **Credit**
AmEx, DC, MC, V. **Map** p306.

The early-1900s pseudo-Moorish Excelsior hosts
hordes of celebrities when the Venice Film Festival
(*see pp202-4*) swings into action each September (the
festival headquarters is just over the road). Demand
a sea-facing room for a view of beach happenings
and the Adriatic beyond. The Excelsior's beach huts
are the last word in luxury. There are tennis courts
and a water taxi to San Marco.
Hotel services *Bar. Conference facilities. Internet
access. No-smoking rooms. Pool (outdoor).
Restaurant. Room service. TV.*

The Lagoon

See also p60 **Sofitel** for Sofitel Venezia
in Isola.

Deluxe

San Clemente Palace ⑥⁶
*Isola di San Clemente (041 241 3484/fax 041 244
5800/www.sanclemente.thi.it).* **Rates** €205-€435
single; €260-€545 double; €610-€980 suite; €2,160-
€3,100 residential suite. **Credit** AmEx, DC, MC, V.
Over time, the island of San Clemente has hosted a
hospice for Holy Land pilgrims, a powder store, an
ecclesiastical prison for unruly priests and, more
recently, a mental hospital. Today, the restored
buildings of the latter house this luxurious 200-room
hotel set in extensive grounds with four restaurants,
a business centre, a beauty farm and all the attendant facilities. There's even a three-hole practice golf
course in the extensive, landscaped grounds. Shuttle
service to piazza San Marco.
Hotel services *Bar (2). Concierge. Conference
facilities. Disabled rooms. Gym. Internet access. No-
smoking rooms. Pool (out). Restaurant (3). Room
service. Spa. TV.*

Expensive

Locanda Cipriani ⑥⁷
*Torcello, piazza Santa Fosca (041 730 150/fax
041 735 433/www.locandacipriani.com. Vaporetto
Torcello.* **Rates** €120 single; €240 double. **Credit**
AmEx, DC, MC, V.
Some people might argue that there's no point in
going to Venice and staying on the island of
Torcello, but this famous green-shuttered inn (still
owned by a branch of *the* Cipriani family) is
special enough to justify the remoteness of the setting, at least for a couple of nights. Some of the six
rooms (done out in understated, elegant country
style) look over the hotel's gorgeous garden; you
might end up in the one where Ernest Hemingway
wrote 'Across the river and into the trees', apparently standing up because of haemorrhoids. The
(expensive) restaurant (*see p164*) enjoys a blissful
setting under a vine-clad terrace; half board costs
an extra €50 per head.
Hotel services *Bar. Internet access. Restaurant.
Room service.*

Sightseeing

Features

Introduction

Behind the postcard image, Venice has plenty to offer – just be careful how you use that map.

For many first-time visitors, the big surprise is finding that Venice really is what you expected. The paintings, films and ice-cream ads were not having you on: the whole city is improbably waterlogged and persistently picturesque.

Of course, certain sights stand out. The **Basilica di San Marco** (*see p79*) is one of Christendom's greatest churches; the **Gallerie dell'Accademia** (*see p129*) contain an unparalleled selection of Renaissance art; and the **Rialto** (*see p75*) is a powerful symbol of mercantile energy as well as a fine bridge. But Venice is much more than this and the best way to get an impression of its full diversity is to leave the main routes.

Most maps of Venice seem to be made with the precise aim of getting you lost. When you do lose your bearings, don't be alarmed: the *calli* will close in around you; you'll come to innumerable dead ends and find yourself returning inexplicably to the same (wrong)

spot over and over. But eventually you'll hit a busy thoroughfare. Until that happens, enjoy the feel of village Venice – or, more appropriately, island Venice. The city is made up of over 100 islands, and every one has something – magnificent or quaint, historic or charming – to offer.

Venice is divided into six *sestieri*. They are worth getting to grips with, firstly because all addresses include the *sestiere* name, and secondly because each district has a different flavour. Cradled by the great lower bend of the Grand Canal is the *sestiere* of San Marco, the heart of the city; east of here is Castello, one of the most lived-in areas; stretching to the west and north is Cannaregio, whose western stretches are among the most peaceful parts of Venice. South of the Grand Canal is San Polo, bristling with churches; to the west is Santa Croce, short on sights but not on atmosphere; while further to the south is Dorsoduro, one of

Santa Maria della Salute. *See p129.*

the city's most elegant and artsy districts, with its wide Zattere promenade looking across to the long residential island of the Giudecca – the honorary seventh *sestiere*.

CHURCHES

Venice began life as a host of separate island communities, each clustered around its own parish church. The bridges were an afterthought. Napoleon, like many other visitors to the city, thought that there were far too many churches, and during his brief rule (*see pp10-21*) cleared away a good 40 or so; but there are still well over 100 of them left. They contain inestimable artistic treasures.

Most of the major churches have reliable opening times; hours in minor churches depend on the goodwill or whim of the priest or sacristan. It's well worth exploring these too, since there is not a single one that does not contain some item of interest, whether it be a shrivelled relic or a glowing Madonna with bambino. In general, early morning and late afternoon are the best times for church-crawling. But it's best never to pass an opportunity by: if you see one open without a service under way, go in and poke around. No Sunday opening times are given in listings for churches that open only for Mass.

MUSEUMS AND GALLERIES

On the whole, Venice's museums and galleries adhere to the basic pre-modern requirement that they should be passive containers for beautiful and/or instructive things. But some of those things are very beautiful indeed, especially in treasure troves such as the Gallerie dell'Accademia. Instruction can be fun too. The **Museo Storico Navale** (*see p97*) provides a colourful introduction to Venice's maritime past, while a grasp of the elaborate mechanisms of Venetian government (*see p12* **Machinery of state**) will turn the slog around the **Palazzo Ducale** (Doge's Palace; *see p79*) into a voyage of discovery.

Then there are the curiosities – **Ca' d'Oro** (*see p103*), where a patchy gallery with the occasional gem is housed inside one of the city's most extraordinary architectural frames; and the eclectic **Museo della Fondazione Scientifica Querini Stampalia** (*see p83*), a private foundation with a fascinating collection of scenes of 18th-century Venetian life and a glorious Bellini (the painter, not the cocktail). If losing yourself in the real Venice is too daunting, visit the **Telecom Italia Future Centre** at San Salvador (*see p87*) and tour the city on a touch-screen computer, with Titian and Marco Polo as your guides. *See also p95* **Back to school**.

ADMISSION AND TICKETS

In summer, expect to queue to enter St Mark's, the Accademia and the Palazzo Ducale. Other sights rarely present any overcrowding problems except during special exhibitions. April and May are traditional months for Italian school trips: this can mean sharing your Titians and Tintorettos with gangs of bored teenagers.

Entry to all state-owned museums is, theoretically, free (or at least reduced) for citizens under 18 and over 65. Charges and concessions at city-run and privately owned museums vary; it pays to carry whatever ID cards you can muster (student card, press card and so on).

For one week each spring – designated the *Settimana dei Beni Culturali* (Cultural Heritage week) – most state-owned (but not city-owned) galleries and museums are free. For more, see www.beniculturali.it for details.

MULTI-ENTRANCE TICKETS

For **Rolling Venice** and the **Venice Card**, *see p292* **Discount cards**.

Many of Venice's landmarks offer multi-entrance tickets, which cut costs if you are planning to visit all the sights covered by any given ticket. Schemes include:

Sightseeing

Handle with care

The Venice tourist board and other public service agencies have plastered vaporetto stops with a rather patronising list of ten obvious/obnoxious guidelines for visitors to the city. Resisting the urge to bounce back with a list of ten things which many Venetians lack when dealing with tourists – including those little things such as manners, patience, goodwill and a fair pricing policy – here are our top ten hints for coping with this extraordinary, unique city.

● Be adventurous and explore the more remote parts of the island; get lost... with a good map to help you resurface. If you want to avoid crowds, stay out of the area around San Marco and the Rialto.

● Venice has an efficient rubbish collection system, including a recycling programme – though it doesn't always look that way at the end of a crowded day in heavily trafficked areas. Hang on to your rubbish until you find a handy (though often well-hidden) bin.

● Wear sensible shoes and appropriate clothing in churches and synagogues. No matter how hot it gets in summer, keep your shirt on: in Italy, bare torsos cause offence unless they're on beaches.

● Follow 'traffic' laws while walking in crowded areas (see p279 **On foot: dry**).

● Don't even *try* to picnic in the almost shade-less, almost bench-less city centre; the Giardini pubblici (see p97), Parco Savorgnan (see p106 **Along the canal**) or a beach on the Lido (see pp137-9) will be far more pleasant.

● Take the sting out of the expense of visiting Venice by using discount cards (see p292), transport passes (see p277) and multi-entrance tickets (see p70). If you really feel you've been ripped off and want to lodge a complaint, contact the Tourist Mediation office at 041 786 236.

● Contribute to cutting pedestrian congestion by using *traghetti* (see p279)... or learning to row your own boat (see p226).

● Small and extremely safe as it is, Venice is not without its pickpockets and street scams, particularly in very crowded areas. Be (reasonably) alert.

● If you're in Venice in autumn or winter, *acqua alta* could interrupt your sightseeing schedule. For how to cope (without annoying the locals), see p278 **On foot: wet.**

● Enjoy the city, be informed, use your common sense and have a great time.

Musei Civici Veneziani

Venice's city-owned museums offer various multi-entrance options, all of which can be bought at participating establishments. The major museums (Musei di Piazza San Marco, Ca' Rezzonico and Ca' Pesaro) accept credit cards (MC, V).

Note that the Musei di Piazza San Marco can **only** be entered on a cumulative ticket. For the others, individual tickets are available. Information at www.museicivicivenezziani.it.

● **Musei di Piazza San Marco** (Palazzo Ducale, Biblioteca Marciana, Museo Correr, Museo Archeologico) €10; €5.50 concessions.

● **Area del Settecento** (museums of the 18th century: Ca' Rezzonico, Palazzo Mocenigo, Casa Goldoni) €8; €4.50 concessions.

● **Musei delle Isole** (Glass Museum and Lace Museum) €6; €4 concessions.

● **Museum Pass** (all the above museums plus Ca' Pesaro/Galleria Internazionale d'Arte Moderna) €15.50; €10 concessions.

State Museums

The Gallerie dell'Accademia (see p129), Ca' d'Oro (see p103) and Museo Orientale (see p116) can be visited on a multi-entrance ticket costing €11 (€5.50 concessions) from participating sights. No credit cards.

Chorus

These churches belong to the Chorus scheme (041 275 0462/www.chorusvenezia.org), which funds upkeep by charging for entry:

San Marco: Santa Maria del Giglio (see p91), Santo Stefano (see p90).
Castello: Santa Maria Formosa (see p92), San Pietro in Castello (see p97).
Cannaregio: Santa Maria dei Miracoli (see p109), Sant'Alvise (see p107), Madonna dell'Orto (see p107).
San Polo & Santa Croce: San Polo (see p115), San Stae (see p116), I Frari (see p120), San Giacomo dell'Orio (see p118), San Giovanni Elemosinario (see p115).
Dorsoduro: Gesuati (see p132), San Sebastiano (see p124).
Giudecca: Il Redentore (see p134).

There's a fee of €2.50 for each church or you can get a multi-entrance ticket (€8; €5 over-65s and students under 30; price includes audioguide in English). Single- and multi-entrance tickets can be bought in participating churches and VeLa shops (see p283). No credit cards.

The Grand Canal

This is no ordinary thoroughfare: hop on a vaporetto and enjoy the world's grandest high street.

The name is no exaggeration. Waterways don't come much grander than this. Three and a half kilometres (two and a half miles) in length, the Grand Canal curls its magnificent way through the centre of the city like a great inverted S, its broad loops giving Venice's *sestieri* (districts) their distinctive shapes.

It is well worth making the vaporetto trip from the railway station to piazza San Marco (about half an hour); it's not only a glittering spectacle but also gives you a better understanding of the city's workings – both at the height of its splendour and today.

The canal is still the main thoroughfare of Venice; in the great days of the city's trading empire it would have been alive with cargo boats from all over the Mediterranean. A Grand Canal address was not only socially but commercially desirable; and the architecture of the *palazzi* that line it is as practical as it was impressive. Most of the notable buildings were built between the 12th and 18th centuries. When a family decided to rebuild a palazzo, they usually maintained the same basic structure – for the good reason that they could build on the same foundations. This resulted in some interesting style hybrids: the Grand Canal offers many examples of *palazzi* in which Veneto-Byzantine or Gothic features are incorporated into the Renaissance or Baroque.

For centuries the *palazzi* generally followed the same plan: a main water entrance opening on to a large hall with storage space on either side; a *mezzanino* with offices; a *piano nobile* (the main floor – sometimes two in grander buildings) consisting of a spacious reception hall lit by large central windows and flanked on both sides by residential rooms; and a land entrance at the back. Over the centuries all kinds of architectural frills and trimmings were added, but the underlying form was stable – and, as always in Venice, it is form that follows function.

In the following description of the most notable *palazzi*, many names recur, for the simple reason that families expanded, younger sons inheriting as well as older ones. Compound names indicate that the palazzo passed through various hands over time. Originally the term 'palazzo' was reserved for the Doge's Palace. Other *palazzi* were known as *Casa* or *Ca'* for short: this is still true of some of the older ones, such as Ca' d'Oro.

This chapter deals mainly with canal-side *palazzi*. Churches and museums facing on to the canal are covered elsewhere in the guide: in these cases, cross references are given. For information on the *vaporetti* that ply the Grand Canal, *see p279*.

Ponte degli
Scalzi.

Left bank

From the railway station to San Marco

1 Vaporetto stop Ferrovia

At the foot of the Ponte degli Scalzi is the fine Baroque façade of the **Scalzi** church (*see p104*), recently restored.

Ponte degli Scalzi

Unusually narrow **Palazzo Flangini** is a 17th-century building by Giuseppe Sardi. Despite picturesque stories of quarrelling brothers, it owes its shape to the simple fact that the family's money ran out.
   Just before

Riva di 1 Biasio

Grand Canal

Ponte degli Scalzi
1 Ferrovia

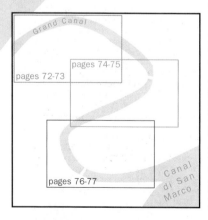

Grand Canal

pages 74-75

pages 72-73

pages 76-77

Canal di San Marco

Right bank

From the railway station to the Salute

Before the Scalzi bridge is the church of **San Simeone Piccolo**, with its high green dome and Corinthian portico. For those arriving in Venice it's a picturesque introduction to the city.
   The Ponte degli Scalzi, which leads across to the station, was built in stone by Eugenio Miozzi in 1934.

Ponte degli Scalzi

1 Vaporetto stop Riva di Biasio

Just before the rio del Megio stands the **Fontego dei Turchi**, a 19th-century reconstruction of the original Veneto-Byzantine building, which was leased to Turkish traders in the 17th century as a residence and warehouse. Some of the original material was used but the effect as a whole is one of pastiche. Once lived in by the poet Torquato Tasso, it's now the **Museo di Storia Naturale** (*see p117*).

the wide Cannaregio Canal is the church of **San Geremia**; from the Grand Canal, the apse of the chapel of Santa Lucia is visible.

Standing with its main façade on the Cannaregio Canal is **Palazzo Labia**, the 18th-century home of the seriously rich Labia family. The story goes that parties ended with the host throwing his gold dinner plates into the canal to demonstrate his wealth; the servants would then be ordered to fish them out again. A famous fancy-dress ball thrown here in 1951 by a Mexican millionaire continued this tradition of conspicuous consumption. The building is now the regional headquarters of the RAI (the Italian state broadcaster). It contains suitably sumptuous frescoes by Tiepolo.

San Marcuola 2

Grand Canal moorings.

The **Depositi del Megio** (state granaries) have a battlemented, plain-brick façade. The sculpted lion is a modern replacement of the original, destroyed at the fall of the Republic. The church of **San Stae** (*see p119*) has a Baroque façade by Domenico Rossi, with exuberant sculpture.

2 Vaporetto stop San Stae

On the rio di Ca' Pesaro, and with a magnificent side wall curving along the canal in gleaming marble, is **Ca' Pesaro** (*see p116*), a splendid example of Venetian Baroque by Longhena.

After two smaller *palazzi* stands the **Palazzo Corner della Regina**, with a rusticated ground floor featuring grotesque masks, some

2 Vaporetto stop San Marcuola

The next building of note is **Palazzo Vendramin Calergi**, an impressive Renaissance palazzo designed by Mauro Codussi (*see p145* **Dark horse**) in the first decade of the 16th century. It uses his characteristic arched windows incorporating twin smaller arches. Porphyry insets decorate the façade. Wagner died here in 1883. It now houses the Venice **Casinò**.

A fairly uneventful stretch ends at the **Ca' d'Oro** (*see p103*), the most gorgeously ornate Gothic building on the Grand Canal. Restoration work on this palazzo came to an end finally in 1984, after 20 years of labour. However, for all its ornaments, it is sober in comparison with its original appearance, when its decorative features were gilded or painted in ultramarine blue and cinnabar red. It has an open loggia on the *piano nobile*, like the Doge's Palace, but unlike any other palazzo after the Byzantine period. ▶

2 San Stae

just above water level. It was built for a branch of the Corner family, who were descended from Caterina Cornaro, Queen of Cyprus; Caterina was born in an earlier house on the site. The present palazzo dates from the 1720s.

The covered fish market or **Pescaria** has occupied a site here since the 14th century. The current neo-Gothic construction, however, was only built in 1907, replacing an iron one. Beyond this is a building with an endless parade of arches along the canal; this is the longest façade on the Grand Canal and belongs to Sansovino's **Fabbriche Nuove**, built in 1554-6 for Venice's financial judiciary; it now houses the Court of Assizes.

Just beyond this stands the **Fabbriche Vecchie** by Scarpagnino, built after a fire in the early 16th century.

Before the Rialto bridge, the **Palazzo dei Camerlenghi** (1523-5) is built around the curve of the canal; the walls lean noticeably. It was the headquarters of the Venetian Exchequer, with a debtors' prison on the ground floor. ▶

Sightseeing

▶ Ponte di Rialto

The Ponte di Rialto was built in 1588-92 by the aptly named Antonio Da Ponte. Until the 19th century it was the only bridge over the Grand Canal. It replaced a wooden one, which can be seen in Carpaccio's painting of *The Miracle of the True Cross* in the Accademia (*see p130*). After the decision was taken to build it, 60 years passed, during the course of which designs by Michelangelo, Vignola, Sansovino and Palladio were rejected. Da Ponte's simple but effective project eventually got the green light, probably because it maintained the utilitarian features of the previous wooden structure, with its double row of shops. The bridge thus acts as a logical continuation of the market at its foot. Palladio's design was far more beautiful, but made no provision for the sale of counterfeit trainers and plastic gondolas.

③ Vaporetto stop San Silvestro

Beyond the San Silvestro vaporetto stop are a few houses with Veneto-Byzantine windows and decorations, including **Ca' Barzizza**, one of the earliest Byzantine houses in Venice.

Before the rio San Polo is the 16th-century **Palazzo Cappello Layard**, once the home of Sir Henry Austen Layard, archaeologist and British ambassador to Constantinople.

A little way before the San Tomà stop is the **Palazzo Pisani Moretta**, a large Gothic palazzo of the 15th century, often hired out for Hollywood-style parties.

④ Vaporetto stop San Tomà

Palazzo Balbi (1582-90), with obelisks (an indication that an admiral lived here), is the seat of the Veneto Regional Council.

The rio Ca' Foscari turns into the rio Novo, a canal dug in the 1930s to provide a short cut to the car park and station; traffic seriously undermined the foundations of the buildings along the canal, so public transport stopped using the rio Novo in the 1980s. Looking down the rio, you can see the archways of the city's fire station. Between the fire station and **Palazzo Balbi** is a minor building, on a site once scheduled to hold Frank

Lloyd Wright's Centre for Foreign Architectural Students. In the end his designs were judged too radical for so conspicuous a spot.

Immediately beyond the rio Ca' Foscari come three magnificent mid 15th-century Gothic *palazzi*. The first and largest is **Ca' Foscari** (being restored as this guide went to press, and hidden behind a huge photographic reproduction of itself). It was at Ca' Foscari that Henry III of France was lavishly entertained in 1574 – so lavishly that his reason seems to have been knocked permanently askew. Doge Francesco Foscari died here of a broken heart after being ousted from office. The palazzo is now the headquarters of Venice's Università Ca' Foscari. The next two are the **Palazzi Giustinian**; Wagner stayed in one of them in the winter of 1858-9, composing part of *Tristan und Isolde*. The horn prelude to the third act was inspired by the mournful cries of the gondoliers.

Ca' Rezzonico (*see p127*) is a Baroque masterpiece by Longhena, begun in 1667 for the Bon family, then sold to the Rezzonico family. Robert Browning died here, while staying with his profitably married but otherwise talentless son Pen, who bought the palazzo with his wife's money. Later guests included Whistler and Cole Porter. The building now contains the museum of 18th-century Venice.

⑤ Vaporetto stop Ca' Rezzonico

Just after the Ca' Rezzonico stop is the 15th-century **Palazzo Loredan**. The last palazzo before the Accademia Bridge housed the British vice-consulate until 2003.

Once the church and monastery of Santa Maria della Carità, the **Gallerie dell'Accademia** now boasts an unrivalled collection of Venetian paintings (*see p130*). ▶

④ San Tomà   Sant'Angelo ⑤

Party palace: the
Palazzo Pisani Moretta.

Ponte di Rialto.

Ponte di Rialto

Rialto

③ San
Silvestro

▶ ③ **Vaporetto stop Ca' d'Oro**
Just before the rio dei
Santi Apostoli is **Palazzo
Mangilli Valmarana**, built
in 1751 for Joseph Smith, the
British consul, who amassed the huge
collection of Canaletto paintings that now
belongs to the Queen. The building is now the
Argentinian Consulate.

Beyond the rio dei Santissimi Apostoli stands
the **Ca' da Mosto**, once the site of the Leon
Bianco (white lion) Hotel, and currently being
returned to its original vocation as a luxury
hotel. This is one of the earliest Veneto-
Byzantine *palazzi* on the Grand Canal. It still
has three of the original five arches of its water-
entrance and a long array of Byzantine arches
on the first floor.

At the foot of the Rialto bridge is the
Fondaco dei Tedeschi, a huge residence-
cum-warehouse leased to the German
community from the 13th century onwards.
The present building was designed by Spavento
and Scarpagnino in 1505-8 after a fire. The

façade once had glorious frescoes by Titian
and Giorgione – now in a sad state of repair in
the Ca' d'Oro gallery (*see p103*). The Fondaco
is now the main post office.

Ponte di Rialto

Just before the Rialto stop is **Palazzo
Manin Dolfin**, with a portico straddling the
fondamenta. The façade is by Sansovino (late
1530s); the rest was rebuilt by Ludovico Manin,
the forlorn last doge of Venice (*see p21*). It now
belongs to the Bank of Italy.

④ **Vaporetto stop Rialto**
Palazzetto Dandolo is a Gothic building
that appears to have been squeezed tight by
its neighbours. Enrico Dandolo, the blind doge
who led the ferocious assault on Constantinople
in 1204 (*see p14*) was born in an earlier palazzo
that stood on this site.

Palazzo Farsetti and **Palazzo Loredan**
are Veneto-Byzantine buildings that now
house the city hall and various municipal
offices. Though heavily restored, these two
adjoining *palazzi* are among the few surviving
examples of the 12th-century Venetian house,
with its first-floor polyforate window.

Palazzo Grimani is one of the largest *palazzi*
on the Grand Canal. Its creator, Michele
Sanmicheli from Verona, was famous for his
military architecture, and this building is
characteristically massive and assertive. The
Grimani family were nouveaux riches, and
the story goes that they wanted each one of
their windows to be larger than the front door
of the palazzo that used to stand opposite.

Seven *palazzi* further on, before the rio Michiel,
stands the pink Palazzo Benzon, home of
Countess Marina Querini-Benzon, a great society
figure at the end of the 18th century. Byron was
charmed by her when she was already in her 60s.
She inspired a popular song, '*La biondina in
gondoleta*', which the gondoliers used to sing
before international tourism imposed the
unfittingly Neapolitan '*O' Sole Mio*'.

Before the Sant'Angelo vaporetto stop is the
small-scale **Palazzo Corner**, built in the last
decade of the 15th century by Mauro Codussi.
It is one of the most beautiful early Renaissance
buildings in Venice, with a rusticated ground
floor, elegant balconies and the characteristic
double-arched windows seen in Palazzo
Vendramin Calergi (*see p73*).

⑤ **Vaporetto stop Sant'Angelo**
A little beyond the traghetto (*see p279*)
station for San Tomà stand the four **Palazzi
Mocenigo,** with blue and white poles in
the water. The central double palazzo (16th
century) was where Byron and his menagerie of ▶

Sightseeing

Ponte dell'Accademia

After four fine Renaissance *palazzi* comes campo San Vio, one of the few *campi* on the Grand Canal. In the corner is the Anglican church of **St George** (*see p289*). To one side of the campo is the 16th-century **Palazzo Barbarigo**, with eye-catching but tacky 19th-century mosaics. Next is the pretty Gothic **Palazzo da' Mula**.

A little beyond that is the single-storey **Palazzo Venier dei Leoni**. Work ground to a halt in 1749 when the family opposite objected to their light being blocked by such a huge pile. Art collector Peggy Guggenheim lived here from 1949-79; she was the last person in Venice to have her own private gondola. The building now contains the **Peggy Guggenheim Collection** (*see p130*). Check out the brass horse and rider (1948) by Marino Marini overlooking the canal.

Next but one comes the pure, lopsided charm of the Renaissance **Ca' Dario**, built in the 1470s, perhaps by Pietro Lombardo, with decorative use of coloured marbles and chimney pots. Venetians say the palazzo is cursed; certainly the list of former owners who have met sticky ends is impressive.

Palazzo Salviati is a 19th-century building with gaudy mosaics advertising the products of the Salviati glass works.

The former abbey of **San Gregorio** is the last building before the Salute stop, with a fine

Sant'Angelo 5

4 San Tomà

▶foxes, monkeys and dogs lived in 1818-9; he wrote to a friend: 'Venice is not an expensive residence... I have my gondola and about 14 servants... and I reside in one of the Mocenigo palaces on the Grand Canal; the rent... is two hundred a year (and I gave more than I need have done).'

Just before the San Samuele vaporetto stop is heavy, grey-white **Palazzo Grassi** (*see p90*), designed by Giorgio Massari. This was the last of the great patrician *palazzi*, built in grand style in 1748-72 when the city was already in terminal decline. It was bought by Fiat in the 1980s and restored at the speed and enormous expense that only huge PR-conscious corporations can allow themselves. With the decline of Fiat's fortunes the future of the palazzo is uncertain, although large-scale exhibitions are still being planned.

San 6 Samuele

5 Ca' Rezzonico

6 Vaporetto stop San Samuele
The **Ca' del Duca** incorporates in one corner a part of the

Accademia
14th-century relief of St Gregory over a Gothic doorway. (Beyond can be seen the apse of the former church of the same name.)

Ponte dell' 5 Accademia

7 Vaporetto stop Salute
In a triumphant position, at the very opening of the Grand Canal, stands the wonderfully curvy church of **Santa Maria della Salute** (*see p132*). Baldassare Longhena's audacious Baroque creation (1671) took 50 years to build. Every year on 21 November (*see p198*) a procession from the basilica di San Marco makes its way across a specially-erected bridge

Palazzo Venier dei Leoni.

aggressively rusticated base and columns of a palace that Bartolomeo Bon was going to build for the Cornaro family; in 1461 the site was bought by Francesco Sforza, Duke of Milan; Bon's project, which was clearly on a massive scale, was never completed.

In 1932 the iron Ponte dell'Accademia built by the Austrians was replaced by a 'temporary' wooden one. When this was discovered to be on the point of collapse in 1984, the Venetians had grown too fond of it to imagine anything else spanning the canal, so it was rebuilt exactly as before.

Ponte dell'Accademia.

Ponte dell'Accademia

At the foot of the bridge is **Palazzo Franchetti**, built in the 15th century but much restored and altered in the 19th; it's now used as a conference centre and occasionally for exhibitions.

Immediately beyond this are two **Palazzi Barbaro**, which have literary associations. The first one – 15th-century Gothic, with a fine but battered Renaissance water entrance – still partly belongs to the Curtis family, who played host to Henry James at intervals between 1870 and 1875. The building was the model for Milly Theale's palazzo in *The Wings of the Dove*.

Just before one of the few Grand Canal gardens comes the bashful **Casetta delle Rose**, set back behind its own small trellised garden. Canova had a studio here; and controversial novelist Gabriele D'Annunzio, who set one of his most sensuous novels, *Il Fuoco* ('Fire'), in Venice, stayed in the house.

The massive rusticated ground floor of the **Palazzo Corner della Ca' Grande** (now the Prefecture) influenced Longhena's Baroque *palazzi*. The highest of High Renaissance, the imposing pile was commissioned in 1537 from Sansovino for Giacomo Cornaro, and built after 1545. Never one to mince words, Ruskin called it 'one of the worst and coldest buildings of the central Renaissance'.

Vaporetto stop Giglio

After campo Santa Maria del Giglio comes the long, 15th-century Gothic facade of **Palazzo Gritti**, now one of Venice's poshest hotels (*see p49*).

Three *palazzi* further on is the narrow Gothic **Palazzo Contarini Fasan**, traditionally, but quite arbitrarily, known as Desdemona's house. It has beautiful balconies with wheel tracery.

The **Europa & Regina** hotel was once the home of Kay Bronson, an American society hostess whose hospitality was much appreciated by Henry James.

The last notable building is **Ca' Giustinian**, built in the late Gothic style of the 1470s, and once a hotel where Verdi, Gautier, Ruskin and Proust stayed. George Eliot's honeymoon here was ruined when her husband fell off the balcony into the Grand Canal and nearly died.

At the corner of calle Vallaresso is the self-effacing **Harry's Bar** (*see p166*), the near-legendary Venetian watering hole, founded by Arrigo Cipriani senior in the 1930s.

Vaporetto stop Vallaresso

Just beyond the vaporetto stop lie the pretty **Giardinetti reali** (*see p79*) and **piazza San Marco**.

Vallaresso

 Giglio

Salute

of boats to the church. Beyond the church is the Patriarchal Seminary. The left bank ends with the **Dogana di Mare** (Customs House, 1677), with its tower, gilded ball, weathervane figure of Fortune and spectacular view out across the Bacino di San Marco towards the Lido.

(Eastward-facing, the view is best savoured, if you can manage it, at sunrise.) Ships wanting to enter Venice would have their cargoes examined by customs officials, who were based here. The warehouses before the Punta della Dogana date from the 19th century.

San Marco

The city starts here.

The **Doge's Palace**. *See p85.*

First-time visitors inevitably concentrate most of their attention on this *sestiere*, which is, and always has been, the city's great and glittering architectural showcase. However, it would be a mistake to think that the magnificent church and piazza that give the name to the *sestiere* are all that is worth seeing. Three main thoroughfares link the key points of this bustling neighbourhood, forming a rough triangle: one from piazza San Marco to the Rialto bridge, one from the Rialto to the Accademia bridge, and one from the Accademia to piazza San Marco. But even when the area is tumultuously teeming with tourists, you can always stray off these congested routes and find quiet corners.

PIAZZA SAN MARCO

Napoleon referred to the square as the 'drawing room of Europe', a description that catches some of the quality of the place: it may not be homey, but it is a supremely civilised meeting place. Byzantine rubs shoulders with Gothic, late Renaissance and neo-classical. Napoleon intended to embellish this open-air salon with a statue of himself in the centre of the western wing. The work (which was recently and controversially acquired by the Museo Correr, *see p83*) remained in front of the Palazzo Ducale for a few years but never made it into the piazza: the Venetians have always kept the square clear of public monuments (sometimes stooping to mendacity to do so – *see p93* Monument to Bartolomeo Colleoni). This is typical of Venice, where individual glory was always kept firmly in second place to communal progress.

The north side of the square dates from the early 16th century. Its 'troops of ordered arches' (to quote John Ruskin, *see p44* **Throwing stones**) take up a motif suggested by an earlier Byzantine building that can be seen in Gentile Bellini's painting *Translation of the Relics of the Cross* in the Accademia gallery (*see p130*). Here resided the procurators of St Mark's, who were in charge of maintaining the basilica – hence the name of this whole wing, the Procuratie Vecchie. At its eastern end is the **Torre dell'Orologio**.

Construction of the Procuratie Nuove on the other side of the square went on for most of the first half of the 17th century; it was built to designs by Vincenzo Scamozzi on the model of the Biblioteca Marciana around the corner. Napoleon, of course, had to join the two wings at the far end – not for the sake of symmetry, but in order to create the ballroom that was lacking in the Procuratie Nuove, which had become the imperial residence. So, in 1807, down came Sansovino's church of San Geminiano and up went the Ala Napoleonica, which now houses the **Museo Correr**. The cafés under the arches have their history too; but before you take the weight off your feet, bear in mind that a cup of coffee at an outside table may double your day's expenses (*see p169* **Sit-down rip-off**).

The **Campanile** and **Basilica di San Marco** close off the square in all its splendour to the east.

PIAZZETTA DEI LEONCINI

On the north side of the basilica is this small square, named after two small marble lions rubbed smooth by generations of children's bottoms. The large palazzo at the far end of the square is the 19th-century residence of the patriarch (cardinal) of Venice.

LA PIAZZETTA

Between the basilica and the lagoon, the Piazzetta, as it is so economically known, is the real entrance to Venice, defined by two free-standing columns of granite. Generations of foreign visitors disembarked here, to be immediately struck by all that pomp and magnificence. The area directly in front of the **Palazzo Ducale** (Doge's Palace) corresponded to the modern-day parliamentary lobby. Known as the *broglio*, it was the place where councillors conferred and connived (hence the term 'imbroglio'). Opposite the palace stands the **Biblioteca Marciana**, now the main city library.

The man who erected the two columns in the 12th century supposedly asked for the right to set up gambling tables between them. The authorities agreed, but soon put a damper on the jollity by using the pillars to string up criminals for public edification – which is why superstitious locals still avoid walking between them. The winged lion on top of the easternmost column is in fact a chimera from Persia, Syria or maybe China; the wings and book are Venetian additions. St Theodore, who tops the other one, was Venice's first patron saint.

BY THE LAGOON

West of the Piazzetta are the Giardinetti Reali (Royal Gardens), created by the French, who had the old granaries pulled down to provide a view for the royal residence they had set up in the Procuratie Nuove. The dainty neo-classical coffee house by Gustavo Selva is now a tourist information office (*see p293*), with a small bookshop attached.

By the Vallaresso vaporetto stop is Harry's Bar (*see p166*), the most famous watering hole in the city, founded in the 1920s. Ernest Hemingway, Orson Welles and many other famous drinkers have contributed to the legend of the place and the price of the food.

Going the opposite way from the Piazzetta, you cross the ponte della Paglia (Bridge of Straw). If you can elbow your way to the side of the bridge, there is a photo-op view of the Bridge of Sighs, famous in legend and poetry linking the Palazzo Ducale to the prisons and thus, supposedly, offering a last glimpse of the outside to the condemned wretches. From the Bridge of Straw there is also a superb view of the Renaissance façade of the Palazzo Ducale, by Antonio Rizzo, which even Ruskin – a fan of the Byzantine and Gothic – was forced to admire against his will.

TICKETS

The museums around piazza San Marco (but not the paying parts of the basilica) must be visited on a multi-entrance ticket. *See p70* **Musei Civici Veneziani/Musei di piazza San Marco**.

Basilica di San Marco

Piazza San Marco (041 522 5205). Vaporetto San Zaccaria or Vallaresso. **Open** *May-Sept* 9.45am-5pm Mon-Sat; 2-4pm Sun. *Oct-Apr* 9.45am-4.30pm Mon-Sat; 2-4pm Sun. Before 9.45am private prayer and Mass only, from the piazzetta dei Leoncini door. **Admission** free. *Loggia & Museo Marciano* €3; €1.50 concessions. *Chancel & Pala d'Oro* €1.50; €1 concessions. *Treasury* €2; €1 concessions. **No credit cards. Map** p312 B1.
Note that large bags or rucksacks must be deposited at no charge in a building in calle San Basso, off the piazzetta dei Leoncini.
Throughout history, the basilica di San Marco has provoked extreme reactions. Some, like John Ruskin, pitch head first into purple prose: 'The crests of the arches break into a marble foam, and toss themselves far into the blue sky in flashes and wreaths of sculpted spray.' Others, resentful of its opulence, take the dissenting view. Mark Twain described it as a 'vast and warty bug taking a meditative walk'.

Often seen as the living testimony of Venice's links with Byzantium, the basilica is also an expression of the city's independence. In the Middle Ages any self-respecting city state had to have a truly important holy relic. So when two Venetian merchants swiped the body of St Mark (though some historians believe they got Alexander the Great's remains by mistake, *see p17* **Illustrious remains**) from Alexandria in 828, concealed from prying Muslim eyes under a protective layer of pork, they were

Sightseeing

Nature trail: the birds of San Marco

There's no getting away from birds as you cross piazza San Marco, and we don't (only) mean the voracious, invasive pigeon variety. The mosaics of St Mark's basilica (*see p79*) are a paeon to our winged brethren: in the creation cupola, anonymous artists brought to life an extraordinary range of birds and fishes, depicted with far more vigour than the prim rows of land-animals. In the scenes from the story of Noah, gorgeously plumaged birds again steal the show, with a peacock entering the ark first. But it is not only the exotic birds that take centre-stage: no bird is represented more convincingly, down to its last ruffled feather, than the scraggy raven released from the ark by Noah and distracted by some gruesomely enticing titbit on the waves.

Three of the column capitals of the Palazzo Ducale (*see p85*) are given over to birds engaged in various activities: preening themselves, fighting snakes or catching fish. In the Museo Correr (*see p83*), Carpaccio's *Two Venetian Noblewomen* await their husbands on a balcony together with a tame menagerie of dogs, doves, a peacock and a pigeon, while in the sacristy of San Salvador (*see p88*) a number of charming birds flit among foliage in 16th-century ceiling frescoes that were only discovered in the 1920s and have been freshly restored.

A much more recent but equally striking bird marks the entrance of the Merceria near campo San Bartolomeo (*see p89*): a spiky metal art deco crane with a long curving neck clutches a multi-coloured ball of open umbrellas in its beak.

St Mark's basilica. *See p79*.

going for the very best – an Evangelist, and an entire body at that. Fortunately, there was a legend (or one was quickly cooked up) that the saint had once been caught in the lagoon in a storm, and so it was fitting that this should be his final resting place.

The Venetians were traders, but they never looked askance at a bit of straightforward looting as well. The basilica – like the city as a whole – is encrusted with trophies brought back from Venice's greatest spoliatory exploit, the Sack of Constantinople in 1204, during the free-for-all that went under the name of the Fourth Crusade.

The present basilica is the third on the site. It was built mainly between 1063 and 1094, although the work of decoration continued all the way through to the 16th century. The church only became Venice's cathedral in 1807, ten years after the fall of the Republic; until then the bishop exerted his authority from San Pietro in Castello (*see p101*).

Next door to the Palazzo Ducale, Venice's most important church was associated with political as much as spiritual power. Venetians who came to worship here were very aware that they were guests of the doge, not the pope, and the basilica was an integral part of the city's self-glorifying mythology.

Exterior

The first view of the basilica from the western end of the square is an unforgettable experience. It is particularly impressive in the evening, when the mosaics on the façade glow in the light of the setting sun (as they are mostly 17th- and 18th-century replacements, the distance improves them). The façade consists of two orders of five arches, with clusters of columns in the lower order; the upper arches are topped by the fantastic Gothic tracery that inspired Ruskin to reach for those metaphors.

The only original mosaic is the one over the north door, *The Translation of the Body of St Mark to the Basilica*, which contains the earliest known representation of the church; it dates from around 1260. Of curiosity value is the 17th-century mosaic over the south door, which shows the body of St Mark being filched from Alexandria and the Muslims reeling back in disgust from its pork wrapping.

The real treasures, though, are the sculptures, particularly the group of three carved arches around the central portal, a masterpiece of romanesque work. The inner curve of the outer arch is the liveliest, with its detailed portrayals of Venetian trades, crafts and pastimes such as shipbuilding, hunting and fishing. The upper order, with its fine 14th-century Gothic sculpture by the Dalle Masegne brothers and later Tuscan and Lombard sculptors, can be seen from the Loggia (*see p82*).

The south façade, towards the Palazzo Ducale, was the first side seen by visitors from the sea and is thus richly encrusted with trophies proclaiming Venice's might. There was a ceremonial entrance to the basilica here as well, but this was blocked by the construction of the Zen Chapel (*see p82*) in the 16th century. At the corner stand the Tetrarchs, a fourth-century porphyry group of four conspiratorial-

looking kings. These come from Constantinople, and are usually accepted as representing Diocletian and his Imperial colleagues. However, popular lore has it that they are four Saracens turned to stone after an attempt to burgle the Treasury.

The two free-standing pillars in front of the Baptistry door, with Syrian carvings from the fifth century, come from Acre, as does the stumpy porphyry column on the corner, known as the Pietra del Bando, where official decrees were read. It bore the brunt of the fall of the Campanile (*see p83*) in 1902, hence its rather battered appearance.

The north façade, facing piazzetta dei Leoncini, is also studded with loot. One example is the carving of 12 sheep on either side of a throne bearing a cross, a Byzantine work of the seventh century. Note the beautiful 13th-century Moorish arches of the Porta dei Fiori, which enclose a Nativity scene.

The narthex (entrance porch) has an opus sectile marble floor; a small lozenge of porphyry by the central door is said to mark the spot where the Emperor Barbarossa paid homage to Pope Alexander III in 1177. The influence of Islamic art comes through in the few remaining grilles that cover the wall niches where early doges were buried. Above, a series of fine 13th-century mosaics by Venetian craftsmen in the Byzantine style shows scenes from the Old Testament.

Interior

Visit every day for the rest of your life and you just might begin to feel that you have seen everything contained in this cave of wonders. Failing that, make more than one visit, preferably at different times of day (with a mini-helicopter), to appreciate the varying effects of light on the mosaics.

The lambent interior exudes splendour and mystery, even when bursting with tourists. It is in many ways an exercise in obsession: for centuries the Venetians continued to add to its treasures, leaving not an inch uncovered.

The form is that of a Greek cross, surmounted by five great 11th-century domes. The surfaces – all the surfaces – are covered by more than four square kilometres (1.5 square miles) of mosaics, the result of 600 years of labour. The finest pieces, dating from the 12th and 13th centuries, are the work of Venetian craftsmen influenced by Byzantine art but developing their own independent style. The chapels and Baptistry were decorated in the 14th and 15th centuries; a century later, replacements of earlier mosaics were made using cartoons by such artists as Titian and Tintoretto. However, most of these later mosaics are fundamentally flawed by the attempt to achieve the three-dimensional effects of Renaissance painting.

In the apse, Christ Pantocrator is a faithful 16th-century reproduction of a Byzantine original. Beneath, in what may be the oldest mosaics in the church, are four saint-protectors of Venice: St Nicholas, St Peter, St Mark and St Hermagoras. The central dome of the Ascension, with its splendidly poised angels and apostles, dates from the early 13th

Sightseeing

century. It is said to have influenced fresco painting in the area as well as the sculptures on the façade. The Passion scenes on the west vault (12th century) are a striking blend of Romanesque and Byzantine styles. The Pentecost dome (towards the entrance) was probably the first to be decorated; it shows the *Descent of the Holy Spirit*. Four magnificent angels hover in the pendentives.

Worth seeking out is the scene of the *Miraculous Rediscovery of the Body of St Mark* in the right transept. This refers to an episode that occurred after the second basilica was destroyed by fire, when the secret of the whereabouts of the body was lost. The Evangelist obligingly opened up the pillar where his sarcophagus had been hidden (it's just opposite and is marked by an inlaid marble panel).

Notice too, the spectacular 12th-century marble, porphyry and glass mosaics on the floor, which have been much restored.

Baptistry & Zen Chapel
The Baptistry contains the Gothic tomb of Doge Andrea Dandolo and some interesting mosaics such as an image of Salome dancing. It is open for private prayer; enter discreetly if you must. The adjoining Zen Chapel, with its bronze 16th-century tomb of Cardinal Zen (Zen is a common Venetian surname), is generally closed; permission (041 522 5202) is needed to visit it.

Chancel & Pala d'Oro
The Chancel is separated from the body of the church by the iconostasis – a red marble rood screen by the Gothic sculptors Jacobello and Pier Paolo Dalle Masegne, with fine naturalistic statues of the Madonna, the apostles and St George. Access to the Chancel is via the San Clemente chapel to the right, with a mosaic showing merchants Rustico di Torcello and Buono di Malamocco, apparently about to send the body of St Mark to Venice. St Mark's sarcophagus is visible through the grate underneath the altar. It was moved here from the 11th-century crypt in 1835; the crypt remains a popular venue for society weddings, though it's closed to the rest of us.

The indigestibly opulent Pala d'Oro (Gold Altarpiece) is a Byzantine work and, for a change, was acquired honestly. It was made in Constantinople in 976 on the orders of Doge Pietro Orseolo I and further enriched in later years with amethysts, emeralds, pearls, rubies, sapphires and topaz, topped off with a Gothic frame and resetting in 1345. It's a worldly corner of the church, this. Set in the frame of the curving sacristy door are bronze busts of its maker, Sansovino, and his friends, Titian and Aretino (*see p89* **Poison pen**), who helped to get him out of prison in 1545. Aretino was a poet and playwright who moved to Venice in 1527 after scandalising Rome with his 'Lewd Sonnets'. A great satirist and hedonist, he is said to have died laughing at a filthy joke about his sister.

The left transept contains the chapel of the Madonna Nicopeia (the Victory Bringer), named after the tenth-century icon on the altar – another Fourth Crusade acquisition. She is still much revered: early in the morning, praying Venetians can often be seen here confiding in her. The St Isidore chapel beyond, with its 14th-century mosaics of the life of the saint is reserved for private prayer and confessions; as with the Baptistry, visitors are asked to show discretion if entering. The same goes for the adjacent Mascoli chapel. The altarpiece in this chapel, featuring Saints Mark and John the Evangelist, with the Virgin between them (in this unusual representation the Virgin has a graceful bend round about her midriff), is a striking piece of Gothic statuary. The chapel's mosaics, dating from 1430-50, have a definite Renaissance look to them, with classical architecture featuring in their backgrounds. They are mostly by Michele Giambono, although some of the figures have been attributed to Jacopo Bellini and to the Florentine Andrea del Castagno (who was in Venice in 1432, working in San Zaccaria, *see p95*).

Loggia & Museo Marciano
Of all the pay-to-enter sections of the basilica, this is definitely the most worthwhile – and moreover it's the only part of the church that can be visited on a Sunday morning. Up a narrow stairway from the narthex are the bronze horses that vie with the book-bearing lion of St Mark as the city's symbol; here too, is Paolo Veneziano's exquisite Pala Feriale, a painted panel that was used to cover the Pala d'Oro on weekdays. The Loggia also provides a marvellous view over the square.

The original bronze horses are now kept indoors. They are the greatest piece of loot – apart from the body of St Mark himself – in the whole city. They were among the many treasures that Venice brought back from the Sack of Constantinople, where they had stood above the Hippodrome. The horses' origins are uncertain. For many years they were attributed to a Greek sculptor of the fourth century BC, but the idea that they may be an original Roman work of the second century AD has recently come into favour: the half-moon shape of their eyes is said to have been a Roman characteristic. They were at first placed in front of the Arsenale (*see p97*), but around 1250 they found their place of honour on the terrace of the basilica, supreme expressions of Venetian pride.

In 1797 it was Napoleon's turn to play looter, and the horses did not return to Venice until after his defeat at Waterloo. Apart from the parentheses of the two world wars, during which they were put away in safe storage, they remained on the terrace until 1974, when they were removed for restoration. Since 1982 they have been on display in a room inside the basilica, with perfect but soulless copies replacing them on the terrace.

Treasury
This contains a hoard of exquisite Byzantine gold and silver work – reliquaries, chalices, candelabras – most of it Crusade plunder. If you can stand the glitter, the highlights are a silver perfume censer in the form of a church and two 11th-century icons of the Archangel Michael.

Venice's tallest **Campanile**.

Campanile

San Marco. Vaporetto San Zaccaria or Vallaresso.
Open *Apr-Sept* 9.30am-30mins before sunset daily.
Nov-Mar 9.30am-3.30pm daily. **Admission** €6;
€3 concessions. **No credit cards. Map** p311 B3.

Venice's most famous landmark – and at almost
99m (325ft) the tallest building in the city – was
originally built between 888 and 912. Its present
appearance, with the stone spire and the gilded
angel on top, dates from 1514.

The Campanile served both as a watchtower and
a bell tower. It provided a site for public humilia-
tions: people of 'scandalous behaviour' were hung
in a cage from the top. More wholesome fun was provided by the *volo dell'anzolo*, when an intrepid
arsenalotto (Arsenale shipwright) would slide down
a rope strung between the Campanile and the
Palazzo Ducale to mark the end of Carnevale (*see
pp196-198* **Festivals and Events**).

In July 1902 the whole thing fell down. Some
blamed old age, weak foundations and lightning
damage; others, such as crusty old British travel
writer Augustus Hare, put it down to 'gross neglect
and criminal misusage'. The Campanile was tidy in
its collapse, imploding in a neat pyramid of rubble;
the only victim was the custodian's cat.

It was rebuilt exactly 'as it was, where it was', to
use the formula of the town council. Holy Roman
Emperor Frederick III rode a horse to the top of the
old version in 1451; these days, visitors take the lift.
The view through the anti-suicide grate is superb,
taking in the Lido, the whole lagoon and the
Dolomites in the distance. Sansovino's little
Loggetta at the foot of the tower, which echoes the
shape of a Roman triumphal arch, was also rebuilt,

jigsaw-fashion, using bits and pieces found in the
rubble. In the 18th century the Loggetta was where
the state lottery was drawn.

Museo Correr, Biblioteca Marciana & Museo Archeologico

*San Marco 52, piazza San Marco/sottoportego
San Geminian (041 240 5211). Vaporetto
Vallaresso.* **Open** *Apr-Oct* 9am-7pm daily
(ticket office closes 6pm). *Nov-Mar* 9am-5pm daily
(ticket office closes 4pm). **Admission** by multi-
entrance ticket (*see p70* **Musei di Piazza San
Marco**). **Map** p311 B3.

These three adjoining museums are all entered on
the same ticket and by the same doorway, which is
situated beneath the Ala Napoleonica at the western
end of piazza San Marco.

Museo Correr
The Museo Correr is Venice's civic museum,
dedicated to the history of the Republic – which
means that it acts as a storeroom for all the bits and
pieces that didn't fit in elsewhere. Based on the
private collection of Venetian nobleman Teodoro
Correr (1750-1830), it is elevated beyond mere curiosity value by the second-floor gallery, which is
essential viewing for anyone interested in Venetian
early Renaissance painting. The museum is housed
in the Ala Napoleonica, the wing that closes off the
narrow western end of the piazza, and in the
Procuratie Nuove. Napoleon demolished the church
of San Geminiano to make way for this exercise in
neoclassical regularity, complete with that essential
imperial accessory, a ballroom. The spirit of these
years is conserved in the first part of the collection,
dedicated to the beautifully soulless sculpture of
Antonio Canova, whose first Venetian commission
– the statue of Daedalus and Icarus, displayed here
– brought him immediate acclaim. Some of the
works on display are Canova's plaster models rather
than his finished marble statues.

The historical collection, which occupies most of
the first floor of the Procuratie Vecchie (*see p78*),
documents Venetian history and social life in the
16th and 17th centuries. Among the globes, lutes,
coins and robes, interesting light is thrown on various aspects of life in the Republic. Room 6, devoted
to the figure of the Doge, features Lazzaro Bastiani's
famous portrait of Doge Francesco Foscari (c1460).
Room 11 has a collection of Venetian coins, plus
Tintoretto's fine *St Justine and the Treasurers*.
Beyond are rooms dedicated to the Arsenale (*see
p97*): a display of weaponry and some occasionally
charming miniature bronzes.

The bulk of one's critical energy should be saved,
however, for the Quadreria picture gallery upstairs
– perhaps the best place in the city to get a grip on
the development of Venetian painting between the
Byzantine stirrings of Paolo Veneziano and the full-
blown Renaissance story-telling of Carpaccio.
Rooms 24 to 29 are dedicated to Byzantine and
Gothic painters – note Paolo Veneziano's fine *St John
the Baptist* and the rare allegorical fresco fragments

St Mark's square: a supremely civilised meeting place. *See p78.*

from a 14th-century private house in Room 27. Room 30 fast-forwards abruptly with the macabre, proto-Mannerist *Pietà* of Cosme Turà.

Room 32, the Sala delle Quattro Porte, is one of the only rooms in the museum that still preserves its 16th-century structure; it contains the famous aerial view of Venice by Jacopo de' Barbari, dated 1500. This extraordinary woodcut is so finely detailed that the architectural details of every single church, palazzo and well head in the city seem to have been diligently copied; also on display are the original matrices in pear wood. Beyond here, the Renaissance gets into full swing with Antonello da Messina's *Pietà with Three Angels*, haunting despite the fact that the faces have nearly been erased by cack-handed restoration. The Bellinis get Room 36 to themselves – note the rubicund portrait of Doge Giovanni Mocenigo, painted by Gentile Bellini just before his departure for Constantinople in 1475.

The gallery's most fascinating work, though, must be Vittorio Carpaccio's *Two Venetian Noblewomen* – long known erroneously as *The Courtesans* – in Room 38. These two bored women are not angling for trade: they're waiting for their husbands to return from a hunt. This was confirmed when *A Hunt in the Valley* in the Getty Museum in Los Angeles was shown to be this painting's other half. Downstairs, the collection continues with rooms dedicated to the state barge, the Bucintoro, to festivities and to trade guilds. The last two rooms have paintings of fairground trials of strength and some portable gambling accessories.

Museo Archeologico

This collection of Greek and Roman art and artefacts is interesting not so much for the quality of the individual pieces as for the light they cast on the history of collecting. Assembled mainly by Cardinal Domenico Grimani and his nephew Giovanni, mainly from Roman finds, the collection is a discerning 16th-century humanist's attempt to surround himself with the classical ideal of beauty; as such these statues were much copied by Venetian artists. Among the highlights are the original fifth century BC Greek statues of goddesses in Room 4, which are among the few such works known to the Italian Renaissance, the Grimani Altar in Room 6, and the intricate cameos and intaglios in Room 7 or Room 12 (depending on temporary exhibitions).

There are free guided tours in English (11am Sat & Sun).

Biblioteca Marciana/Libreria Sansoviniana

For information on use of the library, *see p286.*

In 1468 the great humanist scholar Cardinal Bessarion of Trebizond left his collection of Greek and Latin manuscripts to the state. This time the Venetians didn't lose them, as they seem to have done with Petrarch's library (*see p43*), although they didn't get round to constructing a proper home – a splendid building right opposite the Palazzo Ducale – for them until 1537. Jacopo Sansovino, a Florentine architect who had settled in Venice after fleeing from the Sack of Rome in 1527, was appointed to create the library. Palladio described it as the 'richest and most ornate building since antiquity'.

With this building, Sansovino brought the ambitious new ideas of the Roman Renaissance of Donato Bramante and Michelangelo into Venice. He also appealed to the Venetian love of surface decoration by endowing his creation with an abundance of statuary. His original plan included a barrel-vault ceiling. This collapsed shortly after construction, however, and the architect was immediately clapped into prison. His rowdy friends Titian and Aretino (*see p89* **Poison Pen**) had to lobby hard to have him released from jail.

The working part of Venice's main library is now housed in La Zecca (*see p87*) and contains some 750,000 volumes and around 13,500 manuscripts, most of them Greek.

The main room has a magnificent ceiling, with seven rows of allegorical medallion paintings, produced by a number of Venetian Mannerist artists as part of a competition. Veronese's *Music* (sixth row from entrance), perhaps the least Mannerist in style, was awarded the gold chain by Titian. Beyond this is the ante-room, in which a partial reconstruction has been made of Cardinal Grimani's collection of classical statues, as arranged by Scamozzi (1596). On the ceiling is *Wisdom*, a late work by Titian.

In a room off the staircase landing is Fra Mauro's map of the world (1459), a fascinating testimony to the great precision of Venice's geographical knowledge, with extraordinarily accurate depictions of such places as China and India.

Palazzo Ducale (Doge's Palace)

San Marco 1, piazzetta San Marco (041 271 5911/bookings 041 520 9070). Vaporetto San Zaccaria. **Open** *Apr-Oct* 9am-7pm daily (ticket office closes 6pm). *Nov-Mar* 9am-5pm daily (ticket office closes 4pm). **Admission** with multi-entrance ticket (*see p70* **Musei di Piazza San Marco**). **Guided tours** 11.30am Sun (€6). **Credit** MC, V. **Map** p312 B1.

An unobtrusive side door halfway down the right wall of the nave in San Marco leads straight into the courtyard of the Palazzo Ducale (Doge's Palace). Today's visitors take a more roundabout route, but that door is a potent symbol of the entwinement of Church and state in the glory days of *La Serenissima*. If the basilica was the Venetian Republic's spiritual nerve centre, the Doge's Palace was its political and judicial hub. The present site was the seat of ducal power from the ninth century onwards, though most of what we see today dates from the mid 15th century. Devastating fires in 1574 and 1577 took their toll, but after much debate it was decided to restore rather than replace – an enlightened policy for the time.

The architectural form of the building testifies to Venetian confidence in the impossibility of invasion or attack: whereas Renaissance seats of government in other Italian towns look like castles, this is very definitely a palace. It is the great Gothic building of the city, but is also curiously eastern in style, achieving a marvellous combination of lightness and strength. The ground floor was open to the public; the work of government went on in the more closed part above. This arrangement resulted in a curious reversal of the natural order: the first level has an open arcade of simple Gothic arches, the second a closed loggia of rich, ornate arcading. The top floor is a solid wall broken by a sequence of Gothic windows. And yet somehow it doesn't seem awkward.

The Piazzetta façade was built in the 15th century as a continuation of the 14th-century waterfront façade. On the corner by the ponte di Paglia (Bridge of Straw) is an exquisite marble relief carving, the *Drunkenness of Noah* from the early 15th century, while on the Piazzetta corner is a statue of Adam and Eve from the late 14th century. The capitals of the pillars below date from the 14th to the 15th centuries, although more than a dozen of them are 19th-century copies (some of the originals are on display inside). On the waterfront side (ninth pillar from the left) is what appears to be a boy eating an ice-cream cone; don't disappoint your kids by telling them it's really a chicken leg.

The Porta della carta (or 'Paper Gate' – so called because this was where permits were checked), between the palace and the basilica, is a grand piece of florid Gothic architecture and sculpture (1438-42) by Bartolomeo and Giovanni Bon. The statue of Doge Francesco Foscari and the lion is a copy dating from 1885; French troops smashed the original when they occupied the city in 1797.

Behind the palace's fairy-tale exterior the machinery of empire whirred away with the same kind of assembly-line efficiency that went into the building of ships over at the Arsenale (*see p97*). Anyone really interested in the inner workings of the Venetian state should take the 90-minute *Itinerari segreti* tour (book at least two days in advance, 041 271 5911, tours in English depart 9.55am, 10.45am daily from April to October, €12.50, €7 concessions). This takes you into those parts of the palace that the official route does not touch: the cramped wooden administrative offices; the stark chambers of the *Cancelleria segreta* where all official documents were written up in triplicate by a team of 24 clerks; the chamber of the three heads of the Council of Ten, connected by a secret door in the wooden panelling to the *Sala del Consiglio dei Dieci*, and the torture chambers beyond. The tour ends up in the leads – the sweltering prison cells underneath the roof from which Casanova staged his famous escape (probably by bribing the guard, though his own account was far more action hero).

Following reorganisation, the main visit – for which an audio guide (€5.50) is recommended – now begins at the Porta del Frumento on the lagoon side of the palace, rather than at the main Piazzetta entrance via the Porta della Carta. The Museo dell'Opera, just to the left of the ticket barrier, has the best of the 14th-century capitals from the external loggia; the ones you see outside are copies.

In the main courtyard stands the Arco dei Foscari – another fine late Gothic work, commissioned by Doge Francesco Foscari in 1438, when Venice was at the height of its territorial influence. It was built by Antonio Bregno and Antonio Rizzo. Rizzo also sculpted the figures of Adam and Eve (these, too, are copies; the originals are inside the palace), which earned him gushing accolades and led to his appointment as official architect in 1483, after one of those disastrous fires. Rizzo had time to oversee the building of the overblown Scala dei Giganti (where doges were crowned) and some of the interior before he was found to have embezzled 12,000 ducats; he promptly fled, and died soon after.

The official route now leads up the ornate Scala d'Oro staircase by Jacopo Sansovino, with stuccoes by Vittoria outlined in 24-carat gold leaf.

First floor: Doge's apartments

And to think this is supposed to be the domestic side of the operation. In reality, the doge's private life was entirely at the service of *La Serenissima*, and even his bedroom had to keep up the PR effort. These rooms are sometimes closed or used for temporary exhibitions; when open, the Sala delle Mappe (also known as the Sala dello Scudo) merits scrutiny.

Here, in a series of 16th-century maps, is the known world as it radiated from Venice. Just to the right of the entrance door is a detailed map of the New World with Bofton (Boston) and Isola Longa (Long Island) clearly marked. Further on, it's worth seeking out Titian's well-hidden fresco of St Christopher (above a doorway giving onto a staircase), which, astonishingly, took the artist a mere three days to complete.

Second floor: State rooms

This grandiose series of halls provided steady work for all the great 16th-century Venetian artists. Titian, Tintoretto, Veronese, Palma il Vecchio and Jacopo Bassano all left their mark, though the sheer acreage that had to be covered, and the subjects of the canvases – either allegories or documentary records of the city's pomp and glory – did not always spur them to artistic heights.

The Sala delle Quattro Porte was where the Collegio – the inner cabinet of the Republic – met before the 1574 fire. After substantial renovation it became an ambassadorial waiting room, where humble envoys could gaze enviously at Andrea Vicentino's portrayal of the magnificent reception given to the young King Henry III of France in 1574 (the triumphal arch that you can see in the picture was put up overnight). The Anticollegio, restored in part by Palladio, has a spectacular gilded stucco ceiling, four Tintorettos and Veronese's blowsy *Rape of Europa*. Beyond here is the Sala del Collegio, where the inner cabinet convened.

The propaganda paintings on the ceiling are by Veronese; note the equal scale of the civic and divine players, and the way that both Justice and Peace are mere handmaidens to Venice herself. But for real hubris you have to stroll into the next room, the Sala del Senato, where Tintoretto's ceiling centrepiece shows *The Triumph of Venice*. Here the Senate, which by 1450 had grown from 60 to an unwieldy 300 members, met to debate questions of foreign policy, war and commerce, and to hear the reports of returning Venetian ambassadors.

Beyond are the Sala del Consiglio dei Dieci and the Sala della Bussola, where the arcane body set up specifically to act as a check on the doge considered matters of national security. In the former, note Veronese's ceiling panel, *Juno Offering Gifts to Venice*. By the time this was painted in 1553, the classical gods had started to replace St Mark in Venice's self-aggrandising pantheon.

Here the itinerary (which is liable to change without warning) heads through a bristling armoury, whose ingenious instruments of war impressed early visitors. But, as one 17th-century tourist pointed out, the collection was established so that 'if the People should conspire against the Nobles, and make any Attempt against them while they are sitting, they might be furnished with Arms upon the Spot to defend themselves'.

First floor: State rooms

The Sala dei Censori now leads down to a *liagò* (covered, L-shaped loggia), which gives on to the Sala della Quarantia Civil Vecchia (the civil court) and the Sala del Guariento. The latter's faded 14th-century fresco of *The Coronation of the Virgin* by Guariento (for centuries hidden behind Tintoretto's *Paradiso* in the Sala del Maggior Consiglio) looks strangely innocent amid all this worldly propaganda. The shorter arm of the *liagò* has the originals of Antonio Rizzo's stylised marble sculptures of Adam and Eve from the Arco del Foscari.

Next comes the Sala del Maggior Consiglio – the largest room in the palace. It had to be big, as by 1512, according to historian Marin Sanudo, 2,622 patrician men were entitled to sit on the *maggior consiglio* (Greater Council). This was in effect the Republic's lower house – though with the top-heavy Venetian system of government, this council of noblemen had fairly limited powers. Before the fire of 1577, the hall had been decorated with paintings by Bellini, Titian, Carpaccio and Veronese – a choice collection that was so costly to commission that in 1515 a group of patricians complained about the expense. When these works went up in smoke, they were replaced by less exalted works – with one or two exceptions. Tintoretto's *Paradise* on the far wall, sketched out by the 70-year-old artist but completed after his death in 1594 by his son Domenico, is liable to induce vertigo, as much for its theological complexity as its huge scale. In the ceiling panels are works by Veronese and Palma il Giovane; note, too, the frieze of ducal portraits carried out by Domenico Tintoretto and assistants, with the black veil marking the place where Marin Falier's face would have appeared had he not unwisely conspired against the state in 1356.

On the left side of the hall, a balcony gives a fine view over the southern side of the lagoon. A door leads from the back of the hall into the Sala della Quarantia Civil Nuova and the large Sala dello Scrutinio, where the votes of the maggior consiglio were counted; the latter is flanked by vast paintings of victorious naval battles, including a dramatic *Conquest of Zara* by Jacopo Tintoretto and *Battle of Lepanto* by Andrea Vicentino.

Criminal courts & *prigioni*

Backtracking through the Sala del Maggior Consiglio, a small door on the left leads past the Scala dei Censori to the Sala della Quarantia

Sightseeing

Criminale – the criminal court. The next room retains some original red and gold leather wall coverings. Beyond is a small room that has been arranged as a gallery, with Flemish paintings from Cardinal Grimani's collection, originally hidden from public view. The hysterical religious mysticism of Bosch's *Inferno* strikes an odd note here: though rational, Venice was not always immune to religious fanaticism.

The route now leads over the Bridge of Sighs to the Prigioni Nuove, where petty criminals were kept. Lifers were sent down to the waterlogged *pozzi* (wells) in the basement of the palazzo itself. By the 19th century most visitors were falling for the tour guide legend that, once over the Bridge of Sighs, prisoners would 'descend into the dungeon which none entered and hoped to see the sun again', as Mark Twain put it. But when this new prison wing was built in 1589, it was acclaimed as a paragon of comfort; in 1608, the English traveller Thomas Coryat remarked, 'I think there is not a fairer prison in all Christendom.'

Some of the cells have their number and capacity painted over the door; one has a *trompe l'œil* window, drawn in charcoal by a bored inmate. On the lowest level is a small exercise yard, where an unofficial tavern used to operate. Up the stairs beyond is a display of Venetian ceramics found during excavations, and more cells, one with a fascinating display of cartoons and caricatures left by 19th-century internees.

Back across the Bridge of Sighs, the tour ends on the lower floor in the Avogaria – the offices of the clerks of court. Next to this a bookshop has been set up (open 9am-4pm), with a good selection of works on Venice. On the ground floor is a welcome (though not particularly cheap) cafeteria; beyond the cafeteria are the old kitchens (ask the custodian), where the restored mechanism from the Torre dell'Orologio (Clock Tower, *see below*) can be seen, together with the statues of the Magi and the Angel (usually only seen during Ascension week), all waiting to be replaced in the restored tower.

Torre dell'Orologio
San Marco 147, piazza San Marco (041 522 4951/ www.museiciviveneziani.it). Vaporetto San Zaccaria. **Map** p312 B1.
The clock tower, designed by Maurizio Codussi, was built between 1496 and 1506; the wings were an addition, perhaps by Pietro Lombardo. Above the clock face is the Madonna. During Ascension week and at Epiphany, the Magi come out and bow to her every hour, in an angel-led procession. At other times of year, the burly Moors on the roof, made of gunmetal and cast in 1497, strike the hour. Another Moore – Roger – sent a villain flying through the clock face in the film *Moonraker*. In 1999 the clock was restored. However, the building as a whole has been hidden since 1998 behind a lifesize photograph of itself and, owing to legal wrangling with the proprietors of the adjoining buildings, restoration work

came to a halt until July 2004; it is unlikely to reopen for visitors before 2006. When it does so it will only admit small groups with prior bookings. In the meantime the original mechanism and statues can be seen in the Palazzo Ducale (*see p85*).

La Zecca
San Marco 7, piazzetta San Marco (041 520 8788). Vaporetto Vallaresso. **Open** 8.10am-7pm Mon-Fri; 8.10am-1.30pm Sat. **Admission** free. **Map** p312 B1.
The Mint, designed by Sansovino, was completed by 1547. It coined Venice's famous gold ducats – later referred to as *zecchini*, whence the English 'sequins'. It is more impregnable in appearance than the neighbouring Biblioteca Marciana (*see p83*), though the façade had to accommodate large windows on the *piano nobile* (for relief from heat) and open arches on the ground floor, where the procurators of St Mark's owned a number of cheese shops. The architect's son, author of the first famous guidebook to the city, described the building as 'a worthy prison for all that precious gold'. It now houses most of the contents of the civic library.

Piazza San Marco to the Rialto

Piazza San Marco is linked to the Rialto by the busiest, richest and narrowest of shopping streets: the Mercerie. The name is plural, since it is divided into five parts: the Merceria dell'Orologio, di **San Zulian** (on which stands the church of the same name), del Capitello, di **San Salvador** (with its homonymous church, in the beautiful cloisters of which is the **Telecom Italia Future Centre** visitors' installation) and del 2 Aprile.

Mercerie mean 'haberdashers', but we know from John Evelyn's 1645 account of 'one of the most delicious streets in the world' that in among the luxury textile emporia were shops selling perfumes and medicines too.

Most of the big-name fashion designers are to be found here now, and most of Venice's short-stay tourists too. The ponte dei Baretteri

Classical simplicity at **San Zulian**. *See p88.*

great Titians, the *Annunciation* at the end of the right-hand aisle (with the signature '*Tizianus fecit, fecit*'; the repetition was intended either to emphasise the wonder of his unflagging creativity, or is a simple typo – take your pick) and the *Transfiguration* on the high altar (which conceals a silver reredos, revealed on request).

There's also some splendid Veneto-Tuscan sculpture, including Sansovino's monument to Doge Francesco Venier, situated between the second and third altar on the right. Here too, at the end of the right transept, is the tomb of Cristina Cornaro, the hapless Queen of Cyprus (died 1510), a pawn in a game of Mediterranean strategy that ended with her being forced into abdicating the island to Venetian rule. By way of compensation she was palmed off with the town of Asolo (*see p266*) and the title 'Daughter of the Republic'. In the left aisle, the third altar belonged to the school of the Luganagheri (sausage makers), and has vibrant figures of San Rocco and San Sebastiano by Alessandro Vittoria, influenced by Michelangelo's *Slaves*. The sacristy (ask the sacristan) contains delightful 16th-century frescoes of birds and leafage, discovered in the 1920s and restored in 2003.

Santa Maria della Fava

Campo della Fava (041 522 4601). Vaporetto Rialto. **Open** 8.30-11.30am, 4.30-7pm Mon-Sat. **Map** p312 A1.

St Mary of the Bean – the name refers to a popular bean cake that was turned out by a bakery that used to stand nearby – is on one of the quieter routes between the Rialto and San Marco. This 18th-century church is worth visiting for two paintings by the city's greatest 18th-century artists, which neatly illustrate their contrasting temperaments. Tiepolo's *Education of the Virgin* (first altar on the right) is an early work, painted when he was still under the influence of Giovanni Battista Piazzetta; but the bright colours and touchingly human relationships of the figures are nonetheless in great contrast with the sombre browns and reds of the latter's *Virgin and Child with St Philip Neri* (second altar on the left). In Piazzetta's more earnest painting, which still bears traces of Counter-Reformation gravity, the lily, bishop's mitre and cardinals' hats show the worldly honours rejected by the saint.

San Zulian

Mercerie San Zulian (041 523 5383). Vaporetto Vallaresso or San Zaccaria. **Open** 8.30am-noon, 3-6pm Mon-Sat. **Map** p312 B1.

The classical simplicity of Sansovino's façade (1553-5) is offset by a grand monument to Tommaso Rangone, a wealthy and far from self-effacing showman-scholar from Ravenna, whose fortune was made by a treatment for syphilis, and who wrote a book on how to live to 120 (he only made it to 80 himself). He unilaterally declared his library to be one of the seven wonders of the world, and had himself prominently portrayed in all three of Tintoretto's paintings for the Scuola di San Marco (now in the

Tuscan-feeling **San Salvador**.

(the Hatmakers' Bridge), in the middle of the Mercerie, is, by the way, a minor record holder in Venice: there are six different roads and alleys leading directly off the bridge.

The Mercerie emerge near campo San Bartolomeo, the square at the foot of the Rialto, with the statue of playwright Carlo Goldoni looking amusedly down at the milling crowds. This square, together with the nearby campo San Luca, is where young Venetians meet up and hang out of an evening.

Calle dei Stagneri leads out of the campo to the 18th-century church of **Santa Maria della Fava** (technically in the sestiere of Castello).

San Salvador

Campo San Salvador (041 270 2464). Vaporetto Rialto. **Open** 9am-noon, 4-7.15pm Mon-Sat; 4-6pm Sun. **Map** p311 A3.

If you can't make it to Florence on this trip, come to San Salvador instead, which has one of Venice's most Brunelleschi-esque interiors: a pass-the-baton effort begun by Giorgio Spavento in 1506, continued by Tullio Lombardo and completed by Sansovino in 1534. But even though the geometrical sense of space and the use of soft-toned greys and whites exude Tuscan elegance, the key to the church's structure is in fact a combination of three domed Greek crosses, which look back to the Byzantine tradition of St Mark's. The church contains two

Poison pen

Pietro Aretino, legend relates, died laughing at an obscene joke about his own sister. The story may be apocryphal. True or false, it says much about the larger-than-life character of this outrageous Renaissance man of letters.

Aretino pitched up in Venice in 1527 at the age of 35 and remained there until his death in 1556. (As he wrote to his close friend Duke Federico Gonzaga of Mantua, there was nowhere else in Italy where a writer could keep a grand house and 50 servants at his beck and call.)

His early life had been far less settled. The son of a cobbler (and probably not, as he would have had the world believe, the illegitimate son of a Tuscan nobleman) Pietro had slunk away his native city, Arezzo, under mysterious circumstances while still in his teens and moved to Perugia as an apprentice painter. He didn't stay there – or anywhere else – for long: his scandalous writings – whether pure pornography such as the *Sonetti lussuriosi* (1524) or over-keen satire such as his lampoon on the papal conclave of 1522 – had a habit of making him dangerous enemies. They also, incidentally, made his fortune: many would-be targets were prepared to pay handsomely to be kept out of his vitriolic scribblings. Not for nothing did his contemporaries dub him 'the scourge of princes'.

Aretino travelled from court to court, outstaying his welcome swiftly. Not even his powerful patron Pope Clement VII could guarantee his safety in Rome after publication of the *Sonetti*. An assassination

attempt in the Eternal City – probably ordered by a cardinal who had suffered badly from Pietro's poison pen – persuaded him to leave definitively. He decided to take up residence in Venice.

The lagoon city proved congenial to him. He had the protection of Doge Andrea Gritti. Censorship laws were relatively lax. Hush money continued to flow in, allowing Aretino to live in the riotous style to which he had grown accustomed. So great was his sway that he helped decide the fates of many up-and-coming artists during convivial dinners in his Grand Canal palazzo with his drinking buddies Sansovino and Titian (who painted two portraits of him). The printing presses of open-minded Venice published his *Ragionamenti* – extraordinary dialogues between prostitutes and pimps – his comedies and, later, some rather unconvincingly pious works.

Renaissance Venice comes to vivid life in Aretino's letters; in one to Titian he describes the great spectacle of the Grand Canal beneath his study window, with the bustle of boats and the extraordinary colours of the water and sky: 'In some places the colours appeared green-blue, and in others blue-green, stirred by the caprices of Nature.'

Dangerous as an enemy, Aretino was a loyal and unstinting friend. It was he who secured for Titian the prestigious task of painting Emperor Charles V. And it was Aretino who interceded to get Sansovino out of jail when the ceiling of the Biblioteca Marciana (*see p83*) collapsed.

Sightseeing

Accademia, *see p130*). The interior has a ceiling painting of *The Apotheosis of St Julian* by Palma il Giovane, here in Tintoretto mode, and a more Titianesque *Assumption* by the same painter on the second altar on the right, which also has good statues of St Catherine of Alexandria and Daniel by Alessandro Vittoria. The first altar on the right has a *Pietà* by Veronese. San Giuliano (Zulian to Venetians) is one of only two churches in Venice that you can walk all the way around. (The other is the Angelo Raffaele in Dorsoduro, *see p125*.)

Telecom Italia Future Centre
San Marco 4826, campo San Salvador (www.futurecentre.telecomitalia.it). Vaporetto Rialto. **Open** 10am-6pm Tue-Sun. **Admission** free. **Map** p312 A1.
Though the Italian telephone company acquired the 16th-century cloisters of the monastery of San

Salvador after World War I, it was not until the 1980s that it embarked upon a thorough restoration of the buildings to provide a prestigious showcase for its latest offerings. The Future Centre opened in September 2002 and offers a tour through the latest innovations in information technology. The first cloister contains 100 computers with cutely playful lessons on various aspects of Venetian art and history, in Italian and English. Don't miss the splendid refectory with a 16th-century frescoed ceiling.

The Rialto to the Accademia bridge

The route from the Rialto to the Accademia passes through a series of ever-larger squares. From cosily cramped campo San Bartolomeo, the well-marked path leads to campo San Luca with its bars and cakeshops. Beyond this is campo Manin with its 19th-century statue of Daniele Manin, leader of the 1848 uprising against the Austrians (see p20 **Austrian rule**). An alley to the left of this campo will lead you to the **Scala del Bòvolo**, a striking Renaissance spiral staircase. Back on the main drag, the calle della Mandola leads to broad campo **Sant'Angelo** with its dramatic view of **Santo Stefano**'s leaning tower; off calle della Mandola to the right is the Gothic **Palazzo Fortuny**, once home to the Spanish fashion designer Mariano Fortuny.

Just before the Accademia bridge, campo Santo Stefano is second only to piazza San Marco in the *sestiere* in size. Until 1802, when part of a stand collapsed, this was where *corse al toro* (bullfights) took place. Nowadays, the tables of three bars scarcely encroach on the space where children play on their bikes or kick balls around the statue of Risorgimento ideologue Nicolò Tommaseo, known locally as *Cagalibri* (bookshitter) for reasons that are obvious when the monument is viewed from the rear. At the Accademia bridge end of the square is the freshly restored 18th-century church of **San Vidal**. For information on the bridge, *see p76*.

On the Grand Canal to the north-west of campo Santo Stefano is campo San Samuele, with a deconsecrated 11th-century church and the massive **Palazzo Grassi**, an exhibition centre seeking a future. Nearby, in calle Malipiero (the house is unknown), the 18th-century love machine, Giacomo Casanova, was born. The whole neighbourhood is full of Casanova associations, including the site of the theatre where his actress-mother performed (corte Teatro).

Palazzo Fortuny

San Marco 3780, campo San Benedetto (041 520 0995). Vaporetto Sant'Angelo. **Open** *during exhibitions 10am-6pm Tue-Sun (hours subject to change).* **Admission** *varies.* **No credit cards.** **Map** p311 A2.
With the museum closed for long-term reorganisation (due to reopen in 2005), the only way to see the charming 15th-century palazzo that belonged to Spanish fashion designer Mariano Fortuny (1871-1949) is to catch an exhibition. These are usually photographic, photography being one of Fortuny's interests, alongside theatrical set design, cloth dyes and elegant silk dresses. Also on display are some of Fortuny's paintings of Middle Eastern views.

Palazzo Grassi

San Marco 3231, campo San Samuele (041 523 1680/www.palazzograssi.it). Vaporetto San Samuele. **Open** *during exhibitions 9am-7pm Tue-Sun (hours subject to change).* **Admission** *varies.* **Credit** MC, V. **Map** p311 B1.

This superbly – if boringly – regular 18th-century palazzo on the Grand Canal was bought by Fiat in 1984 and converted by architect Gae Aulenti into a high-profile exhibition space. For over a decade the palazzo hosted a series of blockbuster exhibitions. As Fiat has sunk deeper into financial trouble, the exhibitions have become less frequent and rather less grandiose.

Santo Stefano

Campo Santo Stefano (041 522 5061). Vaporetto San Samuele or Accademia. **Open** *Church 9am-7pm daily. Sacristy 10am-5pm Mon-Sat; 1-5pm Sun.* **Admission** *Church free. Sacristy €2.50 (see also p70* **Chorus**). **Map** p11 B2.
Santo Stefano is an Augustinian church, built in the 14th century and altered in the 15th. The façade has a magnificent portal in the florid Gothic style. The large interior, with its splendid ship's keel roof, is a multicoloured treat, with different marbles used for the columns, capitals, altars and intarsia, and diamond-patterned walls, as on the Palazzo Ducale. On the floor is a huge plaque to Doge Morosini (best known for blowing up the Parthenon) and a more modest one to composer Giovanni Gabrielli. On the interior façade to the left of the door is a Renaissance monument to Giacomo Surian by Pietro Lombardo and his sons, decorated with skulls and festoons. In the sacristy are two tenebrous late works by Tintoretto: *The Washing of the Feet* and *The Agony in the Garden* (*The Last Supper* is by the great man's assistants) and three imaginative works by Gaspare Diziani (*Adoration of the Magi, Flight into Egypt, Massacre of the Innocents*). From the first bridge on the calle that leads from the campo towards piazza San Marco, there's a good view of the apse of Santo Stefano with a canal passing underneath it.

San Vidal

Campo San Vidal (041 522 2362). Vaporetto Accademia. **Open** *9.30am-6pm daily (and for concerts).* **Map** p311 B2.
This early 18th-century church, with a façade derived from Palladio, was for years used as an art gallery. It has now been restored and hosts concerts. Over the high altar is a splendid Carpaccio painting (1514) of St Vitalis riding what appears to be one of the bronze horses of San Marco. The third altar on the right has a painting by Piazzetta (*Archangel Raphael and Saints Anthony and Louis*).

Scala Contarini del Bòvolo

San Marco 4299, corte dei Risi (041 270 2464). Vaporetto Rialto. **Open** *Apr-Oct 10am-6pm daily. Nov-Mar 10am-4pm Sat, Sun. Christmas & Carnevale 10am-4pm daily with guided tour.* **Admission** €3 *with guided tour;* €2.50 *groups.* **No credit cards.** **Map** p311 B3.
Follow the signs for the Scala del Bòvolo from campo Manin and you will emerge in a narrow courtyard entirely dominated by this elegant Renaissance spiral staircase, built c1499 by Giovanni Candi. Spiral staircases are called *scale a chiocciola* (snail staircases) in Italian; *bòvolo* is

Sightseeing

Charming details at **Palazzo Fortuny**. *See p90*.

Venetian dialect for snail. It was beautifully restored in 1986 and has recently been opened to the public; the view from the top makes the climb worthwhile.

From the Accademia to piazza San Marco

The route from Santo Stefano back to piazza San Marco zigzags at first, passing through small squares, including campo **Santa Maria del Giglio** (aka Santa Maria Zobenigo) with the most boastful church façade in Venice. It winds past banks and hotels, along with a few top-dollar antique shops, to end in wide via XXII Marzo, with an intimidating view of the recently restored Baroque statuary of **San Moisè**. To the left is the opera house, **La Fenice**, rebuilt after a fire in 1996.

Press on and you are ready for arguably the greatest view in the world: piazza San Marco from the west side.

Santa Maria del Giglio

Campo Santa Maria Zobenigo (041 275 0462). Vaporetto Giglio. **Open** 10am-5pm Mon-Sat; 1-5pm Sun. **Admission** €2.50 (*see also p70* **Chorus**). **No credit cards**. **Map** p311 B2.

This church's façade drew the censure of Ruskin for its total lack of any Christian symbols (give or take a token angel or two). Built between 1678 and 1683, it's really a huge exercise in defiant self-glorification by Admiral Antonio Barbaro, who was dismissed by Doge Francesco Morosini for incompetence in the War of Candia (Crete). On the plinths of the columns

are relief plans of towns where he served, including Candia; his own statue (in the centre) is flanked by representations of Honour, Virtue, Fame and Wisdom. The interior is more devotional. You may not have heard of the painter Antonio Zanchi (1631-1722), but this is definitely his church. Particularly interesting is *Abraham Teaching the Egyptians Astrology* in the sacristy, while the Cappella Molin has *Ulysses Recognised by his Dog* (an odd subject for a church). The chapel also contains a *Madonna and Child*, which is proudly but probably erroneously attributed to Rubens. Behind the altar there are two paintings of the Evangelists by Tintoretto, formerly organ doors.

San Moisè

Campo San Moisè (041 528 5840). Vaporetto Vallaresso. **Open** 3.30-7pm daily. **Map** p311 B3.

The Baroque façade of San Moisè has been lambasted by Ruskin ('one of the basest examples of the basest school of the Renaissance') and just about everybody else as one of Venice's truly ugly pieces of architecture. Inside, an extravagant piece of Baroque sculpture occupies the high altar, representing not only Moses receiving the stone tablets but Mount Sinai itself. Near the entrance is the grave of John Law, author of the disastrous Mississippi Bubble scheme that almost sank the French central bank in 1720.

Teatro La Fenice

San Marco 1983, campo San Fantin. Vaporetto Giglio. Closed to the public. **Map** p311 B2.

See **p219** **Phoenix from the flames**. For performance information, *see p222*.

Time Out Venice **91**

Castello

Home to some of Venice's grandest buildings, and also her dockyard, this is the city's most diverse district.

Castello is Venice's largest *sestiere* and probably the most disparate in form and tone. It extends almost from the Rialto to the eastern tip of the city, the island of Sant'Elena. In character it ranges from the magnificence of Santi Giovanni e Paolo and San Zaccaria to the more workaday simplicity of the zones around via Garibaldi. It also includes the vast and now mostly desolate expanse of the Arsenale, once the city's pulsing industrial heart.

Northern & western Castello

The *sestiere* of San Marco comes to an abrupt halt with the canal beyond the Doge's Palace. This means that the quaint **Museo Diocesano di Arte Sacra** and stately **San Zaccaria**, although closely associated with San Marco, actually belong to Castello. But the heart of northern and western Castello lies inland: campo **Santa Maria Formosa** (literally 'Shapely St Mary'), a large, bustling, irregular-shaped square on the road to just about everywhere.

This square has all you could possibly need: a fine church, a small market, a couple of bars and an undertaker's. Nearby is the quintessentially Venetian museum-cum-library of the **Fondazione Querini Stampalia**. Constantly buzzing with locals and tourists, the campo is surrounded by *palazzi* that range in style from the very grand to the very homely. It is, in fact, Castello in miniature.

Southward from the campo runs the busy shopping street ruga Giuffa (named after either a community of Armenian merchants from Julfa, or a band of thugs – *gagiuffos* in 13th century dialect – who terrorised the area). The first turning to the left off this street leads to Palazzo Grimani, the grandiose 16th-century home of Cardinal Grimani, whose collection of Greek and Roman antiquities formed the basis of the Museo Archeologico (*see p83*). The palazzo has been under very slow restoration since the 1980s and is to be opened as a museum, offering an example of a splendid patrician residence, in the not too distant future (see www.museicivicivenezian.it for details). When it does finally open its doors to the public, film buffs will recognise it as the setting for the final gory scenes of Nicholas Roeg's film, *Don't Look Now*.

Santa Maria Formosa. See *p95*.

For more grandeur, head north-east from here to campo **Santi Giovanni e Paolo**. This square is second only to piazza San Marco in monumental magnificence. The Gothic red brick of the Dominican church is beautifully set off by the glistening marble on the trompe l'œil façade of the **Scuola di San Marco** and the bronze of the equestrian **monument to Bartolomeo Colleoni** gazing contemptuously down.

It's a short walk through narrow *calli* from Santi Giovanni e Paolo to the fondamenta Nuove, where the northern lagoon comes into view. Murano (*see p141*) and further-flung

Burano (*see p142*) and Torcello (*see p144*) are visible on clear days, as are the foothills of the Dolomites. The cemetery island San Michele is always in sight, acting as a grim memento mori for patients in the hospital.

Eastwards from Santi Giovanni e Paolo runs a long road called Barbaria delle Tole. *Tole* are planks (*tavole* in Italian); various explanations are offered for *barbaria*: the wild appearance of the area, the presence of numerous barbers' shops, the barbaric behaviour of the carpenters, the fact that the planks were destined mainly for 'Barbaria' (the Barbary Coast). The road passes the extraordinary Baroque church of the **Ospedaletto** by Baldassare Longhena, with its alarmingly teetering façade adorned by leering faces. The church now belongs to an old people's home, which contains an exquisite 18th-century music room. Barbaria delle Tole leads into one of the least touristy areas of the city. Here, beyond the old gasworks, is **San Francesco della Vigna**, an austere church whose remoteness is part of its charm.

Monument to Bartolomeo Colleoni

Campo Santi Giovanni e Paolo. Vaporetto Fondamenta Nove. **Map** p309 C3.

Colleoni was a famous *condottiere* (mercenary soldier), who left a legacy to the Republic on the condition that a statue be erected to him in front of St Mark's. Not wishing to clutter up St Mark's square with the statue, but loath to miss out on the money, Venice's wily rulers found a solution to their conundrum in 1479 when they hit upon the idea of giving him a space in front of the Scuola di San Marco. Geddit? In order, perhaps, to make up for this flagrant deception, the Republic did Colleoni proud, commissioning the Florentine artist Andrea Verrocchio to create an equestrian statue that is widely agreed to be one of the world's finest. On Verrocchio's death it was completed, together with the pedestal, by Alessandro Leopardi (1488-96). It is not a portrait, since Verrocchio never saw Colleoni, but a stylised representation of military pride and might. Colleoni's coat of arms (on the pedestal) includes three fig-like objects, a reference to his name, which in Italian sounds very similar to *coglioni* – testicles, of which this soldier was said to possess three. As this guide went to press the statue was under wraps for restoration.

Museo Diocesano di Arte Sacra

Castello 4312, ponte della Canonica (041 522 9166). Vaporetto San Zaccaria. **Open** 10.30am-12.30pm Mon-Sat. **Admission** free (donations accepted). **Map** p309 D1.

A hotchpotch of a collection, which can seem haphazard until you realise its purpose: to act as a storeroom and restoration clinic for works of art from local churches and monasteries. It's difficult to say what will be on view at any time, but items that have nowhere else to go include the 15th-century Cross of the Patriarch from San Pietro in Castello. There is also a series of marble sculptures from the former convent of San Clemente, then one of the abandoned islands of the lagoon (now with a luxury hotel) which were stolen then recovered. The thieves shoved rubber tyres over *Faith* and *Charity* and used a motorboat to drag them along the bottom of the lagoon; you can still see the tyre marks at the back. There is also a pretty Romanesque cloister.

Museo della Fondazione Querini Stampalia

Castello 5252, campo Santa Maria Formosa (041 271 1411/www.querinistampalia.it). Vaporetto Rialto. **Open** *Museum* 10am-6pm Tue-Thur, Sun; 10am-10pm Fri, Sat. **Admission** *Museum* €6; €4 concessions. *Library* free. **Credit** DC, MC, V. **Map** p309 D3.

For library opening times, *see p286.*

This Renaissance palazzo and its art collection were bequeathed to Venice by Giovanni Querini, a 19th-century scientist, man of letters and silk producer. He came from one of the city's most ancient families, which was permanently excluded from running for the dogeship due to involvement in the 1310 Bajamonte Tiepolo plot (*see p16*). Giovanni Querini specified in his will that a library and reading room should also be created here that would open 'particularly in the evenings for the convenience of scholars', and that the foundation should promote 'evening assemblies of scholars and scientists'. The Querini Stampalia still exudes something of its founder's spirit: the first-floor library is a great place to study on misty autumn evenings, and the Foundation organises conferences, debates and concerts (5pm, 8.30pm Fri, Sat; included in admission price). The ground floor and gardens, which were redesigned in the 1960s by Carlo Scarpa, offer one of Venice's few successful examples of modern architecture. On the second floor, the gallery contains some important paintings, including Palma il Vecchio's portraits of Francesco and Paola Querini, for whom the palace was built in the 16th century, a marvellous *Presentation in the Temple* by Giovanni Bellini and a striking *Judith and Holofernes* by Vincenzo Catena. It also has a fascinating series of minor works, such as Gabriele Bella's 67 paintings of Venetian festivals, ceremonies and customs, and a selection of Pietro Longhi's winning scenes of bourgeois life in 18th-century Venice. On the top floor is a gallery designed by Mario Botta, which regularly hosts exhibitions of contemporary art.

San Francesco della Vigna

Campo San Francesco della Vigna (041 520 6102). Vaporetto Celestia. **Open** 8am-12.30pm, 3-6.30pm Mon-Sat; 3-6.30pm Sun. **Map** p312 A3.

San Francesco may be off the beaten track, but the long trek over to the down-at-heel area beyond the gasworks, where the church's Palladian façade is half-concealed by the surrounding buildings, is well worth it. In 1534 Jacopo Sansovino was asked by his friend Doge Andrea Gritti to design this church for the Observant Franciscan order. The Tuscan architect opted for a deliberately simple style to match the monastic rule adopted by its inhabitants. The façade (1568-72) was a later addition by Andrea Palladio; it is the first example of his system of superimposed temple fronts.

The dignified, solemn interior consists of a single broad nave with side chapels, which are named after the families who paid for them – and who held no truck with Franciscan notions of modesty and self-effacement. The Cappella Giustiniani on the left of the chancel holds a marvellous cycle of bas-reliefs by Pietro Lombardo and school, moved here from an earlier church on the same site. In the nave, the fourth chapel on the right has a *Resurrection* attributed to Paolo Veronese. In the right transept is a fruity, flowery *Madonna and Child Enthroned* (c1450), a signed work by the Greek artist Antonio da Negroponte. From the left transept a door leads into the Cappella Santa, which contains a *Madonna and Saints* (1507) by Giovanni Bellini (perhaps assisted by Girolamo da Santacroce). From here it is possible to visit the monastery's two of the church's peaceful Renaissance cloisters (another, generally closed to the public, has a magnificent vegetable garden). Back in the church, the fifth chapel on the left is home to Paolo Veronese's first Venetian commission, the stunning *Holy Family with Saints John the Baptist, Anthony the Abbot and Catherine* (c1551). The second chapel has three powerful statues of saints Roch, Anthony the Abbot and Sebastian (1565) by Alessandro Vittoria.

Santi Giovanni e Paolo (San Zanipolo)

Campo Santi Giovanni e Paolo (041 523 5913).
Vaporetto Fondamenta Nove. **Open** 7.30am-12.30pm, 3.30-7pm Mon-Sat; 3-6pm Sun. **Admission** €2.50. **Map** p309 C3.

Santi Giovanni e Paolo was founded by the Dominican order in 1246 but not finished until 1430. Twenty-five doges were buried here between 1248 and 1778; from the 15th century onwards all ducal funerals were held here. The vast interior – 101m (331ft) long – is a single spatial unit; the simple columns serve to enhance the unity of the whole, rather than dividing the body of the church into separate aisles. The monks' choir was removed in the 17th century, leaving nothing to impede the view. Santi Giovanni e Paolo is packed with monuments not only to doges but also to Venetian heroes. The entrance wall is entirely dedicated to a series of funerary tributes to the Mocenigo family. The grandest – the masterpiece by Pietro, Tullio and Antonio Lombardo – belongs to Pietro Mocenigo, who died in 1476: the doge stands on his own sarcophagus, supported by three warriors representing the three ages of man. The religious reference above – the three Marys at the sepulchre – seems almost an afterthought. Renaissance elegance continues in the second altar on the right, which features an early polyptych by Giovanni Bellini (1465) in its original frame. Continuing down the right side of the church, the huge Baroque mausoleum by Andrea Tirali (1708) has two Valier doges and a *dogaressa* taking a bow before a marble curtain. Tirali also designed the Chapel of St Dominic, notable for its splendid ceiling painting by Giovani Battista Piazzetta of *St Dominic in Glory* (c1727).

The right transept has a painting of *St Antonine Distributing Alms* (1542) by the mystically minded Lorenzo Lotto, who asked only for a decent funeral as payment – but then died far away in Loreto. On the right of the chancel, with its Baroque high altar, is the Gothic tomb of Michele Morosini, which Ruskin (*see p44* **Throwing stones**) loved. Opposite is the tomb of Doge Andrea Vendramin, by the Lombardo family, which the architectural arbiter just as predictably hated. Just to confirm his prejudice, he climbed a ladder and was shocked to discover that the sculptor had not bothered to carve the unseen side of the face.

The rosary chapel, off the left transept, was gutted by fire in 1867, just after two masterpieces by Titian and Bellini had been placed here for safe keeping. It now contains paintings and furnishings from suppressed churches. The ceiling paintings, *The Annunciation, Assumption* and *Adoration of the Shepherds*, are by Paolo Veronese, as is another *Adoration* to the left of the door.

Santa Maria dei Derelitti (Ospedaletto)

Barbarie delle Tole 6691 (041 270 2464).
Vaporetto Fondamenta Nove. **Open** 3.30-6.30pm Thur-Sat. **Admission** (incl guided tour) €2. **No credit cards. Map** p312 A2.

The church was built in 1575 within the complex of the Ospedaletto, a hospice for the poor and aged. There is still an old people's home here. Between 1668 and 1674 Baldassare Longhena gave the church its staggering façade, complete with bulging telamons (architectural supports in the shape of male figures) and leering faces. The interior contains interesting 18th-century paintings, including one of Giambattista Tiepolo's earliest works, *The Sacrifice of Isaac* (fourth on the right). The hospice contains an elegant music room with charming frescoes by Jacopo Guarana (1776), depicting the girl musicians performing for Apollo; the scene is stolen by a dog in the foreground being tempted with a doughnut. There is also a fascinating spiral staircase, apparently unsupported, designed by Sardi and completed by Longhena; the stairs are wide and shallow, to aid the aged inhabitants of the building.

Santa Maria Formosa

Campo Santa Maria Formosa (041 275 0642).
Vaporetto San Zaccaria or Rialto. **Open** 10am-5pm Mon-Sat; 1-5pm Sun. **Admission** €2.50 (*see also p70* **Chorus**). **No credit cards. Map** p312 A1.

In the pre-Freudian seventh century, St Magnus, Bishop of Oderzo, had a rather pleasant vision in which the Virgin appeared as a buxom (*formosa*)

Sightseeing

Back to school

A unique blend of art treasure house and
social institution, Venice's *scuole* (schools)
were devotional lay brotherhoods subject to
the state rather than the Church. The earliest
were founded in the 13th century; by the 15th
century there were six *scuole grandi* and as
many as 400 *minor scuole*. The *scuole grandi*
had annually elected officers drawn from the
'citizen' class (those sandwiched between the
governing patriciate and the disenfranchised
popolani). While members of the *scuole
grandi* (such as Scuola di San Rocco, *see
p123* and Scuola di San Giovanni
Evangelista, *see p119*) were mainly drawn
from the wealthier professional classes,
the humbler *scuole piccole* were either
exclusively devotional groups, trade guilds
or confraternities of foreign communities
(such as Scuola di San Giorgio degli
Schiavoni, *see p101*). When done with
providing funds for dowries and scholarships,
the wealthier confraternities turned to building
and beautifying their own meeting houses
(the *scuole* themselves) in a less-than-humble
spirit of self-promotion.

The *scuole* were dissolved by Napoleon
in 1806, and most of the buildings were put
to new uses. Three – San Rocco, San Giovanni
Evangelista and San Giorgio degli Schiavoni –
survived or were refounded in the mid 19th
century, with their artistic treasures intact.

Scuola di San Marco. *See p96.*

Sightseeing

matron, and a church was built in this bustling
square to commemorate the fact. The present church
was designed by Mauro Codussi in 1492 and has
something fittingly bulgy about it. It has two
façades, one on the canal (1542), the other on the
campo (1604). The Baroque *campanile* has a
grotesque mask, memorably reviled by Ruskin but
now recognised as a portrait of a victim of the
hideously disfiguring Von Recklinghausen's
disease. Codussi retained the Greek cross plan of the
original church in his own Renaissance design; the
spatial effects reveal how strong the Byzantine
tradition remained in Venice. The first chapel in the
right aisle has a triptych by Bartolomeo Vivarini,
Madonna of the Misericordia (1473), which includes
a realistic *Birth of the Virgin*.

The altar in the right transept was the chapel of
the Scuola dei Bombardieri, with an altarpiece of St
Barbara, patron saint of gunners (a heaven-sent stun
gun in the shape of a lightning bolt saved Barbara's
life when it struck her father as he prepared to kill
her), by Palma il Vecchio. The model was apparently the artist's daughter. George Eliot described it as
'an almost unique presentation of a hero-woman'.

Half-hidden by the elaborate high altar is one of the
few works on show in Venice by a woman artist: an
18th-century *Allegory of the Foundation of the
Church, with Venice, St Magnus and St Maria
Formosa* by Giulia Lama. She has been described as
a pupil of Giovani Battista Piazzetta, but Piazzetta's
only known portrait from life (in the Thyssen-
Bornemisza collection in Madrid) is of Giulia Lama:
its tenderness suggests she was more than a pupil.

San Zaccaria

*Campo San Zaccaria (041 522 1257). Vaporetto
San Zaccaria.* **Open** 10am-noon, 4-6pm Mon-Sat;
4-6pm Sun. **Map** p312 B2.
Founded in the ninth century, this church has
always had close ties with the Doge's Palace. Eight
Venetian rulers were buried in the first church on
the site, one was killed outside and another died
while seeking sanctuary inside. This is also a holy
booty church: the body of St Zacharias, the father of
John the Baptist, was brought to Venice in the ninth
century, at the same time as that of St Mark; it still
lies under the second altar on the right. The current
church was begun in 1444 but took decades to

complete, making it a curious combination of Gothic and Renaissance. The interior is built on a Gothic plan – the apse, with its ambulatory and radiating cluster of tall-windowed chapels, is unique in Venice – but the architectural decoration is predominantly Renaissance. Similarly, the façade is a happy mixture of the two styles. Inside, every inch is covered with paintings of varying quality. Giovanni Bellini's magnificently calm *Madonna and Four Saints* (1505), on the second altar on the left, leaps out of the confusion. The Chapel of St Athanasius in the right aisle contains carved 15th-century wooden stalls and *The Birth of St John the Baptist*, an early work by Tintoretto. The adjoining Chapel of St Tarasius (open, together with the sacristy, same hours as the church, admission €1) was the apse of an earlier church on the site; it has three altarpieces (1443) by Antonio Vivarini and Giovanni d'Alemagna – stiff, iconic works in elaborate Gothic frames that are in keeping with the architecture of the chapel. Definitely not in keeping are the frescoed saints in the fan vault by the Florentine artist Andrea del Castagno. Although painted a year before the altarpieces, they have a realistic vitality that is wholly Renaissance in spirit.

Attached to the church was a convent (now a Carabinieri barracks), where aristocrats with more titles than cash dumped female offspring to avoid

French legacy: the **Giardini pubblici**. *See p97.*

having to rake together a dowry. The nuns were not best known for their piety. While tales of rampant licentiousness may have been exaggerated, a painting in Ca' Rezzonico (*see p127*) shows that such convents were more wordly salon than place of contemplation.

Scuola Grande di San Marco (Ospedale Civile)

Campo Santi Giovanni e Paolo (041 529 4111). Vaporetto Fondamente Nove. **Open** 24hrs daily. **Map** p309 C3.

This is one of the six *scuole grandi*, the philanthropic confraternities of Venice (*see p95* **Back to school**). It's now occupied by the city hospital, which extends all the way back to the lagoon. The façade (recently restored) by Pietro Lombardo and Giovanni Buora (1487-90) was completed by Mauro Codussi (1495). It has magnificent trompe l'œil panels by Tullio and Antonio Lombardo representing two episodes from the life of St Mark and his faithful lion. Over the doorway is a lunette of *St Mark with the Brethren of the School* attributed to Bartolomeo Bon.

Southern & eastern Castello

The low-rise, close-clustered buildings of working-class eastern Castello housed the employees of the **Arsenale** – Venice's dockland – most of which now lies poignantly derelict.

Like London's East End or New York's Brooklyn, eastern Castello had its foreign communities, as local churches testify. There's **San Giorgio dei Greci** (Greeks), with its adjoining **Museo dell'Istituto Ellenico** icon museum. (Fans of Donna Leon will recognise the bar at the foot of the Ponte dei Greci as the one where her detective Commissario Brunetti often takes a quick cappuccino; the Questura – police headquarters – is further down the canal on the left.) And there's the **Scuola di San Giorgio degli Schiavoni** (Slavs), with its captivating cycle of paintings by Vittorio Carpaccio. Indeed, the great promenade along the lagoon – the riva degli Schiavoni – was named after the same community.

Inland from the *riva* is the quaint Gothic church of **San Giovanni in Bragora** and, further back in the warren of streets, the church of **Sant'Antonin**, undoubtedly the only church in Venice in which an elephant has been shot. The unfortunate animal escaped from a circus on the *riva* in 1819 and took refuge in the church, only to be finished off by gunners summoned from the Arsenale (a lively dialect poem commemorates the event).

Back on the riva degli Schiavoni is the church of **La Pietà**, where Vivaldi was choir master; concerts once held here are now staged in Palazzo Ca' Papafava (*see chapter* **Performing Arts**). In calle della Pietà, alongside the church, is the **Piccolo Museo della Pietà**, a small museum dedicated to the Pietà (a foundling home) and the composer.

Head on eastwards past the Ca' di Dio, once a hostel for pilgrims setting out for the Holy Land and now an old people's home, and the *Forni pubblici* (public bakeries), where the biscuit (*bis-cotto*, literally 'twice-cooked') – that favourite, scurvy-encouraging staple of ancient mariners – was reputedly invented.

Crossing the bridge over the rio dell'Arsenale, you can see the grand Renaissance entrance to the huge **Arsenale** shipyard, once a hive of empire-building industry and closely guarded secrets, now an expanse of crumbling warehouses and empty docks, parts of which are now regularly brought to life by temporary exhibitions.

Just beyond the rio dell'Arsenale, the model-packed **Museo Storico Navale** charts Venice's shipbuilding history lovingly. A little further on, the wide via Garibaldi forks off to the left. This road, like the nearby *Giardini pubblici*, is a legacy of French occupation in the early 19th century. For proof that Venice is not a dead city, head here in the morning (Mon-Sat) to catch the bustle at the market. Otherwise, take an evening stroll and join Venetians *en masse*, from kiddies on tricycles to old men propping up bars.

Via Garibaldi leads eventually to the island of **San Pietro**, where the former cathedral stands among modest, washing-garlanded houses. For centuries before relocating to St Mark's, the bishop (later patriarch) of Venice was relegated here, at a safe distance from the decision-making centre. Nowadays the island has a pleasant backwoods feel to it; on the feast of Saints Peter and Paul (29 June), locals spill on to the patchy grass in front of the church for the nearest thing Venice offers to a village fête, complete with alfresco dining, dancing, music and gallons of wine. Bring your clogs.

Back on the lagoon, the riva degli Schiavoni changes its name after the rio dell'Arsenale to become the riva dei Sette Martiri, named after seven partisans executed here in 1944 (a statue by the Giardini vaporetto stop recalls the event). Created in 1936, this long, wide section is often dwarfed by moored cruise ships. By the vaporetto stop of the same name, you'll find the shady *Giardini pubblici*, public gardens that took the place of four suppressed convents. A Renaissance archway from one has been reconstructed in a corner.

In another corner lies the entrance to the **Biennale**; the international pavilions, ranging in style from the seedy to the pompous, used to remain locked up except for those few weeks every two years when a major contemporary art bonanza (*see p207*) would be set up; other recently created events such as the Biennale dell'Architettura mean the pavilions get more frequent airings.

The *riva* ends in the sedately residential district of Sant'Elena. This, in Venetian terms, is a 'modern' district. In 1872, work began to fill in the *barene* (marshes) that lay between the edge of the city and the ancient island of **Sant' Elena**, with its charming Gothic church, which now stands just the other side of the football stadium (*see p227*). Sant'Elena has a distinctly suburban feel to it: children play and dogs are walked in grassy expanses dotted with holm oak and pine trees. It's the ideal spot for an evening drink as the sun sets dramatically over the lagoon.

Arsenale

Campo dell'Arsenale. Vaporetto Arsenale.
Map p312 A3/B3, p313 A1/B1.
The word *arsenale* derives from the Arabic *dar sina'a*, meaning 'house of industry': the industry, not to mention the efficiency, of Venice's Arsenale was legendary. When the need arose, the *arsenalotti* could assemble a galley in just a few hours. Shipbuilding activities began here in the 12th

Place of industry: the **Arsenale**.

century, and before long all Venice's galleys were constructed within its confines. At the height of the city's power, 16,000 men were employed here. Production continued to expand until the 16th century, when Venice entered its slow but inexorable economic decline.

The imposing land gateway by Antonio Gambello (1460) in campo dell'Arsenale is the first example of Renaissance classical architecture in Venice, although the capitals of the columns are 11th-century Veneto-Byzantine. The gateway was modelled on a Roman arch in the Istrian city of Pola. The winged lion gazing down from above holds a book without the traditional words *Pax tibi Marce* (Peace to you, Mark), clearly unsuitable in this military context. Outside the gate, four Greek lions keep guard. Those immediately flanking the terrace were looted from Athens by Doge Francesco Morosini in 1687; the larger one stood at the entrance to the port of Piraeus and bears runic inscriptions

on its side, hacked there in the 11th century by Norse mercenary soldiers in Byzantine service. The third lion, whose head is clearly less ancient than its body, came from Delos and was placed here to commemorate the recapture of Corfu in 1716.

Since shipbuilding activity ceased in 1917, the Arsenale has remained navy property. Officers in smart white uniforms cut fine figures against the red brickwork, but appear to put the decaying facilities to no practical use. Exhibitions, theatrical performances and concerts are now occasionally put on in the cavernous spaces within its walls, such as the *Artiglierie* and the grandiose *Gaggiandre*, dockyards designed by Sansovino.

In campo della Tana, on the other side of the rio dell'Arsenale, is the entrance to the *Corderia*, or rope factory, an extraordinary building 316m (1,038 ft) long. In recent years this vast space has been used to house the overflow from the Biennale (*see p207*) and for other temporary exhibitions.

Nature trail glorious mutts

Venice is not a doggy city – too many tramping hordes; not enough green for a good long run – but that doesn't stop Venetians loving dogs. Especially of the painted variety.

Perhaps the most famous dog in Venetian painting is the little white one, gazing up curiously at St Augustine in the Scuola di San Giorgio dei Schiavoni (*see p101*), addressed in Vikram Seth's novel *An Equal Music* as 'glorious mutt'. The tiny creature looks so right here that it comes as a surprise to know that a sketch in the British Museum shows that Vittore Carpaccio had originally planned a cat. Clearly, however, the artist decided his dog was a Good Thing: a fluffier version of the animal appears in a gondola in the foreground of his *Miracle of the True Cross* in the Accademia (*see p130*), its white fur gleaming brilliantly against the dark background.

One of the *Two Venetian Noblewomen* in Carpaccio's painting of that name in the Museo Correr (*see p83*) fondles a melancholy, smooth-haired version. In his *Dream of St Ursula* in the Accademia, the animal is lying at the foot of the saint's bed, looking curiously towards the entering angel. (Two and a half centuries later the same dog crops up in Pietro Longhi's painting of *The Little Concert* in the Accademia. Perched on a table, it appears totally enraptured by the music.)

The retriever in the foreground of Veronese's huge *Last Supper* was one of the elements – along with buffoons, dwarves and Germans – that shocked the Inquisition into declaring the work blasphemous; they demanded, in fact, that the dog be transformed into Mary Magdalene. Undeterred – and presumably fond of his mutt – Veronese simply renamed the painting *Feast in the House of Levi*. It now hangs, dog and all, in the Accademia.

Veronese's deeply religious contemporary Tintoretto had a more reverent way of inserting dogs into his works. No one objected to the bushy-tailed dog in his *Last Supper* in the Scuola di San Rocco (*see p123*). He even managed to sneak one into the *Crucifixion*: it's in the right-hand corner, attentively watching the grave digger.

Two huge frescoes by Tiepolo depicting Antony and Cleopatra in Palazzo Labia (*see p73*) both feature dogs in the foreground, adding a touch of low-life interest to the otherwise pompous pageantry, a role also played by the delightful dog being tempted with a doughnut in Jacopo Guarana's fresco in the music-room of the Ospedaletto (*see p94*) in Castello.

Sculptured dogs abound throughout Venice. Two particularly fine examples are the dog on the façade of a Grand Canal palazzo by the entrance to the Cannaregio Canal and a 15th-century hound with endearingly floppy ears, who turns to stare at passers-by over the entrance to the Palazzo Abadessa hotel (*see p59*).

San Giorgio dei Greci. *See p101.*

Museo dell'Istituto Ellenico

Castello 3412, ponte dei Greci (041 522 6581).
Vaporetto San Zaccaria. **Open** 9am-5pm daily.
Admission €4; €2 concessions. **No credit cards.**
Map p312 B2.

The Byzantine side of Venice is played up in this temple of icons. The adjacent church of San Giorgio dei Greci was a focal point for the Greek community, which was swollen by refugees after the Turkish capture of Constantinople in 1453. There has been a Greek church, college and school on this site since the end of the 15th century, and the museum is an essential adjunct to the centre for Byzantine studies next door. The oldest piece in the collection is the 14th-century altar cross behind the ticket desk. The icons on display mainly follow the dictates of the Cretan school, with no descent into naturalism, though some of the 17th- and 18th-century pieces make jarring and often kitsch compromises with Western art. The best pieces are those that are resolute in their hieratic (traditional-style Greek) flatness, such as *Christ in Glory Among the Apostles* and the Great Deesis from the first half of the 14th century. Also on display are priestly robes and other Greek rite paraphernalia.

Museo Storico Navale

Castello 2148, campo San Biagio (041 520 0276).
Vaporetto Arsenale. **Open** 8.45am-1.30pm Mon-Fri;
8.45am-1pm Sat. **Admission** €1.55. **No credit cards.** **Map** p312 B2.

Housed in an old granary, this museum dedicated to ships and shipbuilding is a treasure trove. It continues an old tradition: under the Republic, the models made for shipbuilders in the final design stages were kept in the Arsenale. Some of the models on display are survivors from that collection. The ground floor has warships, cannons, explosive speedboats and dodgy-looking manned torpedoes, plus a display of ships through the ages. On the walls are relief models in wood and papier mâché, dating from the 16th century to the 18th century, of Venetian fortresses and possessions, including a massive model of the entire island of Crete. On the first floor are ornamental trimmings and naval instruments, plus a series of impressive models of Venetian ships, including a huge 16th-century galleass. Here, too, is a richly gilded model of the Bucintoro, the doges' state barge. The second floor has uniforms, more up-to-date sextants and astrolabes, and models of modern Italian navy vessels. On the third floor there are models of Chinese and Korean junks, cruise ships and liners, and a series of fascinating naïve votive paintings, giving thanks for shipwrecks averted or survived. A room at the back has a display of gondolas, including a 19th-century example with a fixed cabin, and the last privately owned covered gondola in Venice, which belonged to Peggy Guggenheim (*see p130*). The Swedish Gallery on the top floor testifies to links between Venice and Sweden, and also contains a collection of sea shells donated by the fashion designer Roberta di Camerino.

Piccolo Museo della Pietà 'Antonio Vivaldi'

Calle della Pietà 3701 (041 523 9079). Vaporetto
San Zaccaria or Arsenale. **Open** 10am-6pm Mon,
Wed, Fri. **Admission** €3. **No credit cards.**

This small museum was opened in May 2004 and chronicles the activities of the Ospedale della Pietà, the orphanage where Antonio Vivaldi was violin master and choir master. Numerous documents recount such details as the rules for admission of children to the Ospedale and the rations of food allotted them; the 'Daughters of the Choir' received more generous portions of food and wine. Other documents testify to Vivaldi's activities. There is also a selection of period instruments.

La Pietà (Santa Maria della Visitazione)

Riva degli Schiavoni (041 523 1096). Vaporetto
San Zaccaria. **Open** 10am-noon, 4-6pm Mon-Fri.
10am-noon, 4-5.30pm Sat, Sun. **Map** p312 B2.

By the girls' orphanage of the same name, the church of La Pietà was famous for its music. Antonio Vivaldi, violin and choir master here in the 18th century, wrote some of his finest music for his young charges. The present building by Giorgio Massari was begun in 1745, four years after Vivaldi's death. Music inspired its architecture: the interior, reached through a vestibule resembling a foyer, has the oval shape of a concert hall. The ceiling has a *Coronation of the Virgin* (1755) by Giambattista Tiepolo.

Sightseeing

Castello's workaday simplicity.

Sant'Elena

Servi di Maria 3, campo Chiesa Sant'Elena (041 520 5144). Vaporetto Sant'Elena. **Open** 5-7pm Mon-Sat. **Map** off p313 D3.
The red-brick Gothic church of Sant'Elena is reached by a long avenue alongside Venice's football ground (*see p227*). Though it contains no great works of art (the church was deconsecrated in 1807, turned into an iron foundry, and not opened again until 1928), its austere Gothic nakedness is a relief after all that Venetian ornament. In a chapel to the right of the entrance lies the body of St Helen, the irascible mother of the Emperor Constantine and finder of the True Cross. (Curiously enough, her body is also to be found in the Aracoeli church in Rome.)

San Giorgio dei Greci

Fondamenta dei Greci (041 523 9569). Vaporetto San Zaccaria. **Open** 9am-1pm, 3-5pm Mon, Wed-Sat. **Map** p312 B2.
By the time the church of San Giorgio was begun in 1539, the Greeks were well established in Venice and held a major stake in the city's numerous scholarly printing presses. Designed by Sante Lombardo, the church's interior is fully Orthodox in layout, with its women's gallery, and high altar behind the iconostasis. A heady smell of incense lends the church an Eastern mystique, enhanced by dark-bearded priests in flowing robes. The *campanile* is decidedly lopsided. Next to the church are the Scuola di San Nicolò (now the Museo dell'Istituto Ellenico, *see p99*) and the Collegio Flangini (now seat of the Istituto Ellenico di Studi Bizantini e post-Bizantini), both by Baldassare Longhena.

San Giovanni in Bragora

Campo Bandiera e Moro (041 270 2464). Vaporetto Arsenale. **Open** 9-11am, 3.30-5.30pm Mon-Sat. **Map** p312 B3.
San Giovanni in Bragora (the meaning of *bragora* is as obscure as the date of the foundation of the first church on this site) is an intimate Gothic structure. The church where composer Antonio Vivaldi was baptised (the entry in the register is on show), San Giovanni also contains some very fine paintings. Above the high altar is the recently restored *Baptism of Christ* (1492-5) by Cima da Conegliano (which can 'only properly be seen by standing on the altar', according to Victorian traveller Augustus Hare), with a charming landscape recalling the countryside around the painter's home town of Conegliano (*see p270*). A smaller Cima, on the right of the door to the sacristy, shows *Constantine Holding the Cross and St Helen* (1502). To the left of the door is a splendidly heroic *Resurrection* (1498) by Alvise Vivarini, in which the figure of Christ is based on a statue of Apollo, now in the Museo Archeologico (*see p83*).

San Pietro in Castello

Campo San Pietro (041 275 0642). Vaporetto San Pietro. **Open** 10am-5pm Mon-Sat; 1-5pm Sun. **Admission** €2.50 (*see also p70* **Chorus**). **No credit cards. Map** p313 B2.

Until 1807 San Pietro in Castello was the cathedral of Venice, and its remote position testifies to the determination of the Venetian government to keep the clerical authorities well away from the centres of temporal power. The island of San Pietro may be connected to the rest of Venice by two long bridges, but even today it has a distinctly insular feel to it. There has probably been a church here since the 17th century, but the present building was constructed in 1557 to a design by Andrea Palladio. San Pietro's lofty interior looks as if it has seen better days, but it contains some minor gems. The body of the first patriarch of Venice, San Lorenzo Giustiniani, is preserved in an urn elaborately supported by angels above the high altar: a magnificent piece of Baroque theatricality designed by Baldassare Longhena (1649). In the right-hand aisle is perhaps the church's most interesting artefact, the so-called 'St Peter's Throne', a delicately carved marble work from Antioch containing a Muslim funerary stele and verses from the Koran. The Baroque Vendramin Chapel in the left transept was again designed by Longhena, and contains a *Virgin and Child* by the prolific Neapolitan Luca Giordano. Outside the entrance to the chapel is a late work by Paolo Veronese, *Saints John the Evangelist, Peter and Paul.* San Pietro's canal-side 'church green' of scrappy grass under towering trees and a punch-drunk *campanile* in white marble is a charming place to relax and have a picnic.

Scuola di San Giorgio degli Schiavoni

Castello 3259A, calle dei Furlani (041 522 8828). Vaporetto San Zaccaria. **Open** *Apr-Oct* 9.30am-12.30pm, 3.30-6.30pm Tue-Sat; 9.30am-12.30pm Sun. *Nov-Mar* 10am-12.30pm, 3-6pm Tue-Sat; 10am-12.30pm Sun. **Admission** €3; €2 concessions. **No credit cards. Map** p312 B2.
The Schiavoni were Venice's Slav inhabitants, who had become so numerous and influential by the end of the 15th century that they could afford to build this *scuola* or meeting house by the side of their church, San Giovanni di Malta. The *scuola* houses one of Vittore Carpaccio's two great Venetian picture cycles. In 1502, eight years after completing his St Ursula cycle (now in the Accademia, *see p130*), Carpaccio was commissioned to paint a series of canvases illustrating the lives of the Dalmatian saints George, Tryphone and Jerome. In the tradition of the early Renaissance *istoria* (narrative painting cycle), there is a wealth of incidental detail, such as the decomposing virgins in *St George and the Dragon*, or the little dog in the painting of *St Augustine in his Study* (receiving the news of the death of St Jerome in a vision) – with its paraphernalia of humanism (astrolabe, shells, sheet music, archaeological fragments). It's worth venturing upstairs to see what the meeting hall of a working *scuola* looks like. San Giorgio degli Schiavoni still provides scholarships, distributes charity and acts as a focal point for the local Slav community.

Cannaregio

Get away from the bustle and into the Ghetto.

By size, Cannaregio is Venice's second *sestiere*, covering the north-western part of the city from the station almost to the Rialto. The station area has inevitably fallen prey to the demands of tourism with hotels, bars and the tackiest of souvenir stalls predominating. But if the tack is entirely 21st-century, not so the plethora of facilities for incoming travellers: the wide Cannaregio Canal was for centuries the point of entry for visitors from the mainland.

The name of the *sestiere* is said by some to be a contraction of 'Canal Regio' (Regal Canal); others derive it from the *canne* (reeds) that grew along its banks.

The earliest settlements (pre-AD 1000) were around the islands of San Giovanni Crisostomo and Santi Apostoli, close to the Rialto area. The zones alongside the Grand Canal were the next to be built up and urbanisation proceeded gradually northwards, engulfing the convents and monasteries that had been set up earlier

in these remote areas (the Misericordia, the Madonna dell'Orto, the Servi and Sant'Alvise). The construction of the railway bridge in the 19th century changed the configuration of the *sestiere*. Large slaughterhouses (recently converted to University buildings, but the animal-skull friezes are a reminder) were set up at the north end of the Cannaregio Canal, while several abandoned churches and convents were given over to civic and industrial purposes. (Ruskin writes memorably of the smoke rising from the chimney-campanile of San Girolamo.) Roughly parallel to the Grand Canal a wide pedestrian route was carved, the strada Nuova, linking the Rialto to the station. But despite these changes, much of Cannaregio remains pleasingly calm and quiet.

From the station to the Rialto

For those arriving in Venice by train, the first glimpse of the city is truly memorable. Step off the train, and you're practically in the Grand Canal. What comes next, if you decide to walk to the centre, is something of a disappointment: beyond the magnificent Baroque façade of the **Scalzi** church lies a jostling array of souvenir stalls, grotty bars and downmarket hotels on and around the throning lista di Spagna.

The squalor is, mercifully, circumscribed. Heading away from the station towards the Rialto, the *lista* leads to the large campo San Geremia, overlooked by the church of the same name (containing the shrivelled body of St Lucy) and Palazzo Labia, currently occupied by the RAI (Italian state television). The palazzo contains frescoes by Tiepolo, visible by appointment (041 781 277/fax 041 524 0675).

Once over the Cannaregio Canal (*see 106* **Along the canal**) – by way of a grandiose bridge with obelisks – the route assumes more character, taking in lively street markets with Venetians going about their daily business. Off to the right, in a square giving on to the Grand Canal, is the church of **San Marcuola**, with an unfinished façade. A bit further on, the more picturesque church of **La Maddalena**, inspired by the Pantheon in Rome, stands in a small square with an assortment of fantastic chimney pots.

Florid: the **Ca d'Oro**. *See p103.*

Beyond this, the wide strada Nuova begins. Off to the left is the church of **San Marziale**, with whimsical ceiling paintings; on the strada Nuova itself stands the church of **Santa Fosca**, another mainly 18th-century creation. Down a calle to the right is the entrance to the **Ca' d'Oro**, Venice's most splendid Gothic palazzo.

The strada Nuova ends by the church of **Santi Apostoli**; the route to the Rialto soon becomes reassuringly narrow and crooked, passing the church of **San Giovanni Crisostomo** and the adjacent courtyard of the Corte Seconda del Milion, where Marco Polo was born (*see p110* **Il Milion**). Some of the Veneto-Byzantine-style houses in the courtyard would have been there when he was born in 1256. The *corte* also has a splendidly carved horseshoe arch. It was on the well head in the centre of the *corte* that Dirk Bogarde collapsed in Visconti's *Death in Venice*, his hair dye and mascara trickling down his face in the rain.

There's a plaque commemorating Marco Polo on the rear of the Teatro Malibran (*see p223*), formerly the Teatro di San Giovanni Crisostomo, one of Venice's earliest theatres and opera houses. The theatre was reopened in 2001, its slow-moving restoration fast-tracked after the city's main opera house, La Fenice (*see p223*), was destroyed by fire.

Ca' d'Oro (Galleria Franchetti)

Cannaregio 3932, calle Ca' d'Oro (041 523 8790/www.artive.arti.beniculturali.it). Vaporetto Ca' d'Oro. **Open** 8.15am-2pm Mon; 8.15am-7.15pm Tue-Sun. *Courtyard* Apr-Oct 8.15am-6.45pm Tue-Sun. **Admission** €5; €2.50 concessions (*see also p70* **State Museums**). **No credit cards. Map** p309 C1.
In its 15th-century heyday, the façade of this pretty townhouse on the Grand Canal must have looked a psychedelic treat: the colour scheme was light blue and burgundy, with 24-carat gold highlights. Though the colour has worn off, the Grand Canal frontage of Ca' d'Oro – built for merchant Marin Contarini between 1421 and 1431 – is still the most elaborate example of the florid Venetian Gothic style besides the Doge's Palace. Inside, little of the original structure and decor has survived the depredations of successive owners. The pretty courtyard was reconstructed with its original 15th-century staircase and well head a century ago by Baron Franchetti, who assembled the collection of paintings, sculptures and coins that is exhibited on the first and second floors. The highlight of the collection is Mantegna's *St Sebastian*, one of the painter's most powerful late works; the Palladian frame contrasts oddly with the saint's existential anguish. The rest is in parts, though not necessarily the parts you would expect. A small medal of Sultan Mohammed II by Gentile Bellini (a souvenir of his years in Constantinople) is more impressive than the

worse-than-faded frescoes by Titian and Giorgione removed from the Fondaco dei Tedeschi, now the post office. There are some good Renaissance bronzes from deconsecrated churches in the city and small but vigorous plaster models by Bernini for the statues on the fountains in Rome's piazza Navona.

San Giovanni Crisostomo
Campo San Giovanni Crisostomo (041 522 7155). Vaporetto Rialto. **Open** 8.30am-noon, 3.30-7pm Mon-Sat; 3.30-7pm Sun. **Map** p309 C2.
This small church by Mauro Codussi is dedicated to St John Chrysostomos, archbishop of Constantinople, and shows a fittingly Byzantine influence in its Greek cross form. It contains two great paintings. On the right-hand altar is *Saints Jerome, Christopher and Louis of Toulouse*, signed by Giovanni Bellini and dated 1513. This late work is one of his few Madonna-less altarpieces and shows the Old Master ready to experiment with the atmospheric colouring techniques of such younger artists as Giorgione. On the high altar hangs *Saints John the Baptist, Liberale, Mary Magdalene and Catherine* (c1509) by Sebastiano del Piombo, who trained under Bellini but was also influenced by Giorgione. Henry James was deeply impressed by the figure of Mary Magdalene: she looked, he said, like a 'dangerous, but most valuable acquaintance'. On the left-hand altar is *Coronation of the Virgin*, a fine relief (1500-02) by Tullio Lombardo.

San Marcuola
Campo San Marcuola (041 713 872). Vaporetto San Marcuola. **Open** 10am-noon, 5-6pm Mon-Sat. **Map** p309 B1.
There was no such person as St Marcuola; the name is a local mangling of the over-complicated *santi* Ermagora e Fortunato, two early martyrs. The church, designed by 18th-century architect Giorgio Massari, has been beautifully restored (completed in July 2002) and its gleaming interior comes as a surprise after the unfinished brick façade. It contains some vigorous statues by Gianmaria Morleiter and, in the chancel, a *Last Supper* (1547) by Tintoretto, his first treatment of what was later to become one of his favourite subjects. Opposite is a 17th-century copy of another Tintoretto (*Christ Washing the Feet of His Disciples*); the original can be found in Newcastle.

San Marziale
Campo San Marziale (041 719 933). Vaporetto San Marcuola or Ca' d'Oro. **Open** 4-6.30pm Mon-Sat; 8.30-10am Sun. **Map** p309 B1.
The real joy of this church is its ceiling, with its four luminous paintings (1700-05) by the vivacious colourist Sebastiano Ricci. Two of them depict *God the Father with Angels* and *St Martial in Glory*; the other two recount the miraculous story of the wooden statue of the Madonna and Child that resides on the second altar on the left – apparently, it made its own way here by boat from Rimini. The high altar has an equally fantastic Baroque extrav-

aganza: a massive marble group of Christ, the world and some angels looms over the altar while St Jerome and companions crouch awkwardly beneath.

Santi Apostoli

Campo Santi Apostoli (041 523 8297). Vaporetto Ca' d'Oro. **Open** 8.30-11.30am, 5-7pm Mon-Sat. **Map** p309 C2.

According to tradition, the 12 apostles appeared to the seventh-century Bishop of Oderzo, St Magnus, telling him to build a church where he saw 12 cranes together – a not uncommon sight when Venice was little more than a series of uninhabited islands poking out of marshes. The ancient church was rebuilt in the 17th century. Its campanile (1672), crowned by an onion dome added 50 years later, is a Venetian landmark. The Cappella Corner, off the right side of the nave, is a century older than the rest of the structure. It was built by Mauro Codussi for the dispossessed Queen Caterina Cornaro of Cyprus; she was buried here in 1510 alongside her father and brother but subsequently removed to San Salvador (*see p88*). On the altar is a splendidly theatrical *Communion of St Lucy* by Giambattista Tiepolo; the young saint, whose gouged-out eyes are in a dish on the floor, is bathed in a heavenly light. The chapel to the right of the high altar has remnants of 14th-century frescoes while the one to the left has a dramatically stormy painting of *The Guardian Angel* by Francesco Maffei. As this guide went to press this last chapel and the chancel were under restoration.

Gli Scalzi

Fondamenta degli Scalzi (041 715 115). Vaporetto Ferrovia. **Open** 7-11.50am, 4-6.50pm Mon-Sat; 4-6.50pm Sun. **Map** p308 C2.

Officially Santa Maria di Nazareth, this church is universally known as Gli Scalzi after the order of *Carmelitani Scalzi* (Barefoot Carmelites) to whom it belongs. They bought the plot in 1645 and commissioned Baldassare Longhena to design the church. The fine façade (1672-80) is the work of Giuseppe Sardi; it was paid for by a newcomer to Venice's ruling patrician class, Gerolamo Cavazza, determined to make his marble mark on the landscape. The interior is striking for its coloured marble ('a perfect type of the vulgar abuse of marble in every possible way,' wrote Ruskin sniffily) and massively elaborate baldachin over the high altar. There are many fine Baroque statues, including the St John of the Cross by Giovanni Marchiori in the first chapel on the right and the anonymous marble crucifix and wax effigy of Christ in the chapel opposite. An Austrian shell that plummeted through the roof in 1915 destroyed the church's greatest work of art, Tiepolo's fresco, *The Transport of the House of Loreto*, but spared some of the artist's lesser frescoes, *Angels of the Passion* and *Agony in the Garden*, in the first chapel on the left, and *St Theresa in Glory*, which hovers gracefully above a ham-fisted imitation of Bernini's sculpture, *Ecstasy of St Theresa*, in the second on the right. In the second chapel on the left lie the remains of the last doge of Venice, Lodovico Manin.

A mark in marble: **Gli Scalzi**.

Il Ghetto

The word ghetto (like arsenal and ciao) is one that Venice has given to the world. It originally meant an iron foundry, a place where iron was *gettato* (cast). Until 1390, when the foundry was transferred to the Arsenale, casting was done on a small island in Cannaregio. In 1516 it was decided to confine the city's Jewish population to this island; here they remained until 1797.

Venetian treatment of the Jews was by no means as harsh as in many European countries, but neither was it a model of open-minded benevolence. The Republic's attitude was governed by practical considerations, and business was done with Jewish merchants at least as early as the tenth century. It was not until 1385, however, that Jewish moneylenders were given permission to reside in the city itself. Twelve years later, permission was revoked amid allegations of irregularities in their banking practices. For a century after that, residence in Venice was limited to two-week stretches.

In 1509, when the Venetian mainland territories were overrun by foreign troops, great numbers of Jews took refuge in the city. The clergy seized the opportunity to stir up anti-Jewish feeling and demanded their expulsion. Venice's rulers, however, had begun to see the economic advantages of letting them stay, and in 1516 a compromise was reached. In a decision that was to mark the course of Jewish history in Europe, the refugees were given residence permits but confined to the Ghetto.

Restrictions were many and tough. Gates across the bridges to the island were closed an hour after sunset in summer (two hours after in winter), reopening at dawn. During the day, Jews had to wear distinctive badges or headgear. Most trades other than moneylending were barred to them. One exception was medicine, for which they were famous: Venetian practicality allowed Jewish doctors to leave the Ghetto at night for professional calls. Another was music: Jewish singers and fiddlers were hired for private parties.

The Ghetto became a stop on the tourist trail. In 1608 traveller Thomas Coryat came to gaze at the Jews – never having seen any in England – and marvelled at the 'sweet-featured persons' and the 'apparel, jewels, chains of gold' of the women.

The original inhabitants were mostly Ashkenazim from Germany; they were joined by Sephardim escaping from persecution in Spain and Portugal and then, increasingly, by Levantine Jews from the Ottoman Empire. These latter proved key figures in trade between Venice and the East, particularly after Venice lost so many of her trading posts in the eastern Mediterranean. By the mid 16th century the Levantine Jews, the richest community, were given permission to move from the Ghetto Nuovo to the confusingly named Ghetto Vecchio (the 'old Ghetto', the site of an earlier foundry); in 1633 they expanded

into the Ghetto Nuovissimo. Nonetheless, conditions remained cramped, and the height of the buildings in the campo del Ghetto Nuovo shows how the inhabitants, unable to expand in a horizontal direction, did so vertically, creating the first high-rise blocks in Europe. A recent study has calculated that at certain periods overcrowding was such that the inhabitants must have had to take it in turns to sleep. Room was found for five magnificent synagogues, however, each new influx of immigrants wanting its own place of worship. The German, Levantine and Spanish synagogues can be visited as part of the **Museo Ebraico** tour.

With the arrival of Napoleon in 1797, Jews gained full rights of citizenship; many chose to remain in the Ghetto. In the deportations during the Nazi occupation of Italy in 1943, 202 Venetian Jews were sent to the death camps, including the chief rabbi and 20 inmates of an old people's home. The Jewish population of Venice and Mestre now stands at about 500, though only around a dozen Jewish families still live in the Ghetto. The Ghetto remains, however, the centre of spiritual, cultural and social life for the Jewish community: there's a museum, a library, a kosher restaurant, a bakery and a nursery school. Orthodox religious services are held in the Scuola Spagnola in the summer and in the Scuola Levantina in winter.

Spiritual centre: the original **Ghetto**. *See p104.*

Museo Ebraico

Cannaregio 2902B, campo del Ghetto Nuovo (041 715 359). Vaporetto Guglie or San Marcuola. **Open** *June-Sept* 10am-7pm Mon-Fri, Sun; guided tours hourly 10.30am-5.30pm. *Oct-May* 10am-6pm Mon-Thur, Sun; 10am-30mins before sunset Fri; guided tours hourly 10.30am-4.30pm. **Admission** *Museum only* €3; €2 concessions. *Museum & synagogue* €8; €6.50 concessions; €3.50 school groups. **Credit** MC, V. **Map** p308 B3.

Venice's Jewish community has been enjoying a renaissance recently, and this well-run museum and cultural centre – founded in 1953 – has been spruced up accordingly, with the addition of a bookshop. In the small museum itself there are ritual objects in silver – Trah finials, Purim and Pesach cases, menorahs – sacred vestments and hangings, and a series of marriage contracts. To get the most out of the experience, the museum should be visited as part of the guided tours in English and Italian. These take in three synagogues – the Scuola Canton (Ashkenazi rite), the Scuola Italiana (Italian rite) and the Scuola Levantina (Sephardic rite).

North-western Cannaregio

If you're tired of the crowds, there's no better place to get away from it all than the north-western areas of Cannaregio. Built around three long parallel canals, it has no large animated squares and (with the exception of the Ghetto; *see p104*) no sudden surprises – just occasional

Along the canal

For centuries the main route into Venice from the mainland, the Cannaregio Canal is fitted out in suitably impressive fashion with wide *fondamente* on each side (*pictured*) and several imposing *palazzi*. It's spanned by two stately bridges, the ponte delle Guglie (Bridge of the Obelisks, 1823), and the ponte dei Tre Archi, the only three-arch stone bridge in Venice, built by Andrea Tirali in 1688. Heading towards the lagoon from the ponte delle Guglie on the right-hand *fondamenta*, you pass the *sottoportico* leading to the Jewish Ghetto (*see p104*).

Beyond this stands the Palazzo Nani (No.1105), a fine Renaissance palazzo dating from the 16th century. Two hundred metres (700 feet) further on is the Palazzo Surian-Bellotto (No.968): in the 18th century this was the French embassy, where Jean Jacques Rousseau worked – reluctantly – as a secretary. Beyond, Santa Maria delle Penitenti, with its unfinished façade, was formerly a home for the city's fallen women.

On the left bank is the Palazzo Priuli-Manfrin (Nos.342-3), another Tirali creation from 1735, in a neo-classical style of such severe plainness that it prefigures 20th-century purist art.

The imposing 17th-century Palazzo Savorgan (No.349) – now a school – has huge coats of arms and reliefs of helmets. The owners were descended from Federigo Savorgnan who, in 1385, became the first non-Venetian to be admitted to Venice's patrician ruling clique.

Behind it is the Parco Savorgnan, a charming public garden that is one of Venice's better-kept secrets. A little further on, the ponte della Crea spans a canal that was covered over for centuries, only to be re-excavated in 1997.

After passing the ponte dei Tre Archi (with the Renaissance church of **San Giobbe** off to the left) the *fondamenta* continues to the ex-slaughterhouse, built in the 19th century by the Austrians. Long used by a rowing club, it has recently been taken over and revamped by Venice University's economics faculty.

San Giobbe

Campo San Giobbe (041 524 1889). Vaporetto Ponte Tre Archi. **Open** 10am-noon, 3-6pm Mon-Sat; 3.30-6pm Sun. **Map** p308 A2.

Giobbe (Job) – like Moses and Jeremiah – has been raised by Venice to the status of saint, despite his Old Testament pedigree. The church named after him was built to celebrate the visit in 1463 of St Bernardino of Siena, a Franciscan friar and high-profile evangelist. The first Venetian creation of Pietro Lombardo, it introduced a new classical style, immediately visible in the doorway (three statues by Pietro Lombardo that once adorned it are now in the sacristy). The interior of what was probably the first single-naved church in Venice is unashamedly Renaissance. Members of the Lombardo family are responsible for the carvings in the domed sanctuary, all around the triumphal arch separating the sanctuary from the nave, and on the tombstone of San Giobbe's founder Cristoforo Moro, in the centre of the sanctuary floor. The name of this doge has given rise to associations with Othello, the Moor of Venice; some imaginative souls views over the northern lagoon. That's not to say it doesn't have its landmarks, including the *vecchia* (old; 14th-century) and *nuova* (new; 16th-century) Scuole della Misericordia, the 'new' one being a huge building by Sansovino, its façade never completed. Long used as a gym, it now awaits conversion into a new cultural institution of some kind. Plans so far have included an auditorium, a multimedia archive and a music museum.

Behind the *scuole*, the picturesque campo dell'Abbazia, overlooked by the Baroque façade of the **Abbazia della Misericordia** and the Gothic façade of the *Scuola vecchia*, is one of the most peaceful retreats in Venice; on the façade of the latter you can still see the outlines of sculptures (now in London's Victoria & Albert Museum) by Gothic master Bartolomeo Bon. Since 1983 the building has been used as an art restoration workshop.

On the northernmost canal are the churches of the **Madonna dell'Orto** and **Sant'Alvise**, as well as many fine *palazzi*.

The palazzo at the beginning of the *fondamenta* along this canal, Palazzo Contarini dal Zaffo, was built for Gaspare Contarini, a 16th-century scholar, diplomat and cardinal. Behind, a large garden stretches down to the lagoon; in its far corner stands the Casinò degli Spiriti (best seen from fondamente Nuove).

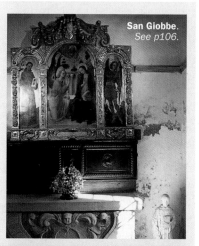

San Giobbe.
See p106.

have even seen the mulberry symbol in his tombstone (a *moro* is a mulberry tree as well as a Moor) as the origin of Desdemona's handkerchief, which was 'spotted with strawberries'. The church's artistic treasures – altarpieces by Giovanni Bellini and Vittore Carpaccio – are now in the Accademia (*see p130*). An atmospheric *Nativity* by Gerolamo Savoldo remains, as does an *Annunciation with Saints Michael and Anthony* triptych by Antonio Vivarini. The Martini Chapel, the second on the left, is a little corner of Tuscany in Venice. Built for a family of silk weavers from Lucca, it is attributed to the Florentine Bernardo Rossellino. The terracotta medallions of Christ and the four evangelists are by the Della Robbia studio – the only examples of its work in Venice.

Designed as a meeting place for the 'spirits' (wits) of the day, the name and the lonely position of the construction have given rise to numerous ghost stories.

The Madonna dell'Orto area may have been the home of an Islamic merchant community in the 12th and 13th centuries, centring on a since-destroyed Fondaco (meeting place and storehouse) degli Arabi. Opposite the church of Santa Maria dell'Orto is the 15th-century Palazzo Mastelli, also known as Palazzo del Camello because of its relief of a turbaned figure with a camel. The Arabic theme continues in the campo dei Mori ('of the Moors') across the bridge, named after the three stone figures set into the façade of a building, all wearing turbans. The one with the comically prominent iron nose – dubbed 'Sior Antonio Rioba' – was the Venetian equivalent of Rome's Pasquino: disgruntled citizens or local wits would hang their rhyming complaints on him under cover of darkness, or use him as a pseudonym for published satires. The three figures are believed to be the Mastelli brothers, owners of the adjacent palazzo, who came to Venice as merchants from the Greek Peloponnese (then known as Morea – which, of course, offers another explanation of the campo's name).

Madonna dell'Orto

Campo Madonna dell'Orto (041 275 0642). Vaporetto Orto. **Open** 10am-5pm Mon-Sat; 1-5pm Sun. **Admission** €2.50 *(see also p70* **Chorus**). **No credit cards. Map** p309 B1.
The 'Tintoretto church' was originally dedicated to St Christopher (a magnificent statue of whom stands over the main door), the patron saint of the gondoliers who ran the ferry service to the islands from a nearby jetty. However, a cult developed around a large, unfinished and supposedly miraculous statue of the Madonna and Child that stood in the nearby garden of sculptor Giovanni de Santi. In 1377 the sculpture was solemnly transferred into the church (it's now in the chapel of San Mauro), and the church's name was changed to the Madonna of the Garden. It was rebuilt between 1399 and 1473, and

Peaceful **campo dell'Abbazia**. *See p107.*

a monastery was constructed alongside. The beautiful Gothic façade is similar to those of the Frari (*see p120*) and Santi Giovanni e Paolo (*see p94*), although the false gallery at the top is unique. The sculptures are all fine 15th-century works. But it is the numerous works by Tintoretto that have made the Madonna dell'Orto famous. Tradition has it that the artist began decorating the church as penance for insulting a doge: in fact, it took very little to persuade Tintoretto to get his palette out, and the urgent sincerity of his work here speaks for itself.

Two colossal paintings dominate the side walls of the chancel. On the left is *The Israelites at Mount Sinai*; some have seen portraits of Venice's artistic top four (Giorgione, Titian, Veronese and Tintoretto himself) in the bearers of the Golden Calf, although there is no documentary evidence for this, nor for the identification of the lady dressed in blue as Mrs Tintoretto. Opposite is a gruesome *Last Judgment*. Like Dante and Michelangelo, Tintoretto had no qualms about mixing religion and myth: note the classical figure of Charon ferrying the souls of the dead. Tintoretto's paintings in the apse include *St Peter's Vision of the Cross* and *The Beheading of St Paul* (or Christopher, according to some), both maelstroms of swirling angelic movement. On the wall of the right aisle is the *Presentation of the Virgin in the Temple*, a calmer, more reverential work. It was painted as a deliberate response to Titian's masterpiece on the same theme in the Accademia, and is more characteristically mystical in tone.

A small treasury, containing reliquaries and other precious objects, has been opened up in a room underneath the bell tower. The room is dedicated to the memory of Sir Ashley Clarke, a former British Ambassador to Italy and chairman of the Venice in Peril organisation which was responsible for the church's restoration.

The Contarini Chapel, off the left aisle, contains the artist's beautiful *St Agnes Reviving the Son of a Roman Prefect*. Once again, it is the swooping angels that steal the show in their dazzling blue vestments. Tintoretto, his son Domenico and his artistically gifted daughter Marietta are buried in a chapel off the right aisle. When the Tintorettos get too much for you, take a look at Cima da Conegliano's freshly restored masterpiece *Saints John the Baptist, Mark, Jerome and Paul* (1494-5) over the first altar on the right. The saints stand under a ruined portico against a sharp, wintry light. There used to be a small *Madonna and Child* by Giovanni Bellini in the chapel opposite, but it was stolen in 1993. The second chapel on the left contains on the left-hand wall a painting by Titian of *The Archangel Raphael and Tobias* (and dog) that has been moved here from the church of San Marziale (*see p103*).

Sant'Alvise

Campo Sant'Alvise (041 275 0642). Vaporetto Sant'Alvise. **Open** 10am-5pm Mon-Sat; 1-5pm Sun. **Admission** €2.50 *(see also p70* **Chorus**). **No credit cards. Map** p309 A1.

Wits met at the lonely **Casinò degli Spiriti**. *See p107.*

A pleasingly simple Gothic building of the 14th century, Sant'Alvise's interior was remodelled in the 1600s with extravagant, if not wholly convincing, trompe l'oeil effects on the ceiling. On the inner façade is a barco, a hanging choir of the 15th century with elegant wrought-iron gratings, formerly used by the nuns of the adjacent convent. Beneath the barco are eight charmingly naïve biblical paintings in tempera, fancifully attributed by Ruskin to the ten-year-old Carpaccio. On the right wall of the church are two paintings by Tiepolo, *The Crowning of Thorns* and *The Flagellation*. A larger and livelier work by the same painter, *Road to Calvary*, hangs on the right wall of the chancel, with rather ill-suited circus pageantry, complete with trumpets and prancing horses.

Anyone looking for a picnic spot will find a garden nearby, complete with picturesque classical 'ruins'.

North-eastern Cannaregio

North-eastern Cannaregio is more intriguingly closed in, with many narrow alleys (including the Venetian record holder, calle Varisco, 52 centimetres (20 inches) wide at its narrowest point), charming courtyards and well heads, but no major sights, with the exception of the spectacularly ornate church of **I Gesuiti**, the **Oratorio dei Crociferi** and, further east, the miniature marvel of **Santa Maria dei Miracoli**. Titian had a house here, with a garden extending to the lagoon; the courtyard where the house was located is raised to the dignity of a 'campo' and named after the artist.

I Gesuiti

Campo dei Gesuiti (041 528 6579). Vaporetto Fondamente Nove. **Open** *10am-noon, 4-6pm daily.* **Map** *p309 B2.*

The Jesuits were never very popular in Venice and it wasn't until 1715 that they felt secure enough to build a church here. Even then they chose a comparatively remote plot on the edge of town. But once they made up their mind to go ahead, they went all out: local architect Domenico Rossi was given explicit instructions to dazzle the Venetians.

The result leaves no room for half measures: you love it or you hate it, and most people do the latter, considering the result the ultimate in church kitsch. The exterior, with a façade by Gian Battista Fattoretto, is conventional enough; the interior (freshly restored) is anything but. All that tassled, bunched, overpowering drapery is not the work of a rococo set designer gone berserk with luxurious brocades: it's plain old green and white marble. Bernini's altar in St Peter's in Rome was the model for the baldachin over the altar, by Fra Giuseppe Pozzo. The statues above the baldachin are by Giuseppe Torretti, as are the rococo archangels at the corners of the crossing. Titian's *Martyrdom of St Lawrence* (1558-9), over the first altar on the left side, came from an earlier church on this site, and was one of the first successful night scenes ever painted. According to writer WD Howells – who labelled the church 'indescribably table-clothy' – the saint seems to be the only person in the building not suffering from the cold.

Oratorio dei Crociferi

Cannaregio 4905, campo dei Gesuiti (041 270 2464). Vaporetto Fondamente Nove. **Open** *Apr-Oct 10am-1pm Sat, Sun. Nov-Mar by appointment.* **Admission** *€2.* **No credit cards. Map** *p309 B2.*

Founded in the 13th century by Doge Renier Zeno, the oratory is a sort of primitive *scuola (see p95* **Back to school**), with the familiar square central meeting hall but without the quasi-masonic ceremonial trappings. Palma il Giovane's colourful cycle of paintings shows Pope Anacletus instituting the

Il Milion

In 1265 brothers Nicolò and Matteo Polo set off across central Asia, eventually making their way to the court of Mongol leader Kubla Khan. The Khan was keen to forge an alliance with the Pope – to form a common front against the expansion-minded Muslims – and sent the Polo brothers back to Italy with messages of goodwill for Clement IV.

At Acre, Nicolò and Matteo learnt that Pope Clement had died and no successor had been appointed and so headed back to Venice, arriving in 1270. Here, Nicolò found his wife was dead and his son Marco almost a man. A year later, the Polos visited Pope Gregory X, then set off once more for the East bearing his embassies. This time, they took 17-year-old Marco with them.

The story of their return, 24 years later, is one of the great Venetian legends: the three men turned up in the old Polo home dressed in shabby Tartar costume. Nobody recognised them until they threw back their hoods. Then, to general amazement, Marco slit open the lining of their rough clothes and out poured a glittering shower of diamonds and precious stones.

Marco's tales of oriental wonders met with some scepticism: he became known as *Il Milion* – apparently he was unable to describe what he had seen using any figure lower than this.

Marco may never have been remembered as anything more than a teller of tall tales if he had not been captured by the Genoese after the naval battle of Curzola and locked up with a Pisan man of letters named Rustichello; the Venetian dictated the story of his travels to his cellmate, and the rest was history.

Recent research has shown that most of the tales related in what remained the West's main source of information on central and eastern Asia until well into the 19th century were accurate. The Polos spent four years crossing Asia, eventually reaching Kubla Khan's summer palace at Shangtu. Marco proved a hit with the Khan, who took him into his service, sending him on missions all over the Empire.

In his book – originally entitled *Le Livre de messer Marco Polo citoyen de Venise, appelé Milion, où sont décrites les merveilles du monde* but soon known more snappily as *Il Milione* – Marco Polo covers everything from the frozen north with its reindeers and dog-sleds to Ceylon, Burma, Siam and Japan and the splendid court of Beijing. Among the fantastic things he describes are fountains on the shores of the Caspian Sea that gush with a dark liquid that can be burnt in lamps.

There are few tangible relics of Marco Polo in Venice. The courtyard where his family lived is named corte seconda del Milion (*see p103*); in one corner is a Byzantine arch that Marco must have been familiar with. The Biblioteca Marciana (*see p83*) preserves his manuscript last will and testament. And, in a homage that must tickle the great traveller's spirit, Venice's airport is named after him.

order of the Crociferi (cross-bearers), and dwells on the pious life of Doge Pasquale Cicogna, who was a fervent supporter of the order.

Santa Maria dei Miracoli

Campo Santa Maria dei Miracoli (041 275 0462). Vaporetto Rialto or Fondamente Nove. **Open** 10am-5pm Mon-Sat; 1-5pm Sun. **Admission** €2.50 (*see also p70* **Chorus**). **No credit cards.** **Map** p309 C2.

Arguably one of the most exquisite churches in the world, Santa Maria dei Miracoli was built in the 1480s to house a miraculous image of the Madonna, reputed to have revived a man who had spent half an hour underwater in the Giudecca Canal, and to have cancelled all traces of a knife attack on a woman. The building is the work of the Lombardo family, early Renaissance masons who fused architecture, surface detail and sculpture into a unique whole. Pietro Lombardo may have been a Lombard by birth but he soon got into the Venetian way of doing things, employing Byzantine spoils left over from work on St Mark's to create a work of art displaying an entirely Venetian sensitivity to texture and colour. There is an almost painterly approach to the use of multicoloured marble in the four sides of the church, each of which is of a slightly different shade. The sides have more pilasters than are strictly necessary, making the church appear longer than it really is. Inside, 50 painted ceiling panels by Pier Maria Pennacchi (1528) are almost impossible to distinguish without binoculars. Instead, turn your attention to the church's true treasures: the delicate carvings by the Lombardi on the columns, steps and balustrade. Look out for the child's head that so distressed Ruskin, who wondered how any sculptor, after creating something this lifelike, could be so 'wanting in all human feeling as to cut it off, and tie it by the hair to a vine leaf'.

Santa Maria dei Miracoli. *See p110.*

Scriba Gallery
Frari Church

VENETIA

Scriba
Paintings Maps Fine Prints
S.Polo 3030   30121 Venice, Italy
Tel.Fax. 0039-041-5236728
E-mail scribave@libero.it
www.scriba-net.com

San Polo & Santa Croce

The centre of the city, with churches, markets, Ponte delle Tette and Titian.

These two *sestieri* encompassed by the pear-shaped bulge of the upper loop of the Grand Canal merge confusingly: Venetian postmen may be the only people who can tell where one starts and the other ends. A more useful dividing line is the rio San Polo, which cuts through the area from north to south, changing its name three times en route. To the east of this canal is the ancient heart of the city, clustered tightly around the Rialto market; there are no imposing buildings here other than the ones on the Grand Canal. To the west of rio San Polo is an area that was settled later; its fulcrum is the great religious complex of the Frari (*see p120*) and the *scuole* of San Rocco (*see p123*) and San Giovanni Evangelista (*see p119*).

The Rialto markets

For information on the Rialto bridge, *see p74*.

Rialto, most experts agree, derives from 'Rivoaltus' (high bank), and it was on this point of higher ground at the mid-point along the

Finishing line: **the Gobbo di Rialto**.

Grand Canal that one of the earliest settlements was founded in the fifth century. The district has been the commercial heart of the city since the market was moved here from campo San Bartolomeo (*see p88*) in 1097. The present layout of the market and adjacent buildings is the result of a reconstruction project by Scarpagnino after a vast fire in 1514 that destroyed the whole area.

As usual in Venice, the project made use of the previous foundations, so the present street-plan probably reflects quite faithfully the earliest urban arrangement, with long, narrow parallel blocks running behind the grand *palazzi* along the riva del Vin, and smaller, squarer blocks further inland for the market workers.

At the foot of the Rialto bridge, where the tourist stalls are thick on the ground, stand (to the south) the Palazzo dei Dieci Savi, which housed the city's tax inspectors but is now used by the ancient but extant lagoon water authority, *Il Magistrato alle acque*, and (to the north) the Palazzo dei Camerlenghi, which housed the finance department.

Beyond, the small church of **San Giacomo di Rialto** (known affectionately as San Giacometto) is generally agreed to be the first of the city's churches – tradition has it that it was founded in 421. All around it stretch the markets, around which commercial and administrative buildings and areas of low-cost housing mushroomed after trade was shifted from across the canal. Despite an over-abundance of souvenir stalls, the Rialto market remains the best place to buy your fruit, veg and seafood.

The larger streets and squares are named after the merchandise that is still sold there (*Naranzeria* – oranges; *Casaria* – cheese; *Speziali* – spices; *Erberia* – vegetables), while the narrower alleys mostly bear the names of ancient inns and taverns – some still in operation – such as 'The Monkey', 'The Two Swords', 'The Two Moors' (fans of Donna Leon's novels will recognise this as one of her detective's favourite bars), 'The Ox', 'The Bell'. Then as now, market traders hated to be too far from liquid refreshment.

On the other side of campo San Giacomo, behind the fruit stalls, is a 16th-century statue of a kneeling figure supporting a staircase leading up to a small column of Egyptian

Sightseeing

Pestilence

Venice's whole way of life was based on trade with the East, but the holds of its merchant ships held more than just luxury goods. Lurking there were also those diseases that were rife in those exotic parts of the world – most terrifyingly, bubonic plague. Reducing its contacts with the Orient was impossible; instead, Venice sought ways to protect itself.

The first – and to a large extent most successful – was the city's system of quarantine centres, using its lagoon islands. The first *lazzaretto* – from Lazarus, the sore-covered beggar of Luke 16:20 – was established in 1423 as a hospital for people already infected. In 1468 a second *lazzaretto* (Lazzaretto Nuovo) was set up; here, ships and crews coming from countries at risk were kept under observation. Liberal quantities of pitch – a powerful disinfectant – were applied. If signs of the disease manifested themselves, the crews were removed to Lazzaretto Vecchio. The system was adopted in other ports under Venetian rule and was soon taken up by Venice's commercial rivals.

Good as they were, these precautions were not always foolproof. In 1575 the city suffered one of its worst epidemics. In less than two years, around 50,000 people died, including the artist Titian and his son. The two islands could no longer hold the plague victims; large boats were moored by the *lazzaretti* to provide room for the overflow. The city's beggars – suspected pestilence spreaders with their personal flea menageries – were rounded up and placed aboard some 2,000 boats anchored in the lagoon.

In the face of such large-scale infection, doctors summoned from the medical school in Padua were powerless. Many Venetians put their faith in *teriaca*, a traditional cure-all elixir containing hundreds of exotic ingredients, including snake-flesh, the livers of deer, eagles and ravens, and a resin extracted from a plant that grew only in Egypt. Exported through Europe, the elixir became a major source of income for the Republic.

When quarantine and *teriaca* failed, divine intervention was the next best thing. Saints Sebastian and Rock (Rocco) were considered the best plague protectors.

This latter, a French saint of the 14th century, was also a handy piece of propaganda material, exploited fervently by Venetian authorities: when Rock found he had plague, he withdrew selflessly deep into a forest, where he would be sure not to infect any of his fellow men... just as it was hoped locals would get themselves to a *lazzaretto* before doing too much damage.

To get back into God's good graces after a clear sign of divine disapproval, the Doge promised that a temple would be constructed to the Redeemer as soon as the plague had ceased. Palladio's magnificent Redentore ('redeemer'; *see p135*) on the Giudecca is one of two major architectural side-effects of devastating disease. Fifty-five years later the plague returned, this time from the land – a legacy of the Thirty Years War. Another church was promised, this time to the Madonna of health or salvation: Santa Maria della Salute (*see p132*).

---

granite, from which laws and sentences were pronounced. It was to this figure – the *Gobbo di Rialto* (the Hunchback of the Rialto, although he is, in fact, merely crouching) – that naked malefactors clung in desperate and bloody relief, since the statue marked the end of the gauntlet they were condemned to run from piazza San Marco as an alternative to gaol.

The ruga degli Speziali leads to the Pescaria (fishmarket; open Tue-Sat morning). The present neo-Gothic arcade (1907) replaced the iron structure of the previous century. Beyond the market extends a warren-like zone of medieval low-rent housing interspersed with proud *palazzi*. This area is traversed by two main pedestrian routes from the Rialto bridge, one running westward, more or less parallel to the Grand Canal, towards campo San Polo, and

the other zigzagging north-westwards via a series of small squares towards campo San Giacomo dell'Orio (*see p118*) and the station.

San Giacomo di Rialto

San Polo, campo San Giacomo (041 522 4745). Vaporetto Rialto. **Open** 9.30am-noon, 4-6pm Mon-Sat. **Map** p309 C2.

The traditional foundation date for this church is that of the city itself: 25 March 421. It has undergone several radical reconstructions since its foundation, the last in 1601. Nonetheless, out of respect for the history of the building, the original Greek cross plan was always preserved, as were its minuscule dimensions. The interior has columns of ancient marble with 11th-century Corinthian capitals. According to Francesco Sansovino (son of the architect and author of the first guide to the city in 1581), the brick dome may have been a model for the domes of St Mark's.

In 1177 Pope Alexander III granted plenary indulgence to all those who visited the church on Maundy Thursday; among the eager visitors every year was the doge. The special role of this church in Venetian history was given official recognition after 1532, when Pope Clement VII bestowed the patronage of the church on the doge, effectively annexing it to the Ducal Chapel of St Mark's.

West from the Rialto

The route to campo San Polo traverses a series of straight, busy shopping streets, passing the recently reopened church of **San Giovanni Elemosinario** and the deconsecrated church of Sant'Aponal, which has fine Gothic sculpture on its façade. To the south of this route, towards the Grand Canal, stands the church of **San Silvestro**, with a good Tintoretto, while to the north is a fascinating network of quiet, little-visited alleys and courtyards.

Curiosities worth seeking out (take calle Bianca Cappello from campo Sant'Aponal) include Palazzo Molin-Cappello, birthplace of Bianca Cappello, who in 1563 was sentenced to death *in absentia* for eloping with a bank clerk but who managed to right things between herself and the Most Serene Republic by subsequently marrying Francesco de' Medici, Grand Duke of Tuscany. Northwestwards from here is campiello Albrizzi, overlooked by Palazzo Albrizzi, which contains one of the most sumptuous Baroque interiors (closed to the public) in Venice.

Nearby is one of Venice's early red-light zones; the district of Ca' Rampana was notorious enough to have passed on its own name (*carampana* means 'slut') to the Italian language. Just round the corner is the ponte delle Tette, or the Tits Bridge, where prostitutes were given unofficial licence to display their wares with the aim of saving Venetian men from less 'acceptable' vices.

After the shadowy closeness of these *calli*, the open expanse of campo **San Polo** – home to the church of the same name – comes as a sudden sunlit surprise. This is the largest square on this side of the Grand Canal and in the past was used for popular occasions such as bull-baiting, religious ceremonies, parades and theatrical spectacles as well as weekly markets. Venue of an open-air film season in the summer, its main day-to-day function is that of a vast children's playground.

The curving line of *palazzi* on the east side of the square is explained by the fact that these buildings once gave on to a canal, which was subsequently filled in. They still have a water entrance, on the other side, which means that when they were first built access was by boat

or bridge only. The two *palazzi* Soranzo (Nos.2169 and 2170-1) are particularly attractive Gothic buildings with marble facing and good capitals. In the 18th century these houses had three bridges leading to them. It was while playing the violin at an aristocratic wedding feast in one of the *palazzi* that Casanova first met Senator Bragadin. The aged senator offered Casanova a ride in his gondola, and on the way home suffered a stroke; showing great coolness Casanova had the gondoliers stop and called a surgeon, saving the man's life. The senator ended up by adopting Casanova.

In the north-west corner is a view of Palazzo Corner (the main façade is on the rio di San Polo), a 16th-century design by Sanmicheli. Novelist Frederick Rolfe stayed here – until his English hosts read the manuscript of his work, *The Desire and Pursuit of the Whole*, which contained vitriolic portraits of their friends. They turned him out of the house, thus earning a place for themselves in this grudge novel.

San Giovanni Elemosinario

San Polo, ruga vecchia San Giovanni (041 275 0462). Vaporetto San Silvestro or Rialto. **Open** 10am-5pm Mon-Sat; 1-5pm Sun. **Admission** €2.50 (*see also p70* **Chorus**). **No credit cards**. **Map** p309 C2.
This small Renaissance church – a Greek cross within a square – was reopened in 2002 after remaining closed for an unexpected 20 years. It was founded in the ninth or tenth century but rebuilt after a fire in 1514, probably by Scarpagnino. On the high altar is a painting by Titian of the titular saint, *St John the Alms Giver*. (The saint's body is preserved in the church of San Giovanni in Bragora, *see p101*.) In the left aisle is a medieval fragment of sculptural relief (12th or 13th century) of the Nativity, which shows an ox and donkey reverently licking the face of the Christ child.

San Polo

Campo San Polo (041 275 0462). Vaporetto San Silvestro or San Tomà. **Open** 10am-5pm Mon-Sat; 1-5pm Sun. **Admission** €2.50 (*see also p70* **Chorus**). **No credit cards**. **Map** p309 D1.
The church of San Polo faces away from the square, towards the canal, although later buildings have deprived it of its façade and water entrance. The *campanile* (1362) has two 12th-century lions at the base, one brooding over a snake and the other toying with a human head, which Venetians like to think of as that of Count Carmagnola, who was beheaded for treachery in 1402. This basically Gothic church was extensively altered in the 19th century, when a neo-classical look was imposed on it. Some of this was removed in 1930, but the interior remains an awkward hybrid. Paintings include a *Last Supper* by Tintoretto to the left of the entrance, and a Tiepolo: *The Virgin Appearing to St John of Nepomuk*. Giambattista Tiepolo's son, Giandomenico, is the

Sightseeing

author of a brilliant cycle of Stations of the Cross in the Oratory of the Crucifix (entrance under the organ), freshly restored. He painted these, and the ceiling paintings, at the age of 20.

San Silvestro
San Polo, campo San Silvestro (041 523 8090). Vaporetto San Silvestro. **Open** 7.30-11.30am, 4-6pm Mon-Sat. **Map** p305 C309 D1.
This church was rebuilt in the neo-classical style between 1837 and 1843. It contains a *Baptism of Christ* (c1580) by Tintoretto over the first altar on the right, with the River Jordan represented as a mountain brook. Opposite is *St Thomas à Becket Enthroned* (1520) by Girolamo da Santacroce, with the saint in startling white robes against a mountain landscape; the other two saints are 19th-century additions. Off the right aisle (ask the sacristan to let you in) is the former School of the Wine Merchants; on the upper floor there's a chapel with 18th-century frescoes by Gaspare Diziani. Opposite the church is the house (No.1022) where Giorgione died in 1510.

North-west from the Rialto

Yellow signs pointing to Ferrovia mark the zigzagging north-western route from the Rialto past the fishmarket, through campo **San Cassiano**. The uninspiring plain exterior of the church here gives no clue to its heavily decorated interior. Across the bridge is campo **Santa Maria Mater Domini** with its

Leaping statues: **San Stae**. *See p119.*

Renaissance church. Before entering the campo, admire the view from the bridge of the curving marble flank of **Ca' Pesaro** – seat of the Museo Orientale and Galleria d'Arte Moderna – on the Grand Canal. On the far side of the square, which contains a number of fine Byzantine and Gothic buildings, the yellow road sign, in true Venetian fashion, indicates that the way to the station is to the left *and* to the right.

The quieter route to the right curls parallel to the Grand Canal. The road towards Ca' Pesaro passes Palazzo Agnusdio, a small 14th-century house with an ogival five-light window decorated with bas-reliefs of the Annunciation and symbols of the evangelists; the house used to belong to a family of sausage makers who were given patrician status in the 17th century.

Many of the most important sights face on to the Grand Canal, including the 18th-century church of **San Stae** and the Fondaco dei Turchi (the Warehouse of the Turks home to the city's **Museo di Storia Naturale**, which has partially reopened after lengthy restoration). On the wide road leading towards San Stae is **Palazzo Mocenigo**, containing a collection of textiles and costumes. A short distance away is the quiet square of San Zan Degolà (**San Giovanni Decollato**), with its well-preserved 11th-century church. From here, a series of narrow roads leads past the church of **San Simeone Profeta** to the foot of the Scalzi bridge across the Grand Canal.

Leave campo Santa Maria Mater Domini by the route to the left, on the other hand, and you'll make your way past the near-legendary Da Fiore eaterie (*see p159*) to the house (No. 2311) where Aldo Manuzio (Aldus Manutius) set up the Aldine Press in 1490, and where the humanist Erasmus came to stay in 1508. To the right, by a building with a 14th-century relief of Faith and Justice above its doorway, the rio terà del Parrucchetta (reportedly named after a seller of animal fodder who used to wear a ridiculous wig, or *parrucca*) leads to the large leafy campo **San Giacomo dell'Orio**. The church has its back and sides to the square; the main entrance was from the water.

Ca' Pesaro – Galleria Internazionale d'Arte Moderna
Santa Croce 2076, fondamenta Ca' Pesaro (041 524 0695). Vaporetto San Stae. **Open** *Apr-Oct* 10am-6pm Tue-Sun. *Nov-Mar* 10am-5pm Tue-Sun. **Admission** €5.50; €3 concessions; includes Museo Orientale (*see also p70* **Musei Civici Veneziani**). **No credit cards. Map** p309 C1.
This museum was reopened in November 2002 after restoration. The grandiose palazzo was built in the second half of the 17th century for the Pesaro family (celebrated in Titian's great painting *La Madonna di Ca' Pesaro* in the Frari), to a project by

Modern art and Oriental *objets* at **Ca' Pesaro**.

Baldassare Longhena. When Longhena died in 1682 the family entrusted the completion of the project to Gian Antonio Gaspari, who concluded it in 1710, sticking largely to the original blueprint. The interior of the palazzo still contains some of the original fresco and oil decorations, although the family's great collection of Renaissance paintings was auctioned off in London by the last Pesaro before he died in 1830. The palazzo passed through many hands until its last owner, Felicita Bevilacqua La Masa, bequeathed it to the city. Into it went the city's collection of modern art, gleaned from Biennale exhibitions (*see p197*). Between 1908 and 1924 its mezzanine floor played host to the renowned Bevilacqua La Masa exhibitions, which gave hanging space to young Italian artists, as well as providing healthy competition for the Biennale. The museum now covers a century of mainly Italian art, from the mid 19th century to the 1950s. On the stately ground floor are a number of 20th-century Italian sculptures, including a monumental *Eve* by Francesco Messina and a bronze *Cardinal* by Giacomo Manzù.

The first rooms on the *piano nobile* contain atmospheric works by 19th-century painters such as Ippolito Caffi and Guglielmo Ciardi and some striking sculptures by Medardo Rosso. In the central hall are works from the early *Biennali* up to the 1930s, including pieces by Gustav Klimt and Vassily Kandinsky, alongside more conventional vast-scale 'salon' paintings. Room 4 holds works by Giorgio Morandi, Joan Mirò and Giorgio De Chirico. After rooms devoted to international art from the 1940s and '50s, the collection winds up with works by postwar Venetian experimentalists such as Armando Pizzinato, Giuseppe Santomaso and Emilio Vedova.

Ca' Pesaro – Museo Orientale

Santa Croce 2070, fondamenta Ca' Pesaro (041 524 1173). Vaporetto San Stae. **Open** *Apr-Oct* 10am-6pm Tue-Sun. *Nov-Mar* 10am-5pm Tue-Sun.

Admission €5.50; €3 concessions; includes Galleria d'Arte Moderna (*see also p70* **Musei Civici Veneziani**). **Map** p309 C1.
If Japanese art and weaponry of the Edo period (1600-1868) are your thing, you'll love this eclectic collection, put together by Count Enrico di Borbone – a nephew of Louis XVIII – in the course of a round-the-world voyage between 1887 and 1890. After the count's death the collection was sold off to an Austrian antique merchant; it bounced back to Venice after World War I as reparations. The Museo Orientale might seem an odd attraction for such a monocultural city as Venice, but if you come here after the Palazzo Ducale and the Museo Correr, all this ceremonial paraphernalia will seem oddly familiar. The collection features parade armour, dolls, decorative saddles and case upon case of curved samurai swords forged by smiths who had to perform a ritual act of purification before putting their irons in the fire. There is a dwarf-sized lady's gilded litter, and lacquered picnic cases that prove that the Japanese obsession with compactness predates Sony. The final rooms have musical instruments and eastern miscellanea, including Chinese crockery and eastern Indonesian shadow puppets.

Museo di Storia Naturale

Santa Croce 1730, salizada del Fondaco dei Turchi (041 275 0206). Vaporetto San Stae. **Open** 10am-4pm Sat, Sun. **Admission** free. **Map** p309 C1.
This museum has long been closed to the public, undergoing slow but steady restoration. As this guide goes to press two rooms have been opened for weekend visits.

The museum is housed in the Fontego dei Turchi, a Venetian-Byzantine building leased to the Turks in the 17th century as a residence and warehouse. The present building is essentially a 19th-century reconstruction of the original. Before restoration the museum displays were the fruit either of Victorian enthusiasm (numerous stuffed animals and varied ethnographic material collected between 1859-60) or of 20th-century-focused research (erudite displays on the lagoon flora and fauna). At present visitors can see the *Acquario delle tegnue*, devoted to the aquatic life of the northern Adriatic and the *Sala dei dinosauri*, a state-of-the-art exhibition chronicling the Ligabue expedition to Niger (1973), which unearthed a fossil of the previously unknown *Auronosaurus nigeriensis* and a giant crocodile.

Palazzo Mocenigo
Santa Croce 1992, salizada San Stae (041 721 798). Vaporetto San Stae. **Open** *Apr-Oct* 10am-5pm Tue-Sun. *Nov-Mar* 10am-4pm Tue-Sun. **Admission** €4; €2.50 concessions (*see also p70* **Musei Civici Veneziani**). **No credit cards. Map** p309 C1.
The Palazzo Mocenigo will not come top of anyone's museum list, but it is a good place to while away half an hour. The museum serves a double purpose. The interior gives a fine illustration of the sort of furniture and fittings an 18th-century Venetian noble family liked to surround itself with. The Mocenigo family (which also owned a complex of *palazzi* on the Grand Canal) provided the Republic with seven doges, and the paintings, friezes and frescoes by late 18th-century artists such as Jacopo Guarana and Gian Battista Canal glorify their achievements. In the rooms off the main *salone* the neo-classical influence already makes itself felt. Here too, are the dusty display cases that serve the museum's other function: to chronicle 18th-century Venetian dress. An andrienne dress with bustles so horizontal you could rest a cup and saucer on them, antique lace and silk stockings, a whalebone corset – it's a patchy but charming collection.

San Cassiano
San Polo, campo San Cassiano (041 721 408). Vaporetto San Stae. **Open** 9am-noon Tue-Sat. **Map** p309 C1.
This church has a singularly dull exterior and a heavily decorated interior, with a striking ceiling (freshly restored) by the Tiepolesque painter Constantino Cedini. The chancel contains three major Tintorettos: *Crucifixion, Resurrection* and *Descent into Limbo*. The Crucifixion is particularly interesting for its viewpoint. As Ruskin puts it, 'The horizon is so low, that the spectator must fancy himself lying full length on the grass, or rather among the brambles and luxuriant weeds, of which the foreground is entirely composed.' In the background the soldiers' spears make a menacing forest against a dramatic stormy sky.

Off the left aisle is a small chapel with coloured marbles and inlays of semi-precious stones. On the wall opposite the altar is a painting by Antonio Balestra, which at first glance looks like a dying saint surrounded by *putti*. On closer inspection it transpires that the chubby children are, in fact, hacking the man to death: the painting represents *The Martyrdom of St Cassian*, a teacher who was murdered by his pupils with their pens. This, of course, makes him the patron saint of schoolteachers.

Relief at **San Zan Degolà**. *See p119.*

San Giacomo dell'Orio
Santa Croce, campo San Giacomo dell'Orio (041 275 0462). Vaporetto Riva di Biasio. **Open** 10am-5pm Mon-Sat; 1-5pm Sun. **Admission** €2.50 (*see also p70* **Chorus**). **No credit cards. Map** p308 C3.
Campo San Giacomo dell'Orio (St James of the wolf, the laurel tree, the rio or the Orio family – take your pick) has a pleasantly downbeat feel, with its trees, bars and children. It's dominated by the church with its plump apses and stocky 13th-century campanile. As with most older Venetian churches, the main entrance faces the canal rather than the campo.

The interior is a fascinating mix of architectural and decorative styles. Most of the columns have 12th- or 13th-century Veneto-Byzantine capitals; one has a sixth-century flowered capital and one is a solid piece of smooth verd-antique marble, perhaps from a Roman temple sacked during the Fourth Crusade. Note, too, the fine 14th-century ship's-keel roof. The *Sacrestia nuova*, in the right transept, was built in 1903 on the site of the Scuola del Sacramento. This was the original home of the five gilded compartments on the ceiling with paintings by Veronese: an *Allegory of the Faith* surrounded by four Doctors of the Church. Among the paintings in the room is *St John the Baptist Preaching* by Francesco Bassano, which includes a portrait of Titian (in the red hat).

Behind the high altar is a *Madonna and Four Saints* by Lorenzo Lotto, one of his last Venetian paintings. There is a good work by Giovanni Bonconsiglio at the end of the left aisle, *St Lawrence, St Sebastian and St Roch*; St Sebastian is conventionally untroubled by his arrow, but St Roch's plague sore has an anatomical precision that is quite unsettling (*see p114* **Pestilence**). The third of these saints, St Lawrence, also has a chapel all to himself in the left transept, with a central altarpiece by Veronese and two fine early works by Palma il Giovane. As you leave, have a look at the curious painting to the left of the main door, a naïve 18th-century work by Gaetano Zompini, showing a propaganda miracle involving a Jewish scribe who attempted to profane the body of the Virgin on its way to the sepulchre.

San Simeone Profeta

Santa Croce, campo San Simeone Profeta (041 718 921). Vaporetto Ferrovia. **Open** 8am-noon, 5-6.30pm Mon-Sat. **Map** p308 C2.

More commonly known as San Simeone Grande, this small church of possibly tenth-century foundation underwent numerous alterations in the 18th century. The interior preserves its ancient columns with Byzantine capitals. To the left of the entrance is Tintoretto's *Last Supper*, with the priest who commissioned the painting standing to one side, a spectral figure in glowing white robes. The other major work is the stark, powerful statue of a recumbent St Simeon, with an inscription dated 1317 attributing it to an otherwise unknown Marco Romano. The prophet has a 'face full of quietness and majesty, though very ghastly', as Ruskin puts it. Outside, beneath the portico flanking the church, is a fine 15th-century relief of a bishop praying.

San Stae

Santa Croce, campo San Stae (041 275 0462). Vaporetto San Stae. **Open** 10am-5pm Mon-Sat; 1-5pm Sun. **Admission** €2.50 (*see also p70* **Chorus**). **No credit cards. Map** p309 C1.

Stae is the Venetian version of Eustachio or Eustace, a martyr saint who was converted to Christianity by the vision of a stag with a crucifix between his antlers. This church on the Grand Canal has a dramatic late Baroque façade (1709) by Swiss-born architect Domenico Rossi. The form is essentially Palladian but enlivened by a number of vibrant sculptures, some apparently on the point of leaping straight out of the façade. Venice's last great blaze of artistic glory came in the 18th century, and the interior is a temple to this swansong. On the side walls of the chancel, all the leading painters operating in Venice in 1722 were asked to pick an apostle, any apostle. The finest of these are: Tiepolo's *Martyrdom of St Bartholomew* (left wall, lower row); Sebastiano Ricci's *Liberation of St Peter*, perhaps his best work (right wall, lower row); Pellegrini's *Martyrdom of St Andrew*; and Piazzetta's *Martyrdom of St James*, a disturbingly realistic work showing the saint as a confused old man in the hands of a loutish youth. The church is often used for temporary exhibitions.

Santa Maria Mater Domini

Santa Croce, campo Santa Maria Mater Domini (041 721 408). Vaporetto San Stae. **Open** 10am-noon Tue-Fri. **Map** p309 C1.

This church, recently restored by the Venice in Peril fund, is set just off the campo of the same name, which has a number of fine *palazzi*. It was built in the first half of the 16th century to a project by either Giovanni Buora or Maurizio Codussi. The façade is attributed to Jacopo Sansovino; the harmonious Renaissance interior alternates grey stone with white marble. The *Vision of St Christine* on the second altar on the right is by Vincenzo Catena, a spice merchant who seems to have painted in his spare time. St Christine was rescued by angels after

being thrown into Lake Bolsena with a millstone tied round her neck; in the painting she adores the Risen Christ, while angels hold up the millstone for her. In the left transept hangs *The Invention of the Cross*, a youthful work by Tintoretto.

San Giovanni Decollato (San Zan Degolà)

Santa Croce, campo San Giovanni Decollato (041 524 0672). Vaporetto Riva di Biasio. **Open** 10am-noon Mon-Sat. **Map** p308 C3.

The church of Headless Saint John, or San Zan Degolà in Venetian dialect, stands in a quiet campo near the Fondaco dei Turchi; it's a good building to visit if you want a relief from Baroque excesses and ecclesiastic clutter. It was restored and reopened in 1994 after being closed for nearly 20 years, and preserves much of its original 11th-century appearance. The interior has Greek columns with Byzantine capitals supporting ogival arches, and an attractive ship's-keel roof. During the restoration a splendidly heroic 14th-century fresco of St Michael the Archangel came to light in the right apse. The left apse has some of the earliest frescoes in Venice, Veneto-Byzantine works of the early 13th century. The church is used for Russian Orthodox services.

From the Frari to piazzale Roma

At the heart of the western side of the two *sestieri* lies the great Gothic bulk of Santa Maria Gloriosa dei Frari (*see p120* **I Frari**), with its 70-metre (230-foot) *campanile*, matched by the Renaissance magnificence of the *scuola* and church of San Rocco. These buildings contain perhaps the greatest concentration of influential works of art in the city outside piazza San Marco and the Accademia (*see p130*).

The monastery buildings of the Frari contain the State Archives, a monument to Venetian reluctance ever to throw anything away. In 300 rooms, about 15 million volumes and files are conserved, relating to all aspects of Venetian history, starting from the year 883. Faced with this daunting wealth of information, ranging from ambassadors' dispatches on foreign courts to spies' reports on noblemen's non-regulation cloaks, grown historians have been reduced to quivering wrecks.

Beyond the archives is the **Scuola di San Giovanni Evangelista**, one of the six *scuole grandi* (*see p95* **Back to school**) which played such an important part in the complex Venetian system of social checks and balances. The courtyard is protected by a screen with a magnificent eagle pediment and a frieze of leaf-sprays by Pietro Lombardo, while the building itself contains a double magnificent staircase by Maurizio Codussi.

North of here runs rio Marin, a canal with *fondamente* on both sides, lined by some fine buildings; these include the late 16th-century Palazzo Soranzo Capello, with a small garden (to the rear) that figures in D'Annunzio's torrid novel *ll Fuoco* and Henry James' more restrained *The Aspern Papers*, and the 17th-century Palazzo Gradenigo, the garden of which was once large enough to host bullfights.

South-west of the Frari is the quiet square of **San Tomà**, with a church on one side and the *Scuola dei Calegheri* (cobblers) opposite; the *scuola* (now a library) has a protective mantle-spreading Madonna over the door and above it a relief by Pietro Lombardo of *St Mark Healing the Cobbler Annanius*, who became bishop of Alexandria and subsequently the patron saint of shoemakers. Directly south of here is campo **San Pantalon** (technically in Dorsoduro); its church has an extraordinary Hollywood-rococo interior. Walking out of the church towards the canal, an alley to the left will take you into little campiello d'Angaran, where there is a carved roundel of a Byzantine emperor, which experts believe possibly dates from the tenth century. Returning to the campo, a slab in the wall by the canal indicates the minimum lengths allowed for the sale of various types of fish.

Just off the square of San Tomà is Palazzo Centani, the birthplace of Carlo Goldoni, the prolific Venetian playwright. The house, which has an attractive Gothic courtyard with a fine well head and staircase, contains a small museum and library (**Casa di Carlo Goldoni**) devoted to the writer and to Venetian theatre.

Nearby are the curiously named fondamenta and ponte della Donna Onesta (honest woman). Explanations for the name abound: the tiny sculptured face of a woman in a house over the bridge was once pointed out as being Venice's only 'honest woman'; a local prostitute was famous for carrying on her trade with singular honesty; the wife of a local sword maker, raped by a client of her husband's, stabbed herself in desperation with one of her husband's daggers.

Heading west from the Frari, the route leads past the **church** and *scuola* of **San Rocco**, treasure troves for Tintoretto lovers, and ends up in a fairly bland area of 19th-century housing, which replaced medieval gardens and orchards. At the edge of this stands the Baroque church of **San Nicolò dei Tolentini**; the adjoining former monastery houses part of the Venice University Architecture Institute.

The rather forlorn Giardino Papadopoli, a small park with Grand Canal views, stands on the site of the church and convent of Santa Croce. The name survives as that of the *sestiere*, but the church is one of many suppressed by the French at the beginning of the 19th century.

All that remains of Santa Croce is a crenellated wall next to a hotel on the Grand Canal. The garden was much larger until the rio Novo was cut in 1932 and 1933 to provide faster access from the new car park to the St Mark's area. The decision was much contested at the time; as the canal had to be closed to regular waterborne traffic in the early 1990s owing to subsidence in the adjacent buildings, it would seem that the protesters had a point.

Beyond the garden there is little but the carbon-monoxide kingdom of piazzale Roma and the multi-storey car parks. One last curiosity is the complex of bridges across the rio Novo known as Tre Ponti (three bridges); there are, in fact, five interlocking bridges.

Casa di Carlo Goldoni e Biblioteca di Studi Teatrali

San Polo 2794, calle dei Nomboli (041 244 0317). *Vaporetto San Tomà.* **Open** *Apr-Oct* 10am-5pm Mon-Sat. *Nov-Mar* 10am-4pm Mon-Sat. **Admission** €2.50; €1.50 concessions (*see also p70* **Musei Civici Veneziani**). **No credit cards. Map** p308 D3.

This museum is really only for specialists, although the attractive Gothic courtyard, with its carved well head and staircase is worth seeing. It is the birthplace of Venice's greatest writer, the playwright Carlo Goldoni, who over the course of his long career, transformed Italian theatre, moving it away from the stultified clichés of the *Commedia dell'arte* tradition and introducing a comedy based on realistic observation. Inevitably he also made a number of enemies – including, at first, some of the actors, who weren't happy with the idea of having to learn lines rather than simply improvise around a skeleton plot. On the first floor there are reproductions of prints based on Goldoni's works and a few 18th-century paintings; the best item is a splendid 18th-century miniature theatre complete with puppets of *Commedia dell'arte* figures. The library on the upper floor has theatrical texts, studies and original manuscripts.

I Frari

San Polo, campo dei Frari (041 522 2637). *Vaporetto San Tomà.* **Open** 9am-6pm Mon-Sat; 1-6pm Sun. **Admission** €2.50 (*see also p70* **Chorus**). **No credit cards. Map** p308 D3.

A gloomy Gothic barn, the brick house of God known officially as Santa Maria Gloriosa dei Frari may not be the most elegant church in Venice, but it is certainly one of the city's most significant artistic storehouses after the Accademia and the Scuola di San Rocco. The Franciscans were granted the land in about 1250 and they completed a first church in 1338. At this point they changed their minds and started work on a larger building which was finally completed just over a century later. The church is 98m (320ft) long, 48m (158ft) wide at the transept and 28m (92ft) high – just slightly smaller than Santi

Nature trail: vicious patere

San Polo and Santa Croce are Venice's most densely packed *sestieri*, their unremitting masonry broken only by a handful of welcome plane trees in campo San Polo and campo San Giacomo dell'Orio, and by the scrappy bit of down-at-heel green that goes by the name of Giardini Papadopoli near piazzale Roma.

Santa Croce *is* home to the Museo di Storia Naturale (*see p117*) but it's a poor tribute to the natural world: closed completely for years, it is now open, occasionally, in parts. Small wonder, then, that even the depictions of animals here display marked hostility in this overwhelmingly urban environment.

On the reconstructed façade of the Museo di Storia Naturale are patere – sculpted ornamentation – showing a veritable menagerie of Byzantine and pseudo-Byzantine beasts: foxes, lions, pheasants, wolves and cats, mostly in the process of ripping one another to pieces. Some (such as the gryphons and peacocks in the arched patere on the two side-towers) are genuine, if heavily restored, 11th or 12th-century works; others are 19th-century imitations.

Near campo San Giacomo dell'Orio are the calle, sottoportico and ponte (and pizzeria) delle Oche – 'of the geese'. The name comes from a remarkable 13th-century patera depicting what in fact appear to be two flamingos with intertwined necks and kissing beaks on a nearby house (Santa Croce 1033); disturbing this bucolic bliss somewhat are two patere below of hares being viciously savaged by eagles.

Altogether more touchingly rustic is the 12th-century relief of the nativity in the church of San Giovanni Elemosinario (*see p115*) near the Rialto market; it shows Christ in his crib being watched over by an ox and donkey, both of which are gently nuzzling him.

San Giacomo dell'Orio.

Giovanni e Paolo (see *p94*) – and has the second-highest *campanile* in the city. And while the Frari may not have as many dead doges as its Dominican rival, it undoubtedly has the artistic edge. This is one church where the entrance fee is not a recent imposition; tourists have been paying to get into the Frari for over a century. At the entrance you are brought face-to-face with the long sweep of church with with Titian's glorious *Assumption* above the high altar.

Right aisle
In the second bay, on the spot where Titian is believed to be buried (the only victim of the 1575-6 plague who was allowed a city burial), is a loud monument to the artist, commissioned nearly 300 years after his death by the Emperor of Austria. On the third altar is a finer memorial, Alessandro Vittoria's statue of St Jerome, generally believed to be a portrait of his painter friend.

Right transept
To the right of the sacristy door is the tomb of the Blessed Pacifico (a companion of St Francis) attrib-

uted to Nanni di Bartolo and Michele da Firenze (1437); the sarcophagus is surrounded by a splendidly carved canopy in the florid Gothic style. The door itself is framed by Lorenzo Bregno's tomb of Benedetto Pesaro, a Venetian general who died in Corfu. To the left of the door is the first equestrian statue in Venice, the monument to Paolo Savelli (died 1405). The third chapel on the right side of this transept has an altarpiece by Bartolomeo Vivarini, in its original frame, while the Florentine Chapel, next to the chancel, contains the only work by Donatello in the city: a striking wooden statue of a stark, emaciated St John the Baptist.

Sacristy
Commissioned by the Pesaro family, this contains one of Giovanni Bellini's greatest paintings: the *Madonna and Child with Saints Nicholas, Peter, Benedict and Mark* (1488), still in its original frame. 'It seems painted with molten gems, which have been clarified by time,' wrote Henry James, his eye, as ever, firmly on the prose structure, 'and it is as

solemn as it is gorgeous and as simple as it is deep.' Also in the sacristy is a fine Renaissance tabernacle, possibly by Tullio Lombardo, for a reliquary holding Christ's blood.

Chancel

The high altar is dominated by Titian's *Assumption*, a visionary work that seems to open the church up to the heavens. In the golden haze encircling God the Father, there may be a reminiscence of the mosaic tradition of Venice. The upward-soaring movement of the painting may owe something to the Gothic architecture of the building, but the drama and grandeur of the work essentially herald the Baroque.

On the right wall of the chancel is the monument to Francesco Foscari, the saddest doge of all. The story of his forced resignation and death from heartbreak (1547) after the exile of his son Jacopo is recounted in Byron's *The Two Foscari*, which was turned into a particularly gloomy opera by Verdi. The left wall boasts one of the finest Renaissance tombs in Venice, the monument to Doge Niccolò Tron, by Antonio Rizzo (1473). This is the first ducal tomb in which the subject is upright; he sports a magnificent bushy beard grown as a sign of perpetual mourning after the death of his favourite son.

Monks' choir

In the centre of the nave stands the choir, with wooden stalls carved by Marco Cozzi (1468), inlaid with superb intarsia decoration. The choir screen is a mixture of Gothic work by Bartolomeo Bon and Renaissance elements by the Lombardi.

Left transept

In the third chapel, with an altarpiece by Bartolomeo Vivarini and Marco Basaiti, a slab on the floor marks the grave of composer Claudio Monteverdi. The Corner chapel, at the end, contains a mannered statue of St John the Baptist by Sansovino; this sensitively wistful figure could hardly be more different from Donatello's work of a century earlier.

Left aisle

Another magnificent Titian hangs to the left of the side door: the *Madonna di Ca' Pesaro*. This work was commissioned by Bishop Jacopo Pesaro in 1519 and celebrates victory in a naval expedition against the Turks, led by the bellicose cleric in 1502. The bishop is kneeling and waiting for St Peter to introduce him and his family to the Madonna. Behind, an armoured warrior bearing a banner has Turkish prisoners in tow. This work revolutionised altar paintings in Venice. It wasn't just that Titian dared to move the Virgin from the centre of the composition to one side, using the splendid banner as a counterbalance; the real innovation was the rich humanity of the whole work, from the beautifully portrayed family (with the boy turning to stare straight at us) to the Christ child, so naturally active and alive, twisting away from his mother (said to be a portrait of Titian's wife) to gaze curiously at the saints clustered around him. The timeless 'sacred conversation' of Bellini's paintings here becomes animated, losing some of its sacredness but gaining in drama and realism.

The whole of the next bay, around the side door, is occupied by another piece of Pesaro propaganda – the mastodontic mausoleum of Doge Pesaro (died 1659), attributed to Longhena, with sculptures by Melchior Barthel of Dresden. Even the most ardent fans of the Baroque have trouble defending this one, with its 'blackamoor' caryatids, bronze skeletons and posturing allegories. 'It seems impossible for false taste and base feeling to sink lower,' wrote Ruskin, and you can see his point.

The penultimate bay harbours a monument to Canova, carried out by his pupils in 1827, five years after his death, using a design of his own that was intended for the tomb of Titian. His body is buried in his native town of Possagno (*see p266*), but his heart is conserved in an urn inside the monument. The despondent winged lion has a distinct resemblance to the one in *The Wizard of Oz*.

San Nicolò da Tolentino

Santa Croce, campo dei Tolentini (041 710 806). Vaporetto Piazzale Roma. **Open** 9.30am-noon, 4-6pm Mon-Sat; 4-6pm Sun. **Map** p308 D2.

This church (1591-5), usually known as I Tolentini, was planned by Vincenzo Scamozzi. Its unfinished façade has a massive Corinthian portico (1706-14) added by Andrea Tirali. The interior (most of which has been recently restored) is a riot of Baroque decoration, with lavish use of stucco and sprawling frescoes. The most interesting paintings – as so often in the 17th century – are by out-of-towners. On the wall outside the chancel to the left is *St Jerome Succoured by an Angel* by Flemish artist Johann Liss. Outside the chapel in the left transept is *The Charity of St Lawrence* by the Genoese Bernardo Strozzi, in which the magnificently hoary old beggar in the foreground easily upstages the rather wimpish figure of the saint. In the chancel hangs an *Annunciation* by Neapolitan Luca Giordano and opposite is a splendidly theatrical monument to Francesco Morosini (a 17th-century patriarch of that name, not the doge) by Filippo Parodi (1678), with swirling angels drawing aside a marble curtain to reveal the patriarch lounging at ease on his tomb. In 1780 the priests of this church handed over all their silverware to a certain 'Romano', who claimed to have a secret new method for cleaning silver and jewellery. He was never seen again.

San Pantalon

Santa Croce, campo San Pantalon (041 523 5893). Vaporetto San Tomà. **Open** 4-6pm Mon-Sat. **Map** p308 D3.

The dedicatee of this church is St Pantaleon, court physician to Emperor Galerius, who was arrested, tortured and finally beheaded during Diocletian's persecution of the Christians. The saint's story is depicted inside the church in one of the most extraordinary ceiling paintings in Italy – a huge illusionist work, painted on 40 canvases, by the Cecil B De Mille of the 17th century, Gian Antonio Fumiani. It took him 24 years to complete the task (1680-1704) and at the end of it all he fell with choreographic

San Rocco.

grace from the scaffolding to his death. Veronese depicts the saint in less melodramatic fashion in the second chapel on the right, in what is possibly his last work, *St Pantaleon Healing a Child*.

To the left of the chancel is the Chapel of the Holy Nail. The nail in question, supposedly from the Crucifixion, is preserved in a small but richly decorated Gothic altar. On the right wall is a fine *Coronation of the Virgin* by Antonio Vivarini and Giovanni d'Alemagna.

San Rocco

San Polo, campo San Rocco (041 523 4864). Vaporetto San Tomà. **Open** *Apr-Oct* 8am-12.30pm, 3-5pm daily. *Nov-Mar* 8am-12.30pm Mon-Fri; 8am-12.30pm, 2-4pm Sat, Sun. **Map** p308 D3.

If you have toured the school of San Rocco and are in the mood for more Tintorettos (perhaps after a shot of whisky or a lie-down), look no further. Built in Venetian Renaissance style by Bartolomeo Bon from 1489 to 1508, but radically altered by Giovanni Scalfarotto in 1725, the church has paintings by Tintoretto, or his school, on either side of the entrance door, between the first and second altar on the right, and on either side of the chancel. Nearly all are connected with the life of St Roch; the best is probably *St Roch Cures the Plague Victims* (chancel, lower right). The altar paintings are all difficult to see; they're high up and not very well lit. Even if you could get a good view, you might not be much the wiser: even Ruskin, Tintoretto's greatest fan, was completely baffled as to their subject matter.

Scuola Grande di San Rocco

San Polo 3054, campo San Rocco (041 523 4864/www.sanrocco.it). Vaporetto San Tomà. **Open** *Apr-Oct* 9am-5.30pm daily. *Nov-Mar* 10am-4pm daily. **Admission** €5.50; €1.50 concessions. **Credit** AmEx, DC, MC, V. **Map** 308 D3.

The Archbrotherhood of St Roch was the richest of the six *scuole grandi* (*see p95* **Back to school**) in 15th-century Venice. Its members came from the top end of mercantile and professional classes. It was dedicated to Venice's other patron saint, the French plague protector and dog lover St Roch/Rock (San Rocco; *see p114* **Pestilence**), whose body was brought here in 1485.

The *scuola* operated out of rented accommodation for many years, but at the beginning of the 16th century a permanent base was commissioned. The architecture, by Bartolomeo Bon and Scarpagnino, is far less impressive than the interior decoration, which was entrusted to Tintoretto in 1564 after a competition in which he stole a march on rivals Salviati, Zuccari and Veronese by presenting a finished painting rather than the required sketch. In three intensive sessions over the following 23 years, Tintoretto went on to make San Rocco his epic masterpiece. Fans and doubters alike should start here; the former will no doubt agree with John Ruskin that paintings such as the *Crucifixion* are 'beyond all analysis and above all praise', while the latter may well find their prejudices crumbling. True, the devotional intensity of his works can shade a touch too much into kitsch for the postmodern soul; but his feel for narrative structure is timeless.

To follow the development of Tintoretto's style, pick up the free explanatory leaflet and the audio guide and begin in the smaller upstairs hall – the Albergo. Here, filling up the whole of the far wall, is the *Crucifixion* (1565), of which Henry James commented: 'It is one of the greatest things of art… there is everything in it.' More than anything it is the perfect integration of main plot and sub-plots that strikes the viewer; whereas most paintings are short stories, this is a novel. Tintoretto began work on the larger upstairs room in 1575, with Old Testament stories on the ceiling and a Life of Christ cycle around the walls, in which the man who possessed what Vasari referred to as 'the most extraordinary mind that the art of painting has produced' experimented relentlessly with form, lighting and colour. Below the canvases is a characterful series of late 17th-century wooden carvings, including a caricature of Tintoretto himself, just below and to the left of *The Agony in the Garden*. Finally, in the ground-floor hall – which the artist decorated between 1583 and 1587, when he was in his 60s – the paintings reach a visionary pitch that has to do with Tintoretto's audacious handling of light and the impressionistic economy of his brush strokes. The *Annunciation*, with its domestic Mary surprised while sewing, and *Flight into Egypt*, with its verdant landscape, are among the painter's masterpieces. Admission is free on 16 August, the feast of St Roch.

Dorsoduro

Wealthy at one end and working-class at the other, with some great bars in between.

Dorsoduro – 'hard back' – constitutes the long, firm southern edge of Venice, stretching from the dockland area of Santa Marta in the west to the Salute church in the east. The distance between its two extremes is social as well as geographical: Santa Marta is unabashedly working-class and decidedly homey, while the highfalutin Salute area oozes international wealth. Halfway between the two lies Dorsoduro's largest square, the wholly democratic campo Santa Margherita, where workers, toffs, shoppers, tourists and students rub shoulders sociably by day and – unusually for Venice – by night.

Western Dorsoduro

This western corner of the city was settled early. The church of San Nicolò was founded as early as the seventh century. The full name of the church is **San Nicolò dei Mendicoli** – 'of the beggars'. The locals have never been in the top income bracket and in the past were mostly fishermen or salt-pan workers. The area gave its name to one of two factions into which

the proletariat was divided: the *nicolotti*. The *nicolotti* were proud enough to maintain a certain form of local autonomy under a figure known as the *gastaldo*, who, after his election, would be received with honours by the doge.

The area is still noticeably less sleek that the centre, although fishing was superseded as a source of employment by the port long ago and subsequently by the Santa Marta cotton mill – now stunningly converted into the Istituto Universitario di Architettura di Venezia (*see p290*). Massive redevelopment schemes are under way for much of this downbeat district, with plans to revitalise it in a vast university-meets-London-Docklands-style project, to a design by the late Catalan architect Enric Miralles Moya. The plans include an auditorium, conference hall, restaurant and huge centralised university library, thus providing Venice university with something approaching a genuine campus.

Moving eastwards, the atmosphere remains unpretentious around the churches of **Angelo Raffaele** and **San Sebastiano**, with its splendid decoration by Paolo Veronese.

Northwards from here, on the rio di Santa Margherita, are some grander *palazzi*, including Palazzo Ariani, with its magnificent Gothic tracery, almost oriental in its intricacy, and, further up, the grand Palazzo Zenobio, now an Armenian school and institute, containing early Tiepolo frescoes (not accessible to the public) and giving on to an elaborate garden where plays are sometimes performed in the summer.

Angelo Raffaele
Campo Angelo Raffaele (041 522 8548). Vaporetto San Basilio. **Open** 9am-noon, 4-6pm Mon-Sat; 9am-noon Sun. **Mass** 10-11am daily. **Map** p310 B3.
This is one of eight churches in Venice traditionally founded by St Magnus in the eighth century, although the present free-standing building – one of only two churches in the city that you can walk right around – dates from the 17th century. The very high ceiling has a lively fresco by Gaspare Diziani of *St Michael Driving out Lucifer*, with Lucifer apparently tumbling out of the heavy stucco frame into the church. There are matching Last Suppers on either side of the organ (by Bonifacio de' Pitati on the left and a follower of Titian on the right). But the real jewels of the church are on the organ loft, whose five compartments, painted by Giovanni Antonio Guardi (or perhaps his brother Francesco), recount the story of *Tobias and the Angel* (1750-3). They are works of dazzling luminosity, quite unlike anything else done in Venice at the time and with something pre-Impressionist about them. The paintings and the story they recount play a significant role in Sally Vickers's novel *Miss Garnet's Angel* (2000).

San Nicolò dei Mendicoli
Campo San Nicolò (041 275 0382). Vaporetto San Basilio or Santa Marta. **Open** 10am-noon, 4-6pm Mon-Sat; 4-6pm Sun. **Map** p310 B2.
San Nicolò is one of the few Venetian churches to have maintained its 13th-century Veneto-Byzantine structure, despite numerous refurbishings. Between 1971 and 1977 the church underwent a thorough restoration by the Venice in Peril Fund, and traces of the original foundations were uncovered, confirming the church's seventh-century origins. Film buffs will recognise this as the church from Nicolas Roeg's dwarf-in-Venice movie *Don't Look Now*. The 15th-century loggia at the front is one of only two extant examples of a once-common architectural feature (the other is on the equally ancient San Giacomo di Rialto, *see p114*); it originally served as a shelter for the homeless. The interior contains no major works of art, but a marvellous mishmash of architectural and decorative styles combines to create an effect of cluttered charm. The structure is that of a 12th-century basilica, with two colonnades of stocky columns topped by 14th-century capitals. Above are gilded 16th-century statues of the Apostles. The paintings are mainly 17th century. There are also some fine wooden sculptures, including a large statue of San Nicolò by the Bon studio.

In the small campo outside the church is a column with a diminutive winged lion. Across the canal is the former convent of the Terese, which is now part of the Architecture University.

San Sebastiano
Fondamenta di San Sebastiano (041 275 0642). Vaporetto San Basilio. **Open** 10am-5pm Mon-Sat; 1-5pm Sun. **Admission** €2.50 (*see also p70* **Chorus**). No credit cards. **Map** p310 B3.
This contains perhaps the most brilliantly colourful church interior in Venice – all the work of one man, Paolo Veronese. One of Veronese's earliest commissions in Venice (in 1555) was *The Coronation of the Virgin* and the four panels of the Evangelists in the sacristy (open 10am-5pm Sat, 1-5pm Sun). From then on there was just no stopping him: between 1556 and 1565 he painted three large ceiling paintings for the nave of the church, frescoes along the upper parts of the walls, organ shutters, huge narrative canvases for the chancel, and the painting on the high altar. The ceiling paintings depict scenes from the life of Esther (*Esther Taken to Ahasuerus*, *Esther Crowned Queen by Ahasuerus* and *The Triumph of Mordecai*). Esther was considered a forerunner of the Virgin, interceding for Jews in the same way that the Virgin interceded for Christians – or (more pertinently) for Venice. These works are full of sumptuous pageantry: no painter gets more splendidly shimmering effects out of clothing, which is probably why Veronese's nude St Sebastians are the least striking figures in the compositions. These huge canvases on the side walls of the chancel depict, on the right, *The Martyrdom of St Sebastian* (who was in fact cudgelled to death – the arrows were just a first attempt) and, on the left, *St Sebastian Encouraging St Mark and St Marcellan*. Other paintings in the church include *St Nicholas*, a late painting by Titian, in the first altar on the right. Paolo Veronese and his brother Benedetto are buried here.

Campo Santa Margherita to the Accademia

A long, irregular-shaped campo with churches at both ends, campo Santa Margherita is full of life by day and night. The morning market (Mon-Sat) is a non-stop bustle of shopping housewives, hurrying students and scavenging pigeons. In the evening, the bars and cafés are invaded by hordes of Venice's under-30s, much to the irritation of local residents. If Venice can be said to have a nightlife hub, this is it.

There are several ancient *palazzi* around the square, with Byzantine and Gothic features. In the middle is the isolated Scuola dei Varoteri, the School of the Tanners. At the north end is the former church of Santa Margherita, long used as a cinema and now beautifully restored as a conference hall for the university; the interior (sneak in the back for a

Wholly democratic **campo Santa Margherita**. *See p125*.

quick gawp if there's a conference going on) is so unashamedly theatrical it's difficult to imagine how it was ever used for religious purposes. St Margaret's dragon features on the *campanile*, and the sculpted saint also stands triumphant on the beast between the windows of a house at the north end of the square. A miraculous escape from the dragon's guts for some reason makes her the patron saint of pregnant women. At the other end of the square are the **scuola** and **church of the Carmini**.

Leaving the campo by the southern end you reach the picturesque rio di San Barnaba. At the eastern end of the fondamenta is the entrance to the swaggering Longhena palazzo of **Ca' Rezzonico**, home to the museum of 18th-century Venice.

The middle of the three bridges across the canal is ponte dei Pugni, with white marble footprints indicating that this was one of the bridges where punch-ups were held between the rival factions of the *nicolotti*, from the western quarters of the city, and the *castellani*, from the east. These brawls, often extremely violent, were tolerated by the authorities, who saw them as a chance for the working classes to let off steam in a way that was not disruptive to the state. However, after a particularly bloody fray, the Council of Ten banned them in 1705.

Past the most photographed greengrocer's in the world (a barge moored in the canal), is campo San Barnaba. The church of **San Barnaba** has nothing special about it except

a picturesque 14th-century *campanile* and a *Holy Family* boldly attributed to Veronese; however, the campo is a good place in which to sit outside a bar and watch the world go by. San Barnaba has never been grand. In the final years of the Republic it was where penniless patricians used to end up, since apartments were provided here by the state for their use. The *barnabotti*, as they were known, could make a few *zecchini* by peddling their votes in the Maggior Consiglio (*see p12* **Machinery of state**); otherwise they hung around in their tattered silk, muttering (after 1789) subversive comments about Liberty, Fraternity and Equality. Katharine Hepburn fell into a nearby canal in the film *Midsummer Madness*, causing permanent damage to her eyesight. In *Indiana Jones and the Last Crusade*, on the other hand, Harrison Ford entered the church (a library in the film) and after contending with most of Venice's rat population, emerged from a manhole on to the pavement outside.

From the campo the busy route towards the Accademia passes alongside the rio della Toletta (where a small plank or *tola – tavola* in Italian – once served as a bridge) towards rio San Trovaso. This handsome canal has twin *fondamente* lined by fine Gothic and Renaissance palaces housing secondary schools and university buildings. Off to the right is the church of **San Trovaso**, with two identical façades, one on to the canal and one on to its own campo. Backing on to the campo

Nature trail: Venice's horses

When that eager proto-sightseer Thomas Coryat visited Venice in 1611 he remarked that he 'saw but one horse in all Venice'. Some 180 years later another British visitor, Dr Johnson's friend Mrs Hester Thrale, reports seeing Venetians queueing to see a stuffed example. But Venice was not always a horseless city.

In the city's early days horses were used regularly, and from 1279 a bell called the *trottera* – a clear horsey reference – would summon the members of the Grand Council. In 1362 the poet Petrarch watched a tournament in piazza San Marco and described the Venetians as a 'nation of horsemen'. Doge Michele Steno in the 15th century kept a stable of 400 horses, all dyed yellow.

However, as Venice became more built-up, restrictions were introduced. In February 1287 a law was passed forbidding the riding of horses in the Merceria; in 1359 it was forbidden to ride faster than a trot near the Rialto area and by the 14th century horses everywhere had to wear warning bells. Riding stables for the rich remained near Santi Giovanni e Paolo but horses were no longer used to move around the city. By the 19th century Byron and Shelley had to head for the Lido for a canter.

As genuine horse-flesh dwindled, there were enough sculptured examples for Venetians to feast their eyes on.

The most famous – the bronze steeds peering down from St Mark's basilica (*see p79*) – became a symbol of the city: looted from their pedestals in the Hippodrome during the sack of Constantinople in 1204, they testified to the city's role as new superpower. They have been attributed to a Greek sculptor of the fourth century BC, though recently scholars have talked of them as a Roman work of the second century AD. They feature frequently in works by Venetian painters: a centurion is mounted on one in Tintoretto's *Crucifixion* in the Scuola di San Rocco (*see p123*) and a miniature one

appears on the mantelpiece in Carpaccio's *St Augustine in his Study* in San Giorgio degli Schiavoni (*see p101*).

After this splendid team, the most superb equestrian statue is Verrocchio's monument to Bartolomeo Colleone in campo Santi Giovanni e Paolo (currently being restored). Verrocchio made the model in Florence then brought it to Venice and was working on it when he died; it was cast in a courtyard near the Madonna dell'Orto (*see p108*), ever since called corte del Cavallo. The statue is a clear attempt to rival both Donatello's equestrian monument to Gattamelata in Padua of 25 years earlier and the ancient statue of Marcus Aurelius on the Capitoline in Rome.

However infrequently they rode, Venetian residents liked to be remembered by posterity as mounted. The church of Santi Giovanni e Paolo (*see p94*) contains four equestrian monuments, of varying degrees of artistic success: two dignified Renaissance statues (monuments to Leonardo da Prato and Nicolò Orsini), one stylised Mannerist work (to Pompeo Giustiniani) and one ostentatiously capering piece in the Baroque style (to Orazio Baglioni). In the right transept of the Frari (*see p120*) is the earliest equestrian monument in the city (after the bronze horses): a Gothic statue in gilded wood to the Roman mercenary Paolo Savelli, who died in 1405. Santo Stefano (*see p80*) has a large monument to Domenico Contarini over the main entrance (1650); the horse looks like an overgrown donkey.

Venice's most flamboyant horse is unquestionably the snorting, prancing animal in bronze ridden by King Vittorio Emanuele on the riva degli Schiavoni, with winged lion, Venice in chains and Venice free clustered around the plinth. And its most daring? At the water entrance to Palazzo Venier dei Leoni, home to the Peggy Guggenheim Collection (*see p131*), a brazen bronze rider by Marino Marini thrusts raised head and erect penis towards passing *vaporetti*.

is a picturesque *squero*, one of the few remaining yards where gondolas are made.

The Accademia (*see p130*), Venice's most important picture gallery, is just a short walk from here, situated at the foot of the reconstructed wooden bridge of the same name over the Grand Canal.

Ca' Rezzonico (Museo del Settecento Veneziano)

Dorsoduro 3136, fondamenta Rezzonico (041 410 100). Vaporetto Ca' Rezzonico. **Open** *Apr-Oct* 10am-6pm Mon, Wed-Sun. *Nov-Mar* 10am-5pm Mon, Wed-Sun. **Admission** €6.50; €4-€4.50 concessions (*see also p70* Musei Civici Veneziani). **No credit cards. Map** p311 B1.

The museum of 18th-century Venice was reopened in July 2001 after careful restoration and is now a gleaming, if somewhat chilly, showcase, complete with bookshop and café, dedicated to the art of the twilight years of the Republic. But for most visitors the paintings on display here will appear less impressive than the palazzo itself, an imposing Grand Canal affair designed by Baldassare Longhena for the Bon family in 1667. Bon ambitions exceeded Bon means, and the unfinished palace was sold on to the Rezzonico family – rich Genoese bankers who bought their way into Venice's register of nobility. The Rezzonicos' bid for stardom was crowned in 1758 by two events: the election of Carlo Rezzonico as Pope Clement XIII, and the marriage of Ludovico Rezzonico into one of Venice's most ancient noble families, the Savorgnan. Giambattista Tiepolo was called upon to celebrate the marriage on the ceiling of the *sala del trono* and he replied with a composition so tumbling and playful that it's easy to forget that this is all about money. Giovanni Battista Crosato's over-the-top ceiling frescoes in the ballroom have aged less well but, together with the Murano chandeliers and the intricately carved furniture by Andrea Brustolon, they provide an accurate record of the lifestyles of the rich and famous at the time. There are historical canvases by Giovanni Battista Piazzetta and Antonio Diziani, plus other gems; detached frescoes, recently restored, of *pulcinellas* (characters from Italian folk theatre, ancestors of the English Punch) by Giandomenico Tiepolo from the Tiepolo family villa capture the leisured melancholy of the moneyed classes as *La Serenissima* went into terminal decline. There are some good genre paintings by Pietro Longhi, whom Michael Levey calls 'the Jane Austen of Venetian art', and a series of smooth pastel portraits by Rosalba Carriera, a female 'prodigy' who was kept busy by English travellers eager to bring back a souvenir of their Grand Tour. On the third floor is the Egidio Martini picture gallery, a collection of mainly Venetian works assembled by a scholar and donated to the city, and a reconstruction of an 18th-century city pharmacy, with fine majolica vases.

A staircase at the far end of the entrance hall leads to the 'Mezzanino Browning', where the poet Robert Browning died in 1889. Tis contain the Mestrovich Collection of Veneto paintings, donated to the city by Ferruccio Mestrovich as a sign of gratitude for the hospitality afforded to his family after they had been expelled from their Dalmatian home in 1945.

Santa Maria dei Carmini
Campo dei Carmini (041 522 6553). Vaporetto Ca' Rezzonico or San Basilio. **Open** 7.30am-noon, 2.30-7.10pm Mon-Sat; 2.30-7.10pm Sun. **Map** p310 B3.
The church officially called Santa Maria del Carmelo has a said *campanile* topped by a statue of the Virgin, a frequent target for lightning. It is richly decorated inside, with 17th-century gilt wooden statues over the arcades of the nave and, above, a series of Baroque paintings illustrating the history of the

Carmelite order. However, the best paintings in the church are a *Nativity* by Cima da Conegliano on the second altar on the right and *St Nicholas of Bari* by Lorenzo Lotto opposite; the latter has a dreamy landscape – one of the most beautiful in Italian art, according to art historian Bernard Berenson – containing tiny figures of St George and the dragon. In the chapel to the right of the high altar is a graceful bronze relief of *The Lamentation Over the Dead Christ*, including portraits of Federico da Montefeltro and Battista Sforza, by the Sienese sculptor, painter, inventor, military architect and all-round Renaissance man Francesco di Giorgio.

San Trovaso
Campo San Trovaso (041 522 2133). Vaporetto Zattere. **Open** 8-11am, 3-6pm Mon-Sat. **Map** p311 C1.
This church overlooking its quiet campo has two almost identical façades, both based on the sub-Palladian church of Le Zitelle (*see p134*) on the Giudecca. The story goes that San Trovaso was built on the very border of the two areas of the city belonging to the rival factions of the *nicolotti* and *castellani*; in the event of a wedding between members of the two factions, each party could make its own sweeping entrance and exit. There was no saint called Trovaso: the name is a Venetian telescoping of martyrs San Protasio and San Gervasio. There are five works by the Tintoretto family in the church; three are probably by the son, Domenico, including the two on either side of the high altar, which are rich in detail but poor in focus. In the left transept is a smaller-than-usual version of one of Tintoretto's favourite subjects, *The Last Supper*, and in the chapel to the left of the high altar is *The Temptations of St Anthony the Abbot*, featuring enough vices to tempt a saint – note the harlot with 'flames playing around her loins', as Ruskin so coyly put it.

On the side wall of this latter chapel is a charming painting in the international Gothic style by Michele Giambono, *St Chrisogonus on Horseback* (c1450); the saint is a boyish figure on a gold background, with a shyly hesitant expression and a gorgeously fluttering cloak and banner. In the right transept, in the Clary Chapel, is a set of Renaissance marble reliefs (c1470) showing angels playing musical instruments or holding instruments of the Passion. The only attribution scholars will risk is to the conveniently named 'Master of San Trovaso'.

Scuola dei Carmini
Dorsoduro 2617, campo dei Carmini (041 528 9420). Vaporetto Ca' Rezzonico or San Basilio. **Open** *Apr-Oct* 9am-6pm Mon-Sat; 9am-4pm Sun. *Nov-Mar* 9am-4pm daily. **Admission** €5; €4 students. **No credit cards**. **Map** p310 B3.
Begun in 1670 to plans by Baldassare Longhena, the building housing this *scuola* (*see p95* **Back to school**) run by the Carmelite order was spared the Napoleonic lootings that dispersed the fittings of most of the other *scuole*. As a result, we have a good idea of what an early 18th-century Venetian confra-

Ca' Rezzonico: gleaming showcase for 18th-century Venice. *See p128.*

ternity HQ must have looked like, from the elaborate Sante Piatti altarpiece downstairs to the staircase with its excrescence of gilded cherubs.

On the upper floor is one of the most impressive of Giambattista Tiepolo's Venetian ceilings. The airy ceiling panels, in the main first-floor hall, were painted from 1740 to 1743 and are best viewed with one of the mirrors provided. Don't even try to unravel the story – a celestial donation that supposedly took place in Cambridge, when Simon Stock received the scapular (the badge of the Carmelite order) from the Virgin herself. What counts, as always with Tiepolo, is the audacity of his off-centre composition. If the atmosphere were not so ultra-refined, there would be something disturbing in the Virgin's sneer of cold contempt and those swirling Turneresque clouds. The central painting fell from the woodworm-ridden ceiling in August 2000 but has been beautifully restored. In the two adjoining rooms are wooden sculptures by Giacomo Piazzetta and a dramatic *Judith and Holofernes* by Giambattista Piazzetta.

Eastern Dorsoduro

The eastern reaches of Dorsoduro, between the **Accademia** and the Salute, is an area of elegant, artsy prosperity, home to many artists and would-be artists, writers and wealthy foreigners. Ezra Pound spent his last years in a small house near the Zattere; Peggy Guggenheim hosted her collection of modern artists in her truncated palazzo on the Grand Canal (now the **Peggy Guggenheim Collection**); and artists use the vast spaces of the old warehouses on the Zattere as studios.

On Sunday mornings, campo San Vio becomes some corner of a foreign land, as British expatriates home in on the Anglican church of St George. Overlooking the campo, the **Galleria Cini** has a collection of Ferrarese and Tuscan art.

It is a district of quiet canals and cosy *campielli*, perhaps the most picturesque being campiello Barbaro, behind pretty, lopsided Ca' Dario (rumoured, after the sudden deaths of owners over the centuries, to be cursed). But all that money has certainly driven out the locals: nowhere in Venice are you further from a simple *alimentari* (grocer's).

The colossal magnificence of Longhena's church of **Santa Maria della Salute** brings the residential area to an end. You can stroll on past the church to the old *Dogana di mare* (Customs House) on the tip of Dorsoduro. There had long been talk of this empty building being taken over by the Peggy Guggenheim Museum and detailed Tate-Modern-style plans drawn up by architect Vittorio Gregotti were confidently presented in 2000. Unfortunately the plans were based on the notion that the museum would be able to spill over into the adjoining Patriarchal Seminary, but the vigorous new Patriarch (bishop) of Venice (installed in 2002) has made it quite clear that not a square foot of any buildings in his keeping will be given up for such purposes. It looks as if the Dogana will remain empty for a good many more years yet.

Crowning the corner tower of the Dogana, a 17th-century weathercock figure of Fortune perches daintily on top of a golden ball. A grand view can be enjoyed from here of St Mark's and the lagoon.

Gallerie dell'Accademia

Dorsoduro 1050, campo Carità (041 522 2247/
www.artive.arti.beniculturali.it). Vaporetto
Accademia. **Open** 8.15am-2pm Mon; 8.15am-7.15pm
Tue-Sun. **Admission** €6.50; concessions €3.25;
EU citizens under 19 and over 65 free (*see also p70*
State Museums). **No credit cards. Map** p311 B1.
The Accademia is the essential one-stop shop for
Venetian painting – and one of the world's greatest
art treasure houses. It is located inside three former
religious buildings: the Scuola Grande di Santa
Maria della Carità (the oldest of the Venetian *scuole*,
founded in the 13th century), the adjacent church of
the Carità, and the Monastery of the Lateran Canons,
a 12th-century structure radically remodelled by
Andrea Palladio (*see pp38-42* **Palladian Villas**).

It was Napoleon who made the collection possible,
first by suppressing hundreds of churches, convents
and religious guilds, confiscating their art-works for
the greater good of the state; and second by moving
the city's Accademia di Belle Arti art school here,
with the mandate both to train students and to act
as a gallery and storeroom for all the evicted art treasures, which were originally displayed as models for
the academy's pupils to aspire to. The art school
moved to a new site, in the Ospedale degli Incurabili
(*see p133*) on the Zattere, in September 2004; the
premises formerly occupied by students are still
waiting to be extensively restored and will eventually provide new exhibition space for the museum;
restoration work is likely to be lengthy.

The collection is arranged chronologically, with
the exception of the 15th- and 16th-century works in
rooms 19-24 at the end. It opens with a group of 14th-
and 15th-century devotional works by Paolo
Veneziano and others – stiff figures against gold
backdrops, still firmly in the Byzantine tradition.
This room was the main hall of the *scuola grande*:
note the original ceiling of gilded cherubim, whose
faces are all subtly different. Rooms 2 and 3 have
devotional paintings and altarpieces by Carpaccio,
Cima da Conegliano and Giovanni Bellini (a fine
Enthroned Madonna with Six Saints).

Rooms 4 and 5 bring us to the Renaissance heart
of the collection: here are Mantegna's *St George* and
Giorgione's mysterious *Tempest*, which has had art
historians reaching for symbolic interpretations for
centuries. In Room 6 the three greats of 16th-centu-
ry Venetian painting, Titian, Tintoretto and
Veronese, are first encountered. But the battle of the
giants gets under way in earnest in Room 10, where
Tintoretto's ghostly chiaroscuro *Transport of the
Body of St Mark* vies for attention with Titian's
moving *Pietà* – his last painting – and Veronese's
huge *Christ in the House of Levi*. Originally commissioned as a *Last Supper*, this painting emerged
so full of anachronistic and irreverent detail that the
artist was accused of heresy and ordered to alter the
painting; instead – and with admirable chutzpah –
he simply changed its name. Room 11 covers two
centuries, with canvases by Tintoretto (the exquisite *Madonna dei Camerlenghi*), Bernardo Strozzi and

Tiepolo. The series of rooms beyond brings the plot
up to the 18th century, with all the old favourites:
Canaletto, Guardi, Longhi and soft-focus, bewigged
portraits by female superstar Rosalba Carriera.

Rooms 19 and 20 take us back to the 15th
century; the latter has the rich *Miracle of the Relic
of the Cross* cycle, a collaborative effort by Gentile
Bellini, Carpaccio and others, which is packed with
telling social details – there's even a black gondolier
in Carpaccio's *Miracle of the Cross at the Rialto*.

An even more satisfying cycle has Room 21 to
itself. Carpaccio's *Life of St Ursula* (1490-5) tells the
story of the legendary Breton princess who
embarked on a pilgrimage to Rome with her
betrothed so that he could be baptised into the true
faith. All went swimmingly until Ursula and all the
11,000 virgins accompanying her were massacred
by the Huns in Cologne (it was the initial 'M' for martyr used in one account of the affair that caused the
multiplication of the number of accompanying maidens from 11 to 11,000, M being the Roman numeral
for 1000). More than the ropey legend, it's the architecture, the ships and the pageantry in these metic-
ulous paintings that grab the attention.

Room 23 is the former church of Santa Maria della
Carità: here are devotional works by Vivarini, the
Bellinis and others. Room 24 – the Albergo Room
(or secretariat) of the former *scuola* – contains the
only work in the whole gallery that is in its original
site: Titian's magnificent *Presentation of the Virgin*.

On Saturdays and Sundays it is possible to ask the
attendants for a guided tour of the *Quadreria*
(no extra ticket required), which is essentially the
museum's storeroom, containing paintings – including some very major works – otherwise not on show.
A free guided tour (without buying a ticket to the
Accademia) of the *Quadreria* can be taken on
Fridays from 11am to noon, or from noon to 1pm;
pre-booking is essential (041 522 2247).

Galleria Cini

Dorsoduro 864, piscina del Forner (041 521 0755).
Vaporetto Accademia. **Open** by appointment only.
No credit cards. Map p312 C2.
This collection of Ferrarese and Tuscan art was put
together by industrialist Vittorio Cini, who created
the Fondazione Cini on the island of San Giorgio
Maggiore (*see p135*). It's small but there are one or
two gems, such as the unfinished Pontormo double
Portrait of Two Friends, on the first floor, and Dosso
Dossi's *Allegorical Scene* on the second, a vivacious
character study from the D'Este Palace in Ferrara.
There are also some delicate, late-medieval ivories
and a rare, 14th-century wedding chest decorated
with chivalric scenes.

Peggy Guggenheim Collection

*Dorsoduro 701, fondamenta Venier dei Leoni
(041 520 6288). Vaporetto Accademia or Salute.*
Open *June, July* 10am-6pm Mon, Wed-Fri, Sun;
10am-10pm Sat. *Aug-May* 10am-6pm Mon, Wed-
Sun. **Admission** €10; €8 over-65s; €5 students.
Credit AmEx, MC, V. **Map** 311 C2.

Well, well

A dense network of narrow alleys, grimy canals and gloomy archways – coupled with the haunting potency of such films as Nick Roeg's psychological thriller *Don't Look Now* (1973) – can lend Venice a menacing air. Yet modern Venice is a remarkably safe city.

It was not always so, as streetnames such as calle dei Assassini and ponte dei Squartai (bridge of the Quarterers) suggest. The innumerable little altars still visible on street corners were one way of seeking divine protection; their constantly tended lamps also ensured that some streetlighting was provided, paid for by pious local residents. But illuminated or not, Venice has had its share of violent crime in the course of its history. And street-names may even hide it.

On 14 June 1779 a serving maid went to draw water from the well in the peaceful square in front of the church of San Trovaso (*see p128*). The bucket would not enter the water. One of the boatmakers from the local *squero* (gondola-maker's yard) climbed into the dark well. In it he found a man's torso: the arms were still attached, but the head was missing.

Some hours later, a pair of legs was fished out of a well on fondamenta del Malcanton, about ten minutes' walk away. News spread, and the search was on for the grisly missing

pieces of the macabre puzzle. Odd bits and bobs were found on the Zattere (*see p132*); a head was pulled out of the Santa Chiara canal next morning.

Entwined in the victim's hair was a small twist of paper, which he had clearly been using as a curler; on it were a few phrases from a letter and the initials 'VFGC'. In the mainland town of Este a certain Giovanni Cestonaro recognised his own signature ('*Vostro Fratello Giovanni Cestonaro*' – your brother...) and hastened to Venice, where he identified the body as that of his brother and informed investigators that Veneranda, his brother's wife, had been having an affair with a footman who lived on the Zattere.

The adulterous couple confessed. The murder had taken place on 12 June and the body sliced up into conveniently disposable in Veneranda's house near campiello dei Squellini at San Barnaba. Veneranda and her lover were executed on 10 January 1780. Veneranda's house was demolished. And the street where it stood was renamed calle della Madonna, either to erase the memory of the crime, or to thank the Virgin for her supposed role in helping to solve the case – floating the body parts to the surface, for instance, or keeping the ink dry on the unfortunate's curling-paper.

This remarkable establishment, tucked behind a high wall off a quite street, is the third most visited museum in the city, after the Palazzo Ducale and the Gallerie dell'Accademia.

It was founded by one of the most colourful of Venice's expat residents, Peggy Guggenheim, whose father went down in the Titanic, leaving her with $460,000. The money came in useful as she set out busily to satisfy her ravenous appetite for men and art. Peggy may have hated her bulbous nose – the result of a botched job by a Cincinnati plastic surgeon, but that didn't stop her running up a list of lovers that read like a who's who of contemporary culture, including Samuel Beckett, Yves Tanguy, Roland Penrose (who liked to tie her up) and Max Ernst, to whom she was briefly married. When asked how many husbands she had had, Peggy replied: 'Do you mean mine, or other people's?'

Ms Guggenheim took the same voracious approach to art as to men.

She turned up in Venice in 1949 looking for a home for her already sizable collection. London had turned her down: a short-sighted Tate curator described her growing pile of surrealist and modernist works as 'non-art'. Venice, still struggling to win back the

tourists after World War II, was less finicky, and Peggy found a perfect, eccentric base in Palazzo Venier dei Leoni (*see p76*), a truncated 18th-century Grand Canal palazzo.

There are big European names here, including Picasso, Duchamp, Brancusi, Giacometti and Max Ernst, plus a few Americans such as Calder and Jackson Pollock, whose career was jump-started by Peggy. Highlights include the beautifully enigmatic *Empire of Light* by Magritte and Giacometti's disturbing *Woman with Her Throat Cut*. Ernst's flamboyant *Attirement of the Bride* often turns up as a Carnevale costume. But perhaps the most startling exhibit of all is the rider of Marino Marini's *Angel of the City* out on the Grand Canal terrace, who thrusts his manhood towards passing *vaporetti*. Never the shrinking wallflower, Peggy took delight in unscrewing the member and pressing it on young men she fancied.

Another wing has been given over to Futurist works on long-term loan from the collection of Gianni Mattioli. The gallery also has a charming garden attached, best surveyed from the terrace of the café-restaurant; temporary exhibitions of contemporary art are held here.

Santa Maria della Salute

Campo della Salute (041 522 5558). Vaporetto
Salute. **Open** *Apr-Sept* 9am-noon, 3-6.30pm daily.
Oct-Mar 9am-noon, 3-5.30pm daily. **Map** p311 C2.
This magnificent Baroque church, queening it over
the entrance of the Grand Canal, is almost as recognisable an image of Venice as St Mark's or the Rialto
bridge. It was built between 1631 and 1681 in
thanksgiving for the end of Venice's last bout of
plague (*see p114* **Pestilence**), which had wiped out
at least a third of the population in 1630. The church
is dedicated to the Madonna, as protector of the city.

The terms of the competition won by 26-year-old
architect Baldassare Longhena represented a
serious challenge, which beat some of the best architects of the day. The church was to be colossal but
inexpensive; the whole structure was to be visually
clear on entrance, with an unimpeded view of the
high altar, the ambulatory and side altars coming
into sight only as one approached the chancel; the
light was to be evenly distributed; and the whole
building should *creare una bella figura* – show itself
off to good effect.

Longhena succeeded brilliantly in satisfying all
these requisites – particularly the last and most
Venetian one. The church takes superb advantage
of its dominant position and pays homage to both
the Byzantine form of San Marco across the Grand
Canal and the classical form of Palladio's Redentore,
across the Giudecca Canal. Longhena said he chose
the circular shape with the reverent aim of offering
a crown to the Madonna. She stands on the lantern
above the cupola as described in the Book of
Revelations: 'Clothed in the sun, and the moon under
her feet, and upon her head a crown of twelve stars.'
Beneath her, on the great scroll-brackets around the
cupola, stand statues of the apostles – the 12 stars
in her crown. This Marian symbolism continues
inside the church, where in the centre of the mosaic
floor, amid a circle of roses, is an inscription, *Unde
origo inde salus* (from the origin comes salvation) –
a reference to the legendary birth of Venice under
the Virgin's protection.

Longhena's intention was for the visitor to
approach the high altar ceremoniously through the
main door. If visitors were able to take this route,
the six side altars would only come into view upon
reaching the very centre of the church, where they
appear framed theatrically in their separate archways. However, the main door is rarely open and
often the central area of the church is roped off, so
you have no choice but to walk round the ambulatory and visit the chapels separately.

The three on the right have paintings by Luca
Giordano, a prolific Neapolitan painter who brought
a little southern brio into the art of the city at a time
(the mid 17th century) when most painting had
become limply derivative.

On the opposite side is a clumsily restored
Pentecost, by Titian, transferred here from the island
monastery of Santo Spirito (demolished in 1656).
The high altar has a splendidly dynamic sculptural

group by Giusto Le Corte, the artist responsible
(with assistants) for most of the statues inside and
outside the church. This group represents *Venice
Kneeling Before the Virgin and Child*, while the
plague, in the shape of a hideous old hag, scurries
off to the right, prodded by a tough-looking putto
with a flaming torch. In the midst of all this marble
hubbub is a serene Byzantine icon of the *Madonna
and Child*, brought from Crete in 1669 by Francesco
Morosini, the Venetian commander responsible for
blowing up the Parthenon.

The best paintings are in the sacristy (open same
hours as church; admission €1.50). Tintoretto's
Marriage at Cana (1551) was described by Ruskin
as 'perhaps the most perfect example which human
art has produced of the utmost possible force and
sharpness of shadow united with richness of local
colour'. He also points out how curiously difficult it
is to spot the bride and groom in the painting.

On the altar is a very early Titian of *Saints Mark,
Sebastian, Roch, Cosmas and Damian*, saints who
were all invoked for protection against the plague;
the painting was done during the middle years of 1509-
14. Three later works by Titian (c1540-9) hang on
the ceiling, violent Old Testament scenes also
brought here from the church of Santo Spirito: *the
Sacrifice of Abraham*, *David Killing Goliath* and *Cain
and Abel*. These works established the conventions
for all subsequent ceiling paintings in Venice; Titian
decided not to go for the worm's eye view adopted
by Mantegna and Correggio, which sacrificed clari-
ty for surprise, and instead chose an oblique viewpoint, as if observing the action from the bottom of
a hill. More Old Testament turbulence can be seen
in works by Salviati (*Saul Hurling a Spear at David*)
and Palma il Giovane (*Samson and Jonah* – in which
the whale is represented mainly by a vast lolling
rubbery tongue).

Le Zattere

From Punta della Dogana, the mile-long stretch
of Le Zattere, Venice's finest promenade after
the riva degli Schiavoni, leads back westwards
past the churches of **I Gesuati** and **Santa
Maria della Visitazione** to the San Nicolò
zone (*see p124*).

This long promenade bordering the Giudecca
Canal is named after the *zattere* (rafts) that
used to moor here, bringing wood and other
materials across from the mainland. The
paved quayside was created by decree in 1519.
It now provides a favourite strolling ground,
punctuated by some spectacularly situated
(if somewhat shadeless) benches for a picnic,
and several bars and *gelaterie*. The eastern
end is usually quiet (restoration work here
was coming to an end as this guide went to
press), with the occasional flurry of activity
around the vast 14th-century salt warehouses,
now used by rowing clubs.

Westward from these is the church of **Spirito Santo** and the long 16th-century façade of the grimly named Ospedale degli Incurabili, long used as a juvenile court but now serving as the new premises of the Accademia di Belle Arti (art school). Volpone's property is confiscated and the character himself sent to this hospital at the end of the 17th-century play of the same name by Ben Jonson; the main incurable disease of the time was syphilis.

The liveliest part of the Zattere is around the church of **I Gesuati**. Venetians flock here at weekends and on warm evenings to savour ice-cream or sip drinks at canal-side tables.

The final and widest stretch of the Zattere passes several notable *palazzi*, including the 16th-century Palazzo Clary – until recently the French consulate – and the Gothic Palazzo Molin, which is now used by the Società Adriatica di Navigazione. Towards the end is the 17th-century façade of the Scuola dei Luganegheri (sausage makers' school), with a statue of the sausage makers' protector, St Anthony Abbot, whose symbol was a hog.

I Gesuati

Fondamenta Zattere ai Gesuati (041 275 0642).
Vaporetto Gesuati. **Open** 10am-5pm Mon-Sat;
1-5pm Sun. **Admission** €2.50 (*see also p70*
Chorus). **No credit cards**. **Map** p311 C1.

Canal-side tables on **Le Zattere**. *See p132.*

The official name of this church is Santa Maria del Rosario, but it is always known after the Gesuati, the minor religious order that owned the previous church on the site. The order merged with the Dominicans – the church's present owners – in 1668. I Gesuati is a great piece of teamwork by a trio of remarkable rococo artists: architect Giorgio Massari (he of the boring but effective Palazzo Grassi on the Grand Canal, *see p90*), painter Giambattista Tiepolo and sculptor Giovanni Morlaiter.

The façade deliberately reflects the Palladian church of the Redentore opposite, but the splendidly posturing statues give it that typically 18th-century touch of histrionic flamboyance. Plenty more theatrical sculpture is to be found inside the church, all by Morlaiter. Above is a magnificent ceiling by Tiepolo, with three frescoes on obscure Dominican themes (a mirror is provided for the relief of stiff necks). These works reintroduced frescoes to Venetian art after two centuries of canvas ceiling paintings. The central panel shows St Dominic passing on to a crowd of supplicants the rosary he has just received from the cloud-enthroned Madonna. Tiepolo also painted the surrounding grisailles, which, at first sight, look like stucco reliefs.

There is another brightly coloured Tiepolo on the first altar on the right, *The Virgin and Child with Saints Rosa, Catherine and Agnes*. Tiepolo here plays with optical effects, allowing St Rosa's habit to tumble out of the frame. In his painting of three Dominican saints on the third altar on the right,

Giovanni Battista Piazzetta makes use of a narrower and more sober range of colours, going for a more sculptural effect.

Santa Maria della Visitazione

Fondamenta Zattere ai Gesuati (041 522 4077).
Vaporetto Zattere. **Open** *Apr-Sept* 8am-noon,
3-7pm Mon-Sat. *Oct-Mar* 8am-noon, 3-6pm Sun.
Map p311 C1.

Confusingly, this has the same name as the Vivaldi church on the riva degli Schiavoni – though the latter is usually known as La Pietà (*see p99*). Santa Maria della Visitazione stands on the Zattere just a few yards from the larger church of I Gesuati (*see above*); it is now the chapel of the Istituto Don Orione, which has taken over the vast complex of the monastery of the Gesuati next door.

Designed by Tullio Lombardo or Mauro Codussi and built in 1423, the church has an attractive early Renaissance façade. It was suppressed (that rascal Napoleon again) at the beginning of the 19th century and stripped of all its works of art with the exception of the original coffered ceiling, an unexpected delight that contains 58 compartments with portraits of saints and prophets by an Umbrian painter of Luca Signorelli's school (mirrors are provided), one of the few examples of central Italian art in Venice. To the right of the façade is a lion's mouth for secret denunciations: the ones posted here went to the *Magistrati della sanità*, who dealt with matters of public health.

La Giudecca & San Giorgio

Home of the 'Garden of Eden' and the splendid San Giorgio Maggiore.

The Giudecca has been many things over time: an idyllic retreat, a place of banishment, a vegetable supplier, an industrial zone and a hop-off place for jet-setting celebrities. Nowadays, it manages to be a little of all these.

It lies to the south of Venice proper, a gondola-shaped strand of eight inter-connected islands once known as Spinalonga, from an imagined resemblance to a fish skeleton (*spina* means fish bone). The present name is attributed by some to an early community of Jews, by others to the fact that troublesome nobles (who had been *giudicati*, judged) were banished here. But plenty of noblemen came of their own free will, building villas as rural retreats. They had illustrious company: Michelangelo, exiled from Florence in 1529, came here to mope; three centuries later Alfred de Musset, during his torrid affair with George Sand, praised the charms of 'la Zuecca'.

During the 19th century the city authorities began to make use of the numerous abandoned convents and monasteries, converting them into factories and prisons, and building over their gardens and orchards (*see p136* **High Walls**). The factories have almost all closed down, while the prisons (one for drug offenders, one for women) remain in use. A great deal of low-rent housing has been created, much of it on Sacca Fisola at the western end, an island created from mud dredged from the lagoon.

Mosts of the factories remain abandoned, contributing to the run-down appearance of the south side of the Giudecca. Much hope was pinned on the transformation of the most conspicuous one, the Molino Stucky – the largest building on the lagoon. This former flour mill was built in 1895 in Hanseatic Gothic style. It was closed in 1954 and stood in rat-ridden Teutonic desolation for over 40 years. At the end of the 1990s an ambitious restoration – a conference centre, a 250-room hotel, 138 apartments and a shopping centre – got under way. In April 2003 a colossal fire destroyed the eastern wing of the building, including the characteristic tower with its Gothic spire, and brought work to a halt. The Giudecca still has a reputation as the city's roughest area, but the *palazzi* along the northern *fondamenta* enjoy a

Conspicuous: **Il Redentore**. *See p135.*

splendid view of Venice and continue to attract well-heeled outsiders (Elton John, for example) in search of picturesque holiday homes.

The main sights of the Giudecca are all on this *fondamenta*: **Santa Eufemia**, the Palladian churches of **Le Zitelle** ('the spinsters'; the convent ran a hospice for poor girls who were trained as lace makers) and **Il Redentore**, as well as several fine *palazzi*.

Near Le Zitelle is the neo-Gothic Casa De Maria, with its three large inverted-shield windows. The Bolognese painter Mario De Maria built it for himself from 1910 to 1913. It is the only private palazzo to have the same patterned brick work as the Doge's Palace.

On the fondamenta Rio della Croce (No.149, close to the Redentore) stands Palazzo Munster, a former infirmary for English sailors. The vitriolic Anglo-Catholic writer Frederick Rolfe received the last sacraments here in 1910, after slagging the hospital off in his novel *The Desire and Pursuit of the Whole*. (He then proceeded to live for two more vituperative years.)

Opposite is another expat landmark, the 'Garden of Eden', pleasure ground of Frederic Eden, a disabled Englishman who, like Byron, discovered that Venice was the perfect city for those with disabilities – particularly if they could afford their own gondola and steam launch. Still in private hands, the Garden of Eden remains verdant – if, reportedly, totally unkempt – behind its high walls.

It is oddly difficult to get through to the southern side of the island, but worth the effort. Take calle San Giacomo, west of the Redentore; at the end turn left along calle degli Orti, and then right. At the end is a small public garden with benches looking out over the quiet southern lagoon and its lonely islands.

Il Redentore

Campo del Redentore (041 275 0642). Vaporetto Redentore. **Open** 10am-5pm Mon-Sat; 1-5pm Sun. **Admission** €2.50 *(see also p70* **Chorus**). **No credit cards. Map** p311 D2.

Venice's first great plague church was built to celebrate deliverance from the bout of 1575-7 *(see p114* **Pestilence**). An especially conspicuous site was chosen, one that could be approached in ceremonial fashion. The ceremony continues today, on every third Sunday of July, when a bridge of boats is built across the canal. Palladio *(see pp38-42* **Palladian Villas**) designed an eye-catching building whose prominent dome appears to rise directly behind the Greek-temple façade, giving the illusion that the church is centrally planned, as was traditional with sanctuaries and votive temples outside Venice. A broad flight of steps leads to the entrance. The solemn, harmonious interior, with its single nave lit by large 'thermal' windows, testifies to Palladio's study of Roman baths. But the Capuchin monks, the austere order to whom the building was entrusted, were not pleased by its grandeur; Palladio attempted to mollify them by designing their choir stalls in a plain style. The best paintings are in the sacristy, which is rarely open; they include a *Virgin and Child* by Alvise Vivarini and a *Baptism* by Veronese.

Santa Eufemia

Fondamenta Santa Eufemia (041 522 5848). Vaporetto Santa Eufemia. **Open** 7.30am-noon, 3-7pm Mon-Sat; 3-7pm Sun. **Map** p3311 C1.

This church has a 16th-century Doric portico along its flank (currently *in restauro*). The interior owes its charm to its mix of styles. The nave and aisles are essentially 11th-century, with Veneto-Byzantine columns and capitals, while the decoration consists mainly of 18th-century stucco (freshly restored) and paintings. Over the first altar on the right is *St Roch and an Angel* by Bartolomeo Vivarini (1480).

Isola di San Giorgio

The island of San Giorgio, which sits in such a strategic position opposite the Piazzetta *(see p79)*, realised its true potential under set designer extraordinaire Andrea Palladio, whose church of **San Giorgio Maggiore** is one of Venice's most recognisable landmarks. Known in the early days of the city as the *Isola dei Cipressi* (Cypress Island), it soon became an important Benedictine monastery and centre of learning – a tradition that is carried on today by the **Fondazione Giorgio Cini**, which runs a research centre and craft school on the island.

Fondazione Giorgio Cini & Benedictine monastery

(041 528 9900/www.cini.it). Vaporetto San Giorgio. **Open** *Monastery* 10.30am-4.30pm Sat, Sun with guided tours every half-hour. **Admission** €12; €10 concessions. **No credit cards. Map** p312 C2.

There has been a Benedictine monastery on the island since 982, when Doge Tribuno Memmo donated the island to the order. The monastery continued to benefit from ducal donations, acquiring large tracts of land both in and around Venice and abroad. After the church acquired the remains of St Stephen (1109), it was visited yearly by the doge on 26 December, the feast day of the saint. The city authorities often used the island as a luxury hotel for particularly prestigious visitors, such as Cosimo de' Medici in 1433. Cosimo had a magnificent library built here; it was destroyed in 1614, to make way for a more elaborate affair by Longhena (now open only to bona fide scholars with references to prove it; for opening times, *see p286*).

In 1800 the island hosted the conclave of cardinals that elected Pope Pius VII, after they had been expelled from Rome by Napoleon. In 1806 the French got their own back, supressing the monastery and sending its chief artistic treasure – Veronese's *Marriage Feast at Cana* – off to the Louvre, where it still hangs. For the rest of the century the monastery did ignominious service as a barracks and ammunition store. In 1951 industrialist Vittorio Cini bought the island to set up a foundation in

The best Views

Getting high enough to appreciate the city in one fell swoop is not easy in Venice. To do so, you'll have to scale one of the following: **Campanile di Torcello** (*see p144*); **Piazza San Marco** (*p83*): the campanile; **San Giorgio Maggiore** (*p136*): the campanile; **Scala Contarini del Bòvolo** (*p80*): the staircase offers beautiful but limited views.

memory of his son, Giorgio, killed in a plane crash in 1949. The Fondazione Giorgio Cini uses the monastery buildings for its activities, including artistic and musical research (it holds a collection of Vivaldi manuscripts, plus illuminated manuscripts), and a naval college. A portion of the complex was given back to the Benedictines; there are currently eight monks in the monastery. The foundation is now open to the public at weekends for guided tours (in Italian, English, French and German). There are two beautiful cloisters – one by Giovanni Buora (1516-40), the other by Palladio (1579) – an elegant library and staircase by Longhena (1641-53), and a magnificent refectory (where Veronese's painting hung) by Palladio (1561). The tour includes the splendid garden behind the monastery.

San Giorgio Maggiore

041 522 7827. Vaporetto San Giorgio. **Open** 9.30am-12.30pm, 2-6.30pm Mon-Sat; 2-6.30pm Sun. **Admission** *Church* free. *Campanile* €3. **No credit cards. Map** p312 C2.

This unique spot cried out for an architectural masterpiece. Palladio provided it. This was his first complete solo church; it demonstrates how confident he was in his techniques and objectives. With no hint of influence from the city's Byzantine tradition, Palladio here develops the system of superimposed temple fronts with which he had experimented in the façade of San Francesco della Vigna (*see p93*). The interior maintains the same relations between the orders as the outside, with composite half-columns supporting the gallery and lower Corinthian pilasters supporting the arches. The effect is of impressive luminosity and harmony, decoration

being confined to the altars. Palladio believed that white was the colour most pleasing to God, a credo that happily matched the demand from the Council of Trent for greater lucidity in church services.

There are several good works of art. Over the first altar is an *Adoration of the Shepherds* by Jacopo Bassano, with startling lighting effects. The altar to the right of the high altar has a *Madonna and Child with Nine Saints* by Sebastiano Ricci.

On the side walls of the chancel hang two vast compositions by Tintoretto, a *Last Supper* and the *Gathering of Manna*, painted in the last years of his life. The perspective of each work makes it clear that they were intended to be viewed from the altar rails. Tintoretto combines almost surreal visionary effects (angels swirling out from a lamp's eddying smoke) with touches of superb domestic realism (a cat prying into a basket, a woman stooping over her laundry). Tintoretto's last painting, a moving *Entombment*, hangs in the Cappella dei Morti (usually closed). It is possible that Tintoretto included himself among the crowd of mourners: he has been identified as the bearded man gazing intensely at Christ's face. In the left transept is a painting by Jacopo and Domenico Tintoretto of the *Martyrdom of St Stephen*, placed above the altar containing the saint's remains (brought from Constantinople in 1109).

Outside the sacristy stands the huge statue of an angel that crowned the bell tower until it was struck by lightning in 1993. To the left of the statue a corridor gives access to the lift which takes you up to the bell tower. The view from the top of the tower is extraordinary: the best possible panorama across Venice itself and the lagoon.

Nature trail: High walls

A glance at maps of Venice by Jacopo de' Barbari (1500) or Lodovico Ughi (1729) reveals a city of exuberant gardens – the former with mainly lush, food-producing plots, the latter with a host of perfect geometric parterres. If many of these have been engulfed by masonry, plenty of others remain, lurking behind high walls. As you pound the unremittingly urban streets of Venice, look up: greenery tumbling over the top of walls signals a hidden garden behind. And use your nose: spring in the lagoon city is a haze of strongly-perfumed pittosporum.

The first – and finest – gardens in Venice belonged to the great monasteries. The ones that still exist are some of Venice's best-kept secrets. The monastery gardens of San Lazzaro degli Armeni (*see p146*), and San Francesco del Deserto (*see p144*) – first created by contemporaries of St Francis

himself – are open to anyone prepared to make their way across the lagoon. To enter the splendid convent gardens of Il Redentore (*see p135*) and San Francesco della Vigna (*see pxxx*), both little changed since the Middle Ages, you'll need to charm one of the monks. Or take a tour.

Venetian monasteries – not to mention owners of the many superb, hidden gardens of noble *palazzi* – are fussy about whom they let in. Few guides hold the keys, and those that do aren't cheap. The formidably knowledgeable, English-speaking Tudy Sammartini arranges half- or whole-day tours – which can include lunch – of many of the best for small groups; call 041 528 8146 for information. The Wigwam Club Giardini Storici Venezia (041 610 791) also provides guides for small groups touring Venice's public and private gardens.

The Lido & Chioggia

Where sedate resort meets lively fishing village.

The Lido is the northernmost of the two strips of land that separate the lagoon from the open sea. If you've come looking for the 'bare strand/ Of hillocks heaped from ever-shifting sand' described by Shelley, you'll be disappointed; it is now a placidly residential suburb of Venice, only stirred to life during the summer and the September film festival (*see p198*).

To feel what the Lido was like before mass tourism and suburbanisation, cross the Porto di Malamocco (one of the three *bocche di porto*, gates from the lagoon to the Adriatic) to Pellestrina, an even narrower sliver of land with straggling fishing villages, kitchen gardens and boatyards. Beyond Pellestrina, after the southernmost *bocca di porto*, is the fishing port of Chioggia, like a miniature working-class version of Venice, rationalised to include cars.

GETTING AROUND

The main Santa Maria Elisabetta stop on the Lido is served by frequent boats from Venice and the mainland. For details of routes, *see pp278-81* **Directory: Getting Around**. The San Nicolò stop to the north is served by the No.17 car ferry from Tronchetto.

Bus routes are confusing. The A (*arancione*, orange) and the B (*blu*) each have two routes, one going south and one north. The southward route of both (marked 'Alberoni') is the same, along the lagoon to Alberoni at the southern tip of the island, via Malamocco. The northward route of each (marked 'San Nicolò' or 'Ospedale') is circular: the A travels clockwise along the lagoon-front and then turns right towards the sea and the Ospedale al Mare and makes its way back to Santa Maria Elisabetta; the B does more or less the same route anticlockwise. In the summer the routes are extended to include popular beaches. The V (*verde*, green) does a shorter route, travelling to the Palazzo del Cinema on the seafront and ending up at via Parri. In summer there's another circular line, the C (*celeste*, light blue), which also travels to the Palazzo del Cinema and back again.

Finally, the No.11, which departs from the Gran Viale opposite the main vaporetto stop also heads down to Alberoni but then continues on to the car ferry across to Pellestrina island. Many No.11 runs (check the timetable) are timed to coincide with the departure of the passenger ferry to Chioggia, from the far end of Pellestrina island – the ferry waits if the bus is

late. The entire journey from the Lido to Chioggia – including the two crossings – takes just over an hour; a ticket providing unlimited travel to and fro along the Venice–Lido–Pellestrina–Chioggia line for 12 hours costs €8.50, while a similar ticket just for the No.11 route (Lido–Pellestrina–Chioggia) costs €5. There is also a coach to Chioggia from piazzale Roma, but the scenery is depressing and the time saved minimal.

Bicycles are a great way to get around the Lido; consider doing the whole 20-kilometre (12-mile) haul down to Chioggia by bike – you can put it on the passenger ferry for €4.10 as long as too many others haven't had the same idea. For bike hire outlets, *see p227*.

TOURIST INFORMATION

From June to September there's a tourist information office at Gran Viale 6A, Lido (041 526 5721/fax 041 529 8720), open 9.30am-1pm, 3-6.30pm daily.

The Lido

Map p306.

If – fired by the example of Dirk Bogarde in *Death in Venice* – you have come to the Lido looking for pale young aesthetes in sailor suits, forget it. These days, Venice-by-the-sea is more dormitory suburb than playground for the idle rich – though there are still a few of the latter in the two big hotels, the Des Bains and the Excelsior, who keep the legend going. On the whole, though, the Lido is an escape from the strangeness of Venice to a normality of supermarkets and cars.

Things perk up in summer when buses are full of city sunbathers and tourists staying in the Lido's overspill hotels. However, the days of all-night partying and gambling are long gone. In January 2001 the Lido Casinò closed. Now the only moment when the place stirs to anything like its former vivacity is at the beginning of September when the film festival rolls into town for two weeks, with its bandwagon of stars, directors, PR people and sleep-deprived, caffeine-driven journalists (*see p198*).

The Lido has few tourist sights as such. Only the church of San Nicolò on the riviera San Nicolò – founded in 1044 – can claim any great antiquity. It was here that the doge would come on Ascension Day after marrying Venice to the sea in the ceremony known as *lo sposalizio del mare* (*see p197* **Festa della Sensa**). Inside is the tomb of Nicola Giustiniani, a Benedictine monk who was forced to leave holy orders in 1172 to assure the future of his illustrious family, of which he was the sole heir. He married the doge's daughter, had lots of kids, then went back to being a monk. After his death he was beatified for his spirit of self-sacrifice.

Fans of art nouveau and deco have plenty to look at on the Lido. On the Gran Viale there are two gems: the tiled façade of the Hungaria Hotel (No.28), formerly the Ausonia Palace, with its Beardsley-esque nymphs; and Villa Monplaisir at No.14, an art deco design from 1906. There are other smaller-scale examples in and around via Lepanto. For full-blown turn-of-the-century exotica, though, it's hard to beat the Hotel Excelsior on lungomare Marconi, a neo-Moorish party piece, complete with minaret.

At the eastern end of the Gran Viale is one of the city's more controversial new architectural offerings, Giancarlo De Carlo's Blue Moon complex, an elaborate building with curious domes, which, to the annoyance of locals, deprives the Gran Viale of its sea view.

Malamocco and Pellestrina

The bus ride south along the lagoon-side promenade of the Lido is uneventful but passes some submerged history. The old town of Malamocco, near the southern end of the island, was engulfed by a tidal wave following a seaquake in the Adriatic in 1107; it had been a flourishing port controlled by Padua. The new town, built further inland, never really amounted to much; today its sights consist of a few picturesque streets and a pretty bridge.

Offshore from Malamocco is the tiny island of Poveglia, once inhabited by 200 families, descendants of the servants of Pietro Tradonico, a ninth-century doge murdered rivals. His servants barricaded themselves inside the Palazzo Ducale and only agreed to leave when safe conduct to this new home was promised.

The Lido ends at Alberoni, with its golf course, Fascist-era bathing establishments, lighthouse and maritime control tower. Beyond the golf course is an attractive area of woodland; it is a well-known gay cruising area.

The channel between the Lido and Pellestrina is the busiest of the three *bocche di porto* between lagoon and sea, and the one used by petrol tankers on their way to and from the refineries at Porto Marghera.

It's a short hop across to Pellestrina – a glorified sandbar so narrow that it has more than once risked being swept away by the sea. The answer to the problem of Pellestrina's

vulnerability can be seen on the left as the bus continues its journey south. The *murazzi*, solid sea walls of wooden piles and landfill clad in Istrian stone, are at their most impressive at the southern end of Pellestrina, where the width of the island dwindles to almost nothing – but the *murazzi*, 14 metres (46 feet) wide at the base, continue to march out towards Chioggia for a distance of four kilometres (two and a half miles). They were built between 1744 and 1782 to replace earlier makeshift wooden defences. Recently, sloping sandy beaches have been created to lessen the impact of waves. On the lagoon side, Pellestrina is a straggle of smallholdings, holiday homes and boatyards, with only two settlements to speak of: San Pietro in Volta and Pellestrina itself, a fishing village with a centre of pastel houses clustered around the 18th-century church of Santa Maria, celebrating an apparition of the Virgin to a local boy named Natalino Scarpa de' Muti. Pellestrina is divided into quarters named after the four families (Scarpa, Zennaro, Vianello and Busetto) sent there by the *podestà* (mayor) of Chioggia after the war against Genoa; it once rivalled Burano as a lace-making island.

At the end of the village is the landing stage for the ferry to Chioggia. Beyond this the island dwindles yet further until there is little more than the wall of the *murazzi* between the open sea and the lagoon; half a mile beyond is the small wooded area of Ca' Roman.

Beaches for city sunbathers on the **Lido.**

Chioggia

Chioggia is older than Venice, being of Roman origin. In the early Middle Ages it had its own grand chancellor and bishop and between 1378 and 1380 it was important enough to have a war named after it even though Venice and Genoa were not fighting over the small fishing port but for control over the eastern Mediterranean shipping routes. During this squabble the Genoese captured the town but were then starved into submission. Chioggia never really recovered from this event.

The town now spreads over a rectangular island split down the middle by the Canal Vena; to the east is the long arm of the beach resort of Sottomarina. Sottomarina has all the big beachfront hotels and supermarkets while Chioggia has the sights, fishing port and low, cramped houses. The topography of this older section of town is linear: from piazzetta Vigo, where the ferry docks, the long, wide corso del Popolo extends the whole length of the island, parallel to the Canal Vena. On either side, narrow lanes lead off towards the lagoon.

The only sight not on the corso is the church of San Domenico (open 8am-noon, 2.30-5.30pm daily), on its very own island at the end of the street that begins across a balustraded bridge from piazzetta Vigo. A barn-like, 18th-century reconstruction, it contains Vittore Carpaccio's last painting, a graceful, poised *St Paul*, signed and dated 1520; as this guide goes to press negotiations are under way to have the painting moved to the Museo Diocesano (*see below*). There is also a huge wooden crucifix – possibly a German work of the 14th century (currently under restoration) – and a Rubens-like Tintoretto. More charming is the collection of naïve ex-voto paintings placed by grateful fishermen in a side chapel.

Midway down the corso, the church of San Giacomo (open 7am-noon, 4-6.30pm daily), with its unfinished façade, looks like a Palladian cowshed. The high altar – an elaborate imitation Baroque structure of 1907 – holds the *Madonna della Navicella*, a miraculous image of the Virgin as she appeared to a Sottomarina peasant in 1508, before making her getaway on a divinely steered boat. Back on the Corso is the Granaio, one of the few buildings in town that predates the War of Chioggia. Built in 1322 but heavily restored in the 19th century, it was the municipal granary; now it hosts the fish market (open 8am-noon Tue-Sun), a photo-op riot of glistening colour.

Across the canal is the church of the Filippine, an 18th-century building (open for services) with an extraordinary Chapel of Reliquaries (third on the right).

Near the end of the corso, two churches stand side by side on the right. The smaller one is San Martino (open only for services), a Venetian Gothic jewel built in 1393. Next door, the huge 17th-century **Duomo** was built to a project by Baldassare Longhena after a fire destroyed the original tenth-century church; there are few indications here that he would go on to design the Salute in Venice. Only the 14th-century 64-metre (210-foot) *campanile* across the road remains from the earlier structure. The chapel to the left of the chancel contains a series of grisly 18th-century paintings depicting the prolonged martyrdom of the two patron saints of Chioggia, Felix and Fortunatus (Happy and Lucky). There is a striking Baroque carved pulpit.

The road to the left of the Duomo leads to the new **Museo Diocesano**. It contains a collection of religious art, including two fine polyptychs by Paolo Veneziano and a series of wooden bas-reliefs of the *Mysteries of the Rosary* by the workshop of Andrea Brustolon. The last rooms are devoted to a 19th-century Chioggia painter, Aristide Naccari, who, among other things, was responsible for the restoration of the Rosary Chapel in the church of Santi Giovanni e Paolo (*see p94*) after a fire in 1867; the collection includes a number of drawings of the chapel both before and after the fire.

The Torre di Santa Maria marks the end of the old town; just beyond, in campo Marconi, is the deconsecrated church of San Francesco, which has been turned into the **Museo Civico della Laguna Sud**. This brand-new collection struggles to fill a huge space. Though patchy, the museum provides a good introduction to aspects of lagoon life. On the top floor is an exhaustive collection of model fishing boats, plus a small gallery, which contains an attractive triptych by Ercole del Fiore (1436), *Justice between Saints Felix and Fortunatus*.

When the museum is open, the front desk also functions as a tourist information office.

Duomo
Calle Duomo 77 (041 400 496). **Open** 8.30am-noon, 4-6pm daily.

Museo Civico della Laguna Sud
Campo Marconi 1 (041 550 0911). **Open** *Sept-mid June* 9am-1pm Tue, Wed; 9am-1pm, 3-6pm Thur-Sat; 3-6pm Sun. *Mid June-Aug* 9am-1pm Tue, Wed; 9am-1pm, 7.30-11.30pm Thur-Sat; 7.30-11.30pm Sun. **Admission** €3.50; €1.75 concessions. **No credit cards.**

Museo Diocesano
Via Sagrato (041 550 7477). **Open** *Sept-May* 8.30-10.30pm Tue, Fri; 9am-noon Thur; 3.30-7.30pm Sun. *June-Aug* 9am-noon Thur; 3-6pm Fri, Sun. **Admission** €3; €1.50 concessions. **No credit cards.**

The Lagoon

This network of islands is home to a secret Venice and a complex ecosystem.

Last stop: **San Michele**.

As you elbow your way across a packed piazza San Marco, it's difficult to imagine quite how much space there is around Venice. If you're feeling hemmed in by holidaying humanity, a day out on the lagoon offers the perfect remedy. Even the classic jaunt to the three main tourist destinations – Murano, Burano and Torcello – on a vaporetto thronging with day trippers provides views enough across the lagoon's empty reaches to steady frayed nerves.

There are 34 islands on the salt-water lagoon, most of them uninhabited, containing only crumbling masonry, home to seagulls and lazy lizards. The lagoon itself covers some 520 square kilometres (200 square miles) – the world's biggest wetland. Painters and photographers are just as well served out here as in the city itself, especially on clear autumn and winter days when the snow-capped peaks of the Dolomites stand starkly out on the horizon.

The wetlands of the lagoon are a wild, fragile environment (*see p142* **Nature trail:**

flora and fauna**); this is where Venetians take refuge from the tourist hordes, escaping by boat for picnics on deserted islands, or fishing for bass and bream. Others set off to dig up clams at low tide (most without the requisite licence), or organise hunting expeditions for duck, using the makeshift hides known as *botte* ('barrels', which is what they were originally, sunk into the floor of the lagoon). Many just head out after work, at sunset, to row.

From the lagoon, the precarious position and the unique urban development of Venice come sharply into focus. Exploring some of the quieter corners of this waterscape is like being wafted back to the sixth-century.

EXPLORING THE LAGOON

To learn more about the lagoon's ecostructure and bird life, catch the blue bus for Chioggia or Sottomarina from piazzale Roma and ask to get off at the WWF's **Oasi Valle Averto** (041 518 5068, open 9am-4pm Mon-Fri & Sun, admission €5, €3 6-16s, free under-6s, guided tours at 10am & 2pm Sun, weekdays by appointment, minimum ten people). Or contact **Limosa** (041 932 003/fax 041 538 4743, www.limosa.it), a group of dedicated environmentalists who will organise day trips by boat or bike, or entire holidays for individuals and groups.

The adventurous can rent a boat for the day. No permit is required for small craft, which can be hired from **Cantiere Lizzio** (Cannaregio 2607, fondamenta della Misericordia, 041 721 655/www.noleggio barchevenezia.it, €115 per day, guide €43 an hour, max six people per boat, no credit cards).

San Michele

Halfway between Venice and Murano, this is the island where tourists begin their lagoon visit. For many Venetians, it's the last stop: San Michele is the city's cemetery (open Apr-Sept 7.30am-6pm daily, Oct-Mar 7.30am-4pm daily). Early in the morning, *vaporetti* (41 or 42) are packed with Venetians coming over to lay flowers. This is not a morbid spot, though: like Père Lachaise in Paris, it is an elegant city of the dead, with more than one famous resident.

An orderly red-brick wall runs round the whole of the island, with a line of tall cypress trees rising high behind it – the inspiration for Böcklin's famously lugubrious painting *Island of the Dead*. The island was originally just a Franciscan monastery, but during the Napoleonic period the grounds that used to extend behind the church were seconded for burials in an effort to stop unhygienic Venetians digging graves in the *campi* around parish churches. Soon it was the only place to be seen dead in. Most Venetians still want to make that last journey to San Michele, though these days it's more a temporary parking lot than a final resting place: the island reached saturation point long ago, and even after paying through the nose for a plot, families know that after a suitable period – generally around ten years – the bones of their loved ones will be dug up and transferred to an ossuary elsewhere.

Before visiting the cemetery, take a look at the church of **San Michele in Isola** (open 7.30am-12.15pm, 3-4pm daily); turn left after the entrance to the cemetery and pass through the fine cloisters. The view of the façade is particularly striking. Designed by Mauro Codussi (*see p145* **Dark horse**) in the 1460s, this white building of Istrian stone was Venice's first Renaissance church.

Next to the church is a dignified archway marked by a 15th-century bas-relief of St Michael slaying a dragon with one hand and holding a pair of scales in the other. In the cloisters, staff hand out maps of the cemetery, which are indispensable for celebrity hunts. In the Greek and Russian Orthodox section of the cemetery is the elaborate tomb of Sergei Pavlovich Diaghilev, who introduced the Ballets Russes to Europe, and a simpler monument to the composer Igor Stravinsky and his wife.

The Protestant section has a selection of ships' captains and passengers who ended their days in *La Serenissima*, plus the simple graves of Ezra Pound and Joseph Brodsky. There's a rather sad children's section and a corner dedicated to the city's gondoliers, their tombs decorated with carvings and statues of gondolas. Visit the cemetery on the *Festa dei morti* – All Souls' Day, 2 November – and the vaporetto is free but seriously packed.

Murano

After San Michele, the number 42 or 41 vaporetto continues to Murano, one of the larger and more populous islands of the lagoon (lines LN and 13 also put in here, but only at the Faro stop). In the 16th and 17th centuries, when it was a world centre of glass production and a decadent resort for pleasure-seeking, wealthy Venetians, Murano had a population of more than 30,000. Now fewer than 5,000 people live here. Many of the glass workers now commute from the mainland.

Murano owes its fame to the decision taken in 1291 to transfer all of Venice's glass furnaces to the island because of a fear of fire in the main city (*see also chapter* **Glass**). Their products were soon sold all over Europe. The secrets of glass were jealously guarded within the island: any glass maker leaving Murano was proclaimed a traitor. Even today, there is no official glass school and the delicate skills of blowing and flamework are only learned by apprenticeship to one of the glass masters.

At first sight Murano looks close to being ruined by glass tourism. Dozens of 'guides' swoop on visitors as they pile off the ferry, to whisk them off on tours of furnaces. Even if you head off on your own, you'll find yourself on fondamenta dei Vetrai, a snipers' alley of shops selling glass knick-knacks, most of which are made far from Murano. But there *are* some serious glass makers on the island and even the tackiest showroom usually has one or two gems.

There's more to Murano, however, than glass. At the far end of fondamenta dei Vetrai is the nondescript façade of the 14th-century parish church of **San Pietro Martire**, which holds important works of art.

Beyond the church, Murano's Canal Grande is spanned by Ponte Vivarini, an unattractive, 19th-century iron bridge. Before crossing, it is worth looking at the Gothic Palazzo Da Mula, just to the left of the bridge; this splendid, 15th-century building has been recently restored and transformed into council offices. In the morning you can stroll through its courtyard, which contains a monumental, carved Byzantine arch from an earlier (12th- or 13th-century) building.

On the other side of the bridge, a right turn takes you along fondamenta Cavour; 200 metres further along, it veers sharply to the left, becoming fondamenta Giustinian. The 17th-century Palazzo Giustinian, situated far from tacky chandeliers and fluorescent clowns, is the **Museo dell'Arte Vetrario**, the best place to learn about the history of glass. Just beyond this is Murano's greatest architectural treasure: the 12th-century basilica of **Santi Maria e Donato**, with its apse towards the canal.

Return to Ponte Vivarini and walk to the end of fondamenta Sebastiano Venier. Here, the church of Santa Maria degli Angeli (open Sun 11am) backs on to the convent where Casanova conducted one of his most torrid affairs, with a libertine nun named Maria Morosoni.

Museo dell'Arte Vetrario
Fondamenta Giustinian 8 (041 739 586).
Vaporetto Museo. **Open** *Apr-Oct* 10am-5pm Mon, Tue, Thur-Sun. *Nov-Mar* 10am-4pm Mon, Tue, Thur-Sun. **Admission** €4; €2.50 concessions (*see also p70* **Musei Civici Veneziani**). **No credit cards. Map** p314.

Housed in the beautiful Palazzo Giustinian, built in the late 17th century for the bishop of Torcello, the museum has a huge collection of Murano glass. As well as the famed chandeliers, which only made their appearance in the 18th century, there are ruby-red beakers, opaque lamps and delicate Venetian *perle* – glass beads that were used in trade and commerce all over the world from the time of Marco Polo. One of the earliest pieces is the 15th-century Barovier marriage cup, decorated with portraits of the bride and groom. In one room is a collection of 17th-century oil lamps in the shapes of animals, some of which are uncannily Disney-like. On the ground floor is a good collection of Roman glass ware from near Zara on the Istrian peninsula.

San Pietro Martire

Fondamenta dei Vetrai (041 739 704). Vaporetto Colonna or Faro. **Open** 9am-noon, 3-6pm Mon-Sat; 3-6pm Sun. **Map** p314.

Behind its unspectacular façade, San Pietro Martire conceals two important works by Giovanni Bellini, both backed by marvellous landscapes: an *Assumption* and a *Virgin and Child Enthroned with St Mark, St Augustine and Doge Agostino Barbarigo*. There are also two works by Veronese and assistants (mainly the latter), and an ornate altarpiece by Salviati that is lit up by the early morning sun. Opening hours are very fluid.

Santi Maria e Donato

Campo San Donato (041 739 056). Vaporetto Museo. **Open** 8.30am-noon, 4-6pm Mon-Sat; 4-6pm Sun. **Map** p310.

Though altered by over-enthusiastic 19th-century restorers, the exterior of this church is a classic of the Veneto-Byzantine style, with an ornate blind portico on the rear of the apse. Inside is a richly coloured mosaic floor, laid down in 1140 at the same time as the floor of the basilica di San Marco, with floral and animal motifs. Above, a Byzantine apse mosaic of the Virgin looms out of the darkness in a field of gold.

Burano & Mazzorbo

Mazzorbo, the long island before Burano, is a haven of peace, rarely visited by tourists. It is worth getting off here just for the sake of the

Nature trail: Flora and fauna

The Venetian lagoon, with its islands, mudflats, salt marshes, fish farms, coastal strips and embankments, covers an area of about 520 square kilometres – the world's most extensive wetland. It's a delicate, complex ecosystem, shaped – and ignored and actively destroyed – by the lagoon's human inhabitants over the centuries.

The lagoon's unique combination of fresh and salt water makes its flora and fauna very particular. The hydraulics necessary for keeping the city above water have been at the centre of non-stop attention over the ages; but for a century and a half after the end of the Venetian republic in 1797, the needs of this special, natural environment went unheeded. Only since the 1970s, in fact, has a series of laws been passed in an effort to curb pollution and reduce *moto ondoso* (the wave movement caused by vibrations from boat engines which so undermines Venice's foundations).

In 2003, Venice's city council created the *Parco della laguna*. Once up and running, this nature reserve will afford much-needed protection to the wildlife, architecture and archaeology of a huge area of the north-eastern lagoon.

Covering much of the lagoon marshes is a Venetian variation on *Salicornia* – samphire – a spongy cactus-like plant with a particular

method of absorbing water from its surroundings; the local variety is taller than the samphire found elsewhere in Europe, and is yellowy-green in colour.

Any boat trip out to Sant'Erasmo (*see p146*) or Torcello (*see p144*) will take you past the marshy outer mudflats and islets which are happy hunting grounds for the *Egretta garzetta*, the egret. With skinny black legs and yellow feet, this white member of the heron family has a long beak perfectly engineered for pulling food out of the mud.

You're more likely to spot some lagoon dwellers on your plate than in the murky waters. *Sparus aurata* (*orata* in Italian; gilt-head bream in English) migrates between the open water and the lagoon, reproducing in the sea's more stable environment from October to December, then transferring in spring to the lagoon, which provides the carnivorous *orata* with a healthy supply of tiny fish and mussels.

The *Zosterisessor ophiocephalus* (*gò* in Venetian; *ghiozzo* in Italian; goby in English) is generally served up as *risotto di gò*. It lives in the Venetian lagoon year-round – you can catch it by hand in the mud at low tide – laying its eggs in holes in the mire between March and July; the males of the species stand guard over the eggs, turfing any sterile ones out of the hole.

quiet walk along the canal and then across the long wooden bridge that connects Mazzorbo to Burano. The view from the bridge across the lagoon to Venice is stunning.

Mazzorbo was settled around the tenth century. When it became clear that Venice itself had got the upper hand, most of the large population simply dismantled their houses brick by brick, transported them by boat to Venice, and rebuilt them there. Today, Mazzorbo is a lazy place of small farms with a pleasant walk to the 14th-century Gothic church of Santa Caterina (opening times vary), whose wobbly looking tower still has its original bell dating from 1318 – one of the oldest in Europe. Winston Churchill, a keen amateur painter, set up his easel here more than once after World War II. Facing Burano is an area of attractive, modern, low-cost housing, in shades of lilac, grey and green, designed by Giancarlo De Carlo.

Don't come to **Burano** with a black and white film in your camera. Together with its lace, its picture-postcard houses make it a magnet for tourists. The locals are traditionally either fishermen or lace makers, though there are increasingly few of the latter, despite efforts by the island's **Scuola di Merletti** (Lace School) to pass on the skills to younger generations. The street leading from the main quay throbs with souvenir shops selling lace, lace and more lace – much of it machine-made in Taiwan. But Burano is big enough for the visitor to meander through its quiet backstreets. It was in Burano that the Venice Carnevale was revived in the 1970s; the modest celebrations here are still far more authentically joyful than the antics of masked tourists cramming piazza San Marco.

Fishermen have lived on Burano since the seventh century. According to local lore they painted their houses different colours so that they could recognise them when fishing out on the lagoon – though in fact only a tiny proportion of the island's houses can actually be seen from the lagoon. Whatever the reason, the *buranelli* still go to great efforts to decorate their houses, and social life centres on the *fondamente* where the men repair nets or tend to their boats moored in the canal below, while their wives – at least in theory – make lace.

Lace was first produced in Burano in the 15th century, originally by nuns, but was quickly picked up by fishermen's wives and daughters. So skilful were the local lace makers that in the 17th century many were paid handsomely to work in the Alengon lace ateliers in Normandy. Today most work is done on commission, though interested parties will have to get to know one of the lace makers

Colour-coded **Burano**.

in person, as the co-operative that used to represent the old ladies closed down in 1995.

The busy main square of Burano is named after the island's most famous son, Baldassare Galuppi, a 17th-century composer who set many of Carlo Goldoni's plays to music and who was the subject of a poem by Robert Browning. The square is a good place for sipping a glass of *prosecco*. Across from the lace museum is the church of San Martino (open 8am-noon, 3-7pm daily), containing an early Tiepolo *Crucifixion*, recently restored, and, in the chapel to the right of the chancel, three small paintings by the 15th-century painter Giovanni Mansueti; the *Flight into Egypt* presents the Holy Family amid an imaginative menagerie of beasts and birds. There's a lively morning fish market (Tue-Sat) on the fondamenta della Pescheria.

Scuola di Merletti

Piazza B Galuppi 187, Burano (041 730 034). Vaporetto LN. **Open** *Apr-Oct* 10am-5pm Mon, Wed-Sun. *Nov-Mar* 10am-4pm Mon, Wed-Sun. **Admission** €4; €2.50 concessions (*see also p70* **Musei Civici Veneziani**). **No credit cards**.
In a series of rooms with painted wooden beams are cases full of elaborate examples of lace work from the 17th century onwards; aficionados will have fun spotting the various stitches, such as the famous *punto burano*. Many of the older exhibits change every few months for conservation reasons, but if it's on display look out for the devout intricacy of

the 17th-century altar cloth decorated with the Mysteries of the Rosary. There are fans, collars and parasols, and some of the paper pattern-sheets that lace makers use. Unfortunately the school that gives the museum its name is now virtually defunct, although occasional courses are offered by some of the older generation of Burano lace makers, who can often be seen at work in a corner of the museum.

San Francesco del Deserto

From behind the church of San Martino on Burano there is a view across the lagoon to the idyllic monastery island of San Franceso del Deserto. The island, with its 4,000 cypress trees, is inhabited by a small community of Franciscan monks. Getting there can be quite a challenge. Burano's one water taxi sits by the main quay, but we haven't always found it easy to locate the driver. Burano's postman may take you across. Either way, expect to pay at least €30 for the return ride. A better, and cheaper, option is to ask one of the local fishermen to give you a lift. They are usually willing to do so for a small fee – perhaps €15 for the return trip.

The other-worldly monk who shepherds visitors around with agonising slowness will tell the story of how the island was St Francis's first stop in Europe on his journey back from the Holy Land in 1220. He planted his stick, it grew into a pine and birds flew in to sing for him; there are certainly plenty of them in evidence in the cypress-packed gardens today. The medieval monastery – all warm stone and cloistered calm – is about as far as you can get from the worldly bustle of the Rialto.

Convento di San Francesco del Deserto

041 528 6863/www.isola-sanfrancescodeldeserto.it.
Open 9-11am, 3-5pm Tue-Sat; 3-5pm Sun.
Admission by voluntary donation.

Torcello

The ferry from Burano to Torcello leaves every half-hour during the day; the crossing takes five minutes. This sprawling, marshy island is where the history of Venice began. At low tide, you could well imagine yourself in the Fens, and there are certainly as many mosquitoes.

Torcello today is a rural backwater with a resident population of less than 20; each time an inhabitant moves away for the bright lights of Burano or Mazzorbo, it is headline news in the Venice press. It's difficult to believe that in the 14th century more than 20,000 people lived here. This was the first settlement in the lagoon, founded in the fifth century by the citizens of the Roman town of Altino on the mainland. Successive waves of emigration from Altino

were sparked off by barbarian invasions, first by Attila and his Huns, and, in the seventh century, by the Lombards. But Torcello's dominance of the lagoon did not last: Venice itself was found to be more salubrious (malaria was rife on Torcello) and more easily defendable. Even the bishop of Torcello chose to live on Murano, in the palace that now houses the glass museum (*see p142*). But past decline is present charm, and rural Torcello is a great antidote to the pedestrian traffic jams around San Marco.

From the ferry jetty the **campanile** can already be made out; to get there, simply follow the main canal through the island. As the guide goes to press, the canal-side street is being restored and a very controversial path in pink concrete has been laid through the fields parallel to it. This path rejoins the canal near the the ponte del Diavolo (one of only two ancient bridges in the lagoon without a parapet), where there is a simple *osteria*, Al Ponte del Diavolo (041 730 401; lunch only except Sat; Nov-Apr closed Wed) with reliable cooking and prices that are almost reasonable. Across the bridge is a private palazzo that occasionally holds extravagant parties.

Torcello's main square has some desultory souvenir stalls, a small but interesting **Museo dell'Estuario** with archaeological finds from around the lagoon, a battered stone seat known somewhat arbitrarily as Attila's throne, and two extraordinary churches.

The 11th-century church of Santa Fosca (open Apr-Oct 10.30am-5.30pm daily, Nov-Mar 10am-5pm daily, free) looks like a miniature version of Istanbul's Santa Sophia, more Byzantine than European with its Greek-cross plan and external colonnade; its bare interior allows the perfect geometry of the space to come to the fore. Next door is the imposing cathedral of **Santa Maria Assunta**.

By the churches, the Locanda Cipriani (*see p164*) is rated as one of Venice's top restaurants, with prices to match. The three big Cipriani concerns in Venice – the Hotel Cipriani (*see p65*), Harry's Bar (run by Arrigo Cipriani, son of the founder; *see p166*) and the Locanda Cipriani (run by Arrigo's sister Carla) have no business links; all have been involved in a long-running legal battle for the right to use the name 'Cipriani'.

A cumulative ticket for the basilica, *campanile* and Museo dell'Estuario is available at the sights themselves and costs €8 (€5.50 groups) or €5.50 (€3 groups) for the basilica and Museo. No credit cards are accepted.

Campanile di Torcello

041 270 2464. **Open** *Apr-Oct* 10.30am-
5pm daily. *Nov-Mar* 10am-4.15pm daily.
Admission €2. **No credit cards**.
The view of the lagoon from the top of the campanile
was memorably described by Ruskin: 'Far as the eye
can reach, a waste of wild sea moor, of a lurid ashen
grey.' And he concluded with the elegaic words:
'Mother and daughter, you behold them both in their
widowhood, Torcello and Venice.' There is no lift,
just a stiff walk up steep ramps.

Museo dell'Estuario

*Palazzo del Consiglio (041 730 761). Vaporetto LN
or T from Burano.* **Open** *Apr-Oct* 10.30am-5pm Tue-
Sun. *Nov-Mar* 10am-4.30pm Tue-Sun. **Admission**
€3. **No credit cards.**
A small but worthwhile collection of sculptures and
archaeological finds from the cathedral and elsewhere in Torcello. Among the exhibits on the
ground floor are late 12th-century fragments of
mosaic from the apse of Santa Maria dell'Assunta,
and two of the *bocche di leone* (lions' mouths) where
citizens with grudges could post their denunciations.
Upstairs are Greco-Byzantine icons, painted panels,
bronze seals and pottery fragments, and an exquisite carved ivory statuette of an embracing couple
from the beginning of the 15th century.

Santa Maria Assunta

041 270 2464. **Open** *Apr-Oct* 10.30am-6pm
daily. *Nov-Mar* 10am-5pm daily. **Admission**
€3 (€1 for audioguide). **No credit cards**.
Dating from 638, the basilica is the oldest building
on the lagoon. The interior has an elaborate 11th-
century mosaic floor that rivals that of San Marco.
But the main draws of this church are the vivid
mosaics on the vault and walls, which range in date
from the ninth century to the end of the 12th. The
apse has a simple but stunning mosaic of a
Madonna and Child on a plain gold background,
while the other end of the cathedral is dominated
by a huge mosaic of the *Last Judgement* (a good
audioguide in English gives a detailed explanation).
The theological rigour and narrative complexity of
this huge composition suggest comparisons with the
Divine Comedy, which Dante was writing at about
the same time, but the anonymous mosaicists of
Torcello were more concerned with striking fear into
the hearts of their audience – hence the wicked
devils pushing the damned into hell.

Sant'Erasmo & Vignole

Sant'Erasmo (served by vaporetto 13) is
the best-kept secret of the lagoon: larger than
Venice itself, but with a tiny population that
contents itself with growing most of the
vegetables eaten in *La Serenissima* – on Rialto
market stalls the sign '*San Rasmo*' is a mark
of quality. Venetians refer to the islanders of
Sant'Erasmo as *i matti* ('the crazies') because of
their legendarily shallow gene pool – everybody
seems to be called Vignotto or Zanella. The
islanders don't think much of Venetians either.
There are cars on this island, but as they are
only used to drive the few miles from house
to boat and back, few are in top-notch condition,
a state of affairs favoured by the fact that the
island does not have a single policeman. It also
lacks a doctor, pharmacy and school, but there
is a supermarket, one fishermen's bar-trattoria
– Ai Tedeschi (lunch only Nov-Mar, closed Tue)

Sightseeing

Dark horse

Mauro Codussi (?1440-1504) is the dark
horse of Venetian architecture: unheard of
until his name (or names – both Codussi
and Coducci are found) emerged from
archives in the late 1900s, his early life
and training remain unsolved mysteries.
He seems, however, to have come from
somewhere near Bergamo and to have
moved to Venice by 1469 when he created
the lagoon city's first Renaissance church,
San Michele in Isola (*see p141*).

Codussi's great gift lay in merging the
characteristic traits of Venetian Gothic
(abundant decoration, three-lobed façades)
with the clean lines and classical features
of the Renaissance.

Flexibility was the keyword for Codussi. For
a glimpse of this architect's genius, visit San
Zaccaria (*see p95*) where classical features
are used on the façade with Gothic profusion.
Santa Maria Formosa (*see p94*) is the most
Tuscan of his churches. In San Giovanni
Crisostomo (built by 1504; *see p103*)
however, he adopted a Greek cross plan
common to the earliest Venetian churches.
His *palazzi*, such as Palazzo Corner Spinelli
or Palazzo Vendramin Calergi on the Grand
Canal, were equally influential but equally
adapted to local traditions.

Other Codussi works in the city include
the Torre dell'Orologio (clock tower; *see
p87*) in St Mark's square, the upper story
of the façade of the Scuola di San Marco
(*see pxxx*) and the grandiose double staircase
in the Scuola Grande di San Giovanni
Evangelista (*see p119*), the only remaining
example of the speciality for which this
maestro was famous.

– hidden away on a small sandy beach by the Forte Massimiliano, an Austrian fort that has recently been restored, and a restaurant, Ca' Vignotto (via Forti 71, 041 528 5329, average €25-€30, closed Tue and mid Dec to mid Jan), where bookings are essential.

The main attraction of the island lies in the beautiful country landscapes and lovely walks past traditional Veneto farmhouses, through vineyards and fields of artichokes and asparagus – a breath of fresh air after all the urban crowding of Venice. For those wanting to get around more swiftly, bicycles can be hired from the guesthouse Lato Azzurro, near the vaporetto stop Capannone (041 523 0642): €3 for an hour, €5 for half a day, €8 for the whole day.

By the main vaporetto stop (Chiesa) is the 20th-century church (on the site of an earlier one founded before 1000; opening hours vary). Over the entrance door is a gruesome 17th-century depiction of the martyrdom of St Erasmus, who had his intestines wound out of his body on a windlass. The resemblance of a windlass to a capstan resulted in St Erasmus becoming the patron saint of sailors.

If you're around on the first Sunday in October, don't miss the *Festa del mosto*, held to inaugurate the first pressing of new wine. This is perhaps the only chance you'll ever get to witness – or even participate in – *gara del bisato*: a game in which an eel is dropped into a tub of water blackened by squid ink. Contestants have to plunge their heads into the tub and attempt to catch the eel with their teeth.

Opposite the Capannone vaporetto stop is the tiny island of Lazzaretto Nuovo. Get off here at the weekend, shout across, and with luck a boat might row over to get you. In the 15th century the island was fortified as a customs deposit and military prison; during the 1576 plague outbreak it became a quarantine centre (*see p114* **Pestilence**). More recently it has become a research centre for the archaeologists of the Archeo Club di Venezia, who are excavating its ancient remains, including a church that may date back to the sixth century.

The number 13 vaporetto also stops at the smaller island of Vignole, where there is a medieval chapel dedicated to St Erosia.

The southern lagoon

The southern part of the lagoon between Venice, the Lido and the mainland has 14 small islands, a few of which are still inhabited, though most are out of bounds to tourists.

San Servolo is home to a private university (*see chapter* **Directory: Study**). La Grazia was for years a quarantine hospital but the structure has now been closed. The huge **San Clemente**, originally a lunatic asylum and later a home for abandoned cats, has been turned into one of the lagoon's plushest hotels.

But pick up vaporetto number 20 from San Zaccaria at 3.10pm (note that only a few each day stop at San Lazzaro), and you will be one of the select few who can say that they made it to the island of **San Lazzaro degli Armeni**.

A black-cloaked Armenian priest meets the boat and takes visitors on a detailed tour of the **Monastero Mechitarista**. This tiny island is a global point of reference for Armenia's Catholic minority, visited and supported by Armenians from Italy and abroad. Near the entrance stand the printing presses that helped to distribute Armenian literature all over the world for 200 years. Sadly, they are now silent, with the monastery's charmingly retro line in dictionaries and school and liturgical texts farmed out to a modern press.

Originally a leper colony, in 1717 the island was presented by the doge to an Armenian abbot called Mekhitar, who was on the run from the Turkish invasion of the Peloponnese. There had been an Armenian community in Venice since the 11th century, centring on the tiny Santa Croce degli Armeni church, just round the corner from the piazza San Marco, but the construction of this church and monastery on the former leper colony made Venice a world centre of Armenian culture.

The monastery was the only one in the whole of Venice to be spared the Napoleonic axe that did away with so many convents and monasteries: the emperor had a soft spot for Armenians and argued that this was an academic rather than a religious institute.

The tour takes in the cloisters and the church, rebuilt after a fire in 1883. The museum and the modern library contain 40,000 priceless books and manuscripts, and a bizarre collection of gifts donated over the years by visiting Armenians, ranging from Burmese prayer books to an Egyptian mummy.

The island's most famous student was Lord Byron, who used to take a break from his more earthly pleasures in Venice and row over three times a week to learn Armenian (as he found that his 'mind wanted something craggy to break upon') with the monks. He helped the monks to publish an Armenian-English grammar, although by his own confession he never got beyond the basics of the language. You can buy a completed version of this, plus a number of period maps and an illustrated children's Armenian grammar, in the shop just inside the monastery gate.

San Lazzaro degli Armeni – Monastero Mechitarista

041 526 0104. **Open** 3.20-5pm daily for guided visits. **Admission** €6; €3 concessions. **No credit cards.**

Eat, Drink, Shop

Features

Eating Out

Eat well? Eat local.

Eat, Drink, Shop

Venice may be the most tourist-infested of Italian cities, but it has a long and glorious culinary tradition based on fresh seafood, game and vegetables, backed up by northern Italy's three main carbohydrate fixes: pasta, risotto rice and polenta. Outside of a handful of top-notch (and top-dollar) hotel restaurants, you will invariably eat better in the lagoon city if you go with the flow of *la cucina veneta*.

This requires a certain spirit of open-minded experimentation. Not everybody has eaten *granseola* (spider crab) before, or *garusoli* (sea snails) or *canoce* (mantis shrimps), but Venice is definitely the place to try these marine curios – plus market garden rarities like *castraure* (baby artichokes) and *fiori di zucca* (courgette flowers).

Unfortunately, eating locally does not necessarily mean eating cheaply. There is a double pricing policy in many local trattorias, with one price for Venetians and another (the one given on the menu, if it exists) for tourists. There is not much you can do about this unofficial congestion charge, unless you take a crash course in Venetian dialect – and even then, you won't fool them. But if you are careful, and don't require the full three-course experience, it is still possible to eat well on the lagoon for €20 a head, including house wine – especially at lunchtime, when prices tend to be less punishing.

BACARO'S BACK

The slow revolution in Venetian dining over the last few years has come from below – from the creative relaunch of the *bacaro*, the city's wine-only equivalent of the British pub. With their blackened beams and rickety wooden tables, *bacari* (accent on the first syllable) are often hidden down backstreets or in quiet *campielli*. Here locals crowd the bar, swiftly downing a glass of wine (*un'ombra*) between work and home, and taking the edge off their appetites with one of the *cicheti* (snacks) that line the counter. The etiquette of *cicheti* is fairly straightforward. Once you've taken up your position at the bar and ordered a glass of soave or cabernet, just reach for the snacks and start eating. It helps if you keep tabs on how many you've consumed – though the barman should keep a fairly accurate count. You pay for drinks and snacks together at the end.

In the 1980s *bacari* began to evolve into full-scale restaurants. The city's top restaurant, **Da Fiore** (*see p159*), began life as a *bacaro* and still wears its entrance bar with pride. But in culinary terms, it was back-to-basics revolutionaries like Claudio Proietto at **Corte Sconta** (*see p154*) who set the agenda, by cutting out the sauces and concentrating on the freshest seafood, simply cooked and marinated in the same way Venetian families do it (or,

Osteria San Marco
See p151.

rather, used to do it) at home. Yesterday's rebels are today's establishment, and the torch has since passed to second-generation players like **Anice Stellato** (*see p155*) and **La Bitta** (*see p162*), which attract a young crowd, yet still look as though they've been around for ever.

Where *bacari* are mainly drinking dens, they have been included in the Cafés, Bars and Pasticcerie chapter (*see pp165-73*). Where food is as much the point as wine, they are listed below.

INS AND OUTS

In more rustic eateries, menus are often recited out loud; waiters are used to doing off-the-cuff English translations, though these can be somewhat approximate. If you are unsure of the price of something you have ordered, ask.

If there is a printed menu, note that fish is often quoted by weight – generally by the *etto* (100 grammes). Steer well clear of those restaurants – mainly around San Marco – that employ sharply dressed waiters to stand outside and persuade passing tourists to come in for a meal: an immediate recipe for rip-off prices. Always ask for a written *conto* (bill) at the end of the meal, as it is, in theory, illegal to leave the restaurant without one.

Finally, bear in mind that there are two timescales for eating in Venice. The more upmarket restaurants follow standard Italian practice, serving lunch from around 1pm to 3pm and dinner from 7.30pm until at least 10pm. But *bacari* and neighbourhood *trattorie* tend to follow Venetian workers' rhythms, with lunch running from noon to 2pm and dinner from 6.30pm to 9pm. In other words, if you want to eat cheaply, eat early.

WHAT'S ON THE PLATE (AND IN THE GLASS)

A writhing, glistening variety of seafood swims from the stalls of the Rialto and Chioggia markets into local kitchens; it's not always cheap, but for dedicated pescivores, there are few better stamping grounds in the whole of Italy. To make sense of the bewildering variety of sea creatures, *see p153* **The menu**.

The once-strong local tradition of creative ways with meat – especially with the more unmentionable parts – is kept alive in a couple of restaurants and one marvellous trattoria, **Dalla Marisa** (*see p157*); it can also be found in bar-counter *cicheti* like *nervetti* (veal cartilage) and *cotechino* (spicy pig's intestine parcels filled with various cuts of pork).

▶ Names of Venetian dishes have been left in Italian, as they appear on the menu; for translations, *see p153* **The menu**.

Vegetarians may be horrified to find that there is not a single veggie restaurant in the city. But Venetian cuisine relies heavily on seasonal vegetables, so it is quite easy to eat a vegetarian meal. *Secondi* are often accompanied by a wide selection of grilled vegetables: aubergine, courgette, tomato or radicchio.

There is something of the Spanish tapas mentality about the Venetian approach to meals: not only in the tasty *cicheti* lined up on *bacaro* counters, but in the way the *antipasti* (hors d'oeuvres) often engulf the whole meal. If you nodded vigorously when the waiter suggested bringing 'one or two' seafood *antipasti*, you may start to regret it when the fifth plate arrives – but it is perfectly OK to just eat a plate of pasta afterwards, or to skip to the *secondo*, or dessert: flexibility is the keyword.

Except in the more upmarket restaurants and one or two born-again *bacari*, wines will mostly be local. Luckily, the wine-growing area that stretches from the Veneto north-east to Friuli is, after Tuscany and Piedmont, one of Italy's strongest, with good whites like tocai and soave backed up by solid reds like valpolicella and cabernet franc (*see p164* **Wines of the Veneto**). This means that even in humbler establishments the house wine is usually drinkable and often surprisingly refined.

PIZZERIE

Like all major Italian cities, Venice has its fair share of pizza joints, though the standard here is not particularly high. Still, prices in *pizzerie* remain reasonably low, which makes them a good standby for a carbohydrate-and-protein injection between more expensive meals.

In the rest of Italy, *pizzerie* are generally open only in the evening; tourist demand, though, means that most Venetian pizza emporia serve the doughy discs at lunch too. Note that beer, rather than wine, is the traditional accompaniment to pizza.

READING THE LISTINGS

Average restaurant prices are based on a three-course meal for one person, with cover charge and house wine. For *pizzerie*, average prices are for one pizza, a medium beer and cover charge; a separate average is given if they also do restaurant meals. In the case of *bacari* that offer both bar snacks and full meals with waiter service, averages are for full sit-down meals; perching at the bar and ordering a plate of nibbles is a whole lot cheaper. For advice on tipping, *see p293*.

Times given in the listings below refer to the kitchen's opening hours – that is, when it's possible to order food; establishments may keep their doors open well after this.

Eat, Drink, Shop

Restaurants for...

Vegetarians
Alla Zucca (*p158*); Bancogiro (*p159*); Cavatappi (*below*); L'Avogaria (*p162*).

Carnivores
Dalla Marisa (*p157*); La Bitta (*p162*); Oniga (*p162*); Vini da Arturo (*p151*).

Wine
Alle Testiere (*p153*); Cavatappi (*below*); Vino Vino (*p151*).

Cicheti (bar snacks)
Ai Vini Padovani (*p161*); Al Bacareto (*below*); Alla Patatina (*p158*); Ca D'Oro (Alla Vedova) (*p155*).

A cheap sit-down meal
Alla Botte (*p150*); Al Portego (*p153*); Dai Tosi (*p154*).

Traditional Venetian
Antiche Carampane (*p158*); Ca D'Oro

(Alla Vedova) (*p155*); Corte Sconta (*p154*); Vini da Gigio (*p157*).

Creative Venetian
Al Covo (*p151*); Alle Testiere (*p153*); Osteria San Marco (*p151*); Osteria di Santa Marina (*p154*); La Mascareta (*see p154*).

A romantic dinner
Al Covo (*p151*); Alla Zucca (outside tables, *p158*); Da Fiore (*p159*); Gran Caffè Quadri (*below*).

Italian regional cuisine
L'Avogaria (Puglia, *p162*); Mistrà (Liguria, *p162*).

International cuisine
Mirai (Japanese, *p157*).

A lagoon lunch
Alla Maddalena (*p163*).

San Marco

Restaurants & *bacari*

Al Bacareto ❶
San Marco 3447, calle delle Botteghe (041 528 9336/ www.paginegialle.it/osteriaalbacareto). Vaporetto Sant'Angelo or San Samuele. Meals served noon-3pm, 7-10.15pm Mon-Fri; noon-3pm Sat. Closed Aug. Average €38. Credit AmEx, MC, V. Map p311 B2.
This rustic family-run trattoria near Palazzo Grassi has tables outside in summer. Inside is a lively bar packed with locals downing wine and sampling the *cicheti*, among which the *polpetta* and the *crochette di patate* (potato and cheese croquettes) stand out; the fried sardines (*sarde fritte*) are also good. The sit-down menu revolves around classics like *bigoli in salsa*. The only drawback is the steep price leap between bar-snack and table service; get around it by turning up around 1pm, when risottos are served piping hot to stand-up customers at the bar.

Alla Botte ❷
San Marco 5482, campo San Bartolomeo (041 520 9775/www.osteriaallabotte.it). Meals served noon-3pm, 7-10pm Mon-Wed, Fri, Sat; noon-3pm Sun. Closed 3wks Jan, 3wks July. Average €23. Credit MC, V. Map p309 D2.
Campo San Bartolomeo is probably Venice's liveliest evening meeting place, and after seeing and being seen, many young Venetians head off to the nearby Botte for a quick *ombra* (glass of wine). At the tiny, barrel-like bar (hence the name: *botte* means

barrel), clients jostle for wine, a seafood *cicheto* or a sandwich made with a slice from the immense mortadella on the counter. There's a back room where simple meals (*seppie in nero, fegato alla veneziana*) are served at prices that are very reasonable this close to Rialto – we managed €15 a head for two courses with wine on a recent visit. It can get extremely packed around aperitivo time, but that's all part of the fun.

Cavatappi ❸
San Marco 525, campo della Guerra (041 296 0252). Vaporetto Vallaresso. Open 9am-midnight Tue-Sat; 9am-3pm Sun. Closed Jan. Average €25. Credit DC, MC, V. Map p311 A3.
One of Venice's brightest new wine bars, the clean-cut, modern Cavatappi ('corkscrew') has more than 30 high-quality wines available by the glass from 9am to midnight. But young owners Marco and Francesca also offer a small lunch and dinner menu, with dishes such as pumpkin and scampi risotto or cinammon potatoes with swordfish, and plenty of creative salads. For snackers or those on a budget, there is also a good range of sandwiches and bar snacks. They also do an excellent €10 offer which covers one hot dish (eg veal scallops in white wine with seasonal side vegetables) and one glass of wine. The *spritz* (*see p166* Bar talk) served here is in the running for one of the best in Venice.

Gran Caffè Ristorante Quadri ❹
San Marco 120, piazza San Marco (041 528 9299/ www.quadrivenice.com). Vaporetto Vallaresso or San Zaccaria. Meals served *Apr-Oct* 12.15-2pm, 7.15-

10.15pm daily. *Nov-Mar* 12.15-2pm, 7.15-10.15pm Tue-Sun. **Average** €100. **Credit** AmEx, DC, MC, V. **Map** p311 B3.

If you want to splash out on a really special meal, book for lunch or dinner at the restaurant above Caffè Quadri on piazza San Marco. The two neo-classical dining rooms upstairs are adorned with huge mirrors, damask wall coverings and imposing Murano chandeliers – even better if you can secure one of the four window tables that look out over the piazza. It would be easy to soft-pedal the food in such surroundings, but chef Graziano Bettiol manages a surprisingly creative take on the Venetian tradition (witness the borlotti bean soup with braised leeks, mussels and – wait for it – gold leaf); there are even one or two clearly marked vegetarian options. And the final reckoning, all things considered, is not excessive – especially if you come at lunch, when the menu is lighter on the stomach and the wallet.

Osteria San Marco ❺

San Marco 1610, Frezzeria (041 528 5242). Vaporetto Vallaresso. **Meals served** 12.30-3pm, 7.30-10.30pm Mon-Sat. Closed 1wk Jan, 1wk Aug. **Average** €45. **Credit** MC, V. **Map** p311 B3.

This smart, modern osteria-wine bar on a busy shopping street is a breath of fresh air in the tourist-oriented San Marco area. The four young guys behind the operation are sometimes run off their feet, but they're serious about food and wine and their attention to detail shows through both in the bar-counter selection of snacks and wines by the glass, and in the sit-down menu, which changes regularly and is based on the freshest local produce. Among the dishes that can be sampled in the long, rustic-minimalist dining area are *crema di piselli nuovi con capesante* (fresh pea soup with scallops), *ossobuco alla menta* (veal shank braised in mint) and *semifreddo allo zenzero* (ginger parfait). Prices are on the high side, but you're paying for the area as well as the quality and the mark-up on bottles is commendably low. A selection of cold dishes is on offer even when the kitchen is closed.

Vini da Arturo ❻

San Marco 3656, calle dei Assassini (041 528 6974). Vaporetto Rialto or Sant'Angelo. **Meals served** *Sept-July* 12.30-2.30pm, 7.30-11pm Mon-Sat. Closed 2wks after Carnevale; Aug. **Average** €75. **No credit cards. Map** p311 B2.

This tiny place just north of La Fenice has a narrow, pannelled interior that has earned it the nickname *il vagone* (the railway carriage). It is a well-kept secret among Venetian gastronomes. There's not a whiff of fish on the menu, which features the best fillet steak on the lagoon, as well as a few less carnivorous (the owner describes them as 'vegetarian') options – including some creative salad tasters, served as an *antipasto*. For dessert, try the creamy tiramisù, or the chocolate mousse. Service is affable and the quality of food is high, but so it should be at these prices – and you should note that they don't take credit cards.

Vino Vino ❼

San Marco 2007A, ponte delle Veste (041 241 7688/ www.vinovino.co.it). Vaporetto Vallaresso or Giglio. **Open** 10.30am-2.30am Mon, Wed-Fri, Sun; 10.30am-12.30am Sat. **Average** €30. **No credit cards. Map** p311 B2.

Overlooking a canal near La Fenice, Vino Vino – an offshoot of the ultra-traditional Antico Martini restaurant – was the city's first authentic wine bar, and it still has one of the best-stocked wine cellars. You can sample vintages from as far afield as Australia, California and Spain, as well as local crus from the Veneto and Friuli regions. Elaborate bar snacks include the likes of quail with polenta, sautéd veal kidneys and *baccalà alla vicentina*; the same menu is on offer for sit-down customers, at a price.

Castello

Restaurants & *bacari*

Al Covo ❽

Castello 3968, campiello della Pescaria (041 522 3812). Vaporetto Arsenale. **Meals served** 12.45-3pm, 7.30-10pm Mon, Tue, Fri-Sun. Closed mid Dec-mid Jan, 2wks Aug. **Average** €75. **Credit** AmEx, MC, V. **Map** p312 B3.

Far from the tourist crowds, Al Covo is in a quiet alley behind the riva degli Schiavoni. Its deservedly high reputation is based on sapient and sapid cooking of the freshest seafood, in creative dishes that range from a warm platter of shrimps and shellfish to *lasagnetta* (mini lasagna) with mussels and aubergines, and grilled whitefish *secondi* – all freshly caught, rather than farmed. The restaurant's charming decor, midway between rustic and elegant, should make it ideal for a romantic dinner, but the atmosphere is more serious foodie than newly wed footsie. The welcome can even verge on the prickly if one turns up outside the kitchen's set-in-stone hours. Chef/owner Cesare Benelli's American wife, Diane, talks non-Italian-speakers through the daily-changing menu; she is also responsible for the delicious desserts. And congratulations Mr Benelli, for finally coming round to credit cards.

Alla Rivetta ❾

Castello 4625, ponte San Provolo (041 528 7302). Vaporetto San Zaccaria. **Meals served** 10am-10pm Tue-Sun. Closed mid July-mid Aug. **Average** €35. **Credit** AmEx, MC, V. **Map** p312 B2.

On an ancient bridge right behind the Hotel Danieli, the Rivetta has managed to preserve its neighbourhood trattoria credentials – and prices – despite the scores of tourists who troop in and out every day. At the bar, owner Stefano serves creamy *polenta con baccalà* for little old ladies to take home for lunch. Gondoliers pile in for a noisy, boozy midday meal, featuring the usual Venetian pasta classics and an unbeatable *fritto misto*. Note the kitchen's non-stop opening times – handy for those who get into town starving at 4pm.

Eat, Drink, Shop

The menu

Antipasti (starters)

Antipasti are so central to the local tradition. The dozens of *cicheti* – tapas-style snacks – served from the counters of the traditional *bacaro* (*see p148*) are essentially *antipasti*; in more upmarket restaurants, these will be joined – or replaced – by an even larger and more refined selection, which will probably include: **baccalà mantecato** stockfish beaten into a cream with oil and milk, often served on grilled polenta; **bovoleti** tiny snails cooked in olive oil, parsley and an awful lot of garlic; **carciofi** artichokes, even better if they are **castrauri** – baby artichokes, served raw in April/May; **canoce** (or **cicale di mare**) delicate, transparent mantis shrimps; **folpi/folpeti** baby octopuses; **garusoli** sea snails, to be winkled out with a toothpick; **moleche** soft-shelled crabs, usually deep-fried; **museto** a boiled brawn sausage, generally served on a slice of bread with mustard; **nervetti** boiled veal cartilage, if you must know; **polpetta** a deep-fried spicy meatball; **polenta** yellow or white cornmeal mush, served either runny or in firm sliceable slabs; **sarde in saor** sardines marinated in a pungent mixture of onion, vinegar, pine nuts and raisins; **schie** tiny grey shrimps, usually served on a bed of soft white polenta; **seppie in nero** cuttlefish in its own ink; **spienza** veal spleen usually served on a skewer; **trippa e rissa** tripe cooked in broth.

Primi (first courses)

bigoli in salsa fat spaghetti in an anchovy and onion sauce; **gnocchi con granseola** potato gnocchi in a spider crab sauce; **pasta... e ceci** pasta and chickpea soup; **...e fagioli** pasta and borlotti bean soup; **spaghetti...**

alla busara in anchovy sauce; **...al nero di seppia** in squid-ink sauce; **...con caparossoli/vongole veraci** with clams; **risotto... di zucca** pumpkin risotto; **...di radicchio** made with bitter red radicchio from nearby Treviso.

Secondi (main courses)

The choice of fish and seafood is almost endless – in addition to the *antipasti* mentioned above you are likely to find the following: **anguilla** eel; **aragosta/astice** spiny lobster/lobster; **branzino** sea bass; **cape longhe** razor clams; **cape sante** scallops; **cernia** grouper; **coda di rospo** anglerfish; **cozze** mussels; **granchio** crab; **granseola** spider crab; **orata** gilt-headed bream; **rombo** turbot; **pesce San Pietro** John Dory; **pesce spada** swordfish; **sogliola** sole; **tonno** tuna; **vongole/caparossoli** clams.

Meat eaters are less well catered for in Venice; the handful of local specialities include: **fegato alla veneziana** veal liver cooked in a slightly sweet sauce of onions; **castradina** a lamb and cabbage broth, traditionally eaten after the Salute festival in November (*see pp196-8*).

Dolci

Venice's restaurants are not the best place to feed a sweet habit – with a few exceptions, there are far more tempting pastries to be found on the shelves of the city's *pasticcerie*. The classic end to a meal here is a plate of **buranei** – sweet egg biscuits – served with a dessert wine such as Fragolino. Then it's quickly on to the more important matter of which grappa to order.

Alle Testiere ⑩

Castello 5801, calle del Mondo Novo (041 522 7220). Vaporetto Rialto. **Meals served** noon-2pm, 7-10.30pm Tue-Sat. Closed last wk Dec; 2wks Jan; last wk July; 3wks Aug. **Average** €55. **Credit** MC, V. **Map** p312 A1.

One of the great success stories of recent years, this tiny restaurant is today one of the hottest culinary tickets in Venice. There are so few seats (22, to be precise) that they do two sittings each evening; booking for the later one (at 9pm) will ensure a more relaxed meal. Bruno, the cook, offers creative variations on Venetian seafood, many of them involving herbs and spices; the *gnocchetti* (mini-gnocchi) with cinammon-flavoured baby squid, and the *branzino* in lime and caper sauce are two mouth-watering examples. Sommelier Luca guides diners around a small but well-chosen wine list and a marvellously recherché cheeseboard.

Al Portego ⑪

Castello 6015, calle Malvasia (041 522 9038/ www.alportego.it). Vaporetto Rialto. **Meals served** noon-2.30pm, 7-9.30pm Mon-Sat. Closed 2wks June. **Average** €23. **No credit cards. Map** p309 D2.

With its wooden decor, this rustic *osteria* smacks of the mountain chalet. Alongside a big barrel of wine, the bar is loaded down with a selection of *cicheti*, from meatballs and tuna balls to fried courgette flowers and *nervetti* stewed with onions. There are also simple but honest pasta dishes, risottos and *secondi*, such as *fegato alla veneziana*, served up for early lunch (noon-2.30pm) and early dinner (7-9.30pm). Eat at the bar or queue for one of the tiny tables, as no reservations are taken.

Antica Trattoria Bandierette 🄬
Castello 6671, barbaria de le Tole (041 522 0619/ www.elmoro.com/bandierette.htm). Vaporetto Ospedale. **Meals served** noon-2pm Mon; noon-2pm, 7-10pm Wed-Sun. Closed 2wks Dec-Jan; 2wks Aug. **Average** €35. **Credit** DC, MC, V. **Map** p312 A2.
The bland trattoria decor leaves a little to be desired, but the locals who cram into this busy place between Santi Giovanni e Paolo and San Francesco don't come for the decor: they're here for the good, reasonably priced seafood and the friendly service. Among the *primi*, the tagliatelle with scampi and spinach, and the spaghetti with prawns and asparagus are especially good.

Corte Sconta 🄭
Castello 3886, calle del Pestrin (041 522 7024). Vaporetto Arsenale. **Meals served** *Feb-Dec* 12.30-2.30pm, 7-10pm Tue-Sat. Closed Jan; mid July-mid Aug. **Average** €55. **Credit** MC, V. **Map** p313 B3.
Claudio Proietto's trailblazing seafood restaurant in the eastern reaches of Castello is now such a firm favourite on the well-informed tourist circuit that it is usually a good idea to book several days in advance. The main act is an endless procession of seafood *antipasti*; the day's catch might include *garusoli*, *schie* and *moscardini* (baby curled octopus). The pasta is home-made and the warm *zabaione* dessert is a delight. Decor is of the modern Bohemian trattoria variety, the ambience loud and friendly. In summer, try to secure one of the tables in the pretty, vine-covered courtyard.

Dal Pampo (Osteria Sant'Elena) 🄮
Sant'Elena, calle Generale Chinotto 24 (041 520 8419/osteriapampo@virgilio.it). Vaporetto Sant'Elena. **Meals served** noon-2.30pm, 7.30-9pm Mon, Wed-Sun. Closed 1wk May; 1wk Aug; 2 wks Christmas. **Average** €32. **Credit** AmEx, V. **Map** p313 D2.
Right at the end of Venice in the residential neighbourhood of Sant'Elena, this rustic trat with tables outside is a good bet for a cheap plate of spaghetti or a mixed seafood grill, especially on sunny summer days. Officially called the 'Osteria Sant'Elena' but known to everyone as Dal Pampo – 'Pampo's Place' – after the jolly owner, it is right by the football stadium, so it can be difficult to get a table on the Sundays when Venezia are playing at home.

La Mascareta 🄾
Castello 5183, calle lunga Santa Maria Formosa (041 523 0744). **Open** 7pm-2am Mon, Tue, Fri-Sun. **No credit cards. Map** p309 D3.
Genial, bow-tied Mauro Lorenzon keeps hundreds of wines – including some rare vintages – in his cellars, serving them up by the bottle or glass along with plates of cheeses, seafood, cold meats or crostini. There are also more filling options – hearty soups, for example – every evening. Dishes are prepared for this cosy *enoteca* by some of the city's most

exclusive restaurants, including Al Covo (*see p151*), while Mariuccia at the Fiaschetteria Toscana (*see p157*) provides mouth-watering desserts. The cost of an evening here will be determined by what you drink. Il Mascaron will soon take credit cards.

Osteria di Santa Marina 🄯
Castello 5911, campo Santa Marina (041 528 5239/ www.osteriadisantamarina.it). Vaporetto Rialto. **Meals served** 7.30-9.30pm Mon; 12.30-2.30pm, 7.30-9.30pm Tue-Sat. Closed 2 wks Jan; 2 wks Aug. **Average** €60. **Credit** MC, V. **Map** p309 D2.
A novelty that looks like its been around for ages, this upmarket Osteria in pretty campo Santa Marina, not far from the Miracoli church, is a welcome addition to the fold. It has the kind of professional service and standards that are too often lacking in Venice, and although it is hardly cheap, the ambience and the high level of the creative, seafood-oriented cuisine justify the price tag. Raw fish feature strongly among the *antipasti*; first courses include some interesting – and successful – dislocations of the local tradition such as *zucca in saor con moeche fritte* (pumpkin in sweet and sour sauce with soft-shell crabs). The joy of this place is in the detail: the way the bread is all home-made, the way a between-course taster turns up just when you were about to ask whatever happened to the *branzino…* The secret is out, though, so book ahead.

Pizzerie

Dai Tosi 🄶
Castello 738, secco Marina (041 523 7102). Vaporetto Giardini. **Meals served** noon-2pm Mon, Tue, Thur; noon-2pm, 7-9.30pm Fri-Sun. Closed 2wks Aug. **Average** €15 pizzeria; €28 full meal. **Credit** MC, V. **Map** p313 C1.
In one of Venice's most working-class areas, in a street festooned with washing, this pizzeria is a big hit with local families and a welcome retreat to normality for visitors to the nearby Biennale dell'Arte (*see p207* **La Biannale**). But beware of the restaurant of the same name on the street: this place (at No.738) is one of the two establishments. The cuisine is humble but filling, the pizzas are tasty (try the Gregory Speck – *speck* is Tyrolean ham), and you can round the meal off nicely with a killer *sgropin* (a post-prandial refresher made with lemon sorbet, vodka and prosecco). In summer, it's a good idea to angle for a table in the garden out back.

Cannaregio

Restaurants & *bacari*

Alla Fontana 🄱
Cannaregio 1102, fondamenta Cannaregio (041 715 077). Vaporetto Guglie. **Meals served** *Apr-Oct* 6.30-11pm Mon-Sat. *Nov-Mar* 7-10pm Mon-Sat. Closed 10 days Nov; 10 days Jan. **Average** €35. **Credit** AmEx, MC, V. **Map** p308 B3.

This traditional osteria just five minutes from the station has recently completed its move from wine-and-snack *bacaro* to bona fide, evening-only restaurant. 'The Fountain' now offers a range of filling trattoria dishes with a creative twist: tagliatelle with eel, gnocchi with turbot and courgettes, *spezzatino* (braised strips of veal) with polenta. In summer, tables line the busy canal pavement outside.

Anice Stellato  ⑱

Cannaregio 3272, fondamenta della Sensa (041 720 744). Vaporetto Guglie or Sant'Alvise. **Meals served** 12.30-2pm, 7.30-10pm Wed-Fri; 12.30-2pm, 7.30-10pm Sat, Sun. Closed 1wk Jan; 3wks Aug. **Average** €35. **Credit** MC, V. **Map** p309 A1.

This nouveau *bacaro* is already a favourite with budget-conscious gourmets. The reason is simple: the ambience is friendly and the food good and reasonably priced. A walk-around bar at the entrance fills up with *cichetari* (locals doing serious snacking) in the hour before lunch and evening meals. Tables take up two oak-beamed rooms around and behind, and spill out on to the canalside walk in summer. The name means 'star anise', but spices have little place in the kitchen, which turns out Venetian classics such as *bigoli in salsa* along with more creative outings like tagliatelle with scampi and courgette flowers. It's hugely popular – so avoid Saturdays, unless you like a scrum, and always book ahead.

Boccadoro ⑲

Cannaregio 5405A, campiello Widman (041 521 1021). Vaporetto Fondamente Nove. **Meals served** 12.30-2.30pm, 8-11pm Mon-Sat. **Average** €52. **Credit** MC, V. **Map** p309 C3.

Helmed by a chef who previously worked at Al Covo (*see p151*), this creative seafood restaurant suffered from the tourist downturn around the time of its 2001 opening. Combined with its out-of-the-way location, this can make for some fairly quiet evenings. But the cuisine is excellent, with a focus on fresh fish – so fresh, in fact, that most of the entrées are raw, a sort of Adriatic sashimi featuring oysters, prawns, scallops, swordfish and tuna. Pasta courses include tasty *spaghetti seppie e pomodorini* (with squid and cherry tomatoes), while *secondi* range from simple grilled fish to more adventurous seafood and vegetable pairings. We were less impressed by the grilled cheese, chocolate and honey dessert… far too heavy for a hot July evening. The original wine list (which was 'being reprinted' on our last visit) includes some Sardinian whites. In summer, tables spill outside on to a small neighbourhood campo – a great play space for bored kids.

Ca D'Oro (Alla Vedova) ⑳

Cannaregio 3912, ramo Ca' d'Oro (041 528 5324). Vaporetto Ca' d'Oro. **Meals served** 11.30am-2.30pm, 6.30-10.30pm Mon-Wed, Fri, Sat; 6.30-11pm Sun. Closed Aug. **Average** €35. **No credit cards**. **Map** p309 C2.

Deservedly famous, this is one of the best-preserved traditional *bacari* in town. Its official name is the Ca' d'Oro, but most Venetians know it as Alla Vedova – the Widow's Place. The widow has now, alas, joined her *marito*, but her family still runs the show and her spirit marches on in the traditional brass-pan and wooden-table decor and the warm, intimate atmosphere. Tourists head for the tables (it's best to

Have a vine time at the cosy wine mecca that is Castello's **La Mascareta**. *See p154.*

Osteria Enoteca Giorgione

Cannaregio 4582/A - 30131 Venezia - Tel. 041 5221725
Email: osteriagiorgione@katamail.com

Closed Mondays

www.alveciobragosso.com

Hosteria Al
Vecio Bragosso

Typical Venetian Cuisine

*Homemade pasta
Fresh fish daily*

*Open 12-midnight
Closed Monday*

*Strada Nuova 4386
S.S. Apostoli
30131 Venezia*

Tel: +39 041 5237277

book), where tasty pasta dishes (like spaghetti in cuttlefish ink) and *secondi* are served, while locals tend to stay at the bar snacking on a range of classic *cicheti*, from *folpeti* to fried artichokes to the best *polpette* in Venice.

Da Alberto ㉑

Cannaregio 5401, calle Giacinto Gallina (041 523 8153). Vaporetto Fondamente Nove. **Meals served** noon-3pm, 7-10pm Mon-Sat. Closed mid July-early Aug. **Average** €35. **Credit** MC, V. **Map** p309 C3.

This *bacaro* with charming trad decor, not far from campo Santi Giovanni e Paolo, has been through a couple of changes of ownership since the eponymous Alberto left to set up the popular Irish-style Innishark pub (*see p213*), but it still maintains a good standard and a well-stocked bar counter. The wide, sit-down menu centres on Venetian specialities such as *granseola* and *seppie in umido* (stewed cuttlefish), along with plenty of seafood pastas and risottos. A favourite with young Venetians, Alberto's is always buzzing and packed – so book ahead if you want to sit down and eat, rather than just snack at the bar.

Dalla Marisa ㉒

Cannaregio 652B, fondamenta San Giobbe (041 720 211). Vaporetto Tre Archi or Crea. **Meals served** noon-2.30pm Mon, Wed, Sun; noon-2.30pm, 8-9.15pm Tue, Thur-Sat. Closed Aug. **Average** €35. **No credit cards. Map** p308 B2.

Signora Marisa, the proud descendant of a dynasty of butchers, is a culinary legend in Venice, with locals calling up days in advance to ask her to prepare ancient recipes such as *risotto con le secoe* (risotto made with a special cut of beef from around the spine). Pasta dishes include the excellent *tagliatelle in drake* (male duck) sauce, while *secondi* range from tripe to roast stuffed pheasant. In summer, tables spill out from the tiny interior on to the fondamenta overlooking the busy Cannaregio canal. Book well ahead – this place is not just *popolare* (proletarian), but popular too. Serving times are rigid: turn up late and you'll go hungry.

Da Rioba ㉓

Cannaregio 2553, fondamenta della Misericordia (041 524 4379). Vaporetto Orto. **Meals served** noon-2.30pm, 7.30-10.30pm Tue-Sun. Closed 3wks Jan. **Average** €35. **Credit** MC, V. **Map** p309 B1.

Taking its name from the iron-nosed stone figure of a turbaned merchant – known as Sior Rioba – which is set into a wall in nearby campo dei Mori, Da Rioba is a nice place for lunch on warm days, when tables are laid out along the edge of the Misericordia canal. A good fall back when nearby Anice Stellato (*see p155*) is full, this nouveau-rustic *bacaro* attracts a predominantly Venetian clientele – always a good sign. The menu ranges from local standards like *schie con polenta* and *spaghetti alla busara* to more adventurous (and not always successful) forays like halibut fillet in pistachio crust on a bed of artichokes and asparagus tips.

Fiaschetteria Toscana ㉔

Cannaregio 5719, salizada San Giovanni Grisostomo (041 528 5281/www.fiaschetteriatoscana.it). Vaporetto Rialto. **Meals served** 7.30-10.30pm Tue; 12.30-2.30pm, 7.30-10.30pm Wed-Sun. Closed mid July-mid Aug. **Average** €60. **Credit** DC, MC, V. **Map** p309 C2.

Don't be fooled by the name: though this was once a depot for wine and olive oil from Tuscany, today only a good selection of steaks and big Tuscan red wines betray its origins. Otherwise, the cuisine, which runs the gamut from meat to fish to game, is true to Venetian tradition, with favourites such as *schie con polenta* and *fegato alla veneziana*. Pasta is not a strong point; better to leap from the fine *antipasti* to delicious *secondi* like grilled John Dory, or a renowned *fritto misto*. The decor is a little tired and the service can be peremptory, but this place is a reliable, though hardly cheap, gourmet standby. Take the sting out of the bill with one of Mamma Mariuccia's fabulous desserts, and a bottle from one of the most extensive wine lists in town. In the evening, they do two sittings; book for the later one (9-9.30pm) for a more relaxed meal.

Vini da Gigio ㉕

Cannaregio 3628A, fondamenta San Felice (041 528 5140/www.vinidagigio.com). Vaporetto Ca' d'Oro. **Meals served** noon-2.30pm, 7.30-10.30pm Tue-Sun. Closed 3wks Jan-Feb; 3wks Aug-Sept. **Average** €42. **Credit** DC, MC, V. **Map** p309 C1.

It's no longer any secret that this is one of the best-value restaurants in Venice, so make sure you book well in advance. Gigio is strong on Venetian *antipasti* such as *crocchette di baccalà* (breaded stockfish) and *canestrelli all griglia* (grilled razor clams); there are also a number of good meat and game options, like *masorini alla buranella* (roasted Burano-style duck). As the name suggests, wine is another forte – there are even bottles from Australia and South Africa, and there is always a good by-the-glass selection. The only drawback in this highly recommended restaurant is the decidedly unhurried service. Allow at least two hours for a complete meal, and don't go in a large group: this is a place that works best with tables of five or six maximum.

International

Mirai ㉖

Cannaregio 227, lista di Spagna (041 220 6517/www.miraivenice.com). Vaporetto Ferrovia. **Meals served** 7.30-11.30pm Tue-Sun. Closed 3wks Jan. **Average** €60. **Credit** AmEx, DC, MC, V. **Map** p308 B3.

One of the few really interesting international options in Venice, this newish Japanese restaurant has already built up a steady local following. It does all the classics – sushi, sashimi of salmon, tuna and bream, tempura – and it does them well. The classy modern decor makes for a cool refuge from the tacky lista di Spagna souvenir hell outside, and they've recently added a garden out back.

Ca D'Oro. *See p155.*

Sahara ㉗

Cannaregio 2519, fondamenta della Misericordia (041 721 077). Vaporetto San Marcuola or Orto. **Meals served** 7pm-2am daily. **Average** €20. **Credit** MC, V. **Map** p309 B1.

At this Syrian-Egyptian restaurant on Cannaregio's trendiest fondamenta, where clients cluster around outside tables on fine summer evenings, friendly owner Mouaffak conjures up a range of unrefined but tasty couscous-and-vegetable dishes, together with grills, shawermas and the usual sticky desserts. Late opening and decent prices make this one of Venice's better non-Italian options, though service can be excruciatingly slow. There's usually a belly dancer on Saturday night.

San Polo & Santa Croce

Restaurants & *bacari*

Alla Madonna ㉘

San Polo 594, calle della Madonna (041 522 3824/ www.ristoranteallamadonna.com). Vaporetto Rialto or San Silvestro. **Meals served** noon-2.30pm, 7-10pm Mon, Tue, Thur-Sun. Closed Christmas, Jan, 2wks Aug. **Average** €42. **Credit** AmEx, MC, V. **Map** p309 D2.

A sort of high-class canteen, this big, bustling fish trattoria with its friendly (though brisk) service and fair (though rising) prices has been piling in loyal locals and clued-up tourists for generations. It's just a minute's walk from the Rialto bridge, and while the cooking will win no prizes, it offers competent versions of old Venetian favourites such as *granse-ola* and *anguilla fritta*. The restaurant can also turn out pan-Italian faves like *cotolette alla milanese* (breaded veal cutlets). Bookings are not taken; you simply join the queue outside, which moves pretty fast – like the meal itself.

Alla Patatina ㉙

San Polo 2741, ponte San Polo (041 523 7238/ www.lapatatina.it). Vaporetto San Tomà. **Meals served** noon-2.30pm, 6.30-9.30pm Mon-Sat. Closed 2wks Aug. **Average** €35. **Credit** AmEx, DC, MC, V. **Map** p311 A2.

A student and workers' haunt with both bar snacks and table service. Officially called Al Ponte, this no-nonsense hostelry is known as Alla Patatina – a reference to the house speciality: chunky chips fried on wooden skewers. Sit-down fare is rough-and-ready Venetian: *seppie fritte* (fried cuttlefish), *polpette al sugo* (meatballs in tomato sauce). If you perch and snack, you can pay under €10; sit-down prices are more in line with the norm. Alla Patatina serves dinner as well as lunch, but note the early kitchen times.

Alla Zucca ㉚

Santa Croce 1762, ponte del Megio (041 524 1570/ www.lazucca.it). Vaporetto San Stae. **Meals served** 12.30-2.30pm, 7-10.30pm Mon-Sat. **Average** €35. **Credit** AmEx, DC, MC, V. **Map** p308 C3.

This was one of the first of Venice's 'alternative' trattorie and it's still one of the best. By a pretty skewed bridge, the vegetarian-friendly Pumpkin offers a welcome break from all that seafood. The menu is equally divided between meat (lamb roasted with fennel and pecorino cheese, ginger pork with pilau rice) and vegetables (penne with aubergine and feta, pumpkin and seasoned ricotta quiche). Women dining alone will feel at home; if any men work here, they're hidden in the kitchen. In summer, book ahead for one of the few outside tables.

Antiche Carampane ㉛

San Polo 1911, rio terà delle Carampane (041 524 0165/www.antichecarampane.it). Vaporetto San Silvestro. **Meals served** 12.30-2.30pm, 7.30-10.30pm Tue-Sat. Closed 1wk Jan, Aug. **Average** €50. **Credit** AmEx, DC, MC, V. **Map** p309 C1.

This compact trattoria between campo San Polo and San Cassiano – in what was once the red-light district – could win the prize for the hardest-to-find restaurant in Venice. The inaccessibility is reinforced by a slightly prickly attitude towards non-Venetians, enshrined in a sign by the door indicating the restaurant's current charge for tourist information. But that's Venetian humour for you; and if you manage to break the ice, the Carampane will deliver a fine (though not cheap) seafood meal in the best local tradition, crowned by an unbeatable *fritto misto*. Inside is cosy, but outside is better for balmy summer evenings.

Bancogiro 32
San Polo 122, campo San Giacometto di Rialto (041 523 2061). Vaporetto Rialto. **Meals served** *Sept-May* noon-2.30pm, 7.30-10.30pm Tue-Sat; noon-2.30pm Sun. *June-Aug* noon-10.30pm Tue-Sun. **Average** €35. **No credit cards. Map** p309 C2.
The location of this updated *bacaro* is splendid: the main entrance gives on to the Rialto square of San Giacometto, while the back door gives access to a prime bit of Grand Canal frontage that until a few years ago was open only to market traders. Downstairs, hirsute player-manager Andrea dispenses excellent wines to an appreciative crowd of locals; above, at a few well-spaced tables squeezed

in under the brick ceiling vaults, a light, creative, almost pasta-less menu is served, which might include *pesce ragno* (weever) fillets with pumpkin and rosemary, squid with radicchio and cinnamon, and sweet ricotta dessert with fresh figs and chestnut honey. Not every dish lives up to its ambitions, but it's certainly a change from *bacalà mantecato*. Allow plenty of time, though, as service can be sluggish. In summer, the ringside view of the Grand Canal from the outside tables makes up for the wait.

Da Fiore 33
San Polo 2202, calle del Scaleter (041 721 308). Vaporetto San Stae. **Meals served** 12.30-2.30pm, 7.30-10.30pm Tue-Sat. Closed Christmas to mid July; Aug. **Average** €95. **Credit** AmEx, DC, MC, V. **Map** p309 C1.
Restaurant critics and local gourmets are almost unanimous in considering the Michelin-starred Da Fiore to be Venice's best restaurant. The façade and the bar at the entrance hark back to its *bacaro* origins; but the elegant, barge-like dining room inside is in quite a different class. Owner Maurizio Martin treats his guests – many of whom are visiting celebrities or local big shots – with egalitarian courtesy. Raw fish and seafood – a sort of Venetian sashimi – is a key feature of the excellent *antipasti*; the pasta dishes and *secondi* such as *filetto di branzino*

Eat, Drink, Shop

A surfeit of apricockes

Thomas Coryat was one of the world's first tourists. In 1608, at a time when almost nobody travelled for pleasure, he set out from Odcombe in Somerset with his baggage, real and cultural, packed in neat trunks, and arrived in Venice some six weeks later. *La Serenissima* left a deep impression on the provincial scholar, whose capacity for amazement remained miraculously intact throughout his travels. Back in Odcombe, Coryat hung up his shoes in the local church (they were still there in the 18th century) and set about writing *Coryat's Crudities*, a proto-Chatwin travelogue which was published by subscription in 1611.

Coryat was fascinated by all he observed in Venice, not least the variety of good things to eat on the lagoon – proof that, even four centuries ago, the city had sophisticated tastes, and a well-developed supply and distribution network.

The Englishman marvels at the 'Grapes, Pears, Apples, Plums and Apricockes' on sale in the 'shambles and market places' (which were far more abundant in those days); he drools over the 'toothsome' melons grown on the 'Litto maggior', or Lido (though he

goes on to warn his readers against 'immoderate eating of them... for it doth often breede... the bloudy fluxe').

He also waxes lyrical about the 'anguria... the pith of which is redde as blood, and full of blacke kernels'. Coryat must have been one of the first Englishmen to have seen a watermelon; the word would not even enter the language for another half-century. Fish too was as important then as it now: 'The abundance of fish, which is twise a day brought into the citie, is so great, that they... doe communicate that commodity to their neighbour townes.'

But one thing shocked the conservative globetrotter – the fact that 'a man worth perhaps two million of duckats, will come into the market and buy their flesh, fish, fruites, and such other things as are necessary for the maintenance of their family'. Like a true Englishman, Coryat disapproved of 'Gentlemen and greatest Senators' taking such a direct interest in the quality of what goes on to their dinner tables, commending his fellow countryman who 'employeth his Cooke or Cator about those inferior and sordid affaires'.

Eat and drink your way around the world

all'aceto balsamico (sea bass fillets in balsamic vinegar) work creative variations on the local tradition. There is also an exceptional selection of regional cheeses – rare in Venice – and a collection of decent desserts. You pays your money, certainly, for what is in the end a good, rather than a superlative, dining experience; but that's Venice for you.

Da Ignazio ㉞
San Polo 2749, calle dei Saoneri (041 523 4852). Vaporetto San Tomà. **Meals served** noon-3pm, 7-10pm Mon-Fri, Sun. Closed 2wks Dec-Jan; 3wks July-Aug. **Average** €45. **Credit** AmEx, DC, MC, V. **Map** p309 D1.
The big attraction of this tranquil neighbourhood restaurant between campo San Polo and the Frari is its pretty, pergola-shaded courtyard. The cooking is safe, traditional Venetian: mixed seafood *antipasti* might be followed by a good rendition of *spaghetti con caparossoli* or *risi e bisi* (risotto with peas), and grilled fish; desserts include a decent tiramisù. Don't expect any frills: just down home Venetian cooking in pleasant surroundings.

Vecio Fritolin ㉟
Santa Croce 2262, calle della Regina (041 522 2881/ www.veciofritolin.com). Vaporetto San Stae. **Meals served** noon-2.30pm, 7-10.30pm Tue-Sun. **Average** €45. **Credit** AmEx, DC, MC, V. **Map** p309 C1.
This old-style *bacaro* hit a low patch a few years ago but has been nursed back to health as a full-on restaurant by the charming present owner. Wooden beams, sturdy tables and the long bar at the back of the main dining room set the mood; but the menu is more creative than one might expect, with a scallop and courgette flower risotto, or a main course of *coda di rospo* (anglerfish) with vegetables and saffron-flavoured potatoes. On our last visit the service was a little uncertain, especially on the wine front; but all in all this is a pleasant enough south-bank option, with prices that are fairly contained for Venice.

Pizzerie

Al Nono Risorto ㊱
Santa Croce 2338, sottoportico di Siora Bettina (041 524 1169). Vaporetto San Stae. **Meals served** noon-2.30pm, 7-11pm Mon, Tue, Fri-Sun; 7-11pm Thur. Closed 2wks Jan, 1wk Aug. **Average** €12 pizzeria; €30 full meal. **No credit cards.** **Map** p309 C1.
There's plenty of attitude in this lively spot. If you want to hang out over a tasty *pizza margharita* in a shady garden courtyard with Venice's bright young things, this is the place to come. It also does traditional Venetian trattoria fare, at traditional Venetian trattoria prices.

Il Refolo ㊲
Santa Croce 1459, campiello del Piovan (041 524 0016/www.dafiore.com). Vaporetto Riva di Biasio or San Stae. **Meals served** *Apr-Oct* 7-11pm Tue; noon-2.45pm, 7-11pm Wed-Sun. Closed Nov-Mar. **Average** €20 pizzeria; €45 full meal. **Credit** MC, V. **Map** p308 C3.

The 'Sea Breeze' has tables outside (and only outside) in one of Venice's prettiest squares, by a canal, with a good view of the church of San Giacomo dell'Orio. Set up by a scion of the **Da Fiore** dynasty (*see p159*), it is Venice's most luxurious pizzeria – a status that is reflected in the prices. Alongside the excellent pizzas, there is also a small international-style restaurant menu featuring high-class deli fare such as marinated salmon, curried chicken and creative salads; the house white wine is an above-average Tocai. Note the four-month winter closure, and be sure to book ahead, even for lunch.

International

Frary's ㊳
San Polo 2559, fondamenta dei Frari (041 720 050). Vaporetto San Tomà. **Meals served** noon-3.30pm, 6.30-11pm Mon, Wed-Sun. **Average** €28. **Credit** AmEx, DC, MC, V. **Map** p308 D3.
A friendly, reasonably priced restaurant specialising in Arab cuisine, though there are some Greek dishes as well. Couscous comes with a variety of sauces – vegetarian, mutton, chicken or seafood. The *mansaf* (Bedouin rice with chicken, almonds and yoghurt) is good, as are the falafel, tsatsiki and taramasalata. The naïve desert murals on the wall make a change from all that Tintoretto.

Dorsoduro

Restaurants & *bacari*

Ai Vini Padovani ㊳
Dorsoduro 1280, calle dei Cerchieri (041 523 6370). Vaporetto Ca' Rezzonico or Accademia. **Meals served** noon-9pm Mon-Fri. Closed 1wk Christmas; Aug. **Average** €30. **Credit** MC, V. **Map** p311 B1.
A difficult place to find, in a quiet calle between the Accademia and San Barnaba. But this friendly neighbourhood *bacaro* is worth the search if good-value, authentic, Venetian cooking in congenial surroundings is your thing – or if you are feeling peckish around mid-afternoon, as the kitchen stays open between lunch and dinner. Either perch at the bar and hit the groaning *cicheto* board or sit down at a table for a filling meal from a menu equally divided between meat – *saltimbocca* (veal and ham strips), *cotechino* sausage – and fish. It's Mondays to Fridays only; and make sure you get here nice and early (in true *bacaro* style) for dinner.

Antica Osteria Al Pantalon ㊵
Dorsoduro 3958, calle del Scaleter (041 710 849/ www.osteriaalpantalon.it). Vaporetto San Tomà. **Meals served** 10am-2.30pm, 6-10pm Mon-Sat. Closed 3wks Aug. **Average** €30. **Credit** AmEx, DC, MC, V. **Map** p311 B1.
This lively *bacaro* near the university lays on a good range of *cicheti*, including *olive ascolane* (like Scotch eggs except with olives inside) and crostini with *bacalà mantecato*. More substantial meals, firmly in

the local tradition, can be ordered from a sitting position. Graduation parties – which tend to get pretty wild in Venice – are a regular feature.

La Bitta 🔢
Dorsoduro 2753A, calle lunga San Barnaba (041 523 0531). Vaporetto Ca' Rezzonico. **Meals served** 6.30-11pm Mon-Sat. Closed Aug. **Average** €35. **No credit cards. Map** p311 B1.
One of the few genuinely lively neighbourhoods left in Venice, with a happy mix of students and trolley-pushing old ladies, the area around San Barnaba has a number of reasonably priced eateries. One of the best is La Bitta, which stands out from the crowd by having virtually no fish on the menu, and has the bonus of a small courtyard out back. Order from a range of pasta dishes like *tagliatelle alla Caruso* (with ham and mushrooms), followed by *fegato alla veneziana* or chicken with chanterelle mushrooms. They also have a good selection of cheeses, served with honey or chutney, and an intelligent by-the-glass wine option.

L'Avogaria 🔢
Dorsoduro 1629, calle dell'Avogaria (041 296 0491/www.avogaria.com). Vaporetto San Basilio. **Meals served** 11.30am-3pm, 7.30-11pm Mon, Wed-Sun. Closed 2wks Jan; 2wks Aug. **Average** €38. **Credit** AmEx, DC, MC, V. **Map** p310 B3.
One of the first sharp, modern design eateries to open on the lagoon, L'Avogaria is neither as pretentious nor as expensive as its appearance might suggest. At lunch you can eat a light two-course meal with wine for around €15 a head; the pricier dinner menu is a little more elaborate. The cuisine is *pugliese*, from the heel of Italy – so the usual Venetian fishy *antipasti* are replaced by vegetable nibbles like stuffed tomatoes or peppers in olive oil. Pasta courses include home-made *cavatelli* pasta with carpet shells and beans, followed by baked lamb and potatoes, or *burrata* (a sort of buttery, half-liquid mozzarella) with grilled vegetables. If you're tired of trad and bored of *baccalà*, L'Avogaria will come as a breath of fresh air – especially if you sit at one of the outside tables.

Oniga 🔢
Dorsoduro 2852, campo San Barnaba (041 522 4410/www.oniga.it). Vaporetto Ca' Rezzonico. **Meals served** noon-2.30pm, 7-10.30pm Mon, Wed-Sun. Closed 2wks Jan; 2wks Nov. **Average** €38. **Credit** AmEx, DC, MC, V. **Map** p311 B1.
A new arrival with tables outside on bustling campo San Barnaba, Oniga has a friendly, local feel. The menu is down-home Venetian with a meaty slant (try the pork chop with potatoes and figs), though Hungarian chef Annika also does an excellent goulash. Her husband Marino, who works the front of the house, is a real wine expert. At lunchtime, a meat or fish two-course menu (including side salad and coffee, but not wine) is offered for €14 a head. Don't miss the desserts – especially the ricotta pie and the chocolate tart.

Pizzerie

Casin dei Nobili 🔢
Dorsoduro 2765, sottoportego del Casin dei Nobili (041 241 1841). Vaporetto Ca' Rezzonico. **Meals served** noon-10.30pm Tue-Sun. **Average** €15 pizzeria; €35 full meal. **Credit** AmEx, DC, MC, V. **Map** p311 B1.
Just off campo San Barnaba, this large pizzeria-restaurant with an artsy-rustic decor serves up tasty pizzas to a mainly student clientele. There is the usual range of Venetian *primi* and *secondi* on offer as well, but you'll eat better, and certainly more cheaply, if you stick to the pizzas. A garden out the back is a summer bonus.

La Giudecca & San Giorgio

Restaurants & *bacari*

Harry's Dolci 🔢
Giudecca 773, fondamenta San Biagio (041 522 4844/www.cipriani.com). Vaporetto Sant'Eufemia. **Meals served** Apr-Oct noon-3pm, 7-11pm Wed-Sun. Closed Nov-Mar. **Average** €75. **Credit** AmEx, DC, MC, V. **Map** p310 C3.
Arrigo Cipriani's second Venetian stronghold (his first is Harry's Bar, *see p166*), towards the western end of the Giudecca, is only open from April to October, when the weather allows diners to enjoy the huge terrace with stupendous views across the Giudecca Canal. The cuisine is supposedly lighter and more summery than chez Harry, but in practice many dishes – such as the flagship risottos – are identical and just as competently prepared. What changes is the cost: prices at Harry II are less than two-thirds of those at the mother ship (though that's still a big dent in the average wallet). Come prepared for mosquitoes on summer evenings.

Mistrà 🔢
Giudecca 212°, fondamenta Ponte Lungo (041 522 0743). Vaporetto Redentore or Giudecca-Palanca. **Meals served** noon-3.30pm Mon; noon-3.30pm, 7.30-10.30pm Wed-Sun. Closed 3wks Jan; 3wks Aug. **Average** €40. **Credit** AmEx, DC, MC, V. **Map** p311 D1.
The unvisited southern side of the Giudecca is about as far as you can get from tourist Venice and it conceals one of the city's most unlikely gourmet treats. Amid a sprawl of boatyards, a fire-escape staircase leads up to this trattoria on the first floor of a warehouse with spectacular views over the southern lagoon. Once patronised exclusively by local shipwrights and gondola makers, Mistrà has become a word-of-mouth success among local foodies for its excellent fish menu (octopus and potato salad, baked fish with potatoes, cherry tomatoes and olives) and range of Ligurian specialities; they also do good steaks, if you're all fished out. Lunch is cheap and worker-oriented, dinner more ambitious and a little more expensive.

L'Avogaria. *See p162.*

Lido

Restaurants & *bacari*

La Favorita

*Via Francesco Duodo 33 (041 526 1626). Vaporetto
Lido.* **Meals served** 12.30-2.30pm, 7.30-10.30pm
Tue; 7.30-10.30pm Wed-Sun. **Average** €55. **Credit**
AmEx, DC, MC, V. **Map** p306.

If you need to clinch a big deal with some industry
maven at the Venice Film Festival, you'll improve
your chances by inviting them to La Favorita. This
is the best restaurant on the Lido, and has a lovely
vine-shaded pergola for summer dining. It's an old-
fashioned and reassuring sort of place that does text-
book exemplars of Venetian seafood classics like
spaghetti ai caparossoli or *scampi in saor* (sweet-and-
sour sauce), plus a few more audacious dishes like
pumpkin gnocchi with scorpion fish and radicchio.
Service is professional, and the wine list has a fine
selection of bottles from the north-east.

The Lagoon

Restaurants & *bacari*

Alla Maddalena

*Mazzorbo 7B (041 730 151). Motonave LN to
Mazzorbo.* **Meals served** noon-3pm Mon-Wed, Fri-
Sun. Closed 20 Dec-10 Jan. **Average** €30. **Credit**
AmEx, DC, MC, V.

The 12 ferry from Fondamente Nove takes a very
pleasant 45 minutes to chug across the lagoon to the
island of Mazzorbo, the stop before Torcello or

Burano. Right opposite the jetty is this rustic lunch-
only trattoria, which serves filling lagoon cuisine.
During the autumn hunting season, there is no better place for wild duck, sourced directly from local
hunters; the rest of the year, seafood dominates the
menu. Book ahead for Sunday lunch in summer,
when the waterside tables and those in the quiet garden behind fill up with Venetian families. The house
wine comes from the family's own island vineyards.

Antica Trattoria Valmarana

*Murano, fondamenta Navagero 31 (041 739 313).
Vaporetto Navagero.* **Meals served** noon-3pm Tue-
Sun. Closed 3wks Jan. **Average** €45. **Credit** AmEx,
DC, MC, V. **Map** p314.

A touch of class on the isle of glass, this elegant
restaurant occupies a historic palazzo opposite the
Museo dell'Arte Vetrario (*see p141*). With its Murano
chandeliers and stuccoed interior, this is a good
lunch option even on a rainy day. The kitchen does
refined versions of seafood classiccs like *risotto alla
pescatora*, with grilled fish starring among the *secondi*. In summer, there are two alfresco options: outside by the canal, or in the quiet garden out the back.

Busa alla Torre

*Murano, campo Santo Stefano 3 (041 739 662/
busaallatorre@virgilio.it). Vaporetto Faro.* **Meals
served** noon-3.30pm daily. **Average** €45. **Credit**
AmEx, MC, V. **Map** p314.

This is Murano's ultimate gastronomic stop-off and
a perfect place for regaining your strength after
resisting the hard sell at the island's many glass
workshops. In summer, tables spill out into a pretty square opposite the church of San Pietro Martire.
The service is deft and professional; the cuisine is

reliable, no-frills seafood cooking, with excellent *primi*. The jovial owner, Lele, is a giant of a man and a real character. Note the lunch-only opening.

Locanda Cipriani 🔟
Torcello, piazza Santa Fosca 29 (041 730 150/ www.locandacipriani.com). Vaporetto LN to Torcello. **Meals served** noon-3pm, 7-9pm Mon, Wed-Sun. Closed Jan. **Average** €70. **Credit** AmEx, DC, MC, V. There is a lot to like about the high-class Locanda Cipriani, which was a haunt of Hemingway. The setting, just off Torcello's pretty square, is idyllic; tables spread over a large vine-shaded terrace during the summer. And although there is nothing remotely adventurous about the cuisine, it's good in anold-fashioned way, as are the waiters. Specialities such as *risotto alla Torcellana* (with seasonal vegetables) or *filetti di San Pietro alla Carlina* (John Dory fillets with capers and tomatoes) are done with competence, and the desserts – including a calorific giant meringue – are tasty treats for rich kids.

Wines of the Veneto

Long typecast as northern Italy's supplier of cheap, dependable plonk, the Veneto region is now in the middle of an image makeover, thanks to a small, energetic cluster of winemakers, spread across the region, who use local grape varieties like corvina and garganega to turn out some fine and complex wines. True, the Veneto area still produces more wine per annum than either Tuscany or Piedmont, and the region's whites still stand in the shadow of their Friulian cousins, especially those from the Collio and Colli Orientali del Friuli appellations. But the best valpolicellas and amarones are now extremely good; and even soave, that two-litre party standby, has its refined, high-class alter ego. The Veneto is also home to Italy's favourite fizz, prosecco – so ubiquitous that the standard term for a glass of sparkling wine is '*un bicchiere di prosecco*'.

The following are the grape varieties you are most likely to come across in wine bars and *bacari*:

RED
Cabernet: When Venetians ask for a glass of cabernet, they generally mean cabernet franc rather than its more famous and well-travelled cousin, cabernet sauvignon. A staple of the Veneto's upland wine enclaves, the grape yields an honest, moreish red with an unmistakeable grassy aroma. Some of the best cabernets in the Veneto come from the up-and-coming Colli Berici area – Mattiello, Costozza and Cavazza are some of the producers to look out for.
Raboso: The classic Venetian winter-warming red, raboso is like the Venetian character – rough, acidic, tannic and entirely lacking in pretension. The best kind is the stuff served from a huge demijohn in your local bacaro.
Valpolicella, Recioto della Valpolicella & Amarone: An often disappointing red from the hills north and west of Verona, standard valpolicella suffers from overstretched DOC boundaries and overgenerous yields. But the best, bottled as valpolicella classico or valpolicella superiore, can be very good indeed. Amarone and recioto, the area's two famous passito wines, are made from partially-dried valpolicella grapes.

Recioto is the sweet version, amarone the dry. In the right hands, the latter can be explosive: powerful, smoky and concentrated, with bags of ripe fruit. The best producers include Allegrini (recioto), Bussola, Cantina Sociale Valpolicella, Corte Sant'Alda, Dal Forno, Masi (amarone), Quintarelli (amarone), Viviani and Zenato.

WHITE & SPARKLING
Soave & Recioto di Soave: In the small soave classico area, a handful of dynamic winemakers is showing that this blend of garganega and trebbiano is capable of greater things than its party-lubricant reputation would suggest: look out in particular for Pieropan's La Rocca or Calvarino selections. In the 1980s a few producers revived the tradition of recioto di soave, a delicious dessert wine made from raisinised garganega grapes. Best producers include Anselmi, Ca' Rugate, Gini, Inama, Pieropan and Suavia.
Prosecco di Conegliano & Valdobbiadene: The classic Veneto dry white fizz, prosecco comes from vineyards around the towns of Valdobbiadene and Conegliano in the rolling hills north of Treviso (*see pxxx*). The grape is subjected to a double fermentation, using the Charmat method; the result is a light, dry, sparkling wine with a bitter finish.

The most highly prized (and expensive) version of prosecco is known as cartizze. A more rustic, unfizzy version – known as prosecco spento – is served by the glass in bacari. Best producers include Bisol, Bortolomiol, Col Vetoraz, Le Colture, Nino Franco and Ruggeri & C.

Cafés, Bars & Gelaterie

There's a drink and a place for every time of day.

Hotel Monaco. *See p166.*

Italian bars and cafés (the terms are pretty much interchangeable) are multi-purpose establishments, and Venice is no exception to this rule. The city offers an abundance of choices catering to everyone from early birds to night owls (for late bars, *see also pp212-7*). Bars serve breakfast, light meals, pastries, wines by the glass… just about everything short of seated and served three-course meals.

Time of day does not dictate what's on offer. Coffee is an all-day pick-me-up; a *spritz* – *the* Venetian tipple (*see p166* **Bar talk**) – can be sipped at any hour; and far from being a mere post-prandial *digestivo*, grappa is what many north-eastern Italian workers use to take the chill off the morning.

If a pre-breakfast grappa doesn't float your boat, then your first daily café- stop will be for coffee. Venice's relationship with this beverage is a long and important one. The city's first *bottega del caffè* opened in 1683 in piazza San Marco. By the late 18th century as many as 24 coffee shops graced this square alone.

San Marco continues to function as the city's most prestigious coffee-sipping drawing room, with two landmark cafés staring each other out across the square: the **Caffè Florian** (*see p166*) and the **Gran Caffè Quadri** (*see p150*), both finely preserved examples of 19th-century café culture.

In most Italian cities, wine is sought out at very specific addresses; in Venice, good wine is as easy to find as the next bridge. The best bars offer an enormous choice of top-quality wines by the glass; bars specialising in wine are called *enoteche* or *bacari* (with the accent on the first a). *Bacari* are typically Venetian wine bars, usually with a range of tapas-like snacks on the counter, called *cicheti*. In some, food has become a key element: these are included in the **Eating Out** chapter on pp148-64. Where drinking remains the focal point, they are listed below.

PASTICCERIE AND GELATERIE

Many of Venice's cake and ice-cream emporia double up as bars, with the usual coffee and liquor offerings in addition to freshly prepared cakes and pastries.

The Venetian day begins with a cappuccino and *brioche* (pronounced the French way), preferably a hot one baked on the premises and kept warm until it is ready to be consumed. Any important meal invitation – and that includes Sunday with family or friends – involves investing in a big tray of sweet things to be shared. But in the lagoon city, cakes also take centre stage at *aperitivo* time: some of the best *spritz* in town are served at Venice's *pasticcerie*. Each *pasticceria* bakes its own specialities, so no two bakeries are ever alike and no two pastries ever taste the same.

Gelato was probably brought down to Venice by the settlers from the icy Dolomite mountains when they fled to the lagoon in ages past. Nowadays ice-cream shops are almost as numerous in Venice as mask shops. And as with mask shops, the quality of product varies greatly from place to place. A quick, foolproof, test of any shop is to eyeball the tub of banana ice-cream – it it's grey in colour, you know it's the real deal: bright yellow screams that it's been made from a mix.

Bar talk

A selection of useful terms to help in ordering any time of the day:

Drinking...

bicchiere glass; **caffè americano** espresso diluted with hot water, served in a larger cup; **caffè** espresso; **caffè corretto** espresso with a shot of alcohol (usually grappa); **caffè doppio** double espresso; **caffè lungo** espresso made with slightly more water; **caffè macchiato** espresso with a dash of milk; **decaffeinato** decaf – can be **caffè decaffeinato** (decaf espresso) or **cappuccino decaffeinato** (decaf cappuccino); **enoteca** wine bar and/or bottle shop; **fragolino** sweet white or red wine made from a particular strawberry-scented grape; **a mescita** (wine) by the glass; **ombra** small glass of wine; **prosecco** light, sparkling white wine;

prosecco spento prosecco with no bubbles; **spritz** classic Venetian aperitivo of white wine, Campari and a shot of selzer or sparkling water; a sweeter version is made with low-alcohol Aperol.

Eating...

baccalà mantecato whipped codfish, usually served on warmed bread or polenta squares; **brioche** croissant, pastry; **cicheto** tapas-like snack; **crostini** bread with a scrumptious spread or topping; **folpeti** tiny octopus; **panino** filled roll; **pizzette** mini-pizzas; **polpetta** deep-fried meatball made with meat and potatoes; **stuzzichino** bite-sized snack; **tramezzino** sandwich.

Paying...

scontrino receipt; **cassa** cash desk.

Eat, Drink, Shop

San Marco

Cafés & bars

See also p213 **Vitae**, *p213* **Centrale Restaurant Lounge** and *p150* **Quadri**.

Bar all'Angolo

San Marco 3464, campo Santo Stefano (041 522 0710). Vaporetto Sant'Angelo. **Open** 6.30am-9pm Mon-Sat. Closed Jan. **No credit cards. Map** p309 D1.
If you're lucky enough to secure a table outside, you'll be well placed to watch the locals saunter through the campo as you enjoy a coffee or *spritz*. Inside you have your choice of standing at the recently expanded bar or relaxing in one of the comfy seats in the back where you'll find a mixed bag of locals and tourists being served good *tramezzini*, fresh salads and *panini* by friendly staff. There are certainly bigger bars in this busy campo, but none match the quality on offer here.

Caffè Florian

San Marco 56, piazza San Marco (041 520 5641/ www.caffeflorian.com). Vaporetto Vallaresso. **Open** *May-Oct* 10am-midnight daily. *Nov-Apr* 10am-midnight Mon, Tue, Thur-Sun. Closed early Dec-Christmas, 1wk Jan. **Credit** AmEx, DC, MC, V. **Map** p309 D2.
Stepping into Florian sweeps you back to 18th-century Venice as you're swallowed into this mirrored, stuccoed and frescoed jewel of a café. Founded by a certain Floriano Francesconi in 1720 as 'Venezia Trionfante', its present appearance, complete with dozens of intimate wooden *séparés*, dates from an 1859 remodelling. Rousseau, Goethe and Byron hung out here – the last in sympathy, no doubt, with those loyal Venetians who boycotted the Quadri (*see*

p150) across the square where Austrian officers used to meet. Times have changed and these days having a drink at Florian is not so much a political statement as a bank statement – especially if you sit at one of the outside tables, where nothing – not even a humble *caffè* – comes in at less than €8 (*see p166* **Sit-down rip-off**).

Harry's Bar

San Marco 1323, calle Vallaresso (041 528 5777/ www.cipriani.com). Vaporetto Vallaresso. **Open** 10.30am-11pm daily. **Credit** AmEx, DC, MC, V. **Map** p311 B3.
This historic watering hole, founded by Giuseppe Cipriani in 1931, has changed little since the days when Ernest Hemingway came here to work on his next hangover... except for the prices and the numbers of tourists. But despite the pre-dinner crush and some offhand service, a Bellini (fresh peach juice and sparkling wine) at the bar is as much a part of the Venetian experience as a gondola ride (and at €13 far cheaper). At mealtimes, the tables upstairs and down are reserved for diners who enjoy the Venetian-themed international comfort food and are prepared to pay very steep prices (€150-plus for three courses) to be seen chez Harry's. Stick with a Bellini, and don't even think of coming in here in shorts or ordering a *spritz*.

Hotel Monaco and Grand Canal Bar

San Marco 1332, calle Vallaresso (041 520 0211/ www.hotelmonaco.it). Vaporetto Vallaresso. **Open** 10am-midnight daily. **Credit** AmEx, DC, MC, V. **Map** p311 B3.
Inviting and welcoming, the newly refurbished Hotel Monaco and Grand Canal Bar, a short walk from piazza San Marco, is truly a special place to sit back and savour *La Serenissima*. There's a cosy,

compact bar inside (it's just a pity they didn't use the stunning Ridotto theatre – available only for private functions – as an additional bar space) and a divine terrace overlooking the punta della Dogana and the Salute church: it really is just like floating along the Grand Canal. Granted, it's an expensive pleasure (a *spritz* will set you back the not insignificant sum of €8.50) but you're paying for sipping in one of the most enchanting points in the city. If the restaurant looks enticing, you'll be lucky to get a table without booking well ahead.

Enoteche & bacari

See also p150 **Alla Botte.**

Osteria ai Rusteghi
San Marco 5520, campiello del Tentor (041 523 2205). Vaporetto Rialto. **Open** 10am-3pm, 5.30-9pm Mon-Sat. **No credit cards. Map** p309 D2.
This small, cosy place serves some excellent wines by both the bottle and the glass to accompany its delicious mini-sandwiches, which come in 30 or more varieties, including bacon and rosemary, egg and asparagus, and prawns and porcini mushrooms. There are also a few outside tables in a hidden square, just a stone's throw from bustling campo San Bartolomeo. A good find.

Pasticcerie

Zanin
San Marco 4589, campo San Luca (041 522 4803). Vaporetto Rialto. **Open** 7.30am-8pm Mon-Sat; 10.30am-7.30pm Sun. **No credit cards. Map** p309 D2.
Zanin has reinvented this popular bar in campo San Luca by stocking it full of their delicious and award-winning pastries and cakes. This is the first Venice outlet for the highly acclaimed bakery in Mestre. In order to counteract the often bitter coffee they sell, add more sugar than normal to your java or feast on multiple mouth-watering sweets. Their miniature-sized pastries simply beg to be tasted, each one a delectable morsel of whatever filling you've chosen – meringue, pistachio, tiramisu, coffee, to name just a few of those available.

Gelaterie

Igloo
San Marco 3651, calle della Mandola (041 522 3003). Vaporetto Sant'Angelo. **Open** *May-Sept* 11am-8pm daily. *Oct, Nov, Feb-Apr* 11.30am-7pm. Closed Dec, Jan. **No credit cards. Map** p309 D1.
Generous portions of handmade, creamy *gelato* in varieties to please everyone is what Igloo is all about. In the summer months, fruit flavours such as fig or blackberry are made from the nearby market's freshest ingredients. In an area where *gelato* is found around every corner, Igloo is a tried and true favourite.

Castello

Cafés & bars

See also p213 **Inishark Pub.**

Angiò
Castello 2142, ponte della Veneta Marina (041 277 8555). Vaporetto Arsenale. **Open** *June-Sept* 7am-12.30am Mon, Wed-Sun. *Oct-Dec, Feb-May* 7am-9pm Mon, Wed-Sun. Closed Jan. **Credit** MC, V. **Map** p309 D3.
Owned by siblings Andrea and Giorgia, Angiò is the finest stopping point along one of Venice's most tourist-trafficked spots – the lagoon-front riva degli Schiavoni. Tables line the water's edge; ultra-friendly staff serve up pints of Guinness, freshly made sandwiches and interesting selections of cheese and wine. Take in the stunning view of San Giorgio with either a morning coffee or an early evening *aperitivo* and enquire about the regular music events that are held here during the summer months on Saturday evenings.

Vincent Bar
Sant'Elena, viale IV novembre 36 (041 520 4493). Vaporetto Sant'Elena. **Open** 7am-10pm Tue-Sun. **No credit cards. Map** p313 D2.
Sant'Elena must be one of Venice's best-kept secrets – it's surely the only place you'll find more trees and grassy expanses than throngs of tourists. So, when you've had your fill of museums and churches, venture over to the eastern edge of the city and

Bar ai Miracoli. *See p170.*

QUADRI

Gran Caffè Ristorante,
since 1683,
in St. Mark's square, n° 121

Restaurant

Light - Lunch,
A' la Carte Restaurant,
Gala Dinner

Onto "the finest drawing-room in the world"
with supreme quality gastronomy

Café

Welcome Coffee,
Cocktail Reception,
Caffè Concerto
After Dinner Drinks

Piazza San Marco, Venezia, Ph. 041 5222105 - 5289299 - Fax 041 5208041
http://www.quadrivenice.com e-mail: quadri@quadrivenice.com
Closed on Monday in the winter season

Sit-down rip-off

After a hard day's church-viewing, you'll need to take a load off your feet. But remember, before collapsing at a café, that the additional cost of sitting down can amount to anything from small change to a major investment. The more famous the bar, the larger the hole burnt in your wallet... and as the palm court orchestras crank up, the surcharges rise further.

Bear in mind, however, that once you decide to take the plunge and enjoy your cappuccino or *spritz* seated, you can linger as long as you wish – no officious waiter will shoo you away. And the everyday life of Venice is rarely more enjoyable than when viewed from a café table, drink in hand.

	Counter	Table
Ai Do Draghi (see p172)		
Cappuccino	€1.10	€2
Spritz	€1.50	€2
Angiò (see p167)		
Cappuccino	€1.10	€4.20
Spritz	€1	€3.50
Caffè Florian (see p166)		
Cappuccino	€4	€7
Spritz	€3	€9
Gran Caffè Quadri (see p150)		
Cappuccino	€2.60	€7.70
Spritz	€3.20	€9.70
Rosa Salva (see right)		
Cappuccino	€1.30	€2.80
Spritz	€1.50	€3

experience a real Venetian neighbourhood. Grab a seat outside this bar and join the locals gazing lazily across the lagoon at passing boats. Ice-cream is made on the premises. There are also several computers inside with high-speed internet connections (€4.50 per hour).

Enoteche & bacari

See also p154 **Alla Mascareta**.

Alle Alpi (Da Dante)

Castello 2877, corte Nova (041 528 5163). Vaporetto Celestia or San Zaccaria. **Open** 8am-9pm Mon-Sat. Closed Aug. **No credit cards**. **Map** p312 A3.
Tourists? Here? Not likely. If you want to hang with the locals in a place that is as Venetian as it is possible to get, head for this out-of-the-way *bacaro* in the depths of Castello, proudly serving its loyal clientele since 1957. There's white and red wine out of demijohns, and Dante's wife serves up specialities such as *bovoleti* – tiny snails in garlic – and *folpeti* (baby octopus).

All'Aciugheta

Castello 4357, campo Santi Filippo e Giacomo (041 522 4292/info@aciugheta-hotelrio.it). Vaporetto San Zaccaria. **Open** 12.30-11.30pm daily. **Credit** MC, V. **Map** p309 D3.
Skip the expensive pizzeria and muscle your way through to the bar to see the other face of the 'Little Anchovy': a bar packed with locals sampling some excellent wines and fuelling up on a selection of *cicheti*. These include *polpette*, filled peppers, and the trademark *pizzette* (mini-pizzas) with anchovies, to be matched with a glass of red or white chosen from the corked bottles lining the shelf.

Pasticcerie

Da Bonifacio

Castello 4237, calle degli Albanesi (041 522 7507). Vaporetto San Zaccaria. **Open** 7.30am-8.30pm Mon-Wed, Fri-Sun. Closed 3wks Aug, 1wk Christmas. **No credit cards**. **Map** p309 D1.
Hidden away in a narrow calle behind the Danieli Hotel, this is a firm favourite with Venetians. As well as a tempting array of snacks and traditional cakes such as *mammalucchi* (deep-fried batter cakes with candied fruit), they are famous for their creative *fritelle* (wild berry, chocolate, almond and apple fillings in addition to the traditional *fritelle* found around the city), which start to appear on the scene in January and remain until Carnevale has come to a close. Each season brings a new pastry to their line-up, so don't be shy, and ask what's special when you're visiting.

Pasticceria Melita

Castello 1000/1004, fondamenta Sant'Anna (no phone). Vaporetto Giardini. **Open** 8am-2pm, 3.30-8.30pm Tue-Sun. **No credit cards**. **Map** p313 B2.
Your senses will reel at the dizzying assortment of pastries on offer here. Don't let the brusqueness of the pastry chef put you off: he made pastries for the Hotel Danieli for 20 years before opening his own piece of sweet paradise here in the 1980s. This is a local favourite, and it's considered a real find by adventurous tourists taking time to explore areas off Venice's beaten path.

Rosa Salva

Castello 6779, campo Santi Giovanni e Paolo (041 522 7949). Vaporetto Fondamente Nove. **Open** 7.30am-8.30pm Mon-Sat. **No credit cards**. **Map** p309 C3.
Take the time and pay the higher prices to sit down and savour the history which surrounds you in campo Santi Giovanni e Paolo – widely considered the most striking after piazza San Marco – while nursing one of the smoothest cappuccini in town and trying one of Rosa Salva's delicious cakes. If it's ice-cream you fancy, all their flavours are made on the premises. The Bartolomeo Colleoni equestrian monument (see p93) was being spruced up as this guide went to press, but the glorious façade of the Scuola Grande di San Marco (see p96) is now back on view.

Eat, Drink, Shop

Boutique del Gelato.

Gelaterie

Boutique del Gelato

Castello 5727, salizzada San Lio (041 522 3283).
Vaporetto Rialto. **Open** *June-Sept* 10am-11.30pm
daily. *Oct, Nov, Feb-May* 10am-8.30pm daily. Closed
Dec, Jan. **No credit cards. Map** p309 D2.
Most Venetians agree that some of the city's best
gelato is served in this tiny outlet on the busy salizzada San Lio. Be patient, though: there's always a
huge crowd waiting to be served. For €1 – the price
of one flavour almost anywhere else in the city –
they'll let you combine two flavours. Otherwise,
their single-scoop, single-flavour cone is 80¢.

Cannaregio

Cafés & bars

See also p213 **Fiddler's Elbow Irish Pub**.

Bar ai Miracoli

*Cannaregio 6066A, campo Santa Maria Nova (041
523 1515). Vaporetto Rialto.* **Open** 6.30am-11pm
daily. **No credit cards. Map** p309 C2.
There is no lovelier place to pass an afternoon than
sitting outside this bar just behind the glorious
church of Santa Maria dei Miracoli (*see p110*). Small
but lively, campo Santa Maria Nova is beautiful,
which makes a drink or snack here taste especially
good. There are cosy booths inside, though you
might want to check the smoke factor.

Enoteche & bacari

La Cantina

Cannaregio 3689, campo San Felice (041 522 8258).
Vaporetto Ca' d'Oro. **Open** 10am-10pm Mon-Sat.
Closed 2wks July-Aug; 2wks Jan. **No credit cards.**
Map p309 C1.
Francesco and Andrea are justifiably proud of their
enoteca, with its warm, cosy ambience indoors and
tables outside set back from the bustling strada

Nuova. The friendly staff will help you to order a
plate (or two or three) piled high with mouth-watering crostini, made on the spot with whatever's in season by food 'artist' Francesco: your plate is his
canvas. Some 30 wines are available by the glass,
costing the same whether you're standing at the bar
or seated – a rarity in Venice. (If it's *spritz* you want,
go elsewhere.)

Pasticcerie

Boscolo

*Cannaregio 1818, campiello de l'Anconeta (041
720 731). Vaporetto San Marcuola.* **Open** *Aug-June*
6.40am-8.40pm Tue-Sun. Closed July; 2wks Feb.
No credit cards. Map p309 B1.
The bar at Maria Boscolo's *pasticceria* is always
packed; locals flock to enjoy an extra-strong *spritz*
al bitter with one of her home-made *pizzette*. There
is also an excellent assortment of Venetian sweets:
frittelle during Carnevale, as well as *zaleti* and *pin-
cia* (a sweet bread that is made with cornflour and
raisins). Chocolates in the form of interesting (and
graphic) kama sutra positions have made this con-
fectioner's famous.

Gelaterie

Il Gelatone

*Cannaregio 2063, rio terà Maddalena (041 720
631). Vaporetto San Marcuola.* **Open** *May-Sept*
10.30am-11pm daily. *Oct-mid Dec, mid Jan-Apr*
10.30am-8.30pm daily. Closed mid Dec-mid Jan.
No credit cards. Map p309 D1.
Follow the trail of overflowing ice-cream cones
between the railway station and the end of strada
Nuova and you'll easily find Il Gelatone, just as
hungry ice-cream seekers have been doing for the
last 17 years. The luscious ice-cream comes in a
number of gorgeous flavours and satisfyingly generous portions: the yoghurt-flavoured variety with
sesame seeds and honey is especially suited to
those with a sweet tooth.

San Polo & Santa Croce

Cafés & bars

See also p214 **Ai Postali**, *p211* **Bagolo** and *p214* **Da Baffo**.

Caffetteria Caffè del Doge

San Polo 609, calle dei Cinque (041 522 7787/ www.caffedeldoge.com). Vaporetto San Silvestro. **Open** 7am-7pm daily. **No credit cards.** **Map** p309 D2.

Italians, it's true, scoff at the idea of drinking cappuccino after 11am, but rules like this go by the board at the Caffè del Doge, a temple to coffee culture, where any time is good for indulging in the richest, creamiest and most luscious cup of coffee you'll taste in Venice. It's a bright, minimalist space designed to eliminate any distractions from the matter at hand: coffee. Thirteen blends, imported exclusively, are available for your tasting pleasure in various preparations from espresso to filtered. Each is also available for purchase. Don't overlook the freshly made pastries, sweets and natural juices, and watch out for the speciality coffees, for which a portion of each sale goes to their own *I bambini del caffè* (The Children of Coffee), a non-profit organisation that assists children who work on coffee plantations around the world.

Muro Vino e Cucina

San Polo 222, campo Cesare Battisti già Bella Vienna (041 523 7495). Vaporetto Rialto. **Open** 9am-3.30pm, 5pm-1am Mon-Sat. **No credit cards.** **Map** p309 C2.

In an area where it's easier to find an *ombra* than a *spritz*, Muro Vino e Cucina has been packed by throngs of thirsty *spritz*-seekers since its recent opening. In the colourful area around the Rialto markets, American architect Michael Foroutan's first project in Italy has become a wild success, drawing a mix of locals, curious onlookers and tourists who make their way to the bar at all hours. The sleek, modern design is complemented by the exceptionally friendly and warm staff. The express lunch is easy on the wallet; snag an upstairs window seat for a front-row view over the theatrics of the markets.

Bar Ai Nomboli

San Polo 2717B, rio terà dei Nomboli (041 523 0095). Vaporetto San Tomà. **Open** 7am-9pm Mon-Fri. Closed 1wk Christmas; 3wks Aug. **No credit cards.** **Map** p308 D3.

This bar, much adored by the student population, has expanded its impressive repertoire of sandwich combinations. You'll need to summon all your decision-making skills when faced with more than 100 sandwiches and almost 50 *tramezzini* choices: try the 'Serenissima' with tuna, peppers, peas and onions or ask them to build your own creation, using any of their fresh ingredients. Take a seat outside, even in inclement weather, when the wide awning will keep you nice and dry.

Caffè dei Frari

San Polo 2564, fondamenta dei Frari (041 524 1877). Vaporetto San Tomà. **Open** 8am-9pm Mon-Sat. Closed 2wks Aug. **No credit cards.** **Map** p308 D3.

A cosy bar with an even cosier mezzanine, which is often packed with students skipping lectures at the nearby university and lawyers from surrounding offices. The walls feature art nouveau interpretations of 18th-century Venice. This is the logical place to frequent after a morning or afternoon spent visiting the nearby Frari church or the Scuola Grande di San Rocco. Sit back and relax in one of their comfortable booths and enjoy a tasty spread of snacks, which accompany all of the *aperivi* and drinks.

Enoteche & bacari

Marcà

San Polo 213, campo Cesare Battisti già Bella Vienna (no phone). Vaporetto Rialto. **Open** 7am-3pm, 6-9.30pm Mon-Sat. **No credit cards.** **Map** p309 C2.

With standing room only in the campo, Marcà has been serving Rialto market goers with their victuals since 1918. Neatly packed into this tiny space is a snack-filled case with meatballs, artichoke hearts and mini-sandwiches in addition to more than 34 different options for panini toppings and a generous selection of wines by the glass.

Do Mori

San Polo 429, calle dei Do Mori (041 522 5401). Vaporetto Rialto or San Silvestro. **Open** 8.30am-8.30pm Mon-Sat. **No credit cards.** **Map** p309 C2.

The Do Mori – in a narrow lane in Rialto market territory – claims to be the oldest *bacaro* in town, dating back to 1462 when Jacopo Tintoretto was leaving his painted mark around town. Batteries of copper polenta pans still hang from the ceiling, and at peak times the narrow bar is a heaving mass of bodies, all lunging for the excellent *francobolli* (mini-sandwiches) and the tremendous selection of fine wines. But don't point to a label at random, as prices can sometimes be in the connoisseur bracket. You won't go far wrong if you stick to a glass of the classic *spento* – prosecco minus the bubbles.

Da Lele

Santa Croce 183, campo dei Tolentini (no phone). Vaporetto Piazzale Roma. **Open** 6am-2pm, 4.30-8pm Mon-Fri; 6am-2pm Sat. **No credit cards.** **Map** p308 D2.

There are plenty of bars to be found around the bus station at piazzale Roma, but most of them are either sleazy or overpriced (or both). Gabriele's (Lele's) place is the first authentic *osteria* for those arriving in Venice – or the last for those leaving; look for the two barrels outside and you've found it. It's so small in here there isn't even room for a phone – but there are local wines from Piave, Lison and Valdobbiadene and fresh rolls are made to order with meat and/or cheese fillings.

Al Prosecco

Santa Croce 1503, campo San Giacomo dell'Orio (041 524 0222). Vaporetto San Stae. **Open** *Sept-Dec, Feb-July* 8am-10pm Mon-Sat. Closed Jan, Aug. **No credit cards. Map** p308 C3.

Sparkling (or still) white prosecco is second only to *spritz* in terms of daily Venetian consumption. The shaded outside tables at this café are at a fantastic vantage point to allow you to observe daily interactions in a lively campo, but the interior is just as convivial on cooler days. Exceptional wines are served by the glass, with a first-rate choice of cheeses, cold meats, marinated fish and oysters to accompany any selection from the bar.

Pasticcerie

Rizzardini

San Polo 1415, campiello dei Meloni (041 522 3835). Vaporetto San Silvestro. **Open** 7am-8.30pm Mon, Wed-Sun. Closed Aug. **No credit cards. Map** p309 D1.

An eye-catching *pasticceria* with pastries, cookies and snacks to match. When owner Paolo is behind the bar, there's never a dull moment. It's especially good for traditional Venetian pastries, and *frittelle* during Carnevale, if you can manoeuvre up to the counter and place your order.

Gelaterie

Alaska Gelateria-Sorbetteria

Santa Croce 1159, calle larga dei Bari (041 715 211). Vaporetto Riva de Biasio. **Open** *Apr-Oct* 11am-midnight daily. *Nov, Feb-Mar* noon-9pm Tue-Sun. Closed Dec, Jan. **No credit cards. Map** p308 C3.

Carlo Pistacchi is passionate about making ice-cream and experimenting with new flavours using only the freshest natural ingredients. If you are feeling cautious, stick to tried and true favourites such as hazelnut or yoghurt; braver types should branch out to sample exotic flavours which change depending on the season, such as artichoke, fennel, celery, asparagus or ginger. Multiple visits are in order, not only to experience a variety of flavours but also to fully enjoy Roma-supporter Carlo's antics.

Dorsoduro

Cafés & bars

See also p214 **Il Caffè**; *p214* **Café Blue**; *p214* **Café Noir**; *p215* **Orange**.

Al Chioschetto

Dorsoduro 1406A, fondamenta delle Zattere (348 396 8466/338 117 4077). Vaporetto Zattere. **Open** *June-Sept* 7.30am-12am daily. *Oct-May* 7.30am-5pm daily. **No credit cards. Map** p310 C3.

A much-loved spot not only for scrumptious panini and nibbles, but also for the tranquillity of sitting outside along the Giudecca Canal with a sweeping

view from industrial Marghera to Palladian San Giorgio Maggiore. Inclement weather poses a problem as seating is strictly outside, so take advantage of any sunny day and head over here for your daily bar needs.

Ai Do Draghi

Dorsoduro 3665, calle della Chiesa (041 528 9731). Vaporetto San Tomà. **Open** *Apr-Oct* 7.30am-2am daily. *Nov-Mar* 7.30am-11pm daily. **No credit cards. Map** p308 D3.

Throngs of cheerful *spritz* drinkers cram into the small calle off campo Santa Margherita where the entrance to Ai Do Draghi is located – and also on to its numerous tables on the square – to enjoy draught beers, strong *spritz al bitter* and approximately 40 wines by the glass. Not only are the staff friendly and courteous, but the outdoor seating provides one of the best vantage points from which to observe the energetic and bustling pace of campo Santa Margherita. The indoor seating, a well-kept secret, is intimate and snug.

Da Gino

Dorsoduro 853A, calle Nuova Sant'Agnese (041 528 5276). Vaporetto Accademia. **Open** 6am-7.30pm Mon-Sat. Closed Aug; 2wks Dec-Jan. **No credit cards. Map** p311 B1.

You'll always be greeted with a smile by the Scarpa family, whether it's your first or your 100th visit; they take customer service seriously in a city where so many tourists make for some cranky hosts. During the warmer months, tables outside along the calle make excellent viewpoints for watching the flow of gallery-goers making their way between the Accademia and the Guggenheim Collection. A recent no-smoking policy means that should you opt to stand inside at the bar (where the Scarpas' dedication to the Inter football team is much in evidence), you won't need to worry about the effects of second-hand smoke. Stop in often and at any time of the day to enjoy breakfast, lunch and late-afternoon drinks. Serves some of the best *tramezzini* and made-to-order panini around.

Enoteche & bacari

Cantinone (già Schiavi)

Dorsoduro 992, fondamenta Nani (041 523 0034). Vaporetto Accademia or Zattere. **Open** 8am-8.30pm Mon-Sat; 9am-1pm Sun. Closed 1wk Aug. **No credit cards. Map** p311 C1.

Two generations of the Gastaldi family work here, filling glasses, carting cases of wine, and preparing huge panini with mortadella or more delicate crostini with, for example, creamy tuna spread with leeks or parmesan and figs. If you're thinking about making this your lunch stop, give yourself ample opportunity to select from the day's offerings by coming before the crowds pour in at 1pm. When the bar itself is full, the steps on the nearby bridge outside make a good background for the Venetian ritual of *spritz* and prosecco consumption.

Gobbetti.

Vinus Venezia

Dorsoduro 3961, calle del Scaleter (041 715 004).
Vaporetto San Tomà. **Open** *June-Sept* 10am-1pm;
3pm-midnight daily. *Oct-May* 10am-midnight daily.
Credit MC, V. **Map** p308 D3.

Come in from the cold to warm up at one of Venice's
newest winebars. The corks piled high in the window are a dead giveaway as to the business at hand
and the young owners will be delighted if you sit
down, taste some wine and help add to the ever-
growing collection. More than 50 wines are available
by the glass, and in addition to some standard crostini on offer, a raw fish bar entices the palate. Despite
first impressions, the cherry-wood seats are surprisingly comfortable. There are few tables, which
makes it a bit of a squeeze when crowded.

Pasticcerie

Gobbetti

Dorsoduro 3108B, rio terà Canal (041 528 9014).
Vaporetto Ca' Rezzonico. **Open** 7am-8pm daily.
Credit AmEx, MC, V. **Map** p308 D3.

Don't judge this *pasticceria* by its size. Though this
shop is tiny, Gobbetti produces some of Venice's
most delicious cakes and sells them in various
outlets throughout the city. Their sought-after
chocolate mousse is their claim to fame and soon
disappears after the day's fresh batch is displayed.
If the whole cakes are sold out, check the display
case for single servings.

Tonolo

*Dorsoduro 3764, calle San Pantalon (041 523
7209). Vaporetto San Tomà.* **Open** 7.45am-8.30pm
Tue-Sat; 7.45am-1pm Sun. Closed Aug. **No credit
cards. Map** p308 D3.

On a busy street that runs into the constantly
bustling campo Santa Margherita, this Venice institution has been operating in this same spot ever
since 1953. The coffee is exceptional, and on
Sundays the place fills up with locals buying sweet
offerings to take to lunch – don't be shy about assert-
ing your rights or you may never get served. All the
delectable pastries – which are candy for the eyes as
well as the stomach – come in miniature sizes to
make sampling that little bit easier.

Gelaterie

Gelateria Lo Squero

*Dorsoduro 989/990, fondamenta Nani (041
241 3601). Vaporetto Accademia or Zattere.*
Open 10.30am-9pm daily. **No credit cards.**
Map p311 C1.

Simone Sambo truly loves his job as maker of some
of the finest ice-cream in Venice. He's hard-pressed
to pinpoint a favourite flavour, but can happily rat-
tle off which are currently in his repertoire – which
always depends on the freshest ingredients available. His mousse series (blueberry, strawberry,
amaretto, chocolate and hazelnut, among others) is
so light and creamy that it's served in a waffle cone
so it doesn't land in the adjacent canal.

Shops & Services

Masks, lace and Body Shop – but practicalities are harder to track down.

Eat, Drink, Shop

In its heyday, the Venetian Republic was the great commercial centre, a sorting house from which an enormous influx of goods from the East was distributed around the Western world. Exotic spices and raw silks were among the goods imported and sold by shrewd Venetian merchants. The luxurious brocades and damasks, Burano lace and Murano glassware still produced and found in the city are the legacy of *La Serenissima*'s prosperous past. Though the prices of such authentic Venetian-made goods can be prohibitive, a recent resurgence of local artisans – shoemakers, jewellers, carpenters, mask makers and blacksmiths – has led to slightly more competitive rates, and has helped to keep traditional techniques alive.

The main retail areas are the **Mercerie** – the maze of crowded, narrow alleyways leading from piazza San Marco to the Rialto – and the streets known collectively as the Frezzeria, which wind between La Fenice (*see p219*) and piazza San Marco. The densest concentration of big-name fashion outlets can be found around the calle larga XXII Marzo, just west of the piazza, where the top names such as Prada, Fendi, Versace and Gucci have all staked their boutiques.

Devotees of kitsch should not miss the stalls and shops near the train station, where plastic gondolas, illuminated gondolas, flashing gondolas, musical gondolas and even gondola cigarette lighters reign supreme.

For more tasteful souvenirs, Venice's glass, lace, fabrics and handmade paper are legendary – as are the made-in-Taiwan substitutes that are passed off as the genuine article by unscrupulous traders. Sticking to the outlets listed below will help you to avoid unpleasant surprises.

With the steady demographic drop has come the demise of 'useful' shops: bread, fruit and veg, milk and meat are increasingly difficult to get hold of. And while new supermarkets have opened in various parts of the city and on the Giudecca, the flip side of this is the threat now posed to the livelihood of those few greengrocers, bakers and butchers that remain.

OPENING HOURS AND TAX REBATES

Most food shops are closed on Wednesday afternoons, while some non-food shops stay shut on Monday mornings. During high season

Madera. *See p179.*

(which in Venice includes Carnevale in February/March, Easter, the summer season from June to October and the four weeks leading up to Christmas) many shops abandon their lunchtime closing and stay open all day, even opening on Sundays.

It pays to be sceptical about the hours posted on the doors of smaller shops: opening times are often determined by volume of trade or personal whim. If you want to be sure of not finding the shutters drawn, call before you set out.

Incomprehensibly – given that summer is Venice's busiest season – some shops close for holidays in August, but the majority of these are smaller ones that cater more for residents than tourists, such as *tabacchi* (*see p291*), photocopying centres and dry-cleaners.

If you are not an EU citizen, remember to keep your official receipt (*scontrino*) as you are entitled to a rebate on IVA (sales tax) paid on purchases of personal goods costing more than €154, as long as they leave the country unused and are bought from a shop that provides this service. Make sure that there is a sign displayed in the window and also ask for the form that you'll need to show at customs upon departure.

One-stop shopping

For obvious reasons, which relate primarily to lack of space, Venice is not shopping-centre friendly. If you are looking for a mall to fill all your needs, you'll have to journey to the mainland. Smart shoppers take the free shuttles from piazzale Roma to Mestre where malls and department stores are a dime a dozen.

Centro Commerciale Valecenter
Via E Mattei 1, Marcon (041 596 9012/ valecenter@tsc4.com). Free bus service to & from piazzale Roma. **Open** 2-9pm Mon; 9am-9pm Tue-Fri; 9am-10pm Sat. **Credit** varies.
One of the largest shopping malls on the Venetian mainland with 70 shops including restaurants, a supermarket, home-improvement and sporting goods shops.

Centro Le Barche
Piazza XXVII Ottobre 1, Mestre (041 977 882/ www.lebarche.com). Bus 4 or 4/ from piazzale Roma. **Open** 2-8pm Mon; 9am-8pm Tue-Sat. **Credit** varies.
With a food court on the top floor, a supermarket in the basement and everything else in between, this centre is the mainland home of the Coin department store. Other shops include Feltrinelli bookshop – with a theatre box office and music store – and smaller clothing boutiques.

Coin
Cannaregio 5787, salizada San Giovanni Crisostomo (041 520 3581/www.gruppocoin.it). Vaporetto Rialto. **Open** 9.30am-7.30pm Mon-Sat; 11am-7.30pm Sun. **Credit** AmEx, DC, MC, V. **Map** p309 C2.
Stylish, above-average department store chain. Prices aren't exactly rock-bottom, but there are bargains to be had during sales. The household goods department is good for unpretentious sheets and linens. Cosmetics and women's intimates can be found at the store in campo San Luca.
Other locations: San Marco 4557, campo San Luca (041 523 8444).

Oviesse
Via Corfu 1, Lido (041 526 5720). Vaporetto Lido. **Open** 9am-8pm Mon-Sat; 9am-4pm Sun. **Credit** AmEx, DC, MC, V. **Map** p307.
Low-cost department store with all the basics – men's, women's and children's apparel, cosmetics and household goods. It's where you go if you've forgotten your swimsuit, need underwear or just a towel for the beach. Convenient supermarket on the ground floor.

Antiques

Antique shops can be found throughout the city, though the concentration is greatest around campo San Maurizio and calle delle Botteghe (near campo Santo Stefano). There is also a *mercatino dell'antiquariato* (antiques fair) twice a year, in the week before Easter and Christmas, in campo San Maurizio (**map p311 B2**). Look for flyers around town advertising markets in via Garibaldi (Castello) or in campo Santa Maria Nova (Cannaregio). Although these markets are organised on the fly, they usually take place on Sundays.

Antiquus
San Marco 2973 & 3131, calle delle Botteghe (041 520 6395/antiquus.ve@tin.it). Vaporetto Sant'Angelo. **Open** 10am-12.30pm, 3-7.30pm Mon-Sat. **Credit** AmEx, DC, MC, V. **Map** p311 B2.
This charming shop has a beautiful collection of Old Master paintings, furniture, silver and antique jewellery, including Moors' heads brooches and earrings. **Other locations**: Dorsoduro 873/A (041 241 3725).

Guarinoni
San Polo 2862, calle del Mandoler (041 522 4286). Vaporetto San Tomà. **Open** 8am-12.30pm, 3-7pm Mon-Sat. **Credit** AmEx, MC, V. **Map** p311 A1.
An assortment of antique furnishings from as early as the 16th century is sold here. The shop also has a workshop that restores gilded ceilings and the like.

Art supplies

Angeloni
Galleria Matteotti 2, Mestre (041 974 236/041 986 264). Bus 4 from piazzale Roma to piazza Ferretto. **Open** 9am-12.30pm, 3.30-7.30pm Mon-Fri; 9am-12.30pm Sat. **Credit** MC, V.

Trade enclaves

Reasonably priced gifts and souvenirs produced by local craftspeople can be found all over the city – often clustered in trade enclaves, a medieval legacy.

Stained glass, wrought iron and wooden sculptures can be found in the *calli* (**map p309 C1**) between campo San Polo and campo San Giacomo dell'Orio. Calle de la Mandola (**map p309 D1**) is the street for paper products and glass beads, while antique shops are thick on the ground around campo Santo Stefano (**map p309 D1**). The Dorsoduro side of the ponte dell'Accademia is one of the best places to go for handcrafted masks.

Pleasant service and a wide range of supplies; this is where *real* artists go. The prices are much better than anything you'll find in island Venice.

Arcobaleno
San Marco 3457, calle delle Botteghe (041 523 6818). Vaporetto Sant'Angelo. **Open** 9am-12.30pm, 4-7.30pm Mon-Sat. **No credit cards. Map** p311 B2.
Arcobaleno stocks a vast assortment of artists' pigments – a virtual rainbow of colours. As well as a variety of art supplies, they carry all the basics in hardware, light bulbs and detergents.

Cartoleria Accademia
Dorsoduro 1044, campiello Calbo (041 520 7086). Vaporetto Accademia. **Open** *Sept-June* 8am-1pm, 3.30-7pm Mon-Fri; 8am-1pm Sat. *July, Aug* 9am-12.30pm, 4-7pm Mon-Fri; 9am-12.30pm Sat. **No credit cards. Map** p311 C1.
This small but well-stocked store carries a wide range of artists' supplies and is conveniently located just behind the Accademia. Cartoleria Accademia has been in the business since 1810, so it must be doing something right.
Other locations: Dorsoduro 2928, campo Santa Margherita (041 528 5283).

Cartoleria Arte e Design
Santa Croce 53, campiello Mosca (041 710 269/ artedesign.ve@libero.it). Vaporetto Piazzale Roma. **Open** 8am-1pm, 3-7.30pm Mon-Fri; 8am-1pm, 3-7pm Sat. **Credit** AmEx, DC, MC, V. **Map** p310 A3.
Art supplies of all kinds, including paper of every imaginable shape, colour and size. Mont Blanc, Waterman and Filofax products are available, as well as an impressive range of computer supplies. A favourite with architecture students.

Testolini
San Marco 1744-1748, fondamenta Orseolo (041 522 9265/www.testolini.it). Vaporetto Vallaresso or Rialto. **Open** 9am-7pm Mon-Sat. **Credit** AmEx, DC, MC, V. **Map** p311 B3.

Testolini carries stationery, backpacks, briefcases, calendars and art/office supplies. Branch stores carry computers and accessories. The staff can be on the cool side but the choice is huge… by Venetian standards.

Bookshops

Alberto Bertoni – Libreria
San Marco 3637B, calle rio terà dei Assassini (041 522 9583). Vaporetto Sant'Angelo. **Open** 9am-12.30pm, 3.30-7.30pm Mon-Sat. **Credit** MC, V. **Map** p311 B2.
Just off calle de la Mandola (look for the display case with sale offers marking the turn-off), this well-hidden cavern is home to art books of all kinds, exhibition catalogues and the like, all with significant reductions off cover prices.

Ca' Foscarina
Dorsoduro 3259, campiello degli Squellini (041 522 9602/www.cafoscarina.it). Vaporetto Ca' Rezzonico or San Tomà. **Open** 9am-7pm Mon-Fri; 9am-12.30pm Sat. **Credit** MC, V. **Map** p311 B1.
The official bookstore of the Università Ca' Foscari, with a large selection of books in English, covering literature, poetry, history and travel.

Fantoni Libri Arte
San Marco 4119, salizada San Luca (041 522 0700/ fantonilibriarte@libero.it). Vaporetto Rialto. **Open** 10am-8pm Mon-Sat. **Credit** AmEx, DC, MC, V. **Map** p311 A2.
Beautifully illustrated art, architecture, design, photography and textile books, mostly in Italian. There's also a small selection of cookbooks and works on Venice in English.

Filippi Editore Venezia
Castello 5284, Casselaria (041 523 6916/ filippi.editore@tin.it). Vaporetto San Zaccaria. **Open** 9am-12.30pm, 3-7.30pm Mon-Sat. **Credit** MC, V. **Map** p312 B2.

The cobbler of Venice

When Rolando Segalin hung up his lasts in 2003, it was the end of a Venetian institution… or nearly. For though 'the Cobbler of Venice', creator of some of the watery city's wildest and weirdest footwear, no longer stitches his hand-made shoes, his legacy lives on through his apprentices.

Shoe leather is a particularly important commodity in a city where the main mode of transport is good old Shanks's pony. Antonio Segalin was, then, fairly well assured of enjoying a good livelihood when he set up his cobbler's shop in 1932. His son Rolando moved the workshop to calle dei Fuseri in

1955. It is still there, though now the inspiration behind it is former pupil Daniela Ghezzo (*see p181*).

Segalin drew inspiration from historical paintings and prints, as well as from his Venetian surroundings, for his creations, which famously included a pair of gondola-shaped shoes still on display in the window of his tiny shop.

Former apprentice Giovanna Zanella (*see p181*), on the other hand, creates firework displays for the feet, glorious colour explosions to match her exquisite clothes and accessories.

Venice's longest-running publishing house is a father-and-son operation with more than 400 titles on Venetian history and folklore – all limited editions in Italian. The evocatively dark and dusty flagship store (address below) is a landmark in Venice. **Other locations**: Castello 5763, calle del Paradiso (041 523 5635).

Laboratorio Blu
Cannaregio 1224, campo del Ghetto Vecchio (041 715 819/laboratorio.blu@libero.it). Vaporetto Guglie. **Open** 4-7.30pm Mon; 9.30am-12.30pm, 4-7.30pm Tue-Sat. **Credit** AmEx, DC, MC, V. **Map** p308 B3.
The only children's bookshop in Venice. Laboratorio Blu carries a good selection of books in English and offers courses for kids – drawing, painting, weaving and story telling.

Libreria Mondadori
San Marco 1345, salizada San Moisè (041 522 2193/www.libreriamondadorivenezia.it). Vaporetto Vallaresso. **Open** 10am-10pm Mon-Sat; 3-8pm Sun. **Credit** AmEx, DC, MC, V. **Map** p311 B3.
Venice's only mega-bookshop sprawls over three floors, including one reserved for exhibits, book signings, events and courses of various kinds. There's a wide selection of English and other foreign language books.

Libreria Toletta & Toletta Studio
Dorsoduro 1214, calle Toletta (041 523 2034/ info@libreriatoletta.it). Vaporetto Accademia or Ca' Rezzonico. **Open** Sept-June 9.30am-7.30pm Mon-Sat; 3.30-7.30pm Sun. July, Aug 9.30am-1pm, 3.30-7.30pm Mon-Sat. **Credit** AmEx, DC, MC, V. **Map** p311 B1.
A good source of cheap books, the Toletta offers 20-40% off its stock from usual retail prices. Italian classics, art, cookery, children's books and history (mostly in Italian) all feature, along with a vast assortment of dictionaries and reference books. Next door is the Toletta Studio, which specialises in books about architecture. Toletta Cube (address below) is their newest shop, just across the calle, and it carries art and photography books as well as posters, cards and gadgets.
Other locations: Dorsoduro 1175, calle Toletta (041 241 5660).

Mare di Carta
Santa Croce 222, fondamenta dei Tolentini (041 716 304/www.maredicarta.com). Vaporetto Piazzale Roma. **Open** 9am-1pm, 3.30-7.30pm Mon-Sat. **Credit** AmEx, DC, MC, V. **Map** p310 A3.
A must for boat lovers, this nautical bookshop carries publications in English as well as Italian. The bulletin board has boats for sale for anyone interested in purchasing a gondola.

Studium
San Marco 337C, calle Canonica (041 522 2382/ libstudium@tin.it). Vaporetto San Zaccaria. **Open** 9am-7.30pm Mon-Sat; 10am-2pm, 3.30-7pm Sun. **Credit** AmEx, DC, MC, V. **Map** p312 B1.
Located just behind St Mark's basilica, this two-room shop has a wide selection of works on Venice,

Arras. *See p179.*

travel books and novels in English. Its speciality is revealed in the back room, which is filled with theology studies, icons and prayer books.

Cosmetics & perfumes

Cosmetics and toiletries can be found in the one-stop stores (*see p175*) or in *farmacie*, although prices tend to be higher at chemists. For designer names try smaller, more specialised *profumerie*. For herbal products of any type, such as aromatherapy oils, head for an *erboristeria*.

Il Bottegon
San Polo 806, calle del Figher (041 522 3632). Vaporetto San Silvestro. **Open** 9am-12.45pm, 4-7.30pm Mon-Sat. **Credit** AmEx, MC, DC, V. **Map** p309 D1.
Make a list before you go because you'll be so overwhelmed with how much stuff is crammed into such a tiny space that you'll have forgotten what you came for. As well as cosmetics and toiletries: you'll find pots, pans, rugs and hardware goods.
Other locations: Castello 1311, via Garibaldi (041 521 0780).

L'Erbania
San Polo 1735, calle dei Botteri (041 723 215). Vaporetto San Silvestro or San Stae. **Open** 9.30am-1.30pm, 3.30-7.30pm Tue-Sat. **Credit** AmEx, DC, MC, V. **Map** p309 C1.

A quaint shop near the Rialto where a herbalist will mix up concoctions for you. Alternatively, choose from a variety of prepared creams and perfumes.

Design & household

Ceramics & china

Ceramiche La Margherita
Santa Croce 2345, sottoportico della Siora Bettina (041 723 120/www.lamargheritavenezia.com). Vaporetto San Stae. **Open** 9.30am-1pm, 3.30-7pm Mon-Sat. **Credit** AmEx, MC, V. **Map** p309 C1.
A wonderful collection of handpainted terracotta designed by the English-speaking owner. Plates, bowls, teapots, ornaments and mugs in a variety of colours and patterns.

Fustat
Dorsoduro 2904, campo Santa Margherita (041 523 8504/cin.cin@virgilio.it). Vaporetto Ca'Rezzonico. **Open** 9.30am-4pm Mon-Fri. **Credit** MC, V. **Map** p311 B1.
The pottery is handmade by the owner in this small workshop-outlet. Raku demonstrations and courses are also offered periodically.

Madera
Dorsoduro 2762, campo San Barnaba (041 522 4181/www.maderavenezia.it). Vaporetto Ca' Rezzonico. **Open** 10.30am-1pm, 3.30-7.30pm Mon-Sat. **Credit** AmEx, DC, MC, V. **Map** p311 B1.
Fusing minimalist design with traditional techniques, the young architect and craftswoman behind Madera creates unique objects in wood. She also sells exceptional lamps, ceramics, jewellery and textiles by other European artists.

Sabbie e Nebbie
San Polo 2768A, calle dei Nomboli (041 719 073). Vaporetto San Tomà. **Open** 10am-12.30pm, 4-7.30pm Mon-Sat. **Credit** MC, V. **Map** p308 D3.
A beautiful selection of Italian ceramic pieces as well as refined Japanese works. Also sells handmade objects (lamps, candlesticks) by Italian designers.

Fabrics & accessories

Antichità Marciana
San Marco 1691, Frezzeria (041 523 5666/marciana@2001.com). Vaporetto Vallaresso. **Open** 3.30-7.30pm Mon; 9.30am-1pm, 3.30-7.30pm Tue-Sat. **Credit** DC, MC, V. **Map** p311 B3.
A tasteful selection of antique baubles can be found in this jewel of a shop; its speciality, however, is the richly painted velvets created by the owner in her workshop. A favourite among interior designers.

Arras
Dorsoduro 3235, campiello Squellini (041 522 6460). Vaporetto Ca' Rezzonico. **Open** 9am-1pm, 3.30-7.30pm Mon-Sat. **Credit** AmEx, DC, MC, V. **Map** p311 B1.

Handwoven fabrics are created here in a vast range of colours and textures using different fabrics such as silk, wool and cotton. These unique textiles are then worked into bags, clothing, scarves. Customised designs can be ordered.

Bevilacqua
San Marco 337B, ponte della Canonica (041 528 7581/www.bevilacquatessuti.com). Vaporetto San Zaccaria. **Open** 10am-7pm Mon-Sat; 9.30am-5pm Sun. **Credit** AmEx, DC, MC, V. **Map** p309 D3.
This small shop behind St Mark's basilica offers exquisite examples of both hand- and machine-woven silk brocades, damasks and velvets. The Venetian textile tradition is kept alive by these weavers, who use original 17th-century looms.
Other locations: San Marco 2520, campo Santa Maria del Giglio (041 241 0662).

Fortuny Tessuti Artistici
Giudecca 805, fondamenta San Biagio (041 522 4078). Vaporetto Palanca. **Open** 8.30am-12.25pm, 2-5.30pm Mon-Fri. **Credit** AmEx, MC, V. **Map** p310 D3.
This pared-back factory showroom space almost glows with the exquisite colours and patterns of original Fortuny prints. At an across-the-board price of €150 a metre, you may not be tempted to buy, but it's worth the trip just to see it.

Gaggio
San Marco 3441-3451 calle delle Botteghe (041 522 8574/www.gaggio.it). Vaporetto San Samuele or Sant'Angelo. **Open** 10.30am-1pm, 4-7pm Mon-Fri; 10.30am-1pm Sat. **Credit** AmEx, DC, MC, V. **Map** p311 B2.
Emma Gaggio is a legend among dressmakers and her sumptuous handprinted silk velvets (from €195 a metre) are used to make cushions and wall hangings as well as bags, hats, scarves and jackets.

Il Milione
Castello 6025, campo Santa Marina (041 241 0722/www.ilmilionevenezia.com). Vaporetto Rialto. **Open** 10am-12.30pm, 3-7.30pm Mon-Sat. **Credit** MC, V. **Map** p309 C2.
Handmade lamps and designer-inspired knock-offs that are a little more affordable.

Trois
San Marco 2666, campo San Maurizio (041 522 2905). Vaporetto Giglio. **Open** 4-7.30pm Mon; 10am-1pm, 4-7.30pm Tue-Sat. **No credit cards**. **Map** p311 B2.
This is one of the best places in Venice to buy original Fortuny fabrics – and at considerable savings on UK/US prices (though this still doesn't make them particularly cheap). Made-to-order bead-work masks and accessories are also available.

Venetia Studium
San Marco 2403, calle larga XXII Marzo (041 522 9281/www.venetiastudium.com). Vaporetto Giglio. **Open** 9.30am-7.40pm Mon-Sat; 10.30am-6pm Sun. **Credit** AmEx, DC, MC, V. **Map** p311 B3.

Eat, Drink, Shop

L'Angolo. *See p181.*

machine made, and if it's very cheap it almost certainly hails from Taiwan rather than from some dark Venetian back room where ancient crones sit hunched over their age-old craft. If you want reliable, top-quality (and exorbitant) lace without the bother of taking the trip all the way across to Burano, stick to big names such as Jesurum and Martinuzzi.

Annelie
Dorsoduro 2748, calle lunga San Barnaba (041 520 3277). Vaporetto Ca' Rezzonico. **Open** 9.30am-12.30pm, 4-7.30pm Mon-Sat. **Credit** AmEx, MC, V. **Map** p310 B3.
A delightful shop run by a delightful woman who has a beautiful selection of sheets, tablecloths, curtains, shirts and baby clothes, either fully embroidered or with lace detailing. Antique lace can also be had at reasonable prices.

Jesurum
San Marco 4857, Merceria del Capitello (041 520 6177/www.jesurum.it). Vaporetto Rialto. **Open** 9.30am-7.30pm Mon-Sat; 10.30am-6.30pm Sun. **Credit** AmEx, DC, MC, V. **Map** p309 D2.
Extremely elegant embroidered linens, towels and fabrics, from a lace company that has been going for more than 100 years. In the 19th century it was considered the only place to come for really good lace; it is still renowned for its sophisticated, traditional lace. Be warned – quality costs.

La Fenice Atelier
San Marco 3537, campo Sant'Angelo (041 523 0578/www.lafeniceatelier.it). Vaporetto Sant'Angelo. **Open** 10.30am-7.30pm Mon-Sat; 11am-7.30pm Sun. **Credit** AmEx, MC, V. **Map** p309 D1.
Slightly more affordable than Jesurum (*see above*), this tiny boutique has its workshop on the opposite side of town. It produces hand-embroidered nightgowns, towels and sheets, as well as a catalogue full of designs for made-to-order items.

Martinuzzi
San Marco 67A, piazza San Marco (041 522 5068/martinuzzi@inwind.it). Vaporetto Vallaresso. **Open** Mar-Oct 9am-7.30pm daily. Nov-Feb 9.30am-7pm Mon-Sat. **Credit** AmEx, DC, MC, V. **Map** p309 D2.
The oldest lace shop in Venice, Martinuzzi has exclusive designs for bobbin lace items such as place mats, tablecloths and linens. If you have an odd-sized bed, not to worry – Martinuzzi will create a sheet set especially for you.

Venetia Studium stocks beautiful, pleated silks, in elegant pillows, lamps, scarves, handbags and other accessories in a marvellous range of colours. They are certainly not cheap, but they do make perfect gifts for those who have it all.
Other locations: San Marco 723, Mercerie San Zulian (041 522 9859).

Hardware & kitchenware

Di Pol
Dorsoduro 3117A, campo Santa Margherita (041 528 5451). Vaporetto Ca' Rezzonico. **Open** 8am-12.30pm, 3-7.30pm Mon-Fri; 8am-12.30pm Sat. **Credit** MC, V. **Map** p311 B1.
This hardware store carries a little bit of everything: paint supplies, gardening tools and detergents. Keys are cut too. Most importantly, you can pick up a pair of high-water boots, even hip-high waders for those exceptionally damp days.

Ratti
Castello 5825, calle delle Bande (041 240 4600/rattisrl@tin.it). Vaporetto San Zaccaria or Rialto. **Open** 9.15am-12.30pm, 3.30-7.15pm Mon-Fri; 9.15am-12.30pm Sat. **Credit** AmEx, MC, V. **Map** p309 D3.
If Ratti doesn't have what you're looking for, it's time to worry. There are kitchen utensils, locks and other security items, household goods, televisions, radios, adapters and all kinds of electronic gadgets. They also cut keys.

Lace & linens

Lace is cheaper on the island of Burano (*see p142*) than in the centre of Venice. Bear in mind in both places, however, that if it's cheap, it's

Fashion

All the big-name boutiques (Armani, Prada, Gucci and so on) are clustered around four streets in the vicinity of San Marco: calle Vallaresso; salizada San Moisè and its continuation, calle larga XXII Marzo; calle Goldoni; and the Mercerie. The shops listed below offer something a little different.

Accessories

L'Angolo

Dorsoduro 2755, calle San Barnaba (041 277 7895).
Vaporetto Ca' Rezzonico. **Open** 10am-12.30pm, 4-
7.30pm Mon-Sat. **Credit** DC, MC, V. **Map** p311 B1.
L'Angolo has bags, hats and scarves in rich, colourful fabrics and unique styles. There's also jewellery
and some clothing.

Balocoloc

Santa Croce 2134, calle longa Santa Croce (041
524 0551/www.balocoloc.com). Vaporetto San Stae.
Open 9am-5pm Tue-Fri; 11am-7pm Sat. **Credit**
MC, V. **Map** p309 C1.
This off-the-beaten-track shop offers a nice selection
of stylish and reasonably priced handmade hats. It
also stocks a line of Carnevale wear too.

Hibiscus

San Polo 1060-1061, ruga Rialto/calle dell'Olio (041
520 8989). Vaporetto San Silvestro. **Open** 9.30am-
7.30pm Mon-Sat; 11am-7pm Sun. **Credit** AmEx, DC,
MC, V. **Map** p309 D1.
Viaggio nei colori – a voyage into colour – is the
Hibiscus motto; it is demonstrated on jewellery,
handmade scarves, bags and ceramics with an ethnic flair. Not cheap, but a refreshing change from
glass and mask shops.

ZaZú

San Polo 2750, calle dei Saoneri (041 715 426).
Vaporetto San Tomà. **Open** 3.30-7.30pm Mon; 10am-
1pm, 3.30-7.30pm Tue-Sat. **Credit** AmEx, DC, MC, V.
Map p308 D3.
Clothing and jewels from the East that are very
wearable in the West. There are handbags and other
accessories as well.

Designers

Araba Fenice

San Marco 1822, Frezzeria (041 522 0664).
Vaporetto Giglio or Vallaresso. **Open** 9.30am-7.30pm
Mon-Sat. **Credit** AmEx, DC, MC, V. **Map** p309 D2.
A classic yet original line of women's clothing made
exclusively for this boutique, plus jewellery in ebony
and mother-of-pearl.

Godi Fiorenza

San Marco 4261, rio terà San Paternian (041
241 0866/www.veneziart.com). Vaporetto Rialto
or Vallaresso. **Open** 9.30am-12.30pm, 3.30-7.30pm
Mon-Sat. **Credit** AmEx, DC, MC, V. **Map** p309 D2.
The London-trained Godi designer sisters sell
exquisite knitwear, stylish coats and chiffon evening
tops. All made on the premises, and complemented
with jewellery and shoes.

Leather goods & shoes

The big names in leather – Bruno Magli,
Fratelli Rossetti and Sergio Rossi, to name but

a few – are all located around piazz
For a more modest investment, you
one of the following places.

Francis Model

San Polo 773A, ruga Rialto/ruga del Ravano (041
521 2889). Vaporetto San Silvestro. **Open** 9.30am-
7.30pm Mon-Sat; 10.30am-7.30pm Sun. **Credit**
AmEx, DC, MC, V. **Map** p309 D1.
Handbags and briefcases are produced in this tiny
bottega by a father-and-son team that has been in
the business for more than 40 years.

Mori & Bozzi

Cannaregio 2367, rio terà Maddalena (041 715
261). Vaporetto San Marcuola. **Open** *June, July,*
Nov-Mar 9.30am-12.30pm, 3.30-7.30pm Mon-Sat.
Apr, May, Aug-Oct 9.30am-12.30pm, 3.30-7.30pm
Mon-Sat; 11am-7pm Sun. **Credit** AmEx, DC, MC, V.
Map p309 B1.
Shoes for the coolest of the cool: whatever the latest
fad – pointy or square – it's here. Trendy names and
the designer-inspired.

Daniela Ghezzo Segalin Venezia

San Marco 4365, calle dei Fuseri (041 522 2115).
Vaporetto Rialto or Vallaresso. **Open** 9.30am-
12.30pm, 3.30-7.30pm Mon-Fri; 9am-1pm Sat.
Credit AmEx, DC, MC, V. **Map** p309 D2.
The shoemaking tradition established by Rolando
Segalin, known as 'the Cobbler of Venice', continues
through his apprentice. Some of the most interesting creations are on display in the window, including an extraordinary pair of gondola shoes… there's
no accounting for taste. A pair of Ghezzo's creations
will set you back anything between €500 and
€1,700. Repairs are done as well. *See p176* **The**
Cobbler of Venice.

Giovanna Zanella

Castello 5641, calle Carminati (041 523 5500/
giovannazanella@yahoo.it). Vaporetto Rialto.
Open 9.30am-1pm, 3-7pm Mon-Sat. **Credit** AmEx,
DC, MC, V. **Map** p309 D2.
Venetian designer-cobbler Giovanna Zanella creates
a fantastic line of handmade shoes in an extraordinary variety of styles and colours. A pair of shoes
costs €350 to €500; clogs are slightly 'cheaper' at a
bargain €280. There are bag, hats and a line of glo-
riously coloured clothes too. *See p176* **The Cobbler**
of Venice.

Second-hand clothes

Laboratorio Arte & Costume

San Polo 2235, calle Scaleter (041 524 6242/
euvenezia@libero.it). Vaporetto San Stae. **Open**
10am-midnight Mon-Sat. **Credit** AmEx, DC, MC, V.
Map p309 D1.
Hidden away behind campo San Polo, this shop is
packed with vintage clothing, toys and a great selection of hats from the traditional panama to stylish
creations by the shop's owner. It's one of the only
shops in Venice you'll find open until midnight.

Eat, Drink, Shop

Laura Crovato

San Marco 2995, calle delle Botteghe (041 520 4170). Vaporetto Sant'Angelo. **Open** 4-7.30pm Mon; 11am-1pm, 4-7.30pm Tue-Sat. **Credit** DC, MC, V. **Map** p311 B2.

Nestling between expensive galleries and antique shops, Laura Crovato offers a selection of used clothes and a sprinkling of new items, including raw-silk shirts and scarves, costume jewellery and sunglasses. Being Venice, the shop's not exactly giving it away – even though it's second-hand.

Trend-setters

BA BA

San Polo 2865, campo San Tomà (041 716 353). Vaporetto San Tomà. **Open** 10am-8pm Mon-Sat. **Credit** AmEx, MC, V. **Map** p308 D3.

All the latest from young Italian designers. Not everyone can wear them.

Diesel

San Marco 5315-5316, salizada Pio X (041 241 1937/www.diesel.com). Vaporetto Rialto. **Open** 10am-7.30pm Mon-Sat; 11am-7pm Sun. **Credit** AmEx, DC, MC, V. **Map** p311 A3.

'For successful living' is the motto of this Veneto-based company, whose kooky, club-wise, lifestyle-based styles and advertising campaigns have invaded Europe and North America. This two-storey hipper than hip store has become a landmark on the Venetian shopping scene.

Ser Angiù

Dorsoduro 868, piscina del Forner (041 523 1149). Vaporetto Accademia. **Open** 2-8pm Wed-Sun. **No credit cards**. **Map** p311 C2.

Probably the only outlet store in Venice that sells discounted designer labels. Local ladies line up on Wednesdays to get first pick.

Food & drink

For the freshest fruit, vegetables, meat and fish at the most competitive prices – plus a slice of everyday Venetian life that should not be missed – the market that's held Monday to Saturday morning at the foot of the Rialto bridge is difficult to beat. For (slightly) less crowded market options, the market that sets up halfway along via Garibaldi in the eastern Castello are every morning (except Sunday) is a more sedate affair; at the far end, make your purchases from one of Venice's few remaining boat-emporia.

Elsewhere, morning markets are once-weekly. Stalls are in operation by 7.30am and

Home thoughts

Suffering from pasta burn out? Longing for a whiff of home? Incredibly, uniquely 'other' as it is, Venice can cater to some extent to your real-world cravings.

If you're dying for sushi and are fortunate enough to have the facilities, take advantage of the Rialto fish market and then head over the bridge to **Giacomo Rizzo**. They have all the fixings – sushi rice, seaweed, soy sauce, pickled ginger, wasabi and sake – as well as imported orange marmalade, Duncan Hines cake mixes and Marmite.

With Venice's growing Chinese population, **Wan Xin**'s shop near piazzale Roma has acquired a large following. In addition to the many Chinese specialities on display, you'll find a fine selection of cheap souvenirs, not to mention a few Western favourites like tang juice mix and peanut butter. Elsewhere, the supermarket in campo Santa Margherita, **Punto Sma** (*see p185*), carries a small selection of Mexican food – tortilla chips, salsa and the like. There's also **Drogheria Mascari** (*see p183*).

For familiar scents, on the other hand, Venice, too, has its **Body Shop** and **Lush**.

Body Shop

Cannaregio 3894, strada Nuova (041 277 0333). Vaporetto Ca'D'Oro. **Open** 9.30am-7.30pm Mon-Sat; 10am-7pm Sun. **Credit** DC, MC, V. **Map** p309 C1.

Lush

San Polo 95, ruga Rialto (041 522 1549/ www.lush.it). Vaporetto Rialto. **Open** 10am-7.30pm daily. **Credit** AmEx, DC, MC, V. **Map** p309 D2.
Other locations: Cannaregio 3822, Strada Nuova (041 241 1200). Vaporetto Ca'd'Oro.

Giacomo Rizzo

Cannaregio 5778, calle San Giovanni Crisostomo (041 522 2824). Vaporetto Rialto. **Open** 8.30am-1pm, 3.45-7.30pm Mon, Tue, Thur-Sat; 8.30am-1pm Wed. **Credit** AmEx, DC, MC, V. **Map** p309 C2.

Wan Xin Store

Santa Croce 155, fondamenta Minotto/rio del Gaffaro (041 710 920). Vaporetto Piazzale Roma. **Open** 9am-1.30pm, 3-8pm Mon-Sat; 9am-1.30pm Sun. **No credit cards**. **Map** p308 D2.

stallholders pack up by 1pm: the early bird definitely gets the best of it. On Tuesday, bargain hunters should head for the Lido's Venice-facing riviera B Marcello waterfront, while there's also a small and endearingly unsophisticated market in campo della Chiesa on Sacca Fisola on Friday. Over in Mestre, stalls selling fruit and vegetables, clothes and basic household goods set up behind piazza Ferretto in via Parco Ponci on Wednesday and Friday.

Grocery shops (*alimentari*) offer all the usual staples from around Italy, as well as the odd Venetian speciality such as *baccalà mantecato* (a delectable spread made with dried cod) and *mostarda veneziana* (a sweet-and-sour sauce made with dried fruit).

Butchers and bakers are sadly becoming thin on the ground as the mushrooming supersize sell-everything malls across on the mainland steal their trade.

Venetians are famous for their sweet tooth. There is, therefore, an extraordinary variety of calorific delights to devour while strolling through the *calli*; see also *pp165-73* **Cafés, Bars & Pasticcerie**.

Alimentari

Aliani
San Polo 654-655, ruga Rialto/ruga vecchia San Giovanni (041 522 4913). Vaporetto San Silvestro. **Open** 8am-1pm Mon; 8am-1pm, 5-7.30pm Tue-Sat. **Credit** MC, V. **Map** p309 D1.
A traditional grocery that stocks a selection of cold meats and cheeses hailing from every part of Italy. Also on offer is an assortment of prepared dishes and roast meats.

Drogheria Mascari
San Polo 381, ruga degli Spezieri (041 522 9762). Vaporetto San Silvestro. **Open** 8am-1pm, 4-7.30pm Mon-Sat. **No credit cards. Map** p309 C2.
Shops like this were quite common in Venice before the onslaught of commercial shopping centres on the mainland; now this is the only one left. It's the best place in the city to find exotic spices, nuts, dried fruit and mushrooms, as well as oils and wines from different regions in Italy.

Confectionery

For ice-cream, *see pp165-73* **Cafés, Bars & Pasticcerie**.

Confetteria Gradella Carlo
San Marco 4814, ponte del Lovo (041 523 4904). Vaporetto Rialto. **Open** 9am-12.30pm, 3-7.30pm Mon-Sat. **No credit cards. Map** p309 D2.
Chocolate is the speciality in this traditional sweet shop. You'll also find hard candy and biscuits sold by the kilo.

Elegant embroidery at **Jesurum**. *See p180.*

Marchini Pasticceria
San Marco 676, calle Spadaria (041 522 9109/ www.golosessi.com/www.fantasychocolate.com). Vaporetto Rialto or San Zaccaria. **Open** 9am-10pm Mon, Wed-Sat. **Credit** AmEx, DC, MC, V. **Map** p312 B1.
Probably Venice's most famous sweet shop, and certainly the most expensive, Marchini has recently moved to this newly remodelled location close to San Marco. Exquisite chocolate, including *Le Baute Veneziane* – small chocolates in the form of Carnevale masks. Cakes can be ordered.

Drink

See also p148 **Bacari** and *pp165-73* **Cafés, Bars & Pasticcerie**.

Bottiglieria Colonna
Castello 5595, calle della Fava (041 528 5137). Vaporetto Rialto. **Open** 9am-1pm, 4-8pm Mon-Sat. **Credit** MC, V. **Map** p309 D2.
Extensive selection of local and regional wines. Helpful staff will give advice on which wines to try, and prepare travel boxes or arrange for shipping.

Vinaria Nave de Oro
Dorsoduro 3664, campo Santa Margherita (041 522 2693). Vaporetto Ca' Rezzonico. **Open** 5-8pm Mon; 8.30am-1.30pm, 5-8.30pm Tue-Sat. **No credit cards. Map** p308 D3.

Bring your own bottles and staff will fill them with anything from Pinot Grigio to Merlot. For something different try Torbolino, a sweet and cloudy first-pressing white wine.
Other locations: Castello 5786B, calle del Mondo Nuovo (041 523 3056); Cannaregio 1370, rio terà San Leonardo (041 719 695); via Lepanto 24D, Lido (041 276 0055).

Vino e... Vini
Castello 3301, fondamenta dei Furlani (041 521 0184). Vaporetto San Zaccaria or Arsenale. **Open** 9am-1pm, 5-8pm Mon-Sat. **Credit** AmEx, MC, V. **Map** p312 B2.
A vast selection of major Italian wines, plus French, Spanish, Californian and even Lebanese wines.

Health foods

Biolandia
Via Andrea Costa 22A, Mestre (041 976 008). Bus 4 from piazzale Roma. **Open** 9am-1pm, 3.30-7.30pm Mon, Tue, Thur, Sat; 9am-1pm Wed; 9am-7.30pm Fri. **Credit** MC, V.
For a better selection and greater savings, head for Mestre. Organic fruit and veg and bread, as well as products for the home and body. Pleasant staff.

Cibele
Cannaregio 1823, campiello dell'Anconetta (041 524 2113). Vaporetto San Marcuola. **Open** 8.30am-12.45pm, 3.30-7.45pm Mon-Sat. **Credit** MC, V. **Map** p309 B1.
A full range of natural health foods, cosmetics and medicines. Staff will also prepare blends of herbal teas and remedies.

Rialto Bio Center
San Polo 366, campo Beccaria (041 523 9515). Vaporetto San Silvestro. **Open** 8.30am-1pm, 4.30-8pm Mon-Sat. **Credit** DC, MC, V. **Map** p309 C1.
A little bit of everything can be found in this small shop, located behind the Rialto fish market, from wholewheat pasta, grains, honey and freshly baked breads to natural cosmetics and incense.

Supermarkets

Billa
Dorsoduro 1491, Zattere (041 522 6187). Vaporetto San Basilio. **Open** 8.30am-8pm Mon-Sat; 9am-8pm Sun. **Credit** AmEx, MC, V. **Map** p311 C1.
The first supermarket in Venice to open seven days a week, Billa stocks fruit, vegetables and other staples at lower prices than most *alimentari*.
Other locations: Cannaregio 3027M, fondamenta Contarini (041 524 4786); Lido, Gran Viale (041 526 2898).

Coop
Giudecca 484, calle dell'Olio (041 241 3381). Vaporetto Palanca. **Open** 8.30am-1pm, 4-8pm Mon-Thur; 8.30am-8pm Fri-Sat; 8.30am-1pm Sun. **Credit** MC, V. **Map** p311 D1.

This supermarket on the Giudecca offers goods at good prices. The branch conveniently located at piazzale Roma is open 8.30am-8pm daily.
Other locations: Santa Croce 1493, campo San Giacomo dell'Orio (041 275 0218); Santa Croce 499, piazzale Roma (041 296 0621).

Punto Sma
Dorsoduro 3017, campo Santa Margherita (041 522 6780). Vaporetto Ca'Rezzonico. **Open** 9am-8pm Mon-Sat. **Credit** DC, MC, V. **Map** p311 B1.
Prices may not be competitive in this small, fully stocked supermarket, but its central location makes it handy.

Jewellery & watches

Shops such as Nardi and Missiaglia in piazza San Marco have the most impressive and expensive jewellery, and Cartier (Mercerie San Zulian) and Bulgari (calle larga XXII Marzo) also have outlets in Venice. The smaller shops on the Rialto bridge offer more affordable silver and gold chains and bracelets sold by weight, and you will find handmade items in workshops far from the chi-chi areas of town.

Laberintho
San Polo 2236, calle del Scaleter (041 710 017/ www.laberintho.it). Vaporetto San Stae or San Tomà. **Open** 9.30am-1pm, 2.30-7pm Tue-Sat. **Credit** AmEx, DC, MC, V. **Map** p309 D1.
A group of young goldsmiths runs this tiny *bottega* hidden away behind campo San Polo. They specialise in inlaid stones. In addition to the one-of-a-kind rings, earrings and necklaces on display, they will produce made-to-order pieces.

Sigfrido Cipolato
Castello 5336, Casselleria (041 522 8437/sigfrido cipolato@yahoo.com). Vaporetto Rialto. **Open** 11am-7.30pm Tue-Sat. **Credit** AmEx, DC, MC, V. **Map** p309 D2.
This jeweller painstakingly carves ebony to recreate the famous Moors' heads brooches and earrings.

Beads

See also pp191-3 **Glass**.

Antichità
Dorsoduro 1195, calle Toletta (041 522 3159). Vaporetto Accademia. **Open** 9.30am-1pm, 3.30-7pm Mon-Sat. **No credit cards. Map** p311 B1.
Beautiful, handpainted antique glass beads that can be purchased individually or made into jewellery. There's also a nice selection of antiques and lace.

Anticlea Antiquariato
Castello 4719A, calle San Provolo (041 528 6946). Vaporetto San Zaccaria. **Open** 10am-1.30pm, 2-7pm Mon-Sat. **Credit** AmEx, MC, V. **Map** p312 B2.
Packed with curious antique treasures, as well as an outstanding selection of Venetian glass beads.

Costantini

San Marco 2668A, campo San Maurizio (041 521 0789/www.costantini-glassbeads.com). Vaporetto Giglio. **Open** 3.30-7.30pm Mon-Fri; 11am-6.30pm Sat. **Credit** MC, V. **Map** p311 B2.

Costantini has a fantastic collection of Venetian glass beads sold by weight or already made up into necklaces, bracelets and brooches.

Perle e Dintorni

San Marco 3740, calle della Mandola (041 520 5068). Vaporetto Sant'Angelo. **Open** 9.30am-7.30pm Mon-Sat; noon-7pm Sun. **Credit** AmEx, DC, MC, V. **Map** p311 B2.

Buy bead jewellery or assemble your own unique-pieces, choosing from a vast assortment of glass beads, most of which are new versions based on antique designs.
Other locations: San Marco 5468, calle della Bissa (041 522 5624).

Masks

See p187 **Masquerading**.

Ca' Macana

Dorsoduro 3172, calle delle Botteghe (041 520 3229/ www.camacana.com). Vaporetto Ca' Rezzonico. **Open** 10am-6pm daily. **Credit** AmEx, DC, MC, V. **Map** p311 B1.

Easy to spot because of the masked statue of a little boy standing at the entrance, this workshop is packed with traditional papier-mâché masks from the *Commedia dell'arte* theatre tradition. A careful explanation of the mask-making process – from the clay model to moulds – is enthusiastically given by the artist in residence, who also organises courses.

MondoNovo

Dorsoduro 3063, rio terà Canal (041 528 7344/ www.mondonovomaschere.it). Vaporetto Ca' Rezzonico. **Open** 9am-6.30pm Mon-Sat. **Credit** AmEx, DC, MC, V. **Map** p311 B1.

Venice's best-known mascheraio offers an enormous variety of masks both traditional and modern. You can also see his work at the recently restored Fenice theatre where he worked on the sculptures.

Papier Mâché

Castello 5175, calle lunga Santa Maria Formosa (041 522 9995/www.papiermache.it). Vaporetto Rialto. **Open** 9am-7.30pm Mon-Sat; 10am-7pm Sun. **Credit** AmEx, DC, MC, V. **Map** p312 A1.

Established for over 20 years, this workshop uses traditional techniques to create contemporary masks. The artists draw inspiration from the works of Klimt, Kandinsky, Tiepolo and Carpaccio. The decoration determines the price, with simple designs starting at €40. Ceramics and painted mirrors too.

Tragicomica

San Polo 2800, calle dei Nomboli (041 721 102/ www.tragicomica.it). Vaporetto San Tomà. **Open** 10am-7pm daily. **Credit** AmEx, MC, V. **Map** p309 D1.

A spellbinding collection of mythological masks, Harlequins, Columbines and Pantaloons, as well as 18th-century dandies and ladies. All are painted by an artist trained at Venice's Accademia di Belle Arti.

Paper products

Ebrû

San Marco 3471, campo Santo Stefano (041 523 8830/www.albertovallese-ebru.com). Vaporetto Accademia or Sant'Angelo. **Open** 10am-1.30pm, 2.30-7pm Mon-Wed; 10am-1pm, 2.30-7pm Thur-Sat; 11am-6pm Sun. **Credit** AmEx, MC, V. **Map** p309 B2.

Beautiful, marbled handcrafted paper, scarves and ties. These are Venetian originals, whose imitators can be found in other shops around town.

Legatoria Piazzesi

San Marco 2511, campiello Feltrina (041 522 1202). Vaporetto Giglio. **Open** 10am-7pm Mon-Sat. **Credit** AmEx, DC, MC, V. **Map** p311 B2.

Venetian paper maker using the traditional wooden-block method of printing: Piazzesi stocks colourful handpainted paper and cards.

Legatoria Polliero

San Polo 2995, campo dei Frari (041 528 5130/ polliero@hotmail.com). Vaporetto San Tomà. **Open** 10.30am-1pm, 3.30-7.30pm Mon-Sat; 10am-1pm Sun. **Credit** AmEx, MC, V. **Map** p311 A1.

This bookbinding workshop, near the Frari church, sells leather-bound diaries, frames and photograph albums. It's not cheap but quality is assured.

Il Pavone

Dorsoduro 721, fondamenta Venier dei Leoni (041 523 4517/fabiopelosin@virgilio.it). Vaporetto Accademia. **Open** 9.30am-1.30pm, 2.30-6.30pm daily. **Credit** AmEx, MC, V. **Map** p311 C2.

Handmade paper with floral motifs in a variety of colours. Il Pavone also stocks boxes, picture frames, key chains and other objects, all decorated in the same style. Quality products at decent prices.

Records & music

Il Tempio della Musica

San Marco 5368, ramo dei Tedeschi (041 523 4552). Vaporetto Rialto. **Open** 9am-7.30pm Mon-Sat. **Credit** AmEx, DC, MC, V. **Map** p311 D2.

A large selection of all musical genres, though classical, jazz and opera is its forte. Check the window display for the latest releases and special offers.

Nalesso

San Marco 5537-5540, salizada fontego dei Tedeschi (041 522 1343/www.vivaldistore.com). Vaporetto Rialto. **Open** 9.30am-7.30pm Mon-Sat; 11am-7pm Sun. **Credit** Am Ex, DC, MC, V. **Map** p309 C2.

You'll hear the music as you approach this small shop located across from the post office. Specialising in classical Venetian music, Nalesso also sells concert tickets for the Fenice and Malibran theatres as well as for concerts in various churches.

Toys & curiosities

Bambolandia

San Polo 1462, calle Madonnetta (041 520 7502/ www.rialto.com/beatrice). Vaporetto San Silvestro or San Tomà. **Open** 9am-noon, 1-5pm Mon-Sat. **Credit** AmEx, DC, MC, V. **Map** p311 D1.
Entering into this Land of Dolls can be a bit unsettling – glass eyes, wigs and limbs of all kinds are

assembled here into perfect porcelain people. You'll find Tom the Gondolier, Pinocchio and many other finely dressed dolls.

Emporio Pettenello

Dorsoduro 2978, campo Santa Margherita (041 523 1167). Vaporetto Ca' Rezzonico. **Open** *Apr-Sept* 9.30am-1pm, 4-8pm Mon-Sat. *Oct-May* 10am-1pm, 4-8pm Mon-Sat; 11am-1pm, 4.30-7.30pm Sun. **Credit** AmEx, MC, V. **Map** p308 D3.

Masquerading

In 1162 Doge Vitale Michiel II won a notable victory over Ulric of Aquileia, and elaborate festivities were held to underscore the Republic's supremacy. Theatre, dances and mask wearing were all part of what was to become a riotous annual celebration that took place in the run-up to Lent, a period of fasting and penitence. Right up until the 18th century, Venice's Carnevale – with its colourful mixture of the sacred and profane – was famous all over Europe.

Perhaps as a result of this event, mask-wearing became common practice in Venice, allowing individual anonymity and privacy in a city where crowded living conditions made these commodities a rarity: patricians could slum it with commoners and vice versa. Mask makers, known as *mascarei*, were officially recognised with their own guild, and by the 15th century wearing costumes and masks had become a well-established tradition.

Of course, masks also provided cover for illegal and immoral activities, forcing the Venetian Republic to issue ordinances curbing masquerading... and, as a result, gambling and prostitution too, as masks were de rigueur for these foibles. But only occasionally: though masks were banned during certain religious festivals and holy days, they were allowed from Ascension Day (40 days after Easter) until June 10 and from October 5 to December 16, as well as during Carnevale from December 26 until Shrove Tuesday.

With the fall of the Venetian Republic in 1797, the mask tradition fell into disuse. It wasn't until Carnevale was revived in the late 1970s that the mask became once again a Venetian symbol. Traditionally the Venetian mask was a simple white face or *volto*. Its variant, 'the plague doctor's mask' had a phallic nose intended to protect the wearer from plague germs. The most common costume (the *baùtta*) was composed of a

black silk hood, a lace cape, a voluminous cloak (*tabarro*), a three-cornered hat and a white mask that completely covered the wearer's face. Today's most common masks are based on characters from the *Commedia dell'Arte* theatre tradition: Harlequin, Pierrot, Columbine and Pantaloon. But *mascarei* have grown more daring with their masks, which are inspired by anything from historical designs to works by Kandinsky and Klimt.

In the early 1980s you could count the number of mask-making workshops on the fingers of one hand. With the local tourist board flogging its revamped Carnevale for all it was worth, these characteristic collectibles became more of a money-spinner, and Venice is now suffering from a plague of uninspired, tourist-oriented mask shops, the worst of which feature some truly nauseating designs. Don't be fooled by cheaper imported versions or those with local decorations painted on to ready-made surfaces.

Run by the same family for more than 100 years, this excellent and fun-filled toy store still has its lovely original furnishings. Choose from good range of marionettes, puppets, wooden toys, dolls and incredible kaleidoscopes.

Molin-Ponte dei Giocatoli

Cannaregio 5899, ponte dei Giocatoli (041 523 5285). Vaporetto Rialto. **Open** 9am-12.30pm, 3.30-7.25pm Mon-Sat. **Credit** DC, MC, V. **Map** p309 C2.

This 'bridge of toys' has everything any kid could possibly need – including Barbies, toy cars, games, models and more.

Wood, sculpture and frames

Cornici Trevisanello

Dorsoduro 662, campo San Vio (041 520 7779). Vaporetto Accademia. **Open** 9am-7pm Mon-Fri; 9am-1pm Sat. **Credit** AmEx, MC, V. **Map** p311 B2.

Strategically located between the Accademia and the Guggenheim (for both, *see p129*), this workshop is home to a father, son and daughter team that makes beautiful gilded frames, many with pearl, mirror and glass inlay. Custom orders and shipping are not a problem.

Dalla Venezia

Santa Croce 2074, calle Pesaro (041 721 276). Vaporetto San Stae. **Open** 8am-noon, 2.30-7pm Mon-Sat. **Credit** AmEx, DC, MC, V. **Map** p309 C1.

Employing the traditional technique of Venetian *tira-oro* (gold leaf decoration), Dalla Venezia creates exquisite gilded frames in his enchanting studio near Ca' Pesaro.

Le Forcole di Saverio Pastor

Dorsoduro 341, fondamenta Soranzo de la Fornace (041 522 5699/www.forcole.com). Vaporetto Salute. **Open** 8am-noon, 2-6pm Mon-Fri. **Credit** MC, V. **Map** p311 C2.

The place to come when you need a new *forcola* or pair of oars for your favourite gondola. Saverio Pastor is one of only three recognised *marangon* (oar makers) in all of Venice; he specialises in making the elaborate walnut-wood rests (*forcole*) that are the symbols of the gondolier's trade. Each gondolier has his very own, specially customised *forcola*, which he guards with his life. Non-rowing visitors may be more interested in purchasing the bookmarks, postcards and some books (in English) on Venetian boatworks.

Livio de Marchi

San Marco 3157A, salizada San Samuele (041 528 5694/www.liviodemarchi.com). Vaporetto San Samuele. **Open** 9.30am-12.30pm, 1.30-5pm Mon-Fri; by appointment Sat. **Credit** AmEx, DC, MC, V. **Map** p311 B1.

Remarkably lifelike wooden sculptures of anything from paintbrushes and books to hanging underwear and crumpled jeans.

Unorthodox sculptures at **Livio de Marchi**.

Gilberto Penzo

San Polo 2681, calle II dei Saoneri (041 719 372/ www.veniceboats.com). Vaporetto San Tomà. **Open** 9.30am-12.30pm, 3-6pm Mon-Sat. **Credit** MC, V. **Map** p311 A1.

This place is a truly fascinating workshop for those that are interested in Venetian boats of all kinds. Gilberto Penzo creates astonishingly detailed models of gondolas, sandolos and topos as well as some remarkable reproductions of vaporettos. Inexpensive kits are also on sale if you would like to practise the fine art of shipbuilding.

Signor Blum

Dorsoduro 2840, campo San Barnaba (041 522 6367/www.signorblum.com). Vaporetto Ca'Rezzonico. **Open** 10am-7.30pm daily. **Credit** AmEx, DC, MC, V. **Map** p311 B1.

Mr Blum's colourful, handmade wooden puzzles of Venetian *palazzi*, gondolas and animals make great gifts for children and adults alike.

Services

Finding conveniences in a city such as Venice can be time consuming, but it's entirely possible. With the growing numbers of university students and tourists flocking to the city, internet access, photocopying and swift film-developing services are easy enough to find. You'll also find other useful services, such as post offices and couriers, listed in the Directory chapter (*see pp275-294*).

Clothing & shoe repairs

Daniela Ghezzo Segalin Venezia and
Giovanna Zanella (for both, *see p181*) also
do shoe repairs.

Calzolaio

Dorsoduro 3799B, calle della Scuola (no phone).
Vaporetto San Tomà. **Open** 10am-noon, 2-6pm
Mon-Fri. **No credit cards. Map** p308 D3.
One of the few remaining shops that repairs shoes:
a heel job will set you back €4.

Ricami Calle del Paradiso

Castello 5754, calle del Paradiso (no phone).
Vaporetto Rialto. **Open** 10am-5.30pm Tue-Sat.
No credit cards. Map p312 A1.
Two ladies carry out minor repairs and alterations,
although embroidery is their speciality. A hem job
starts at €10 and takes about a week. If the work is
urgent, the price goes up.

Carnevale costume rentals

Atelier Pietro Longhi

San Polo 2604B, rio terà Frari (041 714 478/
www.pietrolonghi.com) Vaporetto San Tomà.
Open 10am-12.30pm, 3-7.30pm Mon-Fri;
10am-12.30pm Sat. **Credit** AmEx, DC, MC, V.
Map p308 D3.
It costs between €155 and €600 to rent an outfit for
the first day; each additional day is half-price.
Discounts for groups.

Nicolao Atelier

Cannaregio 5565, rio terà al Bagatin (041 520
7051/www.nicolao.com). Vaporetto Rialto.
Open 9am-1pm, 2-6pm Mon-Fri. **Credit** MC, V.
Map p309 D2.
A very simple costume rents for €80 a day; the more
elaborate ones can go up to as much as €250 a day.
There is, however, a reduction for each additional
day thereafter.

Dry-cleaners & launderettes

In Venice, there are a growing number of self-
service launderettes, but still only a small
number of laundries that will do your wash,
charging by the kilo.

Small, family-run dry-cleaners, offering a
more personal service, are more expensive than
the chains that have opened up in recent years.

Centro Pulisecco

Cannaregio 6262D, calle della Testa (041 522 5011).
Vaporetto Ca' d'Oro. **Open** 8.30am-12.30pm, 3-7pm
Mon-Fri. **No credit cards. Map** p309 C3.
Centro Pulisecco offers dry-cleaning only. Trousers
cost €2.60, jackets €3.20 and sweaters €2. Express
service is available.
Other locations: Cannaregio 1749, rio terà del
Cristo (041 718 020).

Laundry Self-Service

Santa Croce 665A-665B, calle delle Chioverette
(348 301 7457/laundry@laundry.it). Vaporetto
Ferrovia. **Open** 7.30am-10.30pm daily. **No credit**
cards. Map p308 C3.
This coin-operated launderette – open even on public holidays – is a five-minute walk from the station.
€4 for 8kg, €3 for the dryer. Laundry soap can be
purchased and internet access is available.
Other locations: Giudecca 65, fondamenta de le
Zitelle.

Speedy Wash

Cannaregio 1520, rio terà San Leonardo (347
359 3442/www.speedy-wash.it). Vaporetto San
Marcuola. **Open** 8am-11pm daily. **No credit**
cards. Map p308 B3.
This coin-op launderette charges €4.50 for 8kg,
€7.50 for 16kg and €3 for the dryer.

Film & development

Cesana Photo

Dorsoduro 879, rio terà Antonio Foscarini (041 522
2020). Vaporetto Accademia. **Open** *Apr-Sept* 9am-
1pm, 2.30-7pm Mon-Sat. *Oct-Mar* 9am-1pm, 2.30-7pm
Mon-Fri. **Credit** MC, V. **Map** p311 C1.
You won't find low prices but you will find fast,
good-quality service at this shop near the ponte
dell'Accademia: colour developing can be done in
just 25 minutes while slides only take an hour. There
are services also for digital images, passport photos
and photocopies.

Interpress Photo

San Polo 365, campo delle Beccarie (041 528 6978/
mail@interpressphoto.191.it). Vaporetto San
Silvestro. **Open** 9am-12.30pm, 3.30-7.30pm Mon-Sat.
Credit DC, MC, V. **Map** p309 C1.
This is definitely one of the cheapest places in
Venice for film development, and, happily, it's also
probably one of the best: 24 exposures are a mere
€6.50. The shop also provides one-hour service,
passport photographs and photocopies. A small
selection of authentic Murano glass is on sale alongside sunglasses.

Hairdressers

Prices are *à la carte*: each dab of styling foam
or puff of hair spray pushes up the bill. Most
salons are closed on Mondays.

Erminio Scarpa

Dorsoduro 853, piscina Venier (no phone). Vaporetto
Accademia. **Open** 9am-12.30pm, 3-7pm Tue-Sat.
No credit cards. Map p311 C2.
Traditional barber who works only with scissors.
A haircut costs €13, a shave €8.

Stefano e Claudia

San Polo 1098B, riva del Vin (041 520 1913).
Vaporetto San Silvestro. **Open** 9am-5pm Tue-Sat.
Credit AmEx, MC, V. **Map** p309 D2.

The Stefano e Claudia salon is easily the most contemporary in the lagoon. Prices are high and an appointment is a must. The real bonus is that as you're getting styled, you can enjoy a beautiful view of the Grand Canal.

Tocco di Gio'
Santa Croce 661A, campo della Lana (041 718 493). Vaporetto Ferrovia. **Open** 9am-6pm Tue-Sat. **No credit cards. Map** p310 A3.
For men and women. Get a good cut at a reasonable price in a friendly atmosphere.

Opticians

Most opticians will do minor running repairs on the spot and (usually) free of charge.

Ottica Carraro Alessandro
San Marco 3706, calle della Mandola (041 520 4258/www.otticacarraro.it). Vaporetto Sant'Angelo. **Open** 9am-1pm, 3-7.30pm Mon-Sat. **Credit** AmEx, DC, MC, V. **Map** p311 B2.
Get yourself some unique and funky eye wear – the frames are exclusively produced and guaranteed for life. Ottica Carraro Alessandro offers extraordinary quality at reasonable prices.

Punto Vista (Elvio Carraro)
Cannaregio 1982, campiello Anconeta (041 720 453). Vaporetto Ca' Marcuola. **Open** 9am-7.30pm Mon-Sat. **Credit** AmEx, MC, DC, V. **Map** p309 B1.
Eyeglasses, sunglasses, contact lenses and saline solution. Punto Vista also undertakes walk-in eye examinations and repairs.

Photocopies & faxes

Thanks to the Università Ca' Foscari and the University Institute of Architecture (both located centrally in Dorsoduro), finding a place to make a photocopy is neither difficult nor expensive (for more university information, *see p286 & p290*).

Also helpful are the many *tabacchi* (*see p291*) that send faxes and who usually announce the fact in their front windows, as do other service centres. (For couriers, *see p282*; internet points, *see p284*; see also *p189* **Cesana Photo**.)

Ca' Foscarina Puntocopie
Dorsoduro 3224, campiello Squellini (041 523 1814). Vaporetto Ca' Rezzonico. **Open** 9am-12.45pm, 2.30-6pm Mon-Fri. **Credit** MC, V. **Map** p311 B1.
Photocopies, binding and laser printing are offered. Serves stressed-out students with thesis deadlines; 6¢ per photocopy; if you're copying from a book, 18¢ – you have to pay the copyright.

Micoud
San Marco 4581, campo San Luca (041 528 9275/ www.micoud.it). Vaporetto Rialto. **Open** 8.30am-12.30pm, 3-7.30pm Mon-Fri; 8.30am-12.30pm Sat. **Credit** AmEx, DC, MC, V. **Map** p311 A3.

This tiny shop offers a variety of services: colour photocopies, fax, binding, digital images and much more. An A4 photocopy costs 10¢. Reliable, professional service.

Ticket agencies

You can also try **Nalesso** (*see p186*) or **VeLa-HelloVenezia** (*see p278*).

Bassani
Dorsoduro-Santa Marta, San Basilio Fabbricata 17 (041 520 3644/fax 041 520 4009/www. bassani.it). Vaporetto Santa Marta or San Basilio. **Open** 9am-1pm, 2-6pm Mon-Fri; 9.30am-12.30pm Sat. **Credit** AmEx, DC, MC, V. **Map** p310 B2.
Inside the port authority complex at the western end of Dorsoduro, Bassani sells tickets for concerts held in churches around town and organises walking tours, gondola rides and visits to the islands of the lagoon. The company also functions as a regular travel agency.

Travel agencies

You can also try **Bassani** (*see above*).

CTS (Centro Turistico Studentesco)
Dorsoduro 3252, fondamenta del Tagliapietra (041 520 5660/www.cts.it). Vaporetto Ca' Rezzonico or San Tomà. **Open** 9.30am-1.30pm, 2.30-6pm Mon-Fri. **Credit** MC, V. **Map** p311 B1.
This agency caters to its own members (membership costs €28) and also to students in general, offering discount air fares, international train tickets and other useful information for student travellers. ISICs cost €10: bring a passport-sized photo and a document proving you are a student. It also has tickets to concerts, exhibitions and the theatre at discounted prices for members.

Stik Travel
Dorsoduro 3944, calle San Pantalon (041 520 0988/ www.stiktravel.com). Vaporetto San Tomà. **Open** 9am-1pm, 3-7.30pm Mon-Fri. **Credit** AmEx, MC, DC, V. **Map** p311 A1.
The Stik Travel staff are not only friendly but extraordinarily efficient. Stik offers specials to Paris and has a money-changing service too. Purchase train tickets up to 6pm.

Video/DVD rental

Videomat Service
Dorsoduro 3683, campo Santa Margherita (041 522 7960). Vaporetto San Toma. **Open** 10am-1pm, 4-8pm Mon-Sat. **Credit** MC, V. **Map** p311 B1.
DVD sales and rentals at €2.07 a day with membership. A membership card (€10.33) allows you to rent DVDs or videos even when the shop is closed, from the automatic dispenser.
Other locations: San Marco 5249, calle degli Stagneri (041 521 2928).

Glass

The best stuff isn't cheap, but watch out for the hucksters.

Glass and Venice are well-nigh synonymous—the city was famous for its exquisite glassware even before the industry shifted to the island of Murano in 1291, when all glass furnaces except those faking gem stones were ordered to move there to limit the fire hazard in Venice. Glass making – a romance of sand and fire – enthralled visitors in the 15th century for the same reasons that it fascinates today's tourist. And a piece of fine glass captures the spirit of the city in a way no mask or other souvenir can.

Most serious glass works are not open to the public, but opportunities to see glass being blown are ubiquitous. It is impossible to come to Venice and not be accosted by hucksters offering free trips to 'the' glass factory in Murano. These offers are invariably sponsored by one of the large showrooms, which will expect to recoup its investment. If you accept the 'free' trip you will be met by a salesperson with a pitch that's difficult to resist. You are under no obligation to buy, and the 50 per cent discount, like the free lunch, really doesn't exist

Both Murano and Venice are chock full of glass outlets. Prices in Venice are often as low as or lower than on Murano. It's easier to buy glass here then food, but not always easy for the uninitiated to wind their way through the kitsch and clutter to find the gems. The shops, galleries and showrooms identified in this chapter are all reputable outlets. Remember – good Venetian glass is not cheap; anything you find for under €10 is probably made in China.

Several of the Venetian glass artists best known internationally do not regularly show in the city itself. If you are seriously interested in acquiring work by an individual artist and you don't find it in one of the outlets listed, look them up in the phone book and make an appointment. Do it yourself though: hotel staff have formal or informal contracts with the large showrooms and will not willingly direct you to artists, galleries or shops that do not offer them a hefty percentage on anything you buy.

For outlets on Murano, see the map on p307.

Showrooms and glass blowing

These showrooms display a wide selection of all types of traditional Venetian glass – vases, goblets, lighting fixtures, mirrors, sculpture etc

– from some of the best masters currently working on Murano. Mazzega also provides an opportunity to visit adjoining factories engaged in real production, not tourist demonstrations.

CAM Vetri D'Arte
Murano, piazzale Colonna 1B (041 739 944/ www.cam-murano.com). Vaporetto Colonna. **Open** 9am-5pm daily (demonstrations weekdays). **Credit** AmEx, DC, MC, V.

Mazzega
Murano, fondamenta da Mula 147 (041 736 888/ www.mazzega.it). Vaporetto Mula. **Open** 9am-5pm daily (demonstrations weekdays). **Credit** AmEx, DC, MC, V.

Pauly & C.
San Marco 73, piazza San Marco (041 523 5484/ www.paulyglassfactory.com). Vaporetto Vallaresso. **Open** 10am-7pm daily. **Credit** AmEx, DC, MC, V. **Map** p311 B3.
Other locations: San Marco 77, piazza San Marco (041 277 0279); San Marco 316, piazzetta dei Leoni (041 523 5575).

Proprietary outlets

Some of the best in contemporary design and individual art is available only through galleries and shops owned or licensed by the producers. These can range from shops dedicated to the production of internationally famous design houses to small studio ateliers specialised in the work of one artist. Not always easy to find, they are some of finest shops in town, with exceptionally courteous staff. Expect fixed prices and excellent product.

Barovier and Toso
Murano, fondamenta Vetrai 28 (041 739 049/ www.barovier.com). Vaporetto Colonna. **Open** 10am-12.30pm, 1-5pm Mon-Fri. **Credit** AmEx, MC, V.
Lighting and *objets* by one of the oldest and most venerable family owned and operated glass houses on Murano. Their private museum is open by appointment and definitely worth a special trip for fans of historical Murano glass.

Berengo Fine Arts
Murano, fondamenta Vetrai 109A (041 739 453/www.berengo.com). Vaporetto Colonna. **Open** 10am-6pm daily. **Credit** AmEx, DC, MC, V.
Adriano Berengo is establishing a fiefdom producing works in glass – primarily brightly coloured sculpture – designed by international artists.

Other locations: Murano, fondamenta Manin 68 (041 527 6364); San Marco 412/413, calle larga San Marco (041 241 0763).

Canestrelli

Dorsoduro 1173, calle della Toletta (041 277 0617/ www.venicemirrors.com). Vaporetto Accademia. **Open** 11am-1.30pm, 3-7pm Mon-Sat. **Credit** AmEx, MC, V. **Map** p311 B1.
Stefano Coluccio specialises in beautifully framed convex mirrors.

Cesare Sent

Murano, fondamenta Serenella 16 (041 527 4752/ www.cesaresent.com). Vaporetto Colonna. **Open** 10am-6pm daily. **Credit** AmEx, MC, V.
Objects and gifts designed and executed by the artist, often combining multicoloured glass canes in fretwork vessels.

Genninger Studio

Dorsoduro 2793A, calle del Traghetto (041 522 5565/www.genningerstudio.com). Vaporetto Ca' Rezzonico. **Open** 10am-1.30pm, 2.30-7pm Mon-Sat. **Credit** AmEx, MC, V. **Map** p311 B1.
Flame-worked and blown beads, custom jewellery, knick-knacks, lighting and mirrors designed by Leslie Ann Genninger. A contemporary take on Venetian luxury and decadence in beautiful surroundings on the Grand Canal.
Other locations: San Marco 1845, calle del Frutariol (041 523 9494)

L'Isola

San Marco 1468, campo San Moisè (041 523 1973/ www.carlomoretti.com). Vaporetto Vallaresso. **Open** 9am-7pm daily. **Credit** AmEx, DC, MC, V. **Map** p311 B3.
Carlo Moretti's showroom showcases his own elegant clear and coloured glass designs. Some unique pieces and signed and numbered editions by Moretti and a few selected artists working with his factory.

Luigi Camozzo

Murano, fondamenta Venier 3 (041 736 875). Vaporetto Museo. **Open** 11.30am-1.30pm, 2.30-5.30pm Mon-Sat. **Credit** MC, V.
Intricate multicoloured and murrine bowls cut on the wheel, incised glass ware and unique jewellery.

Manin 56

Murano, fondamenta Manin 56 (041 527 5392/ manincinquantasei@tin.it). Vaporetto Colonna. **Open** 11am-6pm daily. **Credit** AmEx, MC, V.
The exclusive Murano outlet for the glass house Salviati features distinctive drinking glasses, and vases designed by Norberto Moretti and others. The selection here is much better, and more elegantly presented, than at the Salviati shop in Venice.

Marina & Susanna Sent

Dorsoduro 669, campo san Vio (041 520 8136/ sent.snc@tin.it). Vaporetto Accademia. **Open** 10am-6pm daily. **Credit** AmEx, MC, V. **Map** p311 B2.

It's easier to buy glass than food on Murano.

Venice's best contemporary glass jewellery is created by the Sent sisters. There's also a good selection of the work of the contemporary design house Arcade, including the new classic 'Bamboo' vases designed by Laura de Santillana.

Micheluzzi

Dorsoduro 1071, calle della Toletta (041 528 2190/ maravege@tin.it). Vaporetto Accademia. **Open** 10am-1pm, 4-7pm Tue-Sat; other times by appointment. **Credit** AmEx, MC, V. **Map** p311 B1.
Massimo Micheluzzi's beautiful cut and murrine vessels will be the sought-after classics of the future. Good design, good workmanship, good prices, good people. You can't go wrong here.

Rossana & Rossana

Murano, riva Longa 11 (041 527 4076/www.ro-e-ro.com). Vaporetto Museo. **Open** 10am-6pm daily. **Credit** AmEx, MC, V.
This new shop is the best place in Venice to find traditional Venetian goblets. They're all made by Davide Fuin, a true master of the craft, and the glass ware is exquisite in colour, design and workmanship. The shop also features braided seed pearl jewellery designed by the two Rossanas in a modern take on a Venetian tradition.

Seguso Viro

Murano, fondamenta Radi 20 (041 527 5353) Vaporetto Museo. **Open** 10.30am-5.30pm Mon-Sat. **Credit** AmEx, MC, V.
Elegant blown filigree vessels by Viro Seguso and his father Gianpaolo. This is modern design in the Venetian tradition, with some unique pieces.

Venini
Murano, fondamenta Vetrai 50 (041 273 7211/ www.venini.com). Vaporetto Colonna. **Open** 9.30am-5.30pm Mon-Sat. **Credit** AmEx, DC, MC, V.
Venini is, well, Venini and the venerable glass house is enjoying a renaissance right now, sparked by pieces designed by glass artists like Philip Baldwin and Monica Guggisberg. Venini continues to produce classic pieces from the past, but your best bet for price appreciation is to pick up one of the new designs.

Vittorio Costantini
Cannaregio 5311, calle del Fumo (041 522 2265/ www.vittoriocostantini.it). Vaporetto Fondamente Nove. **Open** 9.15am-1pm, 2.15-6pm Mon-Fri. **Credit** MC, V. **Map** p309 C3.
Internationally renowned as one of the most original Venetian lamp workers, Vittorio Costantini's animals, insects, fish and birds are instantly recognisable for their beauty and fine workmanship.

A few good shops

Domus Vetri D'Arte
Murano, fondamenta Vetrai 82 (041 739 215/ domusvetri@hotmail.com). Vaporetto Colonna. **Open** 9am-6pm daily. **Credit** AmEx, MC, V.
Domus has over the years continued to select and display a selection of the very best Murano glass, including work by Davide Salvadore and Adriano dalla Valentino.

Ferro
Murano, campo San Stefano 17 (041 527 5398 5398/gianmarco_ferro@hotmail.it). Vaporetto Faro. **Open** 11am-5pm daily. **Credit** MC, V.
This new shop on Murano has a good selection of well-selected uncommon pieces at extremely competitive prices.

Ivano Soffiato
Dorsoduro 1188, calle della Toletta (041 521 0480). Vaporetto Accademia. **Open** 10am-6.30pm daily. **Credit** AmEx, DC, MC, V. **Map** p311 B1.
One of the best places to pick up souvenirs in Venice. Ivano makes about half of the tourist goodies sold in the city and here you can watch him do it.

Il Prato
San Marco 2457/58, calle de le Ostrege (041 523 1148/ilprato@iol.it). Vaporetto Giglio. **Open** 11am-7pm Mon-Sat. **Credit** AmEx, MC,V. **Map** p311 B2.
This new outlet sells well-designed vessels in modern-traditional style by the Vivarini and Padovan glass houses.

Galleries & antiquarians

Antichità Zaggia Claudia
Dorsoduro 1195A, calle della Toletta (041 522 3159). Vaporetto Accademia. **Open** 9.30am-1pm, 3.15-7pm Mon-Sat. **No credit cards. Map** p311 B1.
A large selection of belle epoque Venetian beads.

Caterina Tognon
San Marco 2671, campo San Maurizio (041 520 7859/035 243 300/www.caterinatognon.com). Vaporetto Giglio. **Open** by appointment only. **Credit** AmEx, MC, V. **Map** p311 B2.
This is the Venetian branch of Tognon's larger Bergamo Gallery. She represents the Venetian artist Maria Grazia Rosin and noted international glass artists including Lybensky/Brychtova, Richard Marquis and Sylvia Levenson.

Claudio Gianolla
San Marco 2766, calle Spezier (041 521 2652/ www.gianollavetroantico.it). Vaporetto Giglio. **Open** 10.30am-12.30pm, 3-7pm Mon-Sat. **Credit** AmEx, MC, V. **Map** p311 B2.
Antique and classic Venetian glass.

Galleria Marina Barovier
San Marco 3216, salizada San Samuele (041 523 6748/www.barovier.it). Vaporetto San Samuele. **Open** 9.30am-12.30pm, 3.30-7.30pm Mon-Sat. **No credit cards. Map** p311 B1.
Renowned for her collection of classic 20th-century Venetian glass, Marina Barovier is also the exclusive Venetian representative for Cristiano Bianchin, Dale Chihuly, and Lino Tagliapietra.

Galleria Regina
Murano, riva Longa 25A (041 739 202/ www.galleriaregina.com). Vaporetto Museo. **Open** 10.30am-4.30pm daily. **Credit** AmEx, MC,V.
Contemporary sculpture and vessels. Represents Lucio Bubacco, Vittorio Ferro, Norberto Moretti and other Italian and international artists.

Galleria Rossella Junck
San Marco 2360, calle delle Ostreghe (041 520 7747/www.rossellajunck.it). Vaporetto Giglio. **Open** 10am-12.30pm, 4-7.30pm Mon-Sat. **Credit** AmEx, MC, V. **Map** p311 B2.
Murano glass from the 16th to the 20th century and contemporary artistic glass. Junck represents Massimo Nordio and other international artists, primarily European.
Other locations: San Marco 1997, campo San Fantin (041 521 0759).

Totem – Il Canale
Dorsoduro 878B, campo Carità (041 522 3641/ www.totemilcanale.com). Vaporetto Accademia. **Open** 10am-1pm, 3-7pm daily. **Credit** AmEx, DC, MC, V. **Map** p311 B1.
A treasure trove of glass and wood, the Totem gallery features jewellery made from non-precious materials and some of the most beautifully strung antique trade beads to be found anywhere.

Zancopè
San Marco 2674, campo San Maurizio (041 520 4567/www.jurubeba.it). Vaporetto Giglio. **Open** 10.30 am-1pm, 4-7.30pm Mon-Sat. **Credit** MC, V. **Map** p311 B2.
An eclectic collection of antique, old and contemporary glass at very good prices.

MUSEUM HOURS:
From October 1 to May 31, 10 am / 6 pm
Closed on Saturdays and Jewish holidays

SYNAGOGUE'S TOURS:
In Italian and English, every hour
from 10:30 am until 4:30 pm
(from October 1 to May 31)
Also available:
private thematic tours,
tours in German, French,
Spanish and Hebrew

Information and reservations:
T. +39 041 715 359
F. +39 041 723 007

IN THE WORLD'S FIRST GHETTO
THE ANCIENT SYNAGOGUES AND
THE MUSEUM OF THE JEWISH
COMMUNITY OF VENICE

THE ANCIENT JEWISH CEMETERY ON THE LIDO
GUIDED TOURS:
From October 1 to May 31:
Sunday at 2.30 pm

Information and reservations
T. +39 041 715 359
F. +39 041 723 007

Comunità Ebraica VENEZIA

codess cultura

M U S E O
E B R A I C O
di VENEZIA

Cannaregio 2902/B - 30121 Venezia
T. +39 041 715359 F. +39 041 723007
museoebraico@codesscultura.it
www.museoebraico.it

Arts & Entertainment

Features

Festivals & Events

There's the film festival and La Biennale for culture; water and masks for fun.

La Biennale. See p197.

Since the earliest days of the Republic, festivals, processions and popular celebrations, set against Venice's peerless backdrop, have been an intrinsic part of the city's social fabric. The government used pageantry both to assert the rigidly hierarchical nature of society and to give the lower orders the chance to let loose. The government declared official celebrations in honour of anything from the end of a plague outburst to naval battles or a holy day. With over 100 churches in the city, there was no shortage of local saints' days to celebrate. For the working classes, there were the *corsa al toro* (bullfights) in campo Santo Stefano, or bloody battles between rival sections of the populace.

The frantic festive excesses of the 18th century, when Venice was in terminal decline, were put to an austere end when Napoleon took control. Much of the revelry has only been revived in relatively recent times.

Carnevale (*see below*) is the most successful of these revived revelries in commercial terms; many saints' days have turned into 'village' fairs. But, fittingly, it is on the water that today's Venetians enjoy themselves most: there are more than 120 regattas in the lagoon each year. The **Regata Storica** (*see p198*) may look like it's funded by the tourist board, but Venetians get seriously involved in the boat races immediately following the spectacle; the **Vogalonga** (*see p197*) is a remarkable display of Venetian love of messing about in boats. For public holidays and religious days, *see p294*.

Spring

Carnevale
Date 10 days ending on Shrove Tuesday.
Though it had existed since the Middle Ages, Venice's pre-Lenten Carnevale came into its own in the 18th century: as the Venetian Republic went into terminal decline, the city's pagan side began to emerge. Carnevale became an outlet for all that had been prohibited for centuries by the strong arm of the doge. Elaborate structures would be set up in piazza San Marco as stages for acrobats, tumblers, wrestlers and other performers. Masks served not only as an escape from the drabness of everyday life but to conceal the wearer's identity – a useful ploy for nuns on the lam or slumming patricians (*see p187* **Masquerading**). The Napoleonic invasion in 1797 brought an end to the fun and games; Carnevale was not resuscitated until the late 1970s. The city authorities and hoteliers' association saw the earning potential of all those long-nosed masks, and today the heavily subsidised celebrations draw revellers from all over the world. The party starts ten days before *martedì grasso* (Shrove Tuesday), though plans were afoot to kick off the festivities earlier. Tourist offices (*see p293*) provide full Carnevale programmes.

Su e Zo Per I Ponti
Information *041 590 4717/www.tgseurogroup.it/ suezo/index.htm.* **Date** 4th Sun of Lent.
Literally 'Up and Down Bridges', this privately organised excursion is inspired by the traditional *bacarada* (bar crawl). It is an orienteering event in which you are given a map and a list of checkpoints to tick off in the centre of Venice. Old hands take their time checking out the *bacari* (*see p148*) along the way. Individuals can register at the starting line in piazza San Marco on the morning of the event, while groups should phone ahead.

Benedizione del Fuoco

Basilica di San Marco (041 522 5205). Vaporetto Vallaresso or San Zaccaria. **Date** Easter Saturday. **Map** p312 B1.

At dusk, the lights are turned off inside St Mark's basilica and a fire is lit in the narthex (entrance porch). Communion is celebrated and the four elements are blessed: earth represented by the faithful masses, fire by the large altar candle, water at the baptismal font and air from the surrounding environment.

Festa di San Marco

Bacino di San Marco. Vaporetto Vallaresso or San Zaccaria. **Date** 25 Apr. **Map** p312 B1.

The traditional feast day of Venice's patron saint is a low-key affair. In the morning there is a solemn Mass in the basilica, followed by a gondola regatta between the island of Sant'Elena and the Punta della Dogana at the entrance to the Grand Canal. The day is also known as *La Festa del boccolo* ('bud'): red rosebuds are given to wives and lovers.

Festa e Regata della Sensa

San Nicolò del Lido & Bacino di San Marco. **Information** *041 529 8711/041 274 7737.* **Date** Ascension Day (fifth Thursday after Easter).

Back in the days of the Venetian Republic, the doge would board the glorious state barge, the Bucintoro, and be rowed out to the island of Sant'Andrea, facing the lagoon's main outlet to the Adriatic, followed by a fleet of small boats. Here he would throw a gold ring overboard, to symbolise *lo sposalizio del mare* – Venice's marriage with the sea. Today the mayor takes the place of the doge, the Bucintoro looks like a glorified fruit boat and the ring has become a laurel wreath. The ceremony is now performed at San Nicolò, on the northernmost point of the Lido, and is followed by a regatta. If it rains, local lore says it'll tip down for the next 40 days. ('*Se piove il giorno della Sensa per quaranta giorni non semo sensa.*')

Vogalonga

Information *041 521 0544/www.vogalonga.it.* **Date** one Sunday in May.

Like San Francisco's 'critical mass'– during which bicycles clog downtown once a month to demonstrate against congestion and pollution – Venetians (or at least those with strength enough to complete the 33km/20.5 mile route) protest against motorboats and the damage they do by boarding any kind of rowing craft and making their way through the lagoon and the city's two main canals in this annual free-for-all. They are joined by a host of out-of-towners and foreigners. Boats set off from in front of the lagoon façade of the Doge's Palace at 8.30am.

Venezia Suona

Information *041 275 0049/www.veneziasuona.it.* **Date** Sunday closest to 21 June.

The name means 'Venice plays'… and that it does, with hundreds of bands playing anything from rock to folk to reggae to jazz. Music can be heard from about 4pm onwards in *campi* all over the city.

Summer

Biennale d'Arte Contemporanea & Architettura

Giardini di Castello. Vaporetto Giardini. **Information** *041 521 8711/www.labiennale.org.* **Date** Contemporary art (odd years) June-Nov. Architecture (even years) Sept-Nov. **Map** p312 C2.

The Biennale d'Arte, established in 1895, is the *Jeux Sans Frontières* of the contemporary art world; its architectural counterpart draws a strong local and international crowd. *See p207* **La Biennale**.

Palio delle Antiche Repubbliche Marinare

Bacino di San Marco. Vaporetto Vallaresso or San Zaccaria. **Date** June or July.

This competition falls to Venice once every four years (otherwise it's in Amalfi, Genova and Pisa). Venice stages the 2007 Palio. The race starts at the island of Sant'Elena and finishes at the Doge's palace. Before the race, boats carrying costumed representatives of the four Marine Republics parade along the riva dei Sette Martiri and the riva degli Schiavoni.

Festa di San Pietro

San Pietro in Castello. Vaporetto Giardini. **Date** week ending 29 June. **Map** p313 B2.

The most lively and villagey of Venice's many local festivals in celebration of San Pietro Martire. A week of events centres on the church green of San Pietro (*see p97*): there are competitions, concerts, food stands and bouncy castles.

Festa di San Giacomo dell'Orio

Campo San Giacomo dell'Orio. Vaporetto San Stae or Riva di Biasio. **Date** week ending 25 July.

Concerts, typical Italian barbecue (greasy meat and polenta) and an annual charity raffle make up this local fair: a great occasion to 'do as the Venetians do' in one of the most beautiful campos in the city.

Cinema all'aperto

Campo San Polo. Vaporetto San Silvestro or San Tomà. **Information** *041 524 1320/www.comune. venezia.it/cinema.* **Date** 6wks late July-early Sept. **Map** p309 D1.

A huge outdoor theatre is set up in campo San Polo to show current films, usually dubbed into Italian, occasionally with English subtitles. *See pp202-4*.

Festa del Redentore

Bacino di San Marco, Canale della Giudecca. **Date** 3rd weekend of July. **Map** p312 B1.

The Redentore is the oldest continuously celebrated date on the Venetian calendar. At the end of a plague epidemic in 1576 the city commissioned Andrea Palladio to build a church on the Giudecca – *Il Redentore*, the Redeemer. Every July a pontoon bridge is built across the canal that separates the Giudecca from Venice proper, so people can make the pilgrimage to the church. But what makes this weekend so special are the festivities on Saturday night. Boats of every shape and size gather in the lagoon between St Mark's, San Giorgio, the Punta della Dogana and the Giudecca, each holding merrymakers supplied with food and drink. This party culminates in an amazing fireworks display.

Ferragosto – Festa dell'Assunta
Date 15 Aug.
If you want Venice without Venetians, this is the time to come, as everyone who can leaves the city. Practically everything shuts down and people head to the beach. There is usually a free concert in the cathedral on the lagoon island of Torcello, Santa Maria Assunta (*see p144*), on the evening of the 15th. Tourist offices (*see p293*) have more information.

Regata Storica
Grand Canal. **Date** 1st Sun in Sept.
This event begins with a procession of ornate boats down the Grand Canal, rowed by locals in 16th-century costume. Once this is over, the races start – which is what most locals have come to see. There are four: one for young rowers, one for women, one for rowers of *caorline* – long canoe-like boats in which the prow and the stern are identical – and the last, the most eagerly awaited, featuring two-man sporting *gondolini*. The finish is at the sharp curve of the Grand Canal between Palazzo Barbi and Ca' Foscari: here the judges sit in an ornate raft known as the *machina*, where the prize-giving takes place.

Mostra Internazionale D'Arte Cinematografica (Film Festival)
See pp202-4.

Autumn

Sagra del Pesce
Island of Burano. Vaporetto 12. **Date** 3rd Sun in Sept. **Map** p314.
Fried fish and lots of white wine are consumed in this feast in the *calli* between Burano's brightly painted houses. Those rowers who are not legless then take part in the last regatta of the season.

Sagra del Mosto
Island of Sant'Erasmo. Vaporetto 13 to Chiesa. **Date** 1st weekend in Oct.
This festival is a great excuse for Venetians to spend a day 'in the country' at Sant'Erasmo (*see p145*), getting light-headed on the first pressing of wine. The salty soil does not lend itself to superior wine – which is why it's best to down a glass before the stuff has had much chance to ferment. Sideshows, grilled sausage aromas and red-faced locals abound.

Venice Marathon
Information *041 532 1871/www.venicemarathon.it.* **Date** last Sun in Oct.
This marathon starts in the town of Stra east of Padua, follows the Brenta canal, and then winds through Venice to end on the riva Sette Martiri. The website is in Italian and English.

Winter

Festa di San Martino
Date 11 Nov.
Kids armed with mamma's pots and spoons raise a ruckus around the city centre, chanting the saint's praises and demanding trick-or-treat style tokens in return for taking their noise elsewhere. Horse-and-rider-shaped San Martino cakes, with coloured icing dotted with silver balls, proliferate in cake shops.

Festa della Madonna della Salute
Church of Madonna della Salute. Vaporetto Salute. **Date** 21 Nov. **Map** p311 C2.
In 1630-1 Venice was 'miraculously' delivered from plague, which claimed almost 100,000 lives – one in three Venetians. The Republic commissioned a church from Baldassare Longhena, and his Madonna della Salute (*see p129*) was completed in 1687. On this feast day, a pontoon bridge is strung across the Grand Canal from campo Santa Maria del Giglio to La Salute so that a procession led by the patriarch (archbishop) of Venice can make its way on foot from San Marco. Along the way, stalls sell cakes and candyfloss, and candles that pilgrims light inside the church. Then everybody eats *castradina* – cabbage and mutton stew that tastes nicer than it sounds.

Christmas, New Year & Epiphany (La Befana)
Venice's Yuletide festivities are low-key affairs. There are two events: the New Year's Day swim off the Lido (www.lidovenezia.it) for hardy swimmers, and the *Regata delle Befane* (www.bucintoro.it) on 6 January, a rowing race along the Grand Canal in which the competitors, all aged over 50, are dressed up as *La Befana* – the ugly witch who gives sweets to good children and pieces of coal to bad ones.

Festa del Redentore. *See p197.*

Children

Plenty to do, but if all else fails you can always hop on a gondola.

Venice is an intriguingly ancient place of labyrinthine streets and crooked bridges, guarded by winged lions and offering constant surprises: with its particular intrinsic magic, the city's sheer improbability should go some way to taking your children's minds off their sore feet.

In order to make your offspring see things this way, you'll need to use your imagination when planning the day's activities. A good deal of walking is going to be necessary and few of the major sights are geared towards children. Little ones will be bedazzled by the sheer mechanics of the place: exploit it, and remember that hours hanging over bridges watching for fish-finger delivery boats is part of the Venetian experience too. Older kids may be inveigled into the right frame of mind with a pre-emptive gift of Cornelia Funke's *The Thief Lord* – being made into a film as this guide went to press.

With strategies such as these, it should be possible to keep the kids interested enough not to be clamouring to get back to the satellite TV

at the hotel. And if by the end of a strategically planned day you're clamouring for a romantic candle lit dinner for two, you'll find that the larger hotels have childminders on hand while the smaller ones can probably arrange them.

GETTING AROUND

The frequent absence of barriers between pavement and canal presents a problem for parents travelling with mobile toddlers. Those safety reins you never thought you'd stoop to might not seem such a bad idea here.

Pre-walkers present another dilemma. Remember, the only ways of getting around Venice are by boat or foot, and there are a daunting number of bridges. After heaving a pushchair over the umpteenth bridge in a day, a comfortable baby backpack may begin to look like a gift from heaven.

Vaporetto travel is far from cheap. In theory, kids more than one metre (three foot) tall pay adult fares; children under that height go free. But inspectors don't carry measuring tapes; the general feeling is that you should start paying when they're about six. Still, look on the means of transport as a Venetian experience in itself and the cost will not seem so outrageous. A complete circle on line 82 (red) from the riva degli Schiavoni will take your fascinated offspring across to the Giudecca, then up to the station and port areas, giving them a glimpse of Venice's industrial underbelly as well as a triumphal march down the Grand Canal.

Most children will demand a gondola trip. Remember that this expensive experience (*see p280*) can be substituted by or supplemented with rides on the humbler but more useful *traghetti* (*see p279*) that ply across the Grand Canal at points distant from bridges. Let them stand up in the boat like real Venetians.

Sightseeing

Venice will knock all but the most cynical youngsters sideways, so keeping them amused should not take too much effort. (Of course, you may be able to bore them to death with a surfeit of churches and museums, but you'll have to work hard at it.)

Under-tens, especially, are a pushover. For a start, the city's 400-plus bridges are a joy. Children will love watching boats slipping under one side and emerging from the other.

For a glimpse of illustrious craft of the past, head for the **Museo Storico Navale** (*see p99*), where Venice's maritime history is charted in scale models of the ships built in the Arsenale through the centuries.

When not busy building up their vast empire, the Venetians devoted much time to games and sport, a fact you and your kids can verify with a visit to the **Museo Querini Stampalia** (*see p93*), where a collection of 18th-century scenes of Venetian life includes some very unlikely amusements. Aside from the obligatory hunting parties and antics on the frozen lagoon, one painting, *La Guerra dei Pugni* by Antonio

Strom, shows one of the mass boxing matches that occurred frequently. The fights took place on bridges with no railings, with the initial four competitors – before proceedings degenerated into a free-for-all – starting out with one foot on the white inlaid footprints on the corners of the top step: try it out for yourselves on ponte dei Pugni near campo San Barnaba, ponte della Guerra near campo San Zulian and ponte di Santa Fosca. Don't forget to introduce your kids to the most famous Venetian game of all. With the lagoon behind you, and the lagoon-facing façade of the Doge's Palace in front of you, go to the third column from the left. Place your

The bells, the bells

Venice has 170 eye-catching *campanili* (bell towers). There used to be 200 of them, but over the centuries some (including, of course, the tallest and most august in piazza San Marco, *see p83*) have fallen, some have been prudently dismantled and some have been shortened and put to new uses.

The tallest

San Marco (*see p83*), at 99 metres (324.8 feet). The symbol of the city, it has served as bell tower, watch tower and even, during the War of Chioggia against Genoa, as part of the city's defences with four cannon mounted on top to fend off invaders. In May 1997 a group of clownish secessionists seized the bell tower in a bid to refound the Venetian Republic, before being flushed out by assault troops.

The runner-up

Santa Maria Gloriosa dei Frari (*see p120* **I Frari**), at about 80 metres (262.5 feet).

The oldest

Torcello's *campanile* (*see p145*) dates from the 11th century. It can be climbed: there are no stairs, just steeply sloping ramps.

The most leaning

Santo Stefano (*see p90*). This is the fourth tower on this spot; the first collapsed in 1093, the second in 1347 and the third in 1445 – 24 hours after an architect from Bologna had promised to straighten it. The calle leading out of the north-eastern corner of campo San Maurizio allows an alarming view of the bottom of the tower and the various structures that have been installed in the canal to support it.

More leaners

San Giorgio dei Greci (*see p101*); San Pietro in Castello (*see p101*); San Martino on Burano (*see p143*).

Converted towers

San Boldo, near campo San Giacomo dell'Orio (*see p118*). The church no longer exists; the truncated tower is now part of a block of flats.

Onion-top towers

San Bartolomeo (*see p88*); Santissimi Apostoli (*see p104*); San Lazzaro degli Armeni (*see p146*).

Half-onion (or garlic-head) towers

Gesuati (*see p133*); Santa Maria degli Angeli on Murano (*see p141*); San Pietro Martire on Murano (*see p142*); San Sebastiano (*see p125*).

The most elaborate

Santa Maria Formosa (*see p94*).

The squarest

San Salvador (*see p88*).

The thinnest

San Martino on Burano (*see p143*).

The stumpiest

Santa Margherita (*see p125*): the top half was removed in 1808.

The pointiest

San Giorgio Maggiore (*see p136*) and San Francesco della Vigna (*see p93*).

The newest

Sant'Elena (*see p101*): the church is 15th century but the *campanile* dates from 1958.

back firmly against it, then walk round it, all the way. Can you circumnavigate it without slipping off the shoe-worn marble pavement?

Subjects for I-Spy games are manifold: bell towers (see p200 **The bells, the bells**) are good, as are lions. Piazza San Marco and its adjoining *piazzette* already offer a fine pride, ranging from the ancient and exotic (the Syrian, Persian or Chinese one on the pillar in the Piazzetta) to the pink and cuddly (the porphyry ones in piazzetta dei Leoncini, rubbed smooth by centuries of toddlers' bottoms).

Most of Venice's museums are singularly hands-off, but some may still appeal to kids. If the vast Tintorettos and echoing halls of the **Palazzo Ducale** (see p85) inspire only yawns, combine your visit there with a tour of the palace's secret corridors, the *Itinerari segreti* (see p85), which will take you into dungeons and torture rooms. Only two rooms are currently open at the **Museo di Storia Naturale** (and only at weekends, see p117), but they house an aquarium, and child-impressing dinosaur and giant crocodile fossils.

As far as art goes, try breaking your children in with visits to some of Venice's less demanding exhibits, such as the **Scuola di San Giorgio degli Schiavoni** (see p101), where Vittorio Carpaccio's *St George* cycle is packed with fascinating detail. The grand Tintorettos in the **Madonna dell'Orto** (see p108), particularly *The Last Judgement*, are full of the kind of gruesome details – such as bodies with skulls for heads scrabbling their way out of the earth – likely to appeal to kids.

Don't be scared off from big galleries such as the **Accademia** (see p130): you may link up with one of the gallery's more child-friendly guides, who will bend over backwards to interest your offspring in the collection.

The Musei Civici (see p70) organise occasional events for families; the cost is €8 for a family of four.

To win a little picture-viewing time in churches, try pointing out to your kids that the red marble used in so many church floors contains amazing fossils. While they embark on mini-palaeontological excursions you can concentrate on the artworks.

When the culture all gets too much, take Junior up a campanile for a bird's-eye view of the city. The one in piazza San Marco (see p83) is the highest; the one attached to **San Giorgio Maggiore** (see p136) affords a more detached vantage point. Time your ascent to coincide with the striking of an hour – midday is particularly deafening. The **Scala del Bòvolo** (see p90) is on a smaller scale, but will give the kids the satisfaction of having made their own panting way up to the top.

Parks, beaches & entertainment

Most Venetian kids spend their free time in their local *campi*. Although ball games are officially forbidden there, you will find matches going on in most of them, particularly the larger ones like campo Santa Maria Formosa and campo San Polo. Venetian kids are used to letting foreign visitors join their games, making use of rudimentary school English for essential communication. In campo Santa Maria Formosa and campo Santo Stefano small play areas for toddlers have been set up next to the churches.

Although well hidden, there are public parks in the city too, and most of them – including the **Giardini pubblici** (see p97) and the **Parco Savorgnan** (see p106) – have been fitted up with swings and slides. At Sant'Elena (see p97) things improve with a grassy play area along the lagoon, and a roller skating/cycling rink. Sant'Elena is also where Venice's football team has its home ground (see p227).

On the mainland, the brand new Parco San Giuliano (bus 12 from piazzale Roma) is one of Italy's largest urban parks. The newly planted trees don't offer much shade on a blazing summer day, but there's a roller skating rink, lake, play areas and football pitches.

In summer, break up the culture with a trip to the Lido, where there are some halfway-acceptable beaches. Most of the main ones are sewn up by the big hotels, which will charge you for a small stretch of sand, sometimes with deckchair and umbrella, and always with huge numbers of near neighbours. Sant'Erasmo (see p145) also provides a pleasant break. Green and rural, Sant'Erasmo can be cycled around in an hour or so. There is a small beach straight across the island from the ferry landing stage. Alternatively, head for the Lido di Jesolo (see p216 **Jesolo Night Fever**).

Local feast days may also provide entertainment for your children, usually in the shape of puppet theatres. Watch walls around the city for posters announcing *feste*. Particularly picturesque is the feast of Saints Peter and Paul in the parish of San Pietro in Castello (see p101), culminating on 29 June.

See also p223 **Teatro Toniolo**.

Books

The excellent children's guide (in English) *Viva Venice* by Paolo Zoffoli and Paola Scibilia (Elzeviro, 2002) has games, informative illustrations and interesting facts. *Venice for Kids* by Elisabetta Pasqualin (Fratelli Palombi, 2000) belongs to a series of books on Italian cities.

Arts & Entertainment

Film

It's all about one of Europe's best festivals.

Venice has had film makers falling for its cinematic wiles for decades, but contemporary film-goers are ill-served by the city. Once it was home to a host of cinemas; now many former picture palaces house supermarkets. Though local film buffs complain about the shortage of movie theatres, it is a pretty accurate reflection of local demand, with a diminishing population equalling decreasing numbers of bums on seats.

However, there are two beacons of light shining out on this gloomy landscape. The first is the annual **Film Festival** (*see p203*) at the beginning of September, when the Lido rubs the sand from its eyes to find itself flooded with hordes of journalists and a constellation of international stars.

The second is **Circuito Cinema**, a film promotion initiative established in 1981 by Venice council's film department. Circuito Cinema is a hive of film-related research and activity, but it also runs and programmes a group of local arthouse cinemas, including the **Giorgione Movie d'Essai**, Cannaregio's former porn palace. This has been joined by the **Multisala Astra** on the Lido and two other screens on the mainland – the **Mignon Arthouse** in Mestre and the **Aurora Movie d'Essai** in Marghera. The plush **Sala Perla** on the Lido (Lungomare Marconi, 041 524 1320), previously open only during the Festival, completes the set and now runs a Friday evening series of first-run films, as well as doubling as a Sunday afternoon theatre. The four cinemas show a selection of Festival films in September.

To the chagrin of expats and cinema buffs alike, in Italy the dubber is king. However, both the Giorgione and the Astra offer a limited selection of films in *versione originale*.

SCREENINGS AND TICKETS

Screening times in Venice are limited, and generally there are no performances before 5pm during the week: check local press for details. Tickets cost from €4.50 to €7.

Associations

Circuito Cinema

Palazzo Carminati, Santa Croce 1882, salizada Carminati (041 524 1320/www. comune.venezia.it/cinema). Vaporetto San Stae. Map p309 C1.

'As long as there's cinema, there's hope'. The Circuito Cinema puts its money where its motto is, operating as a publisher, a cine-club organising a series of themed seasons and workshops and as a promoter. Its annual (July-June) Cinemacard gives discounts to all of Venice's cinemas as well as a number of theatres, restaurants, shops and museums. It costs €15 and can be bought from the Giorgione and Astra cinemas as well as the San Polo open-air cinema in the summer.

Cinemas

Giorgione Movie D'Essai

Cannaregio 4612, rio terà dei Franceschi (041 522 6298). Vaporetto Ca' d'Oro. **No credit cards.** Map p309 C2.
This two-screener run by Circuito Cinema (*see above*) combines the usual fare with themed seasons, kids' films (on Saturday and Sunday at 3pm) and English-language offerings on Tuesdays from October to May. While English-language films and blockbusters are in the spacious Sala A, indie material and retrospectives are shown in cinema-cum-living room Sala B.

Multisala Astra

Via Corfù 9, Lido (041 526 5736). Vaporetto Lido. **No credit cards.** Map p307.
Don't be fooled by the name: like its Venetian counterpart, the Giorgione (*see above*), the council-run Astra is a two-screener and has an identical programme to boot, usually offering the same fodder as the Giorgione a day later.

Open-air

Arena di Campo San Polo

Campo San Polo (041 711 024). Vaporetto San Silvestro or San Tomà. **Season** 6wks late July-early Sept. **Tickets** €5-€7; €24 for 6 (excluding special screenings and events). **No credit cards.** Map p309 D1.
This vibrant square in the city centre is home to Venice's second-most important cinematic event of the year. Though the city can barely muster more than one indoor cinema, around 1000 cinema-goers a night brave the mosquitoes to fill this open-air arena. The films are generally re-runs of the previous season's blockbusters and money-spinners, with the odd preview thrown in.

During the Film Festival (*see p203*) you can catch screenings of some original-language films a day or two after their Lido screening.

Arts & Entertainment

Videotheques

Videoteca Pasinetti

Palazzo Carminati, Santa Croce 1882, salizada Carminati (041 524 1320). Vaporetto San Stae. **Open** *Video archive* 9am-1pm Mon-Fri. *Video-projected cinema classics* 6pm, 9pm Tue, Fri. **Admission** by membership card (€13), valid for 4mths (Oct-Jan/Feb-June). **No credit cards.** **Map** p309 C1.

Run by the city council's film office, this video archive was founded in 1991 and given the task of collecting and conserving incredible volume of audiovisual material concerning Venice, in all formats: feature film, TV documentary, newsreel, amateur video. More than 3,000 videos are kept here – around half of them feature films – with a screening room where brief film seasons are held. Members can make reservations for individual consultations.

Festivals

Asolo Art Film Festival

Foresto Vecchio 8, Asolo (0423 520 455/www.asolo filmfestival.it). Dates last wk Oct. **No credit cards.** As well as being a leading protagonist in Liliana Cavani's *Ripley's Game,* Asolo also holds its own film festival, focussing on art and artists. 2004 saw a tribute to Venetian architect Carlo Scarpa. For information on accreditation and prices contact the above number or write to info@asolofilmfestival.it.

Le Giornate del Cinema Muto

Cineteca del Friuli, Palazzo Gurisatti, via Bini 50, Gemona (0432 980 458/www.cineteca delfriuli.org/gcm). Dates 2nd wk Oct. **No credit cards.**

Europe's most prestigious silent movie festival – due to return in 2005 to its home base at the Teatro Verdi in Pordenone after many years in nearby Sacile while the theatre was *in restauro* – is organised by the highly active Cineteca del Friuli. Events include an international forum of musicians for silent movies, retrospectives and delights such as Buster Keaton's *The General* accompanied by music. Accreditation costs €30 and allows unlimited viewings except on the opening and closing nights when a silent movie with musical accompaniment costs €13. Non-accredited viewers pay €5 per screening. The excellent website is in English too.

Venice International Short Film Festival

Circuito Off, Santa Croce 2042, ponte del Cristo (333 423 2749/www.circuitooff.com). Dates 1st/2nd wk May. Admission free.

This short film festival includes competitions, retrospectives and videos. 2004 saw a tribute to Spike Lee and a Dogma 95 retrospective. See the website for information on selection and registration.

Mostra Internazionale d'Arte Cinematografica (Venice Film Festival)

Palazzo del Cinema, lungomare Marconi 90, Lido (041 521 8711/www.labiennale.org). Vaporetto Lido. **Date** 12 days from late Aug. **Tickets** *Season tickets* €50-€150, on sale in 2wks prior to festival from ACTV-VeLa outlets (*see p278*) or online. *Individual screenings* €5-€15, available previous day from ACTV-VeLa outlets or ticket office at the Casinò (lungomare Marconi, Lido, open 8.30am-11pm daily). Same-day tickets occasionally available. **Credit** AmEx, DC, MC, V. **Map** p307.

The Lido comes to life for the **Venice Film Festival.**

'All that glisters is not gold…'

…especially where Hollywood adaptations of Shakespeare are concerned. But some of the Bard's Veneto plays have come up trumps on screen.

Michael Radford directs Al Pacino in a *Merchant of Venice* – first shown, fittingly, at the 2004 Venice Film Festival – that was filmed, appropriately, in the city's Ghetto (*see p104*) and surrounding streets for true authenticity. This period piece pleased the purists, though some baulked at the occasional American accent. A strong supporting cast of Brits includes Joseph Fiennes (Bassanio), Jeremy Irons (Antonio) and Mackenzie Crook (Launcelot Gobbo).

Equally awkward in terms of political correctness is that other Venetian chestnut, *Othello*. Shot in Morocco, Orson Welles' 1951 movie took four years to make, with Welles overcoming huge obstacles to create a dazzling film that revolves around his own towering performance as the jealous husband. Where Welles succeeded, others have failed. Laurence Olivier's stagy 1965 offering was derided in *Time Out* for its 'school of semaphore' acting.

Oliver Parker's 1995 version comes through relatively unscathed: Laurence Fishburne's passionate performance, with top-notch support from Shakespeare veteran Kenneth Branagh and Nathaniel Parker, makes for riveting viewing, which cannot be said for *O* (2001, dir. Tim Blake Nelson), set in a southern boarding school with just one black pupil, Odin (Mekhi Phifer). Trouble ensues when his jealous friend Hugo (Josh Hartnett) formulates a plan to ruin Odin's relationship with the dean's improbably named daughter Desi Brable (Julia Stiles). Tragic.

Stiles also appears in *Ten Things I Hate About You* (1999), based on the Padua/Verona-set *Taming of the Shrew*. Stiles gets to play Kat Stratford opposite Heath Ledger's Patrick Verona. Geddit? (Ledger subsequently remained in Venetian vein playing Casanova in Lasse Hallström's eponymous film.) Again we are in an American high school, but this time it's for laughs with the two Stratford sisters and their potential beaus getting up to high jinks. Franco Zeffirelli gave audiences a voyeuristic thrill when he directed Burton and Taylor in his 1967 version of the play. However, this is not a patch on *Kiss Me Kate* (1953, dir. George Sidney), which combines outstanding Cole Porter tunes, Bob Fosse dance routines and the brilliant concept of a divorced couple of actors reunited to star in the musical version of the play. With songs like 'Too Darn Hot' and 'From This Moment On' performed with gusto by Kathryn Grayson and Howard Keel, Sidney's musical has stood the test of time.

Which isn't the case with *West Side Story*. The truly dynamic dance sequences can't overcome directorial glitches and stilted performances in this 1961 tale on *Romeo and Juliet*. Other R&J films include Zeffirelli's 1968 tale, with a wardrobe to please even the most zealous costume fascist. Baz Luhrmann's 1996 gangsta epic completes the trio of films about the star-crossed lovers. Baby-faced Leo Di Caprio and Claire Danes come a cropper in modern day Verona, Florida, whilst the two feuding family gangs shoot it out on the beach and in the streets. If the film is set in a fast-moving present, the dialogue remains firmly entrenched in the 16th century as Luhrmann spins the pair headlong toward their inexorable tragic end.

The 12-day Venice Film Festival takes place along the main, sea-facing Lido esplanade, between the Hotel des Bains and the Excelsior (for both, *see p65*). Between these two grand hotels is the marble-and-glass Palazzo del Cinema, where official competition screenings take place in the Sala Grande; other festival screens can be found in the gargantuan PalaGalileo and inside the Casinò. Press accreditation guarantees virtually unlimited access; the press pass costs €26 and permits priority entry to a number of special screenings, mostly in the morning and early evening. Arrange this at least two months in advance by contacting the Biennale press office (041 521 8857/fax 041 520 0569).

'Cultural' accreditation is another option; it allows access to a more restricted range of screenings. Again, this should be arranged before the end of June. Failing this, stand in line and buy tickets for single showings. This is best done the day before the screening for competition films. On the same day, try to get there at least an hour before the film you want to see is screened.

Una Settimana da leoni is a special offer for people under 26, offering both a festival pass and accommodation; for details, consult www.venicesystem.com/ita/biennale.htm. Film makers wanting to submit a film for competition should contact cinema@labiennale.org.

Galleries

La Biennale is still the star of the contemporary arts scene.

The new arts and design department at the **IUAV** architecture university.

A shake-up of local cultural institutions over the past five or six years seemed to bode well for the long-forecast, long-awaited flowering of the contemporary art scene in Venice. The results, however, have proved patchy. Sporadic activities that are strong in content but void of any sense of continuity – either in output or management – fail to set the right tone in a city that, if only by virtue of being home to La Biennale, would like to be considered an international leading light for art.

La Biennale di Venezia (*see p207* **La Biennale**) has indeed injected new life into some fields with its revamped theatre, dance and music sector; but it has done little to foster production of contemporary art in the city. The **Accademia delle Belle Arti** (Fine Arts Academy) continues to prove itself unable to forge links between its students and Venice's institutions or citizens. The **Centro Culturale Candiani** (piazzale Candiani 7, Mestre, 041 238 6111, www.comune.venezia.it/candiani, open 9am-7pm Tue-Sun), an enormous venue for exhibitions and cultural activities, has failed miserably to promote the production of visual arts on the Venetian mainland.

The **Fondazione Bevilacqua La Masa** (*see p209*) has stepped up its programmes to support and show local artists, and to keep them in touch with the contemporary art scene beyond the city. However, financial limits prevent its becoming a more active centre for the creation of contemporary art in a city that continues to have difficulty producing artists of its own.

The one truly bright light to have appeared on Venice's contemporary art scene is the new art and design department at the **IUAV** architecture university (www.iuav.it; *see p290*). Its courses, activities and workshops by international artists have provided students – and the rest of the city – with numerous opportunities to get to grips with what is happening in the wider art world. Finally, students are being offered the chance to interact with the city and vice versa in a project that really puts ideas into action.

Although the gallery scene is now largely stagnant, some establishments have widened the scope of their exhibition programmes. However, as yet there is no equivalent in Venice to those New York or London galleries where dealers invest in particular artists or movements, and patrons foster a younger artistic generation experimenting with new media. All of which doesn't mean that there isn't good art out there (*see p208* **VYAs**).

Beware that numerous places calling themselves galleries are really little more than outlets for the artistic output of their owners or for arty knick-knacks. For glass – contemporary and otherwise – *see pp191-3*.

La Biennale

Although arts *biennali* have mushroomed over the past decades in every continent, Venice's remains *the* biennale. Officially called Esposizione Internazionale d'Arte della Biennale di Venezia, it began in 1895 and was the only one of its kind for decades.

A decade or so ago, the dictates of blockbuster exhibiting forced the institution to expand beyond its traditional exhibition site at Giardini to the nearby Arsenale, thus splitting the exhibition in two. La Biennale is complemented by related exhibitions or presentations that turn much of the city into a unique exhibition space.

In the park at the far eastern end of Castello – the Giardini – are a series of nationally owned pavilions: the first one was built by Belgium in 1907; many other countries followed suit, commissioning architects to design suitable containers for the artists chosen to carry their flag every two years. Some of the original buildings were reconstructed or radically altered during the 20th century, in some case by big-name architects. As well as various works by Carlo Scarpa – including the Giardino delle sculture (1952) and the Venezuelan pavilion (1954) – there's Alvar Aalto's 1956 design for Finland, Sverre Fehn's 1961 Scandinavian pavilion, or BBPR's Canadian building (1956).

Unfortunately, these pavilions are only used for Biennali, leaving the Giardini desolate during the rest of the year. Plans to put the buildings to a more regular use have been in the air for some time now.

The recently restored, spectacular and grand spaces of the Arsenale, from the Corderie (rope factory) to the Artiglierie (gun foundry) and the Gaggiandre (dry docks), house the main core of the Biennale exhibition, together with many smaller exhibitions by those countries with no pavilion to host them. Some other countries prefer, or are obliged, by lack of space, to rent exhibition space somewhere else in the city.

Due to a slow-moving restoration programme of the various sites of the Biennale, the offices are divided between Ca' Giustinian (*see below*) and Palazzo Querini Dubois (San Polo 2004, campo San Polo, open 9am-6pm Mon-Fri), while the massive library and archive have recently moved to the mainland (*see p286*).

La Biennale di Venezia

Ca' Giustinian, San Marco 1364, calle del Ridotto (041 521 8711/www.labiennale.org). Vaporetto Vallaresso. **Map** p311 B3. **Venues** Giardini di Castello, vaporetto Giardini (map p313 C & D/1 & 2); Arsenale, vaporetto Arsenale (map p312 B3). **Dates** mid June-early Nov in alternate years (odd for art; even for architecture). **Open** 10am-6pm Tue-Sun. **Admission** (allows access to all official shows) €12; €10 concessions. **No credit cards**.

A+A

San Marco 3073, calle Malipiero (041 277 0466/www.aplusa.it). Vaporetto San Samuele. **Open** 11am-1pm, 2-6pm Tue-Sat. **No credit cards**. **Map** p311 B1.

A non-profit exhibition centre financed by the Slovenian mi nistry of culture. A new director has recently increased its regular programme of shows and events – mostly devoted to Slovenian artists or related projects – to accommodate projects organised in collaboration with other institutions and especially devoted to very young artists. It hosts works by Slovenian representatives to the Biennale.

Bugno Art Gallery

San Marco 1996A, campo San Fantin (041 523 1305/www.bugnoartgallery.it). Vaporetto Vallaresso. **Open** 4-7.30pm Mon, Sun; 10.30am-12.30pm, 4-7.30pm Tue-Sat. **Credit** AmEx, DC, MC, V. **Map** p311 B2.

This large central space situated over two floors is devoted to artists working in all media. Local artists are also included in the gallery's collection. The gallery has recently enlarged into an exhibition space that can be found just a few doors away.

Other locations: San Marco 1655, piscina di Frezzeria (041 528 8135).

A+A.

YVAs

With Titian and Tiepolo hogging the limelight, contemporary artists in Venice struggle for attention. But while not exactly bursting with health, the contemporary Venetian art scene is alive and fairly well. Not only does the city boast some home-grown talent, it also draws artists from around the globe.

Unlike their not-so-YBA (Young British Artists) counterparts – who spread their dirty washing in public and proffer severed carcasses for our visual delight – young Venetian artists tend to stick to more conventional methods while still managing to create new and exciting work. On the whole, painting is the preferred form of many artists based in the watery city.

Local lad Daniele Bianchi (www.daniele bianchi.com) has been churning out great art for 15 years. Looking at his progress, from abstract and ephemeral work at the end of the 1980s through to more personal figurative work at the beginning of the noughties, what stands out is his sublime use of light and shadow. Often working with brown tones illuminated by the infiltration of gold or silver light, Bianchi's work is both atmospheric and romantic.

Carolina Antich (www.carolinaantich.com) was born in Argentina in 1970, but is now happily ensconced in Venice. Antich brings events and moments from her own childhood to her work. In her paintings, which at first glance can seem naïve, children become unwitting witnesses and protagonists of everyday life. There is a sense of silence, with the children often depicted as small figures clutched together against a backdrop of muted colour.

Maria Morganti

Another outsider who has chosen Venice as her base is Milanese artist Maria Morganti (www.italianarea.it). Already well established both in her adopted home and in New York, Morganti concentrates on the development of colour on her canvases. Each painting has been meticulously constructed with layer upon layer of colour. Leaving a corner or a strip of colour from each layer in view, Morganti offers a hint of what the final painting may once have been and demonstrates how a seemingly simple and bold work is actually the result of a persistent and painstaking research.

For an overview of the contemporary scene, head for www.italianarea.it; for Venetian art, check out the Fondazione Bevilacqua La Masa (see p209), which hosts meetings for artists in the city as well as holding collective exhibitions of contemporary work.

Il Capricorno

San Marco 1994, calle dietro la Chiesa (041 520 6920/galleriailcapricorno@libero.it). Vaporetto Giglio. **Open** 11am-1pm, 5.30-8pm daily. **Credit** AmEx, DC, MC, V. **Map** p311 B3.

This small space presents a few shows each year by younger international artists working in a variety of media. Opening hours tend to be fluid.

Contini Galleria d'Arte

San Marco 2765, calle dello Spezier (041 520 4942/ www.continiarte.com). Vaporetto Giglio or Accademia. **Open** 10am-1pm, 3.30-7.30pm daily. **Credit** AmEx, MC, V. **Map** p311 B2.

In a large, recently renovated space, now stretching on two sides of the same street, the Contini stages frequent and well-researched exhibitions of renowned artists, besides keeping a strong collection of 20th-century works. It has sister galleries in Mestre and Cortina d'Ampezzo.

Other locations: piazza Monsignor Vecchi 1, Mestre (041 981 611).

Flora Bigai Arte Moderna e Contemporanea

San Marco 1652, piscina di Frezzeria (041 521 2208/041 241 3799/www.florabigai.com). Vaporetto Vallaresso. **Open** 3.30-7.30pm Mon; 10am-1pm, 3.30-7.30pm Tue-Sat. **Credit** AmEx, DC, MC, V. **Map** p311 B3.

This three-floor space is a recent addition to the gallery scene. Exhibitions are devoted to well-known Italian and international artists and shared with its sister gallery in Pietrasanta.

Fondazione Bevilacqua La Masa

Exhibition space *San Marco 71C, piazza San Marco (041 523 7819/www.bevilacqualamasa.it). Vaporetto Vallaresso.* **Open** during exhibitions only 10am-1pm, 4-7pm Mon, Wed-Sun. **Map** p307 A4.
Offices and exhibition space *Dorsoduro 2826, fondamenta Gerardini (041 520 7797/041 520 8879). Vaporetto Ca' Rezzonico.* **Open** 8am-5.30pm Mon-Fri. **Map** p311 B3.
Founded in the 19th century when Duchess Felicita Bevilacqua La Masa left her palace to the city to give local artists a space in which to explore new trends, the institution has recently been given new direction. Exhibition and office space has been increased, programmes have been expanded, new liaisons with local institutions have been set up and a pool of 'younger' artists has been created; now new studio space is being sought to enlarge its artist-in-residence programme. An annual *Esposizione collettiva* is dedicated to Veneto-based artists under 35.

Fondazione Scientifica Querini Stampalia

Castello 5252, campo Santa Maria Formosa (041 271 1411/www.querinistampalia.it). Vaporetto San Zaccaria. **Open** 10am-6pm Tue-Thur, Sun; 10am-10pm Fri, Sat. **Admission** €6; €4 concessions. **Library** free. **Credit** DC, MC, V. **Map** p312 B1.
The Fondazione Querini Stampalia arrived on the contemporary scene many years ago with Biennale-related projects, seminars and occasional small-scale shows. Although its contemporary programme has been cut back, its *Invito al contemporaneo* seminars remain. The biannual *Premio Querini Stampalia-Furla per l'Arte* is awarded to young artists in any medium, living and working in Italy. Works by shortlisted artists are shown in the upstairs galleries.

Galerie Bordas

San Marco 1994B, calle dietro la Chiesa (041 522 4812/www.galeriebordas.com). Vaporetto Vallaresso. **Open** 11am-1.30pm, 4.30-7.30pm Mon-Sat. **Credit** AmEx, DC, MC, V. **Map** p311 B3.
A small space where international artists who work in graphics are regularly exhibited together with a good selection of illustrated volumes.

Galleria d'Arte L'Occhio

Dorsoduro 181, calle San Gregorio (041 522 6550/ galleria.locchio@tin.it). Vaporetto Salute. **Open** 10am-6pm Mon-Sat; 10am-5pm Sun. **Credit** AmEx, MC, V. **Map** p311 B2.
A tiny, friendly gallery with solo and collective exhibitions devoted to younger national and international artists in various media, mostly figurative.

Galleria Michela Rizzo

Castello 4254, calle degli Albanesi (041 522 3186/ www.galleriamichelarizzo.net). Vaporetto San Zaccaria. **Open** 10am-12.30pm Tue; 4.30-7.30pm Wed-Sat. **No credit cards. Map** p312 B2.
This new gallery (which has a branch in the owner's home, visits by appointment) boasts a packed programme of artists working in various media.

Galleria Traghetto

San Marco 2543, campo Santa Maria del Giglio (041 522 1188/galleria.traghetto@tin.it). Vaporetto Giglio. **Open** 10.30am-12.30pm, 3.30-7.30pm Mon-Sat; by appointment Sun. **Credit** AmEx, DC, MC, V. **Map** p311 B2.
This gallery has long dealt in Venetian abstracts, which are still exhibited, but it also features emerging artists working in various media. Consistent exhibition programme throughout the year.

Galleria Venice Design

San Marco 3146, salizada San Samuele (041 520 7915/www.venicedesignartgallery.com). Vaporetto San Samuele. **Open** 10am-1pm, 3-7pm daily. **Credit** AmEx, DC, MC, V. **Map** p311 B2.
This ambitious gallery deals in all art forms, with a preference for traditional media such as sculpture and painting, besides interior decoration. It represents both Italian and international artists, and organises various shows yearly.
Other locations: San Marco 1310, calle Vallaresso (041 523 9082).

La Galleria

San Marco 2566, calle Calegheri (041 520 7415/ www.galerie.vanderkoelen.de). Vaporetto Giglio. **Open** 10am-1pm, 3.30-7.30pm Mon-Sat. **Credit** AmEx, DC, MC, V. **Map** p311 B2.
A space conceived by international, minimalist standards spreads over various rooms to accommodate artworks, artists' books and scholarly volumes on established artists. The gallery is run by a German curator who is especially active at the sister gallery in Mainz.

Nuova Ikona

Giudecca 454, calle dell'Olio (041 521 0101/ www.nuovaikona.org). Vaporetto Palanca. **Open** during exhibitions 4pm-8pm daily or else by appointment. **No credit cards. Map** p311 D1.
This non-profit cultural association has recently celebrated its tenth anniversary. Initially a solo project, it has now become a larger organisation, promoting and staging visual and performance exhibits and events. Core shows take place in its gallery space on Giudecca. Solo works or performances are held at the tiny Oratorio di San Ludovico (Dorsoduro 2552, corte dei Vecchi), near the church of San Sebastiano (*see p125*). During the Biennale, NI's spaces are offered to countries with no pavilion at the Giardini (*see p207* **La Biennale**) or organisations requiring support to show independently. Nuova Ikona's recent 'by//pass' project promotes cultural exchanges with Middle Eastern countries. The calendar of events is packed though irregular.

San Gregorio Art Gallery

Dorsoduro 165, calle San Gregorio (041 522 9296/ www.sangregorioartgallery.com). Vaporetto Salute. **Open** 10.30am-12.30pm, 3-6pm Mon, Wed-Sat. **Credit** AmEx, DC, MC, V. **Map** p311 C2.
This gallery has three exhibitions a year, focusing on abstract, contemporary Italian art in all media.

Arts & Entertainment

Gay & Lesbian

Take a serene break from the norm, or party in Mestre or Padua.

Exclusively gay or lesbian venues are remarkable only by their absence in Venice. The city itself might appear to be the perfect backdrop for most fantasies – from the blissfully romantic to the one-night stand. But despite tourist hordes that swell the daytime population to unimaginable numbers, the city offers little for gays and lesbians used to a faster-paced scene.

That's the negative aspect. The upside is that this might be just what the doctor ordered for those stressed out by modern urban gay culture. *La Serenissima* has become just that: very, *very* serene. Cruising is as casual and 'venue free' as you can get, and takes place just about anywhere in the city, at any time – discretion, of course, being the bottom line.

There are, however, a few places that, while not catering to exclusively gay or lesbian clienteles, are most definitely gay-friendly or at least frequented by a largely gay clientele.

The **Central Restaurant Lounge** (*see p213*) organises the occasional gay night. During the summer months, the secluded beach and surrounding dunes at **Alberoni** allow sun seekers to indulge in nude sunbathing and cruising. And **Il Muro**, though thronging with mass-tourism day trippers, still attracts a handful of post-midnight cruisers.

Bars in Venice's trendier *campi* range from open-minded to actively gay-friendly and in keeping with Venice's toned-down, bustle-free scene, there has been a recent mushrooming of openly gay-friendly accommodation on the islands of the lagoon.

When the serenity gets too much for you, the Venetian version of the modern world is close by in Mestre or Padua.

ARCIGAY

The national gay rights group ArciGay has local chapters that sponsor activities, festivals, counselling and AIDS awareness. An ArciGay-issued card called Uno Club Card is needed for entry to many venues affiliated with the organisation, including some of those listed below. A one-month *tessera* (membership card) for non-Italian nationals costs €7 (annual membership €14) and can be purchased at the door of venues requiring it, or at the nearest ArciGay chapter, Tralaltro (via Santa Sofia 5, Padua; 340 173 4953 or 049 876 2458; open 9-11pm Mon, 6-8pm Wed).

Catch some rays on **Alberoni** beach.

Venice

Open-air

Il Muro (The Wall)
Map p311 B3.
Behind the Procuratie Nuove, by the Giardinetti Reali, Il Muro has seen better days as the city's after-dark cruising area. Now very rarely frequented from October to May, it can still pull a good crowd during the summer months. Even with almost no one about, the place has a romantic charm, and is worth a visit just for the view it affords of San Giorgio Maggiore across the canal.

Alberoni Beach, Lido
Map p307. For how to get there, *see p137*.
Now an almost exclusively gay beach, Alberoni is *the* place for summer cruising. The dunes and pine forest are where the action is. Cruising starts as early as April, but if you enjoy feeling like a kid let loose in a sweet-shop, go for July weekends.

Accommodation

See also **Casa de' Uscoli** and **Almaviva House** on *p57* **Boat & Breakfast?**.

Il Lato Azzurro
*Via Forte 13, Sant'Erasmo (041 244 4900/348
443 6304/fax 041 523 0642/www.latoazzurro.it).
Vaporetto 13 to Sant'Erasmo-Capannone.* **Rates**
€40-€50 single; €56-€70 double; €75-€90 triple;
€90-€100 quadruple; €20 for each additional bed.
Credit AmEx, DC, MC, V.
This gay-owned and -operated guest house on
Venice's vegetable-garden island of Sant'Erasmo
(*see p145*) is the ideal place to stay if you want a
really quiet retreat. Venice and its flocks of tourists
are a vaporetto ride away. Dinner costs €15.

Lucio Andrich Bed & Breakfast
*Via Borgognoni 4L, Torcello (041 735
292/www.lucioandrich.com). Vaporetto LN to
Burano, then T to Torcello.* **Rates** €60 single;
€80-€120 double; €160 quad. **No credit cards**.
Guest rooms in this B&B on the tranquil island of
Torcello are spread between the main house and a
cason (fisherman's cottage) with incredible views
over the lagoon. Owner Paolo rents boats (€50 per
half day). All rooms for minimum two-night stay.

Eating & drinking

Campo Santa Margherita (*see p125*) is the
focal point for trendier young Venetians. It has
a host of bars and *pizzerie*, all of which buzz
during the summer months when the campo is
invaded by pavement tables and a cacophony
of fast-talking local youth. It's not the cruisiest
of places, but you never know your luck.
See also p158 **Alla Zucca**, long a favourite
with gay and lesbian gourmets.

Bagolo
*Santa Croce 1584, campo San Giacomo dell'Orio
(041 717 584/347 366 5016). Vaporetto Riva
di Biasio or San Stae.* **Open** *Sept-May* 8am-2am
Tue-Sun. *June-Aug* 8am-2am daily. **No credit
cards**. **Map** p308 C3.
This simple, typically Venetian bar is definitely
gay-friendly. Owner Gianni has decided to bring the
Venetian *bacaro* (*see p148*) into the 21st century; the
results are proving very popular with local thirty-
somethings. During the warmer months sit outside,
sip your spritz and watch campo life go by.

Tours etc

Pordenone's silent film festival (*see p203*) is
a popular gay rendez-vous.

Venice à la Carte
(www.tourvenice.org). **Rates** vary according to tour.
Credit AmEx, MC, V.
Tailor-made, personalised tours of Venice and the
villas of the Veneto, catering for a wide variety of
cultural interests and credit limits, organised by
Alvise Zanchi, a native Venetian and expert tour
guide. Member of IGLTA. Bookings and queries are
only accepted through the web page given above.

Mestre

Sauna

Metro Venezia
*Via Cappuccina 82B, Mestre (041 538 4299/
www.metroclub.it). Bus 2 or 7 from piazzale Roma/
train to Mestre, then a five-minute walk.* **Open** 2pm-
2am daily. **Admission** €14 Mon-Sat; €16 Sun with
Uno Club Card (*see p210*). **Credit** MC, V.
Metro has a bar, a dry sauna, steam sauna, private
rooms, darkroom and new solarium. Massage and
hydro-massage are also available. Trade here is very
brisk. Discounts after 9pm and for under-26-year-olds.

Padua

Just a 20-minute drive from Venice, this
city offers the anonymity is sorely missing
on the lagoon. The following list contains only
those gay places that are most easily accessible
by public transport or taxi from Venice (*see
pp274* **Directory: Getting around** and
pp235-45). A word of caution: cruising
continues to be very risky, especially around
and in Padua station, and should be avoided.

Bars & entertainment

Flexo Club
*Via Nicolò Tommaseo 96A (049 807 4707/
www.flexoclub.it).* **Open** 10pm-2am Wed, Thur;
from 10pm until the last guest leaves Fri-Sun.
Admission €8 (1 drink included) Wed, Thur; €10
(1 drink included) Fri-Sun and for special events
with Uno Club Card (*see p210*). **Credit** DC, MC, V.
A private club/disco arranged over four floors, with
bars, and labyrinthine darkrooms downstairs. It's
about ten minutes walk from the station; the front
door (ring the bell) is at the back of a courtyard on
the right side of the road as you approach from the
station (use the handy map on Flexo's website).
Every first Friday (invitation required) and first and
third Saturday of the month Flexo organises
a 'naked party'. The club's clientele is almost
exclusively male; women are not allowed beyond the
downstairs bar area.

Sauna

Metro Sauna
Via Turazza 19 (049 807 5828/www.metroclub.it).
Open 2pm-2am daily. **Admission** €14 Mon-Sat;
€16.50 Sun with Uno Club Card (*see p210*).
Credit MC, V.
Large, modern and well equipped, this place has
a proper work-those-pores Finnish sauna rather
than just the usual warm cabin that smells of pine.
It also has the usual well-earned rest and private
massage, facilities. There are discounts after 9pm
and for under-26-year-olds.

Music & Nightlife

It's not the wildest town in Europe, but there are plenty of nocturnal treats for those prepared to seek them out.

Fondamenta della Misericordia.

Venice was once notorious for its nightlife; nowadays it's deemed a sleeping beauty that slips into a serene slumber by 9pm. Yet if you explore the maze of *calli* and *campi* behind the well-trodden tourist trail, you'll come across a surprising amount of life after dark. Native night owls cluster around Venice's 'alternative' drawing room of campo Santa Margherita, in the heart of the city's southern Dorsoduro district, or on Cannaregio's 'party' fondamenta della Misericordia, but there are myriad late-opening bars secreted away all over town.

MUSIC

The local music scene is small but by no means dormant; home-grown talent includes: Groove Jet producer and DJ Spiller; Pitura Freska, whose unlikely mix of Venetian dialect and reggae shot them to fame and whose most recent spin-off, Ska-J, have shared stages with the Wailers and the Skatalites; the fine jazz musicians Pietro and Marcello Tonolo, who still play in their native city, as does Treviso-born Tolo Marton, 'Italy's Hendrix'. There's also a surprisingly fertile indie-rock scene with One Dimensional Man earning the most success on European circuits.

Unfortunately, stringent noise pollution regulations and lack of adequate venues have effectively pulled the plug on large music events, Carnevale, Venezia Suona (for both, *pp196-8*) and the summer festivals (*see p215* **Summer festivals**) being the exceptions.

Rock 'n' roll royals who do dates in Venice are usually confined to the extremely formal setting of one of the local theatres. Regular series of high-quality jazz and experimental music are organised by local cultural organisations l ike Caligola (www.caligola.it) or Vortice (www.provincia.venezia.it/vortice), which has managed to pull such avant-jazzers as Dave Douglas and Elliot Sharp. Performances usually take place in the more intimate Teatro Fondamenta Nuove.

Venice has not become totally moribund music-wise thanks to the tenacity of the few bar owners still willing to wrestle with red tape, persist in the face of party-pooper petitioning neighbours and offer the chance to play and hear live music in a network of *locali* across the city. Venetian vibes tend to be laid-back and these small, free gigs are almost always reggae, jazz or blues with the occasional rock, Latino or world session. Clubs and venues on the nearby mainland draw bigger acts.

CLUBS

For serious club culture, make for the mainland. In the winter, a short bus or train ride to Mestre or Marghera (just across the bridge and well served by night buses) is all it takes to dance until dawn. In the summer, most of the dance action moves out to the seaside resort of Jesolo Lido (*see p216* **Jesolo night fever**), the place to be for house and techno, with a smattering of Latino to swing your suntan to.

INFORMATION AND TICKETS

Day-to-day listings are carried by the two local papers, *Il Gazzettino* and *La Nuova Venezia*. For a more complete overview of concerts and festivals, with English translations, the monthly listings magazine *Venezia News* is indispensable. Also keep your eyes peeled for the free *Venezia da Vivere* leaflet and around town for notices of gigs and events. Tickets should be available at the venue but can be bought in advance at the CD shop **Parole e Musica**, Castello 5673, salizada San Lio (041 521 2215) or via the national ticket agency www.boxoffice.it. Unless specified, the bars listed below have no extra charge for music.

San Marco

Late bars & bars with music

Bacaro Jazz

San Marco 5546, salizada del Fontego dei Tedeschi (041 528 5249/ bacarojazz@iol.it). Vaporetto Rialto. **Open** 4pm-3am Mon, Tue, Thur-Sun. **Credit** AmEx, DC, MC, V. **Map** p309 D2.

Venice's most central late-night watering hole, Bacaro Jazz is a place to mingle with fellow tourists or foreign students rather than meet the locals. The background jazz and wide range of killer cocktails keep the party going into the early hours.

Centrale Restaurant Lounge

San Marco 1659B, piscina Frezzeria (041 296 0664/ www.centrale-lounge.com). Vaporetto Valaresso. **Open** 7pm-2am Mon, Wed-Sun. **Credit** AmEx, MC, V. **Map** p309 D2.

Only the exposed bricks of the original 16th-century palazzo's walls will remind you you're in Venice: this cool, contemporary restaurant and lounge bar is more New York or London. Owners Franco and Alfredo lay on events like live drum 'n' bass and jazz or a regular international gay night. A full, fresh à la carte is served until closing time. Alternatively, go early for *spritz* and sushi or after dinner to sink into one of the designer armchairs, explore the cocktail menu and chill out to lounge and house sounds.

Malvasia Vecchia

San Marco 2586, corte Malatina (041 522 5883/348 670 8490). Vaporetto Rialto. **Open** 11pm-4am Wed-Sat. Closed July-Sept. **Admission** free with ARCI club card (annual membership €15 at the door). **No credit cards. Map** p309 D1.

A feat to find, this members-only club behind the Fenice is *the* place to party winter nights away.

Torino@Notte

San Marco 4591, campo San Luca (041 522 3914). Vaporetto Rialto. **Open** 8pm-1am Tue-Sat. **No credit cards. Map** p309 D2.

This dreary daytime snack bar switches management after dark and transforms into a happening hotspot. DJ sets and live music on Wednesdays keep

the mix of students and musos grooving to acid jazz, fusion and funky tunes while Carnevale brings a week of live gigs in the campo outside.

Vitae

San Marco 4118, calle Sant'Antonio (041 520 5205). Vaporetto Rialto. **Open** 9pm-2am Mon-Fri; 5pm-2am Sat. **No credit cards. Map** p309 D2.

Known as 'Il Muro' (the wall), this tiny bar behind campo San Luca is busy long into the night with a yuppie set who come for Mojitos, mouth-watering snacks and the background sounds of smooth soul and acid jazz.

Castello

See also **Angiò** *p167*.

Late bars & bars with music

Inishark

Castello 5787, calle del Mondo Novo (041 523 5300). Vaporetto Rialto. **Open** 6pm-1.30am Tue-Sun. **No credit cards. Map** p309 D3.

Tucked away in a small calle near Santa Maria Formosa, this strictly no-smoking Irish-style pub has the best Guinness on tap in town and great snacks to soak up the black stuff – try the roast suckling pig and mustard sandwiches. Satellite TV packs in the fans for Champions League football.

Cannaregio

Late bars & bars with music

Al Parlamento

Cannaregio 511, fondamenta San Giobbe (041 244 0214). Vaporetto Ferrovia or Crea. **Open** 8am-2am daily. **No credit cards. Map** p308 A2.

Prices and position ensure Parliament's popularity. Well off the tourist trail, though just behind the main drag from the station, it's packed during *spritz* hour (6-8pm), is busy until late, and has popular DJ sets on Thursdays.

Fiddler's Elbow Irish Pub

Cannaregio 3847, corte dei Pali già Testori (041 523 9930). Vaporetto Ca' d'Oro. **Open** 5pm-1am daily. **No credit cards. Map** p309 C2.

Expats, locals and tourists all prop up the bar in Venice's oldest Irish pub. Neighbours have put a stop to regular live music, but local bands still play at Hallowe'en and St Patrick's Day. Big sports events are screened in the campo outside.

Iguana

Cannaregio 2515, fondamenta della Misericordia (041 713 561). Vaporetto San Marcuola. **Open** 6pm-1am Tue-Sun. **Credit** AmEx, DC, MC, V. **Map** p309 B1.

With tacos, tequila and tecate, mescal and Margaritas, the Misericordia's Mexican swings to salsa sounds til late. The music comes live on

Thursdays, with Latino, jazz or funk, though this too risks being axed by neighbours, while *spritz* hour (€1 a *spritz* 6.30-8pm) packs in the crowds.

Paradiso Perduto
Cannaregio 2540, fondamenta della Misericordia (041 720 581). Vaporetto San Marcuola. **Open** 7pm-2am Mon, Thur-Sun; noon-2am Sun. Closed 2wks Aug. **No credit cards. Map** p309 B1.
Probably the most famous Venetian haunt after Harry's Bar (*see p166*), this 'Paradise Lost' is well worth finding. The colourful and chaotic mix of seafood and succulent sounds (somewhat impromptu renditions of mainly jazz and blues occur most nights) comes together under the watchful eye of Maurizio: owner, chef and proud possessor of the bushiest beard in town.

Tortuga
Cannaregio 4888, campo dei Gesuiti (041 277 0130/ www.pubtortuga.it). Vaporetto Fondamente Nove or Ca'd'Oro. **Open** 10am-2am daily. **No credit cards. Map** p309 B2.
The decor in this pub behind the fondamenta Nuove is very old sea dog, but the clientele consists of tourists dropping in for a drink and cheap bite to eat on their way back from visiting northern lagoon islands during the day, and young Venetians supping Belgian beer and Murphy's stout later on. Local lads play live on Fridays.

Clubs

Casanova Music Café
Cannaregio 158A, lista di Spagna (041 275 0199). Vaporetto Ferrovia. **Open** *Internet café* 9.30am-11pm daily. *Club* 11pm-4am daily. **Admission** Mon-Fri, Sun free (obligatory 1st drink €7); Sat €10 (incl 1st drink). **Credit** AmEx, MC, V. **Map** p308 B3.
Check your email, then bop till you drop in Venice's only real nightclub, a stone's throw from the train station. Resident ravers, passing tourists and a few of the club's native namesakes all get down to a mix of dance, pop and rock from Sunday to Thursday, hip-hop and R'n'B on Friday and commercial house on Saturday.

San Polo & Santa Croce

See also p171 **Muro Vino e Cucina**.

Late bars & bars with music

Ai Postali
Santa Croce 821, fondamenta Rio Marin (041 715 156). Vaporetto Riva di Biasio or San Tomà. **Open** 7.30pm-2am Mon-Sat. Closed Aug. **No credit cards. Map** p308 C3.
Across the bridge from the train station and down a narrow canal, this long-established *osteria* is a firm Venetian favourite. Locals moor their boats beneath the outside terrace to drop in for a drink or linger long into the small hours.

Altrove
San Polo 1105, campo San Silvestro (041 528 9224). Vaporetto San Silvestro. **Open** 8am-1am Mon-Sat. **No credit cards. Map** p309 D1.
Young and fun, this new bar tucked away in a square behind riva del Vin on the market side of Rialto bridge has DJ sets and/or bands every Tuesday.

Da Baffo
San Polo 2346, campiello Sant'Agostin (041 520 8862). Vaporetto San Stae or San Tomà. **Open** 7.30am-2am Mon-Sat. **No credit cards. Map** p308 D3.
Named after the 18th-century erotic poet whose saucy sonnets are on display inside, this is one of the hippest hangouts in Venice. Locals, students and their profs all come to sample the wide selection of Italian wines, international beers and single malts. Alas, the powers that be have decreed the end of the regular live music slot and gastronomic nights take place instead.

Kler Café
Santa Croce 1539, calle del Tentor (041 244 0324). Vaporetto San Stae. **Open** 11.30am-2am Mon, Wed-Sun. **No credit cards. Map** p308 C3.
In a narrow street behind campo San Giacomo dell'Orio, this innovative haunt is popular with nocturnal natives who come to relax on sofas, work their way through an extensive cocktail menu and admire work exhibited by two different artists a month.

Dorsoduro

Late bars & bars with music

Café Blue
Dorsoduro 3778, calle de la Scuola (041 710 227). Vaporetto San Tomà. **Open** 8pm-2am Mon-Fri; 5pm-2am Sat, Sun. **No credit cards. Map** p308 D3.
This pub-style boozer near campo Santa Margherita bulges with students and an international set well into the small hours. Homesick Scots can enjoy a wee dram in the Whiskeria while lounge lovers can chill out to the Wednesday night DJ set. The music goes live on Fridays with local bands playing rock, blues and folk.

Café Noir
Dorsoduro 3805, crosera San Pantalon (041 710 925/cafenoir@hotmail.com). Vaporetto San Tomà. **Open** 7am-2am Mon-Sat; 7pm-2am Sun. **No credit cards. Map** p308 D3.
Warm and intimate Café Noir is a winter favourite among the university and twentysomething crowd, who while away their days over panini and hot chocolate, and as it livens up later crowd inside and out for *spritz* and alcopops.

Il Caffè
Dorsoduro 2963, campo Santa Margherita (041 528 7998). Vaporetto Ca'Rezzonico. **Open** 7am-1.30am Mon-Sat. **No credit cards. Map** p308 D3.

Summer festivals

Venice Airport Festival.

and films are followed by nightly concerts with salsa, rock, blues, reggae and world music.

Marghera Village Estate
Via Orsato 9, Panorama car park, Marghera (339 671 2187/www.villagestate.it). Bus 6/ from piazzale Roma. **Dates** *June-Aug* 6pm-2am daily; concerts 9.30pm. Closed Sept-May. **Admission** free; €6 for special events. **No credit cards**.
The Village's setting – on the only scrap of grass amid hypermarkets – might not be awe-inspiring, but this is where Venetians and *Mestrini* of all ages spend their summer nights. There's free nightly music, of varying quality, comedy and dancing as well as bars and food stalls to keep the party going.

Venice Airport Festival
Forte Bazzera, via Bazzera, Tessera (349 355 5437/www.srazz.com). Bus 5 from piazzale Roma to Tessera church stop. **Dates** ten days late July/early August; 7pm-2am daily; concerts 9pm. **Admission** free; €5 for special events. **No credit cards**.
Strictly no cover bands: this new festival hosts nightly gigs by top quality Italian and international indie rock bands, drawing fans from all over the region. Concerts are followed by DJ sets and off-beat film screenings.

Villa Pisani Strà Festival
Via Alvise Pisani 1, Strà (049 502 074/ www.zedlive.com). Bus for Padua from piazzale Roma. **Dates** June-Sept; concerts 9.30pm. **Admission** €25-€30. **Credit** MC, V.
Held in the beautiful grounds of 18th-century Villa Pisani, this annual festival organises several dates over the summer by stars including Simple Minds, Dido and Bob Dylan.

As winter loosens its grip, stages are set up in squares, parks and villas to host concerts in Venice and the surrounding mainland area. As well as the following, there is a wealth of other festivals in the region. Look out for the posters around town. See also *pp196-8*.

Festa di Liberazione
San Polo, campo dell'Erberia (www.rifondazionecomunistaveneto.it). Vaporetto Rialto. **Dates** late Aug-early Sept. **Map** p309 D1.
Rally meets rave at Rialto for the Rifondazione Comunista party's festival. Serious debates

Whether for its red exterior, or for the political leanings of its core clientele, the campo's oldest bar is universally known as 'Caffè Rosso'. Relaxed and Bohemian, it attracts a mixed crowd of all ages who spill out from its single room to sip a *spritz* in the campo or to choose from the impressive wine list. Excellent live music, usually on Thursdays.

Orange
Dorsoduro 3054A, campo Santa Margherita (041 523 4740). Vaporetto Ca' Rezzonico. **Open** 7.30am-2am Mon-Sat. **No credit cards**. **Map** p308 D3.
The newest and coolest kid on the campo whose sleek and stylish design, creative list of excellent cocktails, friendly staff and massive, attractive

terrace overlooking the busy square have made it a roaring success with a hip mixture of locals, students and all those who are looking for a slightly more metropolitan feel.

Pane, Vino e San Daniele
Dorsoduro 1722, campo dell'Angelo Raffaele (041 523 7456). Vaporetto San Basilio. **Open** 9am-midnight Mon-Sat. **Credit** AmEx, DC, MC, V. **Map** p310 B3.
As well as having the most romantic table-for-two in town tucked away in the wine cellar and bookable months in advance, this beautiful *osteria* behind Miss Garnet's Angel church serves up great Friulian fare, Sardinian and season-based specialities and monthly live jazz.

Arts & Entertainment

Jesolo night fever

Set sail across the lagoon, with the sun setting behind you over the Most Serene Republic, and land at Lido di Jesolo: the contrast could hardly be greater. From Easter to September, this seaside strip is inundated by an international crowd of holidaymakers in search of sun, sea, low prices and – of course – the party. On offer here is everything you'd expect from a seaside resort: 15km of beach, watersports, crazy golf, plus an opera season and art exhibitions (see www.jesolo.it).

If you are in need of sustenance, all tastes are catered for, from the loud and lairy **Gasoline Pub** (piazza Mazzini 17) to the tiny but beautiful haven for wine connoisseurs **Wine Bar Da Cinzia** (via Bafile 376), trendy **Orange Café** (piazza Marconi/via Dante 5) or the **Garden Pub** (piazza Nember 2) which serves over 200 beers and has grub till 4am.

GETTING THERE

The Lido di Jesolo bus (information 041 520 5530) leaves from piazzale Roma, but it's more fun to get the double-decker motonave from San Zaccaria-Pietà, on the riva degli Schiavoni, to Punta Sabbioni and bus it from there. There are regular boats making the return journey, with a change at Lido between 1am and 6am.

Note that if you drop before dawn you'll need a lift or taxi (call 0421 961 250, €30 approx) back to the boat stop at Punta Sabbioni as no buses link up with the boats between 12.30am and 5.10am.

CLUBS

Most of Jesolo's clubs open at 11pm, but nobody who's anybody shows up until 1am. Save money (rather than face) by picking up flyers offering reduced entrance before 1am.

Right in the centre of Lido di Jesolo, **Matilda**'s resident sounds are house, hip hop and drum 'n' bass, often with top guest DJs on the decks; it's popular with a 'been there done that' older set. A Jesolo legend, **Il Muretto** has been going for over 40 years yet

Clubs

Round Midnight

Dorsoduro 3102, fondamenta dei Pugni (041 523 2056). Vaporetto Ca' Rezzonico. **Open** 9pm-2am Thur-Sat. Closed July-Sept. **Admission** free. **No credit cards. Map** p308 D3.

An absolutely tiny DJ bar behind campo Santa Margherita with no charge on the door and disco sounds that keep its minuscule dancefloor busy with bouncing students all night long.

Further afield

Mestre & Marghera

Area Club

Via Don Tosatto 9, Mestre (041 958 000/ www.areaclub.it). Bus 3 from Mestre. **Open** 11.30pm-4am Fri-Sun. **Admission** €14-€24. **Credit** DC, MC, V.

The first venue in the Venice area to specialise in hardcore techno, Area now brings house mixed by big-name DJs to a well-heeled clique of clubbers.

The Blv Rooms

Via delle Industrie 29, Marghera (041 531 7357). Bus 2, 4, 4/, 6 or 6/ from Piazzale Roma. **Open** Sept-Apr 9pm-4am Fri, Sat. **Admission** €16-€18 (incl pizza and drink). **Credit** AmEx, MC, V.

Just over the bridge from piazzale Roma, this is Venice's nearest mainland dance club. A trendy set don their posh togs and come for aperitifs in the lounge and pizza in the restaurant before getting down to commercial house in the main room.

Kristal Klub c/o Zoo Disco

Via Ca' Zorzi 2, Tessera (041 541 5100). Bus 5 from Piazzale Roma. **Open** 9pm-4am Fri, Sat. **Admission** €10 (incl 1st drink) or €20 (incl pizza & drink). **Credit** MC, V.

Crowds of Venetians head out to this 'dinner and dance' club opposite the airport for pizzas and 1970s and '80s sounds during the winter, and to shake their summer stuff on the open-air dancefloors between May and September.

Magic Bus

Via delle Industrie 118, Marcon (041 595 2151). Venice–Trieste motorway, exit Marcon; follow signs to II zona industriale. **Open** Sept-May 10.30pm-4am Fri, Sat. **Admission** Fri concerts €2; free after 12.30 with ARCI club card (annual membership €6 at the door); Sat free with obligatory 1st drink €8). **No credit cards.**

In a warehouse in the industrial area of Marcon (there's no public transport; Venetians tend to share taxis to get here), this well-known rock club has branched out into new sounds. The indie and rock core remains, while a second room now has reggae and dance on Fridays and house, electronic or new wave on Saturdays. Regular concerts usually feature Italian talent.

remains super-trendy. A mass of ecstatic youth floods the dancefloor for serious house spun by highly respected resident DJs including David Morales and guests who are living legends in clubland: Rampling, Oakenfold, Kevorkian and the Chemical Brothers to name a few.

By the lighthouse at the south-western end of Jesolo Lido, the once-humble **Terrazza Mare** beach bar is more of a cultural space than a club, organising music, exhibitions and theatre as well as house and ambient nights. With free entry (other than on big occasions), no heavy-handed bouncers or label-led dress code, the informal atmosphere attracts a mixed group of groovers, who flock in their thousands for the periodic mega-events that spill over on to the beach.

If you're tired of techno and you've had it with house, the **Sound Garden** is the only real alternative. Rock, punk, new wave and metal is on the turntable and if you're rocked out, you can take a break with a game of pool.

Matilda
Via Bafile 362, Jesolo (0421 370 768/ www.matildaclub.com). **Open** *Apr-July, mid Aug-Sept* 11pm-4am Fri, Sat. *1st 2 wks Aug* 11pm-4am daily. Closed Oct-Mar. **Admission** €25-€50. **Credit** AmEx, MC, V.

Il Muretto
Via Roma Destra 120, Jesolo (0421 371 310/www.ilmuretto.net). **Open** *Apr-Oct* 11pm-4am Wed, Fri, Sat, Sun. Closed Oct-Mar. **Admission** €20-€45. **Credit** MC, V.

Sound Garden
Via Aleardi 18A/piazza Mazzini, Jesolo (info 338 875 2823/www.soundgardencafe.com). **Open** *Apr-Sept* 10pm-4am Tue-Sat. Closed Oct-Mar. **Admission** €6-€8 (incl 1 drink). **No credit cards.**

Terrazza Mare Teatro Bar
Vicolo Faro 1, Jesolo (0421 370 012/www. terrazzamare.com). **Open** *Apr-Sept* 6pm-4am daily. **Admission** free-€10. **No credit cards.**

T.A.G. Club
Via Giustizia 19, Mestre (041 921 970). Train to Mestre. **Open** 10pm-5am Wed, Fri, Sat. **Admission** free to members (annual membership €10). **No credit cards.**
A small but lively club just behind the train station in Mestre that puts on an eclectic range of concerts and exhibitions followed by 'Afterhours', parties that tend to feature house music mixed by well-known DJs – among them local boy Spiller – who keep the joint jumping til dawn.

Paradiso Perduto, *See p214.*

Al Vapore
Via Fratelli Bandiera 8, Marghera (041 930 796/ www.alvapore.it). Train to Mestre, or bus 6 or 6/ from piazzale Roma. **Open** 7am-3pm, 6pm-2am Tue-Sat. **Admission** Tue-Fri free; Sat €10 (incl 1st drink). **No credit cards.**
This music bar just behind the station has been putting on jazz, blues, soul and rock gigs for years and is very active on the local scene. 'Reggae and jazz' nights take place during the week with DJ sets and a free buffet to go with aperitifs; at weekends well-known Italian and international musicians perform on the tiny stage. There's no charge on Fridays, but drinks cost more. During the summer months, Al Vapore moves to Marghera Village (*see p215*).

On the mainland

New Age Club
Via Tintoretto 14, Roncade (Treviso) (0422 841 052/www.newageclub.it). Venice Trieste motorway, exit Quarto d'Altino; follow signs for Roncade. **Open** *Sept-June* 9pm-5am Fri; 11pm-5am Sat. **Admission** *Disco* free after 12.30am for ARCI members Fri (annual membership €8 at the door). *Concerts* €15. **No credit cards.**
You'll need a car to get to this out-of-the-way spot but if you're a pop, rock or metal fan it can be well worth it for some of the big acts that pass through to play on its small stage. Interpol, the Veils, Supergrass, Muse and Graham Coxon have been among recent guests. A rock disco follows the gigs.

Arts & Entertainment

Performing Arts

A rebuilt opera house and revamped theatres provide alternatives to Vivaldi.

Venice's rebuilt opera house, **La Fenice**.

Late 18th-century theatregoers in Venice had a cornucopia of theatres to choose from, with opera and drama on tap. Not content with the popular *Commedia dell'arte* offerings of playwrights Pietro Chiari and Carlo Gozzi, Venetian theatre went into overdrive when the Teatro Sant'Angelo signed up Carlo Goldoni. In the 1750-51 season alone, he wrote 16 major works. Opera was also well served in the 19th century, with composers such as Donizetti and Rossini regularly called upon to provide new works for Venice's opera house, La Fenice.

These days, there are few productions on offer in the city at any given time and the standard of performances sometimes leaves much to be desired, but the growth and revamping in recent years of small theatres has resulted in more drama approaching real avant garde.

The **Teatro Carlo Goldoni** in Venice and the **Teatro Toniolo** in Mestre tend to serve up standard theatrical fare, but you can find more cutting edge work in other theatres in Mestre such as the **Teatrino della Murata**, or in Venice at the **Teatro Fondamenta Nuove**, where contemporary dance heads the bill and the murky territory between technology and dramatic creation is explored.

The **Teatro a L'Avogaria** and **Teatrino Groggia** dedicate their energies to exploring the outer reaches of Venetian and Italian theatre, often using theatre for didactic purposes, while the **Centro Culturale Candiani** in Mestre puts on contemporary pieces.

All things theatrical really take off in the summer months, when performances abound during the Biennale di Venezia, Danza-Musica-Teatro (*see p220*).

DANCE

Dance events are limited until the summer months when the Biennale provides contemporary performances. The **Teatro Toniolo** and **Centro Culturale Candiani** also have fairly mainstream contemporary dance offerings, whereas the **Teatro Fondamenta Nuove** specialises in interactive and multimedia productions. The seasons at **La Fenice** and **Teatro Malibran** always include the obligatory classical ballet features.

CLASSICAL MUSIC AND OPERA

With tourists far outnumbering the local music-going public, Venice has become a victim of its own musical tradition, with Vivaldi topping Venice's classical music chart. An obvious exception is the orchestra of **La Fenice**, one of the best in the country. As well as its opera and ballet seasons, La Fenice has at least two concert seasons a year, and has recently shown a penchant for 20th-century music.

The recent reopening of the **Teatro Malibran** means that La Fenice no longer has to bear the burden of all opera, ballet and classical concerts. Most musical events take place in churches or *scuole* (*see p95* **Back to school**) and every now and then at the **Teatro Toniolo**.

St Mark's basilica only holds a smattering of ceremonial concerts throughout the year, with the patriarch deciding who is to attend.

Phoenix from the flames

When the Teatro San Benedetto burnt down in 1774, it was replaced by a new structure presciently named La Fenice ('the phoenix'). *Nomen est omen*, as Plautus said. Architect Giannantonio Selva won the bid to build the new theatre, only for the runner-up to appeal. Although Selva was stripped of his victory and cash prize, he was left to oversee the building. La Fenice finally opened in 1792 with Paisiello's now virtually forgotten *I giuochi d'Agrigento*.

The phoenix was to burst into flames once again in 1836, its last performance being, fittingly, Rossini's *Cenerentola* (*Cinderella*). The central heating burner had been left on, causing a fire that raged through the theatre. All that was left were the external walls, the atrium and a pile of cinders. Reconstruction work started in February of the following year and after a mere ten months the theatre rose from its ashes, thanks to the Meduna brothers' project that recreated the original, with a few modernising touches.

Fast forward to 29 January 1996. The theatre was closed for restoration work when an electrician lit what he thought would be an insignificant fire intended to earn his company valuable extra time to finish their work. Instead a massive blaze broke out that replicated the theatre's earlier near-total destruction.

Ten Italian and foreign companies competed for the reconstruction job: Milan's Impregilo won; Munich's Philipp Holzmann building giant came second, with a project by Aldo Rossi.

In a bizarre re-enactment of the 1789 competition, the jury's decision was overturned due to irregularities in the winning company's bid. Work on Rossi's project, with adaptations made to incorporate work carried out by the original winners, got underway in March 1998. (Rossi was not to see his work come to fruition; he died in 1997.)

Rebuilding did not go smoothly: after slow progress and mounting costs, the police escorted the Holzmann company out of the worksite in April 2001. Rossi's project then had to be reshaped for the replacement company, Sacaim, due to new regulatory laws. In March 2002 the new works were handed over to Sacaim, and the completion date – originally October 2001 – was reset for November 2003.

On 14 December 2003, after almost eight years camping out in a vast tent on the Tronchetto island, La Fenice began an inaugural musical week, with Riccardo Muti conducting Beethoven's aptly titled *Consecration of the House*.

Although Rossi's project adhered to the idea of maintaining La Fenice 'where it was, as it was', it is undoubtedly a new theatre. It has two new moveable stages, rehearsal spaces beneath the auditorium and state-of-the-art mechanised stage equipment, all hidden from public view. What the audience does see is the Bertolini Arte company's painstaking restoration of the ornate gilding and an abundance of Baroque plush.

November 2004 saw the theatre open its doors to the public with an old La Fenice stalwart: Verdi's *La Traviata*. Rossi said that he worked 'not to remedy a disaster, but to recreate a Venetian monument'. He did. Go and see for yourselves.

Arts & Entertainment

Festivals

Teatro in Campo.

For the cash-strapped traveller, the summer months in Venice offer a variety of drama and live music free of charge. With the advent of warm weather, dramatically lit performances get under way in *campi* and courtyards.

Free festivals include **Venezia Suona**, when live music of every variety floods the city on the third or fourth Sunday in June. Samba, jazz, rock and gospel can be heard in squares throughout the city from 4pm. **Giardini d'Estate** has music (generally ageing Italian rock bands) and ethnic stalls among the trees of the Giardini (*see p97*) in Castello.

The **Teatro in Campo** festival graces campo Pisani near the Accademia during August, with good drama and opera. The programme also includes free performances on the islands of the lagoon (Pellestrina, Giudecca and Murano). Discussions on music and theatre are held at a civilized 6.30pm at the Art Blu Café (campo Santo Stefano) to coincide with *spritz* hour.

Festival Galuppi, from late August to October, is dedicated to the Venetian composer Baldassarre Galuppi. It's an opportunity to hear 18th-century classical music in venues that are otherwise inaccessible, such as the islands of San Francesco del Deserto and Lazzaretto Nuovo; Vivaldi doesn't even get a look in.

The **Biennale di Venezia** has recently allotted new funds to its dance, music and theatre department. The programme remains restricted to the summer months and is staged in two newly restored venues: the Teatro Tese and the smaller Teatro Piccolo Arsenale, both inside the Arsenale (*see p96*) and open only for Biennale performances.

In November, Wagner is the star of a series of world-class concerts organised by the Associazione R Wagner; the **Giornate Wagneriane** also includes conferences on the great man, and visits to the house he occupied while in Venice.

But lovers of church music should catch one of two regular Sunday appointments: the sung Mass at St Mark's (10.30am) and the Gregorian chant on the island of San Giorgio (11am).

THE SEASON

Venice's theatre and dance season stretches from November to June – though La Fenice keeps on going most of the year, closing only for August. Tourist-oriented classical music concerts are held all year. Smaller theatre groups take advantage of the summer temperatures from June and move outdoors into Venice's open spaces (*see p220* **Festivals**). But the colder months are not without their serious attractions: look out for concerts held throughout the city during late December to provide some Christmas sparkle.

Arts & Entertainment

For information on Natale a Venezia and Giardini d'Estate contact local tourist offices (*see p293*).

Biennale di Venezia, Danza-Musica-Teatro

Ca' Giustinian, San Marco 1364A, calle del Ridotto (041 521 8711/www.labiennale.org). Vaporetto Vallaresso. **Venue** Teatro delle Tese, inside the Arsenale (*see p96*). **Tickets** VeLa (*see p278*). **Dates** *dance* Aug; *music* mid-end Oct; *theatre* mid Sept-Oct. **Map** p311 B3.

Festival Galuppi

San Marco 3972, calle Sant'Andrea (041 522 1120/www.culturaspettacolovenezia.it). **Venues** around the city. **Tickets** at venues 2hrs before performance; VeLa (*see p278*). **Performances** 4pm & 8.45pm, days vary. **Dates** Aug-Oct.

Le Giornate Wagneriane

Associazione R Wagner, c/o Associazione Culturale Italo-Tedesca, Palazzo Albrizzi, *Cannaregio 4118, fondamenta Sant' Andrea (041 523 2544).* **Venues** Palazzo Albrizzi (*see above*); Fondazione Cini (Isola di San Giorgio; *see also p135*); Fondazione Levi (San Marco 2893, calle Giustiniani, vaporetto Accademia or San Samuele). **Dates** 17 Nov-30 Dec. **Map** p309 C2.
Concerts are by invite only. Call 041 526 8178 between 9.30am and 12.30pm Mon-Fri.

Teatro in Campo

Pantakin da Venezia, Giudecca 218, fondamenta San Giacomo. **Venue** campo Pisani. *(041 277 0407/www.pantakin.it).* Vaporetto Accademia. **Tickets** at venue from 6pm on performance days; VeLa (*see p278*). **Performances** 9pm, days vary. **Dates** Aug-Sept. **Map** p311 D2.

Venezia Suona

Cannaregio 3546, fondamenta dell'Abbazia (041 275 0049/www.veneziasuona.it). **Venues** around the city. **Date** 3rd or 4th Sun in June. **Tickets** free.

INFORMATION AND TICKETS

Tickets for concerts and performances can usually be purchased at theatre box offices immediately prior to shows; the tourist information office near piazza San Marco (*see p293*) and VeLa offices (*see p278*) sell tickets for 'serious' events; most travel agents and hotel receptions will provide tickets for classical music concerts.

For high-profile or first-night productions at prestigious venues such as La Fenice, Teatro Carlo Goldoni, Teatro Malibran or the Teatro Toniolo, seats will sell out days or even weeks in advance: ideally, tickets should be reserved at the theatres themselves or on their websites at least ten days before performances, and picked up – in most cases – no later than one hour before the show begins. Alternatively you can always book for any concert through a ticket agency (see p199 **Ticket agencies**) or at some tourist information offices (see p293).

Local newspapers *Il Gazzettino* and *La Nuova Venezia* (see pp286-7 **Media**) carry listings of theatrical events, as does the bilingual monthly *Venezia News*. Ticket prices vary according to productions.

Theatres

Teatrino Groggia

Cannaregio 3150, Parco di Villa Groggia (041 524 4665/www.comune.venezia.it/teatrinogroggia). Vaporetto Sant Alvise or San Marcuola. **Open** *Box office* 1hr before start. *Performances* 9pm, days vary. **No credit cards**. **Map** p308 A3.
Tucked away in the trees, this excellent and relatively new little space in the northern part of Cannaregio offers a variety of evenings ranging from a tribute to Emilio Vedova, arguably Venice's greatest living painter, to entertaining cabaret in English for kids.

Teatro a l'Avogaria

Dorsoduro 1606, corte Zappa (041 520 9270/www.culturaspettacolovenezia.it). Vaporetto San Basilio. **Open** *Performances* 8.30pm Mon-Sat; 5pm Sun. **Map** p310 B3.
Freshly restored, this experimental theatre (entry by voluntary donation) was founded in 1969 by renowned director Giovanni Poli. Here he continued the experimental approach he developed in the 1950s. Since his death in 1979, Poli's disciples have pressed on with his experiments, staging works by lesser-known playwrights from the 15th to 19th centuries. Places must be booked at the number above. The theatre opens 15 minutes before performances.

Teatro Carlo Goldoni

San Marco 4650B, calle Goldoni (041 240 2011/www.teatrostabileveneto.it). Vaporetto Rialto. **Open** *Box office* 10am-1pm, 3-7pm Mon-Sat; 1hr before performances. *Performances* 7.30 or 8.30pm Tue, Wed, Fri, Sat; 4pm Thur, Sun. **Credit** MC, V. **Map** p309 D2.
Based in Venice's most beautiful theatre, the Goldoni Teatro Stabile di Venezia company serves up

Around the Veneto

If you're planning a stay outside Venice, you could do worse than the beautiful hillside town of Bassano del Grappa (see p267) where the town council organises the **OperaEstate** summer festival (June-Aug) of dance, theatre, cinema and music in Bassano and other breathtakingly lovely towns such as Asolo (see p266). Jazz and classical music are on offer throughout the summer, with international performers including Sarah Jane Morris. You can also catch dance performances in Bassano and Possagno (see p266), with recent guests including Royal Ballet soloists and Talia Paz, Israel's dance star. Theatre conjures up a bag of treats, such as a tragic-musical interpretation of *Othello* for two performers.

In the sumptuous setting of Palladio's final masterpiece (see p260), you can enjoy Vicenza's annual music festival (throughout May), the **Settimane Musicali al Teatro Olimpico**. The fest focuses on a theme or composer each year, with conferences and concerts as well as films.

Giants of jazz such as Herbie Hancock perform alongside lesser-known talents at the picturesque **Veneto Jazz Festival**. Against a backdrop of the Verona's Arena (see p246) or a small square in Conegliano (see p270), this festival takes you to the principal sites of the Veneto mainland.

OperaEstate

Opera Estate (0424 217 815/fax 0424 217 813/www.comune.bassano.vi.it). **Box office** IAT, largo Corona d'Italia 35, Bassano del Grappa. **Open** 9.30am-12.30pm, 4-7.30pm Mon-Sat. **Dates** June-Aug. **Tickets** prices vary. **Credit** MC, V.
Credit cards are accepted for telephone bookings only, with a €1 booking fee

Settimane Musicali al Teatro Olimpico

Contrà San Pietro 67, Vicenza (tel/fax 0444 302 425/www.olimpico.vicenza.it). **Box office** Apr-mid May at the above address 9.30am-12.30pm, 3.30-6.30pm Mon-Fri. Mid-end May at the Teatro Olimpico (see p262) 9am-5pm Tue-Sun. **Dates** first 2wks June. **No credit cards**.
A season ticket costs €50-€70; students €35-€55; tickets for individual performances €10-€15.

Veneto Jazz Festival

Via Aldo Moro 29, Cavasagra di Vedelago (0423 452 069/fax 0423 451 327/www.venetojazz.com). **Box office** at venues before performances. **Dates** Feb-Apr, June-Aug. **Credit** MC, V.
Credit cards can be accepted for online bookings only.

Venetian classics by Ruzante, Chiari, Selvatico and Gallina, as well as those by Goldoni himself. In the first third of the 20th century, plays by Nobel prize winner Pirandello premiered here. Youth theatre projects, readings and poetry afternoons now take place alongside the usual programme. It has also been the unlikely host of international stars such as Paul Weller and Patti Smith.

Teatro Fondamenta Nuove

Cannaregio 5013, fondamenta Nuove (041 522 4498/www.teatrofondamentanuove.it). Vaporetto Fondamente Nove. **Open** *Box office* 1hr before performances. *Performances* 9pm, days vary. **No credit cards. Map** p309 B2.
Opened in 1993 in an old joiner's shop, the Fondamenta Nuove stages contemporary dance and avant-garde performances, and organises a number of events including film festivals, symposiums, exhibitions and workshops.

Teatro La Fenice

San Marco 1965, campo San Fantin (041 786 575/www.teatrolafenice.it). **Open** *Box office* VeLa (*see p278*). *Performances* 7pm Mon-Fri, 3.30pm Sat, Sun. **Credit** AmEx, MC, V. **Map** p311 B2.
Newly restored and positively gleaming, La Fenice is back in business offering opera, ballet and concert seasons (*see p219* **Phoenix from the flames**). Performance times given above may vary. Rehearsals allowing, tours can be booked on 041 786 611.

Teatro Malibran

Cannaregio 5873, calle dei Milion (041 786 603/box office 899 909 090/www.lafenice.it). Vaporetto Rialto. **Open** *Box office* 1hr before performances; also VeLa (*see p278*). **Performances** 3.30pm Sat, Sun; 7 or 8pm, days vary. **Credit** AmEx, MC, V. **Map** p309 C2.
Inaugurated in 1678 as Teatro San Giovanni Grisostomo, the 900-seater was built on the site where Marco Polo's family palazzo stood; sections of this and older buildings were uncovered during the theatre's recent restoration. In the 17th century, this was the first of Venice's theatres to throw its doors open to anyone who could afford a ticket, rather than to the patrician class exclusively. However, in the 17th and 18th centuries, when other theatres were bringing ticket prices down in order to fill seats, the San Giovanni Grisostomo remained resolutely and expensively elitist. In 1835 the theatre was renamed after Maria Garcia Malibran, the celebrated Spanish soprano who gave a free recital there (then later died in Manchester after falling from a horse). It now shares the classical music, ballet and opera season with La Fenice.

Further afield

Centro Culturale Candiani

Piazzale Candiani 7, Mestre (041 238 6111/ www.comune.venezia.it/candiani). Bus 2 from piazzale Roma, get off at piazza Ferretto.

Open *Box office* 9am-7pm Tue-Sun. *Centre* 9am-10pm Tue-Sun. Ticket prices vary according to productions. **No credit cards.**
This 1970s arts centre includes an auditorium, video library, exhibition space and outdoor arena. Alfresco performances are held June-Sept. Entertainment ranges from Bach to *The Vagina Monologues*, plus mini film festivals (on purchase of the Candiani Cinema Card for €10).

Teatrino della Murata

Via Giordano Bruno 19, Mestre (041 989 879/ www.teatromurata.it). Bus 2 from piazzale Roma, get off at via Einaudi. **Open** *Box office* 30mins before performances. *Performances* 9pm Mon-Sat; 5pm, 9pm Sun. **No credit cards.**
The tiny Murata (60 seats) is situated in a former warehouse under the remains of the ancient city walls. Funded by the city and regional councils, it specialises in multicultural theatre.

Teatro Toniolo

Piazzetta Battisti 1, Mestre (041 274 9070/box office 041 971 666/www.culturaspettacolovenezia.it). Bus 2, 7, 9 from piazzale Roma, get off at the hospital. **Open** *Box office* 11am-12.30pm, 5-7.30pm Tue-Sun. *Performances* 4.30pm Sun; 9pm, days vary. **No credit cards.**
Founded in 1913, the Teatro Toniolo in Mestre is now run by the local council. Serving up an assortment of performances, from vernacular favourites to contemporary plays, new stagings of Italian and foreign classics, cabaret, music, and contemporary dance and ballet, there is definitely something to suit all tastes.

Churches & *scuole*

For information on musical events in Venice's churches, check the local press (*see pp286-7*).

Basilica dei Frari

San Polo, campo dei Frari (041 719 308). Vaporetto San Tomà. **Map** p308 D3.
The lofty Gothic Frari (*see also p120*) is one of the best venues for catching high-standard performances of sacred music. It has regular seasons in the autumn and spring, organ recitals and a number of free or low-cost afternoon concerts, especially over Christmas and the New Year, sponsored by the local paper *Il Gazzettino*. If you go to one of the winter concerts, wrap up warm.

Palazzo Ca' Papafava

Cannaregio 3764, calle Priuli Racheta (041 522 6405/www.vivaldi.it). Vaporetto Ca' d'Oro. **Map** p309 B2.
As this guide went to press, the concerts formerly held in the church of La Pietà (*see p96*) on the riva degli Schiavoni, where Vivaldi was choir master, were being staged temporarily in this 15th-century palazzo overlooking the rio della Misericordia. The prettily costumed groups that perform Vivaldi's music are engaged in a legal

Highly professional renditions at **San Vidal**.

in winter). **Tickets** €22; €17 concessions.
Credit MC, V. **Map** p311 B2.
For highly professional renditions of Venice's
favourite composer, Vivaldi, visit the church of San
Vidal, where the no-frills *Interpreti Veneziani* plays
several times a week.

Scuola Grande di San Giovanni Evangelista

*San Polo 2454, campiello della Scuola (041 718
234/information and bookings 340 546 6965/
www.musicainmaschera.it). Vaporetto San Tomà.*
Open *Box office* at the *scuola* 6pm on performance
days. *Performances* 8.30pm, days vary. **Tickets**
€30-€35; €25-€30 concessions. **Credit** MC, V.
Map p308 C3.
This 14th-century *scuola* with an imposing marble
staircase has in recent years been the venue for an
interesting series of chamber music concerts.
Between May and Sept it has also hosted *Musica in
Maschera*, an orchestra and choir performing
shrink-wrapped opera.

Scuola Grande di San Rocco

*San Polo, campo San Rocco (041 523 4864/
www.scuolagrandesanrocco.it). Vaporetto San
Tomà.* **Map** p308 D3.
The Scuola Grande di San Rocco is best known for
its magnificent interior decoration by Tintoretto (*see
p31*) but it also boasts a musical tradition stretching back over half a millennium: the 16th-century
composer Giovanni Gabrieli was the church's organist, and in 1958 Stravinsky's choral work, *Threni*,
premiered here. Nowadays, musical offerings are
scarce. A free concert at the *scuola* on St Rock's Day
(Aug 16th) is by invitation only, but ask for spare
invites at the *scuola*.

Scuola di San Teodoro

*San Marco 4810, salizzada San Teodoro (041
0294/www.imusiciveneziani.com). Vaporetto
Rialto.* **Open** *Box office* at venue 10am-7pm daily.
Performances 9pm Tue, Wed, Fri-Sun. **Tickets**
€22-€32; €17-€27 concessions. **No credit cards.**
Map p309 D2.
If your heart is set on wigs and silk acetate, head
for the Scuola Grande di San Teodoro, where *I musi-
ci veneziani* dish up Vivaldi every Wednesday,
Friday and Sunday and a medley of opera arias on
Tuesday and Saturday.

wrangle over the rights to use the church as a
concert hall; the palazzo, with its 18th-century
furnishings, provides a suitable alternative.

San Giacomo di Rialto

*San Polo, campo di San Giacomo (041 426 6559/
www.prgroup.it). Vaporetto Rialto.* **Open** *Box
office* at venue from 11am on performance days.
Performances 8.45pm Wed, Fri, Sun. **Tickets** €19;
€16 concessions. **Credit** MC, V. **Map** p309 C2.
The church affectionately known as San Giacometto
hosts concerts by the Ensemble Antonio Vivaldi.

Santa Maria Formosa

*Castello, campo Santa Maria Formosa (041 984 252/
www.collegiumducale.com). Vaporetto Rialto.* **Open**
Box office at venue from 10.30am on performance days.
Performances 9pm Thur, Fri and Sun. **Tickets** €25;
€20 concessions. **No credit cards. Map** p309 D3.
This charming church is home to concerts by
the Collegium Ducale.

San Vidal

*San Marco 2862B, campo San Vidal (041 277 0561/
www.interpretiveneziani.com). Vaporetto Accademia.*
Open *Box office* at venue 9.30am-8.30pm Mon-Sat;
10am-6pm Sun. *Performances* 9pm Mon-Sat (8.30pm

Other music venues

Fondazione Querini Stampalia

*Castello 5252, campo Santa Maria Formosa
(041 271 1411/www.querinistampalia.it).
Vaporetto Rialto.* **Open** *Performances* 5pm, 8.30pm
Fri, Sat. Tickets €6; €4 concessions. **Credit** MC, V.
Map p309 D3.
The soirées that are organised by this enterprising
museum and cultural foundation take the form
of a half-hour recital of lesser-known (usually
Renaissance or Baroque) works. A far cry from your
costumed Vivaldi concert.

Sport & Fitness

The perfect place for messing about in boats.

Venetian R&R on the Grand Canal.

While obesity and exercise slackers hit the headlines, Venice stands proud as the city that constantly puts its inhabitants and tourists through their paces. In return for tramping many miles on foot each day and climbing up and down innumerable flights of steps, Venetians are amply rewarded with longevity and general good health into ripe old age. However, what web-footed Venetians like doing best in their leisure hours is rowing around their watery backyard.

Though many landlocked Venetian sports – such as competitions to build the biggest human pyramids or boxing matches that began with two contestants and ended up involving whole *sestieri* – have fallen into disuse, traditional water-borne competitions have stood the test of time. The Regata Storica (*see p226*) has been taking place since the 15th century and is a clear indicator that Venice's love for all things aquatic is still strong.

LIKE A DUCK TO WATER

Two activities dominate on the mosquito-infested lagoon: Venetian rowing (*voga alla veneta*) and three-sail sailing (*vela al terzo*).

In *voga alla veneta* the rower stands up, facing the direction of travel. There are various types of *voga alla veneta* – team rowing is one, and the impressive solo, cross-handed, two-oar method known as *voga alla valesana* is another. But the most famous type is *voga ad un solo remo* (one-oar rowing) – one of the most difficult rowing strokes of all – as practised by Venetian gondoliers. The gondolier only ever puts his oar in the water on the right side of the boat where it rests in a *forcola*, an elaborate walnut-wood rowlock. Pushing on the oar makes the craft turn to the left. The trick consists in using the downstroke to correct the direction. In theory, a gondolier uses up no more energy rowing a half-ton gondola with three passengers than the average person expends in walking… though that doesn't quite explain how they get those bodybuilder biceps.

Vela al terzo was once the means of transporting goods for trade throughout the length and breadth of Venice's Adriatic dominions. But the city's traditional wooden flat-bottomed sailing craft is now to be found only in the lagoon, being used exclusively for pleasure and sport. Depending upon their

Big fish

Like rowing, fishing is a prevailing Venetian pastime. Anglers can fish just about anywhere, with the Giardini embankment (see p97) and the Zattere (see p132) being two popular haunts. Angling needs can be procured at **Nautica & Pesca** (San Polo 3138, campiello San Rocco, 041 520 0617, www.ferramentadeluca.com), which offers everything from lugworms to thermal wellies, but as yet tackle is not for hire.

So, you've got the tackle, you've got the worms, all you need now is the boat. **Cristiano Brussa** has two hire shops in Cannaregio (fondamenta di Cannaregio 1030, 041 275 0196, www. cristianobrussa.com, open 7.30am-5.30pm Mon-Fri) and Castello (fondamenta dei Greci 5030, 041 528 4333, open 7.30am-5.30pm daily) with boats available by the hour or the day. You don't need a licence, but you'll be taken out on a test run to make sure you know what you're doing. For a six-person boat, prices are €20 per hour or €120 per day, petrol included. A valid document must be left at the hire shop for the duration of the rental period. No credit cards.

If you've been knocking back the hard stuff at Hemingway's old watering hole (see p166 **Harry's Bar**) and envisage yourself battling it out with the big boys on the high seas, contact **Big Game Fishing** (13 campo Stringari, Sant'Elena, 041 528 5123, www.biggamesportfishing.it). Staff will rig you out and escort you to the Adriatic. Smaller catches such as mackerel are the norm but tuna, shark and other monsters of the deep are the real quarry. Day trips cost €100 per person (maximum six people, novices welcome) and staff prefer a week's notice. No credit cards.

length, these boats can hoist one or two square sails, plus the classic triangular jib. They can also be rowed in the traditional standing-up position.

Courses in both are available from some of the clubs listed below.

ROWING RACES

There are more than 120 regattas in the lagoon each year, most of them involving Venetian rowing. The most sumptuous is the **Regata Storica** on the first Sunday in September. The regatta is much more than the extravagant

and picturesque pageant of tourist brochures: rowers of all ages in craft of various classes compete for glory and prizes.

Perhaps even more spectacular is the **Vogalonga**, with a 30-kilometre (18-mile) route around Venice and the northern lagoon. The race is held in May and is open to anyone with a boat and an oar. Rowers of all descriptions come from all over the country and further afield. To participate, contact 041 521 0544 /info@vogalonga.it.

For a taste of history, catch the ceremonial wedding of Venice to the sea on Ascension Day (La Sensa). This is followed by a gondola regatta in which the major rowing clubs compete in multicoloured vessels.

Boating

Canottieri Giudecca
Giudecca 259, fondamenta Ponte Lungo (041 528 7409). Vaporetto Palanca. **Open** 2.30-7.30pm Mon; 8.30am-12.30pm, 2.30-7.30pm Tue-Sat; 9am-12.30pm Sun. **Rates** €26 enrolment; €5 insurance; €156 yearly membership; €13 monthly membership; €6 per lesson. **No credit cards. Map** p311 1D.
A major advantage of this club is that beginners can put their seamanship to the test in the relatively tranquil waters of the lagoon behind the Giudecca. Friendly, experienced rowers offer individual lessons. Options include Venetian rowing in *mascareta* (small, sporty, gondola-like craft), canoes and sailboats, plus use of the gym. Hours vary in winter depending on fog and daylight. All rowers must pay the enrolment and insurance fees; short-stay visitors will be charged the monthly membership fee. A free trial can be arranged at the discretion of the club.

Reale Società Canottieri Bucintoro
Dorsoduro 10, 15 & 261, Zattere (041 520 5630/ 041 523 7933/www.bucintoro.org). Vaporetto Zattere or Salute. **Open** Office 3.30-5.30pm Tue, Sat. Lessons 9am-5pm Tue-Sat; 9am-1pm Sun. **Rates** €65 membership; €85 8 rowing lessons; €85 voga al terzo sailing course. **No credit cards. Map** p311 2C.
Founded in 1882, the Reale Società Canottieri Bucintoro is one of the oldest sports clubs in Italy, and is justly proud of its slew of Olympic rowing records. The club offers canoeing, kayaking and Venetian rowing, plus a well-equipped gym. The club recommends a minimum of two weeks to complete a rowing or sailing course, which consists of outings and theory. Courses do not require payment of membership.

Remiera Canottieri Cannaregio
Cannaregio 732, calle della Cereria (041 720 539). Vaporetto Tre Archi. **Open** 3-7pm Mon-Sat; 8.30am-12.30pm Sun. **Rates** €26 enrolment; €7 monthly membership; individual lessons by arrangement. **No credit cards. Map** off p308 2B.
This boat club does beginners' *voga alla veneta* courses by arrangement. This club around the back

Arts & Entertainment

of the station is one of the friendliest of the lot, and in Giorgio Costantini it has one of the best instructors on the lagoon. There's a good gym too.

Società Canottiere Francesco Querini

Castello 6576D, Fondamenta Nove (041 522 2039).
Vaporetto Ospedale. **Open** 8am-7pm Tue-Sat; 8am-1pm Sun. **Rates** €26 enrolment fee; €80 10 lessons. **No credit cards. Map** p309 D3.
Venice's second-oldest boat club, the Querini now boasts a good gym. The club offers rowing, canoeing and Venetian rowing.

Cycling

Though a recent decree allows kids to whizz around the *campi* to the peril of passers-by, cycling is prohibited for adults and, with a bridge every 50 metres to hike your bike over, prohibitive. However, it is possible – and enjoyable – to hire bikes on the (flat) Lido.

Bruno Lazzari

Gran Viale 21B, Lido (041 526 8019). **Open**
Mar-Sept 8am-8pm daily. *Oct-Feb* 8.30am-1pm, 3-7.30pm daily. **Rates** €3 per hr for the first 3hrs; €9 per day (8am-8pm); €42 per wk; €50 2wks; €60 1mth. *Tandems* €6 per hr/€18 per day. *Two-people 'carriages'* €6 per hr/4-people €12 per hr. **Credit** MC, V. **Map** p307.
Some form of ID must be left with this shop for the entire hire period. Payment is on return of the bike.

Fencing

AS DLF Scherma

Cannaregio 47, Parco di Villa Groggia (041 717 960/dlfven@virgilio.it). Vaporetto Sant'Alvise.
Open 5-9pm Mon-Fri. **Rates** on request. **No credit cards. Map** p309 1A
'Although on the Continent disputes are still occasionally settled by the sword, such affairs of honour may be said to be things of the past'. Though RA Lidstone is right as far as duelling goes, fencing is still fighting fit in Venice. If you want to emulate Zorro (or Madonna), head to the Dielleffe Fencing Club for some fearsome foiling.

Football

Football comes top of the league as far as terra firma sports go. Despite the dearth of playing fields or anything remotely resembling a grass pitch, Venetians are just as *calcio*-crazed as their land-dwelling compatriots. Come Sunday afternoon, supporters sail to the football stadium at Sant'Elena – the only league ground in Europe to be entirely surrounded by water.

The opposing team's supporters are met from the train, herded on to their own steamer and shipped across the lagoon like convicts.

The **football ground**: surrounded by water.

A season of Serie A glory in 2000 still bolsters long-suffering Venezia fans, despite their subsequent wavering second and third division status in the Italian league. Home matches take place on alternate Saturdays or Sundays from September to June.

Tickets cost €10-€55 and are on sale at the ground (follow the fans heading to the tiny island of Sant'Elena in the extreme west of Venice; vaporetto Sant'Elena, map p313 D3), at main ACTV and VeLa (*see p278*) ticket offices, and at two branches of the Banca Antoniana Popolare Veneta: San Marco 5400, campo San Bartolomeo and Cannaregio 3682, strada Nuova. For further information check the club's website at www.veneziacalcio.it.

Golf

Circolo Golf Venezia

Strada Vecchia 1, Alberoni-Lido (041 731 333/ www.circologolfvenezia.it). Vaporetto Lido, then bus B to Alberoni. **Open** *Apr-Sept* 8am-8pm Tue- Sun. *Oct-Mar* 8.30am-6pm Tue-Sun. **Rates** €55 Tue-Fri; €70 Sat, Sun. **Credit** AmEx, DC, MC, V. **Map** p307.
Considered one of Italy's top ten courses, the Lido links have three practice courses as well as an 18-hole one. It is open to non-members, though only to those golfers with proof of membership of golf clubs elsewhere. Rates may rise in 2005.

Gyms

For Venetian rowing clubs equipped with gyms, *see pp226-7.*

Eutonia Club

Dorsoduro 3656, calle Renier (041 522 8618/ www.eutonia.net). Vaporetto San Tomà or Ca' Rezzonico. **Open** 8am-10.30pm Mon-Fri; 10am-1pm Sat. **Rates** €29.50 annual enrolment or €12 daily entrance fee for use of the gym; €60 10 1hr sessions (valid 3mths); €36 per hr with a personal trainer; €299 for 10hrs. **No credit cards. Map** p308 D2.

This gym has three well-illuminated rooms and friendly staff to put you through your paces. Courses on offer range from fit boxing to belly dancing. Kids' courses available.

Running

The best time for '*footing*' along the Venetian streets is early morning. Popular spots include the wider stretches of pavement on the Zattere, the fondamenta by the Giardini vaporetto stop, or further east under the shady *pineta* of Sant'Elena. For a less knee-crunching experience, head for the Lido's long stretches of beach and well-paved roads.

The **Venice Marathon** takes place in October, usually on the fourth Sunday of the month. The starting line for this 42-kilometre (26-mile) run is at the Villa Pisani at Strà (*see chapter* **Padua**); the race passes along the banks of the Brenta Canal, over the road bridge to Venice, then by a specially erected pontoon over the lagoon to the finishing line on the riva degli Schiavoni. For more information, contact the Venice Marathon Club, via Torino 133, Mestre (041 940 644/www.venicemarathon.it).

The less competitive **Su e Zo Per i Ponti** takes place in March in Venice. There are three races in one (14km, 10km and 3km) so that people of all ages and abilities can participate. Entry fee €4; €6 with return vaporetto ticket. For information and entry details, call 041 590 4717 or visit www.tgseurogroup.it.

Shiatsu

Cristina Gemin Zanchi

Dorsoduro 3707, campo San Pantalon (041 528 6154). Vaporetto San Tomà. **Rates** €35 per hr. **No credit cards. Map** p311 A1.

If your energy channels are blocked after traipsing up and down bridges gawping at Venice's treasures, this Japanese finger-pressure therapy will sort out those aching feet and stiff necks. Cristina Gemin, an experienced qualified shiatsu practitioner, will put you to rights for another cultural onslaught.

Swimming

See also right **Tennis Club Ca' Del Moro**. Although it's not exactly enticing, the Lido's lukewarm Adriatic water draws locals in their thousands who come to no harm. For public beaches, *see p137-9*. For more serious swimmers there are three public pools in the city, though Byzantine timetables leave few windows for a spontaneous quick dip. Swimming caps in the water and flip-flops for the journey from changing room to pool are always obligatory.

Piscina Comunale Sant'Alvise

Cannaregio 3163, calle del Capitello (041 713 567). Vaporetto Sant'Alvise. **Open** 1-2.30pm, 9.30-10.15pm Mon, Wed, Fri; 1-4.15pm Tue, Thur; 3-4pm, 5.45-7pm Sat; 10am-noon Sun. **Rates** €5 per session; €43 10 sessions. **No credit cards. Map** p308 A3.

Set in the peaceful grounds of Villa Groggia, this pool offers courses for all, with a warm mini-pool for small fry and lazy adults. The pool's open daily from 9am to 10.30pm; non-course dips can be taken at the hours given above.

Piscina Comunale Sacca Fisola

Giudecca, San Biagio-Sacca Fisola (041 528 5430). Vaporetto Sacca Fisola. **Open** 10.30am-noon, 1-2.30pm, 7.15-8.45pm Mon, Thur; 10.30am-noon, 1-2.30pm, 6.30-7.15pm Tue, Fri; 3.30-5pm, 6.30-7.15pm Wed; 3.30-6pm, Sat; 3-6pm Sun. **Rates** €5 per session; €43 10 sessions (valid 3mths). **No credit cards. Map** p310 C2

Situated in a council estate where a waste dump once stood, this pool is for serious swimmers (no mini-pool here). It's open daily from 9am to 10.30pm; hours given above are for 'free' swimming.

Piscina Ca' Bianca

Ca' Bianca, via Sandro Gallo, Lido. Vaporetto Lido, then bus B towards Malamocco. **Open** 10.45-11.30am, 8.30-9.15pm Mon,Tue, Thur, Fri; 10am-noon, 4.45-5.30pm, 7-7.45pm Sat. **Rates** €4.60 per session; €41 10 sessions. **No credit cards. Map** p307.

The newest pool in town, very popular with the inhabitants of the Lido. No mini-pool. The above hours are for 'free' swimming.

Tennis

Tennis Club Ca' Del Moro

Via Ferruccio Parri 6, Lido (041 770 965/cadelmoro@tiscali.it). Vaporetto Lido, then bus V. **Open** 8.30am-9pm Mon-Sat; 8.30am-8pm Sun. **Rates** €9 per hr per person; €36 per court for 4 people for 90mins. **Pool** €8 half day; €16 full day. **No credit cards. Map** p307.

This sports centre is equipped with ten tennis courts. Other facilities at the Tennis Club Ca' Del Moro include a gym, a swimming pool and pool rooms, as well as football pitches.

Yoga

Yoga Studio di Paola Venturini

San Polo 2006, campo San Polo (041 528 9946/paolaventurini@tiscali.it). Vaporetto San Tomà or San Silvestro. **Rates** €20 2hr session; private lessons by arrangement. **No credit cards. Map** p309 D1.

Though there appears to be a different yoga fad for any celebrity willing to practise it, you'll find the more traditional iyengar yoga in Venice. Though not as energetic-looking as the more dynamic ashtanga, an iyengar session with Paola Venturini will still put you through your paces.

The Veneto

Features

OTEL VILLA CONDULMER
★ ★ ★ ★ ★

Historical residence, in all its beauty set in th
green and peacefulness of the countryside,
only a short distance from Venice (12 Km),
the ideal venue if you are seeking elegance,
quietness and professionalism.

Getting Started

Around Venice you'll find mountains, beaches and villas galore.

Bassano del Grappa. *See p267.*

Roman ruins? Head for Verona (*see p246*).
Renaissance frescoes? Giotto's works in Padua's
Scrovegni chapel (*see p239*) are peerless.
A perfect example of imaginative Renaissance
urban restyling? Head for the Basilica
Palladiana (*see p260*) in Vicenza.

Venice offers so much that it's easy to
forget that there are pieces of the cultural
jigsaw missing. For these, you'll have to look
to the Veneto, the region that extends inland
from the banks of Venice's lagoon.

Venice, moreover, is a little short on natural
beauties. There is the misty, moody lagoon of
course (*see pp140-46*), but for rolling green you
will need to cross to the mainland. If the Veneto
region's landscape was never as striking as,
say, Tuscany's, the environmental ravages of
the economic miracle (*see pp23-25*) have spared

some lovely, untouched and under-visited
corners, particularly in the hills and mountains:
the Colli Euganei beyond Padua, and the Colli
Berici south of Vicenza roll pleasantly above
the industrial sprawl, dotted with their share
of those Palladian villas (*see pp38-42*) that pop
up in the unlikeliest places around the region.

Further north, mountains loom and the scene
changes. Still on the plain, Treviso has frescoed
palazzi and an economic vitality – of which the
Benetton empire is the most famous flag-bearer
– that gives the town a lively, dynamic feel.
In the gentle foothills of the Dolomites are the
wine-producing centres of Conegliano and
Valdobbiadene (for both, *see p270*); Asolo
and Possagno (for both, *see p266*), given up
respectively to the leisured laziness of *il dolce
far niente* and the cold neo-classical visions of

The Veneto

Roman past (*see p272* **Heading east**) – and Grado, one of the pleasantest of the northern Adriatic resorts, with a quiet, island-studded lagoon of its own.

But for many visitors – especially those who don't read the small print on their travel itinerary – the first experience of the Veneto is Mestre (*see p233* **Not Venice but trying**). Part of the Comune di Venezia and situated on the mainland bank of the Venetian lagoon, industrial Mestre – with its plethora of cheaper, modern overspill hotels – is where many unwary tourists end up. Don't despair: Mestre has nightlife, cinemas, theatre… and plenty of transport across the lagoon.

Getting around

By train

For general information on the Italian rail network, *see p281*.

Padua (30 minutes to Padova from Venice), Vicenza (55 minutes) and Verona (85 minutes) are all connected to Venice by frequent fast Intercity or Eurostar trains on the Venice–Milan–Turin line. Padua is where the line to Bologna branches off, with around one fast train an hour during the day stopping at Rovigo (55 minutes) and Ferrara (75 minutes) along the way; slower *interregionali* trains also stop at smaller towns such as Monselice (53 minutes). From the latter, the branch line to Mantua (Mantova) serves the stations of Este (12 minutes from Monselice) and Montagnana (35 minutes from Monselice), though you should study the timetable carefully as these trains are infrequent.

Heading north from Venice is less straight-forward. Treviso (20-30 minutes) and Conegliano (40-50 minutes) are on the main line from Venice to Udine, served mainly by *interregionale* trains. To the north-west, Castelfranco Veneto (40 minutes) and Bassano del Grappa (60 minutes) are served by a local line with around 15 trains a day. Around seven local trains a day make the agonisingly slow but very pretty haul up the Piave valley from Padua to Feltre (90 minutes) and Belluno (two hours); some proceed beyond to Calalzo-Pieve di Cadore (three hours), which is connected by bus to Cortina d'Ampezzo. (Consult www.dolomitisuperski.it for further travel information.)

There are buses from Grado and Aquileia to the station of Cervignano (85 minutes) on the main Venice–Trieste line.

By bus

Italian long-distance buses are usually neither as frequent, cheap nor relaxing as the train. An exception

Loggia Valmarana. *See p258*.

Antonio Canova; and Bassano del Grappa (*see p267*), home of the fiery spirit that keeps the *veneti* going through those foggy winter evenings (and mornings, come to that).

Beyond Belluno (*see p271*) the mountains begin in earnest, bringing hordes of *beau monde* skiers to the elegant resort of Cortina d'Ampezzo and queues of summer hikers to attempt one of the *alte vie* (high-altitude footpaths; for information see www.dolomiti-altevie.it or www.cai.it) that traverse the pink granite Dolomites.

Heading north-east from Venice, a straggle of seaside resorts with high-density beach umbrellas, campsites and discos stretches from Lido di Jesolo (*see p216* **Jesolo night fever**) to the border of the Veneto. Beyond here, in the region of Friuli-Venezia Giulia, are the twin pulls of Aquileia – a tiny village with a glorious

The Veneto

is on mountain routes, where they are often the only mode of public transport. The ski resort of Cortina d'Ampezzo, for example, is best reached by bus from Venice and Treviso (see p273).

Many destinations can be reached by combining train and bus journeys. See individual chapters in the Veneto section for details of bus services to more out-of-the-way destinations. In almost all cases, Sunday services are very limited.

By car

The larger towns in the Veneto are all connected to Venice by fast motorway links: note that Italian motorways (autostrade, prefix 'A' followed by number) are not cheap. Surprisingly, northern Italy's A-roads (strade nazionali or strade statali, prefix 'N' or 'SS' followed by a number) are not always as good as they are further south, and often take a direct route right through the centre of towns (with a high risk of encountering traffic confusion) rather than by-passing them.

For more out-of-the-way destinations and mountain roads, a good map is essential; those in the 1:200,000-scale series published by the Touring Club Italiano (TCI) have plenty of detail and are available in most bookshops and in motorway service stations. For car-hire information, see p280.

Not Venice but trying

The extraordinary beauty of Venice is made all the more striking by the fact that – unlike every other Italian town – it has no outer no-man's-land of unsightly 1950s and '60s residential and/or industrial sprawl. Or rather, it does, but it's across the water. It is called Mestre and it is extremely self-conscious about its role as ugly stepsister to the glamorous queen of the lagoon.

Mestre has no illustrious history to pride itself on. An insignificant walled town from the tenth century (the only notable remnant of these medieval fortifications is the tower in its main piazza, open 4-7pm Mon; 10am-noon, 4-7pm Tue-Sun; admission free), it did not begin to grow exponentially until the last century, with the creation of the industrial port of Marghera (see pp23-25). Then the lure of jobs attracted thousands of workers from all over Italy. From the 1950s, lagoon-dwelling Venetians began to move here too, fleeing high house prices in Venice itself, or simply seeking the convenience of mainland life, with all its luxurious trappings such as cars and supermarkets.

As Venice's population dwindled, Mestre's expanded, galloping outwards and upwards in grim concrete. Defined by what it is not (ie Venice), Mestre has only recently begun to strive for its own identity; the quest is helped by the fact that most younger mestrini have none of the sentimental ties that still bind many of their elders to La Serenissima. And the young in Mestre are a far more significant sector of the population than they are across the lagoon. One evening visit to piazza Ferretto – the attractive square at Mestre's heart – will suffice to get a sense of the extent to which this is a youth-oriented city. Indeed, anyone looking for some active nightlife should consider a trip here, once campo Santa Margherita's (see p125) attractions have been explored and exhausted. Mestre has more cinemas than Venice; both the centre and the environs are home to some great clubs, gay and straight (see pp210-1 and pp212-7).

Pickings are slim in the art and architecture fields: the churches of **San Rocco** (open 10.30am-noon Wed, Fri; 6-7.30pm Thur) with its 18th-century frescoes, and **San Girolamo** (open 9am-noon, 4-6.30pm Mon-Sat) are worth a look, and there are some fine classical villas, particularly in the greener areas northwards on the way towards Carpenedo (which an imaginative Mestre legend says is where Icarus fell to earth).

But, over recent years, Mestre has gone a long way towards establishing some cultural independence: its theatres (see pp218-24) provide musical and theatrical seasons that rival anything Venice has to offer (with the exception of opera). There are lively historical societies and creative writing workshops. In 2001 a long-promised new cultural centre was finally opened: the **Centro Culturale Candiani** (see p223) is a five-storey building with spaces for exhibitions, workshops and multimedia events, not all of which have proved successful (see pp205-9).

In May 2004 dreary Mestre's desire for green space was answered by the opening of **Parco San Giuliano**, a 70-hectare (175 acre) area of former wasteland between the town and the lagoon, with bicycle tracks, woods, canals, play areas, a roller-skating rink and lake; over 3,000 trees and 10,000 shrubs were planted. A 140m (380ft) pedestrian bridge crosses the busy ringroad to connect the park to the city.

The Veneto

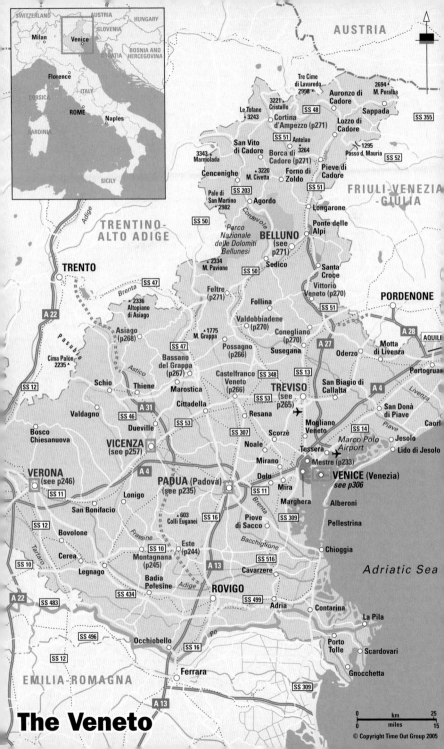

The Veneto

© Copyright Time Out Group 2005

Padua

Once Venice's rival, Padua is a colourful hive of great shops and stunning architecture.

In the **Ghetto**. *See p237.*

Padua (Padova) lays claim to Italy's second-oldest university, a basilica bursting with religious relics and saintly body parts, and one of Italy's most revered artistic treasures: Giotto's frescoes in the Scrovegni Chapel. All right, it doesn't have the architectural riches of its more flamboyant sister on the lagoon, but what it does have is not to be sneezed at.

Although a fishing village was established here some time in the ninth or tenth century BC, it was the Romans who developed this fertile spot into a thriving town, only for the barbarian hordes to knock it all down. However, plucky Padua prospered under Byzantine and Lombard rule, becoming an independent republic in 1164.

The city saw its political and cultural influence reach dizzying heights under the Carrara family (1338-1405), but voracious Venice put a stop to all that in 1405. Padua was governed by *La Serenissima* until its fall in 1797. After a period under Napoleon, Padua fell into Austrian hands (1815-66), and went on to play an active part in the struggle to free northern Italy from foreign dominion.

However, Padua is more than just a historical pageant: its modern status rests on its contribution to the north-eastern economic revival (*see pp23-25* **Venice Today**). Padua now boasts some serious shopping and excellent eateries.

Though Padua's well-heeled young entrepreneurs would look at home in Milan and Rome, the city still bears the traces of an inferiority complex with its more photogenic neighbour. While Venice has exploited its aura of mystery, Padua has, since the 19th century, tried hard to catch up, proudly presenting itself in a sphinx-like riddle as a city possessing 'a meadow with no grass, a café with no doors and a saint with no name'. The meadow is the large urban square of Prato della Valle, and the café with no doors was Pedrocchi's (which never closed). Prato della Valle (*see p237*) has now been turfed and Pedrocchi's now shuts its doors at regular hours (*see p237*). That leaves only the saint with no name, Il Santo, as the locals affectionately still call the basilica of St Anthony (*see p239*).

Sightseeing

Padua has three main *piazze* offering a colourful, dynamic panorama of the city going about its daily life: piazza della Frutta and piazza delle Erbe flank the Palazzo della Ragione, known to locals as **Il Salone**; piazza dei Signori lies a little to the west. In the morning (Mon-Sat) piazza delle Erbe and piazza della Frutta are home to bustling, picturesque fruit and vegetable markets. To the west, **Caffè Pedrocchi** and the **university** stand between the squares and the old **Ghetto**.

Piazza dei Signori is dominated by Palazzo del Capitanio (1532), by Paduan architect Giovanni Maria Falconetto. The clock housed in the palazzo's tower is a replica of the original created in 1344, the first of its kind in Italy.

To the left is the Loggia del Consiglio. This construction, again by Falconetto, housed the Maggior Consiglio, the governing body of the city under Venetian rule. Opposite the Palazzo del Capitanio stands the church of San Clemente.

The Veneto

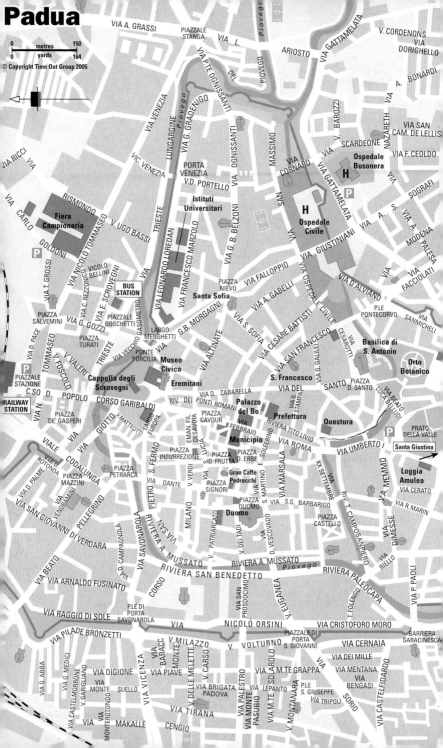

To the south is piazza del **Duomo**, home to Padua's cathedral. Further south, the once-swampy area called **Prato della Valle** was used as a fairground before 1775, when it was turned into an elegant marketplace.

After years of neglect, the canal around the central island has been dredged and cleaned, the statues restored, the lawns replanted and the central fountain repaired. Note the statue of the notable near the southern bridge over to the island: to pre-empt inevitable future indignities, the sculptor provided this statue with its own pigeon. The **Museo del Precinema** is situated in the Prato. Further south towards the river is the beautiful medieval complex housing **La Specola**, the observatory.

Beyond the Prato stands one of Christendom's biggest churches, **Santa Giustina**. To the east, the **Orto Botanico** (Botanical Garden) lies between the Prato and Padua's nameless basilica: **Il Santo**. If the treasures contained in this best-loved of Paduan churches are too awe-inspiring, the little **Scoletta del Santo** and **Oratorio di San Giorgio**, both in piazza del Santo, offer interesting frescoes on a smaller scale… and not a creepy body part in sight. Alongside Il Santo is another fine work by Falconetto, the **Loggia e Odeo Cornaro**.

But if you only see one thing in Padua, make it the **Scrovegni Chapel**: situated to the north of piazza della Frutta, en route to the station, this is the jewel in Padua's artistic crown.

TICKETS

The **Padovacard**, a multi-entrance ticket costing €14, valid for 48 hours, allows free access for one adult and one child under the age of 12 to the Scrovegni Chapel and Musei Civici Eremitani, the Palazzo della Ragione, the first floor of Caffè Pedrocchi, the Oratorio di San Rocco and San Michele, Odeo Cornaro, the Duomo's Battistero and Petrarch's house in Arquà Petrarca (*see p243*). It can be purchased at the sights covered by the ticket, and at the tourist office at the train station. Further discounts on entrance fees for other attractions are included, plus free travel on APS buses. For further information ring 049 876 7927 or see www.turismopadova.it. No credit cards.

Duomo

Piazza Duomo (church 049 662 814/baptistery 049 656 914). **Open** *Church* 7.30am-noon, 3.45-7.30pm. Mon-Sat; 7.45am-1pm, 3.45-8.30pm Sun. *Baptistery* 10am-6pm daily. **Admission** *Church* free. *Baptistery* €2.50; €1.50 concessions. **No credit cards**.
Paduans claim that Michelangelo designed the apse of their city's cathedral; it is obvious, however, that he didn't have much to do with its uninspiring final form. The church is worth visiting mostly for the

paintings in the sacristy, by Bassano, Tiepolo and others, and even more so for the nearby baptistery, containing a series of vivid frescoes by the 14th-century Florentine artist Giusto de Menabuoi.

Gli Eremitani

Piazza Eremitani 9 (049 875 6410). **Open** *Apr-Sept* 8.30am-12.30pm, 3.30-6pm Mon-Sat; 10am-12.30pm, 4-6pm Sun. *Oct-Mar* 8.30am-12.30pm, 3.30-6pm Mon-Sat; 10am-12.30pm, 4-6pm Sun.
The original building, dating from the late 13th century, was bombed on 11 March 1944: the fine trilobate wooden ceiling is a copy of the early 14th-century original. The bombs almost totally destroyed the church's artistic treasure, Andrea Mantegna's frescoes of the *Life and Martyrdom of St James and St Christopher* (1454-7). Fortunately, two panels of the work, together with the main altar-piece, featuring the *Assumption*, had been removed before the raid. Two other panels – the *Martyrdom of St James* and *St Christopher Converts the Knights* – were partially reassembled from the rubble. The work is impressive though the padlocked gate to the chapel makes it difficult to get a good view. Also worthy of note in the church is Bartolomeo Ammanati's tomb of Marco Mantova Benavides (1544-46), on the north wall near the main entrance – a fine allegorical composition with the renowned humanist flanked by statues representing Time, Fame, Immortality, Wisdom and Labour. Another curiosity is the neo-classical bronze medallion on the west wall of the south transept commemorating Protestant hero Wilhelm George Frederick of Orange… in a Catholic church?

Il Ghetto

A stone's throw from piazza delle Erbe and the University of Padua medical faculty – the first in Europe to accept Jewish students (albeit on payment of double fees) – stands what was once the Jewish Ghetto, now a beautifully renovated pedestrian zone. The area only became a ghetto proper at the beginning of the 17th century, when it was shut off. A plaque commemorates the old synagogue, destroyed in 1943 by anti-Semitic *padovani*. The area is not only historically significant, but also offers a host of shops along its cobbled streets.

Gran Caffè Pedrocchi

Via VIII Febbraio 15, entrance from piazzetta Pedrocchi (049 878 1231/www.caffepedrocchi.it). **Open** *Architectural rooms* 9.30am-12.30pm, 3.30-6pm Tue-Sun. **Admission** €4; €2.50 concessions. **No credit cards**.
For café and restaurant opening times, *see p242*. Known as 'the café without doors' because it never closed, Pedrocchi's – a mixture of neo-classical and Victorian Gothic revival – was designed by the early 19th-century architect Giuseppe Japelli. It was the scene of a student uprising in 1848, and later developed a reputation as a Fascist watering hole. After closing for restoration in 1995, it reopened in 1999, with all the renovated theme rooms on show

upstairs. The Greek staircase leads up to a condensed tour of Western culture: the Etruscan room leads into the Roman, then into the Herculaneum room, followed by the Renaissance. The whole culminates in a large white and gold neo-classical room dedicated to Rossini, on the opposite side of which is the Egyptian Room, with squatting dog-gods and starry vaults. Caffè Pedrocchi is also home to the Museo del Risorgimento e dell'Età Contemporanea (included in admission to the Architectural rooms), containing 19th-century uniforms and flags.

Loggia e Odeo Cornaro
Via Cesarotti 37 (049 820 4579). **Open** *Feb-Oct* 10am-1pm Tue-Fri; 10am-1pm, 4-7pm Sat, Sun. *Nov-Jan* 10am-1pm Tue-Fri; 10am-1pm, 3-6pm Sat, Sun. **Admission** €3; concessions €2. **No credit cards**.
Originally the home of Alvise Cornaro, a wealthy Venetian and patron of the arts, this Renaissance gem situated alongside the piazza del Santo was used as a theatre and intellectual salon. Set in tranquil grounds, the real treat is the Cornaro Odeum: a beguilingly plain façade conceals an octagonal room stuccoed and frescoed with mythological motifs by Tiziano Minio and Domenico Campagnola in the 1540s.

Museo del Precinema (Collezione Minici Zotti)
Prato della Valle 1A (049 876 3838/www. precinema.it). **Open** *Mid June-mid Sept* 4-10pm Mon, Wed-Sun. *Mid Sept-mid June* 10am-4pm Mon, Wed-Sun. **Admission** €3; concessions €2; €5 guided tours. **No credit cards**.
This miniscule museum set in the rafters of a building overlooking Prato della Valle has a delightful display of magic lanterns, precursors to photo and film. The collection includes hand-painted glass slides, optical instruments, and a Javanese puppet theatre. Enjoy the diversions of a Victorian slide show and a 360° 'view' of the Piazza, a photographic montage of the square set in a miniscule circus tent.

Orto Botanico (Botanical Garden)
Via Orto Botanico 15 (049 827 2119/www. ortobotanico.unipd.it). **Open** *Apr-Oct* 9am-1pm, 3-6pm daily. *Nov-Mar* 9am-1pm Mon-Sat. **Admission** €4; groups & OAPs €3; students €1; under-6s free. **No credit cards**.
The Orto Botanico started life in the 1540s as a Garden of Simples (medicinal herbs), providing raw materials for the university's medical faculty. It was the first of its kind in Europe. The original layout, with stone borders enclosing the different species, has been maintained in the central section of the garden (a circle within a square) and contains exquisite freshwater habitats. Though not large, it still provides a leafy idyll to counter the stresses of shopping, eating and sightseeing.

Osservatorio Astronomico – Museo La Specola
Via dell'Osservatorio 5 (049 829 3469/www.pd. astro.it/museo-laspecola). **Open** (guided tours only) *Oct-Apr* 11am & 4pm Sat; 4pm Sun.

The economically named **Il Santo**. *See p239.*

May-Sept 6pm Sat & Sun. **Admission** €7; €5 concessions (including Padovacard-holders). **No credit cards**.
Tickets must be purchased in advance from the Oratorio di San Michele, opposite the Specola at piazzetta San Michele 1.
This beautifully situated medieval tower overlooking the river was made into an observatory by the city's Venetian overlords in 1761. A guided tour takes you up the tower (which housed a prison in the 13th century) to a display of telescopes and other heavenly paraphernalia, though no stargazing is included. Check out the 1767 plaque above the door on the right after entering, which reads 'this tower once led to infernal shadows; now, under the auspices of the Venetians, it leads to the stars'.

Il Salone (Palazzo della Ragione)
Via VIII Febbraio (049 820 5006). **Open** *Feb-Oct* 9am-7pm Tue-Sun. *Nov-Jan* 9am-6pm Tue-Sun. **Admission** €8; €4 concessions. **No credit cards**.
The Salone, as locals call it, was built between 1218 and 1219 and served as the law courts. In the early 14th century the building was raised and the external loggia of the *piano nobile* was added, giving it the structure it maintains today. Inside, the Salone is frescoed with signs of the zodiac and representations of the months and seasons; it is claimed that the original frescoes, destroyed in a disastrous fire in 1420, were by Giotto, though contemporary records make no reference to this. The impressive

ship's-keel ceiling is a replacement of the 14th-century original, which was torn off by a whirlwind in 1759. The huge wooden horse was created for a tournament in 1466. Note that there is an extra (variable) charge for temporary exhibitions held in the Salone.

Santa Giustina

Prato della Valle (049 822 0411). **Open** *May-Oct* 8.30am-noon, 3-7pm Mon-Sat; 7am-1pm, 3-7.45pm Sun. *Nov-Apr* 8.30am-noon, 3-7pm daily.

Built in 1532-79, the Basilica di Santa Giustina is the 11th-largest Christian church in the world; its size is best appreciated as you look along its broad, bare transepts. The south transept leads to the small chapel of St Prosdocimo, the first bishop of Padua, with a fine marble iconostasis dating from the sixth century. To the east of the transept is St Luke's Chapel, which contains the tomb of Elena Lucrezia Cornaro Piscopia, the first woman in the world to get a university degree. Visits to the monastery on request.

Il Santo (Basilica di Sant'Antonio)

Piazza del Santo (049 878 9722/www. basilicadelsanto.org). **Open** *Apr-Oct* 6.20am-7.45pm daily. *Nov-Mar* 6.20am-7pm Mon-Fri; 6.20am-7.45pm Sat, Sun.

Popularly known as Il Santo, the Basilica di Sant'Antonio is one of the most important pilgrimage churches in Italy. St Anthony was not a local saint but a Portuguese Franciscan, a powerful preacher against the evils of usury, who died in Padua in 1231. Work on the church began soon after his canonisation in 1232; the main structure remained unfinished until around 1350, when the saint's body was moved to its present tomb in the Cappella dell'Arca. Visited by a steady stream of devotees, this chapel also contains one of the basilica's great artistic treasures: marble bas-reliefs of scenes from the life of the saint by Jacopo Sansovino, Tullio Lombardo and Giovanni Minello. The chapel's ceiling, by Giovanni Maria Falconetto, dates from 1533. The other great art treasures of the basilica are Donatello's bronze panels on the high altar (1443-50). Behind the altar, his stone bas-relief of the Deposition is more visible, as are two of the bronzes – a bull and a lion, representing the evangelists St Mark and St Luke. Other works of interest include Altichiero's late 14th-century frescoes in the Cappella di San Felice (on the south wall), Giusto de Menabuoi's frescoes in the Cappella del Beato Luca Belludi and two fine funeral monuments – to Alessandro Contarini (died 1553) and Cardinal Pietro Bembo (died 1547) – both by the sculptor and military architect Michele Sanmicheli. At the back of the apse is the Baroque Cappella del Tesoro, containing 'miraculous' relics. The reliquary containing the tongue of St Anthony was recently stolen, but then recovered, so legend has it, with the help of Mafia bosses outraged that any of their confraternity could commit such a heinous act.

In the piazza outside the church stands Donatello's famous monument to the *condottiere* (mercenary soldier) Erasmo da Narni, aka Gattamelata.

Scrovegni Chapel & Musei Civici Eremitani

Piazza Eremitani 8 (049 820 4551/049 201 0020/ www.cappelladegliscrovegni.it). **Open** 9am-7pm Tue-Sun. **Admission** *Museum & chapel* €11 (plus €1 booking fee). *Museum only* €9. *Chapel only* €7. **Credit** (website bookings only) MC, V.

Note that booking is obligatory for the Scrovegni Chapel and ideally should be done 72 hours in advance. You can book on the website by credit card or directly at the Musei Civici Eremitani. Although the chapel is included on the Padovacard (*see p237*), the €1 booking fee is extra. If you haven't booked, you may be able to bag an unclaimed place, though in high season you risk disappointment. Ask at the Musei if they can squeeze you in. Note that bookings are not made at the Scrovegni Chapel itself.

After all this complicated procedure, you are allotted a mere 15 minutes to admire this masterpiece after 15 minutes in a 'purification' chamber. But one look at the star-studded ceiling and it will seem worth the hassle.

The Scrovegni Chapel

This externally unassuming building is dedicated to the Virgin of the Annunciation, depicted on either side of the arch leading through to the altar, which contains three statues by Pisano. The wall frescoes – painted in c1304-13 by early Renaissance genius Giotto – relate the story of Christ's life and depict mainly apocryphal stories of Mary's parents Joachim and Anne.

The cycle opens (top right – alongside the Virgin of the Annunciation) with Joachim being driven from the temple because his marriage had so far proved infertile. Banished, Joachim wanders off into the wilderness to make an offering to God. An angel appears to both him and Anne telling them they will have a child and that when Joachim returns to Jerusalem he will encounter his wife at the Golden Gate. In the meeting scene, Giotto reveals the power of his innovative narrative realism: the embracing couple are surrounded by gossiping ladies, carelessly commenting on the coincidence of this meeting between husband and wife. The top row on the wall opposite recounts the childhood and marriage of the Virgin.

The story of Christ unfolds in the middle and lower rows, with the middle of the right-hand wall dominated by the scene of Judas' kiss. The traitor's yellow cloak enfolds Christ – but He is still the dominant figure. Note the fan of spears, clubs and torches around the central couple, leading the eye left down to St Peter as he severs the ear of the high priest's attendant.

The high dado at the base of the walls is decorated with fine grisaille paintings of the seven Virtues and Vices. Particularly striking are the figures of Envy blinded by her own serpentine tongue and Prudence equipped with pen and mirror.

Money ill-gotten by Reginaldo Scrovegni, whose thriving usury business made him a fortune in Padua and earned him a special mention in

Dante's *Inferno* as 'one of the damned, with a blue sow on a white field painted on his bag' (Canto XVII, 64), paid for the chapel. Reginaldo's son Enrico had the chapel built (between 1303 and 1305) and frescoed by Giotto, to atone for his father's mercenary practices and to secure a more comfortable abode in the afterlife than his dad, though Enrico had also dabbled in the usury business. (Enrico is depicted presenting the model of the chapel to the Virgin in the *Last Judgement*.)

By the 19th century the Scrovegni Chapel was crumbling into ruin. The Scrovegni Palace had been demolished in 1827 and this, as well as the removal of the chapel's external plaster, led to further damage to the frescoes. In 2002 after extensive restoration work the chapel reopened to the public looking more magnificent than ever.

Musei Civici Eremitani

Housed in the cloisters of the Eremitani friars, the Musei Civici Eremitani has a moderately interesting public collection and two private collections.

Though small, the Archeological Wing contains some fine pieces. In Room 9 there is a noble female head of the fourth century AD, while in the antechamber to Room 10 is a carved Greek panel. Moving into Room 10 there is an impressive funeral stele of a young girl slave with an inscription informing us that she was happy to elude the disfigurement of age by dying at the age of 19. The room also contains some steles of married couples and interesting floor mosaics.

The Egyptian collection is mainly a tribute to the Paduan GB Belzoni, who moved the massive bust of Ramses II from Thebes to Cairo.

The Picture Gallery opens with two rooms of angels by 14th-century Guariento di Arpo, followed by a Giotto *Crucifixion* that originally hung in the Scrovegni Chapel. What follows includes Squarcione's *Lazarus* polyptych, *Sailing of the Argonauts* by Lorenzo Costa and a fine *Portrait of a Young Man* by Alvise Vivarini. Some marvellous landscapes lurk behind the miserable-looking saints by the anonymous 'Pittore Veneto'. There's an intriguing *Sacra conversazione* by Bernardino Luini

and two marvellous postcard-sized landscapes attributed to Giorgione. There are also fine works by the Bassano family, Pozzoserrato, Luca Giordano, some interesting 16th- and 17th-century Dutch and Flemish works, altarpieces by Romanino and Veronese, portraits by the early 17th-century Chiara Varotari and, to end on a bathetically light-hearted note, a portrait of a portly Venetian captain by Sebastiano Mazzoni (1611-78).

Scuola del Santo & Oratorio di San Giorgio

Piazza del Santo 11 (049 875 5235). **Open** *Apr-Sept* 9am-12.30pm, 2.30-7pm daily. *Oct-Mar* 9am-12.30pm, 2.30-5pm daily. **Admission** €2; €1.50 concessions. **No credit cards.**

The Scuola del Santo contains 16th-century frescoes, some of which Titian is said to have had a hand in. The oratory, constructed in 1377 for the Lupi di Soragna family, contains a cycle of frescoes by Altichiero (1379-84) depicting scenes from the lives of Saints Catherine and George. Altichiero is at his best here, and this place is worth a visit even after the long hike around the basilica.

Università di Padova, Palazzo del Bò (University)

Via VIII Febbraio 2 (049 827 5111/049 827 3047 www.unipd.it). **Open** (guided tours only) *Mar-Oct* 3.15pm, 4.15pm, Mon, Wed, Fri; 10.15am, 11.15am Tue, Thur, Sat. *Nov-Feb* 3.15pm, 4.15pm, 5.15pm Mon, Wed, Fri; 9.15am, 10.15am, 11.15am Tue, Thur, Sat. **Admission** €3; €2.50 groups; €1.50 concessions. Tickets on sale 15mins before tour. **No credit cards.** Note that opening times are liable to change without warning.

The second-oldest university in Italy after Bologna occupies a building – Palazzo del Bò (bull) – named for the butchers' inn that used to stand on the site. The Old Courtyard is decorated with the coats of arms and family crests of illustrious rectors and students. The magnificent oval wooden-benched Anatomy Theatre on the first floor, built by Girolamo

Shopping by saint

The saintly streets of city centre boasts a host of great shops, including big names where you can spend big bucks.

Via San Fermo is home to Cartier and Bulgari, while nearby via Santa Lucia has upmarket frock shops and shoes galore. Via del Santo has everything you could wish for, from quirky clothes to exquisite toiletries. For the more prudent shopper, big department stores, such as Oviesse, Upim and La Rinascente offer less pricey delights,

and are all within spitting distance of central piazza Garibaldi. If you've forgotten to pack the latest Jeffrey Archer, head for Feltrinelli International on via San Francesco, where you can choose from an eclectic range of books and magazines in English. For chic boutiques and antique shops, make for the Ghetto (*see p237*). But beware Paduan opening times: only very few of Padua's largest shops have abandoned the traditional practice of long lunch breaks and Sunday closing.

Fabrizi Aquapendente in 1594, was the first of its kind in the world. Galileo worked here from 1592 to 1610. Past students include Copernicus, Sir Francis Walsingham and Oliver Goldsmith, all of whom are remembered in the Sala dei Quaranta, where you can also see Galileo's lectern. Europe's first ever female graduate, Elena Lucrezia Cornaro Piscopia, studied here; there is a statue dedicated to her on the stairway.

The university also has a gift shop offering such delights as notebooks adorned with Galileo and key rings bearing the university's coat of arms, plus a good selection of classy computer bags and stationery. The shop is open all year round (9am-12.30pm Mon-Sat, 3-7pm Mon-Fri), barring the university's brief summer recess and public holidays.

Where to eat & drink

See also p242 **Gran Caffè Pedrocchi** and **Highlander Pub.**

If you're on a tight budget, the morning markets in piazza delle Erbe or piazza della Frutta and shops in the arcades around them offer a wide range of local produce for picnics.

If DIY sandwiches are not your thing, head for **Bar Maximilian**, on the corner of corso del Popolo and via Nicolò Tommaseo (closed Sat and Sun) for the finest panini in Padua.

Caffè Cavour

Piazza Cavour 10 (049 875 1224/www.caffecavour. com). **Open** 7.30am-8.30pm Mon, Wed-Sun. **Meals served** 12.30-2.30pm. **Average** €18. **Credit** MC, V.
This elegant patisserie is home to world-renowned pastry chef, Emanuele Saracino. Incredibly intricate – and unmissable – cakes and pastries are on offer on the ground floor, while upstairs you can savour a pleasant lunch overlooking the square.

Le Calandre

Via Liguria 1, Sarmeola di Rubano (049 630 303/ www.calandre.com). **Meals served** noon-2pm, 8-10pm Tue-Sat. Closed 3wks Jan, 2wks Aug. **Average** €130. **Credit** AmEx, DC, MC, V.
This restaurant, 4km (2.5 miles) west of the city, boasts the youngest chef to have been awarded three Michelin stars. Local boy Massimiliano Alajmo serves up such delights as saffron risotto with ground liquorice. Though it may sound like hauling coals to Newcastle, try their fish and chips. After washing it all down with wine from a superlative list, a pink pepper crème brûlée with cassis sorbet is all you need to clean the palate. Break the bank (and your diet): Le Calandre is not to be missed.

Graziati

Piazza della Frutta 40 (tel/fax 049 875 1014/ www.graziati.com). **Meals served** noon-2.30pm Tue-Sun. **Average** €20. **Credit** MC, V.
Graziati is essentially a *pasticceria* (open 7.30am-8.30pm Tue-Sun), specialising in a large and calorific range of tantalising millefeuille pastries.

Dynamic **piazza delle Erbe**. *See p235.*

For something more substantial, the subterranean restaurant serves hearty lunches. The decor is simple, the dining room intimate and on display is a beautiful 14th-century wooden door rediscovered during restoration work.

PePen

Piazza Cavour 15 (049 875 9483/www.pepen.it). **Meals served** noon-3pm, 7pm-1am Mon-Sat. **Average** €30. **Credit** MC, V.
A popular haunt for the young and lovely at lunchtime, this quiet corner of piazza Cavour has great outdoor seating in summer. As well as pizza, the menu offers a selection of meat and fish dishes, along with an extensive wine list.

Pinguino Blu

Via Ponte Altinate 6 (049 876 4706). **Open** 11am-1am daily. **No credit cards**.
This friendly ice-cream parlour serves ice-cream and *granite* (crushed water-ice) made on the premises. No artificial preservatives or flavourings are used. Great for those with food allergies, though no soya ice-creams are available. However, vegans can enjoy fruit sorbets and sensational slush puppies.

Zairo

Prato della Valle 51 (tel/fax 049 663 803). **Meals served** noon-2.30pm, 7pm-1am Tue-Sun. **Average** €25. **Credit** AmEx, DC, MC, V.
Its outdoor seating with views over the Prato (*see p237*) and its late-night opening make Zairo a

The Veneto

popular meeting point. This *osteria* has its menu firmly rooted in home territory, with some international cuisine to boot. Pizzas are also served.

Bars & nightlife

For gay and lesbian venues in Padua, *see p211*.

Gran Caffè Pedrocchi

Via VIII Febbraio 15/piazzetta Pedrocchi (049 878 1231/www.caffepedrocchi.it). **Open** *Bar* 9am-9pm Mon, Tue, Sun; 9am-midnight Wed, Sat. *Restaurant* 12.30-3pm, 7-10.30pm daily. **Average** €35. **Credit** AmEx, DC, MC, V.
For centuries Padua's most elegant watering hole, and now restored to its former glory, Pedrocchi's is a landmark in its own right (*see p237*). Savour an early evening aperitif whilst people-watching the Paduans. Booking is essential for dinner.

Highlander Pub

Via Santi Martino e Solferino 69 (049 659 977). **Open** 11am-3pm, 6pm-2am daily. **Average** €10. **Credit** AmEx, DC, MC, V.
One of Padua's biggest pubs, this faux-British nightspot offers a vast selection of beers and bar snacks (though not a pork scratching in sight) and has a restaurant serving cheap meals both day and night. Erasmus students get a 10% discount on food and drink with a valid student card.

Villa Barbieri

Via Venezuela 11 (tel/fax 049 870 3223). **Open** 8.30pm-4am Wed, Fri, Sat. **Admission** €15. **Credit** MC, V.
This summertime haunt for Paduan night owls is set in beautiful grounds buried within the industrial outskirts of the city. It's a fair hike to get there: from the city, follow signs for Padova Est until reaching the Sheraton roundabout, take the motorway towards Bologna, turning off at the corso Stati Uniti exit, which takes you to via Venezuela. The club is so famous that it has released its own sounds on CD (available in local record shops). Music is mainly house and revival, with live music some nights; you'll be turned away at the door if you turn up looking scruffy.

Where to stay

Grand'Italia

Corso del Popolo 81 (049 876 1111/fax 049 875 0850/www.hotelgranditalia.it). **Rates** €145 single; €198 double; €274 suite. **Credit** AmEx, DC, MC, V.
This art nouveau hotel is close to all the major sights of the city centre. The recently restored rooms are quiet and comfortable, and many have balconies.

Hotel Piccolo Vienna

Via Beato Pellegrino 133 (tel/fax 049 871 6331/www.hotelpiccolovienna.it). **Rates** €43 single; €55 double; €66 triple. *Breakfast* €3 extra. **Credit** AmEx, DC, MC, V.

For the cash-strapped traveller, this centrally located hotel provides clean – if cramped – rooms all year round.

Majestic Toscanelli

Via dell'Arco 2 (049 663 244/fax 049 876 0025/ www.toscanelli.com). **Rates** €115 single; €169 double; €215 suite. **Credit** AmEx, DC, MC, V.
All the rooms in this quiet hotel offer attractive views over the quaint streets of the Ghetto. The Majestic Toscanelli is just one minute's walk away from the town's main squares.

Sant'Antonio

Via San Fermo 118 (049 875 1393/fax 049 875 2508/www.hotelsantantonio.it). **Rates** €60 single; €82 double. *Breakfast* €7 extra. **Credit** MC, V.
Sant'Antonio is good value for money, unless you're unlucky enough to get one of the rooms looking out on to what becomes a busy street corner very early in the morning.

Tourist information

IAT

Padua railway station (049 875 2077/fax 049 875 5008/www.turismopadova.it). **Open** 9am-7pm Mon-Sat; 9am-noon Sun.
Galleria Pedrocchi, next to Gran Caffè Pedrocchi (049 876 7927/fax 049 836 3316). **Open** 9.30am-12.30pm, 3-7pm Mon-Sat.
Piazza del Santo, opposite the basilica (049 875 3087). **Open** *Apr-Oct* 9am-1pm, 2-6pm daily. Closed Nov-Mar.

Getting around

City buses are operated by APS (049 20111/ www.apsholding.it/mobilita/index.asp); tickets, which must be bought before boarding, cost 85¢ and are valid for one hour. A block of ten tickets for the city costs €8 and a family day ticket (for two adults and a maximum of three children) costs €2. Destinations outside the city covered in this chapter are served by blue SITA buses (049 820 6811), which depart from the bus station in piazzale Boschetti.

Getting there

By car

Padua is on the A4 La Serenissima motorway.

By train

All trains bound south-west from Venice (on the Bologna line) stop at Padua. Journey time 25-35mins.

By bus

From Venice's piazzale Roma bus terminus, orange ACTV buses saunter slowly to Padua, stopping off near several Palladian villas (*see p38-42*) en route. Blue SITA buses (049 820 6811) speed along the motorway. In Padua, both stop at the bus station in piazzale Boschetti.

The Veneto

Around Padua

South of Padua

To the south of Padua stand the verdant Euganean Hills. Romans enjoyed the restorative powers of the area's volcanic springs and mud: elderly Italians still flock for treatments in the spa resorts of **Abano Terme** and **Montegrotto**. This latter town is home to a butterfly farm: tiny tourists and budding lepidopterists will love **Butterfly Arc**. Admission includes the fairy wood, with a nature trail to help city slickers name their trees with the aid of fairy legends.

If you've packed your walking boots, now is the time to use them: the Monte Grande pathway can be traversed by even the most urban hiker. Starting at **Passo Fiorine**, a two-hour trek takes you on a circuit of wooded public footpaths. You'll be rewarded with a ruined castle and the lushest of panoramas. There's a printable map of the walk on www.padovando.com .

Six kilometres (four miles) west of Abano, in the **Bresso**, is the **Abbazia di Praglia**. Though founded by Benedictine monks in the 12th century, the abbey's present buildings date from the 1400s. The monastery itself consists of an interesting series of cloisters (one of which serves as a botanical garden). A friendly monk offers guided tours every half-hour.

South of Abano lies **Arquà Petrarca**: it was here that the poet Francesco Petrarch (*see p243* **One that loved not wisely**) spent the last years of his life. Still with a delightfully medieval air, the town offers the chance to make a pilgrimage to Petrarch's tomb in the local churchyard and to visit the 14th-century house where the poet lived: the **Casa di Petrarca** has portraits of the poet and some well-preserved friezes. One look at the views from the windows and you'll be waxing lyrical yourself.

Abbazia di Praglia

Via Abbazia 16, Bresseo di Teolo (049 999 9300). **Open** *Jan* 3.30-5.30pm Sat, Sun. *Apr-Oct* 3.30-5.30pm Tue-Sun. *Nov-Mar* 2.30-4.30pm Tue-Sun. **Admission** free (donations welcome).

Butterfly Arc

Via degli Scavi 21bis, Montegrotto Terme (049 891 0189/www.butterflyarc.it). **Open** *Apr-Sept* 9.30am-12.30pm, 2.30-5.30pm daily; *Feb, Mar, Oct, Nov* 9.30am-12.30pm, 2-4pm daily. Closed Jan, Dec. **Admission** €7; €5 concessions. **No credit cards**.

Casa di Petrarca

Via Valleselle 4, Arquà Petrarca (0429 718 294). **Open** *Mar-Oct* 9am-12.30pm, 3-7pm Tue-Sun. *Nov-Feb* 9am-12.30pm, 2.30-5.30pm Tue-Sun. **Admission** €3; €1.50 concessions. **No credit cards**.

Where to eat

Just outside Arquà's town centre is **La Cucina d'Arquà** (via Scalette 1, Arquà Petrarca, 0429 777 170, closed Mon and 3wks Jan, average

One that loved not wisely

"*Blessed may be the day, the month, the year,*
And the season, the time, the hour, the point,
And the course, the place where I was joined
By two fair eyes that now have tied me here."
(Sonnet LXI)
Aah, true love. In the 16th century, Petrarch's fame was such that he influenced Shakespeare's sonnet style, but little is known about the great man himself.

Francesco Petrarch (1304-1347) – whose 700th birthday was celebrated recently – was born in Tuscany, but travelled extensively in his lifetime to Bologna, Padua and Avignon, where in 1327 he first set eyes on his beloved Laura, the object of some of the greatest vernacular love poetry ever written. This first sighting led to an intense 20-year unrequited passion that ended with Laura's death from the plague in 1348. Trying to

take his mind off this devastating event, Petrarch threw himself into his work, dedicating himself to the unification of Italy and pleading for the return of the Papal seat to Rome when he wasn't busy writing endless letters to Cicero.

Crowned Poet Laureate in Rome in 1341, Petrarch was equally at home writing in the vulgar tongue and in Latin (which he mastered as a living language), earning plaudits from his contemporaries.

His delicate and melodious style (it's no coincidence that Petrarch was also a mean musician and great lyre player) became a template for Italian literature for the next three centuries. English translators of his works are not exactly minor characters on the literary scene either: Geoffrey Chaucer, Edmund Spenser and Thomas Wyatt all translated and admired his poetry.

The Veneto

€25), which serves what seem to be endless courses of traditional dishes, with meat being a major protagonist (though fish swims onto the summer menu). Wear loose clothing.

Tourist information

IAT

Terme Euganee Via P d'Abano 18, Abano Terme (049 866 9055/fax 049 866 9053/www.turismo termeeuganee.it). **Open** 8.30am-1pm, 2.30-7pm Mon-Sat; 9am-noon, 3-6pm on alternate Suns.

Getting there

By car

Take the A13 Padua–Bologna motorway, turning off at Padova Sud for Abano, and about 20km (12.5 miles) further south at the Terme Euganee exit for Arquà; Praglia is accessible by minor roads from Abano.

By train

Frequent services (approx every 20mins) to Terme Euganee and Montegrotto for Abano on the Padua–Bologna line.

By bus

ACAP city buses and SITA buses (*see p242*) run approximately every 15mins from Padua to Abano; SITA buses serve Montegrotto, Praglia and Arquà.

Monselice

The most impressive sight in small, industrial Monselice is the **Castello Marcello**, a complex that includes the 13th-century Palazzo di Ezzelino, the Palazzo Marcello, an 18th-century chapel, and a crenellated structure built in the 15th century.

Don't miss the **Santuario delle Sette Chiese** (open 10am-noon, 2-7pm daily), designed by Vincenzo Scamozzi, Palladio's brilliant pupil and erstwhile guide to Inigo Jones. Situated by the town's Porta Romana gate, the church was completed between 1592 and 1593, the chapels coming later in 1605.

Castello Marcello

Via del Santuario 11 (0429 72 931/ roccadimonselice@interfree.it). **Open** *April-mid Nov (*guided tours only) 9am, 10am, 11am, 3pm, 4pm, 5pm Tue-Sun. **Admission** €5.50; €4.50 concessions; €3 6-14 years. **No credit cards**.

Tourist information

APT

Via del Santuario 6 (0429 783 026/ www.comune.monselice.padova.it). **Open** 9.30am-12.30pm daily.

Getting there

By car

Leave the A13 Padua–Bologna motorway at the Monselice exit.

By train

Direct services on the Padua–Bologna line.

By bus

SITA buses (*see p242*) run from Padua.

Este

There is little in the town reflecting the past glories of the Este family, a branch of which was to become the dukes of Ferrara and rule over one of the most artistically prolific courts of the Italian Renaissance. However, the **Museo Nazionale Atestino**'s picture gallery houses a rather lovely *Madonna and Child* by Cima da Conegliano.

Turning west from the museum, you come to the **Duomo** (open 10am-noon, 4-6pm daily), which contains Giambattista Tiepolo's *St Thekla Interceding with God the Father to Free the City from the Plague* (1757).

Museo Nazionale Atestino

Via Guido Negri 9 (0429 2085/www. ceramicadieste.it/museoat/museo.htm). **Open** 9am-8pm daily. **Admission** €2; €1 concessions. **No credit cards**.

Where to eat

For a simple lunchtime snack, try the **Tavernetta Da Piero** (via Pescheria Vecchia 14, 0429 2855, closed Tue & 1wk mid-Aug, average €25). This bustling restaurant full of local characters and colour serves Veneto specialities, including fish.

Tourist information

Pro-Loco

Piazza Maggiore 9A (0429 3635). **Open** *Apr-Nov* 9am-12.30pm, 4-6pm Mon-Fri; 9am-12.30pm Sat, Sun. *Dec-Mar* 9am-12.30pm daily.

Getting there

By car

Take the A13 Padua–Bologna motorway, exiting at Monselice; take the SS10 from here to Este.

By train

Direct services on the Padua–Mantua line, or change at Monselice on the Padua–Bologna line.

By bus

By SITA (*see p242*) bus from Padua.

Montagnana

Montagnana's perfectly preserved defences –
composed of 24 towers and intervening curtain
walls – were built between 1360 and 1362.
Since 1996 the castle has housed the
Museo Antonio Giacomelli with its
modest archeological, medieval and
modern rooms.

The town boasts two other architectural
gems. The first is Palladio's **Villa Pisani**.
The villa is not open to the public but is partly
visible from outside; the rear view from the
road alongside the garden is perhaps the
most impressive.

The second, inside the town walls, is the
Duomo (open 8am-12.30pm, 4-7.30pm daily),
a striking mix of Gothic and Renaissance.
Begun in 1431, it was not consecrated until
1502. The present main portal, attributed to
Jacopo Sansovino, was added in 1530. The
two pilasters alongside it are topped by white
stone spheres that, because of the alignment
of the church, are the first part of the façade
to be lit up by the sun at noon. Above the main
altar is a *Transfiguration* by Paolo Veronese,
while on the second altar along the south wall
is an altarpiece of the *Madonna and Child
Enthroned*, considered one of the masterpieces
of Giovanni Buonconsiglio, who is also credited
with the two damaged panels depicting *David
with the Head of Goliath* and *Judith with the
Head of Holofernes* on either side of the main
portal, though Giorgione is also a contender.

However, the greatest curiosity is in the
Rosary Chapel. In 1959 the Baroque altar was
removed to reveal original 15th-century
frescoes, which form an esoteric astrological
allegory, with two bears (ursa major and ursa
minor) separated by the curls of a dragon (the
draco constellation) alongside a representation
of Pegasus and the ship of the Argonauts.

It has been argued that these astrological
figures represent a particular conjunction of
the heavenly bodies relating to the Feast of
the Annunciation. The iconographical scheme
is similar to one at the Castle of Esztergom
in Hungary, the 15th-century physician
and astrologer Galeotto Marzio da Narni
is known to have lived in both places
for some time.

Museo Antonio Giacomelli

*Castel San Zeno, piazza Trieste 15 (0429 804
128).* **Open** (guided tours only) *Apr-Sept* 11am
Wed; 10.30am, 11.30am, 4pm, 5pm, 6pm Sat;
11am, noon, 4pm, 5pm, 6pm Sun. *Oct-Mar*
11am Wed; 10.30am, 11.30am, 3pm, 4pm, 5pm
Sat; 11am, noon, 3pm, 4pm, 5pm Sun.
Admission €2.10; €1.60 concessions.
No credit cards.

Tourist information

IAT Pro-Loco

*Castel San Zeno (0429 81 320/proloco
montagnana@tiscali.it).* **Open** *Apr-Oct* 4-7pm
Tue; 9.30am-12.30pm, 4-7pm Wed-Sun. *Nov-Mar*
3-6pm Tue; 9.30am-12.30pm, 3-6pm Wed-Sun.

Getting there

By car

Leave the A13 Padua–Bologna motorway at the
Monselice exit, then take the SS10 to Montagnana.

By train

Services on the Padua–Mantua line.

By bus

SITA (*see p242*) buses run from Padua.

The Brenta Canal

Goethe fondly remembered cruising down
the Brenta canal in 1786, enjoying 'the banks
studded with gardens and summer houses;
small properties stretch down to the edge
of the river and now and then the busy
high road beside it'.

Busy, of course, is relative. Nowadays, the
road is a discordant presence and many of the
gardens and summer houses have been replaced
by housing estates and industrial sites. A
number of Palladian Villas still grace the canal,
part of which can be navigated in a boat that
chugs up the Brenta from Venice as far as Strà,
where you are transferred on to a bus to Padua.

The journey includes the villas of
Malcontenta (*see pp38-42*), **Widmann**
and **Pisani**. The boat trip culminates at the
Villa Pisani in Strà, a remarkable villa of the
early-to-mid 18th century. The more
parsimonious traveller can take a similar route
at a fraction of the price by taking the ACTV
No.53 bus from piazzale Roma, leaving at 25
and 55 minutes past the hour.

For information on the Pass Ville *see
p292* **Discount cards**.

SITA – Divisione
Navigazione 'il Burchiello'

*Via Orlandini 3, Padua (049 820 6910/fax 049
820 6923/www.ilburchiello.it).* **Services** *Mar-Oct*
Venice–Padua departure from Pietà boat stop
(near San Zaccaria) at 9am Tue, Thur, Sat;
Padua–Venice departure from piazzale Boschetti
at 8.15am on Wed, Fri, Sun. Closed Nov-Feb.
Rates €62 (incl entrance to Villa Foscari and
Barchessa Valmarana and return SITA bus
journey, but not Villa Pisani or return boat journey);
€36 6-17s; free under-6s. **Three-course lunch**
€24/light lunch €15 extra. **Credit** MC, V.
Information on the website is available in English.

Verona

Forget star-crossed lovers – come to Verona for the magnificent Arena, stay for the *pastissada*.

The **Arena**. See p249.

The world at large may know Verona best as a hotbed of adolescent angst, and many are the visitors standing below Juliet's balcony in the heart of the old town, pondering the meaning of 'wherefore'. Any city, though, whose ruling family had something as prosaic as a ladder on its coat of arms was unlikely to be over-impressed by teenage romance; even today, the citizens of Verona prefer to focus on art, architecture and a history dating back to the Romans.

Not that Verona isn't romantic – a sunset *aperitivo* in the shadow of the Arena (Roman amphitheatre) and an evening stroll through the old town are romantic enough to tinge all your Veronese memories in sepia. But it is real romance, not pubescent pining.

After being colonised by the Romans in 89 BC, Verona became a frequent prize of conquest. Invaders from central Europe and avaricious families from Italy itself coveted the city's position at the mouth of the Adige river valley, about halfway between Milan and Venice. In the late 13th century, the home-grown Della Scala family (they of the ladder – *scala* in Italian means 'ladder'; confusingly,

the family is also called Scaligero) succeeded in controlling a swathe of northern Italy, but they fell in 1387 during a fit of Montague and Capulet-style family feuding. They were replaced by Milan's Viscontis, who were superseded in turn by the Venetian Republic, which ruled until 1797. Only in 1866 did Verona rid itself of foreign rulers, when it joined the newly united Kingdom of Italy.

Sightseeing

Despite a Mittel-European edge to Verona's architecture, ancient Rome is the underlying presence. The **Arena** is the most obvious sign of the ancients, dominating the entrance to the thumb-shaped old town in piazza Brà; but it's not the only one. The streets were laid out according to a grid plan decreed by Emperor Augustus, and the Teatro Romano and ponte Pietra also help set the tone. Even the more modern buildings often have a touch of antiquity. Many of them stand on Roman foundations; some have fragments of Roman marble-work inserted into their fabric.

Verona's medieval architecture dates mostly from after the great north Italian earthquake of 1117. In the building boom that followed this catastrophe, the city was adorned with some of its finest buildings: the basilica of San Zeno, the Duomo and the Gothic churches of Sant'Anastasia and San Fermo.

One of the joys of Verona is the remarkable state of preservation of its monuments. One reason they have withstood the ravages of time is that they have been in constant use through the centuries. Another factor is that the quarry-rich hills outside Verona meant that the kind of 'recycling' so common in medieval and Renaissance Rome was unnecessary here.

The old town, framed by the serpentine Adige River, stretches out from piazza Brà. Overshadowed by the magnificent Arena, this large square is also home to a number of cafés and the Museo Lapidario (1.30-7.30pm Mon, 8.30am-2pm Tue-Sun), a small collection of Greek and Roman fragments and inscriptions.

The heart of the city is the adjoining squares piazza delle Erbe and piazza dei Signori, a short walk north-east from piazza Brà. Once the site of the Roman forum, piazza delle Erbe is today the site of a somewhat tacky food and souvenir market (Mon-Sat mornings). But the knock-off football jerseys and bruised fruit can't detract from the stunning buildings surrounding the square (none of which is open to the public). At the northern end is the huge 14th-century Casa Mazzanti with its splendid late Renaissance frescoes on the outer façade, the highly ornamented Palazzo Maffei and the medieval Torre Gardello, Verona's first clock tower, built in 1370. The basin of the fountain (1368) is of Roman origin, as is the body of the statue known as the 'Madonna Verona', which stands above it; the head is medieval. The tall houses at the southern end once marked the edge of the Jewish ghetto.

A detour south-east out of piazza delle Erbe along via Cappello leads to the **Casa di Giulietta** (Juliet's house). Further down via Cappello is the Porta Leoni, a picturesque fragment of a Roman city gate that is now part of a medieval house; recent excavations, visible from the street, have exposed the full extent of the towered and arched structure. The Gothic church of San Fermo Maggiore stands where via Cappello hits the river.

The heart of medieval Verona's governance and finance, piazza dei Signori, contains the 15th-century Loggia del Consiglio (closed to the public) with its eight elegant arches. (From one of these – Arco della Costa – hangs a whale bone. How it got there and why is a topic for debate; probably it had something to do with the neighbourhood's community of corset-makers who used whale bone to squeeze their clients into shape.) Topped by statues of illustrious Veronese residents (including the poet Catullus, who was exiled from Rome to the shores of Lake Garda, thus making him an honorary citizen), the Loggia del Consiglio marked the beginning of Renaissance architecture in Verona.

While the town seems mildly embarrassed about its connection to English literature, it is quietly boastful about the fact that Dante lived in exile at the court of the Della Scala family from 1304. In fact, piazza dei Signori is also known as piazza Dante because of the statue of the poet in the centre.

Linking *piazze* delle Erbe and dei Signori is the 12th-century **Palazzo della Ragione** (closed to the public). Home until recently to Verona's law courts, the palazzo is soon to be renovated as a 'polyfunctional expositive (sic) centre'. A gateway on the piazza dei Signori side of the palazzo leads into the Mercato Vecchio courtyard, with its huge Romanesque arches and magnificent outdoor Renaissance staircase. The palazzo is dominated by the **Torre dei Lamberti** (1462). At the eastern exit from piazza dei Signori are the Della Scala family tombs (**tombe** or **arche scaligere**).

Moving northwards, the narrow streets are a captivating labyrinth dotted with medieval and Renaissance *palazzi*. In via Pigna, take a look at the carved marble Roman pine cone (*pigna*) placed on a cylindrical Roman tombstone, before heading north down the narrow via San Giacomo alla Pigna towards the **Duomo**, or south towards the imposing church of **Sant'Anastasia**.

Close by, ponte Pietra is Verona's oldest bridge and for centuries was the only link between the city centre and the suburbs beyond. The two stone arches on the left bank of the river are Roman and date back to before 50 BC. The other three brick arches are thought to date from between 1200 and 1500. The bridge was reconstructed using original stones in 1957 (*see p252* **Bridges over the River Adige**).

The ponte Pietra leads across the river to some of Verona's most beautiful churches – including **San Giorgio in Braida** and **Santa Maria in Organo** – as well as the **Museo Archeologico** and the remains of the **Teatro Romano**. In a dominating position on the hills above, the area around Castel San Pietro (closed to the public) – part of the city's medieval and Renaissance fortifications, heavily redesigned by Austrian occupiers in the mid 19th century – offers a bird's-eye view of the city. Head south-east from the bridge along regaste Redentore and its continuations for the pretty **Giardino Giusti**.

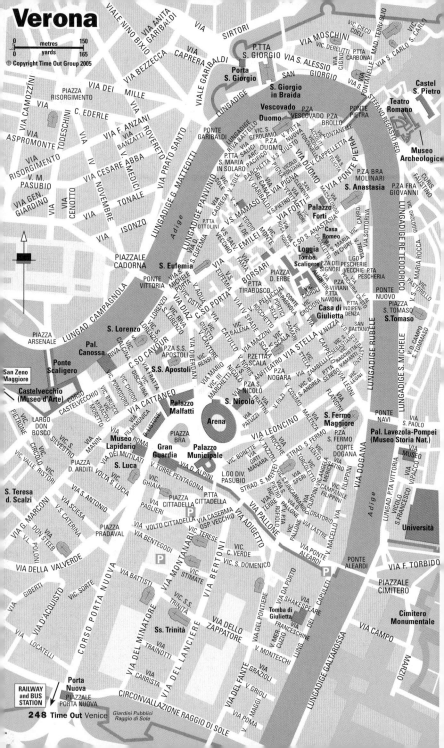

Verona

metres 0 — 150
yards 0 — 165

© Copyright Time Out Group 2005

VIALE NINO BIXIO
VIA ANITA GARIBALDI DI
VIA
SIRTORI
VIA MOSCHINI
VIC. CIECO COELI
VIA MAD. TERRAGLIO
VIC. S. CARLO
VIA S. CARLO
VIA CAPRERA
VIA
P.TTA S. GIORGIO
VIC. DERELITTI
P.TTA CARBONAI
VIA BEZZECCA
VIALE GARIBALDI
VIA S. ALESSIO
VIA CIGNAROLI
VIA STEFANO REGASTO RED
VIA FONTANELLE STO.
PIAZZA RISORGIMENTO
VIA DEI MILLE
Porta S. Giorgio
S. Giorgio in Braida
Castel S. Pietro
C. EDERLE
LUNGADIGE
Vescovado
P.ZA VESCOVADO
PONTE PIETRA
Teatro Romano
VIA CAMOZZINI
VIA TODESCHINI
VIA F. ANZANI
Duomo
P.ZA BROLLO
PONTE GARIBALDI
LUNGADIGE
RIVA BATTELLO
VIA S. GEROLAMO
VIA PIETA
Museo Archeologic
VIA ASPROMONTE
VIA BANZATTI
VIA IV CESARE ABBA
VIA ROVERETO
VIA PRATO SANTO
P.TTA SALICI
ARC. PALLONE
VIA DUOMO
VIA NUOVA
VIA S. GIUSTO
CURTIS FALISTINO
P.ZA BRA GIOVANNI
VIA RISORGIMENTO
V. M. PASUBIO
V. MEDICI
S. MARIA IN SOLARO
P.ZA DUOMO
VICOLO CAPPELLETTA
VIA S. FELICIA
VIA S. MARIA ROCCA
VIA GEN. GIARDINO
VIA CENOTTO
VIA IV NOVEMBRE
TONALE
P.TTA OTTOLINI
ARCHETTIA
V.S. MAFFEO
VIA GARIBALDI
V.S. PIETRO MAR.
VICOLO FONTANELLE
S. Anastasia
P.ZA BRA MOLINARI
LUNGADIGE RE TEODORICO
VIA ISONZO
PIAZZALE CADORNA
Adige
LUNGADIGE PANVINIO
VIA SAV. VECCHIO
VIA S. EUFEMIA
MONTE
CSO S ANASTASIA
V. FORTI
Palazzo Forti
VIC. ORLOGIO
PASTORELLO
S. Eufemia
VIA EUFEMIA
VIA S. MICHELE
Casa Romeo
VIA SOTTORIVA
PONTE NUOVO
LUNGAD. CAMPAGNOLA
PONTE VITTORIA
VIC. S. MATTEO
VIA VADUA
CORSO PORTA
Loggia
Tombe Scaligere
PZA DEI SIGNORI
PESCHERIE VECCHIE
PZA INDIPEN-DENZA
PIAZZA S. TOMASO
PIAZZA ARSENALE
VIA DIAZ
VIA RIVA SAN LORENZO
VIA CATULLO
BORSARI
PIAZZA D. ERBE
CORSO PORTICO BORSA
P.TTA NAVONA
S.Tomaso
S. Lorenzo
VIC. S. LORENZO
VIA CALCINA
P.TTA TIRABOSCO
PELLICCIAI
CASA DI GIULIETTA
VIA INDIPEN-DENZA
LUNGADIGE S. MICHELE
Pal. Canossa
VIA OBERDAN
PZA S.S. APOSTOLI
GUASTO
VIA CAIROLI
VIA NIZZA
V. D. CAMPO
Ponte Scaligero
CORSO CAVOUR
VIA DISCIPLINA
VIA BALENA
VIA MAZZINI
SAN SEBASTIANO
S.S. Apostoli
VIA FRATTA
NICOLO
PZZETTA SCALA
VIA STELLA
VIA LEONI
San Zeno Maggiore
VIA POMODORO
ANFITEATRO
P.ZA NOGARA
LUNGADIGE RUBELE
Castelvecchio (Museo d'Arte)
CASTELVECCHIO
VIA CHIODO
VIA FILARMONICA
VIA III MARCHETTI
V. COSTA
V. S. ANDREA
PONTE NAVI
VIA S. PAOLO
LARGO DON BOSCO
VIA S. SILVESTRO
CORSO
Palazzo Malfatti
S. Nicolò
VIA PATUZZI
V. FILZI
S. Fermo Maggiore
VIA MUSEO
Arena
VIA LEONCINO
Pal. Lavezola-Pompei (Museo Storia Nat.)
Museo Lapidario
Gran Guardia
Palazzo Municipale
VIA ROMA
PIAZZA BRA
VIC. BORLETTI
STRAD. S. FERMO
VIA FERMO
S. FERMO
CORTE DOGANA
PONTE ALEARDI
S. Luca
V. TORRE PENTAGONA
V.D. ALPINI
VIA DOGANA
PIAZZA D. ARDITI
VIA DEI MUTILATI
VIC. GHIAIA
P.TTA CITTADELLA
VIA PALLONE
PIAZZA CITTADELLA
VIA VIPACCO
Università
S. Teresa d. Scalzi
VIA S. ANTONIO
VIA SCIESA
PIAZZA PAGLIERI
VIA VOLTO CITTADELLA
VIA CASERMA VECCHIA
VIA ADIGETTO
VIA MACELLO
PONTE ALEARDI
VIA G. MARCONI
V.S. CATERINA
VIA DON STEEB
PIAZZA PRADAVAL
VIA BENTEGODI
OSP. VECCHIO
VIC. TERESE
VIA LASTRE
LUNGAD. P.TA VITTORIA
VICOLO S. FRANCESCO
PIAZZALE CIMITERO
VIA DELLA VALVERDE
VIA VL. POLONI
VIC. C. VERDE
VIC. S. DOMENICO
VIA DA PORTO
VIA F. TORBIDO
GIBERTI
VIC. SORTE
CORSO PORTA NUOVA
VIA BATTISTI
VIA MONTANARI
VIA BERTONI
VIA SHAKESPEARE
Cimitero Monumentale
VIA D'ACQUISTO
VIA STIMATE
VIC. S.S. TRINITA
Tomba di Giulietta
VIA FRANCESCHINE
VIA LOCATELLI
VIA DEL MINATORE
VIA DEL LANCIERE
VIA DELLO ZAPPATORE
V. MER. CUZIO
VIA CAPULETI
LUNGADIGE GALIAROSSA
Ss. Trinità
VIA TRAINOTTI
VIA DEL PONTIERE
V. MONTECCHI
VIA CAMPO
Porta Nuova
PIAZZALE PORTA NUOVA
VIA ZAPPATORE
V. GRIOLI
MARZIO
RAILWAY and BUS STATION
VIA CARRISTA
CIRCONVALLAZIONE RAGGIO DI SOLE
VIA DEL FANTE
V. GRAZIOLI
V. ROMA
V. MAGGI

248 Time Out Venice

Giardini Pubblici Raggio di Sole

My kingdom for a horse – medium rare

Not to put to fine a spin on it, *pastissada* – Verona's traditional dish – is horse stew and the locals, you'll notice, are proud of it.

It was not until Roman times that anyone questioned horse as a foodstuff. Wild horse was a common dish on Stone Age menus in western Europe. Domestication was left to the nomads on the Asiatic steppes, who valued the horse not as a food source but as transport – it allowed them to travel the large distances needed to support their herds. Nevertheless, horsemeat remained part of the diet, and indeed was often served on special occasions.

Once the domesticated horse reached the Mediterranean, its role changed to instrument of war. Given its value on the battlefield and the high cost of feeding it, it's not surprising that the horse was not viewed as food. For the Romans, though, it was their superiority complex that made horse hard to swallow.

Roman infantry legions were unrivalled in their excellence; their cavalry, however, left much to be desired. In fact the Romans relied on barbarian mercenaries – dirty, uncivilised, horse-eating barbarians – for their mounted troops. After the fall of the Roman Empire, these barbarians were a constant threat to Europe.

An additional mounted threat appeared in AD 711 when Muslim armies crossed the Strait of Gibraltar. In AD 732 the invading army was defeated by Charles Martel and his well-armed cavalry. That close call prompted Pope Gregory III to issue an edict prohibiting the consumption of horsemeat.

The ban was aimed primarily at '*i germani*' – mostly pagan northern Europeans – who had never lost their taste for good horse flesh. The potent combination of 'dirty barbarians', 'pagans', military necessity and cost drove horse eating in Europe underground for more than a thousand years.

Yet horse remained a potent protein source for the poor, and it is this bond with *cucina povera* – as well as affirmation of their 'Germanic' sensibilities – that the Veronese see when they look down at a plate of pastissada. In addition to stew, horse meat appears as cold cuts (*bresaola di cavallo* is a particular favourite) and as steaks.

Corso Porta Borsari, Roman Verona's busy main street, leads out of the north end of piazza delle Erbe towards the Porta Borsari, the best-preserved of the city's Roman gates. Built with blocks of local white marble, it probably dates from the reign of Emperor Claudius (AD 41-54). In a small garden along corso Cavour is the Arco dei Gavi, a triumphal arch attributed to Vitruvius, dating from about 50 BC. Next door, the medieval fortress of **Castelvecchio** hosts a museum and gives on to the ponte Scaligero, the other stone bridge crossing the Adige.

The stunning **basilica di San Zeno**, home to Verona's patron saint, is located a bit outside the centre, to the west of piazza Brà.

TICKETS

An admission fee is charged by some churches and all museums in Verona. Cut costs by purchasing a Verona Card (€8 for one day, €12 for three days), valid for all the sights that charge. It can be bought at the ticket offices of any of the churches or museums participating in the scheme, and includes all bus fares around the city. No credit cards accepted.

A second scheme (the *itinerario completo*) offers entrance to five of Verona's churches (San Zeno, San Lorenzo, Sant'Anastasia, San Fermo and the Duomo) for €5.

Arena

Piazza Brà (045 800 3204). **Open** 1.45-7.30pm Mon; 8.30am-7.30pm Tue-Sun (hours vary during opera season). **Admission** €4; €3 concessions; €1 1st Sun of mth. For opera booking details, *see p255* **A night at the opera. No credit cards.**

The largest Roman amphitheatre in northern Italy, Verona's Arena was capacious enough to seat the city's whole population of 20,000 when it was constructed in about AD 30 from pink marble quarried from nearby hills. The Arena is in remarkably good shape. The 44 tiers of stone seats inside the 139m by 110m (456ft by 361ft) amphitheatre are virtually intact, as is the columned foyer. In large part, this is because the Arena has been taken care of throughout the centuries. After the earthquake of 1117 destroyed most of the Arena's outer ring, the city repaired the damage almost immediately. Verona's Venetian overlords – recognising the historic value of the building – made it illegal to pilfer the ancient stone, and carried out regular maintenance work.

The Arena has served Verona in any number of ways over the last two millennia. Originally the site of gladiatorial games and – filled with water for the occasion – naval battles, post-Roman inhabitants used it as a shelter during fifth- and sixth-century Barbarian invasions. Medieval *veronesi* put it to more prosaic uses – as red-light district and home to the city's cut-throats. Later, city masters used the Arena as law court and site of the occasional

The Veneto

execution. Modern-day theatre promoters were not the first to realise the Arena's attraction – it functioned as theatre in the 17th and 18th centuries, and as a football stadium in the early 20th century.

Casa di Giulietta (Juliet's house)

Via Cappello 23 (045 803 4303). Open 1.30-7.30pm Mon; 8.30am-7.30pm Tue-Sun. Admission €4; €3 concessions. No credit cards.
The *veronesi* may believe that San Zeno (*see p251*) is the city's symbol; hordes of tourists think otherwise, and the good burghers of Verona are pragmatic enough to sacrifice the occasional medieval building to the exigencies of modern tourism. Yes, the Montagues and Capulets were real enough, but no, the Capulets never lived in the so-called Casa di Giulietta (and Juliet most certainly never stepped out on the balcony – a 1920s addition – to capture Romeo's imagination). The exterior walls of the house have long been a blackboard for scribbled protestations of love, and tourists have long crowded underneath this balcony of renown. An admission fee allows you inside for a quick bow on the balcony and a chance to gaze upon garden dwarves (don't ask). Romeo's house – which at least may have actually belonged to the Montague family – is tastefully not open to the public just across from the Della Scala tombs (*see p253*) at Arche Scaligere 4.

Castelvecchio

Corso Castelvecchio 2 (045 592 985/www.comune. verona.it/Castelvecchio/cvsito). Open 1.45-7.30pm Mon; 8.30am-7.30pm Tue-Sun. Admission €4; €3 concessions. No credit cards.
The della Scala family came to power in the 13th century as a result of the Guelf-Ghibelline conflicts that shaped so much of northern Italian politics in

Juliet's balcony, a 20th-century addition.

the Middle Ages. Like many ruling families, the della Scalas looked to patronage of the arts to take the edge off their ruthlessness – patronage paid for by the tax rolls. So by the time Duke Cangrande II began building the castle in 1355, the family needed a fortress for waging war and an unbreachable refuge for avoiding the potential fury of Veronese citizens understandably upset by their hefty tax bills. Cangrande II was nothing if not prudent: ponte Scaligero, the magnificent fortified medieval bridge, was intended as an emergency escape route. The castle is now a museum and exhibition venue, with interiors beautifully redesigned in the 1960s by Venetian architect Carlo Scarpa. The various parts of the castle are linked by overhead walkways and passages offering superb views of the city and surrounding hills. The museum itself contains important works by Mantegna, Crivelli, Pisanello, Giovanni Bellini, Veronese, Tintoretto, Gianbattista Tiepolo, Canaletto and Guardi, as well as a vast collection of lesser-known local artists. On the first floor is a magnificent collection of 13th- and 14th-century Veronese religious statuary. Note the life-sized *Crucifixion with Saints*, a clear indication that Veronese artists were influenced as much by the grittier art from north of the Alps as by the softer, dreamier stuff being produced in Tuscany. An armoury contains a collection of swords, shields and some local jewellery.

Duomo

Piazza Duomo (045 592 813/www.chieseverona.it). Open Mar-Oct 10am-5.30pm Mon-Sat; 1.30-5.30pm Sun. Nov-Feb 10am-4pm Tue-Sat; 1.30-5pm Sun. Admission €2. No credit cards.
Verona's cathedral, begun in 1139, is Romanesque downstairs, Gothic upstairs and Renaissance at the top half of the bell tower. The elegant front portico is decorated with Romanesque carvings of the finest quality, showing Charlemagne's paladins Oliver and Roland (feature players in the medieval epic *Chanson de Roland*) wielding their swords while a fan club of saints looks on. Inside, the first chapel on the left has a magnificent *Assumption* by Titian. To the left of the façade is a gateway leading to a tranquil Romanesque cloister where Roman remains and mosaics are on show. In the same complex is the ancient church of Sant'Elena, with the remains of an earlier Christian basilica and Roman baths. And, at the back of the cathedral, to the right of its graceful apse, is the chapel of San Giovanni in Fonte, with a large, carved, octagonal, Romanesque, baptismal font.

Giardino Giusti

Via Giardino Giusti 2 (045 803 4029). Open Apr-Sept 9am-8pm daily. Oct-Mar 9am-7pm daily. Admission €4.50. No credit cards.
The dusty façades of one of Verona's most traffic-clogged streets hide one of the finest Renaissance gardens in Italy. Tucked in behind the great Renaissance townhouse of the Giusti family – the Palazzo Giusti del Giardino – the statue-packed gardens with their tall cypresses were laid out in 1580. The lower level is typically formal in the Italian

style. The wild upper level climbs the steep slopes of the hill behind, which offers superb views over the city – and good picnic opportunities.

Museo Archeologico

Regaste Redentore 2 (045 800 0360/www.
comune.verona.it/Castelvecchio/cvsito/mcivici2.htm).
Open 1.30-7.30pm Mon; 8.30am-7.30pm Tue-Sun.
Admission €3; €2 concessions (includes Teatro Romano, *see p252*). **No credit cards**.
Across the Adige from the Old Town, this small museum, contains a fine collection of Roman remains. Situated in a former monastery, the museum offers incomparable views over Verona and the river Adige – take the lift from the theatre through the cliffs and up to the museum.

San Fermo Maggiore

Stradone San Fermo (045 592 813/www.
chieseverona.it). **Open** *Mar-Oct* 10am-6pm Mon-Sat; 1-6pm Sun. *Nov-Feb* 10am-4pm Tue-Sat; 1.30-5pm Sun. **Admission** €2. **No credit cards**.
At San Fermo you get two churches for the price of one: the lower church is Romanesque and the upper church, built in the 14th century, is Gothic. While the lower church is intimate and solemn, the upper part is towering and full of light. Its wooden ceiling, resembles an upturned Venetian galleon. Among the important frescoes is an *Annunciation* by Antonio Pisanello to the left of the main entrance.

San Giorgio in Braida

Piazzetta San Giorgio 1 (045 834 0232).
Open 8am-11am, 5-7pm Mon-Sat; 5-7pm Sun.
This great domed Renaissance church, probably designed by the Veronese military architect Michele Sanmicheli between 1536 and 1543, contains some of the city's greatest treasures. Shining in this light-filled Renaissance masterpiece is a *Baptism of Christ* by Tintoretto, above the entrance door, and a moving *Martyrdom of St George* by Paolo Veronese. But even these greats are put in the shade by a serene *Madonna and Child with Saints Zeno and Lawrence* by local dark horse Girolamo dai Libri.

Santa Maria in Organo

Piazzetta Santa Maria in Organo (045 591 440).
Open 8am-noon, 2.30-6pm daily.
The Renaissance church of Santa Maria in Organo has a host of frescoes by local painters. Pass them by and make your way to the apse and sacristy to see what Giorgio Vasari described as the most beautiful choir stalls in Italy. A humble monk, Fra Giovanni da Verona (died 1520), worked for 25 years cutting and assembling these infinitely complex, coloured, wooden images of animals, birds, landscapes, cityscapes, religious scenes and musical and scientific instruments in dozens of intricate intarsia panels.

Sant'Anastasia

Piazza Sant'Anastasia (045 592 813/www.
chieseverona.it). **Open** *Mar-Oct* 9am-6pm Mon-Sat; 1-6pm Sun. *Nov-Feb* 10am-4pm Tue-Sat; 1.30-5pm Sun. **Admission** €2. **No credit cards**.

Giardino Giusti. *See p250.*

This imposing brick Gothic church is best visited early in the morning, when sunlight streams in to illuminate Antonio Pisanello's glorious fresco (1433-38; in the sacristy to the right of the apse) of St George girding himself to set off in pursuit of the dragon that has been pestering the lovely princess of Trebizond. Carved scenes from the life of St Peter Martyr adorn the unfinished façade, while inside, two delightful *gobbi* (hunchbacks) crouch down to support the holy water font; the one on the left was carved by Paolo Veronese's father in 1495.

San Zeno Maggiore

Piazza San Zeno 2 (045 592 813/ www.
chieseverona.it). **Open** *Mar-Oct* 8.30am-6pm Mon-Sat; 1-6pm Sun. *Nov-Feb* 10am-4pm Tue-Sat; 1.30-5pm Sun. **Admission** €2. **No credit cards**.
One of the most spectacularly ornate Romanesque churches in northern Italy, this was built between 1123 and 1138 to house the tomb and shrine of San Zeno, an African who became Verona's first bishop in 362 and is now the city's much-loved patron saint. The façade, with its great rose window and porch, is covered with some of Italy's finest examples of Romanesque marble sculpture. Scenes from the Old Testament and the life of Christ mingle with hunting and jousting scenes, attributed to the 12th-century sculptors Nicolò and Guglielmo. The graceful porch is supported by columns resting on two carved marble lions; they serve as a frame for the great bronze doors of the basilica; the 48 panels have scenes from the Bible and from the life of San Zeno,

Bridges over the River Adige

25 April 1945 was Liberation Day for the Italians. Bologna had been freed a few days before, Milan was in the hands of partisans and the Germans were in full retreat up the peninsula.

But the Germans' line of retreat ran right through Verona. The city offered rail connections, stout walls and direct access to the Brenner Pass (and so on to Innsbruck and Munich). Allied commanders, aware of Verona's importance, made the taking of the city a priority. As soon as troops were across the River Po on the afternoon of the 25th, they surged towards Verona, covering the 50 kilometres from river to city in just over six hours.

There were not enough Germans in Verona to defend it (the speed of the Allied advance had cut off huge numbers of German troops) and by nightfall, the Germans were withdrawing. To cover their retreat, engineers demolished all of the bridges over the Adige, including the Ponte Pietra (*see p247*) and the Ponte Scaligero (*see p249*). In the event, this didn't slow down Allied troops very much – they were across the Adige the next day, and the Germans signed a cease-fire on the 29th.

The Veronese reacted to the destruction of their bridges with quiet determination. While reconstruction of the main transport bridges got under way, they began fishing the original

stones of the Ponte Pietra and Ponte Scaligero out of the Adige. By the 1950s, essential post-war reconstruction had proceeded enough to allow the Veronese to rebuild their scenic historic bridges.

Ponte Scaligero. *See p249.*

and a few that experts have been hard-pressed to pin down, including a woman suckling two crocodiles. The panels on the left-hand door date from about 1030 and came from an earlier church. Those on the right were produced a century later. Inside the lofty church (note the magnificent ceiling built in 1386), the main altar is placed on a raised platform reached by twin staircases. A third staircase descends into the crypt, which contains the tomb of San Zeno. Dominating the altar is a stunning triptych depicting the Madonna and Child with a bevy of saints, an early work by Andrea Mantegna painted between 1457 and 1459. The lower panel, showing Christ on the cross, is a copy: the original was looted by Napoleon and is now in the Louvre .

The enduring love affair between San Zeno and the city that adopted him may have something to do with the huge – and hugely appealing – early 12th-century marble statue of the African bishop having a grand old chuckle, which is to be found in a niche to the left of the apse. His black face, with its distinctly African features, is unique in Italian religious statuary, as is his singularly jovial and not particularly saintly aspect. Covering the inside walls of the

basilica are frescoes dating from the 12th to the 14th centuries, but perhaps more interesting than the paintings themselves is the 15th- to 17th-century graffiti scratched into them by the faithful invoking Zeno's protection from earthquakes and pestilence.

To the right of the church is a massive bell tower, 72m (236ft) high, begun in 1045. To the left is a lower tower, which is all that remains of the Benedictine monastery that stood on the site before the basilica was built, and which, according to local lore, stands over the grave of Pepin, Charlemagne's disinherited hunchback son. Behind is a Romanesque cloister.

Teatro Romano

Regaste Redentore 2 (045 800 0360/www.comune. verona.it/Castelvecchio/cvsito/mcivici2.htm).
Open 1.30-7.30pm Mon; 8.30am-7.30pm Tue-Sun.
Admission €3; €2 concessions (includes Museo Archeologico, *see p251*). **No credit cards.**
The Roman theatre, dating from around the first century BC, was buried under medieval houses until the late 19th century, when the semicircular seating was brought to light. Built into the side of the hill where Verona's earliest pre-Roman and Roman set-

tlements were located, the theatre offers beautiful views over the city and is an evocative venue for an annual festival of theatre (Shakespeare is a perennial favourite), ballet and jazz. For programme and booking details contact Estate Teatrale Veronese (045 807 7201, www.estateteatraleveronese.it). Tickets cost from €4 and can also be purchased at the *teatro* immediately before performances.

Tombe or Arche Scaligere (Della Scala family tombs)

Via Santa Maria in Chiavica. **Open** *June-Sept* 1.30-7.30pm Mon; 9.30am-7.30pm Tue-Sun (also visible from outside). **Admission** €4; €3 concessions (includes Torre dei Lamberti, *see below*). **No credit cards.**
The Gothic tombs of the Della Scala family date from 1277 to the final years of the 14th century and give a good idea of the family's sense of its own importance. Carved by the most sought-after stonemasons of the era – in particular those from the small town of Campione, now an Italian enclave in Switzerland – the more lavish tombs are topped with spires. Note the family's odd taste in first names. The monument to Cangrande (Big Dog, died 1329) above the doorway to the church of Santa Maria Antica, with its equestrian statue, shows the valiant duke smiling in the face of death. (This is a copy; the original is in the Castelvecchio, *see p250*.) Poking out from above the intricate wrought-iron fence surrounding the tombs are the spire-topped final resting places of Cansignorio (Lord Dog, died 1375) and Mastino II (Mastiff the Second, died 1351). Among the less flamboyant tombs is that of Mastino I (died 1277), founder of the doggy dynasty. In summer, you can wander round the small courtyard for up-close examinations of the ornateness.

Next door, the intimate church of Santa Maria Antica (open 7.30am-noon, 3.30-7pm daily) was the Della Scala family chapel. Lit by hundreds of candles, this exquisite building is much loved by the *veronesi*, especially stallholders from the market in nearby piazza delle Erbe.

Torre dei Lamberti

Cortile Mercato Vecchio (045 803 2726). **Open** 1.30-7.30pm Mon; 9.30am-7.30pm Tue-Sun. **Admission** *Lift* €3 (€4 with tombe scaligere, *see above*). *Stairs* €2. **No credit cards.**
This massive medieval tower, 83m (273ft) high, offers superb views of the city and, on clear days, a spectacular panorama of the local mountains and Italian Alps. The 368-step climb is only for the fittest.

Where to eat

Verona's cuisine is an interesting combination of Middle European heft and Italian sensibility. Boiled and roasted meats are popular, served up with *cren*, the local take on horseradish sauce, and *peará*, made of bone marrow, bread and pepper. Braised horse meat (*pastissada de caval*) is another local speciality (*see p249*

My kingdom for a horse – medium rare). Vegetarians take heart, however. *Bigoli*, a sort of thick spaghetti, is often served with meat-free sauces, and the fertile farms to the south of the city yield up excellent vegetables. Pumpkin-stuffed ravioli is also a Veronese speciality.

The vineyards around Verona are responsible for some of Italy's most recognisable wine exports: Soave, Bardolino and Valpolicella. Unfortunately for Verona, however, these names are known more for their undiscerning Bridget Jones-type quaffing qualities than for their heft. In fact, the Veronese take their wine very seriously (the ultra-serious Vinitaly takes place in Verona's fairgrounds every spring; www.veronafiere.it for information), keeping the lightweight export names for everyday use and the better-kept secrets like Amarone and Valpolicella Classico for special occasions.

Al Duomo

Via Duomo 7 (045 800 4505). **Meals served** *Sept-June* 11am-2.30pm, 8pm-midnight Mon, Tue, Thur-Sun. *July, Aug* 11am-2.30pm, 8pm-midnight Mon, Tue, Thur-Sat. Closed 2wks Aug. **Average** €25. **Credit** MC, V.
Elderly mandolin players still congregate here to strum traditional music. Near the Duomo, this osteria is frequented by the people of the quarter who know a well-priced meal when they see one.

Bar Leon d'Oro

Via Pallone 10A (045 590 946). **Open** noon-4am daily. **No credit cards.**

San Zeno Maggiore. *See p251.*

This is a late-night hangout for the city's *glitterati*, with a strong gay element. The bar is situated in a late 18th-century townhouse with a large front garden, where you can sip a drink under the stars on balmy summer nights.

Ostaria La Stueta
Via Redentore 4 (045 803 2462). **Meals served** 7-10pm Tue; noon-2pm, 5-10pm Wed-Sun. Closed July. **Average** €30. **Credit** AmEx, MC, V, DC.
The menu in this tiny restaurant is limited and traditional, but unfailingly delicious. In autumn, mushrooms are a treat; try the polenta with *moscardini* (baby octopus) in summer. Helpful staff and a good wine list add to the experience. Booking advisable.

Papa & Cicia del Caciator
Via Seminario 4A (045 800 8384). **Meals served** noon-2.30pm Mon; noon-2.30pm, 7.30-10.30pm Tue-Fri, Sun; 7.30-10.30pm Sat. Closed 2wks Aug. **Average** €25. **Credit** MC, V.
This small trattoria in the Veronetta area across the river from the *centro storico* serves up a variety of tasty (and economical) lunch menus, and all the grilled meat you can stand in the evenings.

Ristorante La Greppia
Vicolo Samaritana 3 (045 800 4577/www.ristorante greppia.com). **Meals served** noon-2.30pm; 6.30-10.30pm Tue-Sun. Closed 2wks Jan, 2wks June. **Average** €35. **Credit** AmEx, DC, MC, V.
Off via Mazzini, this Verona institution serves up some of the best renditions in town of local classics.

Trattoria Al Pompiere
Vicolo Regina d'Ungheria 5 (045 803 0537). **Meals served** 7.40-10.30pm Mon; 12.40-2pm, 7.40-10.30pm Tue-Sat. Closed 1wk Dec. **Average** €35. **Credit** AmEx, MC, V.

This trattoria may have an address, but the street doesn't appear on Verona's official map. Nevertheless, the restaurant is easy to find – it's down an alley just opposite Juliet's house – and the modern take on Veronese classics is worth the search.

Trattoria Tre Marchetti
Vicolo Tre Marchetti 19B (045 803 0463). **Meals served** 7-10.30pm Mon; 12.15-2.30pm, 7-10.30pm Tue-Sat. Closed 2wks June, 1wk Sept, 2wks Dec. **Average** €50. **Credit** MC, V.
Meals have been served on these premises just round the corner from the Roman Arena since 1291, making it one of the most ancient eating houses in Europe. It has lost none of its allure over the centuries: informal and crowded, with specialities of *bigoli* with duck, *pastissada de caval* and *baccalà* (cod) *alla vicentina*. Booking is advisable, especially during the opera season.

Where to stay

The Verona hoteliers' association **CAV** (via Patuzzi 5, 045 800 9844, fax 045 800 9372, www.cav.vr.it, open Apr-Oct 9am-7.30pm Mon-Sat, 2-7pm Sun; Nov-Mar 9am-6.30pm Mon-Fri) runs a free hotel-booking bureau.

Due Torri Hotel Baglioni
Piazza Sant'Anastasia 4 (045 595 044/fax 045 800 4130/www.baglionihotels.com). **Rates** €239-€367 single; €373-€473 double. **Credit** AmEx, DC, MC, V.
This celebrated hotel (Beethoven and Goethe have been among its illustrious guests) forms one side of the square and is widely considered to be the city's finest. Some of the rooms let guests go eyeball to eyeball with Gugliemo di Castelvarco, whose tomb tops the archway across from the hotel.

Superb views from the **Torre del Lamberti**. See p253.

A night at the opera

All too often in Italy, Roman stones became medieval building materials (the columns in the façade of the building across from the Prada store in corso Porta Borsari are a good Veronese example). Fortunately, Verona's Arena (*see p249*) was spared a similar fate, which means that 21st-century visitors can spend a summer evening there doing what first-century Romans did: being entertained.

The three-month season (mostly, but not exclusively, opera) brings out an eclectic assortment. Down in the orchestra you'll find Armani-clad Italian industrialists showing off their expensive seats (top price €157) and their even more expensive consorts. Up on the unreserved stone steps (bottom price €15) you'll find patched-jeaned music-lovers enjoying a picnic (no glass or cans). Both camps would agree that an evening under the stars in a 2,000-year-old theatre is a good way to spend one's time. Operators on the phone booking line speak Italian, English and German; the Arena also accepts online bookings. Seats are sometimes available on the day of the show, especially in quieter midweek periods. The cheapest seats are not numbered, so get there two hours early to grab a decent spot. Remember to bring a cushion – you'll be sitting on a rock for three hours. And whether you're in the cheap seats or not, don't forget to bring a candle – you'll need it for the atmosphere.

Fondazione Arena di Verona
Via Dietro l'Anfiteatro 6B (045 800 5151/ www.arena.it). **Performances** *June-Aug* 9pm Tue-Sun. **Tickets** €15-€157. **Credit** AmEx, DC, MC, V.

Campeggio Castel San Pietro
Via Castel San Pietro 2 (045 592 037/www.camping castelsanpietro.com). **Rates** €5-€7 per plot; €5.50 per person; €4 under-8s. Closed mid Oct-mid May. **No credit cards**.
In a stunning position 15 minutes' walk from the centre.

Hotel Antica Porta Leona
Corticella Leoni 3 (045 595 499/fax 045 595 214/ htlanticaportaleona@tiscalinet.it). **Rates** €75-€103 single; €95-€150 double. Closed mid Dec-Jan. **Credit** AmEx, DC, MC, V.
This pretty little hotel is in the pedestrian old city.

Hotel Aurora
Piazzetta XIV Novembre 2 (045 594 717/fax 045 801 0860/www.hotelaurora.biz). **Rates** €56-€116 single; €98-€130 double. **Credit** AmEx, DC, MC, V.
In a little nook off piazza delle Erbe, this simple hotel is friendly and efficiently run.

Hotel Bologna
Piazzetta Scalette Rubiani 3 (045 800 6830/fax 045 801 0602/www.hotelbologna.vr.it). **Rates** €110 single; €168 double. **Credit** AmEx, DC, MC, V.
Situated just off piazza Brà, this comfortable hotel is located in a perfect spot for exploring the city.

Resources

Tourist information

IAT
Via degli Alpini 9 (045 806 8680/fax 045 800 3638/ www.tourism.verona.it). **Open** 9am-7pm Mon-Sat; 9am-3pm Sun.

Railway station, piazza XXV Aprile (tel/fax 045 800 0861). **Open** 9am-6pm Mon-Sat; 9am-3pm Sun. *Verona airport (tel/fax 045 861 9163).* **Open** 9am-6pm Mon-Sat.

Getting around

By bus
AMT (045 887 1111/www.amt.it) runs the city bus service (orange buses), most of which start and terminate at Porta Nuova. Tickets can be purchased at any tobacconist's. A 93¢ ticket is valid for one hour and should be punched on each bus boarded.

The **APT Verona bus company** (045 805 7911/ www.aptv.it) runs services (blue coaches) to towns in the area around Verona, including Lake Garda and the Monti Lessini. Buses depart from the bus station, in front of Porta Nuova train station.

By bicycle
El Pedal Scaligero (333 536 7770) is a booth located near the APT office in piazza Brà. Open 9am-8pm Tue-Sun from April to September, it offers a variety of hourly, daily and longer-term rates.

Getting there

By air
See p277.

By train
Regular services from Milan and Venice (75-90mins).

By car
Take the A4 La Serenissima motorway.

Going up

As you travel north from Verona towards the Brenner Pass, you enter the sublime Alpine realm of Trentino-Alto Adige. The floor of the Adige valley is a carpet of apple trees and grape vines, the cliffs of the valley walls are studded with castles, and the Dolomites tower above it all in a study of snow and pink rock: millions of years ago the mountains were coral reefs at the bottom of the sea.

Politically speaking, Trentino and Alto Adige are two separate provinces carved from Austrian territory taken by Italy at the end of World War I. While German is spoken in both (the region is officially bilingual) there are strong differences between the provinces. Trentino has been italianicised for centuries, and saw its cession to Italy as a homecoming. Alto-Adige (or South Tyrol, as it is also known), on the other hand, still views itself as Austrian, and Italian is a decidedly second language.

In the 1970s and 1980s, Alto Adige's secessionists were liberal with their explosives. These days, the *altoatesini* are more interested in tourism than radicalism. The warm welcome and price/quality ratio found here are hard to match anywhere else in Italy. Ski resorts such as Selva Gardena are famous for the quality of their slopes (consult www.val-gardena.com, for more information); during the summer the same mountains offer incomparable hiking.

Though Trentino does not offer the same cachet as Alto Adige, it can certainly hold its own as a tourist destination. In addition to the northern part of Lake Garda, the province boasts the capital city of Trento – where the Council of Trent mapped out the Counter-Reformation which reshaped the Catholic church in the 16th century – and the fin-de-siècle spa resort of Levico Terme.

Around Verona

Verona is a splendid gateway to Lake Garda (*see also* **Time Out Guide to Milan, the Lakes & Lombardy**), the mountains of Trentino-Alto Adige (*see p256* **Going up**) and the rich farmland (and culinary delights) of the Po Valley.

Caldiero

Ancient Verona's inhabitants flocked to Caldiero's hot springs – the **Terme di Giunone** – to splash about in the same stone pool used by today's wallowers. Other more modern pools have been added to accommodate the crowds in this spa 18 kilometres (11 miles) east of Verona, where water bubbles up at a temperature of 28° centigrade (82° farenheit).

Terme di Giunone

Via delle Terme 2 (045 615 1288/www.terme digiunone.it). **Open** *June, July* 9am-8pm daily. *Apr, May, Aug-Oct* 11am-6pm daily. **Admission** €9. **No credit cards**.

Valeggio sul Mincio

This town south of Verona was once the centre of Italy's carriage-building industry. These days it's home to the **Parco Giardino Sigurtà** – one of Italy's prettiest gardens. Valeggio is also famous for serving some of the best food in Italy. After the carriage business slumped, the area's womenfolk opened scores of tiny restaurants serving dishes like *tortelli di zucca* (pumpkin-stuffed pasta) and grilled fish.

Parco Giardino Sigurtà

Via Cavour, Valeggio (045 637 1033/www. sigurta.it). **Open** *Mar-Nov* 9am-6pm daily. Closed Dec-Feb. **Admission** €8.50; €6 6-14s; under-5s free. **No credit cards**.

Where to eat

Alla Borsa

Via Goito 2, Valeggio (045 795 0093/www.ristorante borsa.it). **Meals served** 12.15-2pm, 7.15-10pm Mon, Thur-Sun; 12.15-2pm Tue. **Closed** mid July-mid Aug; 2wks Feb. **Average** €30. **Credit** MC, V.
This family-run trattoria serves perhaps the most delicious pumpkin *tortelli* in existence. Informal and noisy, Alla Borsa also specialises in trout and other fish from nearby Lake Garda, plus stuffed guineafowl, roast pork shanks and duck. Delicious home-made desserts.

Tourist information

See p255.

Getting there

There are regular APTV bus services (045 805 7911/www.aptv.it) for Caldiero and Valeggio sul Mincio from Verona bus station, in front of Porta Nuova train station.

A quick turn right into contrà Battisti (streets in Vicenza's centre are called 'contrà' instead of the usual 'via') leads to the **Duomo**, while a detour to the left leads to the Gothic brick church of **San Lorenzo**. Back on corso Palladio, at No.92, is **Palazzo Pojana** (1564-6), which consists of two separate buildings cunningly joined together by Palladio; where the front door would normally be, the architect left room for a street to run through. **Palazzo Trissino**, at No.98, was designed in 1592 by Palladio's student Vincenzo Scamozzi.

The overwhelming presence of Palladio is to be felt once more in the vast and elegant piazza dei Signori, south of the corso. Apart from the slender, spectacular 82-metre (269-foot) Torre di Piazza clock tower, which dates from the 12th century, the prevailing spirit of the square is definitely late Renaissance. Tacked gracefully onto the square side of the Gothic Palazzo della Ragione assembly hall (known as the **Basilica Palladiana**, in the Roman sense of the word '*basìlica*' – a public place where justice is dispensed) is Palladio's marvellous loggia. Opposite this is his Loggia del Capitanato, a fragment of a building that was intended to continue along most of the northern side of the square. This highly decorated brick arcade was built to celebrate Venice's victory over the Turks in the Battle of Lepanto in 1571; it was the official residence of the powerful Venetian governor of Vicenza. On the same side is the complex of the Monte di Pietà, the city's elegant 16th-century pawn shop, which extends on either side of the Baroquified church of San Vincenzo.

There is a morning clothes and food market in piazza dei Signori on Tuesday and Thursday. Food stalls spill over into piazza delle Erbe, a square dominated by a medieval tower where Vicenza's recalcitrant wrongdoers were taken for a little tongue-loosening torture.

In the labyrinth of streets to the south of piazza delle Erbe is the Casa Pigafetta (contrà Pigafetta 9). Dating from 1444 and built in late Spanish Gothic style, this strange, highly decorated townhouse was the birthplace of Antonio Pigafetta, the adventurous nobleman who was one of only 21 survivors of Magellan's epoch-making circumnavigation of the globe between 1519 and 1522.

Off corso Palladio north of piazza Signori is contrà Porti, which offers a real palazzo feast. The Porto family was rich, influential and clannish; all its members built their houses in one street. At No.11 is the Palazzo Barbaran Da Porto, designed and built by Palladio between 1569 and 1571, with an interior by Lorenzo Rubini. After a 20-year restoration project, the palazzo is enjoying its own little renaissance as the **Museo Palladiano**.

Santuario di Monte Berico. *See p261.*

Basilica Palladiana.

Casa Porto (No.15) is an undistinguished 15th-century building that was badly restored in the 18th century but is of interest as the home of Luigi Da Porto (died 1529), writer of the first known account of the Romeo and Juliet story. At No.19 the exquisite, late Gothic Palazzo Porto Colleoni is a typical 15th-century attempt to beat the Venetians at their own game. Be sure to take a quick peek through the open gateway into the secluded back garden. Palazzo Iseppo Da Porto, at No.21, is one of Palladio's earliest creations.

At the end of the street, across a bridge over the Bacchiglione, contrà San Marco is a wide street lined with fine 16th- and 17th-century *palazzi*, including Palazzo Da Schio, an elegant townhouse designed by Palladio in the 1560s.

Back on corso Palladio, the huge palazzo that stands on the corner with contrà Porti is the Palazzo Dal Toso, a flamboyant Gothic jewel, which once boasted gilded capitals – hence its other name, the Ca' d'Oro. The Gothic theme continues in the church of **Santa Corona** further down the corso. The **Gallerie di Palazzo Leoni Montanari**, in contrà Santa Corona just off the corso, contains charming 18th-century genre paintings by Pietro Longhi. Almost at the end of corso Palladio, tiny Casa Cogollo at No.167 is thought to have been Palladio's home in later life; according to some accounts, he may even have designed it.

The main street ends in piazza Matteotti, where two of Vicenza's real artistic treats await:

Palazzo Chiericati (1550), one of Palladio's finest townhouses, now the city's art gallery (**Museo Civico**); and the architect's final masterpiece, the **Teatro Olimpico**. Towering above the town to the south, the **Santuario di Monte Berico** can be reached on foot in the shade of an 18th-century loggia joining it to the centre.

TICKETS

Admission to the Museo Civico (*see p261*), Museo Naturalistico Archeologico in contrà Santa Corona and the Teatro Olimpico (*see p262*) is by *biglietto unico* only. Tickets – which are valid for three days from the date of purchase – can be bought at the Teatro Olimpico. No credit cards.

The *biglietto unico* is available in three different forms:

Three museums: €7 (Museo Civico, Museo Naturalistico Archeologico in contrà Santa Corona and Teatro Olimpico).
Four museums: €8 (the above plus Museo del Risorgimento e della Resistenza).
Six museums: €12 (the above plus Palazzo Barbaran da Porto and Palazzo Leoni Montanari).

Basilica Palladiana (Palazzo della Ragione)

Piazza dei Signori (0444 323 681). **Admission** during exhibitions only; prices & times vary.
Palladio's most famous piece of urban restyling is a neat alternative to scaffolding. The original Palazzo della Regione, seat of the city government, was built in the 1450s; but the loggia that originally surrounded it – and helped to support it – collapsed in 1496, making it necessary to find an elegant way of shoring up the building. The city fathers canvassed most of the leading architects of the day from 1525 onwards; luckily for Palladio – who was only 17 at this time – they dithered for 20 years before accepting the audacious solution proposed by the home contender in 1546. Palladio's double-tiered loggia, Doric below and Ionic above, encases the original Gothic palazzo in a Renaissance shell. The main *salone* is a barn-like space, with impressive ornate arches holding up the wooden ship's-keel roof. Vicenza now uses the basilica as an exhibition space and it is only open for shows.

Duomo

Piazza Duomo (0444 320 996). **Open** 10.30am-noon, 3.30-5.30pm Mon-Fri; 10.30am-noon Sat; Sun for Mass only.
Founded in the ninth century, the Duomo suffered extensive damage during World War II. The Palladian dome, finished in 1574, has been painstakingly restored to its former splendour, as has the Gothic pink marble façade, attributed to Domenico da Venezia (1467). The brick interior contains an important polyptych by Lorenzo Veneziano, signed and dated 1366.

The Veneto

Gallerie di Palazzo Leoni Montanari

Contrà Santa Corona 25 (0444 991 291/
www.palazzomontanari.com). **Open** 10am-6pm
Fri-Sun. **Admission** €3.50; €2.50 concessions.
No credit cards.
Situated in the recently restored Palazzo Leoni
Montanari, this remarkable collection of 14 master-
pieces by the 18th-century Venetian genre painter
Pietro Longhi, housed together with other important
examples of Venetian art, should not be missed. Also
on display is a collection of Russian icons.

Museo Civico

Palazzo Chiericati, piazza Matteotti 37-9 (0444 321
348/www.comune.vicenza.it/musei/civico/home.htm).
Open *Sept-June* 9am-5pm Tue-Sun. *July, Aug* 9am-
6pm Tue-Sun. **Admission** by *biglietto unico* (*see*
p260).
The art gallery on the second floor of this Palladian
palazzo contains a fascinating collection of works
by local painters, Bartolomeo Montagna (1450-1523)
in particular. It also houses examples of excellent
work by the likes of Van Dyck, Tintoretto, Veronese,
Tiepolo and Giovanni Bellini. Outshining them all
however, is a *Crucifixion* by the Flemish master
Hans Memling, the central part of a triptych whose
side panels are in New York. In the ticket office is
a 16th-century portrait of the Valmarana family
that allows an intimate peek at some of Palladio's
keenest fans and employers.

Museo Palladiano

Palazzo Barbaran Da Porto, contrà Porti 11 (0444
323 014/fax 0444 322 869/www.cisapalladio.org).
Open 10am-6pm Tue-Sun. **Admission** €5; €3
concessions. **No credit cards**.
The main draw of this museum is the palazzo itself,
though temporary exhibitions and occasional workshops are also held here.

Palazzo Trissino

Corso Garibaldi 98 (0444 221 111/www.comune.
vicenza.it). **Open** 9am-1.30pm Mon-Sat; interior by
appointment only. **Admission** free.
Now Vicenza's town hall, this design by Palladio's
student Vincenzo Scamozzi was begun in 1592 but
not completed until 1667. On the corso, a portico
with Ionic columns is surmounted by a Corinthian-
inspired piano nobile. Nobody minds if you stroll
into the courtyard.

San Lorenzo

Piazza San Lorenzo (0444 321 960). **Open** 7am-
noon, 3.30-7.15pm daily.
None of the city's neoclassical or Baroque places of
worship can hold a candle to San Lorenzo's Gothic
glory. The magnificent marble portal encases an
exquisite 14th-century lunette depicting the
Madonna and Child. Inside, three grandiose naves
are lit by high monoforate windows. The Poiana
altar in the right transept is a fine late Gothic assem-
blage of paintings and frescoes by various artists,
while the peaceful 16th-century cloister contains a
pretty, medieval, well head.

Santa Corona

Contrà Santa Corona (0444 321 924). **Open** 4-6pm
Mon; 8.30am-noon, 3-6pm Tue-Sat; 3-5pm Sun.
This Gothic brick church was built between 1260
and 1270, to house a much-travelled stray thorn
from Christ's crown. Its interior, consisting of three
unequally sized naves, contains an *Adoration of the
Magi* (1573) by Paolo Veronese in the third chapel
on the right. In the crypt is the Valmarana Chapel,
designed by Palladio. The church's other artistic
treasure, in the fifth chapel on the left of the nave, is
a *Baptism of Christ* by Giovanni Bellini (1502).

Santuario di Monte Berico

Viale X Giugno 87 (0444 320 998/www.monte
berico.it). **Open** 6am-12.30pm, 2.30-6pm Mon-Sat;
6am-7pm Sun.
It might be hard to imagine as you fight your way
through the clouds of exhaust fumes left by the
countless coaches toting pilgrims up to this spot
where the Virgin is said to have appeared twice – in
1426 and 1428 – but Monte Berico has long been
where *vicentini* come for a breath of fresh air in the
summer. The tree-lined arcade flanking the road
adds another touch of greenery (and some welcome
shade). If you don't feel like slogging up the hill on
foot, there's a regular bus service (no number – ask
at the stop) from the railway station Mon-Sat; on
Sunday take bus 18.
   The church itself was largely rebuilt in the 18th
century. It contains Veronese's *Supper of St Gregory*

The cunning **Palazzo Pojano**. *See p259.*

the Great (1572) in the refectory, as well as a moving *Pietà* by local boy Bartolomeo Montagna and a fine collection of fossils in the cloister.

Teatro Olimpico

Piazza Matteotti 11 (0444 222 101/www.comune. icenza.it/olimpico/teatro.htm). **Open** *Sept-June* 9am-5pm Tue-Sun. *July, Aug* 9am-7pm Tue-Sun. **Admission** by *biglietto unico* (*see p260*).

In 476 the Roman Empire came to an end. In 1579 Palladio began work on the designs of the Teatro Olimpico. In the intervening 1100 years not one permanent indoor theatre had been built in Europe. Palladio died before construction began in 1580, and the project was taken over by his son Silla and his star pupil Vincenzo Scamozzi. The two took considerable liberties with the original blueprint. The decorative flamboyance of the wood-and-stucco interior contrasts notably with its modest entrance and severe external walls. Built on the model of Greek and Roman theatres, it has 13 semicircular wooden steps rising in front of the stage, crowned by Corinthian columns holding up an elaborate balustrade topped with elegant 'antique' sculpted figures. The permanent stage set, with its five *trompe l'oeil* street scenes, represents the city of Thebes in Sophocles's *Oedipus Rex*, which was the theatre's first performance, in 1585.

The elaborately frescoed antechambers to the theatre were also designed by Scamozzi and were used for meetings and smaller concerts of the Accademia Olimpica, the learned society of humanists that commissioned the place. Don't miss the chiaroscuro fresco in the entrance hall depicting a delegation of Japanese noblemen who visited Vicenza in 1585; their presence in Vicenza gives some idea of the city's enduring economic clout.

The theatre has once again begun to realise its potential as a venue for plays and concerts. A season of classical dramas in September and October usually includes a staging of *Oedipus Rex* (in Italian) and may take in various other Greek and Shakespearean tragedies. Concerts tend to be concentrated in May and June. For information, contact the tourist office (*see p264*) or Vicenza's website (www.comune.vicenza.it).

Where to eat & drink

The *vicentini* have been eating *baccalà alla vicentina* – dried cod stewed in milk and oil – since at least 1269. Counter-intuitively, the dish is not made with *baccalà*. There are two ways of preserving cod: it can be salted and partially dried (salt cod, or *baccalà* in Italian) or just dried (stockfish; *stoccafisso*). When stockfish was introduced to the *vicentini* in the 15th century they decided they preferred it to the *baccalà* that was already a firm fixture on their menus. *Stoccafisso*, however, is not an easy word to pronounce in the Vicentine dialect, so they kept on using the word *baccalà*.

De Gobbi

Via Olmo 52, Creazzo (0444 520 509). **Meals served** 12.30-2.30pm, 7.30-10.30pm Mon-Thur, Sun; 7.30-10.30pm Sat. Closed 3wks Aug. **Average** €30. **Credit** AmEx, DC, MC, V.

Located a few kilometres outside Vicenza, this stalwart offers *bollito misto* (*see p263* **Bollito misto**).

I Monelli

Contrà Ponte San Paolo 13 (0444 540 400). **Meals served** 12.30-4pm, 6.30-11pm Tue-Sun. Closed 2wks July. **Average** €30. **Credit** DC, MC, V.

An *osteria* serving *bigoli con sugo di anatra* (fat spaghetti with duck sauce) and *struzzo* (ostrich… really) *all'aceto balsamico* near piazza delle Erbe.

Osteria Il Cursore

Stradella Pozzetto 10 (0444 323 504). **Meals served** *Sept-July* 12.30-3pm, 7.30-10.30pm Mon, Wed-Sat; 7.30-10.30pm Sun. Closed Aug. **Average** €25. **Credit**, MC, V.

Horse about in **Giardino Salvi**. *See p258.*

This old-fashioned *vicentino* drinking den is across the arched ponte San Michele. If you are looking for a quick snack there are bar nibbles; otherwise, for larger appetites, the kitchen turns out excellent versions of local specialities such as *bigoli con sugo di anatra* or *baccalà alla vicentina*.

Pasticceria Sorarù
Piazzetta Palladio 17 (0444 320 915). **Open** 8.30am-1pm, 3.30-8pm Mon, Tue, Thur-Sun. **No credit cards.**
One of Italy's most charming *pasticcerie*, Sorarù is worth a look even if you don't have a sweet tooth. The columns, marble counters and ornate wooden shelves backed with mirrors are all 19th-century originals; the cakes, firmly in the Austro-Hungarian tradition, are a tad fresher. Sit at outside tables in summer drinking coffee as you gaze across to the basilica (*see p260*).

Remo
Contrà Caimpenta 14 (0444 911 007/ristorante daremo@hotmail.com). **Meals served** noon-2.30pm, 8-10.30pm Tue-Sat; noon-2.30pm Sun. Closed Aug; 2wks Dec-Jan. **Average** €35. **Credit** DC, MC, V.
Situated in an old farmhouse a little to the east of the city, this country restaurant offers some of the best cooking that you will find anywhere in the entire Vicenza area. The trolley of boiled and roasted meats is a fixture, and Remo's *baccalà alla vicentina* is spectacular. There are also excellent sweets and house wine.

Ristorante Tre Visi Vecchio Roma
Corso Palladio 25 (0444 324 868/www.trevisi. vicenza.com). **Meals served** 12.30-2.30pm, 7.30-10.30pmTue-Sat; 12.30-3pm Sun. Closed 2wks July. **Average** €35. **Credit** MC, V
A good place to pop into when Palladio's genius gets a bit too much. The outside courtyard is a pleasant place for a summer lunch.

Where to stay

Most of Vicenza's hotels cater more to business travellers than to the tourist market. As long as you don't insist on a room with a view, though, you should be able to get a pleasant night's sleep at a comfortable hotel.

Camping Vicenza
Strada Pelosa 239 (0444 582 311/fax 0444 582 311). **Closed** Oct-Mar. **Rates** €4.10-€7 per person; €8-€13.70 per camper/tent. **Credit** AmEx, DC, MC, V.
Situated near the Vicenza Est exit of the Milan–Venice motorway, this upmarket campsite is well equipped; but be warned that it is a serious hike from the city centre.

Hotel Castello
Contrà Piazza Castello 24 (0444 323 585/fax 0444 323 583). **Rates** €80-€90 single; €90-€100 double. **Credit** AmEx, MC, V.

Bollito misto

Restaurants in the Veneto will occasionally allow intrepid diners a glimpse of feasting as it used to be. As you sit at the table, pleasantly sated by the pasta or risotto you had as a first course, a waiter appears pushing a gigantic trolley. He reaches below to pull out a warmed plate, takes a moment to adjust his knives and cutting board, and then opens the lid. He spears first one cut of meat out of the fragrant steam, then another, then another after that. With each spear he slices enough for your portion, then puts the meat back in its broth. When he is finished, he offers sauces: *salsa verde*, heady with parsley and capers; *mostarda*, spicy preserved fruit; *cren*, horseradish sauce; and *peàra*, made with a combination of bread crumbs and bone marrow.

This is the *bollito misto*, and if the translation (mixed boil) conjures up visions of stringy, dull, grey meats, then you're assuming that Italian chefs cook the way British housewives did in the 1950s. In Italy, the meat used in this dish is plump and savoury, the traditional *cotechino* sausage meltingly soft.

Besides sausage – which is always cooked separately so as to not cloud up the broth – expect to see some combination of whole hen (*gallina*) or chicken (*pollo*), veal's tongue (*lingua*), calf's head (*testina*), a cut of beef (*manzo*) and occasionally a fillet of pork (*maiale*). Boiled potatoes are considered the classic accompaniment to this favourite dish.

This unpretentious hotel with 1980s-style interiors is in the city centre close to corso Palladio and all the main sights.

Hotel Cristina
Corso San Felice 32 (0444 323 751/fax 0444 543 656/hotel.cristina@keycomm.it). **Rates** €98 single; €114 double. **Credit** AmEx, DC, MC, V.
Located just a few steps outside the Porta Castello gate, the recently restructured Hotel Cristina has a mainly business clientele but offers special weekend packages for tourists.

Hotel Giardini
Vialè Giuriolo 10 (tel/fax 0444 326 458/www.hotel giardini.com). **Closed** 2wks Aug. **Rates** €83 single; €114 double. **Credit** AmEx, DC, MC, V.
A small, modern hotel, located across piazza Matteotti from Palladio's Teatro Olimpico (*see p262*).

Resources

Tourist information

UPT
Piazza Matteotti 12 (0444 320 854/fax 0444 327 072/www.vicenzae.org). **Open** 9am-1pm, 2-6pm daily.

Getting there

By car
Take the A4 La Serenissima motorway from Venice towards Milan.

By train
There are regular trains to and from Venice (55mins) and Verona (30mins).

By bus
FTV (0444 223 111/www.ftv.vi.it) buses run from Padua to Vicenza. The terminus is by the railway station.

Around Vicenza

His influence is unmistakeable and lasting, but Andrea Palladio was not the only gainfully employed architect in Vicenza. Throughout the small towns and countryside of the *vicentino*, you can find villas by other noted architects. Below is a selection of the most important country villas in Vicenza province. For villas in which the local architect actually had a hand, *see pp38-42.*

All the destinations listed below are served by FTV buses, which leave from the main terminal outside Vicenza train station; ring 0444 223 115 for timetable information.

Villa Cordellina Lombardi
Via Lovara 36, Montecchio Maggiore (0444 908 141/ www.provincia.vicenza.it/pdv/ville). Bus to Recoaro. **Open** *April-mid Oct* 9am-1pm Tue-Fri; 9am-noon, 3-6pm Sat, Sun. Closed mid Oct-Mar. **Admission** €2.10. **No credit cards**.
This beautifully restored villa, built between 1735 and 1760 in the grand Palladian style, contains some flamboyant frescoes by Giambattista Tiepolo. Painted in 1743, they include one of the painter's favourite Enlightenment allegories, *The Light of Reason Driving out the Fog of Ignorance*. There is also a charming French-style park and garden.

Villa Pisani Ferri 'Rocca Pisana'
Via Rocca 1, Lonigo (0444 831 625). Bus to Lonigo. **Open** Apr-Nov by appointment. **Admission** €5. **No credit cards**.
This magnificent villa perched on a high hill was designed in 1576 on the ruins of a medieval castle, by the architect Vincenzo Scamozzi, Palladio's star pupil. Like La Rotonda (*see p42*), La Rocca has four main windows facing the four points of the compass and a dome with a hole at the top. But whereas the Rotonda hole is covered with glass, and was conceived to allow light into the building, the hole at the Rocca is open, like the Pantheon in Rome, allowing air to circulate.

Villa Trissino Marzotto
Piazza GG Trissino 2, Trissino (0445 962 029). Bus to Recoaro. **Open** by appointment only. **Admission** *Villa* €5. *Garden* €5. **No credit cards**.
This elaborate complex, consisting of two villas (the lower one a romantic ruin), is set in one of the most charming of Italy's private parks. The upper villa and the park were designed by Francesco Muttoni between 1718 and 1722. The garden is a typically 18th-century mixture of art and nature, in which allegorical statues frame tree-lined walks; the lower villa – destroyed by lightning in 1841 – acts as a theatrical focal point.

Villa Valmarana ai Nani
Via dei Nani 2-8, Vicenza (0444 321 803). Bus 8 from viale Roma. **Open** *mid Mar-Nov* 10am-noon, 3-6pm Wed, Thur, Sat, Sun; 3-6pm Tue, Fri. Closed Dec-mid March. **Admission** €6. **No credit cards**.
This delightful villa was designed by Antonio Muttoni in 1688. It still belongs to the Valmarana family. For once it's the interior that is the main attraction, thanks to a remarkable series of frescoes painted by Giambattista Tiepolo and his son Giandomenico in 1757. The statues of dwarfs (*nani*) lining the wall to the right of the main villa are not a sign of the family's lack of taste; they bear witness instead to the sensitivity of a Valmarana father who wished to comfort his own dwarf child by giving him friendly familiars to gaze on.

Where to stay & eat

To turn a visit to the Villa Trissino Marzotto (*see above*) into an indulgence, dine at **Ca' Masieri** (località Masieri, restaurant 0445 962 100, hotel 0445 490 122, www.camasieri.com, closed Mon lunch & Sun, average €50), two kilometres (1.25 miles) west of Trissino town. This charming 18th-century stone *relais* offers serious meat, game and fish cooking at fairly serious prices; it also has 12 rooms (€100 double, €9 breakfast) and suites (€130) and a swimming pool. For the ultimate gastro-treat, head for the village of Montecchio Precalcino, 15 kilometres (9.5 miles) north of Vicenza, where the Michelin-starred **Locanda di Piero** (via Roma 32-4, 0445 864827, closed all Sun, Mon & Sat lunch, 2wks in Mar, Nov, average €55) does a cordon bleu take on the local tradition.

Tourist information

See left.

Treviso & the Northern Veneto

Visit the hills and plains north of Venice for Benetton, Browning and the Bellini.

North of Venice, the Veneto is a land of well-tended well-being. For the tourist, there is no one obvious destination, no definitive must-see. There is, rather, an immersion into what Italians call an 'insieme', a togetherness. Craggy mountains, alpine meadows, potent forests, towered hills, walled towns with one or two points of interest. Taken together, the sites of the northern Veneto create a sense of quality, and offer both physical and metaphysical recreation.

Treviso

Twenty-five kilometres (16 miles) north of Venice, Treviso likes to fashion itself 'little Venice'. The narrow path of the river Sile through town probably won't have you forgetting the Grand Canal, but among the meandering waterways and frescoed porticos of this self-satisfied little sister you'll find an opportunity for idle strolling that's all too rare in Venice.

While the Venetians are responsible for the walls guarding the old town, Treviso was important long before they pitched up here in the 14th century. Originally the Roman town of Tarvisium, the city was also the seat of a Lombard duchy. The Venetian walls, dating back to 1509, protect three sides of the Old Town. The fourth is protected by Sile River, which provides some of the water in the canals – the rest comes from a series of streams that converge outside the walls. Once the canals were used by the city's dyers, tanners and paper mills; today, their mossy walls and small bridges offer a slightly bucolic touch to the casual *osterie* ranged alongside.

Treviso owes its self-satisfaction to the fortunes of its family-run businesses. Its most famous family – the Benettons – have branched out from the home-knitted jumpers of Giuliana Benetton to less-fashionable assets like a sizeable chunk of Italy's motorway system. The oversized Benetton store in piazza Indipendenza is a reminder of the family's connections to the city… just as the *'polenta si, couscous no'* stickers on the nearby lamp-posts are a reminder that all that affluence has led to increased immigration but no increase of inter-racial harmony in this notoriously conservative city.

Around the corner from the Benetton store are piazza dei Signori and the Palazzo dei Trecento, the town hall which dates back to 1217. Across from the palazzo in piazza Duomo, the **Duomo** (open 9am-noon, 3.30-6.30pm daily) contains an *Annunciation* (1570) by Titian and a beautiful *Adoration of the Magi* (1520) by Pordenone. Two other churches in nearby piazza San Vito – **San Vito** and **Santa Lucia** (both open 8am-noon daily) – offer splendid frescoes by Tommaso da Modena, considered by some to be the greatest 14th-century artist after Giotto.

More works by Da Modena, including his masterpiece *The Life of St Ursula*, are tucked away in the deconsecrated church-cum-exhibition space of **Santa Caterina** in piazza Giacomo Matteotti (open during exhibitions only). The privately run **Casa dei Carraresi** (0422 513 161) at via Palestra 33/35 is another exhibition space – one with world-class pretensions. For a fresco fest, head to the church of **San Francesco** (open 7am-noon, 3-7pm daily). Work on the ceiling of the main chapel, including the wonderful *St Francis with Stigmata* and the four evangelists in studious mode, is by an anonymous 14th-century painter, though some argue that this too, should be attributed to Da Modena. Da Modena pops up yet again with a remarkable series of frescoes in the chapter house of the Dominican monastery adjoining the Romanesque-Gothic church of **San Nicolò** (via San Nicolò, open 8am-noon, 3.30-6pm daily). Look closely at the *studiosi* and you'll see the first pair of glasses depicted in art.

Where to stay & eat

Toni del Spin (via Inferiore 7, 0422 543 829, closed Mon lunch, all Sun & mid July-mid Aug, average €25) is a pretty, intimate *osteria* serving local specialities at reasonable prices. **Osteria Al Dante** (piazza Garibaldi 6, 0422 591 897, May-Sept closed Sun, Oct-Apr closed Sun & Wed, average €18) dishes up splendid views and no-frills fare at the foot of the ponte Dante.

Muscoli (via Pescheria 23, 0422 583 390, closed Sunday, average €15) is the place to go for a reviving *ombra* (glass) of wine and outstanding nibbles. **Hotel Campeol** (piazza Ancilotto 4, 0422 56 601, €85 double, breakfast €6) offers good service right in the heart of town.

Tourist information

APT

Piazza Monte di Pietà 8 (0422 547 632/fax 0422 419 092/www.provincia.treviso.it). **Open** 9am-12.30pm Mon; 9am-12.30pm, 2-6pm Tue-Fri; 9.30am-12.30pm, 3-6pm Sat, Sun.

Getting there

By car

Take the Treviso Sud exit from the A27 motorway; alternatively, take the SS13 from Venice–Mestre.

La Divina

Eleonora Duse first made her name on stage at the Arena (*see p246*) in Verona, playing Juliet. The year was 1873 and Duse was only 15. By the time she was in her late 20s she had cemented her reputation as one of the greatest actresses of all time, renowned for her naturalness on stage and the way she avoided the 'make-up' of overblown emotions.

Offstage, Duse had plenty of reasons to blow some emotional steam of her own. Her relationship with poet, playwright and self-styled Nietzschean superman Gabriele D'Annunzio was as dramatic – and public – as the roles she played on stage. He spent her money and cheated on her with equal abandon; while she left him in 1904, their ties continued to bind and later, as she was dying, she would say, 'I forgive him for having used me, ruined me, humiliated me. I forgive him for everything, because I loved.'

Eleonora Duse came to Asolo in 1919, as a house guest. She fell in love with the hills and the peace, and continued to make frequent – if brief – visits. She saw Asolo as a retirement haven, a place of 'lace and poetry'. In poignant fashion, Duse died in Pittsburgh, PA in 1924, while on tour. D'Annunzio petitioned his friend Mussolini to bring the 'adorable corpse' back to Italy ASAP, and Duse was duly laid to rest in the church of Sant'Anna in Asolo.

By train

Regular Venice–Treviso services (25 minutes).

By bus

ACTV and ATVO (for both, *see p278*) buses run regularly from Venice's bus terminus in piazzale Roma.

West from Treviso

The plains and hills of the Po basin west of Treviso are dotted with worthy stop-bys. The **Duomo** (open 9.30-11.45am, 3.15-5.45pm Mon-Sat) in **Castelfranco Veneto** is home to one of the few surviving masterpieces of local boy done good Giorgione. The moats and 13th-century fortified red-brick wall provide a picturesque backdrop to the town.

Another local boy is featured in the tiny village of **Possagno**. Inside the family home of sculptor Antonio Canova (1757-1822) is the **Gipsoteca Canoviana**. The museum has many of Canova's works, including the striking black-tack-studded plaster models for the finished statues. Canoviana's neo-classical statues have been praised as some of the best since Michelangelo, and damned as precursors of Totalitarian Art; the Gipsoteca lets you make up your own mind. Modernist architect Carlo Scarpa is responsible for the museum's extension, built between 1955 and 1957.

Scarpa, the quintessential Venetian, shared his city's traditional fascination with the East, fusing the ancient and modern in functional but striking spaces. His other trademarks were the use of natural elements as raw material and his ability to combine inner and outer space. For further treats, head to the cemetery (open 9am-7pm daily) in **San Vito d'Altivole**. Among the more mundane remembrances is the massive *Tomba Brion* – 2,200 square metres (23,656 square feet) of pure Scarpa, who spent the nine years before his death in 1978 constructing the monster. He is also buried here.

Robert Browning fell so deeply in love with the picture-postcard landscape of **Asolo** that he named his last collection of verse after the town (*Asolando*, 1889). Set among rolling hills covered with cypress trees, olive groves and vineyards, the town is a place for luxuriating, not sight-seeing – a dedicated tourist can cover the town in 20 minutes. Asolo is perfect for window-shopping, a long lunch and a leisurely walk with the town's illustrious ghosts: the exiled Venetian-born Queen of Cyprus Caterina Cornaro, who set up court in Asolo in 1489, and the 19th-century actress Eleonora Duse (*see p266* **La Divina**). When you're through with luxuriating, Asolo is also a good base for exploring the other small gems of the area.

Contemplate 'little Venice' while loading up on coffee at the central **piazza del Signori**.

To the west of Asolo, **Bassano del Grappa** sits astride the Brenta river just as it emerges from the mountains. Monte Grappa, a few kilometres outside of town, offers its name to both the town and Italy's fiery after-dinner drink. Technically a pomace brandy, grappa began life as a way to get the most out of the grapes used for wine-making. After the grapes are pressed, 20 per cent of their total weight still remains, in the form of skins, seeds, stems and so on: this is known as the pomace. Instead of throwing it out, the frugal inhabitants of the Veneto distil it and use it as a sort of internal central heating system during the winter. These days, upscale restaurants come around after dinner with a grappa trolley, but the traditional method of drinking it – pouring a slug into a cup of espresso for a '*caffè corretto*' – still works just fine. The oldest and most famous

name in grappa is Nardini (Ponte Vecchio 2), whose distillery is located in Bassano's main street, just outside the old city gates. Another famous name, Poli, can be found at via Gamba 6, at the foot of Bassano's showpiece, the Ponte degli Alpini. Though the original bridge was probably constructed in the 1150s, what we see now is a faithful copy of Palladio's magnificent covered wooden bridge built in 1586. The copy dates back no further than 1948, Palladio's having been blown up by retreating German troops at the end of World War II.

Bassano is one of Italy's wealthiest cities, a fact easily confirmed by window-shopping in the city centre. The shops are decidedly high-end, with a rich selection of Italian fashion, jewellery, ceramics and gourmet food. In piazza Garibaldi – one of the town's two main squares – is the **Museo Civico**, located inside the

Treviso's **Palazzo del Trecento**. *See p265.*

beautiful convent and cloistered gardens of the 14th-century church of San Francesco. The museum contains a fine collection of ceramics – Bassano is also known for its ceramics industry – and an archaeological section devoted to the city's Roman origins. The other square – piazza Libertà – is dominated by the medieval Palazzo Municipale, which is covered with faded frescoes. The **Museo degli Alpini**, with its collection of World War I memorabilia, stands at the far end of the ponte degli Alpini.

West of Bassano, the town of Marostica with its imposing 14th-century walls stages a huge chess match every second year (*see p270* **Checkmate**). North of Bassano, the mountains are home to the **Altopiano Asiago**. The ride up offers spectacular views of the *pianura* (plain) below and enough hairpin bends to keep the most daring devil happy. The *altopiano* is home to resorts, meadows, forests and cows – Asiago is one of Italy's better-known cheeses. It was also the scene of fierce fighting during World War I (*see p269* **Lest we forget**); cemeteries dotted around the plateau bear witness to British involvement. Asiago is also the name of the most famous of the seven towns on the *altopiano*. Its pretty town centre was a Fascist reconstruction effort of the 1920s and '30s – most of its buildings were destroyed during World War I. Asiago is also home to the massive **Sacrario Militare** (World War I memorial; 1934), resting place for more than 50,000 soldiers from the Great War.

Gipsoteca Canoviana

Piazza Canova 74, Possagno (0423 544 323/ www.museocanova.it). **Open** 9am-noon, 3-6pm Tue-Sun. **Admission** €5; €3.50 concessions. **No credit cards.**

Museo degli Alpini

Via Angarano 2, Bassano (0424 503 662). **Open** 9am-8pm Tue-Sun. **Admission** free.

Museo Civico

Piazza Garibaldi 12, Bassano (0424 519 450/www. museobassano.it). **Open** 9am-6.30pm Tue-Sat; 3.30-6.30pm Sun. **Admission** €4.50; €3 concessions. **No credit cards.**

Sacrario Militare

Viale degli Eroi, Asiago (0424 464 081). **Open** *Mid May-Sept* 9am-noon, 2-6pm daily. *Oct-mid May* 9am-noon, 2-5pm daily. **Admission** free.

Where to stay and eat

In Asolo, the **Hotel Duse** (via Browning 190, 0423 55 241/info@hotelduse.com, €100-€120 double, breakfast €6) is a comfortable three-star option in the centre of town. The **Villa Cipriani** (via Canova 298, 0423 523 411/www. sheraton.com/villacipriani, €307-€466 double) and the **Albergo al Sole** (via Collegio 33, 0423 951 332/www.albergoalsole.com, €170-€255 double) are best for full-immersion luxury. **Ca' Derton** (piazza d'Annunzio 11, 0423 529 648, closed Mon, Sun dinner & 2wks Aug, average €35) is a firm favourite with Italian foodies. In the same piazza, **Ristorante Due Mori** (piazza d'Annunzio 5, 0423 952 256, closed Wed, average €30) offers a more casual but equally delicious repast.

For such a wealthy city, Bassano can be a rather disappointing overnight stay, with few charming hotels and welcoming *osterie*. **Al Castello** (piazza Terraglio 20, 0424 228 665, www.hotelalcastello.it, €70-€82 double) is a reasonably priced three-star. In the centre of town, **Birraria Ottone** (via Matteotti 50, 0424 522 206, closed Mon dinner & Tue, average €25), serving mainly regional and Austrian dishes, is a good bet.

Asiago, as befits a resort town, is chock-full of hotels. One of the most convenient, located just a few steps from the main square, is the **Hotel Croce Bianca** (via IV Novembre 30, 0424 462 642/www.hotelcrocebianca.it, €70-€94 double). Eating is also no problem here, but – with many of the hotels insisting on half- and full-board – eating exceptionally well is. The **Lepre Bianca**, in the nearby town of Gallio (via Camona 46, 0424 445 666, www.laleprebianca.it, closed 2wks Nov, average €45), is one of the area's most highly regarded restaurants.

The Veneto

Tourist information

IAT

Castelfranco Veneto *Via Francesco Maria Preti 66, Castelfranco Veneto (0423 491 416/fax 0423 771 085/iat.castelfrancoveneto@provincia.treviso.it).* **Open** 9am-12.30pm Mon, Wed; 9am-12.30pm, 2-6pm Tue, Thur, Fri; 9.30am-12.30pm, 3-6pm Sat, Sun.
Asolo *Piazza Garibaldi 73, Asolo (0423 529 046/fax 0423 524 137).* **Open** 9am-12.30pm Mon, Wed; 9am-12.30pm, 3-6pm Tue, Thur, Fri; 9.30am-12.30pm, 3-6pm Sat, Sun.

APT

Largo Corona d'Italia 35, Bassano (0424 524 351/fax 0424 525 301/iat.bassano@provincia.vicenza.it). **Open** 9am-1pm, 2-6pm daily.

Uffico del Turismo

Piazza Carli, Asiago (0424 464 081/www.comune.asiago.vi.it). **Open** 9.30am-12.30pm, 3-7pm daily.

Getting there

For airport information, *see p277.*

By car

From Treviso, SS53 goes directly to Castelfranco Veneto. For Asolo, take SS348 to Montbelluna, then take SS248, which continues to Bassano del Grappa and Marostica.

Possagno is a short distance from Asolo on marked minor roads. To get to Asiago from Bassano, take SS47.

By train

Frequent Venice–Bassano trains also stop at Castelfranco.

By bus

La Marca (0422 577 311) runs services from Treviso to Castelfranco and Bassano. Asiago can be reached by bus from Bassano (FTV 0444 223 115).

North from Treviso

The famous Bellini cocktail begins life up the A27 motorway from Treviso in the area of hills and valleys known as the Altamarca Trevigiana. Sheltered from cold northerlies by the nearby Dolomites and enjoying warmer air sweeping up the Adriatic, the area between Conegliano and Valdobbiadene is home to the sparkling *prosecco* necessary for Harry's (*see p166* **Harry's Bar**) signature bubbly-and-peach-juice drink, as well as Italy's oldest *strada del vino* (wine trail – an itinerary around vineyards and wine outlets), the obviously named *Strada del Prosecco*.

Lest we forget

In Italian, *altopiano* refers to the type of mountain meadow that would make Julie Andrews weep with joy. In the Veneto, the Altopiano Asiago refers to a plateau of meadows, but also dense forest and rugged, 1000-metre cliffs. Formerly lying on the border between Italy and Austria, the *altopiano* became the scene of fierce fighting when Italy declared war on Austria in 1915.

By spring of 1916, the Italians had already launched five offensives against the well-fortified Austrian lines and been repulsed every time. Tired of being on the defensive, the Austrians staged an attack designed to push the Italians out of the mountains and on to the plains of the Po – it was also designed to punish the Italians for what the Austrians saw as their duplicity in signing the Treaty of London. Though the Austrians forced the evacuation of the town of Asiago in May, Italian commander Luigi Cadorna was able to stabilise the situation. Stability, however, meant incessant raids and artillery duels, punctuated by the occasional pitched battle... occasional, but memorable, such as the

Battle of Ortigara in June 1917, where the 15,000 men of the 52nd Alpini division suffered more than 12,000 casualties.

British troops were heavily involved in the defence of the *altopiano* towards the end of the war. In June of 1918, Austrian troops began what would be their final offensive. Beginning with an artillery bombardment – which included gas (a rarity on this front where a change of wind could easily push the gas back over the lines) – the Austrians won ground, only to eventually be pushed back by British forces.

The *altopiano* still carries the scars of the fighting, particularly above the timberline where the trenches can be visited. In some areas, shell fragments seem to be as common as stones, and hikers still find artillery shells (and occasionally the remains of a soldier). Throughout the Veneto, you can find memorials to the fallen and the inscription '*per non dimenticare*' ('lest we forget'). Walking in the solitude of the *altopiano*, it seems that nature too, is willing to remember.

The Veneto

The town of **Conegliano** is another in the string of pleasant, unchallenging Veneto towns. The 14th-century **Duomo** is home to a painting of the *Virgin and Child With Saints and Angels* by the town's most famous son, Giambattista Cima, known as Cima da Conegliano. Conegliano's cultural treasures end here, but visit the **Sala dei Battuti** (open Apr-Sept 3.30-7pm Sun; Oct-Mar 3-6.30pm Sun) next to the Duomo: dedicated to a brotherhood of flagellants, it's decorated with some truly odd 15th- and 16th-century biblical frescoes.

The hills change to mountains near **Vittorio Veneto** and the air seems a little fresher, the light a little sharper. Originally the two smaller towns of Ceneda and Serravalle,

Checkmate

Most of the time Marostica, a small town a few kilometres to the west of Bassano (*see p267*), offers the usual contemplative piazza and a bit of rampart leading up to the Veneto hills. But as they sip their cappuccini at one of the cafés in piazza Castello, the sharp-eyed will notice a grid of marble squares on the ground. And therein lies a tale.

In 1454 Taddeo Parisio, lord of Marostica, had a problem. He had a beautiful daughter named Linora and two knights in love with her. Testosterone being what it is, the knights had challenged each other to a duel. Taddeo, though, didn't want to lose either of the knights, so, thinking outside the box, he had Marostica's main square paved into a giant chessboard and ordered the knights to fight it out through a game of chess, using the townspeople as pieces. Vieri da Vallonara won the hand of the boss's daughter, while loser Rinaldo D'Angarano had to settle for Linora's little sister, Oldrada. History does not tell us how either felt about the consolation prize.

The match was such a hit that it was immediately put on ice for close to 500 years. Then, in 1923, two university students suggested a rematch. Again, heady with success, the good people of Marostica waited another 30 years for game three. Finally in the mid 1950s, the game became a regular part of the Marostica landscape. These days, it's played the second Friday, Saturday and Sunday of even-yeared Septembers – see www.marosticascacchi.it for information.

Vittorio Veneto was formed and named in 1866, to commemorate the unification of Italy under King Vittorio Emanuele II. Serravalle boasts a well-preserved medieval *borgo* (quarter), which is unfortunately situated right on the busy *strada statale*. It's worth braving the exhaust fumes for a brief walk through the *borgo* and an admiring glance at the frescoed Loggia Serravallese, which dates from 1462.

Both Conegliano and Vittorio Veneto offer access to Valdobbiadene; the road from Vittorio Veneto (take the SS51 out of town then follow signs) has the advantage of passing through Follina. Here, nestled among the hills of the *prealpi* and the sleepy town centre is one of the jewels of the Veneto, the **Abbazia Santa Maria** (open 6.30am-noon, 2.30-9.30pm daily). The Romanesque abbey dates back to the 12th century and features one of the most peaceful cloisters you'll ever see. A few kilometres before Follina, the **Castello Brandolini** (0438 9761, www.castelbrando.it) is an intriguing mixture of ancient castle (its origins date back to a Roman fortress) and modern health spa. Even if wellness isn't your thing, the trip up the elevator is worth the €1 it costs for the views of the valley.

The town of **Valdobbiadene** is the headquarters for the production of *prosecco*, an autochthonous (it means 'native') grape which fills 33 million bottles a year. The town – in conjunction with the area wine producers – are diligent in their efforts to uphold the reputation of the dry, slightly bitter bubbly, most notably in an annual *Mostra Nazionale degli Spumanti*, which takes place in September – visit www.mostranazionalespumanti.it for more information. The tourist office in the town (*see p273*) will also provide a complete list of producers on request. (Remember to call for an appointment before visiting.) Azienda Bisol, in the neighbouring village of Santo Stefano (via Fol 33, 0423 900 138), produces one of the best *proseccos* you can get.

Hydro-electric power has long been vital to Italy's economy, and the many reservoirs and generating stations you can see along the *Strada d'Alemagna* – the main road (SS51) from Vittorio Veneto to Belluno – are a vivid reminder of this.

It is hard not to rhapsodise about the area. Lago di Santa Croce is a semi-artificial mirror reflecting jagged Dolomite peaks, the thick forests of Bosco di Cansiglio, and the stupendous natural bowl formed by the high valley of the Alpago. There's no shortage of awe-inspiring views, or trails (maps available from the APT in Belluno, *see p273*) to view them from. On top of all the natural beauty there are plenty of reasonable hotels and some

The **Duomo**.
See p265.

wonderful restaurants serving everything from home-cured sausages to Michelin-starred culinary creations.

Like Treviso, the medieval town of **Belluno** invites comparisons with Venice. 'The Venice of the Alps' occupies a rocky terrace overlooking the Piave and Ardo rivers. How high the town is perched is wonderfully illustrated by the escalator that carries visitors from the Lamboi car park to the main piazza. The escalator emerges on to a scene that is pure enchantment. Against a backdrop of mountains and tranquillity, the 15th-century Palazzo dei Rettori (once home to the town's Venetian rulers; not open to the public) and 16th-century **Duomo** (open 7am-12.30pm, 3.30-7.30pm daily) recall the architecture along the Grand Canal. The **Baptistery** (variable hours) across from the Duomo contains an early 18th-century carving of John the Baptist by Andrea Brustolon. Just outside the old city walls is the new heart of the city, piazza dei Martiri. Still called Campadel by locals, this pleasant, open square with plenty of benches for relaxing and breathing in the mountain air had its name changed in 1945, in memory of the four partisans hanged from its lamp-posts.

In the mountains beyond Belluno is the jet-set capital of the Dolomites, **Cortina d'Ampezzo** – beautiful, but expensive. If you're heading there, stop off at **Borca di Cadore** to check

out architect Carlo Scarpa's amazing church (open 9am-noon, 4-6pm daily), built in 1959. Borca itself is a time warp experience. Constructed by the state-owned ENI fuel company as a holiday camp for its sickly workers, this village has remained virtually unchanged since the 1950s. If you're looking for a mountain retreat that bears no resemblance to Heidi's homestead, check in to one of the village apartments or main hotel. To book, contact the Centro Vacanze at Borca di Cadore (Dolomiti Gestioni, on the SS51, 0435 487 500, open 8.30am-12.30pm, 2-6pm Mon-Sat).

To the west of Belluno, **Feltre** was once a Roman fortress on the banks of the river Piave. Today it is a perfectly preserved 16th-century town. Among the cobbled streets and frescoed *palazzi*, the sharp-eyed visitor will notice that many of the lapidaries are chipped clean. *La Serenissima* was a munificent patron to Feltre, and financed a well-endowed rebuilding programme after the town was razed to the ground in 1510 by the troops of the Holy Roman Emperor Maximilian I. Many of the stone markers praised Venice for its aforementioned munificence. When Napoleon rolled in (an event marked by one of the few unchipped lapidaries in town) he took umbrage at all the praise directed towards his enemies, and ordered the words destroyed. Despite Napoleon's enmity, paintings and statues of the lion of St Mark are

Heading east

Friuli-Venezia Giulia, the Veneto's neighbour to the east, is best known for Trieste, the very Mittel European port where James Joyce once taught English. But it is **Aquileia** that draws the attention of Italy's art historians.

Legend has it that an eagle (*aquila*) soared overhead as the outline of the new town of Aquileia was being ploughed up in 181 BC, giving the town its name. In short order, it became one of the most important cities in the Roman Empire, with a population of more than 100,000. By the fourth century, Aquileia was one of Italy's most important patriarchates, but constant harrying by barbarian tribes forced the bishop to shift his residence to nearby Grado.

The 11th-century **Basilica Teodoriana** (piazza Capitolo 1, open 8.30am-12.30pm, 2.30-5.30pm daily) contains 700 square metres (2,333 square feet) of mosaic paving – remains from a fourth-century church that stood on the site – with a mishmash of imagery both Christian (Jonah and the whale, the Good Shepherd) and pagan (tortoises and cockerels). In the apse, frescoes dated 1031 show the patriarch Poppo, who founded the basilica in the 11th century, with Emperor Conrad II and his wife and son, before the Virgin Mary. Twelfth-century frescoes depicting the lives of Christ and Mary are to be found in the crypt beneath the presbytery – entrance is by **Museo Archeologico** ticket; the crypt is a more interesting sight than the museum itself.

Museo Archeologico

Via Roma 1, Aquileia (0431 91 016/ www.museoarcheo-aquileia.it). **Open** 8.30am-2pm Mon; 8.30am-7.30pm Tue-Sun. **Admission** €4; €2 concessions. **No credit cards**.

TOURIST INFORMATION

APT *piazza Capitolo 4, Aquileia (0431 91 087).* **Open** 9am-6pm Mon-Fri; 9.30am-12.30pm, 1.30-6pm Sat, Sun.

---

everywhere. Many of the *palazzi* along Feltre's high street, via Mezzaterra, are frescoed by local artist Lorenzo Luzzo (1467-1512); frescoes on simple merchants' houses down the town's narrow alleyways are often just as striking.

Where to stay & eat

For good-value local cuisine in Conegliano, try the **Trattoria Stella** (via Accademia 3, 0438 22 178, closed Sun & 3wks Aug, average €25). Alternatively, for something more upmarket, head for **Ristorante Al Salisà** (via XX Settembre 2, 0438 24 288, closed Wed, average €35) and take the chance to indulge in a bottle from its excellent wine list.

On the same street you will find the **Hotel Canon d'Oro** (via XX Settembre 131, 0438 34 246, www.hotelcanondoro.it, €100-€110 double). The **Hotel dei Chiostri** in Follina (piazza Municipio 20, 0438 971 805/ www.hoteldeichiostri.com, €130-€150 double) is a very comfortable hotel right across the street from the Abbazia (*see below*); its sister hotel, the up-upscale **Villa Abbazia** (piazza IV Novembre 3, 0438 971 277/www.hotelabbazia.it, double room €220-€230) is one of the fanciest hotels in the region.

At the lovely **Trattoria alla Cima** in Valdobbiadene (via Cima 13, 0423 972 711, closed Mon dinner, Tue, average €30) you can enjoy excellent grilled meats, an incomparable view of the vineyards and the chance to eavesdrop on *prosecco* producers discussing the latest oenological news. East of Belluno, the **Locanda San Lorenzo** in the small town of Puos d'Alpago (via IV Novembre 79, 0437 454 048, www.locandasanlorenzo.it, closed Wed & 3wks Jan-Feb, average €55) offers some of the Veneto's best food, and doubles as an excellent hotel (€90 double). A few kilometres away, the even smaller town of Plois di Pieve d'Alpago (generally shortened to Pieve d'Alpago) is home to Michelin-starred **Dolada** (via Dolada 21, 0437 479 141, www.dolada.it, average €65), also a three-star hotel (€103 double, breakfast €13).

Belluno's rustic **Al Borgo** restaurant (via Anconetta 8, 0437 926 755, closed Mon dinner, Tue & 2wks Jan, average €30) offers smoked ham and sausages, and unusual, filling pasta dishes. For accommodation try the centrally located **Albergo delle Alpi** (via Tasso 13, 0437 940 545, www.dellealpi.it, €102 double).

In Feltre, the **Belle Epoque** (piazza Maggiore, 0439 80193, closed Mon & 2 wks Jan, average €25) serves up comforting food under the porticos of the town's main square.

Tourist information

For information on ski resorts in the region, consult www.dolomitisuperski.it.

APT

Via XX Settembre 61, Conegliano (0438 21 230/fax 0438 428 777/www.comune.conegliano.tv.it). **Open** 9am-12.30 pm Mon, Wed; 9am-12.30pm, 3-6pm Tue, Thur, Fri; 9.30am-12.30pm, 3-6pm Sat, Sun.

UIT

Piazza Marconi 1, Valdobbiadene (0423 976 975/ufficio.turistico@comune.valdobbiadene.tv.it). **Open** 9.30am-12.30pm, 3-6pm daily.

APT

Piazza Duomo 2, Belluno (0437 940 083/fax 0437 958 716/www.infodolomiti.it). **Open** 9am-12.30pm, 3.30-6.30pm daily.

APT

Piazzetta Trento e Trieste 9, Feltre (0439 2540/ fax 0439 2839/www.infodolomiti.it). **Open** 9am-12.30pm, 3.30-6.30pm daily.

Getting there

By car

From Treviso take the SS13 to Conegliano, then the SS51 (*Strada d'Alemagna*) to Vittorio Veneto and Belluno. The three towns can also be reached by the A27 motorway. For the Alpago, turn off SS51 on to SS422d. To get to Feltre from Belluno, take SS50. For Cortina and Borca, continue on SS51.

By train

Fast Venice–Udine trains stop at Conegliano; local Venice–Belluno trains call at Conegliano and Vittorio Veneto as well. There's a local train service from Treviso to Feltre.

By bus

Services from Venice's piazzale Roma to Belluno run during the summer, stopping at Conegliano and Vittorio Veneto. La Marca (0422 577 311) runs services from Treviso's bus station to the three towns, as well as Feltre. Buses to Plois di Pieve d'Alpago and Puos d'Alpago run from Belluno – call Dolomiti Bus, 0437 941 167, for information.

There's an ATVO (041 520 5530) bus from piazzale Roma to Cortina d'Ampezzo at 7.50am (daily through summer; Saturdays and Sundays only for most of the rest of the year, except peak skiing weeks; consult the excellent website www.atvo.it – in English – for details); the journey takes three and a half hours. The return service leaves Cortina at 3.15pm and will, on request, proceed to Venice airport after reaching piazzale Roma at 6.15pm.

Central **Treviso**. *See p265.*

Directory

Features

Directory

Arriving & Leaving

By air – Venice

Venice Marco Polo Airport – SAVE SpA

Viale G Galilei 30/1, Tessera (switchboard 041 260 6111/flight & airport information 041 260 9260/www.veniceairport.it). Located on the northern edge of the lagoon, Venice's airport saw 5.3 million passengers in 2003 and is third in Italy for air traffic volume.

To & from Venice airport

By boat

Società Alilaguna
(041 523 5775/www.alilaguna.com). **No credit cards.**
This ferry service runs hourly between 6.15am and 12.10am from the airport to San Marco and Zattere; and 4.35am (4.20am at Zattere) to 10.50pm in the other direction. Tickets (€10) can be purchased at Alilaguna's counter in the arrivals hall or on board. You should allow 70mins from or to San Marco. The service also stops at Murano, the Lido and Arsenale; after San Marco it proceeds to Zattere. A navetta (shuttle service) to the boat dock departs every 5mins from the airport's main entrance.

Consorzio Motoscafi Venezia
Marco Polo Airport, arrivals hall (041 541 5084). **No credit cards.**
A water-taxi ride from the airport directly to your hotel in Venice will take about 30-40 minutes and cost upwards of €85 depending on the number of people in your party and the stops you make. A navetta (shuttle service) to the boat launch departs every five minutes from the airport's main entrance.

Bucintoro Agency
Marco Polo Airport, arrivals hall (info & reservations 041 521 0632/www.bucintoroviaggi.com). **No credit cards.**
If you book at least 24 hours in advance you can take a shared water taxi to fixed points in Venice. This shuttle system costs €25 per person (minimum two) and is available if your flight arrives between 8am and

7pm – an agency representative will meet you in the arrivals hall with a card with your name on it.

By bus

ATVO
Marco Polo Airport, arrivals hall (041 541 5180/www.atvo.it). **Open** 8am-midnight daily. **Tickets** €3. **No credit cards.**
ATVO runs fast coach services between the airport and piazzale Roma. Tickets can be bought from the ATVO office in piazzale Roma or the ATVO counter in the arrivals hall. The trip takes around 20 minutes; buses leave hourly or more frequently between 8.20am and 12.10am (from airport) and between 5am and 8.40pm (from piazzale Roma); from 10.20am to 7.20pm they're half-hourly.

ACTV
Marco Polo Airport, arrivals hall (041 541 5180/timetable information 041 24 24/www.actv.it). **Open** 8am-midnight daily. Tickets €2. **No credit cards.**
Bus 5 travels between the airport and piazzale Roma, leaving from the airport at 4.08am and 5.10am, and from piazzale Rome at 4.40am, then from both ends at 5.40am, 6.15am, 6.40am, and then every half hour until midnight; journey time 35-40 minutes. Tickets (€2) can be bought at the ACTV counter in the arrivals hall or the ACTV office in piazzale Roma.

By taxi

Cooperativa Artigiana Radio Taxi
Marco Polo Airport, arrivals hall (041 541 6363/info 041 595 1402/switchboard 041 595 2080/taxiapt@radiotaxive.mysem.it). **Credit** AmEx, MC, V.
A traditional taxi ride to piazzale Roma from the airport and vice versa, takes about 20 minutes (depending on traffic) and will cost about €30. Credit cards are only accepted for payments at the arrivals hall.

By bus

Bus services to Venice all terminate at piazzale Roma, which is connected by

vaporetto (*see p278*) to the rest of the city centre. For bus services on mainland Venice and the Lido, *see p280*. For bus services from Venice to other destinations in the Veneto, see individual chapters.

By rail

Most trains arrive at Santa Lucia station in the north-west corner of island Venice (map p308 C2), though a few will only take you as far as Mestre on the mainland, where you will need to change to a local train (every ten minutes or less during the day) for the short hop across the lagoon. *See also p280.*

By road

Venice is connected to other large Italian and European cities by fast motorway links, but prohibitive parking fees make this one of the least practical modes of arrival, especially for stays of more than 24hrs. Note, though, that many Venetian hotels offer their guests discounts at car parks. The main car parks are listed below.

Autorimessa Comunale

Santa Croce 496, piazzale Roma (041 272 7301/www.asmvenezia.it). Vaporetto Piazzale Roma. **Open** 24hrs daily. **Rates** €19 a day. **Credit** AmEx, DC, MC, V. **Map** p310 A3.

Marco Polo Park

Marco Polo Airport, (041 541 5913/www.veniceairport.it). Bus 5 from piazzale Roma/free shuttle bus from main entrance of Venice airport (see above). **Open** 24hrs daily. **Rates** €12 daily (discounts for longer periods). **Credit** AmEx, DC, MC, V.

Parcheggio Sant'Andrea
Santa Croce 465B, piazzale Roma (041 272 7304/www.asmvenezia.it). Vaporetto Piazzale Roma. **Open** 24hrs daily. **Rates** €4.13 2hrs; €49.56 24hrs. **Credit** AmEx, MC, V. **Map** p310 A3.

Parking Stazione
Viale Stazione 10, Mestre (041 938 021). Bus 2 from piazzale Roma or train to Mestre station. **Open** 24hrs daily. **Rates** €4.50 per day. **No credit cards**.

Park Terminal Fusina
Via Moranzani 79, Fusina (041 547 0160/www.terminalfusina.it). Vaporetto 16 from Zattere to Fusina. **Open** *Feb, Mar* 8am-8pm daily; *Apr-mid May, Oct* 8am-10pm daily; *mid May-Sept* 8am-midnight daily; *Nov-Jan* 8am-6pm daily. **Rates** €8 up to 12 hours; €13 up to 24 hours. **Credit** MC, V. **Map** p306.

Venezia Tronchetto Parking
Isola Nuova del Tronchetto (041 520 7555/www.veniceparking.it). Vaporetto Tronchetto. **Open** 24hrs daily. **Rates** €18 a day. **Credit** AmEx, MC, V. **Map** off p308 C1.

Treviso Airport – Aer Tre SpA
Via Noalese, Treviso (airport information 0422 315 111/ www.trevisoairport.it). Ryanair uses this tiny airport with connections to London, Brussels, Frankfurt and Barcelona.

To & from Treviso airport

ATVO
(Timetable information 041 520 5530) Bus services run from Venice's piazzale Roma and back to coincide with flights. The journey takes about one hour ten minutes, and costs €4.50 one way, €8 round trip. Buses leave ridiculously early to ensure your timely arrival – make sure you check the schedule carefully. Alternatively take a train to Treviso and then a bus or taxi (Cooperativa Radiotaxi Padova 049 651 333) to the airport. ACTT (0422 3271) bus 6 does the 20-minute trip from in front of Treviso train station to the airport at 10 and 40 minutes past the hour.

Valerio Catullo Airport
Verona Villafranca (045 809 5666/www.aeroportoverona.it). British Airways and Lufthansa use this airport, in addition to airlines such as Easyjet, Meridiana, Ryanair, Air Dolomiti and Basiq Air.

To & from Verona airport

A shuttle bus runs every 20 minutes between Verona's airport and train station. The 20-minute journey costs €3.62; buy tickets on the bus.

Most major airlines have ticketing counters in Venice's Marco Polo airport. If you need to purchase or change a ticket when your airline's office is closed, use SAVE in the airport departure hall (041 260 6432, fax 041 260 6429, open 5.30am-9pm daily, credit AmEx, DC, MC, V).

Alitalia
Marco Polo Airport, departures hall (international bookings 848 865 642/domestic bookings 848 865 641/www.alitalia.it). **Open** 5.30am-8pm daily. **Credit** AmEx, DC, MC, V.

British Airways
Marco Polo Airport, departures hall, SAVE ticket counter (bookings 199 712 266/www.britishairways.com). **Open** 5.30am to 9pm daily. **Credit** AmEx, DC, MC, V. Note that if you a ticket direct from BA online or by phone, you must have a credit card issued, and with a billing address, in Italy. With cards issued elsewhere, you'll need to buy BA tickets from SAVE (*see p276*).

Easyjet
Marco Polo Airport, departures hall, SAVE ticket counter (848 887 766/ www.easyjet.com). **Open** 5.30am to 9pm daily. **Credit** AmEx, DC, MC, V. Easyjet services London and the East Midlands from Marco Polo airport.

Ryanair
Treviso Airport (0422 315 331). **Open** *Office* 7am-1pm, 3-10pm daily. *Booking line* 8am-6pm Mon-Fri. **Credit** MC, V.

Cutting costs

The privilege of seeing Venice from the Grand Canal does not come cheap: a single ticket for a ride down this grandiose high street on routes number 1 and 82 will set you back a whopping €5 – the fact that this ticket is valid for 90 minutes, allowing multiple journeys along the Grand Canal in that time, does little to ease the pain. If you're heading for the islands, the Lido or any stops not on the Canal itself, take one of the outside routes (41, 42, 51, 52, 61, 62) for which you'll pay the normal price of 'only' €3.50.

If you're staying for longer than a few hours and planning to make good use of public transport, cut costs by investing in a 24hr ticket (€10.50) or a three-day ticket (€22). The Venice Card (*see p292* **Discount cards**) too, gives discounts on transport.

For even longer stays, an *abbonamento* is a sound investment. Available from main ACTV-VeLa offices (*see p278*), this three-year travel ID card allows you to pay the same, much lower, rates as residents of the Veneto region. A one-off charge of €8 is made for the card, for which you will need one passport photo and valid photo ID. You must buy a monthly season ticket (€25; €17 students) when applying for the *abbonamento*; after the month is up, you can buy single tickets for €1 or a carnet (ten tickets) for €9 – a considerable saving.

Getting Around

Public transport – including *vaporetti* (water buses) and buses – in Venice itself and in some mainland areas is run by **ACTV** (Azienda Comunale per il Trasporto di Venezia).

ACTV's recently-created marketing wing is called **VeLa**; VeLa outlets sell tickets for concerts and events in addition to selling transport timetables (60¢), vaporetto tickets and *abbonamenti* (passes and season tickets; for further information *see p277* **Cutting costs**). VeLa's extremely helpful **Hello Venezia!** (041 24 24) call centre provides ACTV vaporetto and bus schedule, events and tourist information, in English.

ATVO runs more extensive bus services to many destinations on the mainland. These services, along with those of many other local companies, are described in The Veneto section of this guide which begins on page 229.

On foot: wet

Photos and film footage make *acqua alta* (high water) look more dramatic than it really is. Except in truly exceptional tides, all that happens is that a couple of inches of water laps into the lowest parts of the city for an hour or two at most, then recedes. The *acqua alta* season is between September and April. How often a high tide occurs depends on several factors: a high tide in itself is not enough. What's needed is a stiff breeze forcing water up the Adriatic, plus particularly high pressure. Some years it doesn't happen at all. When it does, sirens sound five ten-second blasts two hours before the water rises.

During the *acqua alta* season, trestles and wooden planks are stacked up along flood-prone thoroughfares, ready to be transformed into raised walkways by the city rubbish department workers. If the tide rises more than 120cm (47 inches) above its average level, even the walkways float.

Acqua alta has an etiquette all of its own. It is most evident on the raised walkways where Venetians wait their turn patiently, then proceed along the narrow planks slowly and with consideration for other users. They expect tourists to do the same, or risk an angry telling-off for their lack of manners.

The etiquette extends beyond the walkways. The *calli* and *campi* may be waterlogged, but they continue to function as a municipal road network; local road-users are understandably peeved if thoughtless tourists doing Gene Kelly impersonations prevent them from reaching their destination in as dry a state as possible. Remember too, that during *acqua alta* you can't see where the pavement stops and the canal begins.

A map posted at each vaporetto stop shows flood-prone areas and routes covered by raised walkways. If you don't want to get your feet wet, stick to higher ground. Alternatively, sit out those couple of damp hours in your dry hotel room or bar.

The tide office (Centro Maree) provides *acqua alta* forecasts in Italian only (recorded message 041 241 1996/www.comune.venezia.it/maree).

ACTV-VeLa

Santa Croce 509, piazzale Roma (information 041 24 24/ www.hellovenezia.it). Vaporetto Piazzale Roma. **Map** p308 C3. *Public transport tickets* **Open** 7am-8pm daily. **No credit cards**. *Event tickets* **Open** 8.30am-6.30pm daily. **Credit** DC, MC, V.

ACTV-VeLa

San Marco 1810, calle dei Fuseri (information 041 24 24/ www.hellovenezia.it). Vaporetto Vallaresso or Rialto. **Map** p309 D2. *Public transport tickets* **Open** 7.30am-7pm Mon-Sat. **No credit cards**. *Event tickets* **Open** 8.30am-6.30pm Mon-Sat. **Credit** DC, MC, V.

ATVO

Santa Croce 497, piazzale Roma (041 520 5530/www.atvo.it). Vaporetto Piazzale Roma. **Open** 6.40am-7.30pm daily. **No credit cards**. **Map** p308 C3.

By bicycle

Bikes are banned – and otiose – in Venice itself. One of the best ways to explore the Lido is by bicycle but be prepared to fight off hordes of sleep-deprived, caffeinated journalists and film critics during the Film Festival in early September (*see* chapter **Film**).

Giorgio Barbieri

Gran viale Santa Maria Elisabetta 79A, Lido (041 526 1490). **Open** *Mar-Oct* 8.30am-7.30pm daily. Closed Nov-Feb. **Rates** €3hr; €9 a day. **No credit cards**. **Map** p307.

Bruno Lazzari

Gran viale Santa Maria Elisabetta 21B, Lido (041 526 8019). **Open** *Mar-Sept* 8am-8pm daily. *Oct-Feb* 8.30am-1pm, 2.30-7pm. **Rates** €3hr; €9 a day. **Credit** MC, V. **Map** p307.

Directory

By boat

Vaporetti

Venice's ferries – *vaporetti* (*see p281* **Vaporetti**) – run to a tight schedule, with sailing times marked clearly at stops for each line that puts in there. Strikes, however, are not infrequent. To avoid being left high and dry – especially if you have a plane or train to catch – check the ACTV website where strikes (*sciopero*) are announced, or contact the Hello Venezia! call centre (041 24 24) for updates.

Regular services run from about 5am to shortly after midnight, after which a frequent night service follows the route taken by Line 82 during the day.

Venice

The main lines ply the Grand Canal, or circle the island. Without a clear idea of Venetian topography, taking the wrong boat in the wrong direction is alarmingly easy. It is worth picking up a timetable (60¢) and route map from the central ACTV-VeLa office (*see p278*), tourist offices (*see p293*) or any large ACTV booth.

Remember – if you're standing with your back to the station and want to make your way down the Grand Canal, take Line 1 (slow) or Line 82 (faster) heading left. During peak season, ACTV runs express vaporetti 3 and 4 to San Marco from Tronchetto, piazzale Roma and the train station (Ferrovia). The express round-trip tickets cost €7 if you take the boat to San Marco via the Grand Canal and return via the Giudecca Canal. The stop called San Zaccaria is closest to piazza San Marco.

Southern islands

To get to the islands in the lagoon south of Venice (San Servolo, San Lazzaro degli

On foot: dry

Venice is one of the Western world's only cities where walking is the main means of locomotion. With millions of tourists coursing through its narrow thoroughfares every year, it's easy to understand why the Venetians take a dim view of tourists who obstruct narrow streets as they stand to gawp, or – worse still – spread out their picnics on busy bridges. A few 'road rules' will help you manoeuvre through the streets of Venice.

Think of your body as a car. Traffic tends to flow in loosely divided lanes (always keep to the right) with potential for passing. A quick acceleration to the left with a polite '*scusate*' or '*permesso*' will help part the crowds. Slow down and pull off to the right side – or, better still, into an untrafficked side-street – to consult a map or admire a building, instead of suddenly stopping, causing disruption to the traffic flow.

As in any city, rush hour for Venetians is in the mornings and afternoons going to and from work. During the high season this blends into an all-day-long traffic jam clogging the main arteries of the city, especially near San Marco and Rialto, and along the road that joins them. Be adventurous and explore the more remote parts of the island if you want to avoid these situations.

Armeni) take the 20 from San Zaccaria. The 1, 51, 52, 61, 62, 82 all terminate at the Lido.

Northern islands

The DM line (Diretto Murano) departs every half hour from Tronchetto, Piazzale Roma and Ferrovia for Murano. Between 10.15am and 4.55pm Line 5 departs from San Zaccaria for Murano every 20 minutes (with a break between 12.15 and 1.15pm); the journey takes just under half an hour. Line 51 leaves every 20 minutes from San Zaccaria passing via the Lido and takes much longer.

All other services to islands in the northern lagoon depart from Fondamente Nove.The LN (Laguna Nord) Line leaves about every 30 minutes from Fondamente Nove for Faro (Murano), Mazzorbo, Torcello, Burano, Treporti and Punta Sabbioni. Certain boats call at Torcello after Burano; others skip Torcello altogether; check the timetable or call 800 845 065 for information. Line

13 leaves hourly from Fondamente Nove to Faro (Murano), Vignole, Lazzaretto Nuovo, Capannone (Sant'Erasmo), Chiesa (Sant'Erasmo) and Vela (Sant'Erasmo). Some boats continue for Treporti. Lines 41 and 42 from Fondamente Nove stop at the island of San Michele (cimitero) before continuing to Murano.

TICKETS

Individual and visitors' fixed-period vaporetto tickets can be purchased at most vaporetto stops, at *tabacchi* and at ACTV-VeLa offices (*see p278*). They can also be bought on board at a slightly higher price. Tickets must be stamped in the yellow machines at the entrance to the jetty before boarding a vaporetto. *See also p277* **Cutting costs**.

Traghetti

The best way to cross the Grand Canal when you're far

Directory

from a bridge is to hop on a *traghetto*. These large, unadorned *gondole* are rowed back and forth at fixed points along the canal. At 40¢ (though prices were expected to rise in 2005), this is the cheapest gondola ride in the city; Venetians make the three-minute hop standing up.

Traghetti ply between the following points:

San Marcuola-Fontego dei Turchi: *June-Sept* 9am-12.30am Mon-Sat. *Oct-May* 7.45am-1pm Mon-Sat. **Map** 309 B1.
Santa Sofia-Pescheria: 7.30am-7.30pm Mon-Sat; 8.30am-6pm Sun. **Map** p309 C2.
Riva del Carbon-riva del Vin: 8am-2pm Mon-Sat. **Map** p309 D2.
Ca' Garzoni-SanTomà: 7.30am-7.45pm Mon-Sat; 8am-7.15pm Sun. **Map** p309 D2.
San Samuele-Ca' Rezzonico: 7.30am-1.30pm Mon-Sat. **Map** p311 B1.
Santa Maria del Giglio-Santa Maria della Salute: 9am-6pm daily. **Map** p311 B2.
San Marco-Dogana: 9am-2pm daily. **Map** p311 B3.

Water taxis

Venetian water taxis are jaw-droppingly expensive: expect to pay €85 from the airport directly to San Marco and only slightly less from San Marco to the railway station or piazzale Roma. A quick cruise along the Grand Canal will set you back upwards of €60-€70. Between the hours of 10pm and 7am there is a surcharge of €10.

Beware of unlicensed taxis, which charge even more than authorised ones. The latter have a black registration number on a yellow background.

Cooperativa San Marco
Information 041 240 6711/switchboard 041 522 2303/www.motoscafivenezia.it. **Open** 24hrs daily. **No credit cards**.

Gondole
See above **Gondole**.

Gondole

What can you say about the Venetian gondola? They're over-hyped, overpriced, hopelessly kitsch... and hopelessly romantic. Even the hardest-hearted cynics may find themselves melting at the unique and unforgettable experience.

Official gondola stops can be found at the following locations:
Fondamenta Bacino Orseolo (map p311 B3)
In front of the Hotel Danieli on the riva degli Schiavoni (map p312 B2)
By the Vallaresso vaporetto stop (map p311 B3)
By the railway station (map p308 C2)
By the piazzale Roma bus terminus (map p308 C2)
By the Santa Maria del Giglio vaporetto stop **(map** p311 B2)
At the jetty at the end of the piazzetta San Marco (map p3312 B1).
At campo Santa Sofia (map p309 C2) near the Ca' d'Oro vaporetto stop
By the San Tomà vaporetto stop (map p308 D3)
By the Hotel Bauer in campo San Moisè (map p311 B3)
On the riva del Carbon at the southern end of the Rialto bridge (map p309 D2).

Fares are set by the Istituzione per la Conservazione della gondola e tutela del gondoliere (Gondola Board; 041 528 5075/www.gondolavenezia.it); in the event that a gondolier tries to overcharge you – and it does happen: be prepared to stick to your guns – complain to the Ente. Prices below are for the hire of the gondola, regardless of the number of passengers (up to six). Having your own personal crooner will push the fare up.

8am-8pm: €73 for 50mins; €37 for each additional 25mins.
8pm-8am: €91 for 50mins; €47 for each additional 25mins.

By bus

Orange ACTV buses serve both Mestre and Marghera on the mainland, as well as the Lido, Pellestrina and Chioggia. Services for the mainland depart from piazzale Roma (map p308 C2).

From midnight until 5am, buses N1 (every 30 minutes) and N2 (every hour) depart from Mestre for piazzale Roma and vice versa. There are also regular Lido night buses (departing at least hourly) to Malamocco, Alberoni and Pellestrina.

TICKETS
Bus tickets, costing €1 (also available in blocks of 10 tickets for €9), are valid for 60 minutes, during which you may use several buses, though you can't make a return journey on the same ticket. They can be purchased from ACTV ticket booths or from *tabacchi* (*see p291*) anywhere in the city. They should be bought before boarding the bus and stamped on board.

By car

For car parks, *see p276*.

Avis
Santa Croce 496G, piazzale Roma (041 523 7377/www. avisautonoleggio.it). **Open** *Apr-Oct* 8am-6pm Mon-Fri; 8am-12.30pm Sat,

Sun. *Nov-Mar* 8.30am-12.30pm,
2.30-6pm Mon-Fri; 8am-12.30pm Sat,
Sun. **Credit** AmEx, DC, MC, V.
Map p308 C2.
Other locations: Arrivals hall,
Marco Polo Airport (041 541 5030).

Europcar
*Santa Croce 496H, piazzale Roma
(041 523 8616/www.europcar.it).*
Open *Apr-Oct* 8.30am-1pm, 2-
6.30pm Mon-Fri; 8.30am-12.30pm
Sat, Sun. *Nov-Mar* 8.30am-12.30pm,
2.30-6pm Mon-Fri; 8.30am-noon Sat.
Credit AmEx, DC, MC, V.
Map p308 C2.
Other locations: Arrivals hall,
Marco Polo Airport (041 541 5654).

Hertz
*Santa Croce 496F, piazzale Roma
(041 528 4091).* **Open** *Apr-Oct* 8am-
6pm Mon-Fri; 8am-1pm Sat, Sun.
Nov-Mar 8am-12.30pm, 3-5.30pm
Mon-Fri; 8am-1pm Sat. **Credit**
AmEx, DC, MC, V. **Map** p308 C2.
Other locations: Arrivals hall,
Marco Polo Airport (041 541 6075).

Maggiore National
*Mestre railway station (041 935
300/www.maggiore.it).* **Open** 8am-
1pm, 2.30-7pm Mon-Fri; 8am-1pm
Sat. **Credit** AmEx, DC, MC, V.
Other locations: Arrivals hall,
Marco Polo Airport (041 541 5040).

Mattiazzo
*Santa Croce 496E, piazzale Roma
(041 522 0884/www.mattiazzo.it).*
Open 8am-8pm daily. **Credit**
AmEx, DC, MC, V. **Map** p308 C2
Chauffeur-driven limousine hire.

By train

Santa Lucia (map p308 C2)
is Venice's main station. Most
long-distance trains stop here,

bringing travellers right into
the historic city. Some, though,
only go as far as Mestre on the
mainland. Local trains leave
Mestre for Santa Lucia every
ten minutes or less.

TICKETS AND INFORMATION
The information office in
the main hall of Santa Lucia
railway station is open 7am-
9pm daily. Train tickets can
be purchased from windows
(open 6am-9pm daily, all major
credit cards are accepted),
from cash and credit card
vending machines in the
station, or from travel agents
around the city displaying
the Trenitalia logo.

The Club Eurostar office
(open 7.30am-8.30pm Mon-Fri,
9am-1pm, 2-4.30pm Sat, Sun,
041 785 547), located in a glass
hut near platform 2, dispenses
information about high-speed
Eurostar trains (not to be
confused with the British
cross-channel service of the
same name).

The national rail
information and booking
number is 89 20 21, or 199
166 177 from mobile phones
(both services operate 7am-
9pm daily). From a land line,
press 1 after the recorded
message, then say '*altro*' to
be connected to an operator
(who may or may not speak
English).

The user-friendly website
www.trenitalia.com gives
complete information on
schedules, in English as
well as Italian. Tickets can
be booked through the website
with a credit card and picked
up from automated dispensers
in the station; for a surcharge
of €3.35, you can have tickets
delivered to your home (takes
4-6 days, only in Italy). Some
Eurostar routes are ticketless;
take your email booking
printout with you and show
it to inspectors on board.

Note that the website has
details of Trenitalia's special
offers and of discount cards
for the under-26s (*Carta verde*)
and over-60s (*Carta argento*).

Supplements are charged
for high-speed trains: ES
(Eurostar), IC (Intercity) or EC
(Eurocity, the same as Intercity
except that it goes across a
national border). Seat bookings
are obligatory (and included in
the ticket price) on ES trains;
tickets can be purchased until
departure time (but may sell
out before). Reserving a seat
on IC and internal EC routes
costs €3 and is well worth it
to avoid standing in a packed
corridor at peak travel times,
especially on Friday and
Sunday evenings. If your ES
or IC train arrives more than
30 minutes late and you have
a seat booking, up to 50% of
the cost of your ticket will be
reimbursed, either at booths
marked '*rimborsi*' or at
information offices at your
destination; it's a long process.

Remember that **you must
stamp your ticket** – and
any supplement – in the yellow
machines at the head of each
platform before boarding the
train. Failure to do so can
result in a fine, though looking
foreign, confused and contrite
usually gets you off the hook.
If you are running for your
train and forget to stamp your
ticket, locate the inspector as
soon as possible after boarding
and s/he will waive the fine.

Vaporetti

Though even the locals tend to lump them together, not all
Venetian passenger ferries are, strictly speaking, *vaporetti*.
Disabled travellers, in particular, should learn to spot the
different boats as wheelchairs can be accommodated on
vaporetti and *motonavi* but not on *motoscafi*.
Vaporetto a larger, slower, more rounded boat with
more room for luggage and much sought-after outside
seats at the front.
Motoscafo a sleeker, smaller and faster boat with
outside seats only at the back.
Motonave a charming double-decker steamer that crosses
the lagoon regally to Lido and Torcello.

Resources A-Z

Accommodation

It's best not to come to Venice without a hotel reservation. But if your spontaneous romantic weekend getaway so demands, the **Associazione Veneziana Albergatori** (Venice Hoteliers' Association, (041 522 8004 or 800 843 006 in Italy) can make on-the-spot reservations. Booths can be found at locations listed below:
Santa Lucia train station (041 715 288).
Arrivals hall, Marco Polo airport (041 541 5133).
Autorimessa Comunale (*see p276*; 041 522 8640).

Addresses

Postal addresses in Venice consist of the name of the *sestiere* (*see p68*) plus the house number. With only this information, you will never reach your destination.

For convenience, we have also given the name of the *calle* (street) or *campo* (square) etc each place is located. But finding your way around remains a challenge, especially as matters are sometimes complicated by there being an official Italian and several unofficial Venetian dialect names in use for the same location. When asking for directions, make sure you ascertain the nearest vaporetto stop, church, large square or other easily identifiable landmark.

Age restrictions

You must be 16 to buy cigarettes and alcohol legally. Alcohol can be consumed in bars from the age of 16. Anyone aged 18 or over can ride a 50cc moped or scooter; so can 14-18 year olds if they have a special licence. You must be over 18 to drive and over 21 to hire a car.

Business

If you are planning to do business in Venice, a call to your embassy's commercial sector in Rome (*see p283*) is always a good idea.

Conferences

Venice has many options for business conferences and congresses. Palladian villas and other historic landmarks in the surrounding areas also make great venues for all sorts of events. For information on trade fairs in Venice, contact **Venezia Fiere** (San Polo 2120, campo San Polo, 041 714 066/fax 041 713 151/ www.veneziafiere.it).

Most of the organisers listed below are able to book transportation and hotels as well as the usual facilities.

Codess Settore Cultura
San Polo 2120, campo San Polo (041 710 200/fax 041 717 771/ www.codesscultura.it). **Map** p309 D1.

Endar
Castello 4966, fondamenta de l'Osmarin (041 523 8440/fax 041 528 6846/www.endar.it). **Map** p312 B2.

Nexa
San Marco 3870, corte dell'Albero (041 521 0255/fax 041 528 5041/ www.nexaweb.it). **Map** p309 D1.

Studio Systema
San Polo 699, calle del Paradiso (041 520 1959/fax 041 520 1960). **Map** p309 D1.

Venezia Congressi
Dorsoduro 1056, calle Gambara (041 522 8400/fax 041 523 8995/www.veneziacongressi.com). **Map** p311 B1.

Couriers

Local
Bartolini *041 531 8944/fax 041 531 8943/www.bartolini.it*
Executive *041 999 506/800 331 393/www.executivegroup.com*
Pony Express *041 532 1077/www.pony.it*

National and international
DHL *199 199 345/www.dhl.it*
Federal Express *(toll free) 800 123 800/www.fedex.com/it*
Mail Boxes Etc *041 275 9534/www.mbe.it*
UPS *(toll free) 800 877 877*

Interpreters

Most of the conference organisers listed above will also provide interpreters.

Travel advice

For up-to-date information on travel to a specific country – including the latest news on safety and security, health issues, local laws and customs – contact your home country government's department of foreign affairs. Most have websites packed with useful advice for would-be travellers.

Australia
www.dfat.gov.au/travel

Canada
www.voyage.gc.ca

New Zealand
www.mft.govt.nz/travel

Republic of Ireland
www.irlgov.ie/iveagh

UK
www.fco.gov.uk/travel

USA
www.state.gov/travel

Directory

Lexicon Translations
Via Caneve 77, Mestre (041 534 8005/www.lexitrad.it).

TER Centro Traduzioni
Cannaregio 1076C, ramo San Zuane (041 717 923/www.ter-traduzioni.com). Map p308 C3.

Customs

If you arrive from an EU country you are not required to declare goods imported into or exported from Italy if they are for personal use.

For people arriving from non-EU countries the following limits apply: 200 cigarettes or 100 cigarillos or 50 cigars or 250 grams of tobacco; one litre of spirits or two litres of wine; one bottle of perfume (50 grams/1.76 oz), 250 millilitres of eau de toilette or various merchandise not exceeding €175. Anything above these limits is subject to taxation at the port of entry. There are no restrictions on cameras, watches or electrical goods. For more information call customs (*dogana*) on 041 269 9311.

Drugs

As this guide went to press, Italy's drug laws were under review.

Current laws state that anyone caught in possession of drugs of any kind must be taken before a magistrate. If you can convince him or her that the tiny quantity you were carrying was for personal use then you will be let off with a fine or possibly ordered to leave the country. Habitual offenders will be offered rehab. Holders of Italian driving licences may have them temporarily suspended. Proposals for new legislation define the difference between *leggere* (light) and *pesanti* (heavy) drugs, with different punishments depending on the circumstances of each case.

Couriering or dealing can land you in prison for up to 20 years. If you are a foreigner you will be made to serve your prison sentence and then be expelled from the country.

It is an offence to buy drugs or even to give them away. Sniffer dogs are a fixture at most ports of entry into Italy. Customs police will take a dim view of visitors entering with even the tiniest quantities of narcotics, and are likely to allow them to stay no longer than it takes a magistrate to expel them from the country.

Electricity

Italy's electricity system runs on 220/230v. To use British or US appliances, you will need two-pin adaptor plugs: these are best bought before leaving home, as they tend to be expensive in Italy and are not always easy to find. If you do need to buy one here, try any electrical retailer (look for *casalinghi* or *elettrodomestici* in the yellow pages).

Embassies & consulates

There are a handful of diplomatic missions in Venice. For most information, and emergencies, you will probably have to contact offices in Rome or Milan.

British Consulate
Piazza Donatori di Sangue 2, Mestre (041 505 5990). Bus 7 from Piazzale Roma. **Open** 10am-1pm Mon-Fri.
The British consulate has moved recently to the mainland. Outside of these hours refer to the duty officer at the Milan consulate on 335 810 6857.

South African Consulate
Santa Croce 466G, piazzale Roma (041 524 1599). Vaporetto Piazzale Roma. **Open** 9.30am-12.30pm Mon-Fri. **Map** p308 C2.
In emergencies contact the Milan consulate (*see below*).

Embassies in Rome

Australian 06 852 721
British 06 4220 0001
Canadian 06 445 981
Irish 06 697 9121
New Zealand 06 441 7171
South African 06 852 541
US 06 46 741

Consulates in Milan

Australian 02 777 041
British 02 723 001
Irish 02 5518 7569
Canadian 02 675 81.
New Zealand 02 4801 2544
South Africa 02 885 8581
US 02 290 351

Emergencies

See also p290 **Safety & security** *and p284* **Insurance**.

Thefts or losses should be reported immediately at the nearest police station (either the Polizia di Stato or the nominally military Carabinieri).

Report the loss of your passport to the nearest consulate or embassy (*see above*). Report the loss of a credit card or travellers' cheques to your credit-card company (*see p287*).

National emergency numbers
Ambulance 118
Carabinieri 112
Car breakdowns (Automobile Club d'Italia) 803 116
CISS road information 1518
Coastguard 1530
Fire brigade 115
Guardia Forestale 1515
Infant emergency 114
Polizia di Stato 113

Local emergency numbers
Ambulance 041 523 0000.
Carabinieri *Castello 4693A, campo San Zaccaria (041 274 111). Vaporetto San Zaccaria.* **Map** p312 B2.
Coastguard (Capitaneria di Porto) 041 520 5600 / 041 520 3044.
Fire brigade 041 257 4700.
Polizia di Stato *Santa Croce 500, piazzale Roma (041 271 5511/ www.poliziadistato.it). Vaporetto Piazzale Roma.* **Map** p308 C2.

Domestic emergencies

To report a malfunction in any of the main public services, call the following:
Electricity (ENEL) 800 900 800
Gas (Italgas) 800 900 777
Telephone (Telecom Italia) 187
Water (Vesta) 041 729 1111/www.vestaspa.net

Health & hospitals

The *pronto soccorso* (casualty department) of all public hospitals provides free emergency treatment for travellers, but it is also worth taking out private health insurance (*see p284*).

If you are an EU citizen and need minor treatment, take your E111 form with you to any doctor for a free consultation. Drugs they prescribe can be bought at chemists at prices set by the health ministry.

Tests or specialist examinations carried out in the public system (*Sistema sanità nazionale*, SSN), will be charged at fixed rates (*il ticket*) and a receipt issued.

For urgent medical advice from local health authority doctors during the night call 041 529 4060 in Venice, 041 526 7743 on the Lido and 041 534 4411 in Mestre (8pm-8am Mon-Fri; 10am Sat-8am Mon).

Contraception

Condoms are on sale near the checkout in supermarkets, or over the counter at chemists. The contraceptive pill is freely available on prescription at any pharmacy.

Dentists

Dental treatment in Italy is expensive; your insurance may not cover it. For urgent dental treatment at weekends, go to the **Ambulatorio Odontostomatologico** at the Ospedale Civile (*see below*).

Hospitals

The public relations department of Venice's **Ospedale Civile** (041 529 4588) provides general information on being hospitalised in Venice.

The hospitals listed below all have 24-hour *pronto soccorso* (casualty) facilities. For an ambulance boat, call 041 523 0000.

Ospedale Civile

Castello 6777, campo Santi Giovanni e Paolo (041 529 4111/casualty 041 529 4516/668). Vaporetto Ospedale. **Map** p312 A2.
Housed in the 15th-century Scuola di San Marco, Venice's main hospital has helpful staff and doctors who are quite likely to speak English.

Ospedale al Mare

Lungomare D'Annunzio 1, Lido (041 529 4111/casualty 041 529 5234). Vaporetto Lido. **Map** p307.
Smaller than the Ospedale Civile, and offering a smaller range of services, but with fine sea views.

Ospedale Umberto I

Via Circonvallazione 50, Mestre (041 260 7111).
A modern hospital on the mainland.

Ospedale di Padova

Via Giustiniani 2, Padova (049 821 1111).

Ospedale di Verona

Piazzale Stefani 1, Verona (045 807 1111).

Pharmacies

Pharmacies (*farmacie*), identified by a red or green cross above the door, are run by qualified chemists who will dispense informal advice on, and assistance for, minor ailments, as well as filling doctors' prescriptions. Over-the-counter drugs such as aspirin are more expensive in Italy than in the UK or US.

Most chemists are open 9am-12.30pm, 3.45-7.30pm Mon-Fri and 9am-12.45pm Sat. A small number remain open on Saturday afternoon, Sunday and at night on a duty rota system, details of which are posted outside every pharmacy and published in the local press (*see p286*).

Most pharmacies carry homeopathic medicines. All will check your blood pressure. If you require regular medication, bring adequate supplies of your drugs with you. Ask your GP for the generic rather than the brand name of your medicine: it may only be available in Italy under a different name.

Insurance

EU citizens are entitled to reciprocal medical care in Italy provided they leave their own country with an E111 form, available from local health authorities. If used for anything but emergencies (which are treated free anyway in casualty departments, *see above*), it will entail dealing with the intricacies of the Italian state health system. For short-term visits, it may be advisable to take out private health insurance.

Non-EU citizens should review their private health insurance plans to see if they cover expenses incurred while travelling. If not, travel insurance should be obtained before setting out from home. If you are a student, you may want to check with your student travel organisation: some offer basic health cover with the purchase of their IDs.

If you rent a car, motorcycle or moped while in Italy, make sure you pay the extra charge for full insurance cover.

Internet

A number of Italian service providers offer free internet access, including **Caltanet** (www.caltanet.it), **Libero** (www.libero.it), **Tiscali** (www.tiscalinet.it), **Kataweb** (www.kataweb.com) and **Fastweb** (www.fastweb.it).

Directory

Cyber-cafés have mushroomed but are not cheap; if you plan to check email from a hotel or private house, check that the phone jack on the end of the cable works in an Italian phone socket; US jacks (RJ11) are fine, British ones not. Buy suitable adaptors before leaving home. Some places still have old-fashioned three-pin phone sockets; adaptors for these can be found in supermarkets, and phone and electrical shops.

Net House
San Marco 2958, campo Santo Stefano (041 520 8128/ www.nethousecafes.com). Vaporetto Accademia or San Samuele. **Open** 9am-midnight daily. **Rates** *non-*

members €3 for 20mins. *Members* €1 for 20mins; €3 per hour (membership €16). *Students* €2 for 20mins. **Credit** AmEx, MC, V. **Map** p311 B2. Filled with teenage video-game junkies, this place offers student discounts (proper student ID required) and special deals for members. Services include fax, photocopying facilities, web cam, word-processing, scanner, printing, CD burning and computer courses.

Left luggage

Most hotels will look after your luggage even after you have checked out.

Marco Polo airport
Arrivals hall (near Post Office) (041 260 5043). **Open** 5.30am-9pm daily. **Rates** €4.50 per item per day. **No credit cards**.

Piazzale Roma bus terminus
041 523 1107. **Open** 6am-9pm daily. **Rates** €3 per item per day. **No credit cards**. **Map** p308 C2.

Santa Lucia railway station
041 785 531. **Open** 6am-midnight daily. **Rates** €3.50 per item per 5hrs; 30¢ every additional hour. **No credit cards**. **Map** p308 C2.

Legal aid

If you are in need of legal advice, your first stop should always be your consulate or embassy (*see p283*). For diplomatic missions not listed here, look for *Ambasciate* in the phone book.

Disabled travellers

The very things that make Venice unique – narrow streets, hundreds of bridges, no barriers between pavements and canals – make the city an extra-difficult destination for disabled travellers.

Despite this, Venice should not be crossed off the holiday list altogether, as there has been an effort in recent years to provide facilities and make at least some areas of the city viable for disabled travellers.

Information

The Comune di Venezia's **Informahandicap** service (*see below*) is a vital one-stop shop for information.

APT offices (*see p293*) provide maps showing bridges with wheelchair ramps (five in the *sestiere* of San Marco, one on the island of Burano and one on Murano) and accessible public toilets, though the APT will be the first to tell you that these latter don't always work. The map can also be download from the Informahandicap site. Keys for operating the automated ramps are also available at APT offices.

Informahandicap
Ca' Farsetti, San Marco 4136, riva del Carbon (041 274 8144/www.comune. venezia.it/handicap). **Open** 9am-1pm, 3-5pm Thur. **Map** p309 D1.
Centro Culturale Candiani, piazzale Candiani 5, Mestre (041 274 6144).
Open 3-5pm Tue, Thur; 9am-1pm Wed, Fri.

Set up by the city council, this service has an excellent website with travel information for the disabled, though it's in Italian only. English-speaking staff will provide information on accessible hotels, restaurants and museums in Venice and the Veneto. Call the numbers given above or send inquiries to informahandicap@comune.venezia.it

CO.IN
062 326 9231/www.coinsociale.it.
This Rome-based organisation provides nationwide information on the wheelchair-friendliness of hotels, museums and other disabled facilities.

Transport

Public transport is one area where Venice scores higher than many other destinations, as standard *vaporetti* and *motonavi* (but not *motoscafi* – see p281) **Vaporetti**) have a reasonably large, flat deck area and there are no steps or steep inclines on the route between quayside and boat. The vaporetto lines that currently guarantee disabled access (though peak times should be avoided) are 1, 82, 3, 4, 13, T, LN and N. Some of the buses that run between Mestre and Venice also have wheelchair access.

For further information consult the Informahandicap site or call these numbers:
Bus and vaporetti: ACTV 041 24 24.
Trains: Trenitalia 041 785 570.
Planes: Marco Polo Airport 041 260 9260.

Libraries

Most of the libraries below have online catalogues. For in-depth research at national level consult the **Servizio bibliotecario nazionale** website at www.sbn.it.

Archivio di Stato

San Polo 3002, campo dei Frari (041 522 2281/www.archivi. beniculturali.it). Vaporetto San Tomà. **Open** 8.30am-6pm Mon-Thur; 8.30am-2pm Fri, Sat. **Map** p311 A1.
The state archives house all official documents relating to the administration of the Venetian Republic, and a host of other historic manuscripts. Material must be requested between 8.30am and 1pm. ID is required; a letter of presentation is a good idea but not mandatory.

Archivio Storico delle Arti Contemporanee (ASAC)

Vega-Lybra, via delle Industrie 17A, Porto Marghera (041 521 8700/ www.labiennale.org/it/asac).
The archive of the Venice Biennale contemporary art festival (see p207 **La Biennale**) has moved to Marghera and all services are temporarily suspended, though scholars may find they can get in by appointment. More information can be found on their web page.

Biblioteca Centrale Istituto Universitario di Architettura di Venezia

Santa Croce 191, fondamenta Tolentini (041 257 1106/ http://iuavbc.iuav.it). Vaporetto Piazzale Roma. **Open** 9am-midnight Mon-Fri; 2pm-midnight first Mon of the month. **Map** p308 C2.
The library of one of Italy's top architecture faculties has a vast collection of works on the history of architecture, town planning, art, engineering and social sciences. ID is necessary to enter the library; only students of the university can borrow books.

Biblioteca Fondazione Giorgio Cini

Isola di San Giorgio Maggiore (041 271 0255/www.cini.it). Vaporetto San Giorgio. **Open** 9am-4.30pm Mon-Fri. **Map** p312 C2.
Specialises in art history, with sections dedicated to the history of Venice and the Venetian state and society, literature, theatre and music. There's a large archive of microfilms and photographs as well as

individual archive collections of scholar's and historical figures. The library is a reading room only; you'll be asked to deposit a valid document at the entrance.

Biblioteca Fondazione Scientifica Querini Stampalia

Castello 5252, campo Santa Maria Formosa (041 271 1411/ www.querinistampalia.it). Vaporetto Rialto or San Zaccaria. **Open** 10am-midnight Tue-Sat; 10am-7pm Sun. **Map** p309 D3.
The Querini Stampalia library is attached to the museum of the same name (see p93) and has a fine collection of books with an emphasis on Venice and all things Venetian. You will need to fill out an application and present valid ID to access the library.

Biblioteca Generale dell'Università di Ca' Foscari

Dorsoduro 3199, calle Bernardo (041 234 6111/www.biblio.unive.it). Vaporetto Ca' Rezzonico. **Open** 8.30am-7.30pm Mon-Fri; 8.30am-1pm Sat. **Map** p311 B1.
The university library is strong on the humanities and economics. ID is necessary to enter the library; only students of thee university can borrow books.

Biblioteca Museo Correr

San Marco 52, piazza San Marco (041 240 5211/www.comune. venezia.it/museicivici). Vaporetto Vallaresso. **Open** 8.30am-1.30pm Mon, Wed, Fri; 8.30am-5pm Tue, Thur. **Map** p311 B3.
Part of the Museo Correr (see p83), this small library contains prints, manuscripts and books on Venetian history and art history. To access the library you will need to fill out an application form, and show your passport and a letter of presentation from your university or faculty advisor.

Biblioteca Nazionale Marciana

San Marco 7, piazzetta San Marco (041 240 7211/www. marciana.venezia.sbn.it). Vaporetto Vallaresso. **Open** 8.10am-6.45pm Mon-Fri; 8.10am-1.30pm Sat. **Map** p311 B3.
The city's main public library, the Marciana has medieval manuscripts and editions of the classics dating back to the 15th century. The library is, in fact, now housed in the Zecca (see p87); the original Biblioteca Marciana can be visited through the Museo Correr (see p83). ID will get

you access to the reading rooms; proof that you are connected to any Veneto university might get you permission to borrow books.

Lost property

Your mislaid belongings may end up at one of the *uffici oggetti smarriti* listed below. You could also try the police (*see p283* **Emergencies**), or ring VESTA, the city's rubbish collection department, on 041 729 1111.

ACTV

Santa Croce, piazzale Roma (041 272 2179). Vaporetto Piazzale Roma. **Open** 9am-8pm daily. **Map** p308 C2.
For items found on *vaporetti* or buses.

Comune (City Council)

San Marco 4136, riva del Carbon (041 274 8225). Vaporetto Rialto. **Open** 8.30am-12.30pm Mon-Fri; 2.30-4.30 pm Mon, Thur. **Map** p311 D2.

FS/Stazione Santa Lucia

Santa Lucia railway station, next to track 14 (041 785 531). Vaporetto Ferrovia. **Open** 6am-midnight daily. **Map** p308 B2.
All items found on trains in the Venice area and in the station itself are brought to this deposit.

Marco Polo Airport

Arrivals Hall (lost bags) (041 260 9222). Bus 5 to Aeroporto. **Open** 9am-8pm daily.
Arrivals Hall (lost objects) (041 260 9260) **Open** 24hrs daily.

Media

National dailies

Sometimes lengthy and with indigestible political stories, Italian newspapers can be a frustrating read. On the plus side, papers are delightfully unpretentious and happily blend serious news, leaders by internationally known commentators, and well-written, often surreal, crime and human-interest stories.

Sports coverage in the dailies is extensive and thorough, but if you're not sated there are the mass-circulation sports papers

Directory

Corriere dello Sport, *La Gazzetta dello Sport* and *Tuttosport*.

Corriere della Sera
www.corriere.it
To the centre of centre-left, this solid, serious but often dull Milan-based daily is good on crime and foreign news. Online there is an English section called 'Italian Life' which has international news and Italocentric editorials.

Il Manifesto
www.ilmanifesto.it.
Although the Cold War may be a distant memory, there is still some corner of central Rome where hearts beat Red.

La Repubblica
www.repubblica.it.
The centre-ish, left-ish *La Repubblica* is good on the Mafia and the Vatican, and comes up with the occasional scoop on its business pages.

Il Sole-24 Ore
www.ilsole24ore.com
This business, finance and economics daily has a great arts supplement on Sunday.

Venice dailies

Il Gazzettino
www.gazzettino.it.
Il Gazzettino is one of Italy's most successful local papers. It provides national and international news on the front pages and local news inside, with different editions for towns around the Veneto region.

La Nuova Venezia
www.nuovavenezia.it.
This popular, small-circulation daily – known to locals as *La Nuova* – contains lively editorials, crime stories, Venetian news and event listings.

Foreign press

The *Financial Times*, *Wall Street Journal*, *USA Today*, *International Herald Tribune* and most British and European dailies can be found on the day of issue at news stands all around town – especially those at the station, within striking distance of St Mark's and the Rialto, and at the large *edicola* at the Accademia vaporetto stop. US dailies sometimes take a day or two to appear.

Magazines

News weeklies *Panorama* (pro-Berlusconi) and *L'Espresso* (anti-Berlusconi) provide a general round-up of the week's events, while *Sette* and *Venerdì* – respectively the colour supplements of *Corriere della Sera* (Thursday) and *La Repubblica* (Friday) – have nice photos, though the text often leaves much to be desired.

For tabloid-style scandal, try *Gente* and *Oggi* with their weird mix of sex, glamour and religion, or the execrable scandal sheets *Eva 3000*, *Novella 2000* and *Cronaca Vera*.

Internazionale (www.internazionale.it) provides an excellent digest of interesting bits and pieces gleaned from the world's press the previous week. *Diario della Settimana* (www.diario.it) is informed and urbane with a flair for investigative journalism.

But the biggest-selling magazine of them all is *Famiglia Cristiana* – available from news-stands or in most churches – which alternates Vatican line toeing with Vatican baiting, depending on the state of relations between the Holy See and the idiosyncratic Paoline monks who produce it.

Listings & classified ads

Aladino
Issued every Thursday, it has classified ads for everything from flats for rent to gondole for sale.

Boom
A small-ads paper thrust free through every letterbox each week. The place to look for flats, jobs and lonely hearts.

Gente Veneta
This weekly broadsheet, produced by the local branch of the Catholic church, blends cultural and religious listings with reports on Venetian social problems.

Venezia News
This info-packed bilingual magazine, which comes out on the first of each month, includes music, film, theatre, art and sports listings, plus interviews and features.

Television

Italy has six major networks (three are owned by state broadcaster RAI, three belong to Silvio Berlusconi's Mediaset group). Dancing girls, variety shows, music and beauty competitions predominate. The standard of TV news and current affairs programmes varies; most, however, offer wide-ranging international news coverage.

Local radio
Radio Venezia (FM 92.4)
Pop music, pop music, pop music.
Radio Capital (FM 98.5)
Heavy on advertising, but generous with information on events and news in the city. In between you'll hear 1980s and '90s classics and a sprinkling of current hits.
Radio Padova (FM 103.9 & 88.4)
Popular chart music and concert information for the Veneto area.

Money

Italy's currency is the euro (€). There are euro banknotes of €5, €10, €20, €100, €200 and €500, and coins worth €1 and €2 as well as 1¢ (*centesimo*), 2¢, 5¢, 10¢, 20¢ and 50¢. Notes and coins from any euro-zone country are valid.

ATMs

Most banks have cash dispensers and the vast majority of these accept cards with the Maestro, Cirrus and Visa Electron symbols. Most cashpoint machines will dispense cash to a daily limit of €250.

Banking hours

Most banks are open 8.20am-1.20pm and 2.45-3.45pm Mon-Fri. All banks are closed on

Directory

public holidays and work reduced hours the day before a holiday, usually closing at 11am. Banks are listed under *Banche ed istituti di credito* in the Yellow Pages.

Foreign exchange

Banks usually offer better exchange rates than bureaux de change (*cambio*). Commission rates in banks vary considerably. Don't be fooled by 'no commission' signs in exchange offices: these usually mean that the exchange rate is dire.

It's a good idea to take your passport with you, especially if you want to change travellers' cheques or draw money on your credit card.

American Express

San Marco 1471, salizada San Moisè (041 520 0844/ travel.tso. venice@aexp.com). Vaporetto Vallaresso. **Open** 9am-5.30pm Mon-Fri. **Map** p307 B4.
Exchange with no commission, travellers' cheque refund, card replacements, 24-hour money transfers, plus extra services such as hotel reservations, car rentals, train and plane tickets and tour organisation. There is also an ATM.

Travelex

San Marco 5126, riva del Ferro (041 528 7358/www.travelex.it). Vaporetto Rialto. **Open** *May-Oct* 9am-7pm Mon-Fri; 9am-5.50pm Sat; 9.30am-4.50pm Sun. *Nov-Mar* 9am-6pm Mon-Fri; 9.30am-4.30pm Sat, Sun. **Credit** MC, V. **Map** p305 C3.
Cash and travellers' cheques exchanged with no commission. Mastercard and Visa cardholders can also withdraw cash.
Other locations: Service San Marco 142, piazza San Marco (041 277 5057); Marco Polo Airport, arrivals (041 541 6833).

Credit cards

Most hotels of two stars and over will take most major credit cards.Report lost credit or charge cards to the appropriate emergency number listed below. All the lines are toll-free, operate 24 hours a day and have English-speaking operators.

American Express 800 864 046.
American Express (cheques) 800 872 000.
Diners' Club 800 864 064.
Mastercard 800 870 866.
Visa 800 819 014.

Postal services

Posta Centrale (Central Post Office)

San Marco 5554, salizada del Fontego dei Tedeschi (041 271 7208). Vaporetto Rialto. **Open** 8.30am-6.30pm Mon-Sat. **Map** p309 C2.
The main post office is housed in the 16th-century Fontego dei Tedeschi, once a base for German merchants in the city and formerly frescoed by Giorgione. You can purchase stamps, and send packages or MoneyGrams, faxes or telegrams. The office also provides information for stamp collectors and a *fermo posta* (poste restante) service.
Each district has its own sub-post office, open 8.30am-2pm Mon-Fri, 8.30am-1pm Sat. There is also a branch at Marco Polo Airport open 8.30am-2pm Mon-Fri, 8.30am-1pm Sat (041 541 5900).

Stamps & charges

Italy's postal service (www.poste.it) is generally reliable and you can be more or less sure that your letters will arrive in reasonable time. Postage supplies – such as large mailing boxes and packing tape – are now available at most post offices.

Italy's equivalent to first-class post, *posta prioritaria*, works very well: it promises to get letters to their destination within 24 hours in Italy, three days for EU countries and four or five for the rest of the world; more often than not, it delivers. A letter of 20g or less in Italy is 60¢, within the EU 62¢, and to the rest of the world 80¢ by *posta prioritaria*; prioritaria stamps can be bought at post offices and *tabacchi* (*see p291*) and posted in any letter box.

A 20g *posta ordinaria* letter costs 45¢ to Italy or the EU, 80¢ to North America, Africa & Asia and the rest of the world. These stamps, too,

are sold at post offices and *tabacchi* only.

The Postacelere service (up to 3kg €8) promises (though doesn't always achieve) 24-hour delivery to major cities in Italy. Paccocelere (for packages) has one- three- and five-day services within Italy. Paccocelere Internazionale, Quick Pack Europe and EMS Corriere Espresso Internazionale move packages internationally, charging according to destination.

Letterboxes are red and distributed throughout the city. They have two slots: *Per la città* (for Venezia, Mestre and Marghera), and *Tutte le altre destinazioni* (for all other destinations).

Telegrams

The main post office provides a telegram service during business hours; it's not cheap and not always quick, however. Telegrams to any destination can be sent and dictated over the phone by dialling 186 from a private phone or 49186 from a mobile phone, which will be billed automatically for the service. Or you can speed things up by sending a telegram via the post office's website (www.poste.it; in English).

Faxes

The main post office will send faxes during regular business hours. The service is costly, however. Most photocopy and *tabacchi* shops offer fax services too; ask for prices before you send your fax, as they vary significantly.

Religion

Mass times vary from church to church and are posted by front doors: services are usually held between 9am and 11am and again at 6.30pm on Sundays; most churches have

Saturday Mass at 6pm. *Un Ospite di Venezia*, free in hotels, has Mass times. The church of San Zulian (041 523 5383; map p307 A4) has Mass in English from May to September at 9.30am on Sunday. Listed below are the non-Catholic denominations in the city:

Anglican

St George's, Dorsoduro 870, campo San Vio (041 520 0571). Vaporetto Accademia. **Services** *Sung Mass* 10.30am Sun. **Map** p311 C2.

Greek Orthodox

San Giorgio dei Greci, Castello 3419, fondamenta dei Greci (041 522 5446). Vaporetto San Zaccaria. **Services** 9.30am, 10.30am Sun. *Vespers* 6pm Sat. **Map** p312 B2.

Jewish

Cannaregio 2899, campo del Ghetto Nuovo (041 715 012/www. jewishvenice.org). Vaporetto San Marcuola. **Services** after sunset Fri; 9.30am Sat. **Map** p308 B3. Shabbat meals are held at the restaurant Gam Gam and are free for tourists. You may be asked to show ID.

Lutheran

Cannaregio 4448, campo Santi Apostoli (041 524 2040). Vaporetto Ca' D'Oro. **Services** 5pm on 2nd & 4th Sat of mth. **Map** p309 C2.

Methodist (Valdese)

Castello 5170, fondamenta Cavagnis (041 522 7549/www. chiesavaldese.org). Vaporetto Rialto or San Zaccaria. **Service** 11am Sun. **Map** p312 B3.

Relocation

Accommodation

Student-type shares are abundant in Venice and can be found on little paper announcements around the city, through the notice boards at Ca' Foscari university (*see p291*) or through local listings magazines (*see p287*).

For short-term rentals expect to pay upwards of €600 a week for a very basic apartment in Venice. Online you can try www. veniceapartment.com, www.venice-rentals.com or

www.interflats.it. For longer stays, an agency is your best bet; it will take the equivalent of one month's rent as a commission. Landlords will demand at least one month's (and sometimes as much as three months') rent as a deposit.

Giaretta

San Marco 514, campo della Guerra (041 528 6191/ www.giaretta.com). Vaporetto Rialto. **Open** 9am-1pm, 2-7pm Mon-Fri. **Map** p309 D2. Well organised and pleasant, they offer pricey, long-term rentals and sales.

Immobil Veneta

San Polo 3132, campiello San Rocco (041 524 0088/www.immobil venetasnc.com). Vaporetto San Tomà. **Open** 9am-12pm, 4-7pm Mon-Fri. **Map** p308 D3. A reliable agency with short-term apartment rentals, monthly rentals and apartments for sale.

Bureaucracy

You may need any or all of the following documents if you plan to work or study in Venice. Be prepared for multiple office visits, long, unruly queues and irritable people who have been waiting longer than you.

Permesso di soggiorno (permit to stay)

The crucial document for anyone staying in Italy for more than a short period, the *permesso di soggiorno* can be obtained from the Questura in Marghera. Get there by 7am. Take your passport and a photocopy of every page; three passport photos; proof that you are enrolled in a course or that you are in Italy on a scholarship and have health insurance (for students); and a statement from your employer;. Feelancers and students should take a certified bank or tax statement showing you have means of support; everyone needs to take their *contratto di locazione* (apartment contract) or a *lettera di ospitalità* (hospitality letter); and a €10.33 *marca da bollo* (official stamp) available from *tabacchi* (*see p291*) or the post office. EU citizens are given their *permesso*, usually valid for ten years, directly; as this guide went to press, the waiting period for renewal for non-EU citizens was 12 months.

Questura *via Nicolodi 22, Marghera (ufficio stranieri 041 271 5802/ 041 271 5761/switchboard 041 271 5511). Bus 6/ from piazzale Roma.* **Open** 8.30-9.30am Tue, Thur, Fri; 8.30-9.30am, 2.30-3.30pm Wed.

Carta d'Identità (identity card)

This official Italian ID card is not strictly necessary for foreigners, who can use their own national IDs and passports as a means of identification. It can be obtained from the Ufficio anagrafe of the town hall. Take ID, your *permesso di soggiorno* and three passport photographs.

Ufficio anagrafe *San Marco 4061, calle del Carbon (041 274 8221). Vaporetto Rialto.* **Open** 8.45am-1pm Mon-Sat. **Map** p309 D2.

Codice fiscale & partito IVA (tax code & VAT number)

A *codice fiscale* is required to work legally in Italy, or to open your own business. You will need one to open a bank account or get a phone line, and for treatment under the Italian national health service. Take your passport or equivalent.

The same office also issues the *partito IVA* (VAT number). Freelancers or company owners may need a VAT number for invoicing. There is a form to be filled in, but no charge.

Agenzia delle Entrate *ufficio locale Venezia 1 San Marco 3538, campo Sant'Angelo (041 271 8111). Vaporetto Sant'Angelo.* **Open** 8.45am-12.45pm Mon, Wed, Fri; 8.45am-12.45pm, 2.45-4.45pm Tue, Thur. **Map** p309 D1.

Certificato di residenza (residence permit)

Necessary if you want to buy a car or import your belongings without paying customs duties, the *certificato di residenza* can cause diplomatic stand-offs with your landlord: to obtain it, the tax on rubbish collection (*nettezza urbana*) must have been paid for the property you reside in – which means that either you have to volunteer to pay it (and landlords renting out property but not paying taxes on the income run the risk of being discovered), or you have to persuade the owner to. In either case, you'll need to present your passport and *permesso di soggiorno*.

Ufficio anagrafe *San Marco 4142, calle Loredan (041 274 8221). Vaporetto Rialto.* **Open** 8.45am-1pm Mon-Sat. **Map** p309 D2.

Directory

Permesso di lavoro (work permit)

Non-EU citizens must have a work permit to be legally employed in Italy. Employers will usually arrange this; if not, pick up an application form at the address given below, get it signed by your employer and return it with a photocopy of your *permesso di soggiorno*.
Ufficio Direzione Provinciale del lavoro di Venezia *via Ca' Marcello 8/9, Mestre (041 531 8880/fax 041 531 8866). Train to Mestre or ACTV bus 4.* **Open** 9am-noon Mon, Wed, Fri; 9am-noon, 3-5pm Tue, Thur.

Work

Falling in love with Venice is easy; living in the city (unless you have independent means of support) is difficult. Openings for casual employment in Venice are few, though language schools (*Scuole di lingua* in the Yellow Pages) are sometimes on the lookout for native English speakers, especially with TEFL experience. Women *di bella apparenza* (as the advertisements put it) – and with some knowledge of Italian – might try conference organisers (*see p282*), or the smart boutiques in the Frezzerie area around San Marco, which sometimes advertise for *commesse* (sales assistants). The more exclusive hotels may have openings for experienced babysitters.

The main Ca' Foscari university building at Dorsoduro 3246, calle Foscari (vaporetto San Tomà) often has employment opportunities posted on the notice boards. Alternatively, try the following agencies:

Manpower
Via Piave 120, Mestre (041 935 900/fax 041 936 666/ www.manpower.it). Bus 2 from piazzale Roma. **Open** 9am-11am; 2.30-4.30pm Mon-Fri.

Temporary
Via Manin 38A, Mestre (041 979 048/www.temporary.it). Bus 7 from piazzale Roma. **Open** 10.30am-12.30pm, 3-6pm Mon-Fri.

Safety & security

Venice is, on the whole, an exceptionally safe place at any time of day or night, and violent crime is almost unknown. Lone women would be advised to steer clear of dark alleyways late at night, though even there they are more likely to be harassed than attacked (*see p293* **Women**). Bag-snatchers are a rarity, mostly because of the logistical difficulties Venice presents for making quick getaways. However, pickpockets operate in crowded thoroughfares, especially around San Marco and the Rialto, and on public transport, so make sure you leave passports, plane/train tickets and at least one means of getting hold of money in your hotel room or safe.

If you are the victim of theft or serious crime, call one of the emergency numbers listed under Emergencies, *see p283*. The following rules will help avoid unfortunate incidents:

● Don't carry wallets in back pockets, particularly on buses or boats. If you have a bag or camera with a long strap, wear it across your chest and not dangling from one shoulder.
● Keep bags closed, with your hand on them. If you stop at a pavement café or restaurant, do not leave bags or coats on the ground or the back of a chair where you cannot keep an eye on them.
● Avoid attracting unwanted attention by pulling out large wads of cash to pay for things at street stalls or in busy bars. It's a good idea to keep some small bills and change easily accessible.
● Crowds in general offer easy camouflage for pickpockets. Be especially careful when boarding buses or boats, and entering museums.

If you have your bag or wallet snatched, or are otherwise a victim of crime,

go immediately to the nearest police station to report a *scippo* (*see p283* **Emergencies**). A *denuncia* (written statement) of the incident will be made for you.

Give police as much information as possible, including your passport number, holiday address and flight numbers. The *denuncia* will be signed, dated and stamped with an official police seal. It is unlikely that your things will be found, but you will need the *denuncia* for making an insurance claim.

Smoking

Smoking is not permitted in public offices or on public transport and is becoming a rarity in bars and restaurants. For where to buy cigarettes, *see p291* **Tabacchi**.

Study

All lectures and exams – the majority of which are oral in the Italian system – at Venice's two main universities are in Italian, making a thorough knowledge of the language essential if you wish to get the full benefit of studying here.

To find out about entrance requirements and contact numbers, consult the faculty websites at **www.iuav.it** (Istituto Universitario di Architettura di Venezia) or **www.unive.it** (Università degli Studi di Venezia Ca' Foscari).

EU citizens have the same right to study at Italian universities as Italian nationals. You will need to have your school diplomas translated and authenticated at the Italian consulate in your own country before presenting them to the *ufficio studenti stranieri* (foreign students' department) of any university.

Both universities run exchange programmes with foreign institutions and participate in the EU's Erasmus scheme. The **Venice International University** (041 271 9511/www. univiu.org), housed on the island of San Servolo, is a consortium of seven universities, the Cassa di Risparmio Foundation of Venice and the Province of Venice. Students currently registered at one of the Venice International member universities (Duke University, Ca' Foscari, Istituto Universitario di Architettura di Venezia, Universitat Autònoma de Barcelona, Ludwig Maximilians Universität of Munich, Waseda University of Tokyo and Tel Aviv University) are eligible to apply for VIU undergraduate activities. There are also Masters and PhD programmes available.

Less academic but very Venetian, American gondola-maker Thom Price organises courses of one week or longer in basic boat-building at his *squero*. See **www.squero. com** for details.

Language courses

ASCI-Onlus – Associazione Socio-Culturale Internazionale

Corso del Popolo 117, Mestre (041 504 0433/www.ascionlus.com). Bus 4/ to Mestre. **Open** 3.30-8.30pm Mon-Thur. **No credit cards.**
This association offers courses in Italian, French, German, Spanish, Greek, Arabic, Hindi and Chinese. If languages aren't your thing, try computing, tango or belly dancing.

Centro Linguistico Interfacoltà

Palazzo Bonvicini, Santa Croce 2161, ramo dell'Agnello (041 234 9711/www.unive.it/cli/). Vaporetto San Stae. **Open** (office hours) 10am-noon Mon, Wed, Fri; 10am-noon, 3-5pm Tue, Thur.
No credit cards. Map p309 C1.
This school offers good courses in French, English, Italian, Spanish and German with access to audio and video equipment.

Tabacchi

Tabacchi or *tabaccherie* (identified by signs with a white T on a black or blue background) are the only places where you can legally buy tobacco products.

They also sell stamps, telephone cards, individual or season tickets for public transport, lottery tickets and the stationery required when dealing with bureaucracy.

Most of Venice's *tabacchi* pull their shutters down by 7.30pm. If you're gasping for nicotine late in the evening or on Sunday, you'll have to try one of the automatic cigarette vending machines in campo Santa Margherita, piazzale Roma, next to the train station, on strada Nuova near Ponte della Guglie and near Santi Apostoli, fondamenta della Misericordia, Scuola di San Giorgio degli Schiavoni (*see p101*) and via XXII Marzo.

Telephones

Phone numbers

All Italian landline numbers must be dialled *with* their prefixes, even if you are phoning within the local area. Numbers in Venice and its province begin 041; numbers in Padua province begin 049; in Vicenza they begin 0444; in Verona 045.

Phone numbers generally have seven or eight digits after the prefix; some older ones still have six, and some switchboards five. If you try a number and cannot get through, it may have been changed to an eight-digit number. Check the directory (*elenco telefonico*) or ring directory enquiries (12 or 412).

Numbers beginning with 800 are freephone lines. Numbers beginning 840 and 848 are charged at a nominal rate. These numbers can be

called from within Italy only, and some are available only within certain regions.

Cellphone numbers begin with a 3. Until recently they began with 03; you may still find them written with the zero.

Rates

Italy's telephone company (Telecom Italia) is still costly despite tough competition.

The minimum charge for a local call from a private phone is about 6¢ (8¢ from a public phone). Calling a mobile phone from a fixed line is almost triple and phoning abroad remains expensive. You can keep costs down by:
● phoning off-peak (10pm-8am Mon-Sat, all day Sun).
● not using phones in hotels, which usually carry extortionate surcharges.
● using international phone cards, purchasable at *tabacchi* (*see above*). Operators such as Happiness, Planet, Welcome and Europa offer €5 and €10 cards, which can be used from public, cell or landline phones and will cut costs significantly.
● not calling cellphones from landlines and vice versa.

Public phones

There are some public phones in Venice along the tourist routes but many are out of service. Some bars also have payphones. Most public telephones operate only with phone cards (*schede telefoniche*). Some newer models take major credit cards, while the few remaining old-style ones take 10¢, 20¢ and 50¢ coins. Phonecards costing €2.50, €5 and €7.50 can be purchased at post offices, *tabacchi* and some newsstands. To use your card, tear off one corner as marked, insert it into the appropriate slot and dial. Your credit balance will be displayed on the phone.

Directory

Discount cards

If you plan to spend your time in Venice doing some serious sightseeing a discount card is the remedy for extortionate transport costs and multiple museum entrance fees. Remember that ICOM members (with ID), Venetian residents, children under five, disabled people with escorts, authorised guides, journalists (with ID), interpreters accompanying groups and group leaders receive free admission to many churches and museums; be sure to check policies before you invest in one of the following cards.

Other multi-entrance cards for Venice's museums and churches include the **Museum Pass**, various themed multi-entrance tickets to Venice's city-owned museums, and the **Chorus** ticket. For all, *see p70*.

Venice Card

www.venicecard.it
Produced by the city council, this is a one-, three- or seven-day card that gives discounts and access to services around the city. You must book your ticket at least 24 hours in advance: do this on-line or by calling 041 24 24 24 (8am-7.30pm daily). There are two types of cards, blue and orange: the blue card allows you to use public transport, toilets and baby-changing facilities while the orange card also includes admission to the Musei Civici (*see p70*) circuit. For a surcharge of around €10 (depending on the ticket) you can opt to include Alilaguna service to the airport. Tickets can be collected at any VeLa office (*see p278*), from Alilaguna or from the ATVO office in the airport (*for both see p276*).

The following prices are without the Alilaguna surcharge:
Blue One-day €14; €9 under-30s.
Three-day €29; €22 under-30s. Seven-day €51; €49 under-30s.

Orange One-day €28; €18 under-30s. Three-day €47; €35 under-30s. Seven-day €68; €61 under-30s.

Further discounts are given if you book online. Many car parks (*see p276*) offer significant discounts to Venice card holders.

Rolling Venice

www.comune.venezia.it/rol2/
Visitors between the ages of 14 and 29 can sign up for the **Rolling Venice** programme. Holders of a Rolling Venice card are eligible for discounts at selected hotels, museums (up to 50 per cent) and restaurants and shops (10-15 per cent) around the city, as well as cut-price (€15), three-day vaporetto passes and 50 per cent off tickets for concerts (not operas) at La Fenice. The card costs €3 and is valid until 31 December of the issue year; to get it, take a valid document to any VeLa (*see p278*) or APT office (*see p293*).

Pass Ville

From April to October the villas along the Riviera del Brenta (*see chapter* **Padua**) open their doors and gardens to visitors. The tourist office offers a ticket to five of the finest: Villa Pisani, Villa Widmann, the Barchessa of Villa Valmarana, the Barchessa of Villa Alessandri and the Barchessa of Villa Foscarini Rossi.

The ticket, available from APT offices (*see p293*) costs €19; €16 EU citizens 18-25; €17.50 non-EU citizens under 18 and over 65; €12 EU citizens under 18 and over 65. All the villas can be reached on bus 53 which departs from piazzale Roma at 25 and 55 minutes past each hour. By car take the SS11 from Mestre-Venezia to Padova, then the A4 motorway.

International calls

To make an international call from Venice dial 00, then the country code (Australia 61, Canada and USA 1, Ireland 353, New Zealand 64, UK 44, South Africa 27), then the area code (usually without the initial 0) and the number. International directory enquiries are on 4176. When calling an Italian landline from abroad, the whole prefix, including the 0, must be dialled, so dial 00 39 041… for Venice from the UK.

For operator-assisted calls abroad or reverse-charge calls (collect) dial 170.

Other services provided by Telecom Italia include:
170 operator-assisted national and International calls.
4176 international call information.
4114 alarm call.
186 telegrams.

4161 speaking clock.
4197 interrupts a conversation on an engaged line.
412 international calls information (892 412 from a mobile phone).

Mobile phones

Owners of GSM phones can use them in Italy on both 900 and 1800 bands, though reception in Venice can be patchy. American phones operate on a 1900 band and are therefore useless in Europe. Some phones now have a tri-band system, which operates on all three frequencies.

Time

Italy is one hour ahead of London, six ahead of New York, eight behind Sydney and 12 behind Wellington.

Tipping

There are no hard and fast rules on tipping in Italy, though Venetians know that foreigners tip generously back home and therefore expect them to be liberal. Some upmarket restaurants (and a growing number of cheaper ones) will add a service charge to your bill: feel free to ask *il servizio è incluso?* If it isn't, leave whatever you think the service merited (and remember that Italians rarely leave more than five to ten per cent).

Bear in mind that all restaurants charge a cover fee (*coperto*), which is a quasi-tip in itself.

Toilets

Public toilets (*servizi igienici pubblici*) are numerous in Venice can be found by following the blue and green signs marked WC. They are relatively clean and cost 50¢ to use.

Tourist information

Several free publications provide comprehensive tourist information in Venice, available at APT and VeLa (*see p278*) offices, and some bars. Most hotels will provide you with a copy of *Un Ospite di Venezia/A Guest in Venice*, a bilingual booklet compiled by hoteliers, which contains useful addresses, night pharmacies, Mass times and

transport timetables. It is published every fortnight in high season and once a month in winter.

The local press is another source of useful information on events (*see p286*), as are the posters plastered on walls all over the city. *Leo*, available at the APT, has unique, well-written features and a tear-out, easy to consult, listing booklet of events by day.

Information offices

See chapters in **The Veneto** section for information offices outside Venice.

Azienda di Promozione Turistica (APT)

San Marco 71F, piazza San Marco (041 529 8711/fax 041 523 0399/www.turismovenezia.it). *Vaporetto Vallaresso.* **Open** 9am-3.30pm daily. **Map** p311 B3.
The APT website is worth looking at before you arrive in Venice. The offices provide information on sights and events, a list of hotels, and walking itineraries with maps for sale. They'll also put you in touch with registered guides and give details of official fees for guided tours (also available on their website). The Palazzina Santi branch (map p311 B3) has a selection of books, sells concert tickets, and provides internet access too. In high season supplementary kiosks are set up around the city.
Direct any complaints to the Tourist Mediation Counter 041 529 8710, fax 041 523 0399 or complaint.apt@turismovenezia.it
Other locations: Palazzina Santi, San Marco 2, Giardinetti Reali (041 522 5150). **Open** 10am-6pm daily. Venice-Santa Lucia railway station (041 529 8727). **Open** 8am-6.30pm daily. San Marco 71F, piazza San Marco (041 529 8740). **Open** 9am-3.30pm daily. Marco Polo Airport arrivals hall (tel/fax 041 541 5887). **Open** 9.30am-7.30pm daily. Autorimessa Comunale, Santa Croce 465B, piazzale Roma (041 529 8746). **Open** 9.30am-6.30pm daily. Viale Santa Maria Elisabetta 6A, Lido (041 526 5721). **Open** June-Sept 9am-12.30pm, 3.30-6pm daily.

Tours & guides

The APT site (*see below*) provides information on guides by language and area.
Venice Walks and Tours (www.tours-italy.com) offers a selection of themed tours. For guides specialising in Venice's gardens, *see p136* **High walls**.

Cooperativa guide turistiche

San Marco 750, calle Morosini de la Regina (041 520 9038/fax 041 521 0762/www.guidevenezia.it). *Vaporetto San Zaccaria.* **Open** 9am-5pm Mon-Fri; 9am-1pm Sat. **Rates** €121 for 2hr tour for groups of up to 30 people; €4 for every extra person. **No credit cards. Map** p312 B2.
This cooperative has around 65 guides on its books, and offers made-to-measure tours in English and other languages. In high season, book at least a week in advance.

American Express

San Marco 1471, salizada San Moisè (041 520 0844/travel-tso-venice@aexp.com). *Vaporetto Vallaresso.* **Open** 9am-5.30pm Mon-Fri. **Credit** AmEx, DC, MC, V. **Map** p311 B3.
American Express offers daily guided tours in several languages from €30.

Visas

For EU citizens, a passport or a national identity card valid for travel abroad is sufficient. Non-EU citizens must have full passports. Citizens of the US, Canada, Australia and New Zealand do not need visas for stays of up to three months. In theory, visitors are required to declare their presence to the local police within a few days of arrival, unless they are staying in a hotel, where this will be done for them. In practice, you will not need to report to the police station unless you decide to extend your stay and you apply for a *permesso di soggiorno* (permit to stay, *see p289*).

Directory

Average temperatures

Month	High (°F/°C)	Low (°F/°C)
January	42/5.5	30/-1
February	47/8.3	33/0.5
March	54/12.2	39/3.9
April	61/16.1	46/7.8
May	70/21.1	54/12.2
June	77/25	61/16.1
July	82/27.8	64/17.8
August	81/27.2	63/17.2
September	75/23.9	58/14.4
October	65/18.3	49/9.4
November	53/11.7	40/4.4
December	44/6.7	32/0

Water & drinking

Forget *Death in Venice*-style cholera scares: the water is safe to drink and checked regularly. For information visit www.vestaspa.net.

When to go

Holidays

See also chapter **Festivals & Events**.

On public holidays (*giorni festivi*) public offices, banks and post offices are closed. So, in theory, are shops – but in tourism-oriented Venice, this rule is often waived, especially in high season. Some bars and restaurants may observe holidays: if in doubt, call ahead. You'll be hard pushed to find much open on Christmas Day and New Year's Day.

Public transport is reduced to a skeleton service on 1 May, Christmas Day and New Year's Day, and may be rerouted or curtailed for local festivities (*see chapter* **Festivals & Events**); details are posted at vaporetto stops and at the bus terminus in piazzale Roma.

Holidays falling on a Saturday or Sunday are not celebrated on the following Monday. By popular tradition,

if a public holiday falls on a Tuesday or Thursday, many people will also take the Monday or Friday off as well, a practice known as *fare il ponte* (doing a bridge). The public holidays are:
1 January New Year's Day (Capodanno).
6 January Epiphany (Befana).
Easter Monday (Pasquetta).
25 April Liberation Day (Festa della Liberazione) and patron saint's day (San Marco).
1 May Labour Day (Festa del Lavoro).
15 August Assumption (Ferragosto).
1 November All Saints' Day (Ognissanti).
21 November Festa della Salute (Venice only).
8 December Immaculate Conception (L'Immacolata).
25 December Christmas Day (Natale).
26 December Boxing Day (Santo Stefano).

Weather

Venice's unique position gives the city a bizarre mix of tropical European weather conditions. During the winter, high levels of humidity often make winter days seem colder than their average few degrees above zero, and summer days become humid as soon as the thermometer rises above 25°C. Strong north-easterlies in winter, coming off snow in the mountains (snow in the city is rare) may have bone-chilling

effects but turn the sky an incredible shade of turquoise-blue. In the summer months a hot southerly wind called the scirocco makes the heat more intense. Autumn and spring are generally mild with occasional pea-soup fog; November and March are the rainiest months. *Acqua alta (see p278* **On foot: wet**) is mainly a winter and spring event.

Women

Although Venice is a relatively safe place for women travellers, it is always best to apply common sense while travelling alone.

At night, keep away from quieter, more outlying areas and from the Tronchetto car park. Stick to main through-routes to avoid getting lost in dark alleyways; if in doubt, cut walking to a minimum by taking the vaporetto to as near to your destination as possible.

Tampons (*assorbenti interni*) and sanitary towels (*assorbenti esterni*) are cheaper in supermarkets, but can also be found in pharmacies and in some *tabacchi* shops.

Women suffering gynaecological emergencies should make for the *pronto soccorso* (emergency ward) at the Ospedale Civile (*see p284*).

Family planning

Consultori familiari are run by the local health authority, and EU citizens with an E111 form are entitled to use them, paying the same low charges for services and prescriptions as locals. Non-EU citizens may use the service and, depending on their insurance plan, claim refunds. The *consultori* are staffed by good gynaecologists – book ahead for a visit.

The pill is available on prescription. Abortions are legal when performed in public hospitals.

Glossary

Amphitheatre (*ancient*) oval open-air theatre.

Apse large recess at the high-altar end of a church.

Baldachin canopy supported by columns.

Barrel vault a ceiling with arches shaped like half-barrels.

Baroque artistic period from the 17th-18th centuries, in which the decorative element became increasingly florid, culminating in the Rococo (*qv*).

Basilica ancient Roman rectangular public building; rectangular Christian church.

Byzantine Christian artistic and architectural style drawing on ancient models developed in the fourth century in the Eastern empire (capital Byzantium/Constantinople/Istanbul) and developed through the Middle Ages.

Campanile bell tower.

Campo Venetian for piazza or square.

Capital head of a column, generally decorated according to classical orders (*qv*).

Caryatid column carved in female shape.

Chiaroscuro painting or drawing technique using no colours, but shades of black, white and grey.

Cloister exterior courtyard surrounded on all sides by a covered walkway.

Coffered ceiling decorated with sunken square or polygonal panels.

Cupola dome-shaped roof or ceiling.

Decumanus (*ancient*) main road, usually running east-west.

Ex-voto an offering given to fulfil a vow; often a small model in silver of the limb/organ/loved one cured as a result of prayer.

Fan vault vault formed of concave semi-cones, meeting at the apex; from beneath, gives the appearance of four backwards-leaning fans meeting.

Festoon painted or carved swag or swathe decorated with fruit and/or flowers.

Fresco painting technique in which pigment is applied to wet plaster.

Gothic architectural and artistic style of the late Middle Ages (from the 12th century), of soaring, pointed arches.

Greek cross (church) in the shape of a cross with arms of equal length.

Grisailles painting in shades of grey to mimic sculpture.

Iconostasis rood screen; screen in Eastern-rite churches separating nave from the sanctuary.

Intarsia form of mosaic made from pieces of different-coloured wood; also know as **intaglio**.

Latin cross (church) in the shape of a cross with one arm longer than the other.

Loggia gallery open on one side.

Lunette semi-circular surface, usually above a window or door.

Mannerism High Renaissance style of the late 16th century; characterised in painting by elongated, contorted human figures.

Monoforate with one opening (cf biforate, triforate, polyforate *qv*), usually used of windows.

Narthex enclosed porch in front of a church.

Nave main body of a church; the longest section of a Latin cross church (*qv*).

Ogival (of arches, windows etc) curving in to a point at the top .

Opus sectile pavement made of (usually) geometrically shaped marble slabs.

Orders classical rules governing the proportions of columns, their entablatures (*qv*) and their capitals (*qv*), the most common being the less ornate Doric, the curlicue Ionic and the Corinthian in which capitals are decorated with stylised acanthus leaves.

Palazzo large and/or important building (not necessarily a palace).

Pendentives four concave triangular sections on top of piers supporting a dome.

Piano nobile showiest floor of a palazzo (*qv*), containing mainly reception rooms with very high ceilings.

Pilaster column-shaped projection from a wall.

Polyforate with more than one opening (cf monoforate).

Polyptych painting composed of several panels (cf dyptych with two panels and triptych with three).

Porphyry hard igneous rock ranging from dark green to dark purple; this latter was most commonly used, and known as *rosso antico*.

Presbytery the part of a church containing the high altar.

Reredos decorated wall or screen behind an altar.

Rococo highly decorative style fashionable in the 18th century.

Romanesque architectural style of the early Middle Ages (c500 to 1200), drawing on Roman and Byzantine (*qv*) influences.

Rusticated large masonry blocks with deep joints between them used to face buildings or monuments.

Sarcophagus (*ancient*) stone or marble coffin.

Stele upright slab of stone with commemorative inscription and/or decorative relief scupture.

Transept shorter arms of a Latin cross church (*qv*).

Trilobate with three arches .

Triumphal arch arch in front of an apse (*qv*), usually over the high altar.

Trompe l'oeil decorative painting effect to make surface appear three-dimensional.

Vocabulary

In hotels and restaurants you'll generally find someone who speaks English; further off the tourist track, however, some Italian is useful (and appreciated). Italian is pronounced as it is spelled. Stresses usually fall on the penultimate syllable; a stress on the final syllable is indicated by an accent.

There are three 'you' forms: the formal singular *lei*, the informal singular *tu*, and the plural *voi*. Masculine nouns and their accompanying adjectives generally end in 'o' (plural 'i'), female nouns and their adjectives end in 'a' (plural 'e').

VENETIAN

The distinctive nasal Venetian drawl is more than just an accent: locals have their own vocabulary, too, some of it from Byzantine roots. Venetians tend to ignore consonants, running vowels together in long diphthongs (explaining how *vostro schiavo* – 'your servant' – became *ciao*.) Xè is pronounced 'zay'; *gò* sounds like 'go' in 'got'. For further information consult www.veneto.org/language.

PRONUNCIATION

Vowels
a – as in ask
e – like a in age (closed e) or e in sell (open e)
i – like ea in east
o – as in hotel (closed o) or in hot (open o)
u – as in boot
Consonants
c before a, o or u is like the c in cat
c before an e or an i is like the ch in check (sh as in ship in Venetian)
ch is like the c in cat
g before a, o or u is like the g in get
g before an e or an i is like the j in jig
gh is like the g in get
gl followed by an i is like lli in million
gn is like ny in canyon
qu is as in quick
r is always rolled
s has two sounds, as in soap or rose
sc before an e or an i is like the sh in shame

sch is like the sc in scout
z has two different sounds, like ts and dz

USEFUL WORDS & PHRASES
(Italian/*Venetian*)
Hello and goodbye – ciao; used informally in other parts of Italy; in any and all social situations in Venice
Good morning, hello – buongiorno
Good afternoon, good evening – buonasera
I'm sorry – mi dispiace/*me dispiaxe*
I don't understand – non capisco, non ho capito/*no gò capìo*
Do you speak English? – parla inglese?
Please – per favore, per piacere
Thank you – grazie
You're welcome – prego
Open – aperto/*verto*
Closed – chiuso
When does it open? – quando apre?
It's closed – è chiuso/*xè serà*
What's the time? – che ore sono?
Excuse me – mi scusi (polite), scusami (informal) *scusime/me scusa*
Entrance – entrata; **exit** – uscita
Do you have a light? – hai d'accendere?/*ti gà da accender, ti gà fógo?*
Would you like an ice-cream? – Vuoi un gelato?/*ti vol un geàto?*

Transport
Car – macchina; **bus** – autobus; **taxi** – tassi, taxi; **train** – treno; **plane** – aereo; **stop** (bus or vaporetto) – fermata; **station** – stazione; **platform** – binario; **ticket/s** – biglietto, biglietti; **one way** –solo andata; **return** – andata e ritorno; **I'd like a ticket to...** – Vorrei un biglietto per…

Communications
Phone – telefono; **cellphone** – cellulare; **fax** – fax; **postcard** – cartolina; **stamp** – francobollo.

Directions
Where is...? – dov'è…?/*dove xè?*
(Turn) left – (giri a) sinistra
(It's on the) right – (è sulla/a) destra
Straight on – sempre dritto
Could you tell me the way to...? – mi può indicare la strada per…?
Is it near/far? – è vicino/lontano?

Accommodation
I'd like to book a single/twin/double bedroom – vorrei prenotare una camera singola/doppia/matrimoniale

I'd prefer a room with a bath/shower/window over the courtyard – preferirei una camera con vasca da bagno/doccia/finestra sul cortile

Eating & drinking
I'd like to book a table for four at eight – vorrei prenotare una tavola per quattro alle otto
That was poor/good/delicious – era mediocre/buono/ottimo
The bill – il conto
Is service included? – è incluso il servizio?
I think there's a mistake in this bill – credo che il conto sia sbagliato

Shopping
I'd like to try on the blue sandals/black shoes/brown boots – vorrei provare I sandali blu/le scarpe nere/ gli stivali marroni
I take (shoe) size – porto il numero…
I take (dress) size – porto la taglia…
It's too loose/too tight/just right – mi sta largo/stretto/bene
100 grammes of – un etto di; **200 grammes of** – due etti di
One kilo of – un kilo di; **two kilos of** – due kili di
A litre – un litro
Ha delle monete? – do you have small change?

Days & times
Monday – lunedì; **Tuesday** – martedì; **Wednesday** – mercoledì; **Thursday** – giovedì; **Friday** – venerdì; **Saturday** – sabato; **Sunday** – domenica; **yesterday** – ieri; **today** – oggi/*ancuo*; **tomorrow** – domani; **morning** – mattina; **afternoon** – pomeriggio; **evening** – sera; **this evening** – stasera; **night** – notte; **tonight** – stanotte

Numbers, money & shopping
0 zero; **1** uno; **2** due; **3** tre; **4** quattro; **5** cinque; **6** sei; **7** sette; **8** otto; **9** nove; **10** dieci; **11** undici; **12** dodici; **13** tredici; **14** quattordici; **15** quindici; **16** sedici; **17** diciassette; **18** diciotto; **19** diciannove; **20** venti; **21** ventuno; **22** ventidue; **30** trenta; **40** quaranta; **50** cinquanta; **60** sessanta; **70** settanta; **80** ottanta; **90** novanta; **100** cento; **1,000** mille; **2,000** duemila
Money – soldi/*schei*
Shop – negozio/*botéga*
How much does it cost/is it? – quanto costa?, quant'è?/*quanto xè?*
Do you accept credit cards? – si accettano le carte di credito?

Further Reference

Books

Non-fiction

Paolo Barbaro *Venice Revealed: an Intimate Portrait*
An engineer provides fascinating facts on the city's physical structure.
Robert Davis and Garry Marvin *Venice: The Tourist Maze*
A well-documented study of problems connected with Venice's role as a tourist mecca.
Deborah Howard *The Architecture of Venice; Venice and the East*
Howard's *Architecture* is the definitive account.
WD Howells *Venetian Life*
US consul's (1861-5) account of Venetian life before mass tourism.
Peter Humfrey *Painting in Renaissance Venice*
Informative and compact enough to carry with you.
Frederick C Lane *Venice: A Maritime Republic*
The best single-volume scholarly history of Venice.
Mary Laven *Virgins of Venice: Broken Vows and Cloistered Lives in the Renaissance Convent*
The title says it all.
Michelle Lovric *Venice: Tales of the City*
The best compendium of writers on Venice.
Mary McCarthy *Venice Observed*
Witty account of Venetian art.
Damiano Martin *The Da Fiore Cookbook*
How to cook like they do at Da Fiore (*see p159*).
Francesco Da Mosto *Francesco's Venice*
Coffee-table guide by a scion of an aristocratic Venetian family.
Jan Morris *Venice*
Impressionistic history.
John Julius Norwich *A History of Venice; Paradise of Cities*
The *History* is engagingly rambling; *Paradise* deals with 19th-century visitors to Venice.
John Pemble *Venice Rediscovered*
On the 19th-century obsession with things Venetian
Andrea Di Robilant *A Venetian Affair*
Steamy love affair between Di Robilant's noble forbear and an Englishwoman in the 1750s.
David Rosand *Painting in 16th-Century Venice*
A great book to read before your trip.
John Ruskin *The Stones of Venice*
Ruskin's hymn to the Gothic.
Gary Wills *Venice: Lion City*
Fascinating blend of history and art criticism.

Fiction & literature

Lord Byron *Childe Harold's Pilgrimage; Beppo*
Venice as a dream (*Harold*) and at Carnevale (*Beppo*).
Giacomo Casanova *My Life*
The great seducer's escapades in mid 18th-century Venice.
Michael Dibdin *Dead Lagoon*
Aurelio Zen returns to his native city.
Ernest Hemingway *Across the River and into the Trees*
Aka Across the Canal and into the Bar.
Henry James *The Wings of the Dove*
Melodrama concealed behind a wall of elegant prose.
Donna Leon *Acqua Alta* (and many others)
Series featuring detective *commissario* Guido Brunetti.
Thomas Mann *Death in Venice*
Disease, decadence, indecision, voyeurism.
Ezra Pound *The Cantos*
Full of abstruse Venetian details.
William Rivière *A Venetian Theory of Heaven*
Atmospheric novel set among the 1980s English community in Venice.
William Shakespeare *The Merchant of Venice; Othello*
The bard's Venetian offerings.
Sally Vickers *Miss Garnett's Angel*
Elderly English lady's staid life is overturned by angelic encounters.

Film

Casanova (Lasse Halstrom, 2005?)
Heath Ledger plays the legendary lover in Halstrom's new film.
The Comfort of Strangers (Paul Schrader, 1990)
Dysfunctional couple have salt rubbed in their emotional wounds.
Death in Venice (Luchino Visconti, 1971)
Dirk Bogarde chases sailor-suited boy around cholera-plagued Venice.
Don't Look Now (Nick Roeg, 1973)
Chilling tale of a couple (Donald Sutherland and Julie Christie) in Venice after the death of their daughter.
Eve (Joseph Losey, 1962)
Budding novelist Stanley Baker is ensnared by temptress Jeanne Moreau.
The Merchant of Venice (Michael Radford, 2004)
Al Pacino is Shylock in this star-studded adaptation.
Senso (Luchino Visconti, 1954)
Venetian countess Alida Valli falls violently in love with sadistic Austrian soldier Farley Granger, betraying her husband and her country in her blinding passion.

Music

Lorenzo Da Ponte (1749-1838)
Expelled from Venice for his loose behaviour, Father Lorenzo Da Ponte fled to Vienna, where he penned *libretti* for Mozart's *Marriage of Figaro*, *Don Giovanni* and *Così fan tutte*.
Andrea Gabrieli (c1510-1586)
Organist of St Mark's basilica, Gabrieli senior's madrigals were Venetian favourites.
Giovanni Gabrieli (c1556-1612)
Nephew and student of Andrea, Gabrieli junior composed sacred and choral music, particularly motets for a number of choirs stationed at different points around churches to create a stereophonic effect; *In ecclesiis* is perhaps his masterpiece.
Antonio Vivaldi (1678-1741)
There's no escaping his *Four Seasons* in Venice. But there are nearly 500 more concertos and 16 surviving operas to choose from too.

Websites

The first port of call for information on museums and exhibitions in Venice is the cultural heritage ministry's informative site at www.beniculturali.it. Other useful sites include:
www.venezia.net Everything from apartment rents to information on renting a carnevale costume (English & Italian).
www.venetia.it History, useful phone numbers and good links (English).
www.doge.it Cultural information, courses and online hotel booking (English).
www.comune.venezia.it City council's site with useful practical information (English).
www.regione.veneto.it/cultura Cultural offerings and happenings around the Veneto region. Parts (including museum info) in English.
www.meetingvenice.it Hotel booking service in the city and surrounding areas, plus news on events and tourist attractions (English).
www.agendavenezia.it Events in Venice for an entire calendar year (English).
www.veniceword.com News magazine with current events and entertainment (English).
www.venice-ghetto.com/ This is the website for the Jewish Community and very helpful.
www.venetianlegends.it A great collection (in English) of ghost stories and grisly legends (better than boring tourist-advice sites!).

Directory

Index

Advertisers' Index

Please refer to the relevant sections for full contact details.

	Church
	Airport
H	Hospital
	Vaporetto stop
	Palazzo

Maps

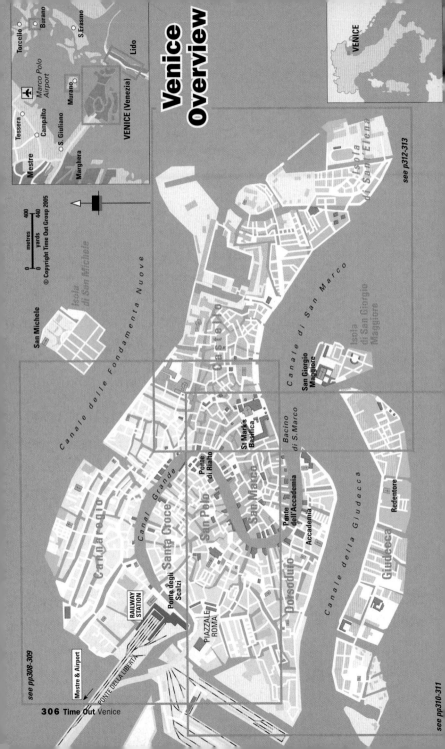

Venice Overview

VENICE

VENICE (Venezia)

Marco Polo Airport ✈

Torcello Burano
S. Erasmo
Lido

Tessera Canpalto S. Giuliano
Mestre Marghera
Murano

see pp312-313

Isola di San Michele
San Michele

Isola di Sant'Elena

Canale delle Fondamenta Nuove

metres 0 400
yards 0 440
© Copyright Time Out Group 2005

Castello

Canale di San Marco

Isola di San Giorgio Maggiore
San Giorgio Maggiore

Bacino di S.Marco

Cannaregio

Canal Grande

Ponte di Rialto

Santa Croce

San Polo

St Mark's Basilica

San Marco

Ponte dell'Accademia
Accademia

Ponte degli Scalzi

Dorsoduro

Canale della Giudecca

Giudecca

Redentore

RAILWAY STATION

PIAZZALE ROMA

PONTE DELLA LIBERTÀ

see pp308-309

Mestre & Airport

see pp310-311

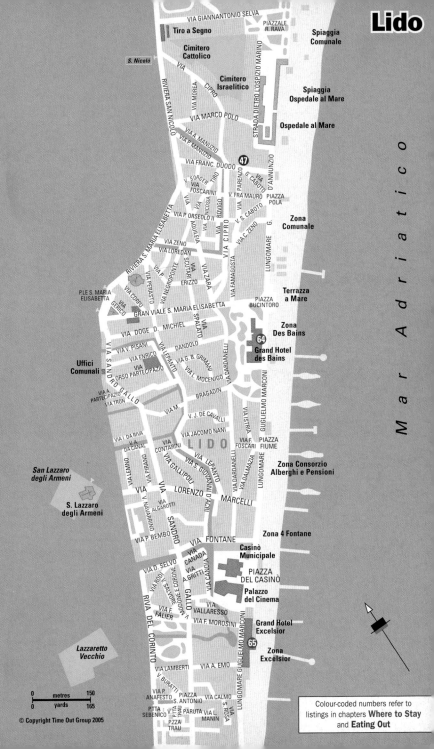

1   **2**   **3**

A

Ospedale
Umberto I **H**
Villa
Groggia

FONDAM. DI SACCA S. GIROLAMO

Tre Archi

Le Cappuccine

CANNAREGIO

S. Giobbe

22

CAMPO
S. GIOBBE

17

CAMPO DI
GHETTO
NUOVO **37**

B

S. Giobbe

Pal.
Nani

CAMPIELLO
PESARO

Pal.
Savorgnan
Pal. Venier

Guglie

Tempio
Israelitico

Pal.
da
Mosto

39 **26** **38**

Pal.
Zeno

Pal.
Labia

CAMPO
S. GEREMIA

Pal.
Emo

Pal.
Gritti

**RAILWAY
STATION
S. LUCIA**

Gli Scalzi

Ex Scuola
dei Morti

Pal.
Flangini

Riva di
Biasio

Pal.
Giovanelli

Pal. Calbo
Crotta

Ferrovia

CAMPO
S. SIMEON
PROFETA

30

C

**P.le
Roma**

Ferrovia

Pal.
Emo-Diedo

Campo
Gradenigo

CAMPO
N. SAURO

S. Giacomo
dell'Orio

37

**P.le
Roma**

PIAZZALE
ROMA

Pal.
Papadopoli

Giardini
Papadopoli

41

Pal.
Soranzo
Cappello

S. Giovanni
Evangelista

Scuola di
San Rocco

S. Maria
dei Frari **38**

Pal.
Michiel

CAMPIELLO
TRE PONTI

CAMPIELLO
LAVADORI

S. Nicolò
da Tolentino

Pal.
Marcello

48

CAMPO
S. ROCCO

D

Ex Chiesa di
S.M. Maggiore

RIO TERRÀ DEI PENSIERI

45

44

S. Pantalon

CAMPO
S. PANTALON

S. Tomà

S. Tomà

Pal.
Foscarini

CAMPO
SANTA
MARGHERITA

Ca' Foscari

Pal.
Balbi

Pal. Contarini
d. Figure

Pal.
Giustinian

3

Pal.
Grassi

S. Samuele

1 **308** Time Out Venice

Pal.
Cicogna

See p310

Coll.
Armeno

Carmini

Pal.
Rezzonico

Pal.
Malipiero

Ca' Rezzonico

S. Angelo
Raffaele

S. Barnaba

Colour-coded numbers refer to
listings in chapters **Where to Stay**
and **Eating Out**

Northern Venice

0   metres   150
0   yards   165

© Copyright Time Out Group 2005

Canale delle Fondamenta Nuove

S. Alvise

Orto

S. Alvise

Madonna
dell'Orto

Casino
d. Spiriti

Pal. Contarini
d. Zaffo

Sacca della
Misericordia

Pal. Longo

Cappella d.
Volto Santo

S. Maria
Valverde

Pal.
Diedo

Pal. Lezze

Ex Chiesa
di S. Caterina

Gesuiti

Fondamenta
Nove

S. Fosca

Pal.
Papafava

Pal.
Vendramin

FONDAMENTA NUOVE

Pal.
Soranzo

Pal.
Giovanelli

Pal.
Molin

Marcuola

Pal.
Vendramin
Calergi

Pal.
Erizzo

Ca' Tron

S. Stae

Pal.
Boldu

Pal.
Fontana

S. Sofia

Pal.
Sagredo

Ss. Apostoli

Pal.
Widman

Pal.
Grifalconi

Ospedale
Civile

Ca' d'Oro

Pal. Foscari

Ca'
da Mosto

Pal. Michiel
d. Colonne

Pal. Mangili

S. Canciano

Santa Maria
dei Miracoli

Pal. Sanudo
Von Axel

S. Giovanni
e Paolo

Fabbriche
Nuove

Teatro
Malibran

Pal.
Pisani

Ospedaletto

CAMPO S.
GIACOMO
DI RIALTO

Fondaco
d. Tedeschi
(Post Office)

Pal. Cavazzi
Foscari

Pal.
Dona

Pal.
Morosini

Pal.
Corner

CAMPO
S. POLO

S. Polo

Ponte
di Rialto

S. Lio

Pal.
Ruzzini

Pal.
Bragadin

Pal.
Cavagnis

S. Maria
Formosa

Pal.
Albrizzi

Pal.
Rava

Rialto

Pal. Bembo

Pal. Dolfin-
Manin

Pal.
Gussoni

Pal. Dina

Pal.
Cappello

S. Silvestro

Scuola Gr.
S. Teodoro

S. Maria
della Fava

Pal.
Grimani

Questura

Pal. Corner

Pal.
Papadopoli

Pal.
Grimani

S. Salvador

Pal. Tasca
Papafava

Fondazione
Querini
Stampalia

Pal.
Zorzi

Pal. Layard

Teatro
Goldoni

S. Angelo

Pal.
Volpi

Pal. Benedetto

Salizz.
S. LUCA

Teatro
Rossini

CAMPO
MANIN

S. Luca

Pal.
Avogadro

Pal.
Soranzo

S. Giorgio
dei Greci

Pal.
Corner
Spinelli

Pal.
Pesaro

Teatro
Rossini

Pal. Contarini
d. Bovolo

S. Gallo

S. Zaccaria

See p312

S. Stefano

S. Fantin

Procuratie
Vecchie

St Mark's
Basilica

Pal.
Trevisan

Pal.
Priuli

Pal.
Patriarc.

Pal. Zorzi

PIAZZA
S. MARCO

Campanile

Palazzo
Ducale
(Doge's Palace)

S. Maurizio

La Fenice

Procuratie Nuove

PIAZZETTA
S. MARCO

Libreria
Sansoviniana

Bridge of
Sighs

Pal.
Dandolo

La Pietà
(Santa Maria
d. Visitazione)

See p311

DEGLI SCHIAVONI

Southern Venice

See p308

↑

1

Bacino della Stazione Marittima

Canale Scomenzera

Santa Marta

Calle Larga S. Marta
FOND. S. MARTA

RIO TERRA
DEI SECCHI

*Quartiere
Santa Marta*

S. Nicolò
dei Mendicoli

2

P.le
Roma

C. NUOVA O. TABACCHI

FONDAMENTA S. ANDREA

PIAZZALE
ROMA

FONDAMENTA FABBRICA TABACCHI
FONDAMENTA DELLE BURCHIELLE

RAMO
BERNARDO

RIO TERRA DEI PENSIERI

CORTE
CORRERA

Rio della Cazziola

Ex Chiesa di
S.M. Maggiore

Pal.
Cicogna

S. Angelo
Raffaele

Pal.
Foscarini

Coll.
Armeni

Carmini

S. Sebastiano

3

Emo-Diedo

Pal.
Papadopoli

*Giardini
Papadopoli*

S. Nicolò
da Tolentino

Pal.
Marcello

CORTE
CONTARINI

CORTE
CRISTO

CORTE
MALCANTON

CORTE
ROSA

CORTE
D'AVOGARIA

CALLE LUNGA

42

Ospedale
G. B. Giustina
Ognissanti

H

CORTE
ZAPPA

SALIZZADA SAN BASEGIO

BANCHINA DI S. BASEGIO

S. Basilio

Stazione
Marittima

FONDAMENTA ZATTERE

Canale di Fusina

Sacca Fisola

BEATA

GIULIANA

C. DE LA SCUOLA

Sacca Fisola

CAMPO DELLA
CHIESA IN SACA

S. Gerardo

CAMPO
S. GERARDO

*Sacca
S. Biagio*

Fisola S. Biagio

Canale

CAMPO
DEI
LAVRANERI

PONTE
LAVRANERI

Canale dei Lavraneri

Mulino
Stucky

FONDAMENTA SAN BIAGIO

Sant' Eufemia

GIUDECCA

45

CAMPIELLO
SANT' EUFEMIA

Sant' Eufemia

CAMPIELLO
PRIULI

FONDAMENTA DELLE CONVERTITE

CAMPIELLO
MONTORIO

CAMPO
S. COSMO

Penitenziario
Femminile

Ex Chiesa dei
SS. Cosma e
Damiano

CAMPAZZO
DI DENTRO

0 — metres — 150
0 — yards — 165
© Copyright Time Out Group 2005

Southern
Venice

Colour-coded numbers refer to
listings in chapters **Where to Stay**
and **Eating Out**

A

B

C

D

1   **2**   **3**

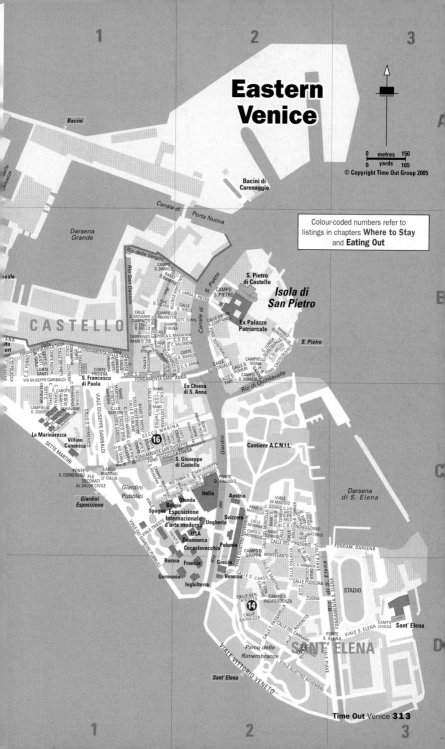

Eastern Venice

© Copyright Time Out Group 2005

```
0    metres    150
0    yards    165
```

Colour-coded numbers refer to listings in chapters **Where to Stay** and **Eating Out**

Bacini

Bacini di Carenaggio

Canale di Porta Nuova

Darsena Grande

Rio delle Vergini

Rio San Daniele

CAMPO S. DANIELE

RAMO S. DANIELE

CALLE LARGA S. PIETRO

S. Pietro

S. Pietro di Castello

Isola di San Pietro

CAMPO S. PIETRO

Canale di S. Pietro

CALLE DIETRO IL CAMPANILE

Ex Palazzo Patriarcale

S. Pietro

CALLE S. GIOVANNI

CAMPIELLO FIGARETTO

CALLE D. FIGHER

CALLE D. TERCO

SOTT. ZURLIN

CAMPO D. RUGA

CALLE DA PORTO

C. QUINTAVALLE

RAMO QUINTAVALLE

C. DELLE VIGNA

CAMPIELLO D. VIGNA

CALLE D. POMERI

FOND. CASTELFORTE D.

C. QUINTAVALLE

CALLE D. MEZO

CAMPO D. POMERI

CASTELLO

CALLE D. ERBE

R. RIELLO

C. MARAFANI

E. D. OLE

C. S. SALOMON

C. DEL RIELLO

SOTT. D. RIELLO

CORTE BIANCO

CALLE S. ANNA

CALLE QUINTAVALLE

CALLE D. FARI

Rio di Quintavalle

S. Francesco di Paola

CORTE FRISIERA

FOND. S. GIOACCHINO

FONDAMENTA SANT'ANNA

Ex Chiesa di S. Anna

VIA GIUSEPPE GARIBALDI

La Marinarezza

Villino Canonica

SETTE MARTIRI

VIALE GIUSEPPE GARIBALDI

SECCO MARINA

16

FOND. BIANCO LA CHIESA

S. Giuseppe di Castello

Giardini

Cantiere A.C.N.I.L.

PONTE S. DOMENEGO

PLE DECORATI AL VALOR CIVILE

LARGO MARINAI D'ITALIA

RIO TERRA DI SAN GIUSEPPE

PONTE D. PALUDO

RIO DI S. GIUSEPPE

Darsena di S. Elena

Giardini Pubblici

Giardini Esposizione

VIALE TRIESTE

VIALE TRENTO

VIALE DEI GIARDINI PUBBLICI

Italia

Olanda

Belgio

Spagna

Esposizione Internazionale d'arte moderna

USA

Danimarca

Cecoslovacchia

Russia

Francia

Germania

Inghilterra

Austria

Svizzera

Ungheria

Polonia

Grecia

Venezia

VIALE 24 MAGGIO

RAMO D. MONTELLO

CALLE ASIAGO

RAMO C.I.D.

C. DEL PASUBIO

CALLE DEL NEVEGAL

CORTE D. CONGREGAZIONE

RAMO 1° ORATORIO

CALLE DEL PASUBIO

C. MONTESANTO

CALLE OSLAVIA

CALLE D. HERMADA

CALLE PODGORA

FONDAM. DARSENA

VIALE PIAVE

CALLE DEL CARSO

CALLE SABOTINO

ZUGNA

STADIO

CAMPO CHIESA

Sant'Elena

14

CALLE GEN. CHINOTTO

CALLE BAINSIZZA

CAMPO D. INDIPENDENZA

CALLE D. CARSO

CALLE SARDEGNA

CALLE D. CASTELLO

CALLE PASUBIO

CALLE DEL NOVEGNO

PONTE S. ELENA

VIALE S. ELENA

RIO DI S. ELENA

FONDAMENTA S. ELENA

SANT' ELENA

Parco delle Rimembranze

Sant'Elena

VIALE VITTORIO VENETO

VIALE QUATTRO NOVEMBRE

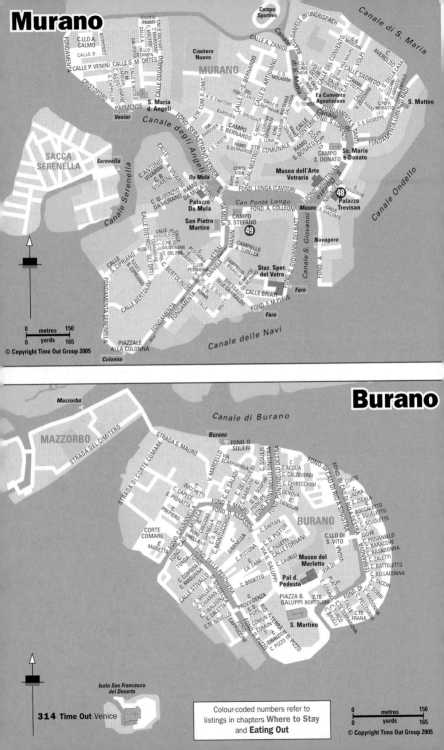

Murano

Campo Sportivo

Canale di S. Maria

C.LLO G PUIATI
CALLE D. LOREDAN
C.LLO SALVATI
CALLE D.
Canale Grande
C.G. ORTES
CALLE D.
CALLE D.
BRIDGE
C.LLO A. CALMO
CALLE D.
FONDAMENTA
CRISTOFORO
PARMENSE
CALLE P. VENINI
CALLE G. M. ORTES
CALLE D'ODOARDO
CALLE MULALBONO
C.G. CAPPELLINI
C.M. AGOSTINIANE
C.T. DARDUINI
C.LLO STAMPA
CALLE D.
CALLE S. NICOLO

Cimitero Nuovo
CALLE A. ZANIOL

BEATRICE

CAMPO S. BERNARDO
CALLE DE FORCELLANTE
CALLE D. SUPIADOR
CALLE D. BRUSSA
CAMPO BERNARDO
VIA BAROVIER
RAMO S. CRISTO
STR. COMUNALE
RAMO S. BERNARDO
CORTE VIDA
CALLE DEL MISTRI

MURANO

S. Maria d. Angeli
Venier

Canale degli Angeli

FOND. SEBASTIANO VENIER
CALLE A. VIVARINI
C. ANTONIO VIVARINI
C. B. VIVARINI
RAMO DA MULA
C. QUIRINZIO DA MURANO
Da Mula
FOND. DA MULA
CALLE DA MULA
Palazzo Da Mula
San Pietro Martire
CALLE FOSCOLO
C. P.O. GIUSTINIAN
C. ROSETE
CALLE DIETRO GLI ORTI
CALLE S. CIPRIANO
RAMO S. CIPRIANO
FONDAMENTA SERENELLA
CALLE BERTOLINI
FONDAMENTA

SACCA SERENELLA

Serenella

Canale Serenella

PIAZZALE ALLA COLONNA
Colonna

DANIELE DI UNGRISPACH
CALLE DE CONVENTO
CALLE D. ARTIGIANO
C.D. MOLADOR
CALLE D.
CALLE CALLE
Ex Convento Agostiniane
FOND. S. LORENZO
CALLE D. CONTERI
RAMO S. DONATO
CAMPO S. DONATO
Ss. Maria e Donato
Museo dell'Arte Vetraria

C.G. MOSCHIN
AVEROLDO
CALLE SAGREDO
FOND.TA L. RADI
S. Matteo
C.S. GIUSEPPE
FONDAMENTA LORENZO RADI

Canale Ondello

FOND. GIUSTINIAN
FOND. NAVAGERO
48
Palazzo Trevisan
PASSERINI

Can. Ponte Longo
FOND. A. COLLEONI
Museo
CAMPO S. STEFANO
49
Navagero

FOND. S. GIOVANNI DEI BATT
Canale S. Giovanni
FOND. A.

CAMPIELLO A. TURELLA
PESCHERIA
C. DEL PROSPETTO
CALLE DANIELE
CAMPIELLO DI BIGAGLIA
BRESSAGIO
IV LE GARIBALDI
C.D. OLIO
FORNO
Staz. Sper. del Vetro
CALLE BRIATI
Faro
FOND. F. M. PIAVE
Faro

Canale delle Navi

metres 150
yards 165

© Copyright Time Out Group 2005

Burano

Mazzorbo

Canale di Burano

Burano

MAZZORBO
STRADA DEL CIMITERO
STRADA S. MAURO
STRADA DI CORTE COMARE

FOND. D. SQUERI
VIA SCARPARIOLA
V. MARCELLO
C. SALADI
C. DEI SQUERI
FOND. S. MAURO
C. ABBAZIA
FOND. PONTINELLO SINISTRA
FOND. PONTINELLO DESTRA
C. SOSSPIR
C. PRINCIPE
C. GENOVA
C. DAFFAN
C. D. PISTOR
C. PITTORA
FOND. DI RIO A SINISTRA
FOND. DI CAO DI RIO A DESTRA
FOND. DI CAO DI RIO A DESTRA

ZUCCHETTI
C. CAPECE
C. PIGNATTA
PREPIERO
CORTE COMARE
C. MANETTA
FOND. CAVANELLA
FIURE
C. GMELA
C. GMELA
C. GIANELLA
C. D. BOTE
C. MONTLUCHICHIO
GIMINELLA
CA ZANE
VIA G. GALUPPI
CALLE FORNANI
C. CAVALLI
C. BROETTO
FOND. DELLA PESCHERIA
C. COMBRA'
C. MADONA
CALLE STIVALLO
C. MALEO
C. CHIARAN
C. TIBALDON
C. CALETTA
C.TE NOVELLO
PROVVIDENZA
RIO COMUN
C. POPE
FOND. PIZZO
C. TIBALDON
C. PIZZO
C. D. PIZZO
CAPUCCINE

FOND. DI CAO DI RIO A DESTRA
CORTE
C. JADRA
C. ZIGALA
C. BOCCALETTO
C. SQUELETTO
C. SCUOLETTE
C.LLO DI S. VITO
GIOVE
C. PIOVANELLO
C. BARACCHE
C. BASADONNA
C. ZALETTI
C. BATTELETTO
C. BELLADONNA
C. TACCHI
C. CORBI
VIA DI
C. MADONA
C. PELLEGRIN
C.TE TERRANOVA
C.TE FRANA
C.TE BROLI

C. CALZEVERDI
C. CHIBECCHINI

BURANO

Museo del Merletto
Pal d. Podestà
PIAZZA B. GALUPPI BORTOLONI
S. Martino

Isola San Francesco del Deserto

314 Time Out Venice

Colour-coded numbers refer to listings in chapters **Where to Stay** and **Eating Out**

metres 150
yards 165

© Copyright Time Out Group 2005

Street Index

C.	CALLE
C.LLO	CAMPIELLO
C.TE	CORTE
FOND.	FONDAMENTA
P.LE	PIAZZALE
SAL.	SALIZADA
V.LE	VIALE

Vaporetti

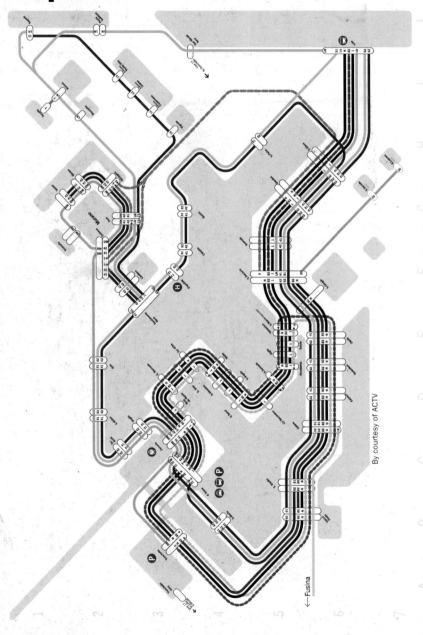

By courtesy of ACTV